# CURRICULUM PLANNING
## *A New Approach*

### FIFTH EDITION

## GLEN HASS
*University of Florida*

## Allyn and Bacon, Inc.
*Boston     London     Sydney     Toronto*

**Library of Congress Cataloging-in-Publication Data**

Curriculum planning.

    Bibliography: p.
    Includes index.
    1. Curriculum planning—United States.  2. Child development—United States.  3. Learning.  4. Educational psychology.  I. Hass, Glen.
LB1570.C944   1987      375'.001       86-28769
ISBN 0-205-10457-6 (pbk.)

Series editor: Susanne F. Canavan
Production coordinator: Helyn Pultz
Editorial-production service: Publication Services
Cover administrator: Linda K. Dickinson
Cover designer: Richard Hannus

Printed in the United States of America

10 9 8 7 6 5 4 3 2 1    90 89 88 87 86

# Contents

# Preface

The fifth edition of *Curriculum Planning: A New Approach* is a guide for the development of the knowledge, performance competencies, and alternative strategies needed by curriculum planners and teachers at all levels of education from early childhood to adulthood. As a resource for generating skill in curriculum planning and teaching, the book offers a variety of learning experiences for students with wide-ranging interests, learning styles, and backgrounds.

The previous editions of this book presented many methods and approaches for studying curriculum planning and improvement that provided much flexibility in the ways that it could be used by instructors and students. Recent studies emphasize the importance of alternative strategies, designs, models, processes, curricula, and schools in providing for interests, learning styles, and needs. Appropriately, a goal in preparing this edition has been to continue to increase the options, alternatives, and resources for both teachers and learners.

Part I presents vital curriculum planning components: values and goals, the four bases of the curriculum, and curriculum criteria. Thirty criterion questions are presented and activities are provided to help to develop skill in their use in curriculum planning. Part II emphasizes application of the skills developed in Part I and identifies the many curriculum innovations and trends that can currently be found at educational levels from early childhood through adulthood. A final section summarizes the multidimensional, rather than linear, approach emphasized throughout the book. This method of studying curriculum planning and teaching utilizes all of our knowledge about the individual, the society, and the group. The multi-dimensional approach should distinguish the professional in curriculum planning from specialists in fields such as human development or learning or group sensitivity, while acknowledging the importance of their contributions and assimilating their findings. When engaging in several of the learning activities in the final section, the student will need to summarize and synthesize the knowledge developed through working with the preceding sections of the book.

The place of educational philosophy in curriculum planning and teaching is given major attention in the first of the eleven sections in the book. This has been accomplished by including important vintage articles by key figures representing each of the four philosophical positions that have had major influence on curriculum planners and teachers during the past fifty years. These noted past leaders' statements show the sharp contrast in viewpoint among the philosophical positions, and they highlight the values in each that are significant for curriculum planning now and in the future. Statements of article length from John Dewey's books, *The Sources of a Science of Education* and *Experience and Education,* are also included in sections 1, 5, and 6 because of the way in which they help bring current issues and opportunities into clear focus. Other articles provide contemporary views. In this way past, present, and future perspectives on curriculum planning are provided.

Since the publication of the fourth edition of this book in 1983, *A Nation at Risk,* the report of the National Commission on Excellence in Education, and fourteen other national reform reports have been issued regarding the schools and the university. This onslaught of recommendations is having major impact on curriculum planning. Seven new articles in sections nine and ten are devoted to these reports. They deal with educational excellence and its implications for our work as curriculum planners.

This edition pays increased attention to *future planning* and includes several articles by key leaders in that field. Topics covered include methods of studying the future, education in the microelectronic-information age, the changing work place, the future of the family, schools of the future, and the future university. The microcomputer in the classroom is also the focus of several articles.

Other topics which receive increased emphasis are active learning, learning style, recent brain research, television and values, international education, and new programs for adult learners.

As in the previous editions, the ten major topics are presented as "modules" including prerequisites for the topics, the rationale, objectives stated as performance competencies, a preassessment (which can be used as a diagnostic self test), a postassessment, and alternative additional learning activities. This modular approach allows you to pursue each topic substantially through independent study. However, most college teachers have used this book as the textbook for either large or small group instruction. When used in this way, the numerous additional learning activities provide many alternative resources for class discussion and group or individual research, which are often not so readily available to either the teacher or the students.

Each module is highlighted by carefully selected readings representing the viewpoints of over ninety contributing authors. The readings elaborate on the ten major topics, conveniently offering the reader competing or special perspectives, and expanding on the positions presented in each of the rationales. All of the rationales have been rewritten for this edition, and forty-one new articles are included, most of which have been published during the past two years. Five articles have been written especially for *Curriculum Planning* or have been rewritten by their authors for this book and have not been published elsewhere in their present form. The other articles have been retained for one of two reasons—either they are classics that continue to have unusual merit, or nothing of equal merit on the same topic has been published recently.

Incorporated into each section of the book is an optional case study method of learning that involves the student with real curricula, teaching practices, and school programs. The study of working educational plans, along with the theory and research presented, will facilitate *development of the following performance competencies:*

1. the ability to describe and analyze a curriculum or teaching plan with respect to its relationship to objectives; current and future social aims, forces, and problems; human development knowledge and theories; knowledge about learning styles and how learning occurs; and knowledge of the nature of knowledge and cognition;
2. the ability to formulate and justify a set of criteria for evaluating a curriculum or teaching plan;
3. the ability to identify the various roles in curriculum planning, including the role of the teacher; and
4. the ability to identify, describe, and evaluate currently characteristic features, trends, and innovations of programs of education at all age levels.

Students can demonstrate to themselves the degree to which they have achieved the competencies, either in the preassessment prior to study or in the postassessment for each of the ten major topics.

Each section concludes with problem-oriented, competency-developing additional learning activities for each topic, including a broad selection of problems and projects. Some are intended to stimulate discussion and application of ideas presented in this book. Others identify valuable new sources and resources not available in this book and develop issues that may be explored through their use. The author has encouraged his own students to make selections from these problems and projects for independent study and small-group discussions. These activities then often become the basis for class discussion and presentations.

Also featured are extensive lists of related films, books, and articles that provide additional references on each of the topics covered as well as the most recent sources of particular value. Articles in these lists are largely those that were considered for inclusion in this edition but had to be excluded for want of space. For the most part they too were published during the past two or three years and are therefore excellent choices for additional reading. Books whose titles are included are selected for the additional depth that they can provide on particular topics. A method for making it possible to more easily identify the additional readings related to recent innovations and trends at each curricular level is used in sections 7, 8, 9, and 10.

Acknowledgment is given to the many authors who have granted access to their writings. Their willingness to permit others to republish their ideas is an indication of their dedication to the continuous improvement of curriculum and instruction as a field of study. I wish also to recognize the help given me in many ways in the preparation of this book by my wife, Margaret.

*Curriculum Planning: A New Approach* may be used as a textbook to provide support for many different approaches to curriculum planning at all levels, from elementary to university and adult education. It may also be used as a guide to independent study, with the instructor available as a consultant, adviser, or resource person.

# I

# Bases and Criteria for the Curriculum

# 1

# *Values and Goals*

## RATIONALE

The purpose of the fifth edition of *Curriculum Planning: A New Approach* is to help you develop many of the performance competencies that you need in order to engage in curriculum planning and decision making as a teacher, principal, supervisor, or other curriculum leader. The competencies that you may attain through the resources offered in this book are as follows:

1. To describe and analyze a curriculum or teaching plan with respect to its relationship to (a) current social aims, forces, and problems; (b) human development knowledge and theories; (c) knowledge about how learning occurs; and (d) knowledge of the nature of knowledge.
2. To formulate and justify a set of criteria for evaluating a curriculum or teaching plan.
3. To explain and use the roles of various persons in curriculum planning and change, including teachers, parents, other citizens, specialists in the disciplines, school principals, etc.
4. To identify, describe, and evaluate characteristic features, trends, and innovations of programs of education at all age levels, preschool through the university.
5. To develop skill in integrating the knowledge and using the processes that are required for effective curriculum planning.

Part I, "Bases and Criteria for the Curriculum," will help you perfect the first three performance competencies. Part II, "The Curriculum," will help you attain competency four and continue the development of the first three. The entire book is devoted to the accomplishment of competency five.

You must be a student of society, human development and learning, and knowledge and cognition if you are to be competent in curriculum planning and decision making. You must be able to interrelate your understandings in each of these areas appropriately as you plan programs of education for groups of learners or for an individual learner.

Because this procedure is difficult until you have mastered the knowledge involved, Part I presents social forces, human development, learning, and knowledge and cognition as separate topics. Part I concludes with a section on curriculum criteria that will help to teach you how to interrelate the competencies learned with the objectives of a curriculum or teaching plan.

Part II will help you to use objectives of education, curriculum bases and criteria, and current trends in education in evaluating curriculum plans at all levels of education including elementary, middle, and high school, as well as those in community colleges, universities, and adult education. Even though this may be your first opportunity to study curriculum planning, you should find it possible to begin to develop the competencies involved so that you can describe and analyze curriculum plans at each level and suggest improvements.

At the beginning, you should have answers to the following questions:

1.   What is meant by the term *curriculum?*
2.   What is meant by instruction?
3.   Why are social forces, human development, the nature of learning, and the nature of knowledge and cognition called the "bases of the curriculum"?
4.   What is the purpose of goals and objectives in curriculum planning?
5.   What is meant by "curriculum criteria"?

Each of these questions will now be discussed.

## Curriculum and Instruction: Definitions and Discussion

The word *curriculum* has been used in a variety of ways. It has been used to mean:

1.   A school's written courses of study and other curriculum materials
2.   The subject matter taught to the students
3.   The courses offered in a school
4.   The planned experiences of the learners under the guidance of the school.

The definition of curriculum in this book incorporates all of those definitions and more.

When the term *curriculum* includes all of the planned experiences of the learners under the school's guidance, curriculum and instruction cannot be regarded as separate entities. The learners' planned experiences in the school will, of course, include the planning of instruction by the teachers and the methods used by them in teaching. This is a helpful conceptualization of *curriculum* and *instruction* because it shows clearly that the curriculum bases are important both for guiding decision making in teaching and for curriculum planning and evaluation. The planning of a curriculum and teaching are part of the same process: the planning of learning opportunities and engagements. And the most creative teachers are often those who engage in all the steps of the process—the preplanning of the curriculum and the planning of instruction as well.

When the curriculum is defined as "all of the planned experiences that learners have under the school's guidance," it includes, of course, all school activities and planned school services such as the library, health care, assemblies, the food services and lunchrooms, and field trips. Indeed the school is then seen as a social system designed to provide planned learning experiences for the students who attend the school. All aspects of the learners' school experiences should be examined in terms of the appropriate curriculum bases—social forces, human development, learning, and knowledge and cognition—by the school principal, the teachers, other staff members, and the learners themselves.

But none of these definitions are adequate in terms of present needs and trends. The definition of curriculum we use is this: *The curriculum is all of the experiences that individual learners have in a program of education whose purpose is to achieve broad goals and related specific objectives, which is planned in terms of a framework of theory and research or past and present professional practice.*

The phrase *program of education* has major significance in this definition. It means that the curriculum is a planned program based in part on prepared curriculum materials and planning by teachers and other professional staff members. The words *program of education* are utilized instead of *under the direction of the school* to indicate that the planned experiences may take place in the community, in the learner's home, in a school, or in any other suitable place. This definition emphasizes that all of the following factors should be included in our thinking when we consider the meaning of *curriculum:*

1. The curriculum is preplanned.
2. Planned objectives, and theories and research concerning social forces, human development, learning, and knowledge and cognition should guide the preplanning at all levels including the school system, the school, the instructional group, and the individual learner.
3. Planning of instruction by teachers is a major part of curriculum planning, since it often has greater influence on the learners than the preplanned curriculum, which may be used in part or ignored by the teacher. This is as it should be, since the teacher is usually in a better position to know the learner and the learner's needs than the other persons who engage in preplanning at the na-

tional, state, school system, or school levels. But in planning the instruction, the teacher should be guided by his or her knowledge of planned objectives and of theories and research concerning the four bases of the curriculum and curriculum criteria.

4.      For each learner, the actual curriculum is the learner's experiences as he or she participates in the learning opportunities provided, and as he or she shares in the planning of the program of education.

5.      As the curriculum focuses to a greater extent on programs of education rather than programs of schooling, the teacher's role in the planning becomes increasingly important, since the uniqueness of each individual and of the local community as a classroom becomes more important. In such programs of education, the importance of preplanning flexible arrangements and learning alternatives also increases. To make skillful, professional decisions in such a setting, the teacher should make them in terms of the objectives, bases, and criteria of the curriculum. Programs have failed in the past when teachers and other curriculum planners have failed to recognize the need for adequate planning.

The *framework of theory and research or past and present professional practice* is made part of the definition of the curriculum because it is the presence or absence of this framework of theory that may determine the quality of the curriculum or teaching. Implicit ideas and views about social forces, human development, knowledge and cognition, and learners and learning should be made explicit by each person who engages in curriculum planning. What is implied is professional accountability in the planning of both curricula and instruction.

Definitions of *planned curriculum, instruction, experienced curriculum,* and *curriculum planning* may also be helpful as you use this book:

- *Planned curriculum* is the set of experiences, based on theory, research, and past professional practice, that are designed with and for learners with the purpose of achieving the objectives of the curriculum.
- *Instruction* is the processes, based on theory, research, and past and present professional practice, that are utilized in implementing the curriculum.
- *Experienced curriculum* is the set of actual experiences and perceptions of the experiences that each individual learner has of his or her program of education.
- *Curriculum planning* is the process of gathering, sorting, selecting, balancing, and synthesizing relevant information from many sources in order to design those experiences that will assist learners in attaining the goals of the curriculum. It involves the consideration and use of planned goals and objectives, the four bases of the curriculum, and other curriculum criteria on a multi-dimensional basis.

## The Bases of the Curriculum: Definition and Discussion

In this book we will study the four bases of the curriculum as a major source of guidance for decision making in curriculum planning and the planning of teaching. The four bases are *social forces, human development, the nature of learning,* and *the nature of knowledge and cognition.* Most of Part I is devoted to the study of these four bases and how they should be used in the planning of curricula and teaching.

All civilized societies establish schools and programs of education in order to induct the young into the culture and to transmit the society's culture and values. But today the work of the school must be constantly conducted in the midst of social and economic pressures and changes. Thus, one of the major areas of consideration in all curriculum planning must be *social forces* as reflected in (1) social goals, (2) cultural uniformity and diversity, (3) social pressures, (4) social change, (5) future planning, and (6) concepts of culture.

The graded school and the curriculum organization based on it were adopted in the United States before we knew about human development and individual differences. However, *human development* knowledge and scientific research have been accumulating for more than eighty years. Children are not small adults, we have learned. Human beings are qualitatively different at the different age levels for which we must provide in curriculum planning and in the planning of teaching. Knowledge of human development helps the curriculum planner provide for both age and individual differences among learners. Therefore, knowledge of human development research is an essential aspect of curriculum planning.

Knowledge about the *ways human beings learn* has also been accumulating for approximately eighty years. Because of the complexity of learning and because of individual differences in learning, a number of *theories of learning* have been developed and tested through scientific studies and research during this period. Today the curriculum planner is guided by several approaches to learning that have been described in the theories. Each of the scientific learning theories appears to describe a different kind of learning. There are many differences among learners, and the various learning theories support the development of approaches to curriculum planning that can help to provide for these differences.

Today *knowledge and cognition* must be considered one of the bases of the curriculum. A major question is, What knowledge is of most worth? What to exclude from the curriculum is as difficult to determine as what to include. How shall knowledge be organized in the curriculum? How does each learner seek meaning? How does he or she process information? Curricula should include alternative paths for learning that provide for these differences in cognitive style. A number of theories about knowledge and cognition can assist the curriculum planner in making these decisions.

In the planning of curricula and instruction, we should use what we know about society, human development, learning, and knowledge and cognition. That is why Part I is devoted to assisting you to develop the performance competencies needed to do this planning. This *multi-dimensional approach* to planning will distinguish you, as a professional in curriculum and instructional planning, from other professionals in education such as specialists in human development, learning, the areas of social structure, group sensitivity, knowledge, or educational philosophy (all of whom assist the curriculum planner).

## EMPHASIS ON EACH OF THE BASES IN PLANNING

What degree of emphasis should be placed on each of the four *curriculum bases—social forces, human development, learning,* and *knowledge and cognition*—in curriculum planning? This question should be clearly and carefully examined and regularly reexamined by each curriculum planner and teacher. Most of this section of the book is given to considering this question.

During the past eighty years some curriculum theorists have placed major emphasis on some one of the four bases to the exclusion of the others. The emphasis preferred by particular curriculum leaders has often been determined by that person's value positions or philosophy, or by historical developments.

One of the four curriculum bases has been emphasized to the exclusion of the others at different intervals and periods. Up to the beginning of this century, knowledge and subject matter were the focus of planning. After 1900 the research and study in the new fields of child development, anthropology and sociology, and learning gave rise to an emphasis on each of these areas as the basis of curriculum planning and teaching. The curriculum base emphasized today is sometimes related to the level of the school or the subject-matter being taught. (For a historical treatment of the development of the four bases of curriculum planning, see "Eighty Years of Curriculum Theory" by Hass in Section 6.) In a multi-dimensional approach to planning all four of the bases are considered for their possible contributions toward improving the plan, but they are not necessarily given equal weight or emphasis.

### Curriculum Criteria

A *criterion* is a standard on which a decision or judgment can be based; it is a basis for discrimination. Curriculum criteria are guidelines or standards on which curriculum and instructional decisions can be made.

The planned objectives are among the most significant criteria for developing and evaluating any curriculum plan. This is true regardless of what the objectives are or how they are stated. The four bases of the curriculum should also be used as curriculum criteria in curriculum and instruction planning.

Other criteria are often suggested. Among those most frequently suggested are individual differences, continuity, balance, flexibility, cooperative planning, student-teacher planning, teaching of values, systematic planning, self-understanding, relevance, personalization of instruction, and problem solving. The importance of most or all of these criteria can be derived from the bases of the curriculum. For instance, understanding of social forces, human development, learning theories, and knowledge theories all support the need to provide for individual differences in planning the curriculum.

All four curriculum bases are needed for making decisions that will result in a balanced curriculum. Knowledge about human development is necessary to provide a basis for continuity in learning and for the development of self-understanding.

Knowledge about the nature of knowledge enables the curriculum planner to provide for learning that is useful, or problem oriented, or that can be transferred by the learner from one situation to another. It also assists the planner in providing for individual differences and for balance in the curriculum. Understanding the large and small scale cultures (see "Our Two-Story Culture" in Section 2), as well as social forces, helps the curriculum planner to provide for relevance and the teaching of values. As you study the four bases of the curriculum in the next four sections of this book, you will learn how each of these criteria is related to social forces, human development, learning, and knowledge and cognition.

This variety of emphases should suggest to you the need to develop your own set of criteria for use in planning. Your criteria should reflect your own thinking as well as the particular subject or area of the curriculum with which you are concerned. This should be one of your goals as you study *Curriculum Planning: A New Approach.* You will give more attention to this task as you study the rest of Part I.

## Objectives of a Curriculum Plan or Teaching Plan

The purposes of a curriculum or teaching plan are the most important curriculum criteria. They should provide the first guidelines for determining the learning experiences to be included in the curriculum. Unfortunately, schools commonly lack a comprehensive and reasonably consistent set of objectives on which to base curriculum decisions, and teachers often fail to use a set of objectives to guide their planning for teaching.

Without having a set of objectives clearly in view, teachers and curriculum planners cannot make sound professional judgments. They cannot use their knowledge of the curriculum bases to make choices of content, materials, or procedures that will further student learning toward intended ends. To choose among curriculum alternatives or instructional strategies, educators must know the goals they are seeking and the curriculum bases on which they may make their choices. Otherwise, their selections will be little more than random; the decisions cannot be termed professional in the light of today's knowledge of cultural and social forces, human development and learning, and knowledge and cognition.

Learners should be clearly aware of the objectives being sought by teachers and by the curriculum they are experiencing. In the process of instruction, learners should share in defining the objectives. While the objectives the teacher uses to guide his or her planning and those sought by the learners need not be identical, there should be much overlapping. The teacher's and learners' goals for a learning experience certainly must be understood by both the teacher and the learners, and they must be compatible or they are not likely to be achieved. This sharing of objectives by teachers, curriculum planners, and learners can only be achieved by student-teacher planning. In the article, "Who Should Plan the Curriculum?" in Section 6, Hass states that the student is the "major untapped resource in curriculum planning."

Broad, general goals are needed in planning the objectives of a program of education and for teaching it. Such objectives can then be used to define the need for various courses, activities, and experiences in the community. I have found it useful to think of the broad, general goals as necessarily including goals in four areas: education for *citizenship, vocation, self-realization, and critical thinking*. These four goals can be placed in two broad areas, both of which should always be considered in curriculum planning: *the goals that relate to the society and its values; the goals that relate to the individual learner and his or her talents, needs, interests, and abilities in a changing society.*

In this section Raywid, Tesconi, and Warren identify the school's primary purpose as the "development of intellectual power"; in this they reflect the current dominant demand for excellence in education. They describe the ways in which, since the early 1950s, schools have been through four different eras of reform and criticism—each pulling public education toward purposes different from and sometimes at odds with the purposes of the others. They identify two major sources of educational purpose: values and what we know about the development of individual human beings. By contrast in Section 2, Cremin describes a new "ecology of education" (changes in families, in the domain of work, and in the influence of television), which makes five agenda for the schools more important than ever: literacy in language, numbers, and computers; essential knowledge of the humanities, natural and social sciences, and the arts; the ability to reason, inquire and criticize; a shared awareness of the views and values of others; and the motivations and methods of educational autonomy.

Goals and objectives are properly determined through consideration of the demands of society, the characteristics of the students, and the potential contributions of the various fields of knowledge. Because society, learners, and knowledge are all constantly changing, goals and objectives must change and be restated. The four bases of the curriculum, which you will be studying in the next four sections of this book, should be considered in planning curriculum and instructional goals and objectives.

## Values in Curriculum Planning

In selecting goals and objectives curriculum planners make choices regarding the relative importance given to society, human development, learning and knowledge, and cognition in planning the curriculum. Philosophy enters into every curriculum decision that is made. There is rarely a moment in the school day when a teacher is not confronted with situations in which philosophy is a part of determining the choices that are made. It is one's (usually covert) answers to such questions as "What is the good person?" "What is the good society?" "What is the good life?" that determine action. All curriculum thinking and work is value based.

Four philosophical positions have had major influence on curriculum planners and teachers during the past fifty years—*perennialism, essentialism, progressivism,* and *reconstructionism.* Forty years ago the struggle for influence among these philosophical positions was much more visible than it is today. Because of the significance of values in formulating curriculum goals and selecting learning experiences, and in deciding how to evaluate learning, a statement of each philosophical position by an *influential historical leader for that position* in curriculum planning is included in this section. Robert M. Hutchins represents the perennialists, William C. Bagley the essentialists, William H. Kilpatrick the progressivists, and Theodore Brameld the reconstructionists. The conflict and contrast in their positions will become clear as you read their statements.

John Dewey combined in his *concept of experience* all the elements of curriculum planning—the learner (human development and learning), the society (social forces), and knowledge. In the 1940s, and even at the present time, his followers have tended to emphasize one or another of these bases to the exclusion of the others. In 1938 Dewey was concerned about the ways in which some progressive schools were then focusing on the learner while giving little or no attention to knowledge or the society. In his statement in this section he rejects these "either-or" positions.

Can a curriculum planner be eclectic in using the four philosophical positions? Harold Shane and Bernadine Tabler examine this question in the excerpt from their book.

There must be more than a grain of truth in each of the four philosophical positions, or three of them would have been dropped by scholars long ago. One approach might be to pay more attention to areas of agreement among the positions and less to areas of controversy. Bagley, the essentialist, frequently referred to Dewey as "the greatest educational leader of modern times." Until curriculum planners have established convictions, they should consider all schools of thought. They can better afford to be eclectic and right in some things than to be partisan and wrong in many.

It seems clear to me that the learner, learning, and knowledge should all be considered in curriculum planning since each represents values that are important in a democratic society.

## Curriculum Criteria for Section 1

As previously stated, curriculum criteria are guidelines or standards for curriculum decision making, and the objectives of a curriculum or teaching plan are the most important curriculum criteria, since they should be used in selecting learning experiences and in evaluating learning achievement. Stating the criteria in the form of questions is a good way to bring them into clear focus, and we shall use this method in Sections 1 through 6 of this book. The criterion questions for this section on the objectives of a curriculum or teaching plan are as follows:

1.  Have the goals of the curriculum or teaching plan been clearly stated; and are they used by the teachers and students in choosing content, materials, and activities for learning?
2.  Have the teachers and students engaged in student-teacher planning in defining the goals and in determining how they will be implemented?

3.   Do some of the planned goals relate to the society or the community in which the curriculum will be implemented or the teaching will be done?
4.   Do some of the planned goals relate to the individual learner and his or her needs, purposes, interests, and abilities?
5.   Are the planned goals used as criteria in selecting and developing learning activities and materials of instruction?
6.   Are the planned goals used as criteria in evaluating learning achievement and in the further planning of learning subgoals and activities?

If most of these questions cannot be answered affirmatively, the curriculum planning has probably been inadequate, and steps should be taken to correct the identified deficiencies. The criterion questions again bring into clear focus the fact that teachers are important partners in curriculum planning and that the planning of a curriculum cannot be completed until there are engagements with the learners.

### Summary of Rationale for Section 1

This introduction raises many topics and questions that will be treated in detail throughout the book. The introduction is intended not to settle the questions, but to help you see where we are going together. It is intended also to suggest the ways in which we can professionalize decision making in curriculum planning and teaching.

If excellence is the public's current dominant demand for education (see Raywid, Tesconi, and Warren), then the professional educator must raise questions like the following: What is excellence? Excellence for what purpose? How can it be achieved? How can it be measured? Which is more important—the pursuit or the achievement of excellence? The goal of excellence will be examined in further depth in Section 6 (see article by Duke) and Section 9 (see "Excellence and Standards" in the article by Passow).

If excellence is to be a major goal, its attainment will depend substantially on decisions made by curriculum planners and teachers. A goal of *Curriculum Planning: A New Approach* is to enable you to be professionally accountable when you make these decisions. Such accountability requires that you use objectives, the bases of the curriculum, curriculum criteria, and critical knowledge of trends in decision making. One who is professionally accountable has the ability to use the knowledge, methods and skills that the profession has developed through past experience, theories and research. You are about to begin, or to continue, the development of some of the necessary performance competencies. The first of these competencies is the development and use of curriculum objectives in curriculum planning. Clarifying one's own values in relation to objectives is a part of this competency.

## OBJECTIVES

Your objectives in studying this introduction to *Curriculum Planning: A New Approach* should be as follows:

1. To develop an understanding of the terms *curriculum, instruction, bases of the curriculum,* and *curriculum criteria* that will be of help to you as you study the rest of this book.
2. To begin to examine your own value positions in relation to the perennialist, essentialist, progressivist, and reconstructionist philosophies.
3. To begin to develop the skills and understandings that are needed to use objectives, bases, and curriculum criteria in curriculum and instruction planning, decision making, and evaluation.
4. To be able to analyze a curriculum plan with respect to its statement of goals and objectives for the learners.
5. To be able to suggest changes and improvements in a curriculum plan that are based on an understanding of the functions of statements of goals and objectives in curriculum planning and evaluation.

## PREASSESSMENT

The purpose of the preassessment is to enable you to determine whether you already possess the performance competencies in curriculum planning that are listed in the objectives just mentioned. The following activities will aid you in your evaluation:

1. Develop and defend a statement of the broad goals of education that you would consider appropriate at this time. You can, of course, change your list as your understanding of curriculum planning grows.
2. Explain ways in which the goals you have listed might change the curriculum of a school with which you are familiar.
3. Select any curriculum plan of your choice, at any school level, and examine it in the light of the list of goals and objectives that you have developed. This could be done by visiting and studying a school or by analyzing a written statement regarding the school's program.
4. Examine your list of broad goals in the light of the perennialist, essentialist, progressivist, reconstructionist, and eclectic philosophical positions regarding education. Which position is most compatible with your list of goals?
5. Suggest improvements or changes in the curriculum plan as a result of your analysis in number 3.

Do not be surprised if the curriculum plan of your choice does not appear to have a clear statement of its objectives or goals. Many curriculum plans do not. Suggest improvements in the plan based on the objectives that you believe should be considered in today's world for today's learners.

In answering number 3, you might choose to read "Getting a Headstart on Career Choices" in Section 7 in order to identify the goals of the program as they are stated or implied in the article. Then compare them with your own statement of broad goals. If your list of goals was used in planning the program, would it change it? Would it improve it? How?

## LEARNING ACTIVITIES

To assist you in becoming familiar with current thinking about educational philosophies, goals, and objectives, seven articles are included in this section that present contrasting viewpoints about the goals and objectives of education and changes that may be needed in them. Other learning activities are suggested at the end of this section.

## POSTASSESSMENT

After attempting the preassessment you may do one or more of the following:

1. See your instructor to determine whether he or she believes that you are ready for a postassessment evaluation on goals and objectives of the curriculum. Most students will need further work on this topic.
2. Read the articles in this section and try to determine how the values and goals discussed in each article might be used in curriculum planning and teaching.
3. Prepare a list of the broad goals of the curriculum as you think they might be stated by (1) Hutchins, (2) Kilpatrick, (3) Bagley, and (4) Brameld in this section. After preparing the lists identify the ways in which they differ.
4. Choose additional activities and readings from those listed at the end of this section.
5. With your fellow students, discuss the reading and the work that you have done. The key questions: How would the values and goals you have studied affect a school's curriculum? How do you think they should affect planning for teaching?
6. Summarize the five philosophical positions regarding curriculum values and goals presented in this section—perennialism, essentialism, progressivism, reconstructionism, and eclecticism. Then try to identify your own position and give your reasons for it.
7. When you are ready, ask your instructor for advice on a suitable postassessment for you for this topic. Satisfactory completion of number 1 under Problems and

Projects at the end of this section might be one possibility. Written completion of the preassessment for this section, after completing other learning activities, might be another satisfactory postassessment. Consult your instructor about this. Try to determine whether you can do either or both of these activities before seeing the instructor.

# The Challenge of Purpose

## MARY ANNE RAYWID, CHARLES A. TESCONI, JR., AND DONALD R. WARREN

The purposes of the public school tend to be unarticulated and to exist *ad hoc*, the residue of changes induced by periodic shifts in public preference. Since the early 1950's, in just three decades, public schools have been through no fewer than four different eras of criticism and reform, each pulling the school toward purposes different from, sometimes at odds with the purposes of others.

The first era, the early 1950's, was dominated by a "back to basics" purpose intended to rescind school practices of an earlier period. The second era, launched by Sputnik in 1957, was dominated by math and science innovations which pushed schools in directions different from those of the early 1950's. "Excellence" became our mission then also. The third period, beginning in the mid 1960's, brought a brand of humanism and social consciousness which centered the school in social reform, while seeking to eradicate the practices of the 1950's. With this new orientation, school functions were expanded dramatically. Now in the fourth era, begun in the mid-1970's, we are witnessing a return to the earlier 1950's sort of reforms.

Schools respond as dominant interests demand. More often than not the changes are piecemeal and additive, rather than thoroughgoing. Add-ons to the curriculum surface here and there as part of each new reform cycle. New requirements are invoked and new options made available. New support services are developed and delivered. New school professions are created. Programs which educate school professionals expand accordingly. Because each of these developments represents a constituency, little, if anything, is eliminated. The consequence is a continuing, evolving expansion of school functions and responsibilities, and a mounting confusion of purpose for schools and their critics alike.

Beyond the problems posed by additive reform, another of a different order stems from the way we perceive purpose itself. Schools have always served two logically different types of purpose for people, two distinct orders of intention. The first relates to educational goals as endstates or outcomes to be achieved by students and is the more familiar of the two. Here, school purposes are construed as goals like learning to read

From *Pride and Promise: Schools of Excellence for All the People*. Westbury, New York, American Educational Studies Association, 1984. Used by permission of the authors. Copyright, 1984 by Mary Anne Raywid, Charles A. Tesconi, Jr., and Donald R. Warren.

or knowing about the Civil War or being able to solve algebraic problems at certain levels of intricacy. These kinds of goals or purposes are the sort whose attainment is demonstrated through student performance on standardized tests of academic achievement.

The second kind of purposes we want schools to meet are of quite a different sort, They have to do not with outcomes, but with circumstances along the way, with particular experiences we want youngsters to undergo and with the qualities we want to see reflected in the arrangements and processes the school administers.

Although very prominent in the way Americans feel about schools, this second kind of educational purpose is less understood and discussed than the first. We can all readily understand educational goals as desired outcomes to be achieved. The concept of educational purposes as exposure to particular qualities of experience is more elusive. It addresses not only what one does in school, but the spirit in which it is done, what it means to participants, and priorities to be applied in judging it. When people ask that schools reflect order or discipline or civility or compassion—or excellence—they are enunciating this second kind of educational purpose.

We err in overlooking either of these two types of goals. Both are important to good schools and both are important to public approval of schools. Neither can be reduced to the other, although different eras may seem to try. For example, most current improvement plans call almost exclusively for measurable results, more credits in math and science or higher standardized test scores. In the 1960's, many of the reform designs sought to suffuse schools with humanistic qualities of experiences. Two decades later, increased concern with schools' livability and responsiveness is very much needed. Neither sort of purpose ought to be sacrificed to the other. We do not want "nice" school experiences which lead nowhere and produce little learning; neither, however, do we want pedagogically efficient activities which are physically, psychologically, or morally injurious to children.

The need is now great to identify the necessary and appropriate contributions of the school to the individual and to society. A sense of central and directive purpose is necessary to such a task. Otherwise, it is impossible to decide what schools are supposed to do, unfair to evaluate and judge their performance, difficult to hold their personnel accountable, foolhardy to educate professionals to staff them, and illusory to initiate reforms. *Accordingly, the articulation of an overall purpose for the public school is the most important educational challenge of the day.*

Purpose must not evolve and endure *ad hoc.* That, we have seen, leads to disaster. Purpose must be framed by principles which derive from values and ideals central to the public that supports and consumes schooling. In the United States, democracy is the most important among all the possible philosophical and political sources from which public school purpose can be derived. American public schools have not always satisfied democracy's needs nor aided fully in the realization of its promise. But surely past lapses cannot absolve schools of responsibility for continually and aggressively pursuing the goals of democracy. After all, American public schooling was born out of democracy, and without it our democracy is inconceivable.

American democracy's major goal is to encourage and support individuals in becoming the best persons they are capable of becoming. This goal derives from those central tenets of democracy most pertinent to education. These include:

- freedom to be an individual, to dissent, to grow and to pursue one's own dreams are inalienable human rights.

- human capacities and freedoms are realizable in a society which seeks to protect and nourish them.
- humans have the capacity to devise institutions which honor the equal rights of all.
- a society which nourishes and protects human capacities and freedoms depends upon individual commitment to responsible participation in it.
- humans have the capacity to learn from and to improve themselves as a result of experience.
- it is both possible and morally obligatory to think for oneself.

From these tenets derive several commitments: to individual autonomy; to tested knowledge and experience in preference to the edict of vested authority; to earned, not inherited, social position; to individual dignity and personal liberty; and to responsible citizenship. A society founded on these principles and beliefs must sustain institutions which ensure the development of valued human capacities, the primacy of the individual, and a consensual commitment to democracy and to its way of life. Hence, public schooling.

The commitments of democracy suggest a number of directions for public schools. Freedom to be an individual, to realize personal autonomy, to develop and exercise one's capacities, to grow and pursue one's dreams, to develop one's distinct identity, to relate responsibly to others, and to exercise responsible citizenship— all of these speak to the need for cultivating individuality. None of this denies the need for extensive commonality. It does not mean that schooling must or can satisfy *all* of the needs and develop *all* the capacities unique to each student. Nor can schooling be left simply as a matter of personal preference. Indeed, many of the skills and learnings important to realizing individual potential are acquisitions important for all. Also,

the importance of shared knowledge and values, relatedness and concern for others, and the exercise of responsible citizenship reveal the imperative need for some commonality, some shared attributes of the schooling experience.

Moreover, a democratic commitment demands a pedagogy which does more than effectively transmit the cultural heritage, extant bodies of knowledge, or vocational skills. It must teach students how to think, how to order their own affairs rationally, how to function as competent citizens and how to accept, value, and respect others. It must develop the exercise of those capacities central to understanding one's own interests, those of others, and how to effect decisions.

It is not only our socio-political commitments which must undergird American education. What we know about the development of individual human beings must also play a formative role in the shaping of educational purpose.

All people need to acquire and exercise those *cognitive capacities* associated with understanding. The ability to extract data from experience—from vicarious experience such as books, or from direct experience—is acquired fairly early in life. The more sophisticated intellectual processes—the ability to reflect on, to interpret, and to analyze the data one has acquired—appear to depend even more on specific cultivation. These more intricate intellectual skills do not emerge naturally or automatically simply as a product of human growth. The school must deliberately foster them or trust that some other institution will. The evidence suggests that only half our population is arriving at the full set of adult intellectual capacities that should become available to all during adolescence. If the school is to equip all young people to understand and respond appropriately to the practical challenge of managing their own lives, it must concentrate on the development and expansion of intellectual capacity. Thus, curricula, policy, and practice in schools must be prominently associated with cognitive development.

Establishing an *identity,* and an awareness of that identity, is also a fundamental task of human development. It is during adolescence that one's sense of self is likely to take near final shape. This is a matter of both personality and character formation. One's personal vision of the world, which frames the individual as a moral actor, tends to become set during the years that mark schooling. At this stage young adults should arrive at a realistic sense of what they are, want, and need, what they are obligated to, and what their prospects are. The sense of self thus forged will subsequently serve as the individual's personal criterion for decisions and life choices. If they have a stake in what individuals become, schools cannot try to evade responsibility for helping youngsters achieve and accommodate to a realistic sense of who they are. Curricula, policies, and practice should all reflect the major contribution of the school to this particular aspect of development.

One's essential *relatedness* to other human beings is another crucial phase of development fairly well completed by the entrance to young adulthood. The success with which this dimension of growing up is accomplished will determine not only the individual's capacity for forming close personal associations; it will also govern his or her sense of connectedness to other human beings. This has become one of the most serious challenges of our time. There are few individual achievements more important to the survival of our way of life, perhaps, indeed, to *any* way of life, than a cultivated sense of connectedness to other human beings. It is the absence of just such a sense which is reflected in the most brutal of adolescent crimes; and on a larger scale, it is the absence of such a sense that enables mature adults to entertain serenely the possibility of surviving global nuclear war. Formal education has a vital part to play in the development of the emerging adult's relatedness to

other human beings. Fulfillment of that role constitutes a major function of the school.

A final task of growing up which deserves serious attention in schools is the challenge of helping individuals to establish themselves as *autonomous human beings*. It involves the development of an individual sense of appropriate behavior, and the deliberate cultivation of judgment. It is unreasonable to expect school graduates to behave responsibly unless they have learned to exercise the judgment that yields such behavior and to practice the examining and choosing of alternative courses of action. Regrettably, the ability to make wise decisions is not an automatic developmental accomplishment. If we want adults who can arrive at and execute informed decisions, the ability to do so must be systematically nurtured and tried out. If we want adults who can outgrow the bonds of their own personal dependency, and who are capable of the freedom a democratic society expects them to exercise, the school must explicitly concern itself with the development of individual autonomy.

Clearly, there are numerous other developmental tasks which human beings must accomplish. The development of cognitive power, identity, relatedness, and autonomy are, however, the most central to the school's purpose. Two fundamentally important characteristics must be noted about these four tasks. The first is that they constitute a set. Consider the connection between the development of cognitive ability and individual identity, relatedness, and autonomy: human intelligence is the connecting thread. Cultivation of the individual's ability as meaning-maker, analyst, and synthesizer makes possible the self-consciousness to explore and articulate an identity; generates the awareness of others that permits the role shift that is identification with other human beings; and facilitates the deliberation that is the core of genuine autonomy. Thus it appears that the cultivation of intelligence is a cornerstone or common denominator of these four key developmental tasks.

The second characteristic to be noted about these four dimensions of maturation is that they complement those central tenets of democracy identified earlier. The pride of the democratic tradition is that it need force no choice in principle between the interests of the individual and those of society. It seeks to serve *both* and to serve the one *by* serving the other. It is the sense of just this mutuality of individual and social interest which is perhaps one of the greatest losses of the late 20th century. The school could do much to restore it, as both faith and reality, and indeed, this should be a central part of public education's mission.

Both individual interests and the nation's most fundamental commitments recommend that the school's primary purpose be the development of intellectual power. This transcending goal must infuse the culture of the school. It must be translated into curricula which acknowledge that student performance below certain levels of literacy means lifelong disadvantage, that skill acquisition below certain levels means limited opportunities and mortgaged futures. It must be reflected in the way schools are organized and the way in which *all* people therein are treated. It must also suffuse the content and the activities through which schools seek to carry out the several quite different functions parents want them to fulfill:

- *academic* functions, which address the transmission and creation of knowledge and the acquisition of intellectual skills;
- *social/civic* functions, which address preparation for responsible citizenship and participation in society;
- *personal* functions, which address the development of responsible individuality, creativity and freedom of expression; and
- *vocational* functions, which address preparation for productive work and economic self-sufficiency.

John Goodlad found parents to want schools to fulfill all four of these sets of functions, with no more than half being willing to agree on any one of them as primary. As Goodlad concluded, the American public "wants it all." Given the demands life imposes on each of us, such expectations make sense. It is possible, however, and necessary to find a connecting thread to permeate our treatment and guide our approach to all of them. We find that thread in the unifying purpose of contributing to human fulfillment by enriching and strengthening the intellectual power of our children and young people.

*Mary Anne Raywid* is Professor of Foundations of Education at Hofstra University, Hempstead, New York.
*Charles A. Tesconi, Jr.* is Dean of the College of Education and Social Services at the University of Vermont.
*Donald R. Warren* is Chairman of the Department of Educational Policy, Planning, and Administration at the University of Maryland.

# The Organization and Subject-Matter of General Education

## ROBERT M. HUTCHINS

I assume that we are all agreed on the purpose of general education and that we want to confine our discussion to its organization and subject-matter. I believe that general education should be given as soon as possible, that is, as soon as the student has the tools and the maturity it requires. I think that the program I favor can be experienced with profit by juniors in high school. I therefore propose beginning general education at about the beginning of the junior year in high school. Since I abhor the credit system and wish to mark intellectual progress by examinations taken when the student is ready to take them, I shall have no difficulty in admitting younger students to the program if they are ready for it and excluding juniors if they are not.

The course of study that I shall propose is rigorous and prolonged. I think, however, that the ordinary student can complete it in four years. By the ingenious device I have already suggested I shall be able to graduate some students earlier and some later, depending on the ability and industry that they display.

General education should, then, absorb the attention of students between the ages of fifteen or sixteen and nineteen or twenty. This is the case in every country of the world but this. It is the case in some eight or nine places in the United States.

If general education is to be given between the beginning of the junior year in high school and the end of the sophomore year in college and if a bachelor's degree is to signify the completion of it, the next question is what is the subject-matter that we should expect the student to master in this period to qualify for this degree.

I do not hold that general education should be limited to the classics of Greece and Rome. I do not believe that it is possible or desirable to insist that all students who should have a general education must study Greek and Latin. I do hold that tradition is important in education; that its primary purpose, indeed, is to help the student understand the intellectual tradition in which he lives. I do not see how he can reach this understanding unless he understands the great books of the western world, beginning with Homer and coming down to our own day. If anybody can suggest a better method of accomplishing the purpose, I shall gladly embrace him and it.

Nor do I hold that the spirit, the philosophy, the technology, or the theology of the Middle Ages is important in general education. I have no desire to return to this period any more than I wish to revert to antiquity. Some books written in the Middle Ages seem to me of some consequence to mankind. Most Ph.D.'s have never heard of them. I should like to have all students read some of them. Moreover, medieval scholars did have one insight; they saw that in order to read books you had to know how to do it. They developed the techniques of grammar, rhetoric, and logic as methods of reading, understanding and talking about things intelligently and intelligibly. I think it can not be denied that our students in the highest reaches of the university are woefully deficient in all these abilities

From an address presented at the annual convention of the National Association of Secondary School Principals at Atlantic City, New Jersey, February 26, 1938. Used by permission of the National Association of Secondary School Principals.

today. They cannot read, write, speak, or think. Most of the great books of the western world were written for laymen. Many of them were written for very young laymen. Nothing reveals so clearly the indolence and inertia into which we have fallen as the steady decline in the number of these books read in our schools and colleges and the steady elimination of instruction in the disciplines through which they may be understood. And all this has gone on in the sacred name of liberalizing the curriculum.

The curriculum I favor is not too difficult even for ordinary American students. It is difficult for the professors, but not for the students. And the younger the students are the better they like the books, because they are not old enough to know that the books are too hard for them to read.

Those who think that this is a barren, arid program, remote from real life and devoid of contemporary interest, have either never read the books or do not know how to teach. Or perhaps they have merely forgotten their youth. These books contain what the race regards as the permanent, abiding contributions its intellect and imagination have made. They deal with fundamental questions. It is a mistake to suppose that young people are interested only in football, the dramatic association, and the student newspaper. I think it could be proved that these activities have grown to their present overwhelming importance in proportion as the curriculum has been denatured. Students resort to the extracurriculum because the curriculum is stupid. Young people are interested in fundamental questions. They are interested in great minds and great works of art. They are, of course, interested in the bearing of these works on the problems of the world today. It is, therefore, impossible to keep out of the discussion, even if the teacher were so fossilized as to want to, the consideration of current events. But these events then take on meaning; the points of difference and the points of similarity between then and now

can be presented. Think what a mine of references to what is now going on in the world is Plato's "Republic" or Mill's "Essay on Liberty." If I had to prescribe an exclusive diet for young Americans, I should rather have them read books like these than gain their political, economic, and social orientation by listening to the best radio commentators or absorbing the *New York Times*. Fortunately, we do not have to make the choice; they can read the books and listen to the commentators and absorb the *New York Times,* too. I repeat: these important agencies of instruction—the radio and the newspaper—and all other experiences of life, as a matter of fact—take on intelligibility as the student comes to understand the tradition in which he lives. Though we have made great advances in technology, so that the steam turbine of last year may not be of much value in understanding the steam turbine of 1938, we must remember that the fundamental questions today are the same with which the Greeks were concerned; and the reason is that human nature has not changed. The answers that the Greeks gave are still the answers with which we must begin if we hope to give the right answer today.

Do not suppose that in thus including the ancients in my course of study I am excluding the moderns. I do not need to make a case for the moderns. I do apparently need to remind you that the ancients may have some value, too.

Do not suppose, either, that because I have used as examples the great books in literature, philosophy and the social sciences, I am ignoring natural science. The great works in natural science and the great experiments must be a part and an important part of general education.

Another problem that has disturbed those who have discussed this issue is what books I am going to select to cram down the throats of the young. The answer is that if any reasonably intelligent person will conscientiously try to list the one hundred most important books that have ever been written I will accept his list. I feel safe in doing this because (a) the books would all be worth reading, and (b) his list would be almost the same as mine. There is, in fact, startling unanimity about what the good books are. The real question is whether they have any place in education. The suggestion that nobody knows what books to select is put forward as an alibi by those who have never read any that would be on anybody's list.

Only one criticism of this program has been made which has seemed to me on the level. That is that students who can not learn through books will not be able to learn through the course of study that I propose. This, of course, is true. It is what might be called a self-evident proposition. I suggest, however, that we employ this curriculum for students who can be taught to read and that we continue our efforts to discover methods of teaching the rest of the youthful population how to do it. The undisputed fact that some students can not read any books should not prevent us from giving those who can read some the chance to read the best there are.

I could go on here indefinitely discussing the details of this program and the details of the attacks that have been made upon it. But these would be details. The real question is which side are you on? If you believe that the aim of general education is to teach students to make money; if you believe that the educational system should mirror the chaos of the world; if you think that we have nothing to learn from the past; if you think that the way to prepare students for life is to put them through little fake experiences inside or outside the classroom; if you think that education is information; if you believe that the whims of children should determine what they should study—then I am afraid we can never agree. If, however, you believe that education should train students to think so that they may act intelligently when they face new situations; if you regard it as important for them to understand the tradition in which they live; if you feel that the present educational program leaves something to be desired because of its "progressivism," utilitarianism, and diffusion; if you want to open up to the youth of America the treasures of the thought, imagination, and accomplishment of the past—then we can agree, for I shall gladly accept any course of study that will take us even a little way along this road.

*Robert M. Hutchins* was both President of the University of Chicago and Head of the Center for the Study of Democratic Institutions. He edited the *Great Books of the Western World* (1952) and championed the need to preserve the intellectual traditions of Western culture.

# The Case for Essentialism in Education
## WILLIAM C. BAGLEY

What kind of education do we want for our children? Essentialism and Progressivism are terms currently used to represent two schools of educational theory that have been in conflict over a long period of time—centuries in fact. The conflict may be indicated by pairing such opposites

From *Today's Education: Journal of the National Education Association* 30, no. 7 (October 1941): 201–202. Used by permission of the publisher.

as: effort vs. interest; discipline vs. freedom; race experience vs. individual experience; teacher-initiative vs. learner-initiative; logical organization vs. psychological organization; subjects vs. activities; remote goals vs. immediate goals; and the like.

Thus baldly stated, these pairings of assumed opposites are misleading, for every member of every pair represents a legitimate—indeed a needed—factor in the educative process. The two schools of educational theory differ primarily in the relative emphasis given to each term as compared with its mate, for what both schools attempt is an integration of the dualisms which are brought so sharply into focus when the opposites are set off against one another.

The fundamental dualism suggested by these terms has persisted over the centuries. It appeared in the seventeenth century in a school of educational theory the adherents of which styled themselves the "Progressives." It was explicit in reforms proposed by Rousseau, Pestalozzi, Froebel, and Herbart. It was reflected in the work of Bronson Alcott, Horace Mann, and later of E. A. Sheldon and Francis W. Parker; while the present outstanding leader, John Dewey, first came into prominence during the 1890s in an effort to resolve the dualism in his classic essay, now called "Interest and Effort in Education."

## PROBLEMS OF AMERICAN EDUCATION

The upward expansion of mass education first to the secondary and now to the college level, has been an outcome not alone of a pervasive faith in education, but also of economic factors. Power-driven machinery, while reducing occupations on routine levels, opened new opportunities in work for which general and technical training was essential. That young people should seek extended education has been inevitable. In opening highschools and colleges to ever-increasing

numbers, it was just as inevitable that scholastic standards should be reduced. Theories that emphasized freedom, immediate needs, personal interest, and which in so doing tended to discredit their opposites—effort, discipline, remote goals—naturally made a powerful appeal. Let us consider, in a few examples, these differences in emphasis.

**1.** *Effort against Interest*—Progressives have given the primary emphasis to interest, and have maintained that interest in solving a problem or in realizing a purpose generates effort. The Essentialists would recognize clearly enough the motivating force of interest, but would maintain that many interests, and practically all the higher and more nearly permanent interests grow out of efforts to learn that are not at the outset interesting or appealing in themselves. If higher interests can grow out of initial interests that are intrinsically pleasing and attractive, well and good; but if this is not the case, the Essentialists provide a solution for the problem (at least, with some learners) by their recognition of discipline and duty—two concepts which the Progressives are disposed to reject unless discipline is self-discipline and duty self-recognized duty.

**2.** *Teacher against Learner Initiative*—Progressive theory tends to regard teacher-initiative as at best a necessary evil. The Essentialist holds that adult responsibility for the guidance and direction of the immature is inherent in human nature—that it is, indeed, the real meaning of the prolonged period of necessary dependence upon the part of the human offspring for adult care and support. It is the biological condition of human progress, as John Fiske so clearly pointed out in his essay, "The Meaning of Infancy." The Essentialists would have the teachers responsible for a systematic program of studies and activities to develop the recognized essentials. Informal learning through experiences initiated by the learners is important, and abundant opportunities for such experiences should be provided; but informal learning should be regarded as supplementary rather than central.

**3.** *Race against Individual Experience*—It is this plastic period of necessary dependence that has furnished the opportunities for inducting each generation into its heritage of culture. The cultures of primitive people are relatively simple and can be transmitted by imitation or by coming-of-age ceremonies. More highly organized systems of education, however, become necessary with the development of more complicated cultures. The need of a firmer control of the young came with this development. Primitive peoples pamper and indulge their offspring. They do not sense a responsibility to provide for their own future, much less for the future of their children. This responsibility, with its correlative duty of discipline, is distinctly a product of civilization. The Progressives imply that the "child-freedom" they advocate is new, whereas in a real sense it is a return to the conditions of primitive social life.

**4.** *Subjects against Activities*—The Essentialists have always emphasized the prime significance of race-experience and especially of organized experience or culture—in common parlance, *subject-matter*. They have recognized, of course, the importance of individual or personal experience as an indispensable basis for interpreting organized race-experience, but the former is a means to an end rather than an educational end in itself. The Progressives, on the other hand, have tended to set the "living present" against what they often call the "dead past." There has been an element of value in this position of the Progressives, as in many other of their teachings. Throughout the centuries they have been protestants against formalism, and especially against the verbalism into which bookish instruction is so likely to degenerate. Present-day Essentialists clearly recognize these dangers.

**5.** *Logical against Psychological Organization*—The Essentialists recognize, too, that the organization of experience in the form of subjects involves the use of large-scale concepts and meanings, and that a certain proportion of the members of each generation are unable to master these abstract concepts. For immature learners and for those who never grow up mentally, a relatively simple educational program limited in the earliest years of childhood to the most simple and concrete problems must suffice. This the Essentialists (who do not quarrel with facts) readily admit. The tendency throughout the long history of Progressivism, however, has been to discredit formal, organized, and abstract learnings *in toto,* thus in effect throwing the baby out with the bath, and in effect discouraging even competent learners from attempting studies that are "exact and exacting."

## WHAT ABOUT FAILURE?

The Essentialists recognize that failure in school is unpleasant and that repetition of a grade is costly and often not effective. On the other hand, lack of a stimulus that will keep the learner to his task is a serious injustice to him and to the democratic group which has a stake in his education. Too severe a stigma has undoubtedly been placed upon school failure by implying that it is symptomatic of permanent weakness. By no means is this always the case. No less a genius than Pasteur did so poorly in his efforts to enter the Higher Normal School of Paris that he had to go home for further preparation. One of the outstanding scientists of the present century had a hard time in meeting the requirements of the secondary school, failing in elementary work of the field in which he later became world-famous.

## WHAT ARE THE ESSENTIALS?

There can be little question as to the essentials. It is no accident that the arts of recording, computing, and measuring have been among the first concerns of organized education. Every civilized society has been founded upon these arts, and when they have been lost, civilization has invariably collapsed. Nor is it accidental that a knowledge of the world that lies beyond one's immediate experience has been among the recognized essentials of universal education, and that at least a speaking acquaintance with man's past and especially with the story of one's country was early provided for in the program of the universal school. Investigation, invention, and creative art have added to our heritage. Health instruction is a basic phase of the work of the lower schools. The elements of natural science have their place. Neither the fine arts nor the industrial arts should be neglected.

## ESSENTIALISTS ON DEMOCRACY

The Essentialists are sure that if our democratic society is to meet the conflict with totalitarian states, there must be a discipline that will give strength to the democratic purpose and ideal. If the theory of democracy finds no place for discipline, then before long the theory will have only historical significance. The Essentialists stand for a literate electorate. That such an electorate is indispensable to its survival is demonstrated by the fate that overtook every unschooled democracy founded as a result of the war that was "to make the world safe for democracy." And literacy means the development and expansion of ideas; it means the basis for the collective thought and judgment which are the essence of democratic institutions. These needs are so fundamental that it would be folly to leave them to the whim or caprice of either learner or teacher.

## SUMMARY OF THE CASE FOR ESSENTIALISM

To summarize briefly the principal tenets of the present-day Essentialists:

**1.** Gripping and enduring interests frequently, and in respect of the higher interests almost always, grow out of initial learning efforts that are not intrinsically appealing or attractive. Man is the only animal that can sustain effort in the face of immediate desire. To deny to the young the benefits that may be theirs by the exercise of this unique human prerogative would be a gross injustice.

**2.** The control, direction, and guidance of the immature by the mature is inherent in the prolonged period of infancy or necessary dependence peculiar to the human species.

**3.** While the capacity for self-discipline should be the goal, imposed discipline is a necessary means to this end. Among individuals, as among nations, true freedom is always a conquest, never a gift.

**4.** The freedom of the immature learner to choose what he shall learn is not at all to be compared with his later freedom from want, fraud, fear, superstition, error, and oppression—and the price of this latter freedom is the effortful and systematic mastery of what has been winnowed and refined through the long struggle of mankind upward from the savage—and a mastery that, for most learners, must be under guidance of competent and sympathetic but firm and exacting teachers.

**5.** Essentialism provides a strong theory of education; its competing school offers a weak theory. If there has been a question in the past as to the kind of educational theory that the few remaining democracies of the world need, there can be no question today.

*William C. Bagley* was Professor of Education, Teachers College, Columbia University. He believed that education should preserve a body of essential knowledge. His philosophy is contained in *Education and Emergent Man* (1934).

# The Case for Progressivism in Education
## WILLIAM HEARD KILPATRICK

The title of this article is the editor's. The writer himself questions whether labels as applied to a living and growing outlook may not do more harm than good. Still, for certain purposes, a name is desirable. In what follows the writer tries to state his own position in a way to seem fair and true to that growing number who approve the same general outlook.

**1.** The center and nub of what is here advocated is that we start with the child as a growing and developing person and help him live and grow best; live now as a child, live richly, live well; and thus living, to increase his effective participation in surrounding social life so as to grow steadily into an ever more adequate member of the social whole.

Among the signs that this desirable living and consequent growth are being achieved, two seem especially significant. One is child happiness—for best work is interested work, and to be zestfully interested and reasonably successful is to be happy. The other, less obvious, but highly desirable is that what is done now shall of itself continually sprout more of life, deeper insights bringing new suggestions with new desires to pursue them.

**2.** The second main point has to do with learning and how this best goes on so as most surely to come back helpfully into life. For the test of learning is whether it so builds mind and character as to enhance life.

Two types of learning must here be opposed, differing so much in degree as to amount to a difference in kind. In one the learner faces a situation of his own, such that he himself feels inwardly called upon to face it; his own interests are inherently at stake. And his response thereto is also his own; it comes out of his own mind and heart, out of his own very self. He may, to be sure, have had help from teacher or book, but the response when it comes is his.

With the other kind of learning, the situation is set by the school in examination or recitation demands. This accordingly seems to the typical learner as more or less artificial and arbitrary; it does not arise out of his own felt needs. Except for the school demands there would be no situation to him. His response to this hardly felt situation is itself hardly felt, coming mainly out of words and ideas furnished by the textbook or, with older students, by the professor's lectures.

This second, the formal school kind of learning, we all know. Most of us were brought up on it. Except for those more capable in abstract ideas, the learning thus got tends to be wordy and shallow. It does little for mind or heart, and possibly even less for character, for it hardly gets into life.

The first kind has great possibilities. We may call it life's kind. It furnishes the foundation for the type of school herein advocated. Since what is learned is the pupil's own response to a situation felt to be his own, it is at once both heartfelt and mind-created. It is learned as it is lived; in fact, it is learned because it is lived. And the more one's heart is in what he does, the more important (short of too painful solicitude) it is to him, the more impelling will be the situation he faces; and the stronger accordingly will be his response and in consequence the stronger the learning. Such learning comes from deeper

From *Today's Education: Journal of the National Education Association* 30, no. 8 (November 1941):231–232. Used by permission by the publisher.

down in the soul and carries with it a wider range of connection both in its backward and in its forward look.

If we take the verb "to live" in a full enough sense, we may then say that, by definition, *learning has taken place when any part or phase of experience, once it has been lived, stays on with one to affect pertinently his further experience*. And we assert that *we learn what we live and in the degree that we live it*.

A further word about the school use of this life-kind of learning may help. Suppose a class is studying Whittier's "Barefoot Boy." I as teacher cannot hand over appreciation to John, nor tell it to him, nor can I compel him to get it. He must in his own mind and heart see something in the poem that calls out in him approval and appreciation. He must first respond that way before he can learn appreciation. Learning here is, in fact, the felt appreciation so staying with John as to get into his mind and character and thence come out appropriately into his subsequent life.

It is the same way with any genuinely moral response attitude. I cannot compel it. John must first feel that way in his own heart and accept it as his way of responding. Such an acceptance on John's part fixes what is thus learned in his character there to stay till the right occasion shall bring it forth again in his life. As it is accepted, so is it learned.

It is the same with ideas. These can be learned only as they are first lived. I cannot simply give John an idea, no matter how skillful I am with words. He may read and I may talk, but he has to respond *out of his own mind* with the appropriate idea as his own personal insight. He has to *see it* himself; something has to *click* inside him; the idea has to come from within, with a certain degree of personal creative insight, as his response to the problematic situation. Otherwise he hasn't it even tho he may fool himself and us by using the appropriate words. I as teacher may help John to see better than otherwise he would, and his fellow pupils and I may help him make

up his own mind and heart more surely to the good, but he learns only and exactly his own response as he himself accepts this as his way of behaving.

We may sum all this up in the following words: *I learn my responses, only my responses, and all my responses, each as I accept it to act on. I learn each response in the degree that I feel it or count it important, and also in the degree that it interrelates itself with what I already know. All that I thus learn I build at once into character.*

The foregoing discussion makes plain once more how the presence of interest or purpose constitutes a favorable condition for learning. Interest and felt purpose mean that the learner faces a situation in which he is concerned. The purpose as aim guides his thought and effort. Because of his interest and concern he gets more wholeheartedly into action; he puts forth more effort; what he learns has accordingly more importance to him and probably more meaningful connections. From both counts it is better learned.

**3.** Each learner should grow up to be a worthy member of the social whole. Thus to grow up means to enter more fully and responsibly into the society of which one is a member and in so doing to acquire ever more adequately the culture in terms of which the group lives.

The school exists primarily to foster both these aspects of growing up. The older type school, holding itself relatively secluded within its own four walls, shut its pupils off from significant contact with actual surrounding life and instead had them learn words about life and about the actual culture. The newer school aims explicitly to have its pupils engage actively in life, especially in socially useful work within the community, thus learning to manage life by participation in life, and acquiring the culture in life's varied settings where alone the culture is actually at work.

**4.** The world in which we live is changing at so rapid a rate that past-founded knowledge no longer suffices. Intelligent thinking and not mere habit must henceforth rule. Youth must learn better to think for themselves. They must understand the why of our institutions, of our system of legal rights, of moral right and wrong—because only then can they use these essential things adequately or change them intelligently. The newer school thus adds to its learning by living the further fact of pervasive change and undertakes to upbuild its pupils to the kind of thoughtful character and citizenship necessary for adequate living in such a changing social world. The older school cared little either for living or for change. Stressing book study and formal information and minimizing presentday problems, it failed to build the mind or character needed in modern life.

5. The curriculum, where pupil and teacher meet, is of necessity the vital focus of all educational theory.

The older curriculum was made in advance and given to the teacher who in turn assigned it as lessons to the pupils. It was a bookish content divided into separate subjects, in result remote from life. The pupils in their turn "learned" the lessons thus assigned and gave them back to the teacher in recitation or examination, the test being (in the main) whether what was given back was the same as what had been given out. Even the few who "succeeded" on this basis tended to get at best a pedantic learning. The many suffered, being denied the favorable opportunity for living sketched above. The lowest third suffered worst; such a curriculum clearly did not fit them, as becomes now more obvious with each advance of school leaving age.

The newer curriculum here advocated is first of all actual living—all the living of the child for which the school accepts responsibility. As we saw earlier, the child learns what he actually lives and this he builds at once into character. The quality of this living becomes then of supreme importance. The school, as we say, exists precisely to foster good living in the children, the

kind of living fit to be built into character. The teacher's work is to help develop and steer this desirable living. This kind of curriculum, being real child living, cannot be made in advance and handed down either to teachers or to pupils. Living at the external command of another ceases by that much to be living for the person himself and so fails to meet desirable learning conditions.

The curriculum here sought is, then, built jointly by pupils and teacher, the teacher remaining in charge, but the pupils doing as much as they can. For these learn by their thinking and their decisions. The teacher helps at each stage to steer the process so as to get as rich living and, in the long run, as all-round living as possible. The richness of living sought includes specifically as much of meaning as the children can, with help from teacher and books, put into their living, meanings as distinctions made, knowledge used, considerations for others sensed, responsibilities accepted. The all-roundedness refers to all sides and aspects of life, immediately practical, social-moral, vocational, esthetic, intellectual. To base a curriculum on a scheme of set subjects is for most children to feed them on husks; the plan here advocated is devised to bring life to our youth and bring it more abundantly.

6. Are we losing anything in this new type school?

a. Do the children learn? Yes. Read the scientific studies (Wrightstone's, for example, and Aikin's report on the Thirty Schools*) and see that the evidence is overwhelming. The "tool subjects" are learned at least as well, while the others depending on initiative and creative thinking are learned better. Honesty is much better built.

b. Does the new plan mean pupils will not use books? Exactly no; they do now show far

---

* See Books and Articles to Review at the end of this section.

more actual use of books. Textbooks as such will decrease perhaps to nothing, but the use of other books will appreciably increase, as experience already well shows.

**c.** Will children be "spoiled" by such a regime? Exactly no. For character building, this kind of school far surpasses the old sit-quietly-at-your-desk type of school. Modern psychology is well agreed that one cannot learn what one does not practice or live. The school here advocated offers abundant opportunity to associate on living terms with others and to consider them as persons. The schoolroom of the older school, in

the degree that it succeeded with its rules, allowed no communication or other association except through the teacher. Accordingly, except for a kind of negative morality, it gave next to no chance to practice regard for others. The discipline of the school here advocated is positive and inclusive, consciously provided by the school, steered by the teacher, and lived by the pupils. Prejudiced journalists have caricatured the liberty as license; intelligent observation of any reasonably wellrun school shows exactly the contrary. This discipline is emphatically the constructive kind.

*William H. Kilpatrick* was Professor of Education, Teachers College, Columbia University. He has often been called "the father of progressive education." His philosophy was presented in several books including *Education for a Changing Civilization* (1926) and *Selfhood and Civilization* (1941).

# A Cross-Cutting Approach to the Curriculum: The Moving Wheel

## THEODORE BRAMELD

A number of presuppositions must underlie a cross-cutting approach to the curriculum. Let me merely sketch several of these presuppositions.

**1.** The prime responsibility of the curriculum on any level, but most focally on the lagging senior high school and undergraduate college levels, is the confrontation of young people with the array of severe, indeed ominous, disturbances that now beset the "naked ape" himself.

**2.** These disturbances are by no means of exclusive concern to the "social studies." Rather, they pervade every aspect of human life across

the planet—whether we are thinking either of the political, economic, esthetic, moral, and religious, or of the so-called "objective" sciences and skills of, say, chemistry, botany, and mathematics. Nothing that man has begun to understand or to utilize can any longer be considered as separable from the crucial roles that he now plays, and the extraordinary obligations that these roles entail.

**3.** The interpenetrating, interfusing, and evolving character of nature, including human nature, compels us to recognize the universality of the critical period through which we are pass-

Excerpted from *Phi Delta Kappan* 51, no. 7 (March 1970):346–348. © 1970, Phi Delta Kappa, Inc. Used by permission of the publisher.

ing. And education, in turn, is compelled to create new models of the curriculum that express and dramatize this universality.

**4.** By the same token, the new curriculum models and applications of them in experimental practice repudiate and supersede the entire conventional structure of subjects and subdivisions of knowledge that, for much too long a time, have reflected a grossly outworn, atomistic model of both the universe and man.

**5.** The legitimate place that special subjects and skills occupy in transformed conceptions of the curriculum undergoes its own metamorphosis. The part no more remains merely a part than does the heart or the hand when it becomes dissevered from the total human body.

**6.** To follow the same metaphor another step, the human species requires abundant opportunity to reach inward, outward, and upward toward increasing fulfillment of its ever-developing powers both individually and cooperatively. To the degree that men are denied this opportunity, life becomes a failure for them. When education is not completely geared to this same purpose, it too becomes a failure.

**7.** The necessarily comprehensive presuppositions that we have made above apply, as norms, to any period of culture and history. But they apply with peculiar urgency to our own period. Fearful warnings, often heard, that the birth of the twenty-first century may never be attended by any historian, because no historian will have survived on our planet thirty years hence, are not warnings that any serious-minded citizen, much less any serious-minded educator, can conscientiously ignore. Unless, of course, he chooses to scoff at such an absurdity.

I am aware that each of these bald statements could be refined and supplemented almost endlessly. Nevertheless, for purposes of discussion, I intend to point directly toward one prospective design for a secondary school curriculum constructed upon the bases that they provide. This is not at all to claim that only one defensible curriculum is possible. It is to claim, however, that models at least comparable to this model should be pulled off the drawing boards and put to the test.

What are the interrelated problems and issues that illustrate the educational agenda inherent in our several presuppositions? I shall state them, again baldly, and without pretense of either order of priority or novelty. They do, however, serve as catalysts for the model to follow.

1. Can the ordinary human being conceivably hope to approach anywhere near optimal fulfillment of his own capacities in the face of accelerating technologized and depersonalized forces?

2. Can the ordinary human being develop a sense of inner personal tranquility and harmony amidst the alienating, divisive, disillusioning experiences by which he is constantly bombarded?

3. Does one (that is, you or I) hold substantial expectations of maintaining any deep sense of relationship with others (that is, with one's mate or family, with one's friends or associates) either amidst chronic instabilities or under the aegis of the folk belief of modern Western culture that self-interest (however "enlightened") still remains the only "realistic" justification for one's daily conduct?

4. Can neighborhoods and other relatively homogeneous communities learn to work together in attacking their own difficulties, in acting concertedly to remove them, and in achieving even a modicum of well-planned, cooperatively organized programs of constructive change?

5. Can racial, ethnic, and other disadvantaged minorities learn to act similarly both among themselves and with other groups of differing backgrounds?

6. It is actually plausible to expect that hu-

man conflicts—for example between the sexes, the generations, and socio-economic classes—can be ameliorated by more humane, viable patterns of living and working?

7. Can religious institutions, with all their rigidities of custom and tradition, still find ways to emulate the same general processes suggested above?

8. Can we reasonably aspire to the expectation that nations will find powerful means to conquer and control the ever-advancing threat of human annihilation?

9. Can the fine arts become a vastly wider, richer experience of unique as well as communal creativity for people across the globe, to be shared freely and openly among diverse cultures?

10. Can communication, in every form (such as travel) and through every medium (such as television), occur without restriction or intimidation not only within but between nations?

11. Can the sciences become equally available to all men, devoted to their welfare and advancement (for example, through the sciences of human health or of the control and growth of natural riches), without depletion and decay?

12. Can economic and accompanying political establishments be rebuilt so that people in every part of the earth have access to and become the exclusive directors of (through their chosen representative) physical and human resources?

13. Can a converging awareness and unity of mankind as one species—a species with unique, life-affirming, life-controlling powers—be achieved, and will this awareness and unity prove translatable into workable guidelines for political, scientific, esthetic, religious direction and renewal?

14. Can education, finally, direct its attention and energy not only toward the past or toward the present of man's experience, but even more persistently and painstakingly toward man's future as well?

That this agenda is far from all-inclusive is surely obvious. Each question could proliferate into dozens of others; indeed, students themselves, stimulated by mankind-oriented teachers, could and should raise innumerable others. All of these questions, moreover, invite explorations into learning not only by means of books and laboratories; above all, they invite firsthand involvement in the experiences of people in nearby or more distant communities who frequently share the same kinds of questions and seek the same kinds of answers.

To approach the problem somewhat more directly, what does all this mean for the organization and operation of the cross-cutting curriculum? It is possible again to summarize only a number of potentialities. According to this normative model:

1. A minimum of one-half of the entire time devoted to the curriculum is spent outside the classroom—in the laboratory of direct participation with people and institutions, and always with the close support of teacher-consultants equipped to deal with whatever situations or issues have been selected for analysis and prognosis.

2. The circumference of this kind of participation is as wide as the earth, extending all the way from the family and neighborhood outward to the region, nation, and eventually to distant nations. Learning therefore occurs *directly* through intra- and international travel (let us not be deluded by financial bugaboos; more than adequate funds are available if we insist upon them enough), and *vicariously* through films, the fine arts, and contact with experts such as anthropologists. There are countless other resources.

3. "Team teaching," so often applied adventitiously these days, is supplanted by flexible part-

nerships of interdisciplinary study, research, and field involvement.

4. The structure of the curriculum may be symbolized (I have developed this proposal at length elsewhere) in the form of a moving "wheel." The "rim" is the unifying theme of mankind—its predicaments and its aspirations. The "hub" is the central question of any given period of learning (perhaps extending over one week, perhaps a semester), while the "spokes" are the supporting areas of concentrated attention that bear most directly upon each respective question. The "spokes" may thus be termed "courses" in art, science, foreign language, or any other pertinent subject or skills. But these are not to be construed as *mere* courses. At all times they are as supportive of the "hub" as it is of them.

5. To the extent that a particular student discovers whatever special interests and talents he may possess, the individual is given every opportunity to develop fields of concentration in his own "spoke." Never is he encouraged to do so, however, for the sake of completing a "major" or passing "college entrance examinations," or other dubious appendages of conventional school systems.

The normative target of this theme is, I contend, far more "practicable" than are most of those advocated in the name of "practicality."

This is so because a cross-cutting curriculum of the kind I urge meets the ever more insistent demands of young people for audacious, unconventional, but directly meaningful experiences in both learning and action.

If it is to succeed, students themselves should, of course, share throughout in the planning and implementation of each year's program. Jointly with their teachers, they should decide what issues are most significant to concentrate upon in a selected period. They should help to pre-plan each successive year. They should take heavy responsibilites for all field involvements both in arranging and in following them through. They should support the deviant student who may not always be interested in "problems" at all, but rather in his own "thing" (music, for example). They should engage in the dialogic process of learning that demonstrates (as Martin Buber has so brilliantly urged) how it is possible to face the profound dilemmas of human existence through the mutualities of shared emotion, reflection, and aggressive action.

I suggest, in short, that the time is long overdue when theories of the integrative curriculum should be revived and reconstructed. The trend among influential curriculum experts who have managed during the post-progressive-education period to reverse those theories should itself now be reversed.

*Theodore Brameld* is Emeritus Professor of Education, Boston University, and the leading proponent of the reconstructionist philosophy, which encourages schools to take an activist position regarding social problems. His "wheel curriculum" was originally described in his book, *Patterns of Educational Philosophy* (1950). He also coined the terms, "perennialism," "essentialism," "progressivism," and "reconstructionism" and introduced them in that book.

# Traditional vs. Progressive Education

## JOHN DEWEY

Mankind likes to think in terms of extreme opposites. It is given to formulating its beliefs in terms of *Either-Ors,* between which it recognizes no intermediate possibilities. When forced to recognize that the extremes cannot be acted upon, it is still inclined to hold that they are all right in theory but that when it comes to practical matters circumstances compel us to compromise. Educational philosophy is no exception. The history of educational theory is marked by opposition between the idea that education is development from within and that it is formation from without; that it is based upon natural endowments and that education is a process of overcoming natural inclination and substituting in its place habits acquired under external pressure.

At present, the opposition, so far as practical affairs of the school are concerned, tends to take the form of contrast between traditional and progressive education. If the underlying ideas of the former are formulated broadly, without the qualifications required for accurate statement, they are found to be about as follows: The subject-matter of education consists of bodies of information and of skills that have been worked out in the past; therefore, the chief business of the school is to transmit them to the new generation. In the past, there have also been developed standards and rules of conduct; moral training consists in forming habits of action in conformity with these rules and standards. Finally, the general pattern of school organization (by which I mean the relations of pupils to one another and to the teachers) constitutes the school a kind of institution sharply marked off from other social institutions. Call up in imagination the ordinary schoolroom, its time-schedules, schemes of classification, of examination and promotion, of rules of order, and I think you will grasp what is meant by "pattern of organization." If then you contrast this scene with what goes on in the family for example, you will appreciate what is meant by the school being a kind of institution sharply marked off from any other form of social organization.

The three characteristics just mentioned fix the aims and methods of instruction and discipline. The main purpose or objective is to prepare the young for future responsibilities and for success in life, by means of acquisition of the organized bodies of information and prepared forms of skill which comprehend the material of instruction. Since the subject-matter as well as standards of proper conduct are handed down from the past, the attitude of pupils must, upon the whole, be one of docility, receptivity, and obedience. Books, especially textbooks, are the chief representatives of the lore and wisdom of the past, while teachers are the organs through which pupils are brought into effective connection with the material. Teachers are the agents through which knowledge and skills are communicated and rules of conduct enforced.

I have not made this brief summary for the purpose of criticizing the underlying philosophy. The rise of what is called new education and progressive schools is of itself a product of discontent with traditional education. In effect it is a criticism of the latter. When the implied criticism is made explicit it reads somewhat as follows: The traditional scheme is, in essence,

From John Dewey, *Experience and Education,* pp. 1–10 (New York: The Macmillan Co., 1938), a Kappa Delta Pi Lecture. © Kappa Delta Pi. Used by permission.

one of imposition from above and from outside. It imposes adult standards, subject-matter, and methods upon those who are only growing slowly toward maturity. The gap is so great that the required subject-matter, the methods of learning and of behaving are foreign to the existing capacities of the young. They are beyond the reach of the experience the young learners already possess. Consequently, they must be imposed; even though good teachers will use devices of art to cover up the imposition so as to relieve it of obviously brutal features.

But the gulf between the mature or adult products and the experience and abilities of the young is so wide that the very situation forbids much active participation by pupils in the development of what is taught. Theirs is to do—and learn, as it was the part of the six hundred to do and die. Learning here means acquisition of what already is incorporated in books and in the heads of the elders. Moreover, that which is taught is thought of as essentially static. It is taught as a finished product, with little regard either to the ways in which it was originally built up or to changes that will surely occur in the future. It is to a large extent the cultural product of societies that assumed the future would be much like the past, and yet it is used as educational food in a society where change is the rule, not the exception.

If one attempts to formulate the philosophy of education implicit in the practices of the newer education, we may, I think, discover certain common principles amid the variety of progressive schools now existing. To imposition from above is opposed expression and cultivation of individuality; to external discipline is opposed free activity; to learning from texts and teachers, learning through experience; to acquisition of isolated skills and techniques by drill, is opposed acquisition of them as means of attaining ends which make direct vital appeal; to preparation for a more or less remote future is op-

posed making the most of the opportunities of present life; to static aims and materials is opposed acquaintance with a changing world.

Now, all principles by themselves are abstract. They become concrete only in the consequences which result from their application. Just because the principles set forth are so fundamental and far-reaching, everything depends upon the interpretation given them as they are put into practice in the school and the home. It is at this point that the reference made earlier to *Either-Or* philosophies becomes peculiarly pertinent. The general philosophy of the new education may be sound, and yet the difference in abstract principles will not decide the way in which the moral and intellectual preference involved shall be worked out in practice. There is always the danger in a new movement that in rejecting the aims and methods of that which it would supplant, it may develop its principles negatively rather than positively and constructively. Then it takes its clew in practice from that which is rejected instead of from the constructive development of its own philosophy.

I take it that the fundamental unity of the newer philosophy is found in the idea that there is an intimate and necessary relation between the processes of actual experience and education. If this be true, then a positive and constructive development of its own basic idea depends upon having a correct idea of experience. Take, for example, the question of organized subject-matter—which will be discussed in some detail later. The problem for progressive education is: What is the place and meaning of subject-matter and of organization *within* experience? How does subject-matter function? Is there anything inherent in experience which tends towards progressive organization of its contents? What results follow when the materials of experience are not progressively organized? A philosophy which proceeds on the basis of rejection, of sheer opposition, will neglect these questions. It will tend to suppose that because the old education was based on ready-made organization, therefore it suffices to reject the principle of organization *in toto*, instead of striving to discover what it means and how it is to be attained on the basis of experience. We might go through all the points of difference between the new and the old education and reach similar conclusions. When external control is rejected, the problem becomes that of finding the factors of control that are inherent within experience. When external authority is rejected, it does not follow that all authority should be rejected, but rather that there is need to search for a more effective source of authority. Because the older education imposed the knowledge, methods, and the rules of conduct of the mature person upon the young, it does not follow, except upon the basis of the extreme *Either-Or* philosophy, that the knowledge and skill of the mature person has no directive value for the experience of the immature. On the contrary, basing education upon personal experience may mean more multiplied and more intimate contacts between the mature and the immature than ever existed in the traditional school, and consequently more, rather than less, guidance by others. The problem, then, is how these contacts can be established without violating the principle of learning through personal experience. The solution of this problem requires a well thought-out philosophy of the social factors that operate in the constitution of individual experience.

What is indicated in the foregoing remarks is that the general principles of the new education do not of themselves solve any of the problems of the actual or practical conduct and management of progressive schools. Rather, they set new problems which have to be worked out on the basis of a new philosophy of experience. The problems are not even recognized, to say nothing of being solved, when it is assumed that it suffices to reject the ideas and practices of the old education and then go to the opposite extreme. Yet I am sure that you will appreciate what is meant when I say that many of the newer schools tend to make little or nothing of organized subject-matter of study; to proceed as if any form of direction and guidance by adults were an invasion of individual freedom, and as if the idea that education should be concerned with the present and future meant that acquaintance with the past has little or no role to play in education. Without pressing these defects to the point of exaggeration, they at least illustrate what is meant by a theory and practice of education which proceeds negatively or by reaction against what has been current in education rather than by a positive and constructive development of purposes, methods, and subject-matter on the foundation of a theory of experience and its educational potentialities.

*John Dewey* was Professor of Philosophy, Emeritus, Columbia University. He was the most influential American thinker of his time, and his philosophy, writing, and teaching profoundly affected educational theory and practice, philosophy, psychology, law, and political science. His ideas were adopted and often distorted by the "progressive education" movement. He protested these distortions in the book from which this article was taken, *Experience and Education* (1938).

# Complexities of Curriculum Planning for Tomorrow's World

## HAROLD G. SHANE WITH M. BERNADINE TABLER

Educators responsible for the climate of learning in our schools are charged with the unique and challenging task of developing and revising curriculum content in a time of turbulence. Therefore, we hope that this inventory of basic concepts for coping with the future will prove useful.

*The spectrum of choices before us.* We present and interpret six options, any one of which might serve as a value base for curriculum development. The six alternative approaches to curriculum planning that we have selected are:

1. The regressive option—return to some of the values and practices that have been discarded.
2. The conservative option—leave things as they are.
3. The liberal option—adopt changes that are mandated by a changing society.
4. The experimental option—create new educational designs.
5. The regenerative option—adopt new approaches to learning experiences.
6. The eclectic option—any one or any combination of the above might be the best option.

*The regressive option* is based on the assumption that discipline and intellectual rigor, which will be required for the future, have deteriorated and that cognitive development has been superseded by a concern for social and affective development. Furthermore, motivation has been lost because "hard" subject matter and competitive grading have been replaced by equalitarian, life-adjustment programs where presumably everyone is a winner. One outcome has been impairment in the quality of secondary education, as reflected in declining test scores. Colleges have, as a result, become less intellectual in their emphases.

The regressive option would seek to restore the high standards associated with an intellectually elitist era, which prevailed in the British grammar schools of yesteryear or in U.S. private schools, where programs were rigidly determined by college admission requirements. Its proponents argue that the projected outcome of this option would be a higher output of persons prepared to cope with tomorrow because of their substantive knowledge and leadership abilities.

*The conservative option* is designed to preserve those qualities that its supporters suggest are the best of present instructional practices—"to try nothing for the first time." Also included in this option is the continuing quest for basic literacy skills. The major difference between the regressive and the conservative positions is that the former stresses an elitist approach while the latter emphasizes basic education for all.

*The liberal option* is sometimes accused by its critics of deemphasizing academic content. However, its proponents stress practices that improve the performance of all learners by recognizing individual differences, psychosocial needs, and meaningful learning. Advocates of

Excerpted from *Educating for a New Millennium*, a Phi Delta Kappa Special Publication, pp. 6–12, 138. © 1981, Phi Delta Kappa Educational Foundation. Used by permission of the authors and the publisher.

liberal option education often tend to utilize innovative and sometimes untested practices.

*The experimental option,* in addition to accepting liberal option practices, encourages the creation and validation of novel approaches to the improvement of teaching and learning, attempts to design curriculum around real world needs, and seeks to bring about certain social reforms to assure equitable educational opportunity.

The advocates of both liberal and experimental approaches tend to reject the elitist and competitive stance of the regressive option as well as the "status quo policy" of the conservatives. Instead, they methodically seek new or promising ideas and endeavor to generate and implement experimental or innovative practices.

*The regenerative option* is concerned with radical change. The term implies a substantial reform or reestablishment of educational practices and learning experiences. While advocates of the liberal and experimental options are likely to conceptualize good education as today's education with its problems removed, the proponents of the regenerative option see education for the future in radically new or different forms.

*The eclectic option* selects a combination of various doctrines, beliefs, or practices, depending on the age of the learners, their individual differences, the subject matter, or the socioeconomic and cultural background of the group. Thus, in a given situation, it is conceivable that an eclectic option might comprise aspects of regressive, experimental, and regenerative practices! Such a blending of seemingly contradictory options is actually consistent, according to its proponents, because an eclectic approach inherently involves selecting what appears likely to comprise the best combination.

Curriculum literature is rife with in-group terminology. Figure 1 and its accompanying notes are intended to clarify the curriculum options in the form of a taxonomic chart that compares the above classification with three additional classifications by well known persons in the field of curriculum theory.

This summary of curriculum options is offered to help educators extend their thinking about curriculum change and to begin thinking in terms of appropriate options to foster better learning for living on a rapidly changing planet.

## CHOOSING AMONG CONFLICTING CURRICULUM CONCEPTIONS

In view of the educational directions for the 1980s, some choice seems almost inevitable. It probably will be the eclectic option, one that uses the best positive aspects of all five of the alternatives presented.

Indeed, there is much to support the eclectic option for a future-focused curriculum. The cultural heritage from the past, represented by the durable perennialist choice, cannot be discarded. At the same time, there are many positive aspects of U.S. education today that should be retained as noted by Ralph Tyler[1] in his 1981 essay on academic performance. What is working well in the curriculum should be retained.

Nor is it mere conciliatory rhetoric to point out that there is a place for the liberal position with its psychosocial, humanistic view of the learner, and for the experimental position that, during the twentieth century, has helped to enrich the teaching profession through the work of such able practitioners as Helen Parkhurst, Flora Cook, Carleton W. Washburne, and the staff of the Eight Year Study conducted by the Progressive Education Association. It is also simple common sense to recognize that an all-out drive to remodel U.S. education totally in the short-term future is impossible. Changes during the next decade that will endure are likely to be made by those who already are working within

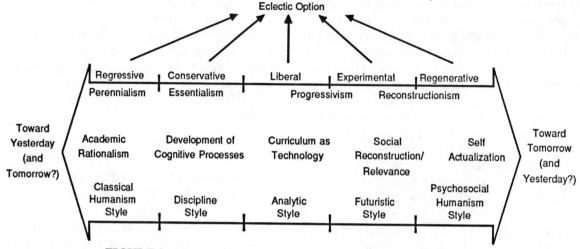

**FIGURE 1**
The taxonomy of curriculum options

Theodore Brameld identified the following options some thirty years ago: 1) perennialism, to designate those who see "perenially contemporary" values in the cultural heritage (e.g., Robert M. Hutchins, Mortimer Adler, Stringfellow Barr); 2) essentialism, which emphasizes basic education (e.g., William Bagley, Henry C. Morrison, Arthur Bestor); 3) progressivism, to label the early proponents of open education (e.g., Carleton W. Washburne); and 4) reconstructionism, which considers schooling as a means of developing a "new social order" (e.g., George S. Counts, Theodore Brameld, and more recently such prophets of reform as Ivan Illich).

Elliot Eisner and Elizabeth Vallance (1974) use the following terms to distinguish conflicting curriculum conceptions: 1) academic rationalism, 2) development of cognitive processes, 3) curriculum as technology, 4) social reconstruction/relevance, and 5) self-actualization/consummatory experience.[2]

Donald E. Orlosky and B. Othanel Smith (1978) use the following terms: 1) the classical humanism style, 2) the discipline style, 3) the analytic style and 4) the futuristic style, and psychosocial humanism style (associated with Abraham H. Maslow and Carl Rogers).[3]

the established educational community. This leaves us with the eclectic choice that permits the educator to create a desirable amalgam of the several virtues of all the curriculum conceptions.

In summary, there is need for a reasonably paced and continuous educational transformation based on the best features of past and present practices recast and supplemented by the demands the future will impose.

## ENDNOTES

1. See Ralph W. Tyler, "The U.S. versus the World: A Comparison of Educational Performance," *Phi Delta Kappan*, January 1981, pp. 307–310.
2. Eisner, Elliot and Vallance, Elizabeth (Eds.). *Conflicting Conceptions of Curriculum*. Berkeley, CA: McCutchen Pub. Corp., 1974.
3. Orlosky, Donald E. and Smith, B. Othanel (Eds.). *Curriculum Development: Issues and Insights*. Chicago: Rand McNally College Pub. Co., 1978.

*Harold G. Shane* is University Professor of Education, Indiana University, Bloomington.
*M. Bernadine Tabler* is Project Associate, Phi Delta Kappa Diamond Jubilee Project.

## ADDITIONAL LEARNING ACTIVITIES

### Problems and Projects

1. Begin to develop a "case problem" about one school and the curriculum and teaching in that school. (You will find a suggested outline for the writing of such a case problem in the Appendix of this book.) Try to identify the school's objectives as they now are (whether they are clearly stated or not). Then try to write the objectives as you think they should be. You can add to this case study as you work on each of the bases of the curriculum and the criteria in the next five sections of this book.

2. List the broad general goals of education as you think they might be listed by each of the following authors in this section: Hutchins, Bagley, Kilpatrick, and Brameld. Compare each of these lists of goals to the "school's primary purpose" and the four "quite different functions parents want school to fulfill," as they are described in a current statement by Raywid, Tesconi, and Warren in this section. How are they alike? How do they differ?

3. After reading the articles in this section, prepare your own statement of the broad general goals of education. Which of the philosophical positions best represents your statement of goals?

4. Review the discussion and the definitions of curriculum and instruction in this section. Then look for definitions of these terms in other books. It is suggested you see the following:
   Beane, James A.; Toepfer, Jr., Conrad F.; and Alessi, Jr., Samuel J. *Curriculum Planning and Development* (Boston: Allyn and Bacon, Inc., 1986): 30–35.
   J. Galen Saylor, William M. Alexander, and Arthur J. Lewis, *Curriculum Planning for Better Learning and Teaching*, 4th ed. (New York: Holt, Rinehart and Winston, 1981): 3–8.
   Schubert, William H., *Curriculum: Perspective, Paradigm, Possibility* (New York: Macmillan Publishing Co., 1986): 26–34, 40–43, 46–51.

5. According to Raywid, Tesconi, and Warren, there are two major sources to be considered in the formation of educational purpose. What are these two sources? They also identify two "logically different types of purpose" that schools serve. Which type do they consider to be most important? Examine your own position. Do you share their views about the sources and types of purpose?

6. Contrast the sources of goals as they are defined by Cremin in Section 2 with the sources as they are explained by Raywid, Tesconi, and Warren in this section. Which of the four curriculum bases are emphasized in each article?

7. Study the objectives of any curriculum plan of your choice and try to determine whether they seem to be "subject-centered," "society-centered," or "learner-centered." Which do you think they should be? Which philosophical position is closest to each of these three approaches to curriculum goals? Discuss your thinking on this with other students.

8. There have been many important statements about the goals of education in the past forty or fifty years, each of which has influenced thinking on this topic. The best-known past statement of broad goals has been called the "Seven Cardinal Principles of Education," which was issued by the Commission on Reorganization of Secondary Education, U.S. Office of Education, *Cardinal Principles of Secondary Education,* Bulletin No. 35 (Washington, D.C.: Government Printing Office, 1918). The seven goals in that statement included the following: health; command of fundamental processes; worthy home membership; vocation; civic education; worthy use of leisure; ethical character. Other leading statements of broad goals from the past include the following:

   • Educational Policies Commission, *The Unique Function of Education in American Democracy* (Washington, D. C.: National Education Association, 1937).
   • Educational Policies Commission, *The Purposes of Education in American Democracy* (Washington, D.C.: National Education Association, 1938).
   • Educational Policies Commission, "Imperative Educational Needs of Youth," in *Education for All American Youth* (Washington, D.C.: National Education Association, 1944), pp. 225–226.
   • John W. Gardner, "National Goals in Education," in *Goals for Americans, The Report of the President's Commission on National Goals* (Englewood Cliffs, New Jersey: Prentice-Hall, 1960), pp. 81–103.

   Find these books in your library and compare these statements of goals and objectives with those found in this section. How have the goals changed? In what respects have they remained the same?

9. In 1936, the National Education Association and the American Association of School Administrators created the Educational Policies Commission "to clarify the major current issues facing public education and direct the efforts toward their solution." One of its first publications, *The Purposes of Education in American Democracy* (see Books to Review at the end of this section), listed four major purposes for education: the objectives of self-realization, human relationship, economic efficiency, and civic responsibility. Next to the "Seven Cardinal Principles," this is the best-known of the goal statements of the past. It has been described as "reflecting eclecticism at its best." Review the statement in a copy of the book and then relate it to the four philosophies of education that are presented in this section. Then explain why this statement of purposes is described as eclectic.

10. *Education for Freedom,* by Harold M. Schroder et al. (New York: John Wiley & Sons, 1973), argues that education must prepare learners to deal with freedom if

democracy is to survive in this age. It can do this only by teaching them *how to think*—a capacity not to be confused with the amount of knowledge they acquire. The authors have developed a model for process learning in which learners move from level one thinking—categorical thinking—to level six, which is multi-conceptual thinking. Read this book to determine how a curriculum might be planned to seek this objective of education according to this model. (One student who read this book recently commented: "This book should be read as a whole; it is brief and compelling.")

11. In 1970 *Crisis in the Classroom* was published (New York: Random House), in which Charles E. Silberman charges that a chief problem regarding education is the refusal by society as well as educators to think seriously about educational purposes—that schools today are characterized by mindlessness. Read the first chapter of this book (pp. 3–12) to determine what Silberman believes the goals of education should be. Then you might wish to read *Reactions to Silberman's "Crisis in the Classroom,"* edited by A. Harry Passow (Worthington, Ohio: Charles A. Jones Publishing Co., 1971), in which seven educators examine Silberman's ideas, and Silberman responds. After reading these sources, write your own critique of Silberman's ideas on objectives and goals and relate it to your own goals statement.

12. The Appendix of this book includes a list of books, each of which describes a school or school program. Select one that interests you and determine the goals and objectives of the curriculum described. Suggest changes you think should be made in the objectives of that school or school program.

13. Have your personal views about the goals and objectives of education changed as a result of your experience with this section? If so, state what change has taken place, and relate it to one or more of the activities in this section (the rationale, an article, a postassessment activity, etc.) Compare your ideas with those of the other members of your class.

## Books and Articles to Review

*On Curriculum Goals and Objectives*

Aikin, Wilford M. *The Story of the Eight-Year Study.* New York: Harper and Brothers, 1942.

Bailey, Stephen. *The Purposes of Education.* Bloomington, IN: Phi Delta Kappa Educational Foundation, 1976.

Bakalis, Michael J. "Power and Purpose in American Education." *Phi Delta Kappan* 65, no. 1 (September 1983): 7–13.

Blanke, Virgil; and Grady, Marilyn. "On Schooling for a Well Society." *Educational Forum* 47, no. 4 (Summer 1983): 445–452.

Bloom, Benjamin, ed. *Taxonomy of Educational Objectives: The Classification of Educational Goals, Handbook I: Cognitive Domain.* New York: David McKay Co., 1956.

Butts, R. Freeman. "The Search for Purpose in American Education." *Today's Education* 65 (March-April 1976): 77–82, 84–85.

Commission on the Reorganization of Secondary Education. *Cardinal Principles of Secondary Education.* Washington, D.C.: U.S. Government Printing Office, 1918, Bulletin No. 35.

Cross, K. Patricia. "The Rising Tide of School Reform Reports." *Phi Delta Kappan* 66, no. 3 (November 1984): 167–172.

Derr, Richard L. *A Taxonomy of Social Purposes of Public Schools.* New York: David McKay Co., 1973.

Educational Policies Commission, National Education Association. *The Education of Free Men in American Democracy.* Washington, D.C.: NEA, 1941.

———— *The Purposes of Education in American Democracy.* Washington, D.C.: NEA, 1938.

———— National Education Association. *Social Responsibility in a Free Society.* Washington, D.C.: NEA, 1963.

———— *The Unique Function of Education in American Democracy.* Washington, D.C.: NEA, 1937.

Eisner, Elliot. "The Kind of Schools We Need." *Educational Leadership* 41, no. 2 (October 1983): 48–55.

Fantini, Mario D. "Adapting to Diversity—Future Trends in Curriculum." *NASSP Bulletin* 69, no. 481 (May 1985): 15–22.

Goodlad, John. "The Great American Schooling Experiment." *Phi Delta Kappan* 67, no. 4 (December 1985): 266–271.

Harrow, Anita J. *A Taxonomy of the Psychomotor Domain.* New York: David McKay Co., 1972.

Krathwol, David; Bloom, Benjamin; and Masia, Bertram. *Taxonomy of Educational Objectives: The Classification of Educational Goals, Handbook II: Affective Domain.* New York: David McKay Co., 1956.

McDaniel, Thomas R., "Inquiries Into Excellence: A Reexamination of a Familiar Concept." *Educational Forum* 49, no. 4 (Summer, 1985): 389–396.

Ornstein, Allan C. "How Do Educators Meet the Needs of Society: How Are Education's Aims Determined?" *NASSP Bulletin* 69, no. 481 (May 1985): 36–47.

Sewall, G. T. "Against Anomie and Amnesia: What Basic Education Means In the Eighties." *Phi Delta Kappan* 63, no. 9 (May 1982): 603–606.

Swanchek, John; and Campbell, James R., "Conservatives and the Curriculum." *Educational Forum* 47, no. 2 (Winter 1983): 175–189.

Wrightstone, J. Wayne. *Appraisal of Experimental High School Practices.* New York: Teachers College, Columbia University, 1936.

Wrightstone, J. Wayne. *Appraisal of Newer Elementary School Practices.* New York: Teachers College, Columbia University, 1938.

## On Educational Philosophers and Philosophies

Bagley, William C. *Education and Emergent Man.* New York: The Macmillan Co., 1934.

Bode, Boyd H. *Democracy as a Way of Life.* New York: The Macmillan Co., 1937.

Brameld, Theodore. *Patterns of Educational Philosophy.* Yonkers-on-Hudson, N. Y. World Book Co., 1950.

Counts, George S. *Dare the Schools Build a New Social Order?* Carbondale, Ill.: Southern Illinois University Press, 1978 (originally published in 1932).

Dewey, John. *Democracy and Education.* New York: The Macmillan Co., 1916.

———— "My Pedagogic Creed." pp. 629–638 in Ulich, Robert (Ed.). *Three Thousand Years of Educational Wisdom: Selections from Great Documents,* 2nd Ed. Cambridge, MA: Harvard University Press, 1954.

Dykhuizen, George. *The Life and Mind of John Dewey.* Carbondale, Ill.: Southern Illinois University Press, 1973.

Gutek, Gerald L. *Basic Education: A Historical Perspective.* Phi Delta Kappa Fastback no. 167. Bloomington, Ind.: Phi Delta Kappa, 1981.

Handlin, Oscar. *John Dewey's Challenge to Education.* New York: Harper and Brothers, 1959.

Hook, Sidney. *Education for Modern Man.* New York: The Dial Press, 1946.

Hutchins, Robert M. *The Learning Society.* New York: F. A. Praeger Co., 1968.

Kandel, I. L. *William Chandler Bagley: Stalwart Educator.* New York: Bureau of Publication, Teachers College, Columbia University, 1961.

Kilpatrick, William H. *Remaking the Curriculum.* New York: Newson and Co., 1936.

Kliebard, Herbert M. *The Struggle for the American Curriculum, 1893–1958.* New York: Routledge and Kegan Paul/Methuen, Inc., 1986.

Lauderdale, William B. *Progressive Education: Lessons from Three Schools.* Phi Delta Kappa Fastback no. 166. Bloomington, Ind.: Phi Delta Kappa, 1981.

Schubert, William H. *Curriculum: Perspective, Paradigm, and Possibility.* New York: Macmillan Publishing Co., 1986.

Sewell, G. T. "Against Anomie and Amnesia: What Basic Education Means in the Eighties." *Phi Delta Kappan* 63, no. 9 (May 1982): 603–606.

Wallace, James M. "The Assault on Public Education: A Deweyan Response." *Phi Delta Kappan* 64, no. 1 (September 1982): 57–58.

# 2

# *Social Forces: Present and Future*

## PREREQUISITE

Reading Section 1 of this book.

## RATIONALE

To understand schools and school systems, one must relate them to the surrounding cultural, economic, historical, philosophical, and political circumstances. Since education is always an expression of a civilization and of a political and economic system, schools must harmonize with the lives and ideas of people in a particular time and place. Since the social environment today is in a state of change, descriptions of society in the nineteenth century or in the sixties or seventies no longer suffice. As a major element in curriculum planning and teaching, present social forces and future trends must be regularly reconsidered.

Today we are faced with a crisis of purpose such as we never faced in the past. Perhaps it is because of our seeming inability to control our technology or the weight of corporate or bureaucratic power that often seems to override individual rights and public interests. The western democracies seem to have moved from a climate of continuity and certainty ("the future belongs to us") to one of danger and recurrent crisis.

Behind these dilemmas are other major issues and trends: environment, changing values and morality, the family, the microelectronics revolution, the changing world of work, equal rights, urban and suburban crises, crime and violence, alienation and anxiety, and international tensions. All of these changes and trends have profound implications for education, curriculum planning, and teaching.

**1.** *Environment.* People have become increasingly proficient in their attempt to control and use nature for their safety, comfort, and convenience. Scientific and technological advances and the increased industrialization of America led many to believe that people could indeed control and use nature as they pleased. We are now realizing that such is not the case. A computer at M.I.T. predicted that we are doomed if we don't make some drastic changes. Ecological experts disagree about the seriousness of the problem. Some believe that we have already passed the "point of no return"—that we have so polluted our air and water and plundered our natural resources that it is only a matter of time before we perish, regardless of what corrective measures we now take. The federal government has admitted that beginning the clean-up in earnest will produce the following results: expenditure of billions of dollars, rise in unemployment, increase in the price of products, the closing of many plants, and a seriously damaging impact on the economic welfare of many communities. In this period of severe economic strain, we have actually reduced the amounts spent on protecting the environment.

**2.** *Changing Values and Morality.* We are losing faith in many of our institutions, including government, schools, religion, and the professions. The fast pace of events pushes aside values almost as rapidly as styles come and go in the fashion world. For example, in a short period of time we have undergone a shift in values ranging from frugality to conspicuous consumption to ecologically-oriented frugality to renewed conspicuous consumption. There is much unrest in today's middle-aged generation because of its inability to pass its values on to the young. Our fluctuating moral standards contribute to adult and child drug abuse, teen alcoholism, and the divorce rate. Our private lives are played out in a world where much of the landscape seems threatening and constantly changing. There is an increasing feeling on the part of many educators that the school program should include extensive experiences in the process of valuing and values clarification. Other educators, who support their position with extensive research, assert that the processes of moral judgment can and should be taught at all school levels to raise the future level of morality in our society (see "The Cognitive-Developmental Approach to Moral Education" and "Now then, Mr. Kohlberg, about Moral Development in Women . . ." in Section 3, and "Children's Literature and Moral Development" in Section 7). In this section Shane asserts that a good curriculum for the 1990s will be one that helps learners understand the nature of an "era of value conflicts." Yet our society often seems to be in headlong retreat from our commitment to education. Many parents and teachers oppose the inclusion of values and morals as part of the curriculum. They believe this is an area of instruction that should be reserved for the home and church or synagogue. Certainly our various social institutions—the schools, the media, the government, the churches, the family—must redefine and clarify their responsibilities for instruction in values and ethics.

**3.** *The Family.* The family has traditionally been one of the most important institutions in American society. But in many cases today, the family no longer functions as a closely-knit unit. There is great mobility among a large segment of the population—the family is not tied closely to the community, and family members are spread out over a wide geographical area. More and more children are raised without benefit of their natural father's or mother's presence. The roles of the father and mother have undergone change. There is, however, no evidence of a large-scale rejection of marriage among us; family ties remain a central part of American life. For a recent summary of current social forces that are affecting families and the children in them see "The American Family in the Year 2000" in this section.

According to Uri Bronfenbrenner, Professor of Child Development and Family Studies at Cornell University, the social forces now affecting the family in this country are "a social time bomb and our children are the casualties of the fallout." Viewing the same social forces, Edward Zigler, Director of Yale University's Center for Early Childhood Education, calls for a new model of "the community school" which would serve as a center for information and child care from children's earliest years. In this section, Cremin sees changes in the family as a major factor in the "revolution in American education."

**4.** *The Microelectronics Revolution.* According to four articles in this section (Cremin; Shane; Cetron, Soriano, and Gayle; Raffa) the microelectronics revolution (including video and TV) is affecting all parts of society today. This includes the times and places where work is done; the range of food available; the ways in which we are entertained; the ways and places in which we learn; the role of the teacher; the time of life in which we engage in formal study; the values we hold; our increased mobility and mode of transportation; and health care and longevity. The changes being wrought today by computers, interactive video, video recorders, and TV are endlessly startling and are probably now about where automobiles were in the 1920's. All four of the articles describe the profound effects that this revolution is having and will have on education, the curriculum, and teaching.

**5.** *The Changing World of Work.* The new microelectronics revolution is radically changing work and the workplace. We are in the midst of a revolution that will leave virtually no form of work unchanged. Even when a person prepares for a job well, it never stays constant; it may not even continue to exist. The issue is not whether these changes are occurring, but the rate and shape of them. Illustrations of these changes may be found in articles by Cremin and Shane in this section.

A major responsibility for curriculum planners and teachers now and in the future will be to prepare students for a rapidly changing job market. Curriculum planners from the preschool to the graduate school and beyond must be alert to these demands. Vocational education will no longer be a narrow field of study. Everyone needs to develop strong analytic, expressive, communicative and computational skills. Extensive discussion of these topics may be found in "Schools of the Future" in this section as well as in the articles by Cremin and Shane.

**6.** *Equal Rights.* Women and minority groups in America have become more vocal and more active in demanding equal rights. Blacks, Chicanos, Indians, Puerto Ricans, and other racial groups often do not agree among themselves about how to proceed, but they share in a common cause of fighting back against years of inequality, inferior status, and often inhumane treatment. Those who know poverty, regardless of race, also clamor for a better life. Some middle-class Americans rebel against such groups and feel that their own "hard earned" rights are being violated in favor of other groups. The women's equality movement, which for a time made significant gains, may now be losing some of them.

After years of neglect the needs of the five million children in the United States who come to school speaking a language other than English were finally recognized by several acts of Congress, a Supreme Court decision (Lau vs. Nichols, 1974), and legislation in two-thirds of the states supporting bilingual education. Before these governmental actions, such children were considered marginal and barely worth educating; their drop-out rates were as high as 50 or 60 percent. Recent significant social forces are also assisting four million handicapped boys and girls to begin to obtain the educational program they need (see "Another Look at Mainstreaming" in Section 6).

But there are other problems. According to "Barriers to Excellence: Our Children at Risk" (report of the National Coalition of Advocates for Students, 1985), many students who are not handicapped now end up in special education classes because of a lack of adequate education options designed to meet the needs of children with diverse learning styles. With its emphasis on higher standards, the current education reform movement increases the risk that many low achieving and minority students will be inappropriately labeled as handicapped.

7. *Urban and Suburban Crises.* An increasingly higher percentage of the American population has moved into the urban areas. Whites have been moving to the suburbs, leaving the inner city to minority groups. The tax base for the inner city has been seriously eroded, making it difficult for the government to provide adequate services. Crime has continued to rise at a seemingly unstoppable pace, spreading from the central city into the suburbs. Slums and ghettos are evident in every major city, and providing adequate housing is a major problem. The transportation system has also become a problem of major proportions, as it relates to both the inner city and the suburban commuter.

8. *Crime and Violence.* Crime rates are rising rapidly, in part because of the increase in juvenile delinquency. Violence and vandalism in schools have become problems of shocking proportions. The Surgeon General issued a five-volume report in 1972 indicating that TV carnage can cause aggressive behavior in some children. The National Association for Better Broadcasting has estimated that a child may see some 13,000 violent deaths on television between the ages of five and fifteen. Other reports, including one by the National Institute of Mental Health, conclude that there is a significant link between TV violence and children's behavior. (See "Television and Values: Implications for Education" in this section.)

9. *Alienation and Anxiety.* The inability of many individuals to develop and pursue goals they consider worthwhile has led to increasing alienation and anxiety. If you like your job, you've got it made—maybe. If you don't, you may not be able to quit and find another job. Changes in family structure, the seeming immorality of many leaders, injustice, income disparities, society's gradualism in dealing with problems of technological change, sharp fluctuations in the economic system, inflation, unemployment, our loss of faith in science and the "experts'"—all contribute to anxiety and alienation. According to a 1985 report by the Education Commission of

the States, "Reconnecting Youth: The Next Stage of Reform," a growing proportion of our young people are not making successful transitions to productive adult lives. More than 2.5 million young people between the ages of 16 and 19 (10–15 percent of the age group) have become disconnected from society at large. The Education Commission of the States believes that this calls for "a profound restructuring of the schools and a thorough rethinking of our priorities" (see "Our Two-Story Culture" in this section, "Today's Children Are Different" in Section 3, and "High School Reform: The Need for Engineering" in Section 9).

10. *International Tensions.* A major war remains an ever-present possibility. International terrorism is a constantly recurring reality. According to Tonkin and Edwards in "A World of Interconnections," our fate is inextricably bound up with the fate of the rest of the world. They assert that the "single most important task" now facing education may be the cultivation of an understanding of other people's motives and the social, psychological, and historical settings that cause them to think and act as they do. Today interdependence is a simple fact. The choice is between destruction and survival. (See also "Multicultural Education and Global Education: A Possible Merger" in Section 7, and "International Education's Expanded Role in Higher Education" in Section 10).

The articles in this section, dealing with these and other social forces, should help you examine your own views regarding social forces that you regard as important as, or more important than, the ones discussed.

## Social Forces and the Individual

One way to see the close relationship between an understanding of the social environment and the development of an appropriate educational program is to view the social setting from the standpoint of the individual. Some claim that in our society the role of each person is determined by his or her *occupation*. Friends are often drawn from those with whom a person works, and the whole tone of life is related to this reference group. Moreover, a democratic society requires *citizens* who are prepared to deal with the current issues of government. Finally, each person faces problems of *self-fulfillment* and *self-development*. Thus, from the individual learner's standpoint, the rationally developed school program must provide for his or her *vocational demands and requirements,* the *demands of citizenship,* and the *demands of self-fulfillment*. In every society the nature of these demands on the individual is different. And because all industrial civilizations are undergoing rapid change, the demands are subject to constant modification within each society.

One of the difficult problems is that all of these social forces are constantly changing, and the curriculum and teaching should change with them. Few of the social forces exist independent of each other. They are interrelated to a large degree, and each individual in the society has most, and sometimes all, of them acting upon him or her to a greater or lesser degree at the same time. This point can be illustrated by the following hypothetical situation.

Liza is a black girl who lives in the ghetto of a large city. She is fourteen years old, the oldest of a family of nine children. Her father left the family five years ago because he could not find employment and knew that his children could receive more financial support from the government if he left home. Liza's mother works during the evening, so Liza is expected to care for the apartment and children when she gets home from school. The apartment has only two rooms and is infested with rats. It has poor plumbing and toilet facilities, and the heating system works only occasionally. The children get only one real meal a day and have no money to spend at school. Their clothing is old and worn.

Kevin is a white boy who lives in a middle-class suburb. He is fourteen years old, and has a seventeen-year-old sister. His father is a lawyer who works downtown and commutes daily, often arriving home very late in the evening. Kevin's mother attends many social functions and has a serious drinking problem. His parents often have loud arguments and are openly talking about divorce. Kevin's sister smokes marijuana and takes LSD. She often spends the weekend with her boyfriend. Kevin is well fed, lives in an attractive home with a good-sized yard, and is given a generous allowance.

Roy is a white boy who lives near a factory on the outer fringe of the city. He is fourteen years old, and he has one older brother and one older sister. His father is employed at the nearby factory as a blue collar worker. Roy lives in a small but comfortable house. His family does not have many luxuries, but their needs are well satisfied. His parents are deeply religious and take Roy to church with them twice on Sunday and again on Wednesday evening. His father is a veteran and proudly displays several medals. He also belongs to the local VFW. Roy's parents spend much time with their children. He often hears them talk about how radicals and the minority groups are taking over the country.

All three of these young people attend the same school and most of the same classes. Roy walks three blocks to school, but both Liza and Kevin ride the bus. Consider these questions and try to formulate some answers to them in your own mind.

1. How are all three of these young people alike?
2. How are they different?
3. What social forces have played a significant part in their lives?
4. How can the school curriculum plan for meeting the needs of these students, considering the social setting from which they come?
5. How would you, as the teacher of these three students, deal with the similarities and differences they bring from diverse social backgrounds?

It is obvious that each person is unique in the way that social forces have affected his or her life, and the school curriculum is challenged to deal with that individuality. But the curriculum is also asked to meet the needs of the total society. This problem can be seen as you consider the following questions:

1. How actively involved should the school become in dealing with social forces? (Should the faculty lead the students in picket lines?)
2. What percentage of the curriculum should be devoted to learning about and discussing social issues?

**3.**    How should the school respond to parents who feel that the curriculum is either overemphasizing or underemphasizing particular social issues?

## Levels of Social Forces

There are actually several levels at which social forces should be considered by the curriculum planner and teacher. There is the *national and international level* where concerns like those just discussed should be discerned and utilized in planning.

There is also the level of social forces found in the *local community,* including family structure, class structure, the ethnic, racial, and religious backgrounds, and the values of the community in which the teaching is to be done. These social forces affect the learners and heavily influence their perceptions.

There is the *social context in which the teaching occurs*—the social forces characteristic of a particular curriculum or school. The many social influences here include the individual learner's social status, the teacher's role in the school, the teacher's role in relation to the principal, the relationships between the school and community, and the extent of role and school-community conflict. Sensitivity to the ways in which these social forces influence learners is of major significance in curriculum planning and teaching.

## Concepts from the Social Disciplines

A number of concepts from sociology, anthropology, and social psychology are of great value to curriculum planners and teachers in defining and describing the social forces that should be considered as they do their planning. Among these concepts are *humanity, culture, subculture, cultural pluralism, social structure, socialization,* and *roles in settings.* This list of concepts could be greatly extended, but those listed have major significance in considering social forces in curriculum planning.

The concept of *humanity* can be a significant organizing element in curriculum planning, and it is one that is particularly needed as the world becomes a smaller and smaller community sharing problems of pollution, energy and food shortages, and increasing violence. Instead of trying to understand the social forces affecting American society or Canadian society, curriculum planners might focus attention on the forces that affect humanity and society as a whole. The materials investigated and the problems considered would be placed in a frame of reference going well beyond national boundaries. The arts might be utilized to a greater extent to enlarge the learners' understanding. "Cultural universals" would be a major focus in planning and teaching. Tonkin and Edwards, in "A World of Interconnections" in this section, cite evidence that Americans receive less exposure to foreign countries than any other people in the world with the possible exception of China!

A *culture* is the sum total and organization of all the patterned ways by which a people live. Because there are hundreds of different cultures, nobody can hope to learn about them all. But in spite of their specific differences, all cultures are basically alike, and all serve essentially the same functions. There must be ways of getting food, clothing, and shelter. There must also be ways of dividing up the work and some patterning of the relationships of men, women, and children, and of old and young. A person is immersed in a culture or in cultures from birth to death. *Culture is learned behavior*—learned in early life and invested with a great deal of emotion. Learning the first culture is called *enculturation* or *socialization*. As more mothers are employed, a variety of agencies take over the process of socializing and enculturating the child. "Through the Cultural Looking Glass" in this section will help you to understand *culture* as a concept that has particular significance for curriculum planners when they are defining the social forces that must be considered for adequate planning. This article asserts that "ignorance of others is not bliss and what you don't know *can* hurt you."

A *subculture* is a division of a cultural group consisting of persons who share special cultural characteristics at the same time that they share some of the major characteristics of the whole culture. American and Canadian societies consist of many subcultures. Many children representing subcultures come to school without many of the experiences that are "normal" for the kinds of children the schools and teachers are used to teaching. It is very important that teachers and curriculum planners under-stand the differences and similarities among the subcultures found in a particular community, as well as those found in our national culture. The individual learner should have positive feelings about his or her own culture. The task of creating positive feelings toward the different cultures and subcultures in our society should be a primary objective of teachers and curriculum planners. This is one of the goals of citizenship and self-realization in curriculum planning. "Our Two-Story Culture" in this section makes it clear that our two levels of culture must not get too far "out of phase"; we must learn to cherish a "whole spectrum" of subcultures.

A culture that includes many subcultures is called a *pluralistic society*. *Cultural pluralism* refers to a co-mingling of a variety of ethnic and generational lifestyles, each grounded in a complexity of values, linguistic variations, skin hues, and perhaps even cognitive world views. The term *pluralism* implies that, theoretically at least, no one cultural style takes precedence over any other, although many persons would be uncomfortable with this affirmation of "equality." Cultural pluralism means that each person, regardless of self- or group-identification, is entitled to the respect, dignity, freedom, and citizen rights promised by law and tradition.

The concept of cultural pluralism places a responsibility on curriculum planners and teachers to develop learning experiences and environments in which each group's contribution to the richness of the entire society is held up to view with a sense of gratefulness and appreciation. It means that a community survey must be conducted to determine which cultures and subcultures are present and which are conspicuously absent. Then curriculum planners should determine which of the absent subcultures should be included so that learners receive exposure to a more generalized view of the whole society's multiple-culture composition. An advisory group of teachers, adminis-trators, parents, and other citizens should oversee this survey and the incoming data.

Next, a list of community resources should be collected, including places to visit and persons to invite into the classroom to assist in developing cross-cultural awareness and appreciation. Printed resources must now be created. The shape and content of the resources should grow out of an inservice education workshop designed specifically to produce these materials. The resource materials should contain practical suggestions for integrating multiple-cultural awareness into the existing, ongoing curriculum of language arts, social studies, computation, art, music, and physical education already laying claim to the teachers' and learners' time. When the resources are ready, teachers should be trained to use them. It is folly to assume that anyone has a knowledge of and an appreciation for cultural distinctiveness simply because they have a curriculum guide. Since cultural pluralism is one of the keys to America's continuing social vitality, anything less than what is described here in curriculum planning is likely to be woefully inadequate. Schools that facilitate understanding of cultural pluralism radiate a mood of pluralism in policies, practices, and programs—the academic curriculum, and cocurricular activities, the organizational structure and staff, and the informal program (hall decorations, assemblies, clubs, and lunch programs). "Through the Cultural Looking Glass" and "Our Two-Story Culture" in this section, "Multicultural Education and Global Education" in Section 7, and "International Education's Expanded Role in Higher Education" in Section 10 examine the implications of cultural pluralism for curriculum planning.

*Social structure* has a great impact on the members of a culture or subculture. Examples are the learnings that accrue from growing up in a society with particular qualities of institutional life, such as the authoritarian family or self-conceptions acquired from learning the behavior roles assigned by some social structures to one's social class or race. Social structure includes *roles in settings,* such as the structured interacting roles of teacher, student, principal, and parent involved in educational transactions that take place in a school. The actual onsite definitions of these roles (as opposed to the ideal versions of them) are part of the curriculum and shape the behavior of all of the participants. Teachers, principals, and curriculum leaders are often subject to severe role strain. Lack of clarity regarding roles adversely affects leadership, productivity, and morale. Clarity regarding roles is a result of attention to their clarification. If we want learners to learn such things as individual responsibility and social reciprocity, we must make the practice of these behaviors part of the student's role and part of the curriculum in all school situations. To initiate change, teachers, students, parents, and other citizens should be involved from the outset. The greatest possible awareness of what is involved should be developed.

## Future Planning

Future planning is an active process of conceiving the future in terms of many possibilities and assuming that the future can be mediated. This is another way in which curriculum planners are using social forces in curriculum planning and teaching. Future planners project present social forces into the future in order to try to identify and develop alternative ways of coping with them. Unlike past futurists, today's future planners do not predict any one outcome. Future planning of the curriculum is needed in relation to social forces in order to develop curriculum and instruction strategies that are more than hindsight remedies for today's problems. Edward Cornish, in "Why Study the Future," describes the available methods for studying the future and provides a number of forecasts for the 1980s and 1990s.

In using the processes of future planning, curriculum planners and teachers work with students, parents, and other members of the community in identifying and discussing present trends, forecasting and projecting the effects of one trend as compared with another. Alternative scenarios may be developed that describe outcomes of efforts to "change the future" by some intervention, or by doing nothing.

For example, the need for planning for the future in the curriculum in the light of present social forces may be seen in the current "computer revolution." For thirty years, there has been constant improvement in digital electronic components and growth in the power of computers built with them. In the last five years, computers have moved from the laboratories and big companies into the mainstream of everyday life. They are at the grocery checkout counter, the neighborhood garage, and in many offices. Hundreds of thousands of personal computer units are now sold each year at low cost. It is predicted that the entire Library of Congress may soon be available to anyone on his or her personal microcomputer which may be used at home, at school, or at work during the day or night. Perhaps the illiterates of the 1990s will not be those who cannot read, but those who cannot program computers and use them for learning and solving problems. If these projections are correct, what may be the implications of this "computer revolution" be for the planning of today's curriculum? Two articles in this section—those by Shane and Papert—examine the future effects of microprocessors on schooling, education, learning, and world society. They use such expressions as the "wired planet," the "computer as pencil," and "dynabook."

Successful living today and in the future demands that we learn much more. The curriculum should prepare children, youth, and adults for the present as well as for the new century. Learning to look ahead—to see local, national, and worldwide forces and trends in terms of alternative futures and consequences—is becoming an increasingly necessary part of the curriculum. We must be wise enough to plan for the *next* rather than the *past* twenty years.

Today, the curriculum should help the learner to participate in the development of the future by involvement in the real world of events, by provision of many decision-making opportunities, and by illumination of alternative choices and consequences.

## Curriculum Criteria

As noted in the rationale in Section 1, curriculum criteria are guidelines or standards by which decisions can be made in curriculum planning and teaching. What guidelines for such planning may be derived from the social forces that are discussed and described in this rationale and in the articles and additional learning activities in this section? Providing for *the individual differences of learners, the teaching of values, the development of self-understanding,* and *the development of problem-solving skills and abilities* are curriculum planning criteria that all depend in important ways on the use of social forces in curriculum planning.

Many *individual differences of learners* are related to family and home background, subculture, or community background. The descriptions of Kevin, Liza, and Roy in the rationale, and the articles in this Section by Fersh and by Cherlin and Furstenberg, illustrate the ways in which social forces are one of the keys to an understanding of individual differences for which teachers and curriculum planners should provide. The criterion questions for curriculum planners and teachers are as follows:

1.  What social or cultural factors contribute to the individual differences of learners?
2.  How can the curriculum or teaching provide for these differences?

The school program has a social climate and programs that *teach values* that are often not clearly stated, or about which curriculum planners and teachers may be unaware. Schools teach values whether they intend to do so or not. The discussion of cultural pluralism in this rationale and the articles in this section by Shane, Fersh, and Raffa all illustrate the relation of social forces to the teaching of values. The criterion questions are as follows:

3.  What values *are* we teaching?
4.  What values do we *wish* to teach?

*Self-understanding* as a curriculum criterion is related to cultural pluralism and to various social forces such as changing values, changes in family life, and contrasting educative environments. The criterion question for curriculum planners and teachers is the following:

5.  What can the school program do to assist learners in their goals of social self-understanding and self-realization?

Articles by Fersh and by Cherlin and Furstenberg are related to this criterion.

*Problem solving* as a curriculum criterion asks whether the curriculum and the planned teaching assist the learners in confronting problems and in developing problem-solving skills. The criterion questions for curriculum planners and teachers are as follows:

6.  How can the curriculum and teaching be planned and organized so that learners are assisted in confronting personal and social problems?

7.  How can learners be helped to develop the problem-solving skills needed to cope with problems which they face or they will face in the future?
8.  Is provision made in the curriculum and teaching for the development of the skills of future planning?

Articles by Cremin, Shane, Raffa, Cornish, and Papert in this section, and the article entitled "Problem Solving: Encouraging Active Learning" in Section 7, are all related to problem solving as a curriculum criterion.

### Summary of Rationale for Social Forces

When planning curricula and teaching, we should consider the various levels and types of social forces, pertinent concepts from the social disciplines, and future planning. One key word suggests something that the school and its educators must have in order to deal with social forces: *awareness*. The point is somewhat general, but it surely must be the starting place. The school and its faculty should know and understand intimately the social setting of the surrounding community, and a strong effort should be made to know and understand each of the students. If such awareness is lacking, it is unlikely that positive constructive action can be taken. Curriculum plans should be made that will assist teachers in doing these things.

Do you agree?

## OBJECTIVES

Your objectives in studying social forces as one of the bases of curriculum planning should be as follows:

1.  To be able to analyze a curriculum plan with respect to its relationships to the various levels and types of social forces.
2.  To be able to suggest changes and improvements in a curriculum plan or teaching that are based on an understanding of the various levels and types of social forces.
3.  To be able to consider and use social forces, future planning, cultural and social concepts, and knowledge about the community in planning for teaching.

## PREASSESSMENT

The purpose of the preassessment is to enable you to determine whether you already possess the performance competencies in curriculum planning that are listed under the objectives just mentioned. The following activities will aid you in your evaluation:

1.    List no more than ten social forces and/or cultural and social concepts that have implications for planning the curriculum of today's public schools. For example, rapid population growth is said to have meaning for curriculum planning. It is assumed that this will be your own list, and that it may not have precisely the same social forces as those listed in the preceding rationale.

2.    Taking each of the social forces you have listed, tell how you believe it should influence or change curriculum planning and planning for teaching in the 1980s and 1990s.

3.    Select any curriculum plan of your choice, at any school level, and examine it in light of the social forces you have selected and its own local community. This could be done by visiting and studying a school or by analyzing a written statement regarding the school's program or the instruction in one classroom. You might choose some part of the school's curriculum, such as the science curriculum, if you prefer to do so.

4.    Suggest improvements or changes in the curriculum plan as a result of your analysis in number 3.

Do not be surprised if the curriculum plan of your choice does not appear to consider social forces. Many curriculum plans do not. Suggest improvements in the planning on the basis of social forces that you believe should be considered in today's curriculum.

In answering number 3, you might choose to consider the use of social forces in the curricula described in "The Young Reach Out to the Old in Shaker Heights" and "Getting A Headstart on Career Choices" in Section 7, or "James Madison High: A School for Winners" in Section 9.


## LEARNING ACTIVITIES

The articles in this section will assist you in defining many of the current and future social forces of importance in curriculum planning. They may cause you to ask whether a curriculum focused only on planning for experiences in schools can adequately meet the needs of learners who must cope with many social forces outside of school.

Other learning alternatives are suggested at the end of this section.


## POSTASSESSMENT

After attempting the preassessment you may do *one or more* of the following:

1.    Ask your instructor's opinion to determine whether you are ready for a postassessment evaluation on social forces and the curriculum. Most students will need further work on this curriculum base.

2. Read the articles on social forces in this section and try to determine how the social forces discussed in each article should be considered in curriculum planning and teaching.
3. Choose additional activities and readings or films from those listed at the end of this section.
4. Look for other films, books, or articles on social forces in your library or media center.
5. With your fellow students, discuss the reading you have done and the films you have viewed. The key questions: How should the social forces you've studied affect a school's curriculum? How should they be considered in planning for teaching?
6. When you are ready, ask your instructor for advice on a suitable postassessment for you for this topic. Satisfactory completion of number 1 under Problems and Projects at the end of this section might be one possibility. Or written completion of the preassessment for this section, after completing other learning activities, might be a satisfactory postassessment. Consult your instructor about this. Determine whether you can do either or both of these activities before seeing the instructor.

# The Revolution in American Education

## LAWRENCE A. CREMIN

I believe we are living through a revolution in our time that represents the most fundamental change in American education since the rise of public popular schooling during the nineteenth century. The revolution is compounded of many elements, but I would like to dwell on three in particular: the changes in our American families, the changes wrought by television, and the changes in the nature of work in the United States.

American families have become smaller, less stable, and more varied during the past twenty years. Moreover, two-parent families are increasingly dual-career families; i.e., there has been a steady increase in the number of married women, including mothers of young children, engaged in full-time paid employment outside the home. Given that the family initiates most early education and inevitably mediates much education that goes on elsewhere, these changes have profoundly affected what American children learn and how they learn it.

Television was in 10 percent of American homes in 1950; today it is in virtually all of them. We know that television entertains; we know that it sells products; and we know that it influences elections. I would assert that it also educates and miseducates relentlessly. It informs via news broadcasts and documentaries. It teaches people to want via commercials. It teaches values via soaps and situation comedies. And it teaches styles via the star system. For

From *Educational Forum* 47, No. 2 (Winter 1983): 29–30. © Kappa Delta Pi. Used by permission of the publisher.

years before youngsters come to school and during all the time they are in school, television profoundly affects what they learn and how they learn it.

In the domain of work, we have become a society in which intellectual technology based on knowledge and information holds the key to productivity and progress. Many of the jobs in a modern hospital or communications agency or computer software firm have only come into existence during the past twenty-five years. Simultaneously, traditional roles in banks, insurance companies, and government agencies have been dramatically altered. Moreover, even when a person learns a job well, the job itself never stays constant. One no longer makes a single decision to prepare for a single career; one makes a series of decisions involving a series of preparations for a series of careers. And, increasingly, systematic education within the workplace is involved in the process.

What does all this mean for schooling? I continue to believe that schools remain society's preeminent institutions for systematic teaching and learning tied to humane and cosmopolitan values. Nevertheless, schools are working in a radically changed ecology of education and they must adapt their instruction to that changed ecology. They can expect less from families by way of common teaching; they face a cacophony of conflicting teaching and misteaching via television; and they cannot avoid the rapidly shifting educational demands of the workplace.

Within this new ecology of education, I think five agenda for the schools become more important than ever: first, teaching literacy with respect to language, numbers, and computers; second, teaching the essential knowledge, values, and skills of the humanities, the natural and social sciences, and the fine and applied arts; third, teaching the ability to reason and especially to inquire and criticize; fourth, teaching a sense of community, by which I mean a shared awareness of and respect for the views and values of others; and fifth, teaching the motivations and methods of self-education, or, of educational autonomy.

In addition, schools require a better sense of their part in the overall education of their students, and particularly a better sense of the possibility of their linking with other educators to carry on certain kinds of instruction. There are some educational tasks schools are uniquely equipped to carry out; there are others that are better done in collaboration with other educating agencies; there are still others that are best left entirely to the other educators.

Finally, schools need to do whatever they do with a greater intensity than ever before, largely because they are facing more spirited competition than ever before. Rather than eschew the new instructional technology, schoolteachers ought to seize upon the best of it and use it to create the sort of influential teaching that can hold its own in the face of the power and dynamism of the other educators.

*Lawrence A. Cremin* is Professor of Education, Teachers College, Columbia University. He was President of Teachers College, 1974 to 1984. He is the author of *American Education: The National Experience,* 1980 (for which he was awarded the Pulitzer Prize).

# The Silicon Age II: Living and Learning in An Information Epoch

## HAROLD G. SHANE

Some years ago Daniel Bell, the Harvard sociologist, coined the term "post-industrial society" to describe an era based on services, into which our industrial age was being transformed. More recently, however, it has become clear that the post-industrial world is not just a service society; it is an "information society"—one in which knowledge and the handling of information have elbowed aside the smokestack and the assembly line as symbols of America's prowess.[1]

When did the U.S. enter the information epoch? John Naisbitt argues persuasively that the "megashift" from industrial to information society occurred in 1956 and 1957. In 1956 white-collar workers—managerial, technical, clerical, and professional—for the first time outnumbered blue-collar workers. And 1957 "marked the beginning of the globalization of the information revolution: The Russians launched Sputnik, the missing technological catalyst in a growing information society."[2]

The unique opportunities (and demands) that accompany the information epoch require us to explore and to understand more clearly the myriad ways in which society is being influenced by the information sciences and microtechnologies. We must determine what social inventiveness and institutional repair work may be required because of 1) the enormous impact of the microprocessor and of telecommunications networks, 2) ergonomic[3] responses to increasingly robotized workplaces and computerized homes, and 3) ubiquitous 24-hour television, which, in some areas, now allows access to more than 100 channels.

## LEARNING TO LIVE WITH NEW REALITIES

Change in our modern age takes place with bewildering speed. In recent decades the life sciences have produced clones of mammals, oral contraceptives, artificial life forms, heart transplants, and gene splicing. The physical sciences have given us lasers and holography, the computer, and landings on our moon and on Mars; they have even sent a probe into the infinite reaches of space that lie beyond the orbits of the outermost planets in our solar system.

One outcome of this rapid change has been social disorientation. The disorientation manifests itself in many ways—from worldwide assassinations, political kidnappings, and terrorism to alienation, drug and alcohol abuse, and teenage pregnancies and suicides. Correcting problems such as these—and a host of others—will be a prime task for humans to undertake in the information age.

Another challenge in an era of information overload or "infoglut"[4] is meeting the demands that will be placed on education. As Bentley Glass put it in 1968, "The educated man of yesterday is the maladjusted, uneducated man of today and the culturally illiterate misfit of tomorrow." Consequently, educated humans need to acquire much more knowledge than they needed to have 25 or 30 years ago. Traditional curriculum content and instructional practices are certain to change as educators begin to master the art of using knowledge to react promptly

From *Phi Delta Kappan* 65, No. 2 (October 1983): 126–129. Used by permission of the author and the publisher.

and wisely to the difficulties created by the demands that accompany an era of infoglut.

In the remainder of this article I plan to outline some of the ways in which the world community is being transmuted by the electronic environment. Since "knowledge potential" is our one infinite resource, I have also suggested some ways in which we need to modify certain personal and educational values as we use this potential to thread our way through the maze of information that Daniel Bell estimated will soon be doubling every two years.

## THE ELECTRONIC ENVIRONMENT

The implications of microelectronic phenomena go far beyond the microcomputers that have captured popular attention. The steam-powered technology of the 18th and 19th centuries and the internal combustion/electrical technology that shaped the early decades of the 20th century greatly reduced the need for arduous physical labor. However, because microelectronic technology has begun to supplant both physical *and* intellectual labor in the 1980s, significant changes are taking place at all levels of society throughout the world.

The effect of the microelectronic revolution on the military, for example, is dramatic and rather alarming. On the one hand, many of the most advanced developments in microelectronics lend themselves readily to military applications. On the other hand, the rapid development in sophisticated communications and weaponry could further destabilize the nuclear arms race. Devastatingly accurate targeting, guidance, and damage assessment devices have been developed. A report from the Worldwatch Institute suggests that the new technology may make first strikes more tempting to an enemy that hopes to score a nuclear knockout.

One other factor adds a devastating element of uncertainty in a society that has begun to de-

pend heavily on the power of microelectronics: the electromagnetic pulse (EMP) effect. Scientists believe that a nuclear device exploded over, say, Nebraska—even though detonated 250 miles above the earth's surface—would blanket the entire United States with an electromagnetic pulse that could completely paralyze much of the equipment powered by electricity—some of it permanently.[5] This EMP effect renders electronic gear—from toasters and telephones to transistors, computers, and even our airborne command posts—dysfunctional. Imagine the catastrophic effect on a society that is coming to depend ever more heavily on microelectronics of all kinds.

The changes wrought by the microelectronic revolution go far beyond the military, however; they affect all parts of society today, including the times and places where work is done, the range of foods available, the bewildering array of video- and audiocassette equipment, our increased mobility and choice of mode of transportation (more than 700 models of cars and trucks were on the U.S. market in 1982), and even new patterns of personal relationships. The microchip has created living quarters in which mail, information sources such as videotext and viewdata, security control, and the selection and ordering of goods and services are all handled electronically.

Health and longevity are also being influenced in our microelectronic epoch. Computerized prosthetic devices have already helped the paraplegic to walk, the voiceless to speak, and the brain-injured to function. It has even become technically possible to use brain-dead bodies, housed in a "neomortorium," to provide storage for living organs until they are harvested to replace the lungs, kidneys, hearts, or livers of those who need transplants.[6]

The growing use of laser-beam surgery represents yet another dramatic advance in medicine. Doctors can now snake a laser through tubing and reach organs in locations that heretofore were inoperable because they are out of the reach of traditional surgical tools and techniques.

And then there are the electronic media (particularly television)—possibly the most pervasive manifestation of the silicon age. The "tube" brings us visual mobility and instant information, as well as the phenomenon of "interactive TV," which enables viewers in some communities to express opinions on various issues and questions merely by pressing a button. TV also barrages us with manic ads, increasingly explicit sex, and gore-in-detail during the *1½ billion* hours Americans spend daily in televiewing.

Until recently, the TV programs available to European audiences were for the most part limited, and to some extent controlled, by the governments of the various countries. One cannot avoid speculating about the socioeconomic and political implications of a vastly increased public exposure to American-style TV with multiple stations and dozens of program choices. One European official, who requested anonymity, suggested that, to protect the public from garbage on TV, his government might consider forbidding the use of receiving dish antennae that pick up signals from satellites.

Charles Owen of the Illinois Institute of Technology is among a growing group who forecast the proliferation of in-the-home electronic equipment that ranges far beyond television. Among his images: robots to perform routine household chores; appliances responsive to voice commands; force fields to detect intruders; high-tech food processors to chop, mix, cook, and store victuals; and "holographic" TV to project three-dimensional scenes *outside* the confines of the tube.

Though experts disagree as to the merits and demerits of video games, it seems safe to conclude that they have pervaded our lives. In 1982 alone, 38 billion quarters clinked into coin slots, and home video vendors grossed $4.5 billion in sales. Some communities have felt obliged to set a minimum age for admission to video arcades. Others have forbidden their youths to enter such arcades during school hours, in an effort to stem absenteeism on the part of pupils who had become "video junkies." The most unusual—and alarming—information that testifies to the possible effects of "videomania" indicates that prolonged play—five or six hours at a stretch—has triggered epileptic seizures (both grand and petit mal) in young addicts.[7]

## THE CHANGING WORKPLACE

The new microelectronic age is radically changing the workplace. This transformation has implications for education that we are only now beginning to understand.

The long-term impact of rapid technological change is nearly impossible to forecast accurately. The technological changes reported almost daily tend to threaten us with technogenic unemployment even as they open new employment vistas. In July, for instance, *Robotics World* announced that scientists at the Nippon Telegraph and Telephone Public corporation had created a robot that could read the news with 99.5% accuracy. The robot's computer (programmed with a dictionary) can scan print, check its memory banks, and deliver a properly inflected sentence. The report suggests a future for news-reading robots on the radio and for robots as telephone operators and as readers for the blind.[8] Some innovations are already creating technogenic unemployment, as when, for instance, a factory is retooled and automated. Consider this example:

> The General Electric Company is investing $316 million over the next three years to revitalize its locomotive plant in Erie, Pennsylvania. When all of the robots, computerized machine tools, and other automation systems are in place, the Erie "factory with a future" will have increased its production capacity by one-third.[9]

Obviously, such investments should strengthen the nation's economy. As far as the workforce is concerned, however, *two* workers in the future will do in 16 *hours* at General Electric what *70* employees did in 16 *days* before the plant received its electronic facelift.

Developments of this nature promise more major job-market shifts for the Eighties and Nineties. For instance, electronic mail promises to reduce the need for postal workers; linotype workers, elevator operators, and farm laborers will probably continue to dwindle in number; and our homes, as they become "electronic cottages," are likely to take less time to maintain.

On the other hand, the ranks of computer operators, office machine technicians, and tax-form specialists should swell, along with those of child-care personnel, geriatric nurses, social workers, and fast-food distributors. A volume prepared for the World Future Society forecasts a sampling of new occupations, the number of workers likely to be required, and average salaries as of 1990: energy technicians, 1.5 million at $26,000; housing rehabilitation technicians, 1.75 million at $24,000; genetic engineering technicians, 150,000 at $30,000; holographic inspection specialists, 200,000 at $28,000; bionic-electronic technicians, 200,000 at $32,000; and many more.[10] Educators from the preschool to the graduate school will need to be increasingly alert to shifting demands posed by a rapidly changing workplace.

Automated offices and an increase in stay-at-home workers have added two new buzz words to our vocabularies: 1) *telecommuters,* to describe people who "commute" to work via TV or computer terminals, and 2) *flexiplaces,* which refers to flexibility in the sites where one earns a living. The terms also suggest that new employer/employee relationships will continue to emerge and that many of our long- and dearly held images of work are obsolete. As Alvin Toffler observes in his most recent book, *Previews and Premises,*[11] the nature of work in the emerging Third Wave information sector that is superseding the industrial society mandates enriching and enlarging jobs, increasing employee participation in policy making, devising more varied organizational approaches to the tasks performed in our workplaces, and—of particular importance to educators—graduating workers who are knowledgeable, literate, resourceful, empathic, and innovative.

The increasingly widespread deployment of industrial robots may prove to be the most important phenomenon to restructure industry since steam engine technology appeared in the 18th century. James Albus, chief of the industrial systems division at the National Bureau of Standards, estimates that, as of early 1983, there were perhaps 5,000 robots in U.S. factories and that their numbers would increase by at least 20,000 and perhaps by as many as 60,000 installations *per year* between 1990 and the year 2000 if present trends continue. Since two to four person-years of work go into the installation of a system of industrial robots, a robot/electronic economy could be a welcome source of employment. However, these "steel-collar workers" will take jobs from a substantial number of human blue-collar workers. As Vary Coates noted, "[S]ince robots have neither flexibilities nor the restrictions of humans, a work environment organized for humans is not necessarily the environment that is best for robots. . . . to use robots most efficiently, the flow of work and the factory floor may have to be completely redesigned."[12]

Consider the challenge to education presented by 1) meeting new skill requirements of workers and of managers and 2) retrofitting or retraining the personnel displaced. In fact, as Toffler sees it, educators need to begin revamping our present system of mass education:

> Today's schools are turning out still more factory-style workers for jobs that won't exist. Diversify. Individualize. Decentralize. Smaller, more local schools. More education in the home. More parental involvement. More creativity, less rote (it's the rote jobs that are disappearing the fastest).[13]

Another development that may create spectacular changes in the workplace is examined by Colin Norman in his study of science and technology in the Eighties.[14] The potential impact of microtechnology and biotechnology is so tremendous that it seems unlikely that any new industries will even begin to approach the wallop that these two fields promise to have on our lives by the end of the century. Gene splicing, for instance, permits the gene for human interferon to be fished out of a cell possessing tens of thousands of other genes. Among other possible biochem/microtech contributions to the information epoch are self-fertilizing corn and wheat that draw nitrogen from the air. Other innovations include new ways to produce drugs and chemicals at modest cost, to produce fuel from waste materials, and to produce bacteria that clean up oil spills.

Let me mention one final development of the silicon age that could soon affect all our lives. Kenneth Hanck and Keith DeArmond, chemistry professors at North Carolina State University at Raleigh, have been working for more than four years to replace microchips with individual molecules. Such molecules would be capable of storing readable, coded information in approximately *one-millionth* of the space that even today's tiny computer chips require. To date, Hanck and DeArmond have identified chemical compounds with molecules that retain six electrons potentially useful as memory devices. Computers using molecular memory devices would be incredibly more powerful, tinier, and more efficient than anything now available.

## EDUCATION IN AN ELECTRONIC AGE

In recent months our entire system of education—kindergarten through college—has come under harsh scrutiny. In part, this is because governments, institutions, and individuals are discovering that dynamic developments in electronic information technologies, in biotechnologies, and in complex global communications are rapidly changing what they do, how they do it, and how they relate to one another. But the onrushing silicon age is already changing the entire landscape of education. According to the Office of Technology Assessment:

> The so-called *information revolution,* driven by rapid advances in communication and computer technology, is profoundly affecting American education. It is changing the nature of *what needs to be learned, who needs to learn it, who will provide it, and how it will be provided and paid for.*[15] (Emphasis added)

We cannot improve our schools without first determining how to cope with the silicon age; we need to develop strategies—both as professional educators and as private citizens—for living and learning in an electronic epoch, as well as future-oriented administrative policies, curriculum content, instructional practices, links with parents and community and other educational agencies—including the omnipresent TV set and its video-appendages.

## ALTERNATIVES AND CONSEQUENCES

As the microelectronic boom enhances the information explosion, I see no cause for "technophobia" in public school classrooms or on the college campus. However, we must recognize that in an information society the schools seem fated to find themselves no longer cloistered retreats but lively arenas in which an increasing array of conflicting social, economic, moral, and political ideas will collide. A good curriculum for the 1990s will be one that, among other things, helps learners understand the nature of an era of value conflicts.

Basic skills, clearly defined, are of even greater importance in the new knowledge society that we are entering. As we define "basic skills," we find that, in addition to the basic computer skills necessary to an information epoch, familiar basic elements—e.g., reading and writing, which have constituted traditional literacy—will acquire new meanings. In the language arts, for instance, an understanding of propaganda and the nature of and reasons for selected news is now basic. So is an understanding of ecological relationships, toxic waste problems, and the subtle meanings of entropy in the natural sciences. As for the social sciences (e.g., history, political science, economics, sociology, anthropology), all must acquire new meanings that will be compatible with the demands of the era in which our young learners will spend their lives.

Perhaps above all, one of the basic qualities of good schools will be their ability to teach skills that are transferable from one job to another in a rapidly changing world of work. This has become an important direction for traditional career and vocational education to take.

In addition, the "mind workers" of tomorrow—many of them already enrolled in our kin-dergarten-to-university continuum—must be exposed to value choices by wise and courageous teachers who are themselves aware of contemporary ideological crises and who have clarified their *own* values. Educators must understand that the nature of the world of tomorrow cannot be forecast with precision; what tomorrow brings will depend on where our insightful, humane values—or their absence—will lead us as we move into the future of the information society. This is what living and learning in a high-tech/microteach age involves.

The societal tensions generated by microtechnologies and their impact on our world will not grow less. Schools must begin living in the future now, just as their young charges will have to do. Even amid rapid and often bewildering changes, I remain optimistic. I believe we are passing the crest of our Third Wave malaise and are ready to debate and to determine what the "microkids" of today and tomorrow need to know and how U.S. schools can best educate the "microelectronic generation."

## ENDNOTES

1. See, for example, Yoseji Masuda, *The Information Society as Post-Industrial Society* (Tokyo: Institute for the Information Society, 1980).
2. John Naisbitt, *Megatrends* (New York: Warner Books, 1982), p. 12.
3. "Ergonomics" originally referred to the study of worker/machine relationships with the aim of reducing fatigue, strain, or discomfort. In the computer era, it has begun to be used to encompass psychological and social relationships. For example, the computer may begin to take the place of the imaginary playmate in the affections of some children; hence it has become the object of psychosocial analysis.
4. To the best of my knowledge, "infoglut" is a useful coinage by Michael Marien, editor of *Future Survey.*

5. For a more detailed report on EMP, see William J. Broad, "the Chaos Factor," *Science 93,* January/ February 1983, pp. 41–49.
6. For compelling arguments supporting this rather unsettling proposal, see Willard Gaylin, "Harvesting the Dead," *Harper's,* September 1974, pp. 23–30.
7. T. K. Daneshmend and M. J. Campbell, "Dark Warrior Epilepsy," *British Medical Journal,* 12 June 1982, pp. 1751–52.
8. *Indianapolis Star,* 4 July 1983, p. 10-A.
9. The June 1983 issue of *Futurist,* from which this illustration is taken (p. 18), notes that further information can be obtained from the news Bureau, General Electric Company, P.O. Box 5900, Norwalk, CT 06856.
10. Marvin Cetron and Thomas O'Toole, "Careers

with a Future: Where the Jobs Will Be," in Edward Cornish, ed., *Careers Tomorrow: the Outlook for Work in a Changing World* (Bethesda, Md.: World Future Society, 1983), pp. 10–18.

11. Alvin Toffler, *Previews and Premises* (New York: William Morrow, 1983).

12. Vary T. Coates, "The Potential Impact of Robotics," *Futurist*, February 1983, pp. 28–32.

13. Toffler, p. 58.

14. Colin Norman, *The god That Limps: Science and Technology in the Eighties* (New York: W. W. Norton, 1981).

15. Office of Technology Assessment. *Informational Technology and Its Impact on American Education* (Washington, D.C.: OTA, Autumn 1982), p. 3.

*Harold G. Shane* is University Professor of Education, Indiana University, Bloomington.

# A World of Interconnections

## HUMPHREY TONKIN AND JANE EDWARDS

The very science and technology that brought U.S. society to its present peak of achievement have inexorably brought us into competition with the other peoples of the world. Science and technology, of course, have also brought us new opportunities for human advancement and, conversely, new dangers of nuclear annihilation. The critical choice is no longer between stagnation and progress but between destruction and survival. Whether, through education, we can go beyond survival to forge a new sense of ourselves and others as global partners remains to be seen.

In many ways the pace of change in the world is faster than the pace of change in higher education. Academic institutions are not keeping up with changing needs. Consider, for example, the matter of integration of national economies. Between 1960 and 1977 direct foreign investment in the U.S. rose by 77 percent and our investment abroad by 123 percent. Imports of goods and services went up 246 percent and exports 202 percent.

Consider, too, the matter of global human contact—through both transportation and electronic communications. In the brief space of thirty years or less they have revolutionized our lives: The first regularly scheduled jet service across the Atlantic dates from 1958, a year after the launching of the world's first artificial satellite. In 1965 only five countries possessed satellite antennas; by 1979, 114 countries had antennas in the Intelsat satellite system.[1] In 1950 Americans made 900,000 overseas telephone calls; twenty-five years later that annual figure exceeded sixty million.

To what extent has American education adapted to these new realities? We refer not only to the need to teach American students how to use these new machines but to the need to consider the changes they have wrought on human institutions, the new institutions that will be needed in the future to exploit and regulate them, and the implications they carry for the organization of societies and individual freedom.

We speak of competition for natural resources. Americans, who make up 5 percent of the world's population, consume 27 percent of the world's production of raw materials. Of the 30,000 gallons of petroleum consumed worldwide per second, the U.S. uses 10,000. The natural resources of the world are finite, though we may disagree on just *how* finite. A 1977 United Nations report concluded that the world could run out of certain minerals such as lead and zinc as early as the year 2000. Half of America's recoverable oil reserves have probably already been used.

We speak of raising the poor out of misery. Yet human misery goes on. The world cannot feed its people. An annual increase in food production of 4 percent would be necessary to insure that by 1985 the world was adequately fed, but actual food production increases by only about 2 percent each year. Of the 4.5 billion inhabitants of this planet, some 1.3 billion remain chronically undernourished. There are 250 million children in the world who have never seen, and will probably never see, the inside of a classroom. Quite apart from the massive human cost involved (a cost almost beyond our ability to comprehend), misery breeds instability, despair breeds violence, and no belief in the decency of democratic institutions can prevail against the imperatives of personal, human survival. This is not a new problem, but it is one that strikes at the very heart of our way of life in a world in which the United States, like all the other nations in their various ways, can no longer so easily call the shots or predetermine the outcomes.

Our fate is bound up with the fate of others. The acid rain that falls on Scandinavia is primarily produced in the industrial plants of Britain and the Low Countries. Our own nuclear testing in the South Pacific during the 1940s so damaged the homeland of the people of Eniwetok that not even the biggest cleanup project ever attempted, at a cost of over $100 million,

could make the island habitable again. In the Baltic Sea the residuals discharged by many bordering countries have already come close to destroying the sea's ecology. Only an unprecedented cooperative effort of the nations surrounding the Mediterranean Sea seems likely to prevent that body of water from dying. Every nation is at fault because every nation has tended to put its own concerns first. Yet to a greater and greater extent we are discovering that it is in our best interest to consider others' interests and to create instruments and institutions of cooperation to take the place of the confrontation politics of the past.

Although the world has made immense progress in recent years in governing itself and in husbanding its resources—in the face of growing difficulties and complexities—the road is rutted with failures. For every dollar spent on education worldwide, sixty are spent on armaments. Nuclear confrontation, across the Bering Strait and arching over Europe, continues. It has been joined by a problem that promises to increase in urgency: nuclear proliferation. The trade in so-called conventional weapons feeds dozens of local wars. In 1975, 5.5 percent of the world's gross national product was devoted to military expenditures. While that ratio is dropping slightly in the industrialized world, it is rising in the developing nations. New wealth generated by foreign investment and aid in the developing countries has been slow to filter down to all levels of the population. In fact, it may have done more to raise the expectations of the poor through the contiguity of riches than to fulfill these expectations. And some of the best-intentioned efforts have had undesirable side effects. The much-vaunted Green Revolution, which raised crop yields dramatically, did nothing to address the problems of food distribution and tended to put agriculture at the mercy of machines and fossil fuels.[2] While aid pours into Southeast Asia from the industrialized world to ward off starvation for millions of people, that world continues to sell infant formula to Cambodian refugees, though formula feeding in unhygienic and impoverished surroundings may actually contribute to infant mortality.

These problems are in no sense the exclusive fault and burden of the United States. Nor will a dramatic improvement in our awareness of the world bring change overnight. But there is much that we can do to increase our own awareness and our students' awareness of such issues. *It may be the single most important task now facing higher education.* We must help our students come to grips with what is increasingly perceived to be a single set of interlocking concerns of almost indescribable complexity. Are our fragmented knowledge institutions and modes of thought adequate to the need?

We should remember that the increase in international contact over the past thirty years has been accompanied by unprecedented growth in the scope and impact of international institutions. It has even included some voluntary surrender of sovereignty on a regional basis—in the European Community, for example. In this regard the importance of the massive consultative and cooperative mechanism born in the United Nations Charter of 1945 should not be underestimated. The UN may not always do what we would like it to do, and it may sometimes seem a mere political talking-shop. But talk is better than war, and relations between states are, by definition, political. The elimination of smallpox was the work of a "political" body, the World Health Organization, but that in no sense diminishes the importance of the task or the need to support it.[3] Supplementing such formal organizations as the UN, the Organization of American States, or the Organization of African Unity is a host of less formalized structures promoting the free exchange of information across national boundaries and supporting international cooperation in myriad ways. These are structures in which all participants have a stake; to that extent

they help to diminish conflict and promote dialogue.

We may choose to divide world affairs into numerous problem areas—war and peace, hunger, disease, illiteracy, and so on. But we must not forget that these problems manifest themselves in human populations. Indeed, we ourselves are often actors in the problems we study. Not only have the problems of the world changed in scope and complexity in recent years, and not only have advances in technology created new difficulties and helped solve old ones, but the ideas and aspirations of much of the world have changed—our own included. One of the greatest challenges facing education in world affairs is the cultivation in our students of an understanding of the motives of other people and of the social and psychological (and historical) settings that cause them to think and act as they do. We must also learn to understand our own motives with greater sophistication.

As technology flows outward from the industrialized nations, and as knowledge of these nations becomes more widespread in the developing countries (accelerated by advances in mass communications), the aspirations of the developing peoples grow to keep pace. This should come as no surprise, nor should it necessarily be a cause for dismay. But it is the biggest single change in the complexion of world power in the last twenty years, and it is a process little understood in the U.S. There is a dilemma at the heart of these new stirrings of political will. On the one hand, the new nations want to share in the wealth of the industrialized countries. On the other, they are eager to preserve many of their traditional values.

Cultural autonomy and interdependence are in part the results of recent spectacular advances in communications technology—a field that the United States continues to dominate.[4] Currently the U.S. controls more than half the world market in computer hardware; its hold on the software market is even firmer. Two of the world's four major news agencies are American; the other two are in the hands of ex-colonial powers. Films and television series earn $200 million in exports annually for the U.S.; four of the five largest record distributors are American. The U.S. also dominates in the production and use of artificial satellites. Many in the developing world feel that the flow of communications is all in one direction—from the developed to the developing world. The new nations feel tied to the intellectual apron strings of the old, and they resent the intrusion of Western (and particularly American) ways of thinking on societies that have their own values and ways of doing things.

Nevertheless, the predominance of economic power in the world continues to lie in the northern hemisphere, among the large industrialized nations. Here, too, the situation has changed dramatically in recent years. At the core of Western Europe, in the European Community, lies a partially integrated economy, pulled this way and that by internal rivalries but integrated in many respects. The Community is now expanding to take in new members. Its external trade is increasingly enmeshed with the nations of Eastern Europe, who have pulled away from the Soviet Union and now often pursue independent courses, though constantly held in check by their master to the east. Japan, South Korea, Singapore, and others have taken their places among the major industrialized powers. China, the great enigma, clouds the foreign policy considerations of everyone. And through it all the rivalry between the U.S. and the USSR continues, and the squabbles and quarrels of individual nations take place in the constant shadow of the nuclear threat.

Though the East-West rivalry may be a constant in the world array of power, recent events have shown with startling clarity that neither grouping of nations is monolithic. Nor is the Soviet Union winning the hearts and minds of the developing world. In fact, there is every indication that a new pluralism, a new polycentrism,

is entering the relations among nations. The old residual alliances are breaking up and a new pragmatism is emerging. This confirms the importance of an understanding of people and their motives. At the best of times one nation can only hope to have an inkling of the motives behind the actions of another. We must learn to understand how people feel about us, about one another, about their places in the world; and we must *act* on this understanding—whether as specialists in world affairs, as leaders and opinion makers, or as ordinary citizens.

When we turn from consideration of other countries' attitudes toward the United States (and they are obviously far more complex and diverse than our brief comments could suggest) and look at our own attitudes toward the rest of the world, the record is mixed. The 1970s were puzzling years for the U.S., beginning and ending with events of ironic significance. The decade began with our invasion of Cambodia on 30 April 1970, as the U.S. tried vainly to contain a war by expanding it. On 29 December 1979 the Soviet Union invaded Afghanistan, prompted by motives seemingly as self-contradictory as those of its archrival ten years earlier. In 1970 the United States vetoed in the UN Security Council the economic isolation of Rhodesia; in 1980 it actively supported Zimbabwean independence. And in November 1979, fifty-three Americans were taken hostage in Tehran; fifty-two of them suffered 444 days of captivity.

While there are those who delight in pointing out the ineptitudes of the U.S. in one country after another, our record is no worse, and may be considerably better, than that of other nations. The fact remains, however, that we are insufficiently prepared to cope with the complexities of the new world order that is gradually and inexorably coming upon us. Edward Keller and Ronald Roel point out that "studies in television suggest that Americans receive less exposure to foreign countries than any other people in the world" with the possible exception of

China.[5] Content analysis of the popular press produces comparable results. In 1945 some 2,500 staff correspondents from the American press were stationed abroad; thirty years later the number had dropped to 429. There may be many reasons for this, not all of them indicating a decline in interest or quality, but the figures are disturbing.

Educational statistics are also worrisome—at every level. The teaching of foreign languages in elementary schools, an expanding sector in the mid-sixties, has now more or less stopped altogether. While 24 percent of American high school students were studying a language in 1965, by 1976 the figure had fallen to 18 percent. Between 1968 and 1977 enrollment in college language courses fell by 17.7 percent. Nor do the statistics show a rise in interest in other aspects of international studies. As for the federal government, its funding of international studies in colleges and universities has declined steadily over the past ten or fifteen years—by as much as 50 percent in real dollars over a ten-year period.[6]

It is worthy of note that this lack of awareness of international affairs and this decline in international expertise are taking place at a time when the need is greatest. The negative effects are several. First, there is a shortage of skilled experts in international affairs—experts trained in leading universities, with specialized knowledge of particular fields or geographical areas. Second, relatively little attention is given to the international dimension in the general education of our school and college students. This means that the public is less conscious than it might be of the degree and nature of U.S. involvement with the world beyond its borders and of the options and constraints involved. Third, and related to this, the relative lack of attention to world events in the mass media tends to reinforce and compound the problem.

Historically, as many scholars have pointed out, U.S. society is assimilationist and integrationist.

Over the years America has absorbed a vast range of nationalities and races whose overriding desire has been to become American, to differentiate themselves from those they left behind and break the old ties. This process of absorption has led inevitably to a concentration on American ideas and values[7]—ideas and values which, because of the very fact that they are not the natural heritage of many of those who espouse them, must be repeatedly articulated, written down, recited, and reaffirmed.

This long-standing tradition of the melting pot may now be weakening. We place more emphasis on ethnicity than we once did—with results disquieting to many who value a sense of American cultural homogeneity. U.S. society increasingly recognizes the importance of cultural diversity and differing personal roots. There is at least some effort to learn more about the countries from which our ancestors came and even to revive and maintain their customs and languages in a new setting. Of course, ethnicity may simply produce what Bruce LaBrack, in a different context, has called "dual ethnocentrism"—dedication to the imagined virtues of a single nation or people in addition to the United States.[8] Nevertheless, the new emphasis on ethnicity does admit the possibility of diversity and can lead us to appreciate diversity in others. With twelve million native speakers of Spanish in our midst, most of them born and reared in the United States, we are now one of the world's largest Spanish-speaking countries.[9] However, it is only in recent years—through the bilingual education movement (with all of its own vicissitudes) and an increasing awareness of the legal rights of Spanish speakers—that we have begun to appreciate this fact.

Other factors also aid our efforts. More Americans are traveling abroad. More and more foreigners are visiting the U.S. The influence of other nations on the U.S. economy and way of life is observable at every turn. To a greater and greater extent we are obliged to deal with other peoples as equals. It is not exactly that the

United States is shifting from a condition of isolation into active participation in world affairs but that it is learning, or must learn, how to become a *partner* rather than a dominant power. What Sen. William Fulbright called the "arrogance of power"—a sense of manifest destiny concerning America's role in the world—has always been an improper way of handling international relations, but it has now become impractical as well.

Education is not the only element needed in the adaptation of the U.S. to this new view of the world, but it is one of the most important. If educators do not take the lead in making the public more aware of the world and in creating a sense of world responsibility and global values among our citizens, it is difficult to know who will. And if our teachers are not ourselves, they may ultimately prove to be our rivals, whose mode of education is more abrupt, more painful, more demoralizing. The place to start, then, is in school and college curricula, in the attitudes of educators, and in their prescriptions for their students.

It is fashionable, and has been for a number of years, to suggest that the world is becoming increasingly complicated. But such a view is an oversimplification. It is not that the world is more complicated but that we have cultivated a more complicated approach to it, as we become more aware of the limits of power and as greater participation in decision making (again, largely a consequence of the revolution in communications) gives more voices the power to be heard. Above all, the ever-present awareness that we possess the power to destroy ourselves—through environmental as well as nuclear catastrophe—adds to each decision a new dimension of agony. "A democracy" wrote Alexis de Tocqueville, "cannot get at the truth without experience, and many nations may perish for lack of the time to discover their mistakes." What was once true of nations is now true of humanity itself. As noted in a recent Club of Rome report that argued for a new type of learning, we can no longer hope to learn only from experience, for the experience may be fatal.[10]

Many feel that the old battles of national sovereignty are, or ought to be, outdated and that world loyalties will gradually outstrip national loyalties. But another, largely unspoken, attitude sharpens resistance to this view. Many people fear that the inculcation of "global" values, of a world view of things, will somehow weaken the national resolve of our own society and expose us to the manipulation of other nations. But neither innocence nor ignorance provides protection against manipulation. Lack of knowledge may on occasion make action easier, but it also heightens the probability that such action will prove self-defeating. We must have the courage to seek out and act upon the international facts of life.

The realities of interdependence are with us all. Interdependence is not so much an ideal as a very simple fact. Even those who fear it must learn to understand it, if only to set limits to it. At issue is whether we shall manage interdependence effectively, not whether we have the collective capability to wish it away.

## ENDNOTES

1. International Commission for the Study of Communication Problems, *Interim Report on Communication Problems in Modern Society* (Paris: Unesco, 1978), p. 41; and *Many Voices, One World: Toward a New, More Just, and More Efficient World Information and Communication Order* (London: Kogan Page, New York: Unipub, and Paris: Unesco, 1980).
2. Paul R. Ehrlich, Anne H. Ehrlich, and John P. Holdren, *Ecoscience: Population, Resources, Environment* (San Francisco: Freeman, 1977); Vernon Ruttan, "The Green Revolution: Seven

Generalization," *International Development Review,* vol. 19, no. 4, 1977, pp. 16–23; and Cheryl Christensen, "World Hunger: A Structural Approach," in Raymond F. Hopkins and Donald J. Puchala, eds., *The Global Political Economy of Food* (Madison: University of Wisconsin Press, 1978), pp. 171–200.

3. Robert Muller, *The Need for Global Education* (Philadelphia: Global Interdependence Center, n.d. [1976]).

4. Jeremy Tunstall, "The American Role in Worldwide Mass Communication," in George Gerbner, eds., *Mass Media Policies in Changing Cultures* (New York: Wiley, 1977), pp. 3–12; idem, *The Media Are American* (New York: Columbia, 1977).

5. Edward Keller and Ronald Roel, "Foreign Languages and Culture in the Media: Report to the Task Force on Public Awareness," in Richard I. Brod, ed., *Language Study for the 1980's: Reports of the MLA-ACLA Language Task Forces* (New York: Modern Language Association, 1980), pp. 78–94.

6. President's Commission on Foreign Language and International Studies, *Strength Through Wisdom: A Critique of U.S. Capability* (Washington, D.C.: U.S. Government Printing Office, 1979).

7. Frederick Rudolph, *Curriculum: A History of the American Undergraduate Course of Study Since 1636* (San Francisco: Jossey-Bass, 1977), p. 65.

8. Bruce LaBrack, "Results of International Experience for U.S. Students: Bi-Culturalism or Dual Ethnocentrism," paper presented at the 21st annual convention of the International Studies Association, Los Angeles, 1980.

9. Rose L. Hayden, "Funding International Education Programs: An Unmet Agenda," statement before the U.S. Senate Appropriations Subcommittee on Labor HEW, 21 September 1977.

10. James W. Botkin, Mahdi Elmandjra, and Mircea Malitza, *No Limits to Learning: Bridging the Human Gap* (Oxford, England: Pergamon, 1979).

*Humphrey Tonkin* is Professor of English and Coordinator of International Programs, University of Pennsylvania, Philadelphia.
*Jane Edwards* is Foreign Student Advisor, International Programs Office, University of Pennsylvania, Philadelphia.

# Through the Cultural Looking Glass . . .

## SEYMOUR FERSH

Within the next hour about 7,200 babies will be born. At the moment of birth, the infants will be more like each other than they ever will be again. Their differences will grow because each of them is born into a different family and into a different culture—into a way of living that has developed in a particular place over a long period of time. From birth onward, each child is encouraged to be *ethnocentric*—to believe that his homeland, his people, his language, his everything is not only different but also superior to that of other people. The elders teach that the ways in which we do thing are the natural ways, the proper ways, and the moral ways. In other places, they—"barbarians" and "foreigners"—follow a strange way of life. Ours is *the* culture; theirs is *a* culture.

This kind of behavior in favor of one's own culture occurs most frequently when groups of people live in relative isolation from each other.

From *AAUW Journal* 68, no. 6 (April 1975): 9–12. Used by permission of the author and the publisher.

Survival of the group is believed to depend mainly on each person's acceptance of and loyalty to the group's traditional patterns of life and thought. People from outside the group are unwelcome because their manners and morals, being different, might by example threaten the existing system. These outsiders, in almost all languages, are designated by a word which means "stranger"—one whose beliefs and behavior are, to the insider, strange, peculiar, eccentric, erratic, odd, queer, quaint, or outlandish.

This hatred of foreigners has a name; it is xenophobia. The anthropologists even have a name for this kind of behavior; it is misoneism, a deep and unreasoned hatred of new ideas. The traditional distrust of foreigners has been intensified by the news media where usually, as Marshall McLuhan observes, "real news is bad news—bad news *about* somebody or bad news *for* somebody." We have been generally conditioned to think of other national groups as either threats or burdens. Terms such as "trouble spots," "powder kegs," and "points of conflict" are often used to describe situations and conditions outside the United States. Such terms carry the feeling that the rest of the world has become a "burdensome" and "troublesome" place which creates a continuous series of problems for us.

Deaths and population decreases among foreigners are often unconsciously welcomed as "good news" because of the feeling that there will be fewer of "them" with whom to compete for worldly resources, which are assumed to be limited. Because each nation tends to exaggerate its own achievements, people everywhere tend not to appreciate how much of their own development—in ideas and in physical survival—has been contributed by "foreigners."

In some ways, however, the ethnocentric view of life is "right"; the pattern of responses that evolved in a particular place may make relatively good sense—for *that* particular people and place.

This generalization was especially true in the past when, according to Professor Elting E. Morison:

For generations—for centuries—men did their work with the natural resources and energies lying ready at hand—the earth, the beast of burden, the wind and falling water. These materials and sources of power remained on the whole constant and stable; therefore the conditioned reflexes, habits of mind, customary emotional responses—in short, the culture—built up around these agencies remained on the whole relatively constant and stable.

## SEPARATE AND RELATED

As human beings become aware of their relatedness, they need not necessarily cease being ethnocentric. When a person begins to identify with a nation, he does not cease being a member of his immediate family; he learns to apportion and extend his loyalties. Ethnocentrism is important and useful because it helps a person to develop a local cultural pattern that is appropriate for specific conditions. It would be unfortunate if the richness of cultural variety were lost to us. In learning about other cultures, the objective is not to discover a "universal culture" suitable for all people, in all places, and for all times. Rather, the objective is to learn the lesson that Aldous Huxley described following his first around-the-world trip in 1926:

So the journey is over and I am back again, richer by much experience and poorer by many exploded convictions, many perished certainties. For convictions and certainties are too often the concomitants of ignorance. . . . I set out on my travels knowing, or thinking I knew, how men should live, how be governed, how educated, what they should believe. I had my views on every activity of life. Now, on my return, I find myself without any of these pleasing certainties. . . . The better you understand the significance of any question, the more difficult it becomes to answer it. Those who attach a high importance to their own opinion should stay at home. When one is traveling, convictions are mislaid as easily as spectacles, but unlike spectacles, they are not easily replaced.

A person's awareness of his own ethnocentricity does not mean that he therefore must consider all cultures equally acceptable to him. Awareness can, however, help an observer to realize that what he "sees" is largely already "behind his eyes." Marshall McLuhan says, "Our need today is, culturally, the same as the scientist's who seeks to become aware of the bias of the instruments of research in order to correct that bias." A similar warning comes from Pierre Teilhard de Chardin: "When researchers reach the end of their analysis, they cannot tell with any certainty whether the structure they have made is the essence of the matter they are studying, or the reflection of their own thoughts."

Today, humankind is living in a world where groups are becoming more and more interrelated, less and less isolated. Ignorance of others is *not* bliss and what you don't know *can* hurt you. Moreover, many inventions and styles of life created by individual groups can help others. Each culture does not have to reinvent the wheel or depend exclusively on its own scientists, philosophers, and artists. Learning about other cultures is not something done as a favor to the people who live in them—as an expression of goodwill. Such knowledge can be of immediate and profound benefit and pleasure to the learner.

We should, in the words of James Thurber, "not look back in anger or look forward in fear but look around in awareness." It is too late for us to be unprejudiced, but we can recognize and become alert to our condition. The unprejudiced mind is not without prejudices; it is, says Hans Selye, "a mentality that has control over its numerous prejudices, and is always willing to reconsider them in the face of contrary evidence."

For example, in the United States the currently popular way of dividing the world is in terms of Western and non-Western cultures. In the so-called non-Western parts of the globe are people as different from each other as Chinese, Indians, Nigerians, Egyptians, and Iranians. But these differences are minimized or, more often, overlooked or ignored. In a similar way, all the peoples who were living in the Americas when Columbus landed were identified by the Europeans as "Indians." The so-called Indians never thought of themselves as one people but considered themselves, more correctly, to be Iroquois, Hopi, Aztecs, Incas, and other tribal groups.

The major purpose, therefore, of learning about other cultures is to discover the ways in which other groups of human beings have organized their lives to answer the perennial questions of survival and fulfillment. Confucius said, "The nature of people is always the same; it is their habits which separate them."

## FACTS AND FEELINGS

Each culture has its own kinds of achievements and problems. In comparing his country to the United States, an educated person from India, for example, would not deny that his country is backward with reference to the number of automobiles, amounts of electrical power, and supplies of food and medical services. But he would rightfully resent the conclusion, by inference, that he and his people are less human. Why, for instance, should a photograph of an Indian woman and her children in an American textbook have a caption which reads, "Even in mud huts, Indian parents love their children"? Does love increase with an increase of material goods? A *New York Times* reporter wrote:

The Easterner seems heartlessly unconcerned about the misery of those to whom he is not related by some tie. But to his family and friends, the

Asian commits himself in a way that makes the American appear heartless. The thought of packing one's parents off to some old-age home or retirement colony is shocking to him.

The features and qualities admired in one culture may bring hostility and suspicion in another. What image does the United States present in a world where our people, who number six percent of the population, have half of the material wealth and spend an average of about $90 per person for liquor and tobacco in a year—more than the average *total* income of many of the world's people? How do others see us in a world where most people have too little to eat, while in the United States some of our major health problems come from overeating? It is not really likely that such gaps between the world's rich and poor peoples will be narrowed if conditions continue as they have.

And should the peoples of the so-called "backward" or "undeveloped" countries be impressed with the so-called "developed" countries, which in recent years have spent more money on military matters than on health and education? Their total annual war-related expenditures, if divided among the world's population, would amount to more than $50 for every person. It has been estimated that the elimination of military spending could double the income of the 1.2 billion people who make less than $100 annually. It could also release 25 million soldiers and 75 million workers for constructive work.

It should become clear that choices between cultural patterns need not be rigidly restricted between the "spiritual East" and the "materialistic West." In the United States, many are beginning to learn that people do not live by gross national product alone. Similarly, in countries such as India, there is a growing dissatisfaction with the relatively low material standard of living. As people learn more about cultures other than their own, they begin to apply a variety of measurements in judging their own culture. The result is that waves of "spiritualism" and "materialism" flow around the world, mixing ingredients from one culture into another. It is no longer rare to see an Arab camel driver listening to a transistor radio or to see American students listening to lectures on Hinduism.

But to the overwhelming majority of the world's people, their own culture is still the one against which all others are measured. There is still a strong habit of accepting one's own culture as superior. The need is for alertness to assumptions. What is a person implying when, with apparent goodwill, he says, "Although the people of Asia and Africa are backward, there is no reason for us to feel superior"?

## WINDOWS AND MIRRORS

When we become alert to our cultural conditioning, we are ready to continue our study of other peoples. The next concern is one of *cultural contexts*. New information and experiences are likely to be perceived within the framework of one's own cultural background rather than that of the one being studied. Contexts, after all, are invisible. How can the "outsider" possibly hope to create for himself the same cultural contexts which the "insider" carries effortlessly and unconsciously in his head? Here again, the need is for humility and strong motivation.

Until recently, for most people of the world, it really did not matter if understanding stopped at national boundaries, if indeed it stretched that far. Now, however, when international travel is so fast and so frequent, it is hazardous to base our actions solely on our own views. Moreover, ignorance about others perpetuates ignorance about ourselves because it is only through comparisons that we can discover personal differences and similarities. The glass through which we view other cultures serves not only as a window but also as a mirror in which we can see a reflection of our own way of life.

The achievement and maintenance of a dual vision, sometimes called *empathy* (the capacity to imagine what it is like to have the ideas and feelings of another person), is not, however, easily accomplished. Professor Ralph K. White explains that empathy requires us to hold two interpretations of the same facts, the other fellow's interpretation and our own. Because the human mind seeks simplicity and certainty, he feels, it rebels at the complexity and uncertainty of holding two points of view.

For example, most of the reporting in American newspapers about "cow worship" in India has been factually correct but contextually false. Few Americans understand the practical importance of cows in nonindustrial countries such as India. A cow gives milk and provides dung—a dependable source of fuel. The cow also delivers other cows and bulls. And those bulls which are castrated become bullocks (oxen), which are the main work animals in rural India. After they die, the cow, bull, and bullock provide skins for leather. The cow may have become "sacred," as Gandhi suggests, because she has been one of the most useful and docile creatures on earth.

This consideration of the cow's utility within the traditional Indian context is not meant to suggest that the cow will or should continue to be "sacred." In every culture, there are reasons why certain things are done in certain ways. When the reasons are no longer relevant, changes can be introduced without serious damage to the cultural pattern. Many times, however, the relevance of traditional customs is not understood by outsiders. Changes introduced under these conditions are often harmful.

As another example of a point of view based on cultural context, consider that in the United States the automobile holds a special (some would say "sacred") position, even though almost two million Americans have died in motor vehicle crashes—almost twice the number killed in all of our wars. Each year, about 55,000 people in this country die in car accidents—a rate of one every nine minutes. The number seriously injured annually is about five million. The total economic loss is estimated at $50 billion yearly.

If a "non-Western" consultant were to study "the problem of the automobile in the United States" he might start out by considering it basically as a means of transportation. After all, this is how Henry Ford started out when he produced all of his earliest cars in one color and changed models only when there were technological advances. In terms of transportation, the consultant might recommend that we have fewer cars and more express trains and that in fact we should consider "birth control" of cars because they are increasing so rapidly in number. But in making this recommendation, the foreign consultant would reveal that he did not understand the car's place in American culture. The American economy currently depends overwhelmingly on widespread auto transportation, and the car is believed to be an essential part of an American's "pursuit of happiness."

Today, more people throughout the world are trying to understand each other but a willingness is not enough. It takes careful attention and concern. Never before have we had the opportunity to know so much about the world we inhabit—its peoples, its natural resources, its technological potential. But it is also true that the quality of life, and respect for the individual worth of each person may be lessening. We need to reaffirm that the proper study of humankind is still humans.

*Seymour Fersh* is Professor of Education, College of Education, Fairleigh Dickinson University, Rutherford, New Jersey.

# Our Two-Story Culture

## PAUL BOHANNAN

Only a few years ago it was stylish to say that we could not prepare our children and our students to live in the world because we did not know what their world would be like. Today that world is becoming clear. They will live with—they already live with—a two-story culture. There is a large-scale world, with its common culture. It is primarily economic and political, mediated by dollars and votes, by consumer products and televised national political conventions. There is, at the same time, a small-scale world of family and community, mediated by sympathy and trust in face-to-face relationships. To different degrees, we all live in both.

Both the large-scale and the small-scale world have become complicated; the first by sheer size, the second by sheer variety. All of us must learn to deal with the large-scale culture. We may not seek to participate actively in it, but we cannot ignore it. We must also deal with the fact that most people today—at least those of us who live in an industrialized society—belong to many small intimate groups, and that these are no longer space-bound territorial groups.

We might call ourselves, with our two-story culture, post-peasants. For a long time social scientists have recognized that the essence of the peasant society is that it is divided into two parts; that is, the peasant culture is not capable of survival without joining with other part-cultures to make up a larger entity. Peasants, although they are self-sufficient in many ways, depend on traders to bring them products (salt, perhaps) that they cannot produce themselves, and on political authorities (earls, perhaps) to protect them.

The large-scale culture—the upstairs culture—revolves around power. There are only a few distinct cultures in the large-scale world: the varieties of democracy, the varieties of communism, and the various socialisms. All the cultures of the large-scale world are interconnected. They are part-cultures in one big world-culture.

The small-scale cultures—downstairs, if you will—are based on intimacy. They are many and varied, and they are *not* interconnected. Or, rather, they are interconnected by individuals who participate in several of them, rather than by institutions in which each individual is a recognizable entity. Some are still tribal; others still peasant. Some are based on religion, some on propinquity. But even more are based on the choice or subscription of individuals and are in that sense "voluntary." The basis for the choice may be rock music, pot, or Masonic ritual. Some small-scale cultures are limited by race or (that most mystical of all concepts) ethnicity.

Small-scale cultures are not usually in touch with one another. Between them are invisible boundaries (or unspoken or disputed boundaries) rather than the overt and known boundaries established between nations or corporations. Indeed, the only reason that the people of small-scale groups should get to know one another is to reduce fear. But they can go on without one another. They are connected only within the experience of individuals—in the bits of culture that each of us packs within himself.

Obviously, we need both large- and small-scale groups. Consumption aside, the economic and political tasks cannot be done by small-scale groups; welfare aside, providing care and inti-

From *Saturday Review* 55 (September 2, 1972): 40–41. © 1972, Saturday Review, Inc. Used by permission of the author and the publisher.

macy cannot be done by large-scale groups. The problem is to successfully negotiate the stairs between the two stories.

The two levels of culture with which each of us lives must not get too far out of phase; that is, the stairs between levels must not be allowed to collapse or to be overused. The small-scale cultures, for example, are sometimes dragged into the worldwide framework of large-scale culture. The church in the late fifteenth century had concerned itself with power and hence became a political institution. Nationalism—the practice of building a state on the basis of a nation (a word derived from the Latin word meaning "to be born")—led to a new kind of colonialism and to the widespread problems of minorities because, via the complex idea of "nation," the state could invade ethnic cultures. When power derived from a large-scale culture seeks to destroy or isolate microcultures by controlling entree into the large-scale culture, strife inevitably results.

One of the most common strategies for squeezing people out of the large-scale culture is powerful condemnation of their small-scale cultures. On the other hand, some small-scale cultures are isolated (sometimes voluntarily) in such a way that their members are systematically held back from learning the principles of the large-scale culture.

The most characteristic aspect of what is called the Establishment is that the people in it have no difficulties with the stairs. They can go easily from macroculture to microculture. Their microcultures contain people who run or move easily in the institutions of the large-scale culture. They have a built-in third level that gives easy access to both the others. They often despise people who lack the ability to pass between the two and thus shut themselves off from most microcultures.

We all know that today there are many young people (usually referred to as "middle-class" because of the socioeconomic position of their parents) who can, when they choose, manipulate the large-scale culture very well (but who may consider it immoral to do so) and who feel empty—"alienated"—because they have been "robbed" of the intimacy of a small-scale culture. The countercultures are attempts to create viable and rewarding microcultures, because living only within the large-scale culture is not enough. However, living within the small-scale culture alone is not enough either, as most people in most experimental communities come to realize.

The size of the world population and the excellence of our communications means that we are necessarily living in a world that is truly fraught with danger, danger to our power structures on the one hand, danger to our tribalism on the other. All of us are both running scared and longing for community. So we join the John Birch Society or "the counterculture"—it is the same thing. Yet we are also living in a world potentially fraught with delight. Never have so many people had so wide a choice of cultures open to them.

The goal for America must be to make its two-story culture overt. We must recognize it and learn how to use it toward humane ends. The large-scale culture of America—the culture that accompanies and vivifies our economic and political institutions—must be based on our historically validated doctrines of equality, doctrines that we are still struggling to define. In this context equality means one man, one vote and equal economic opportunity.

At the same time we must cherish a whole spectrum of microcultures. We all know that the melting pot didn't, in fact, melt anything. It was a myth for dealing with the overwhelming migration of "foreigners." The early immigrants to the New World were not foreigners to anyone except the red Americans. But late in the eighteenth century, when America was becoming an independent state, it also sought to become a nation—a cultural unity based on a common history.

America was probably the first to achieve nation-statehood backward. Whereas Portugal, Britain, France, Spain, and Holland were all nations that founded states, America first made herself a state, and then had to struggle to make herself a nation. Except for the blacks, immigrants before 1776 did indeed merge more or less into "old stock Americans." The first European "foreigners" were the Irish fleeing the famine—the earlier Irish began to call themselves "Scotch-Irish" to keep their "nationality" (a strange new American concept) at the same time they kept their nonforeignness in America.

Equality in small-scale cultures means something very different from what it means in the large-scale culture. Fundamentally, it means a respect for "differentness," without envy and without fear. In these microcultures we can "be ourselves," relax and enjoy with "our own," struggle with the external problems of birth, sex, and death, eat and dance, love and hate, all to the limit of the human capacity for these things.

And what does that mean for people? It means that we have a lot of people who are competent in the large-scale culture and, at the same time, in one or more microcultures. It is happening: One need only look at the variety of people in the televised portion of the Democratic National Convention. There were a lot of two-story people there, their microcultures showing, working together in the large-scale culture with determination and skill.

But what about a new vision to replace the melting pot? The black revolution has brought black small-scale cultures (the "s" is important) to the attention of everyone, as blacks work to regain rights in the large-scale culture that they almost grasped after the Emancipation Proclamation. And blacks are not the only groups in the public eye. Today we hear of red power, brown power, Greek power, Italian power, Irish power, Polish power, Jewish power, and, feebly but nevertheless audibly, WASP power.

But most microcultures are not, strictly speaking, ethnic. They center upon the hordes of voluntary associations that industrialized people create. This is especially true of Americans, probably as a function of mobility.

There are two great difficulties in the world: communication between the two stories and fear among microcultures. But surely the goals are obvious: civil rights laws based on equality and justice, and sufficient intercultural education so that the differences among microcultures need no longer frighten us. Confusion between the large-scale culture and the microcultures often leads one small group to believe that by putting another group down they thereby control the large-scale culture. They do not reckon that, even if they succeed momentarily, the forces within the total system will destroy them. It is the same kind of futility as the War of the Roses. There can be no victory worth the price.

*Paul Bohannan* is Dean, Social Sciences and Communications, University of Southern California, Los Angeles.

# Television and Values: Implications for Education

## JEAN BENEDICT RAFFA

In recent years the moral development of youth has received increasing attention. Many social commentators suggest that an erosion of traditional values is taking place in society and that educational institutions must accept a portion of the responsibility for enhancing moral growth. In any list of variables that are seen as contributing to this value erosion, the medium of television is invariably included. Research data are beginning to accumulate that suggest that television may indeed be a significant factor. As a consequence, educators need to understand the potential impact of television on children and look for ways to counteract any negative influences of this medium. What follows is a summary of the prevailing concerns about the impact of television on the formation of values in youth, and some resultant implications for curriculum and instruction.

There are at least two major classifications under which we could discuss the many variables that can contribute to value formation and change. The first category includes all the characteristics of the medium itself, and the second is comprised of the many aspects of the content (such as words, sounds, and images) that combine to convey messages.

## THE MEDIUM

McLuhan asserted that it is the form of the medium and not its messages that is the critical element in understanding the consequences of media exposure.[1] Following his lead, others have advanced several hypotheses, but it will take years of research and observation before we will know for certain which of the postulated characteristics are truly capable of influencing value change in a negative manner. In the meantime, educators should be aware of the implications of these possibilities.

1. *Television preempts the traditional development of childhood by replacing active daily play.*[2] Children's play is serious business. It enhances physical skill development, affords children the opportunity to become active users instead of passive receivers of experience, provides outlets for psychological tension, and is the means of acquiring social skills and impulse control. Above all, the ability to play enables one to enjoy living.

What then are the consequences of play deprivation? In one famous experiment, Suomi and Harlow found that young monkeys who were play-deprived were significantly more aggressive in their social behavior than monkeys who had adequate play opportunities.[3] Could there be a human correlation between reduced play time and the increase in normal childish aggression observed by so many parents and teachers? Could this be the reason for the link between television viewing and aggressive behavior reported by the Surgeon General in 1972?[4] An implication for the thesis of an erosion of values in this society is that with increased television viewing and a commensurate decrease in opportunities for social interaction, children may be less apt to develop such social skills as sharing, cooperating, getting along peacefully with

From *Education Forum* 49, No. 2 (Winter, 1985): 189–198. © 1985, Kappa Delta Pi. Used by permission of the author and the publisher.

others, losing gracefully, and learning to give in. In an age in which we have developed the capability of destroying the human race with nuclear weapons, violence and aggression as a means of problem solving are values we can ill afford to perpetuate.

The implication for education is that we provide more opportunities for children to learn through play. While most schools include physical education in the curriculum, too often these classes stress skill development and competition to the exclusion of cooperative social interaction and the sheer pleasure of play. It is essential that educators search for ways to make both indoor and outdoor play attractive. Perhaps we can interest children in physical activity by allowing them to be active all day long in their learning instead of only during one short period when all must play the same game and learn the same skills. Perhaps we can also make those games and skills desirable and fun by stressing each child's physical strengths and not his or her weaknesses. At the preschool and primary levels we can allow children many opportunities to engage in unstructured play throughout the day. At all levels we can provide group learning activities that necessitate the development of social skills. Finally, we can, perhaps simultaneously, attain our educational objectives and provide opportunities for fun through play, when we use such instructional techniques as role-playing, dramatic play, simulations, and games. As we teach children to value play and social interaction, we will also be establishing behavior patterns that lead to a deeply satisfying way of life.

2. *The passive nature of television viewing instills an attitude of spectatorship and withdrawal from direct involvement in real life experiences.*[5] Some observers deny that watching television is a passive experience and cite as proof the obvious signs of involvement and enjoyment that can be witnessed in any child viewer. Yet, as compared with talking, writing, running, working, and playing, we must consider sitting, watching, and

listening as passive activities. Unfortunately, the traditional school also tends to instill an attitude of spectatorship. Children are often forced at very early ages to sit still for long periods of time, listen to lengthy lectures, and read about or watch scientific experiments instead of actually conducting them. If schools instill passivity and television does the same, what opportunities remain for the growing child to learn to value active involvement in life? Very few, especially for children who spend most of their out-of-school time watching television.

The implication for schools is clear. We must provide more opportunities for children to become actively involved in their learning: to make choices, to solve problems, to conduct their own experiments, to learn from their own mistakes. The ultimate consequences of passivity must be a dehumanized society in which the majority of interactions are with machines, most pleasurable experiences are vicarious, and the psychological norm is a sense of isolation, alienation from nature and other human beings, and chronic frustration and depression caused by the numbing awareness of one's powerlessness.

3. *The technical specifications of television dilute plots, characters, and ideas to deemphasize the complexity of life.*[6] Time demands based on standard half-hour or one-hour formats, small screen size (which does not allow for visual complexity), and an emphasis on visualization place constraints on television writers that (a) result in stereotyped and simplistic characters and plots, and (b) preclude the presentation of complex ideas or verbalization. Thus, we may be subtly teaching children to value the easy answer; the surface judgment; the quickly-grasped, simple concept; and only the most common, everyday language. This could contribute to a lack of commitment to language as a vehicle for complex thought and expression.

Of course, television is only one factor in the life of a child. But when we combine the powerful impact of this medium with absentee parents and a watered-down curriculum taught by teachers with lowered expectations for students, we have reason for concern. If teachers are required to spend so much time coaching children to pass minimum competency tests that they must forego the daily reading of fine literature or the involved, time-consuming discussion that necessitates clear thinking and abstract reasoning, children will get the message. While scores on tests requiring factual recall and simple comprehension go up, the emphasis on the skills of analyzing complex ideas, creating new ones, or evaluating the ideas of others will be diminished.

Children must have more experience in the expressive forms of language, i.e., writing and speaking, and more exposure to good literature containing multi-faceted characters and profound ideas expressed in complex ways. We cannot totally blame television for the emergence of a new minority, that of the linguistically and conceptually deprived, but educators can avoid presenting children with the same type of simple-minded mediocrity that comprises the average child's daily television consumption!

4. *The highly visual aspect of the medium discourages the formation of individual, creative images.*[7] The concern is that if children are provided with all the pictures, they will have no need to create their own and thus will rely less upon their imaginations. I believe this argument is too simplistic and tends to ignore the true nature of the faculty of imagination. A unique characteristic of the human is his or her awareness of the vast range of possibilities in any given situation, as well as the ability to run through in imagination the different ways of reacting that she or he can possibly consider in any given situation. Television, like movies and books, can open up the range of alternatives for viewers. I do not believe that these modes of communication necessarily limit one's capacity for imagination or creativity; on the contrary, they may expand it.

However, having a larger repertoire of alternatives is only helpful when one has many opportunities to make choices and interact with the environment. Children who absorb excessive numbers of ready-made television images at home and who passively follow teacher directions at school will not learn to value personal choices or self-originated visual experiences. This is where schools can make a difference—they can provide children with opportunities to originate and experiment with their own visual images. When viewed from this perspective, we can see that art education, far from being a "frill," is actually essential to the healthy development of children in today's world. Experiences in art provide outlets for creativity, opportunities to experiment with a variety of alternatives, and direct involvement with one's physical environment. They force the individual to produce mental images that gradually take physical shape as material and equipment are manipulated.

Moreover, children must be read to on a regular basis from the preschool years through elementary grades, and they themselves must be continually encouraged to read. When we listen to or read a book, we create our own images, derived from our own experiences and organized in ways that help us make sense in our world. Good literature also exposes children to some traditional values that are often absent from standard television fare, thus providing them with moral alternatives as well as visual ones.

5. *The time demands of television result in an emphasis on speedy conflict resolution, creating the impression that all problems can be solved easily and quickly.*[8] This is especially true of commercials. It is suggested that this produces a low tolerance for any frustration in the learning process and discourages children from activities that promise less than instant gratification. Although many experienced teachers have noted with concern that today's children seem much more impatient with delayed gratification than ever before, I am

again not convinced that television is solely responsible. Our nation's unparalleled affluence and the common practice of buying now and paying later have led most of us to expect to obtain what we require quickly and relatively painlessly. But regardless of the cause of this phenomenon, it is true that television tends to perpetuate subtly the value of quick and easy answers. In contrast, for instance, with reading a literary classic, debating with a learned, articulate adult, or experimenting with a difficult problem for which there is no easy answer, television viewing is less likely to teach children to value persistence, patience, and perseverance.

Implications for education are many. Teachers can employ instructional techniques that require inductive reasoning, problem solving, and prolonged involvement. Talented adults in such fields as sports and business may be brought into classrooms to describe the years of preparation and practice that went into the development of their skills. Biographies of famous, successful people whose achievements came only after patience and persistence, can be read to students. Finally, students themselves can be involved in attempts to solve actual school and community problems that have no simple solutions.

## THE CONTENT

Most television research to date has dealt with content or, more specifically, with the types of characters portrayed and their words and actions. Other aspects of content, such as sound effects, music, facial expressions, and camera techniques have been less often studied. We now know that the portrayal of aggressive behavior on television contributes to the learning of such behavior in some children. Nevertheless, we can as yet do little more than guess about the possible impact of the more subtle aspects of television content. The following are some concerns that have educational implications.

1. *The visual techniques employed by television are so poorly understood by the majority of our population that we are vulnerable to subtle manipulation.*[9] Television uses a wide variety of visual techniques such as fades, zooms, cuts, pans, close-ups, and slow motion. Each of these is deliberately employed to convey certain messages and evoke certain viewer reactions. Most of us pay no attention to these techniques, yet they can be the very factors that make a scene unsettling, memorable, and conducive to modeling effects.

Bandura asserts that most human behavior is learned observationally through modeling, and the types of models that prevail within a given social setting affect which human qualities, from many alternatives, will be selectively activated.[10] Thus, the visual images we are exposed to can have a tremendous impact on the learning of values. Television offers an unprecedented source of visual stimulation, but because our society has traditionally emphasized the skills that deal with the verbal, logical, and sequential (the so-called left-brain functions), we largely ignore the visual inputs to learning. Accordingly, children and adults are vulnerable to visual propaganda because they are unaware of the "grammar" of these images.

If children are not made aware of these visual stimuli, or taught to interpret and analyze them, they are very much apt to model the inappropriate behavior they see on television. They won't have developed the ability or the awareness necessary to combat negative visual influences or the emotional responses that accompany them. In the long run, it is possible that youth may adopt the very values (aggression, violence, the desire for simple solutions, and inanity, to name a few) that are least conducive to personal and societal growth. I know of no better argument for the inclusion of aesthetic education and television literacy in today's curriculum.

2. *Emotionally disturbed children are more apt to*

*be harmed by televised content than are well-adjusted children.*[11] Because of this, it is especially important for our school counselors and teachers of the emotionally disturbed to understand the impact of television. One suggestion is for teacher preparation programs to include courses, or portions of courses, that examine television literacy and recent research pertaining to the effects of television on youth. Teachers of disturbed children can make special use of this knowledge to counsel parents as to appropriate viewing for their children, and to initiate discussions and activities with these children in an effort to counteract some of the possibly negative influences in television viewing.

3. *The television depiction of violence in the hands of the righteous gives the impression of its acceptability.*[12] Violent behavior exhibited by law enforcement officers and other heroes convey the idea that it is alright for the police and other "good" characters to use violence and break laws when their motives are socially acceptable ones. While well-adjusted children may not actually model such behavior, they may be subtly absorbing a belief in violence as the only way of solving difficult problems. If we want to teach children the value of nonviolence, we must find ways to counteract this message.

One suggestion is for teachers to view popular television shows with their students and then to lead discussions about the rightness and wrongness, or desirability and undesirability of aggressive behavior. Teachers can ask such questions as, "Is there another way the hero could have solved the problem without fighting?" Having children devise peaceful methods of resolving televised problems should heighten their awareness of the necessity for doing the same in their real lives. Furthermore, using television programs as sources of issues for classroom discussion can be an interesting way of enhancing responsible moral development in students.

4. *Advertisements foster a belief in "things" or materialism.*[13] If there is any one predominant

value that can be seen to characterize the American public today, it is probably our overwhelming trust in technology and its resultant products. We truly seem to believe that our problems will be solved if only we use the better toothpaste, coffee, soap, or deodorant; wear the name blue jeans; drive the right car; or buy the best computer. Rarely do media emphasize invisible qualities, or all the standards, character traits, values, and religious beliefs that were such an important part of our nation's history. Today our society looks to highly visible "things" to provide us with answers.

Is this totally the fault of television? Certainly not. However, the medium does perpetuate the message. Fortunately, these commercial messages with which every child is familiar provide excellent examples from which to extract lessons about the value of materialism and how it is conveyed. Children can be offered courses in consumer education in which they are taught to recognize sales techniques, propaganda, half-truths, bias, and exaggeration. But more than this, they can be reminded again and again by thoughtful teachers that it is not the visible "things" of the world that provide true happiness, but the much more elusive, much more desirable, invisible qualities. This understanding can also be conveyed through exposure to great literature, religion, ethics, history, and philosophy. These should be offered in some form to all children in order to insure that as many young people as possible, and not just the smarter or richer ones, are made aware of this important message.

## SUMMARY

Television is a powerful medium of communication that appears to be fostering and perpetuating some values that have been traditionally considered undesirable. There are many things schools can do to counteract the formation of these negative values in children, and several specific suggestions have been offered.

Throughout the foregoing discussion, however, a disturbing coincidence appeared again and again. It is not enough to say that television is causing problems and that education must respond, for I believe that both television *and* schools are the culprits. If television instills passivity, so does education. Television devalues active learning, but so do schools. The average television diet is comprised of simple-minded mediocre fare. The same charge has repeatedly been leveled against schools. Television likes the quick and easy answer; so do schools! Few teachers have the time to explore complexity and ambiguity. The analogy can be extended, but the point is clear—the medium of television and the institution of education are both outgrowths of the same values of society. It may thus be that television is merely a mirror reflecting back to us who is really responsible for eroding values.

There are not many ways of altering the form of the television medium, and it is highly unlikely that television content will ever rise above the intellectual and moral level of the majority of those who watch it. However, schools do not have to suffer from the same limitations. Education has the capability, nay, the responsibility of changing itself and society for the better. The final and major implication for education, therefore, is that we develop a theory of change and learn how to apply this theory to schools that are becoming outmoded in our rapidly changing, technologically sophisticated society. A dynamic, growth-oriented society requires an educational system that grows with it: a system that develops the skills necessary for helping its citizens adjust to technological change, creatively solve the problems that result from it, think independently, analyze social input from television and other sources, and form their own values and opinions. If educators can accomplish this, it may well be that television, in forcing us to reexamine our values and the ways our schools contribute to their development, will turn out to be a benefactor and not a polluter of society.

## REFERENCES

1. Marshall McLuhan, *Understanding Media* (New York: McGraw-Hill, 1964).
2. H. Himmelweit, A. N. Oppenheim, and P. Vince, *Television and the Child: An Empirical Study of the Effects of Television on the Young* (New York: Oxford University Press, 1958); J. Lyle, and H. R. Hoffman, "Explorations in Patterns of Television Viewing by Preschool-age Children," in *Television and Social Behavior,* Vol. 4, ed. E. A. Rubinstein, G. A. Comstock, and J. P. Murray (Washington, D.C.: Government Printing Office, 1972); Wilbur Schramm, J. Lyle, and E. B. Parker, *Television in the Lives of Our Children* (Stanford, Calif.: Stanford University Press, 1961).
3. S. J. Suomi and Harry F. Harlow, "Monkeys at Play," *Natural History* 80 (December 1971): 72–75.
4. Surgeon General of the United States, *Report on Television and Social Behavior* (Washington, D.C.: U.S. Government Printing Office, 1972).
5. J. Ellul, *The Technological Society* (New York: Vintage, 1964); J. Mander, *Four Arguments for the Elimination of Television* (New York: William Morrow, 1978); H. F. Waters, "What TV Does to Kids," *Newsweek* (February 21, 1977): 62–66; M. Winn, *The Plug-in Drug: Television, Children, and the Family* (New York: Viking Press, 1977).
6. R. Adler, "Television as a Cultural Force," in *Television as a Cultural Force,* ed. Douglas Cater and R. Adler (New York: Praeger, 1976); Neil Postman, "TV's 'Disastrous' Impact on Children," *U.S. News & World Report* (January 19, 1981): 43–45.
7. Winn, *The Plug-in Drug.*
8. Postman, "TV's 'Disastrous' Impact"; Waters, "What TV Does."

9.  Harry S. Broudy, *The Whys and Hows of Aesthetic Education* (St. Louis: CEMREL, 1977; ERIC Document No. ED 167 458); Elliot W. Eisner, *The Educational Imagination* (New York: Macmillan, 1979).
10. Albert Bandura, *Social Learning Theory* (Englewood Cliffs, N.J.: Prentice-Hall, 1977).
11. F. Wertham, "School for Violence: Mayhem in the Mass Media," in *Where Do You Draw the Line? An Exploration into Media Violence,* ed. V.B. Cline (Provo, Utah: Brigham Young University Press, 1974).
12. S. Arons and E. Katsh, "How Cops Flout the Law: A Critical Report on Crime Shows," *Saturday Review* (March 19, 1977): 10–18; J. H. Bryan, and N. H. Walbek, "Preaching and Practicing Generosity: Children's Actions and Reactions," *Children Development* 41 (June 1970): 329–353; Jean B. Raffa, *"Values on Television Shows Watched by Elementary School Aged Children: The Development and Implementation of a Methodology,"* Ed.D. diss., University of Florida, 1982 (*Dissertation Abstracts International 43* (6A), 1982: 1830).
13. George Comstock, S. Chaffee, N. Katzman, M. McCombs, and D. Roberts, *Television and Human Behavior* (New York: Columbia University Press, 1978); Robert Liebert, "Television Advertising and Values: The Surprising Impact on Television Commercials," in *Television Awareness Training,* ed. B. Logan (New York: Parthenon Press, 1977); A. A. Sheikh, V. K. Prasad, and T. R. Rao, "Children's TV Commercials: A Review of Research," *Journal of Communication* 24 (Autumn, 1974): 126–36.

*Jean Benedict Raffa* is Adjunct Instructor, College of Education, University of Central Florida, Orlando.

# Why Study the Future?

## EDWARD CORNISH

### WHY STUDY THE FUTURE?

Both the past and the present are unchangeable; only the future is still subject to human will. Thus, if we want to be practical, we must focus our attention on the future. The very near future—the next five hours, say—is very difficult to change, but the more distant future can be changed a great deal because we have adequate time to make plans, implement them, and see them take effect. Futurists claim that almost anything can be done in twenty years! (If that seems incredible, remember that it took only four years to make the first atomic bomb and eight to put a man on the moon.)

In recent years, the serious study of future possibilities has become increasingly important because the pace of change has accelerated: In the past forty years, man has entered the atomic age, the space age, and the computer age; more than eighty new nations have appeared; the global population has nearly doubled; and the gross world product (GWP) has doubled and redoubled.

To plan and act effectively, businessmen, government officials, and others must understand what may happen in the years ahead. It is not possible to know exactly what is going to happen and when, but it is possible to learn about new technologies that may become practical,

From a paper prepared by Edward S. Cornish, 1979, for the World Future Society, Bethesda, MD 20814. Reprinted by permission of the World Future Society.

significant changes that may occur in the world's economic and political structures, and possible shifts in human values and goals. Knowing what may happen in the decades ahead is now essential for wise decision making.

## METHODS OF STUDYING THE FUTURE

Many people fail to recognize that they constantly make forecasts and think about the future. Common methods that everyone uses include:

1. *Trend extrapolation.* We can make a forecast about the future by simply assuming that things will remain what they are now—or will continue to change in the same way as we now perceive them to be changing. This method allows us to forecast that New York City will still be located between Boston and Philadelphia ten years from now. We can also forecast that the United States will have a larger population in 1990 than it has today.
2. *Scenarios.* A scenario is simply a series of events that we imagine happening in the future. We may begin a scenario by asking, "What would happen if we went to the movies on Saturday?" Once the question is posed, we can proceed to imagine what would have to happen for that event to occur: Do we need a baby-sitter? Will we miss our favorite TV program? Our imaginative venture into the future allows us to identify potential problems and opportunities so that we can make wise decisions.
3. *Getting advice.* When we want to make an important decision, we often ask the opinions of others. They can tell us what they think might happen in the future, and their opinions help us to form our own.

In recent years, scholars have refined these methods (along with many others) so that today

there is an impressive number of scientific or rational ways to study the future. Serious scholars do not, of course, claim they can infallibly predict the future; what they say is that the emerging discipline of futuristics (future studies) offers valuable assistance for good decision making and management.

## CRITICAL ISSUES OF THE NEXT TWENTY YEARS

- *Preventing World War III:* This issue will not go away and nuclear weapons are steadily spreading to other countries. What can be done to remove the threat of world war?
- *Overpopulation:* Underlying all kinds of problems is the fact that many countries have birthrates that overwhelm their resources. What can be done to reduce birthrates in the poor countries?
- *The distribution of wealth:* Living standards have risen greatly during the twentieth century, but wealth remains very unequally distributed both among countries and among individuals within a given country. What can or should be done about this inequality?
- *Financial disorder:* Inflation and fluctuating currencies have led to widespread uncertainty in international finance. Billions of dollars flash across the world beyond the control of central banks, and a sudden movement could trigger a global economic crisis. What can be done to restore order to the world's financial system?
- *Terrorism:* Many political groups have found that they can get their way through bombings, assassinations, and kidnappings. How can terrorism be curbed?
- *Energy:* Petroleum and natural gas are becoming increasingly expensive, yet alternatives, such as nuclear and solar energy, pose many problems. What mix of energy sources should be used so that the world can have adequate power without unacceptable costs or risks?

- *Protectionism:* Many workers are losing their jobs as a result of imported goods. What can be done to protect the interests of these workers and at the same time maintain the free trade that promotes low prices and international harmony?
- *Intergroup tensions:* Most countries contain a number of racial, religious, or cultural groups. Tension, even violence, often breaks out between such groups. What can be done to make intergroup relations more harmonious?
- *Decline of the family:* The family has traditionally had the function of producing and rearing tomorrow's citizens. Soaring rates of divorce, runaway children, and child abuse suggest that the family now is experiencing difficulties. What can or should be done to strengthen the family?
- *Reforming education:* Despite rising expenditures, increasing numbers of young people emerge from the educational system without the basic skills to function effectively in modern society. How can the educational system be improved?

## A FEW ANTICIPATIONS FOR THE DECADES AHEAD

(Note: These forecasts are designed simply to give *a sense of the possible.* They are offered as a stimulus to thinking, not as an authoritative guide to the future.)

### 1980–89

A difficult decade, especially in the economic area. World population growth and industrial development have been overwhelming the earth's resources. Many nations will be hard-pressed to provide food and jobs. Economic difficulties will lead to political unrest, with revolu-

tions likely not only in the poor countries but also in the rich.

- Pocket-sized computers turn the average person into a walking encyclopedia.
- Artificial heart is perfected.
- Choosing the sex of one's children becomes a widespread practice.
- Computers transcribe spoken speech into typed letters.
- Campers must reserve two years in advance at some U.S. national parks.
- Most new university graduates are "overqualified" for the jobs they get.
- Twenty nations have nuclear weapons or can readily obtain them.
- A license is required for parenthood in some countries.
- Videocassette recorders, videodisc players, and cable TV threaten the survival of TV networks.
- A "slim pill" effectively reduces obesity without forced dieting.
- Automobiles equipped with microcomputers can drive themselves to pre-selected destinations.
- Computers function as psychiatrists, asking questions, diagnosing problems, and prescribing therapies.
- Synthetic skin is used in treating burns.
- Underground housing becomes popular.
- Communications satellites become a multibillion-dollar industry.
- Brain grafts are successfully performed, curing some neurological ailments.
- First moon base is established.
- Abortion-inducing drugs replace surgical abortions.
- Bus and train transportation revives.

### 1990–99

Political disorders worsen. Democratic regimes dwindle. Security measures and military build-ups intensity. Severe danger of major wars, with World War III a possibility. Economic decline is slowed or halted.

- First "submotel" opens, offering underwater views and parking for mini-subs used on pleasure cruises.
- Machines scan foreign-language newspapers and journals and make rough translations, which are automatically stored for later retrieval.
- The blue whale, the largest animal that ever lived, is declared extinct; the bald eagle, symbol of the U.S., is almost gone.
- The average person does more work (for pay) at home than at his formal workplace (office, factory, etc.).
- Men visit Mars for the first time.
- Synthetic blood is in wide use.
- Automobiles must have mechanical "brains" (microcomputers) that prevent most collisions and other accidents.
- Synthetic foods are manufactured from chemicals.
- Total nudity is accepted on many public beaches.
- Computer outclasses man on standard intelligence tests.
- Communications from extraterrestrial civilization are received and translated.
- Legislatures and governments battle over weather control—who should get the rain or snow, etc.
- Most large enterprises are managed largely by artificial intelligence.
- Electricity is produced by fusion.
- Most countries have strict population control measures, including parenthood licenses, compulsory contraceptive injections, and forced abortions.
- More than half of all Americans hold white-collar jobs.
- World population passes the six billion mark.
- The Age of Petroleum draws to a close; petroleum furnishes a declining percentage of man's energy needs.
- All sizeable nations and many private groups have nuclear weapons or can readily purchase them.

## 2000–2019

The world may be in a subdued mood at the beginning of the twenty-first century due to a general exhaustion after the turbulent 1980s and 1990s. However, conditions could improve rapidly and the world might enter a new Golden Age starting about 2010. Thanks to new scientific discoveries, the colonization of outer space, and the establishment of effective computerized management systems, the human race might soon be enjoying a life-style that would have seemed utopian in 1980.

- A world government is functioning, though imperfectly. An international currency, postal system, and police force are operative, but disputes between nations continue.
- Senility is controlled through chemicals. People now can look forward to living 200 years or more.
- People take vacations in space. "Grand tour" includes several space stations and the moon.
- Many grocery and department stores are almost completely automated; few sales clerks remain.
- Better education—through memory-assisting pills—makes it easy to learn vast amounts of material.
- Tourism becomes world's biggest industry, with two billion people traveling for pleasure each year.
- Some automated factories now operate in orbit around the earth.
- Ocean farming produces 5 percent of world's food needs.

## Beyond 2020

Only a few speculations can be offered about this distant period, which may see the flourishing of a new Golden Age of peace, prosperity, and progress.

- A lunar hotel complex is now a major convention center. Golfers enjoy the power of being able to hit a ball more than a mile in one swing.
- World government—based heavily on artificial intelligence—now monitors most human activities, intervening where necessary to control malefactors (both military adventurers and ordinary criminals).
- Large numbers of people live in airborne mobile homes that move around the world, stopping here and there to enjoy local scenery and sights.
- Most work is voluntary—or almost so. Automated robots mine coal, grow crops, drive buses, clean houses—and even provide companionship by playing games and conversing with people.
- Individuals now are incredibly intelligent (thanks to chemicals and computers), beautiful (cosmetic surgery and other beautifying techniques), good (computerized monitoring of brain waves with automated intervention to prevent misdeeds), and happy (slow-release chemicals provide a permanent glow of tranquility and pleasure).

*Edward Cornish* is President, World Future Society, Washington, D.C.

# The American Family in the Year 2000
## ANDREW CHERLIN AND FRANK F. FURSTENBERG, JR.

- At current rates, half of all American marriages begun in the early 1980s will end in divorce.
- The number of unmarried couples living together has more than tripled since 1970.
- One out of four children is not living with both parents.

The list could go on and on. Teenage pregnancies: up. Adolescent suicides: up. The birthrate: down. Over the past decade, popular and scholarly commentators have cited a seemingly endless wave of grim statistics about the shape of the American family. The trends have caused a number of concerned Americans to wonder if the family, as we know it, will survive the twentieth century.

And yet, other observers ask us to consider more positive developments:

- Seventy-eight percent of all adults in a recent national survey said they get "a great deal" of satisfaction from their family lives; only 3% said "a little" or "none."
- Two-thirds of the married adults in the same survey said they were "very happy" with their

From *The Futurist* 17, No. 3 (June 1983): 7–14. Used by permission of the publisher, The World Future Society.

marriages; only 3% said "not too happy."
- In another recent survey of parents of children in their middle years, 88% said that if they had to do it over, they would choose to have children again.
- The vast majority of the children (71%) characterized their family life as "close and intimate."

Family ties are still important and strong, the optimists argue, and the predictions of the demise of the family are greatly exaggerated.

Neither the dire pessimists who believe that the family is falling apart nor the unbridled optimists who claim that the family has never been in better shape provide an accurate picture of family life in the near future. But these trends indicate that what we have come to view as the "traditional" family will no longer predominate.

## DIVERSE FAMILY FORMS

In the future, we should expect to see a growing amount of diversity in family forms, with fewer Americans spending most of their life in a simple "nuclear" family consisting of husband, wife, and children. By the year 2000, three kinds of families will dominate the personal lives of most Americans: families of first marriages, single-parent families, and families of remarriages.

In first-marriage families, both spouses will be in a first marriage, frequently begun after living alone for a time or following a period of cohabitation. Most of these couples will have one, two, or, less frequently, three children.

A sizable minority, however, will remain childless. Demographer Charles F. Westoff predicts that about one-fourth of all women currently in their childbearing years will never bear children, a greater number of childless women than at any time in U.S. history.

One other important shift: in a large majority of these families, both the husband and the wife will be employed outside the home. In 1940, only about one out of seven married women worked outside the home; today the proportion is one out of two. We expect this proportion to continue to rise, although not as fast as it did in the past decade or two.

## SINGLE-PARENT FAMILIES

The second major type of family can be formed in two ways. Most are formed by a marital separation, and the rest by births to unmarried women. About half of all marriages will end in divorce at current rates, and we doubt that the rates will fall substantially in the near future.

When the couple is childless, the formerly married partners are likely to set up independent households and resume life as singles. The high rate of divorce is one of the reasons why more men and women are living in single-person households than ever before.

But three-fifths of all divorces involve couples with children living at home. In at least nine out of ten cases, the wife retains custody of the children after a separation.

Although joint custody has received a lot of attention in the press and in legal circles, national data show that it is still uncommon. Moreover, it is likely to remain the exception rather than the rule because most ex-spouses can't get along well enough to manage raising their children together. In fact, a national survey of children aged 11 to 16 conducted by one of the authors demonstrated that fathers have little contact with their children after a divorce. About half of the children whose parents had divorced hadn't seen their father in the last year; only one out of six had managed to see their father an average of once a week. If the current rate of divorce persists, about half of all children will spend some time in a single-parent family before they reach 18.

Much has been written about the psychological effects on children of living with one parent, but the literature has not yet proven that any lasting negative effects occur. One effect, however, does occur with regularity: women who head single-parent families typically experience a sharp decline in their income relative to before their divorce. Husbands usually do not experience a decline. Many divorced women have difficulty reentering the job market after a long absence; others find that their low-paying clerical or service-worker jobs aren't adequate to support a family.

Of course, absent fathers are supposed to make child-support payments, but only a minority do. In a 1979 U.S. Bureau of the Census survey, 43% of all divorced and separated women with children present reported receiving child-support payments during the previous year, and the average annual payment was about $1,900. Thus, the most detrimental effect for children living in a single-parent family is not the lack of a male presence but the lack of a male income.

## FAMILIES OF REMARRIAGES

The experience of living as a single parent is temporary for many divorced women, especially in the middle class. Three out of four divorced people remarry, and about half of these marriages occur within three years of the divorce.

Remarriage does much to solve the economic problems that many single-parent families face because it typically adds a male income. Remarriage also relieves a single parent of the multiple burdens of running and supporting a household by herself.

But remarriage also frequently involves blending together two families into one, a difficult process that is complicated by the absence of clear-cut ground rules for how to accomplish the merger. Families formed by remarriages can become quite complex, with children from either spouse's previous marriage or from the new marriage and with numerous sets of grandparents, stepgrandparents, and other kin and quasi-kin.

The divorce rate for remarriages is modestly higher than for first marriages, but many couples and their children adjust successfully to their remarriage and, when asked, consider their new marriage to be a big improvement over their previous one.

## THE LIFE COURSE: A SCENARIO FOR THE NEXT TWO DECADES

Because of the recent sharp changes in marriage and family life, the life course of children and young adults today is likely to be far different from what a person growing up earlier in this century experienced. It will not be uncommon, for instance, for children born in the 1980s to follow this sequence of living arrangements: live with both parents for several years, live with their mothers after their parents' divorce, live with their mothers and step-fathers, live alone for a time when in their early twenties, live with someone of the opposite sex without marrying, get married, get divorced, live alone again, get remarried, and end up living alone once more following the death of their spouses.

Not everyone will have a family history this complex, but it is likely that a substantial minority of the population will. And many more will have family histories only slightly less complex.

Overall, we estimate that about half of the young children alive today will spend some time in a single-parent family before they reach 18; about nine out of ten will eventually marry; about one out of two will marry and then divorce; and about one out of three will marry, divorce, and then remarry. In contrast, only about one out of six women born in the period 1910 to 1914 married and divorced and only about one in eight married, divorced, and re-married.

Without doubt, Americans today are living in a much larger number of family settings during their lives than was the case a few generations ago.

The life-course changes have been even greater for women than for men because of the far greater likelihood of employment during the childbearing years for middle-class women today compared with their mothers and grandmothers. Moreover, the increase in life expectancy has increased the difference between men's and women's family lives. Women now tend to out-live men by a wide margin, a development that is new in this century. Consequently, many more women face a long period of living without a spouse at the end of their lives, either as a widow or as a divorced person who never remarried.

Long-lived men, in contrast, often find that their position in the marriage market is excellent, and they are much more likely to remain married (or remarried) until they die.

## CONVERGENCE AND DIVERGENCE

The family lives of Americans vary according to such factors as class, ethnicity, religion, and re-gion. But recent evidence suggests a conver-gence among these groups in many features of family life. The clearest example is in childbear-ing, where the differences between Catholics and non-Catholics or between Southerners and Northerners are much smaller than they were 20 years ago. We expect this process of convergence to continue, although it will fall far short of eliminating all social class and subcultural differ-ences.

The experiences of blacks and whites also have converged in many respects, such as in fer-tility and in patterns of premarital sexual behav-ior, over the past few decades. But with respect to marriage, blacks and whites have diverged markedly since about 1960.

Black families in the United States always have had strong ties to a large network of ex-tended kin. But in addition, blacks, like whites, relied on a relatively stable bond between hus-bands and wives. But over the past several dec-ades—and especially since 1960—the propor-tion of black families maintained by a woman has increased sharply; currently, the proportion exceeds four in ten. In addition, more young black women are having children out of wed-lock; in the late 1970s, about two out of three black women who gave birth to a first child were unmarried.

These trends mean that we must qualify our previously stated conclusion that marriage will remain central to family life. This conclusion holds for Americans in general. For many low-income blacks, however, marriage is likely to be less important than the continuing ties to a larger network of kin.

Marriage is simply less attractive to a young black woman from a low-income family because of the poor prospects many young black men have for steady employment and because of the availability of alternative sources of support from public-assistance payments and kin. Even though most black women eventually marry, their marriages have a very high probability of ending in separation or divorce. Moreover, they have a lower likelihood of remarrying.

Black single-parent families sometimes have been criticized as being "disorganized" or even "pathological." What the critics fail to note is that black single mothers usually are embedded in stable, functioning kin networks. These net-works tend to center around female kin—moth-ers, grandmothers, aunts—but brothers, fathers, and other male kin also may be active. The mem-bers of these networks share and exchange goods and services, thus helping to share the burdens of poverty. The lower-class black extended family, then, is characterized by strong ties among a network of kin but fragile ties between husband and wife. The negative aspects of this family system have been exaggerated greatly; yet it need not be romanticized, either. It can be difficult and risky for individuals to leave the network in order to try to make it on their own; thus, it may be hard for individuals to raise themselves out of poverty until the whole network is raised.

## THE DISINTEGRATING FAMILY?

By now, predictions of the demise of the family are familiar to everyone. Yet the family is a resilient institution that still retains more strength than its harshest critics maintain. There is, for example, no evidence of a large-scale rejection of marriage among Americans. To be sure, many young adults are living together outside of marriage, but the evidence we have about cohabitation suggests that it is not a life-long alternative to marriage; rather, it appears to be either another stage in the process of courtship and marriage or a transition between first and second marriages.

The so-called "alternative lifestyles" that received so much attention in the late 1960s, such as communes and lifelong singlehood, are still very uncommon when we look at the nation as a whole.

Young adults today do marry at a somewhat older age, on average, than their parents did. But the average age at marriage today is very similar to what it was throughout the period from 1890 to 1940.

To be sure, many of these marriages will end in divorce, but three out of four people who divorce eventually remarry. Americans still seem to desire the intimacy and security that a marital relationship provides.

Much of the alarm about the family comes from reactions to the sheer speed at which the institution changed in the last two decades. Between the early 1960s and the mid-1970s, the divorce rate doubled, the marriage rate plunged, the birthrate dropped from a twentieth-century high to an all-time low, premarital sex became accepted, and married women poured into the labor force. But since the mid-1970s, the pace of change has slowed. The divorce rate has risen modestly and the birthrate even has increased a bit. We may have entered a period in which American families can adjust to the sharp changes that occurred in the 1960s and early 1970s. We think that, by and large, accommodations will be made as expectations change and institutions are redesigned to take account of changing family practices.

Despite the recent difficulties, family ties remain a central part of American life. Many of the changes in family life in the 1960s and 1970s were simply a continuation of long-term trends that have been with us for generations.

The birthrate has been declining since the 1820s, the divorce rate has been climbing since at least the Civil War, and over the last half century a growing number of married women have taken paying jobs. Employment outside the home has been gradually eroding the patriarchal system of values that was a part of our early history, replacing it with a more egalitarian set of values.

The only exception occurred during the late 1940s and the 1950s. After World War II, Americans raised during the austerity of depression and war entered adulthood at a time of sustained prosperity. The sudden turnabout in their fortunes led them to marry earlier and have more children than any generation before or since in this century. Because many of us were either parents or children in the baby-boom years following the war, we tend to think that the 1950s typify the way twentieth-century families used to be. But the patterns of marriage and childbearing in the 1950s were an aberration resulting from special historical circumstances; the patterns of the 1960s and 1970s better fit the long-term trends. Barring unforeseen major disruptions, small families, working wives, and impermanent marital ties are likely to remain with us indefinitely.

A range of possible developments could throw our forecasts off the mark. We do not know, for example, how the economy will behave over the next 20 years, or how the family will be affected by technological innovations still at the conception stage. But, we do not envision any dramatic changes in family life resulting solely from technological innovations in the next two decades.

Having sketched our view of the most probable future, we will consider three of the most important implications of the kind of future we see.

## GROWING UP IN CHANGING FAMILIES

Children growing up in the past two decades have faced a maelstrom of social change. As we have pointed out, family life is likely to become even more complex, diverse, unpredictable, and uncertain in the next two decades.

Even children who grow up in stable family environments will probably have to get along with a lot less care from parents (mothers in particular) than children received early in this century. Ever since the 1950s, there has been a marked and continuous increase in the proportion of working mothers whose preschool children are cared for outside the home, rising from 31% in 1958 to 62% in 1977. The upward trend is likely to continue until it becomes standard practice for very young children to receive care either in someone else's home or in a group setting. There has been a distinct drop in the care of children by relatives, as fewer aunts, grandmothers, or adult children are available to supplement the care provided by parents. Increasingly, the government at all levels will be pressured to provide more support for out-of-home daycare.

How are children responding to the shifting circumstances of family life today? Are we raising a generation of young people who, by virtue of their own family experiences, lack the desire and skill to raise the next generation? As we indicated earlier, existing evidence has not demonstrated that marital disruption creates lasting personality damage or instills a distinctly different set of values about family life.

Similarly, a recent review on children of working mothers conducted by the National Research Council of the National Academy of Sciences concludes:

> If there is only one message that emerges from this study, it is that parental employment in and of itself—mothers' employment or fathers' or both parents'—is not necessarily good or bad for children.

The fact that both parents work *per se* does not adversely affect the well-being of children.

Currently, most fathers whose wives are employed do little childcare. Today, most working mothers have two jobs: they work for pay and then come home to do most of the childcare and housework. Pressure from a growing number of harried working wives could prod fathers to watch less television and change more diapers. But this change in fathers' roles is proceeding much more slowly than the recent spate of articles about the "new father" would lead one to expect. The strain that working while raising a family places on working couples, and especially on working mothers, will likely make childcare and a more equitable sharing of housework prominent issues in the 1980s and 1990s.

## FAMILY OBLIGATIONS

Many of the one out of three Americans who, we estimate, will enter a second marriage will do so after having children in a first marriage. Others may enter into a first marriage with a partner who has a family from a previous marriage. It is not clear in these families what obligations remain after divorce or are created after remarriage. For one thing, no clear set of norms exists specifying how people in remarriages are supposed to act toward each other. Stepfathers don't know how much to discipline their stepchildren; second wives don't know what they're supposed to say when they meet their husbands' first wives; stepchildren don't know what to call their absent father's new wife.

The ambiguity about family relations after divorce and remarriage also extends to economic support. There are no clear-cut guidelines to tell adults how to balance the claims of children from previous marriages versus children from their current marriages. Suppose a divorced man who has been making regular payments to support his two small children from a previous marriage marries a woman with children from her previous marriage. Suppose her husband isn't paying any child support. Suppose further that the remarried couple have a child of their own. Which children should have first claim on the husband's income? Legally, he is obligated to pay child support to his ex-wife, but in practice he is likely to feel that his primary obligation is to his stepchildren, whose father isn't helping, and to his own children from his remarriage.

Our guess, supported by some preliminary evidence from national studies, is that remarriage will tend to further reduce the amount of child support that a man pays, particularly if the man's new family includes children from his new wife's previous marriage or from the current marriage. What appears to be occurring in many cases is a form of "childswapping," with men exchanging an old set of children from a prior marriage for a new set from their new wife's prior marriage and from the remarriage.

Sociologist Lenore J. Weitzman provides a related example in her book *The Marriage Con-*

*tract.* Suppose, she writes, a 58-year-old corporate vice president with two grown children divorces his wife to marry his young secretary. He agrees to adopt the secretary's two young children. If he dies of a heart attack the following year:

> In most states, a third to half of his estate would go to his new wife, with the remainder divided among the four children (two from his last marriage, and his new wife's two children). His first wife will receive nothing—neither survivors' insurance nor a survivor's pension nor a share of the estate—and both she and his natural children are likely to feel that they have been treated unjustly.

Since the rate of mid-life divorce has been increasing nearly as rapidly as that of divorce at younger ages, this type of financial problem will become increasingly common. It would seem likely that there will be substantial pressure for changes in family law and in income security systems to provide more to the ex-wife and natural children in such circumstances.

## INTERGENERATIONAL RELATIONS

A similar lack of clarity about who should support whom may affect an increasing number of elderly persons. Let us consider the case of an elderly man who long ago divorced his first wife and, as is fairly typical, retained only sporadic contact with his children. If his health deteriorates in old age and he needs help, will his children provide it? In many cases, the relationship would seem so distant that the children would not be willing to provide major assistance. To be sure, in most instances the elderly man would have remarried, possibly acquiring stepchildren, and it may be these stepchildren who feel the responsibility to provide assistance. Possibly the two sets of children may be called upon to cooperate in lending support, even when they have had little or no contact while growing up. Currently, there are no clear guidelines for assigning kinship responsibilities in this new type of extended family.

Even without considering divorce, the issue of support to the elderly is likely to bring problems that are new and widespread. As is well known, the low fertility in the United States, which we think will continue to be low, means that the population is becoming older. The difficulties that this change in age structure poses for the Social Security system are so well known that we need not discuss them here. Let us merely note that any substantial weakening of the Social Security system would put the elderly at a great disadvantage with regard to their families, for older Americans increasingly rely on Social Security and other pensions and insurance plans to provide support. A collapse of Social Security would result in a large decrease in the standard of living among older Americans and a return to the situation prevailing a few decades ago in which the elderly were disproportionately poor.

The relations between older people and their children and grandchildren are typically close, intimate, and warm. Most people live apart from their children, but they generally live close by one or more of them. Both generations prefer the autonomy that the increased affluence of the older generation has recently made possible. Older people see family members quite often, and they report that family members are their major source of support. A survey by Louis Harris of older Americans revealed that more than half of those with children had seen them in the past day, and close to half had seen a grandchild. We expect close family ties between the elderly and their kin to continue to be widespread. If, however, the economic autonomy of the elderly is weakened, say, by a drop in Social Security, the kind of friendly equality that now characterizes intergenerational relations could be threatened.

One additional comment about the elderly: Almost everyone is aware that the declining birthrate means that the elderly will have fewer children in the future on whom they can rely for support. But although this is true in the long run, it will not be true in the next few decades. In fact, beginning soon, the elderly will have more children, on average, than they do today. The reason is the postwar baby boom of the late 1940s and 1950s. As the parents of these large families begin to reach retirement age near the end of this century, more children will be available to help their elderly parents. Once the next generation—the baby-boom children—begins to reach retirement age after about 2010, the long-term trend toward fewer available children will sharply reassert itself.

Were we to be transported suddenly to the year 2000, the families we would see would look very recognizable. There would be few unfamiliar forms—not many communes or group marriages, and probably not a large proportion of lifelong singles. Instead, families by and large would continue to center around the bonds between husbands and wives and between parents and children. One could say the same about today's families relative to the 1960s: the forms are not new. What is quite different, comparing the 1960s with the 1980s, or the 1980s with a hypothetical 2000, is the distribution of these forms.

In the early 1960s, there were far fewer single-parent families and families formed by remarriages after divorce than is the case today; and in the year 2000 there are likely to be far more single-parent families and families of remarriage than we see now. Moreover, in the early 1960s both spouses were employed in a much smaller percentage of two-parent families; in the year 2000, the percentage with two earners will be greater still. Cohabitation before marriage existed in the 1960s, but it was a frowned-upon, bohemian style of life. Today, it has become widely accepted; it will likely become more common in the future. Yet we have argued that cohabitation is less an alternative to marriage than a precursor to marriage, though we expect to see a modest rise in the number of people who never marry.

*Andrew Cherlin* is Associate Professor of Sociology, The Johns Hopkins University, Baltimore, Maryland.
*Frank F. Furstenberg,* is Professor of Sociology, University of Pennsylvania, Philadelphia.

# Schools of the Future: Education Approaches the Twenty-First Century

## MARVIN J. CETRON, BARBARA SORIANO, AND MARGARET GAYLE

Nearly 30 reports issued by commissions, task forces, and individuals have made it clear to the American people that their nation will be "at risk" unless they pay attention to their schools.

Most of these reports emphasize the need to better prepare students for entering college. Yet three-fourths of U.S. kids don't graduate from college. A major responsibility of schools in the future will be to prepare students to enter a rapidly changing job market. If the United States is to continue to compete in the worldwide marketplace, American workers will need to be more highly trained than at present. This means a greater emphasis on high-tech vocational education will be needed—an issue most educational reformers have ignored.

Schools will be responsible for preparing students who are adaptable and able to respond quickly to the changing requirements of new technologies. In the near future, workers' jobs will change dramatically every 5 to 10 years. Schools will train both youths and adults; adult workers will need re-education and retraining whenever business and industry update their operations. In the future, workers will be displaced frequently and will be moving constantly from one occupation to another. They will need periodic retraining because each new job will be different from the previous one.

### SCHOOLS OF THE FUTURE

By 1990, most adults will be working a 32-hour week. During the time that they are not at work, many will be preparing for their next job. While the adult workweek is getting shorter, the student schoolweek will be getting longer.

Not only will the normal academic day be longer for children, but the buildings themselves will be open a minimum of 12 hours a day. Schools will be providing services to the community, to business, and to young students who will use the recreation facilities, computer labs, and job simulation stations—modules that combine computers, videodiscs, and instrumentation to duplicate job-work environments.

Many schools may be open 24 hours a day. They will be training centers for adults from 4 p.m. to midnight; some will also serve business through their computer and communication facilities from midnight until the next morning when young students arrive again.

Individual communities may conduct classes that include both adults and high-school students. But if for some reason this combination is unsuccessful, the groups can separate and work independently. In some communities, adults might take over portions of school buildings that have been closed because of declining school enrollments.

At present, most schools are in session for approximately 180 days a year. A number of reform reports recommend an increase to 210 days a year or 240 days to match schools abroad, but many people have objected. Funds have not been available; some students and teachers feel they do not have the mental energy for a longer year; and families want free time to make summer plans. Also, school buildings generally are not air-conditioned.

Schools in the 1990s, however, increasingly will extend the time that buildings are in service. Air conditioning and modifications in the size and structure of classrooms will accommodate the changing purposes of school programs.

Some students will have the option of accelerating their progress through the school year in order to graduate and enter college or the job market earlier. Others may spend time at school in the summer to enrich their academic backgrounds through telecommunications coursework with another school district, state, or country.

Adults may find summer months a good time to train for a new phase of their careers. The core academic year will lengthen to 210 days, but students will not necessarily be in the school building at all times during this period.

## GOOD-BYE, LITTLE RED SCHOOLHOUSE?

Interactive cable television and computer communication links with the school may allow school districts to close down costly old buildings even if enrollments are increasing. As the workweek shortens from 32 hours a week in 1990 to 20–25 hours a week in the year 2000, families will want to make plans for the periods children would previously have been in school. Students will be able to time their study hours to fit these family schedules.

Computers will be used for the drill and practice of skills introduced by the teacher; they will also be used for helping students explore creative and problem-solving situations. Today's educational software, however, rarely does either job very well.

Teachers will effect some of the biggest changes in educational software. Their experience with computers in the classrooms during the late 1980s will give them insight into the ways such software will need to change. The teachers who are particularly good at making modifications may even leave the classroom and launch their own software-writing businesses.

## PLANNING INDIVIDUALIZED EDUCATION

Many teachers will operate in teaching teams, which will be able to use frequently updated information on their students to design individual education plans (IEPs). IEPs are simply plans for instruction. Each student will have a plan tailored to his or her own background, interests, and skills.

The IEPs in today's schools list skills in reading or math, for example, and suggest how the teacher should test the student to see if the skills have been mastered. IEPs in the future will also recommend whether students should learn each skill in a small or a large group, independently, one-on-one with a teacher, or a combination of these formats. They will suggest which senses the student should use more frequently to develop them further—for example, visual (reading books or computer screens) rather than aural (listening to tapes).

Once the quality of educational software improves, schools will be able to teach and drill students in basic skills more efficiently and also increase the percentage of students achieving certain minimum competencies.

Students who work relatively well without a great deal of supervision will be assigned to teachers who work well with large groups. Often, lessons will be introduced and skills developed through teacher-managed computer systems. Teachers will be responsible for setting up the instructional schedules, reviewing progress with the students, and seeing that students have opportunities to participate in a broad range of learning situations: problem-solving groups; independent information-gathering activities in the school or the community; music, art, or drama activities led by professionals from these disciplines; or computer-based drill routines.

For students who need to work in small groups, teachers skilled in handling and coordinating small-group experiences will move these students from teacher-student interaction to student-student interaction. Students will teach each other, not because the teacher does not have time and is trying to find a way to keep these student teams busy but because effective learning can take place in these teams.

Teachers will be assigned students based on the kind of teaching they do best. Students will be assigned to groups based on the way they learn best, according to what learning researchers feel they need to be successful. Students will not be assigned by grade level but by the developmental level they have reached in each area. Neither teachers nor parents will be concerned with pupil-teacher ratios.

## NO MORE PENCILS, NO MORE BOOKS?

As software improves, computers will begin to replace some kinds of textbooks; they already can replace drillbooks. Software can be tailored to meet individual student needs and can be updated more quickly and inexpensively than textbooks. The writing and computing deficiencies that national educational reform groups have noted among today's students may often be remedied by simple practice—something computers do tirelessly.

Computers themselves could even provide income for the school: Parents might come to school to learn how to use computers in their businesses, and companies could use school computer facilities to run their data at night. And computers can be linked with videodiscs or with equipment that simulates the job environment.

Computers linked with videodiscs will provide sight, sound, and movement. Some lessons in history, language, politics, psychology, math, word problems, and music, art, or dance could be taught or reinforced from one video-disc. Software, written by a member of a teaching team, will program sequences of visual images from a disc. The computer program will stop and start the disc every so often to ask the student questions.

Widespread use of computer-linked equipment will not be a major feature of schools until the twenty-first century, but certain schools will use computers in this way long before 1995.

Computer simulations of certain job procedures have been used to train employees for 10 years in certain industries. Because sophisticated workplace simulation equipment is expensive, it will probably be placed only in regional centers where students will be sent for short periods of time to study and live in supervised dormitories attached to the public school system. Finally, individual high schools will begin to offer simulation as a means of job training.

## TEACHERS AND BUSINESS

Before the mid-1990s, teachers will receive higher pay—raised to at least 90% of comparable professionals' salaries. The current, popular concept of merit pay is not as relevant as the concept of pay equity, or parity. Teachers are the lowest paid of all professionals. In 40 out of the 50 states, a starting garbage collector earns more money than a starting teacher. Something must be done now.

Funding required to raise teacher's salaries will come in large part from businesses contracting with schools to retrain their workers; from private individuals studying skills for their next jobs; from selling computer time, day-care, and geriatric services to the community; and from other ways of using school buildings more efficiently.

As business becomes more closely connected with schools, it is possible that skilled teachers will join private business in even greater numbers than they do today. Teachers may choose to continue their careers as trainers of employees for private businesses. Many times, however, businesses will find that teachers are valuable employees in other respects. Some of the services that teachers will be able to sell to businesses include communication skills, performance evaluation skills, group management abilities, and information management skills.

Schools that wish to keep their most skilled teachers will probably offer flexible work schedules so that teachers can participate in both worlds and will not be forced to make a choice. In this way, schools will not passively let businesses raid their personnel.

## ALL STUDENTS WILL TRAIN FOR JOBS

Training for the job world does not keep people from going to college. One indication is that, from 1974 to 1979, part-time college enrollment increased by 25.8%. More students are now prolonging the period between when they graduate from high school and when they enter college. Some of that delay is caused by the fact that federal loans and grants for college students have declined dramatically.

As schools provide more resources for teaching adults, they will be able to offer job training based on jobs that are actually available, not those that are becoming obsolete.

From eighth grade on, many students may actually be placed in different businesses that use the skills they are learning. If businesses that might provide a wide range of experience are not immediately available to the school, students will be able to travel to a learning center staffed with instructors and containing the latest equipment suited to students' career fields.

In either location, students will have their work supervised and graded by employers' standards. A trainer will watch them at the work site or via a television hookup. The trainer will be able to talk with the student. After this experience at the work site, students will return to the school to have their performance reviewed. The school will then judge whether the students need additional attention, practice at a simulator, or study.

Taking the last two years of high school for job preparation does not mean that the advanced-course needs of students bound for college must be put aside. Schools will, however, be forced to become more effective in teaching English, mathematics, history, and science courses before the tenth grade. Students who plan to enter professions requiring intermediate or advanced skills in foreign languages, science, or math could sample jobs in related fields while studying those subjects.

Vocational education will no longer be a narrow field of study. Rather than the quickly legislated, quickly funded, inadequate remedy for a stalled economy that it has been in the past, vocational education will prepare students for ca-

reers of challenges and changes—not just for a first job.

We can forecast a basically positive, progressive future for America's schools based on current international and national economic and social trends. These trends could change direction, however, thereby altering our predictions.

But nothing will alter these forecasts as greatly as inaction. If America's citizens ignore these warnings about their educational and industrial future, the nation's economic stability and preeminence will be jeopardized.

*Marvin J. Cetron* is President of Forecasting International, Ltd., Arlington, Virginia. He is author of *Encounters With the Future* (1982), and *Jobs of the Future* (1984).
*Barbara Soriano* is a Washington, D. C.-based consultant on future planning.
*Margaret Gayle* is Associate Director, Vocational Education, North Carolina State Department of Public Instruction, Raleigh.

# Society Will Balk, but the Future May Demand a Computer for Each Child

## SEYMOUR PAPERT

It is now universally accepted that every school should own at least one computer. The more adventurous schools even accept the idea that there ought to be a computer in every classroom.

I believe that the image of a computer per classroom is quite unrealistic for the future. A more accurate formula will be one computer per child. The computer can and should come to be as commonplace as the pencil.

The metaphor "computer as pencil" captures several aspects of the vision of computers I develop in my book, *Mindstorms: Children, Com-*

*puters and Powerful Ideas.* The pencil is universal: everyone uses it, starting with babies too young to know not to scribble on the walls and going all the way up to include poets and mathematicians, engineers and artists, judges and criminals. The pencil never dictates what we do with it, but enhances our ability to do anything we want it to do. So, from my vision, does the computer. The computer of the future will be as small as a paperback book. In fact it will be used as a book by loading a small cartridge or charging it through a telephone line. But this book will do

From *Electronic Education* 1, no. 1 (September 1981): 5–6, 31. © Electronic Communications, Inc. Used by permission of the publisher.

more than display print and pictures. It will talk, its pictures will be animated, it will allow interaction. It will serve as a sketch pad, one that will allow doodling in motion as well as in form. It will serve as a writing pad, as an electric game, as a terminal to information networks, as a newspaper, as a music synthesizer. It is futile to continue the list. Most of the purposes served by the computer of the future are as much beyond our imagination as the computer itself was beyond the imaginations of our grandfathers.

The presence of these personal computers, for which Alan Kay has proposed the name, "dynabook," will change human lives in many ways. They will change work and play, but the most important change will not come through what the computers can do for us, but through their effect on how people learn. In fact, even without waiting for the super computers of the future, the computer presence is already beginning to revolutionize the way children learn. For me the most dramatic example came in a project through which we gave three- and four-year-old children access to computers designed to simulate just enough of the power of the "dynabook" to become a personal instrument for a child. By typing on a keyboard the children could put shapes on the screen, assign and change colors, set them in motion, and program animation sequences. In doing so they learned concepts normally considered beyond the reach of children their ages: principles of logic, mathematics, and, of course, simple principles of computer programming. But what seemed to me of greatest importance is that they learned the alphabetic language. They were learning to type—at first single letters, then words, and finally sentences and the computer language, Logo.

Watching these children reminded me how fragile our knowledge is about what children can do and what they cannot do. For example, we take for granted that there should be a gap between the spoken and written language. Children learn to speak as babies without formal in-struction. But the written language comes much later, if at all, and seems to require deliberate professional teaching. But why should this be so? Is writing really harder than speaking? I believe not and that the computer presence will close the gap. Perhaps it will even reverse the order in that mastery of writing may develop faster once it starts, than mastery of speech. Let me mention two reasons for this belief.

The first reason is a motor one. Hitting keys is a less complex skill than calligraphy and so more easily accessible to the very young. But if this were a major factor, the typewriter would have made writing accessible to infants.

The second reason is weightier. The major reason why children do not write at the age they talk is social. Talking is an important part of the most important task of an infant—relating to other people—while writing serves no purpose at all in a child's life. My expectation of change is based on a vision of how the computer presence will enter the fabric of a child's life becoming, in a very real sense, part of the culture into which the child grows.

At present writing serves no purpose in the lives of young children. But the children I saw using the Logo computer had found several very important uses for it. First, it allowed them to produce exciting effects on the computer screen. Secondly, it gave them an exhilarating sense of power and control over the machine. And, thirdly, it allowed them to achieve one of the principal desires of children: to master what is perceived as an adult activity.

It is easy to project a future where typing at a computer keyboard could open doors to vast worlds of unlimited interest to children. These could be worlds of games, of art forms, of access to libraries of video materials and of access to communication with people. Thus, the principal social factor that makes writing more difficult to learn than speaking would disappear. Let me mention two ways in which these children's relationship to language would be different. Many children of five or six still do not have clear notions about constituents of language. For example, they seldom understand the concept of words. It is quite possible to speak without any such explicit notion but to be able to write, one must grasp some basic language concepts. The children working with the computer develop at the very beginning a concept of words and accept the idea that each word has a definite spelling. Secondly, and perhaps most important of all, these children have an *emotional* relationship with alphabetic language very different from the relationship most people have. A serious obstacle to learning to write is the alienation to language most people form early and few ever change. A spoken language *feels* like a natural activity, a direct expression of one's self. Very few people ever develop this feeling for the written language. The children learning the written language in a well-motivated, self-directed situation develop warm feelings toward it.

In many schools computers are being used to give children drill and practice in spelling and other formal language skills. The computer is used as part of an "unnatural" teaching process that is only necessary because children do not learn the written language in a natural way. No drill and practice is needed to teach children to talk. The vision of the computer I am presenting is not one of improving present day instructional practices. It leads to a fundamental change in the way in which certain knowledge, such as written language, is acquired. In *Mindstorms* I argue that the same will be true in other areas, for example, mathematics and science. Children will learn mathematics as they learned to talk because they will learn mathematics as a living language: it is the language of the computers that they will find all around them. Learning mathematics will be more like learning English in America or French in France than like the very difficult process of learning French in an American classroom.

In such a future what will happen in school?

It is impossible to predict. But one thing is sure: schools as we know them today will be obsolete before the end of this century. I hope it will still be considered necessary to have places where children meet and interact. We will at last be able to invent places for children designed for their development as full human beings without having to compromise this noble social purpose by also serving the need to force unwilling children to learn phonics and multiplication tables. One might say that the computer presence will abolish the need for school or one might say that it will liberate the school to be able to fully serve its true social purpose.

Inevitably this picture of the future raises questions about cost. How will society afford all these computers? The answer is quite simple. Not only are computers becoming less and less expensive, but even today the formula of a computer for every child would be amply cost-effective. Personal computers which can be bought in the stores for $2000 would not cost more than $500 if mass produced for distribution to every child. The cost of educating a child is at least $30,000 for the thirteen years from kindergarten through high school. Thus, on the assumption that the computer will be replaced several times but that prices will fall, it is reasonable to estimate that keeping every child supplied with a personal computer will not cost more than 5 percent of what we are today spending on education. It needs little imagination to see how teaching costs would be reduced by at least that much and probably by very much more. It would be sad to think that society would choose to recuperate the 5 percent in lower teaching costs rather than spend more money for the better education that is now possible. But in either case, it is clear that the obstacle to giving every child a computer is not economics. This formula would reduce the cost of education. The obstacle is of a different nature. It is partly political in that our society seems to have no way in which to make such a decision. It is partly psychological in that people who have grown up with a century old image of schools and paper and pencils cannot easily bring themselves to visualize a very different image of how children learn. Ultimately they will be forced to. When one country moves into the computer future it will sweep aside all competitors who lag too far behind. And when the disadvantaged of the world discover that there is at last a practical means to give their children access to knowledge and a sense of personal intellectual mastery, they will raise morally or violently irresistible pressures.

*Seymour Papert* is Professor of Mathematics, Massachusetts Institute of Technology, Cambridge.

## ADDITIONAL LEARNING ACTIVITIES

### Problems and Projects

1.  Continue to develop a "case problem" about one school and the curriculum and teaching in that school. Select a real school that you know well, and describe how its social setting affects the school and individual learners in that school. Then try to suggest how these forces should be reflected in the curriculum and teaching. You will, of course, be suggesting changes both in the curriculum and in teaching. You can add to this study as you work on each of the bases of the curriculum and the criteria.

2.  Describe the social forces in one community that *do affect* and those that *should affect* the school curriculum and teaching in the community. Discuss them with your fellow students, community leaders, school principals, and others.

3.  In this section, the authors of "A World of Interconnections" assert that the most important task now facing education is to develop students' understanding of other people's motives and of the social and psychological settings that cause them to think and act as they do. Why do the authors assert this? What curriculum directions do they suggest? What would you propose to do in curriculum planning to address the problems they describe?

4.  The rationale for this section states that forecasts of alternative futures should be developed and used by curriculum planners in order to create curriculum and instruction strategies that are more than hindsight remedies to today's problems. Several of the articles in this section—e.g., those by Shane, Cornish, Cherlin and Furstenberg, Cetron et al., and Papert—present future forecasts in which the nature of the curriculum and the status of teachers and learners and what they do will change radically. Select several of the forecasts from one or more of the articles. Then identify the objectives and some appropriate learning activities for both a present and a future curriculum in the light of those anticipated future social forces.

5.  The first scheduled radio program was on November 2, 1920—the returns of the Harding-Cox presidential election. Less than thirty years later, in 1949, there were eighty million radio sets in use in the United States with twelve

million in automobiles. In 1949, fewer than 5 percent of American homes had television sets. Today the figure has leveled off at around 96 percent. One or more members of the average household today watches television more than six hours out of every twenty-four, with the greatest amount of viewing being done by the very young, the very old, and the very poor. Is this a major social force? Should it influence curriculum planning and teaching? In what ways? You may be wise to review "Television and Values: Implications for Education" in this section before answering this question.

6. "The American Family in the Year 2000" in this section describes and predicts many changes in family life. If these predictions are correct, how should they affect school curricula? Do you agree with Cremin (in "The Revolution in American Education") that these changes "have profoundly affected what children learn and how they will learn it"?

7. "Schools of the Future" in this section predicts many changes in the ways that schools are organized, the content of the curriculum, the ways that learners are grouped, the learners that are served, and the relationship of the schools to the community. How will these changes affect the role of the teacher? How may they affect the role you now have or hope to have in the future?

8. Herbert Thelen has developed a plan or model for teaching called the "Group Investigation Model." The model combines the democratic process and the process of problem solving. You can read about this teaching model in Chapter 13 of *Models of Teaching*, Second Edition, by Bruce Joyce and Marsha Weil (Englewood Cliffs, New Jersey: Prentice Hall, 1980). Think about how you might use this approach to teaching in relation to some social force. Discuss your plan with other members of your group.

9. During a vacation in Colorado some years ago, Mayor John Lindsay of New York City quipped that he "wasn't used to breathing air he couldn't see." Times have changed, for today Denver has the highest level of carbon monoxide pollution in the nation. In 1972, however, Colorado's aroused voters overwhelmingly rejected plans to host the 1976 Winter Olympics in their state. To read about the problems of environment and pollution in Colorado, see "Goodbye Colorado" by Hugh Gardner in *Harper's* (April 1974), pp. 14–23.

10. Examine several recent curriculum guides to determine what, if any, provision has been made to consider changing social forces in the curriculum (changing values, changes in family life, urban and suburban crises, etc.). What changes or additions along these lines would you suggest in these curriculum guides?

11. The rationale for this section states that the concept of "humanity" should guide curriculum planning and teaching. To gain a perspective on this concept get a copy of *The Family of Man*, which has been called the greatest photographic exhibition of all time and was created by Edward Steichen (New York: Museum of Modern Art, 1955). You can probably find it in your library or bookstore. What does one learn by viewing these 503 pictures from sixty-eight countries? How can this learning be applied to curriculum planning and teaching?

12. The Appendix of this book includes a list of books, each describing a school or

school program. Select one that interests you and then determine how its social setting affects the school, individual learners in that school, and the present curriculum and teaching. Then suggest ways in which the school's program should, in your opinion, be influenced by the various levels of social forces. What changes would you suggest in the curriculum and teaching at the school in the light of social forces? You can add to your study of this school's program as you work on each of the bases and the criteria.

**13.** Have your personal beliefs or values about social forces changed as a result of your experience with this section? If so, state what change has taken place and relate it to one or more of the activities in this section (an article, a postassessment activity, an additional reading, a film, etc.). Compare your ideas with those of the other members of your class.

## Films, Video and Audiocassettes:

*Changing Occupational Trends in the 1990s.* Features Marvin Cetron. Forecasts a great explosion of new occupations and says that school curricula should be changed now. Audiocassette, 75 min., 1984. Four other audiocassettes on occupational trends and school curricula are also available. Association for Supervision and Curriculum Development, 225 North Washington Street, Alexandria, Virginia 22314.

*Multicultural Education: Goals, Teaching Strategies, and Evaluation.* Explains what multicultural education is about and why it is an essential part of educating today's youth. Videocassette (Beta or VHS), 53 min., 1984. Association for Supervision and Curriculum Development, 225 North Washington Street, Alexandria, Virginia 22314

*Planning Curriculum with a Futures Perspective.* Five futurist educators discuss what the future may be like and how schools can help students look ahead to life in the 21st century. Videocassette (Beta or VHS), 21 min., 1984. Association for Supervision and Curriculum Development, 225 North Washington Street, Alexandria, Virginia 22314.

*The Math Science Connection: Educating Young Women for Today.* Presents four exemplary programs for girls and women who are considering scientific or technical study. 16 mm, 18 min., 1980. Education Development Center, 55 Chapel Street, Newton, Massachusetts 02160.

*It's Her Future.* Provides information regarding women in the labor force, the benefits of pursuing nontraditional careers, and current training opportunities. 16 mm, color, 17 min., 1980. Education Development Center, 55 Chapel Street, Newton, Massachusetts 02160.

*Toward the Future: A Film That Animates Tomorrow.* 16 mm, color, 20 min., 1978. What does the future hold: a garden earth, a technology world, or the end of civilization as we know it? The film offers a compelling look at the fascinating field of alternative futures and shows how everyone can benefit from the methods of futuristics such as scenarios, Delphi polls, and relevance trees. Films Service, World Future Society, 4916 St. Elmo Avenue, Washington, D.C. 20014.

*Century III—Man and His Environment.* 16 mm film No. 0100631 G. B., color, 28 min., 1978. Illustrated here are efforts toward a stabilization of the ecosphere through architecture, industrial and urban conservation, and solar energy. Dr. Loren Eiseley comments on man and his environment now and in the future. National Audio-Visual Center, National Archives and Records Trust Fund Board, Washington, D.C. 20409.

*Gift of the Black Folk.* 16 mm, color, 15 min., 1975. An expression of the "quality of humanism" that black people have given to the nation. Centers around three impressive people: Denmark Vesey, Harriet Tubman, and Frederick Douglass. Pyramid Films, Box 1048, Santa Monica, California 90406.

*Mexican-American: Viva La Raza.* 16 mm, black and white, 47 min., 1974. Grievances of the Mexican-American community in Los Angeles are discussed from several viewpoints, both moderate and militant. Contemporary/McGraw-Hill Films, 1221 Avenue of the Americas, New York, New York 10020.

## Books and Articles to Review

### On Communications and Society
Cater, Douglass. *TV Violence and the Child*. Washington, D.C.: Russell Sage Foundation, 1975.
Cohen, Richard. "Television Teaches Violence." *Educational Leadership* 39, no. 8 (May 1982): 614.
Doerken, Maurine. *Classroom Combat: Teaching and Television*. Englewood Cliffs, N.J.: Educational Technology Publications, 1983.
Flannery, Gerald V.,; Hillman, R. E.; McGee, J. R.; and Rivers, W. L. "Communications and Society." In ASCD Yearbook, *Improving the Human Condition*. Washington, D.C.: Association for Supervision and Curriculum Development, 1978.
Judd, Wallace. "A Teacher's Place in the Computer Curriculum." *Phi Delta Kappan* 65, no. 2 (October 1983): 120–122.
Mander, Jerry. *Four Arguments for the Elimination of Television*. New York: William Morrow and Co., 1977.
Postman, Neil. *Amusing Ourselves to Death: Public Discourse in the Age of Show Business*. New York: Viking Penguin Inc., 1985.

### On Cultural Pluralism
Appleton, Nicholas. *Cultural Pluralism in Education*. New York: Longman, Inc. 1983.
Banks, James A. (ed.). *Multiethnic Education*. Washington, D.C.: National Education Association, 1981.
Claydon, Leslie; Knight, Tony; and Rado, Marta. *Curriculum and Culture: Schooling in a Pluralistic Society*. Winchester, MA: Allen and Unwin, 1978.
Deal, Terence; and Kennedy, Allan A. "Culture and School Performance." *Educational Leadership* 40, no. 5 (February 1983): 14–15.
Kramer, M.; and Schmalenberg, C. *Path to Biculturalism*. Wakefield, MA: Contemporary Publishing, Inc., 1977.
Sedlacek, W. E.; and Brooks, G. C., Jr. *Racism in American Education*. Chicago: Nelson-Hall, Inc., 1976.
Sennett, R. (ed.). *The Psychology of Society*. New York: Vintage Books, 1977.
Tesconi, Charles A. "Multicultural Education: A Valued But Problematical Ideal." *Theory Into Practice* 23, no. 2 (Spring 1984): 87–92.
Thomas, M. Donald. "The Limits of Pluralism." *Phi Delta Kappan* 62, no. 8 (April 1981): 589, 591–592.

### On the Family
Anthony, E. J.; and Chiland, Colette (eds.). *Children and Their Parents in a Changing World*. New York: Wiley, 1978.
Apple, K. W. *America's Changing Families: A Guide for Educators*. Phi Delta Kappa Fastback no. 219: 7–45, 1985.
Bane, Mary Jo. *Here To Stay*. New York: Basic Books, 1979.
Bettelheim, Bruno. "The Family: Then and Now." *New York University Education Quarterly* 8, no. 3 (Spring 1977): 2–8.
Bigner, Jerry J. *Parent-Child Relationships: An Introduction to Parenting*. New York: Macmillan, 1979.
"Changing Family: Where Is It Destined?" (A Symposium). *Educational Horizons* 59, no. 1 (Fall 1980): 2–53.
Green, Maureen. *Fathering*. New York: McGraw-Hill Book Co., 1976.
Jurich, Anthony P.; Polson, Cheryl J.; Jurich, Julie A.; and Bates, Rodney A. "Family Factors in the Lives of Drug Users and Abusers." *Adolescence* 20 (Spring 1985): 143–159.
Keniston, Kenneth. *All Our Children*. New York: Harcourt, Brace, Jovanovich, 1977.
Kenkel, W. F. *The Family in Perspective*. (4th ed.) Santa Monica, CA: Goodyear Publishing Co., 1977.
Rich, Dorothy. "The Forgotten Factor in School Success—The Family." Washington, D.C.: The Home and School Institute (1201 16th St., N.W.), 1985.
Rich, John Martin. *Discipline and Authority in School and Family*. Lexington, MA: Lexington Books/D. C. Heath, 1982.

Schubert, William; Schubert, Ann; and Schubert, Heidi Ann. "Familial Theorizing and Literature That Facilitates It," *Journal of Thought* 21, No. 2 (Summer 1986): 61–73.

## On Future Planning and the Information Society

Apple, Michael W. "Curriculum in the Year 2000: Tensions and Possibilities." *Phi Delta Kappan* 64, no. 5 (January 1983): 321–326.

Cetron, Marvin; and O'Toole, Thomas. *Encounters With the Future: A Forecast of Life in the 21st Century.* New York: McGraw-Hill, 1982.

Cornish, Edward. "The Race for Artificial Intelligence." *Futurist* 19, no. 3 (June 1985): 2, 54.

Etzioni, Amatai. *An Immodest Agenda: Rebuilding America Before the Twenty-First Century.* New York: McGraw-Hill, 1983.

Evans, Christopher. *The Micro Millennium.* New York: The Viking Press, 1979.

Harris, Robert D. "The Information Economy: Exploiting an Infinite Resource." *The Futurist* 15, no. 4 (August 1981): 25–30.

Papert, Seymour. *Mindstorms: Children, Computers and Powerful Ideas.* New York: Basic Books, Inc., 1980.

Ravitch, Diane. "On Thinking About the Future." *Phi Delta Kappan* 64, no. 5 (January 1983): 317–320.

Shane, Harold G.; with M. Bernadine Tabler. *Educating for a New Millennium.* Bloomington, IN: Phi Delta Kappa Education Foundation, 1981.

Toffler, Alvin. *Reviews and Premises.* New York: William Morrow and Company, 1983.

———. *The Third Wave.* New York: William Morrow and Company, 1981.

## On the Realities We Face

Albus, James S. "Robots and the Economy." *Futurist* 18, no. 6 (December 1984): 38–44.

ASCD Yearbook. *Education for Peace, Focus on Mankind.* Washington, D.C.: Association for Supervision and Curriculum Development, 1973.

*Barriers to Excellence: Our Children At Risk.* Report of the National Coalition of Advocates for Students. Boston: NCAS, 1985.

Best, Fred. "Technology and the Changing World of Work." *Futurist* 18, no. 2 (April 1984): 61–62, 64–66.

Boyer, Ernest L. "Seeing the Connectedness of Things." *Educational Leadership* 39, no. 8 (May 1982): 582–584.

Coates, Joseph F. "Population and Education: How Demographic Trends Will Shape the U.S." *Futurist* 12, no. 1 (February 1978): 35–36, 38, 40–42.

Harris, Marvin. "Why It's Not the Same Old America." *Psychology Today* 15, no. 8 (August 1981): 22–51.

Ianni, A. J.; and Reuss-Ianni, Elizabeth. "What Schools Can Do About Violence." *Today's Education* 69, no. 2 (April–May 1980): 20–23.

Kozol, Jonathon. *Illiterate America.* New York: Anchor/Doubleday, 1985.

Molnar, Alex. "Nuclear Policy in a Democracy: Do Educators Have A Choice?" *Educational Leadership* 40, no. 8 (May 1983): 37–39.

Morf, Martin. "Eight Scenarios for Work in the Future." *Futurist* 17, no. 3 (June 1983): 24–29.

Naisbitt, John. *Megatrends: Ten New Directions Transforming Our Lives.* New York: Warner Books, 1982.

Schubert, William K. "Knowledge About Out-of-School Curriculum." *Educational Forum* 45, no. 2 (January 1981): 185–198.

Simon, Julian. "Life on Earth is Getting Better, Not Worse." *Futurist* 17, no. 4 (August 1983): 7–14.

Stokes, Bruce. "Water Shortages: The Next Energy Crisis." *Futurist* 17, no. 2 (April 1983): 37–47.

## On Sex Roles

Auersher, Dorothy. "Wanted: A More Realistic Education for Women." *Educational Leadership* 33, no. 2 (November 1975): 118–122.

Boulding, Elise. *The Underside of History: A View of Women through Time.* Boulder, Colorado: Westview Press, 1976.

Gutentag, Marcia; and Bray, Helen. *Undoing Sex Sterotypes: Research and Resources for Educators*. New York: McGraw-Hill, 1976.

McLure, G. T.; and McLure, J. W. *Women's Studies*. Washington: National Education Association, 1977.

Mussen, P.; and Eisenberg-Berg, N. *Roots of Caring, Sharing and Helping*. San Francisco: W. H. Freeman Co., 1977.

Newland, Kathleen. *The Sisterhood of Man*. New York: Norton, 1979.

Stannard, Una. *Mrs. Man*. San Francisco, California: Germainbooks, 1977.

Tiedt, Iris M. *Sexism in Education*. Morristown, New Jersey: General Learning Press, 1976.

Zaret, Esther. "Women/Schooling/Society." In ASCD Yearbook, *Schools in Search of Meaning*. Washington, D. C.: Association for Supervision and Curriculum Development, 1975.

# 3

# *Human Development*

PREREQUISITE

Reading Sections 1 and 2 of this book.

RATIONALE

Human development is now generally accepted as one of the bases of the curriculum. For the past fifty years, the study of child and adolescent development has been regarded as one of the basic sciences underlying elementary and secondary education. With the increasing significance of lifelong education, it becomes necessary for curriculum planners to focus attention on human development during early adulthood, middle age, and later maturity for learners at these stages of development.

The human development approach to the curriculum and to teaching includes a body of knowledge about human growth. It also includes a point of view with reference to learners: they should be studied as individuals, so that the program of instruction can be shaped, in part, by the individual's own nature and needs. In the first three articles in this section, the uniqueness and educability of each human being is emphasized from the perspective of three disciplines, by anthropologist Ashley Montagu, biochemist Roger J. Williams, and sociologist Gerald Grant (with John Briggs).

In "The Biology of Behavior" Roger J. Williams describes the biological basis of each individual's uniqueness. Each learner has an inborn individuality and an innate uniqueness. The facts of biological individuality indicate the very great need for the provision of many alternatives in educational programs. Montagu emphasizes that the human person is capable of learning anything, under the appropriate environmental conditions. He states that we need to "grow up into children" and not into adults—that is, we need to preserve some of the traits that children so conspicuously exhibit. Gerald Grant and John Briggs, in "Today's Children Are Different," tell us that socialization strongly influences the kinds of persons we become. They describe how the processes of socialization have changed from the times of our grandparents (and even our parents) and state that today there is a particular need for us to share socializing tasks with adolescents and young adults.

The generally accepted stages of human development include infancy, childhood, early adolescence, middle adolescence, late adolescence, and adulthood. The elementary school years correspond roughly to the stage known as childhood. Early, middle, and late adolescence correspond roughly to the middle school, high school, and community college levels of education. And now the later stages which include adult and senior learners are of increasing importance to community colleges and universities. The stage concept is useful as a rough rule of thumb, but it cannot define the development of any one learner at a particular age.

Several theorists and their research studies have had particular influence on curriculum planning. They include Havighurst and the "developmental tasks" concept; Erikson and his stages of "growth toward a mature personality"; and Piaget and his four stages of growth in intelligence through "assimilation" and "accommodation." Articles concerning all three of these theorists and their theories are included in this section.

Curriculum planning should be guided by five aspects of development:

1. The biological basis of individual differences
2. Physical maturation
3. Intellectual development and achievement
4. Emotional growth and development
5. Cultural and social development

Havighurst's and Piaget's theories consider the biological, psychological, and cultural aspects of development. Erikson's theory emphasizes emotional growth and development.

Ausubel's article in this section discusses several concepts of significance in curriculum planning that he relates to human growth and development: *readiness,* which is based on both maturation and learning; *breadth and depth of the curriculum;* the *learner's voice in curriculum planning;* and *organization and cognitive development.*

Maturation and change in human development occur over the whole life span, providing one of the bases for curriculum and instruction planning at all age levels, including university and adult education. Havighurst's developmental tasks include those of adult and later life. Erikson's theory also examines human development during adult and later life.

Maturation follows different courses of development for different individuals. One of the guidelines for curriculum planning derived from the study of human development is the *"problem of the match."* Some sort of fitting or matching between the development stage and the program of learning is needed by each individual. The goal of curriculum makers and teachers is to see that the proper match is accomplished.

Recent research on brain growth periodization may have special significance for curriculum planning and the "problem of the match" at various age levels. The research shows that there are five periods of growth spurt, which alternate with intervals of growth lag, in the development of the human brain from birth to about the age of seventeen. The implications of this research for curriculum planning are discussed in "Brain Periodization: *Challenge,* Not Justification" in Section 8.

All four of the human development theorists whose work you will study in this section—Havighurst, Erikson, Piaget, and Kohlberg—hold that the development stages they describe have a fixed order, and that each person passes through these stages in this order. Successful achievement of each stage is necessary if the individual is to proceed with vigor and confidence to the next stage. There is a "teachable moment" or time of special sensitivity for each task or stage.

Should moral education be one of the aspects of human development to which curriculum planners and teachers give attention? Perhaps the best answer to this question is that we are moral educators whether we wish to be or not. Education simply is not value-free. Learners cannot attend school for twelve or more years and avoid its influence in the way they think about moral issues and the way they behave.

Today there are several curricular and teaching approaches to values and moral education. Kohlberg's cognitive-developmental approach to moral education is being widely discussed now by curriculum planners. It is a human development approach that is based on Piaget's stages of cognitive development and John Dewey's levels of moral development. Like the ideas of Havighurst, Erikson, and Piaget, Kohlberg's six stages of moral development involve a "problem of the match" between the learner's developmental stage and the curriculum and teaching.

In his article in this section, Kohlberg states that moral principles are ultimately "principles of justice," and that at each stage of moral development the concept of justice is reorganized. Carol Gilligan, a colleague of Kohlberg's, believes that his research has depended too heavily on studies of men and that women's moral judgments are more likely to be based in care and concern for others. A brief review of research on sex differences in moral development is presented in "Now Then, Mr. Kohlberg, About Moral Development in Women . . ." at the end of this section.

## Curriculum Criteria

Curriculum criteria are guidelines by which decisions can be made in curriculum planning. What guidelines for planning can be derived from the human development theories discussed in this rationale and in the articles and additional learning activities in this section? *Individual differences and continuity in learning* are the criteria that depend in important ways on knowledge about human development.

Although stages of human development can be identified, no two individuals of the same age are necessarily alike in physical, emotional, intellectual, or social development. Knowing how development occurs in each of these areas assists curriculum planners and teachers in providing for individual differences and continuity. Providing for continuity in learning means that teaching and learning must start for each learner "where the learner is." The criterion questions are as follows:

1. Does the planned curriculum provide for the developmental differences of the learners being taught?
2. Does the planned curriculum include provisions so that learning may start for each learner where he or she is?
3. Has the significance of developmental tasks, stages of growth toward a mature personality, and the four successive models of intelligence been considered in planning?
4. Do the curriculum planners and teachers attempt to provide for earlier tasks inadequately achieved, and for their maintenance when successfully achieved?
5. Has the curriculum planning been adjusted to the biological, social, cultural, and intellectual changes that are occurring and that have occurred in recent years at each stage of human development?
6. Do the curriculum planning and teaching allow for the inborn individuality and innate uniqueness of each learner?

Cognitive and personality stages, developmental tasks, and the biological uniqueness of each individual should have a meaningful relationship to the content of the curriculum. If no such relationship can be found, the curriculum's appropriateness should be questioned by curriculum planners and teachers.

## OBJECTIVES

Your objectives in studying human development as one of the bases of curriculum planning should be as follows:

1. To be able to analyze a curriculum plan with respect to its relationship to human development research and theories.
2. To be able to suggest changes and improvements in the curriculum plan that are based on an understanding of human development theories and research.
3. To be able to plan for teaching in terms of human development stages and individual needs and development.

## PREASSESSMENT

The purpose of the preassessment is to enable you to determine whether you already possess the performance competencies in curriculum planning that are listed under the objectives just mentioned. The following activities will aid you in your evaluation:

1. Select three aspects of human development, and tell how each can be applied to planning a curriculum or teaching.
2. Describe each of the following human development concepts and how they may be applied to curriculum planning and teaching: stages of development, developmental tasks, readiness, assimilation and accommodation, growth toward a mature personality, and biological uniqueness of each learner.
3. Select any curriculum plan, at any school level, and examine it in the light of human development concepts, theories, and research. This could be done by visiting and studying a school, or by analyzing a written statement regarding a school's program or the instruction in one classroom. You might choose some part of the school's curriculum, such as the social studies curriculum.
4. Suggest improvements or changes in the curriculum plan as a result of your analysis in number 3.

In answering number 3, you might analyze the curricula described in "Problem Solving: Encouraging Active Learning" or "Children's Literature and Moral Development" in Section 7, or "Model Programs for Adult Learners in Higher Education" in Section 10, in the light of ideas expressed by Williams, Havighurst, Erikson, Piaget or Kohlberg.

If you find that the school of your choice does not consider human development in its curriculum planning, suggest improvements in the planning on the basis of knowledge about human development. Begin by checking the developmental tasks of the age group in the school (in terms of Havighurst's theory described in "Developmental Tasks" in this section). Then see what other theories, such as Erikson's and Piaget's (see their articles in this section), suggest for this age level. Remember that individual variations must be considered in providing for individual learners.

## LEARNING ACTIVITIES

The articles in this section will assist you in identifying and understanding human development concepts, theories, and research that are important in curriculum planning and in planning for teaching.

Other learning activities are suggested at the end of this section.

## POSTASSESSMENT

After attempting the preassessment you may do *one or more* of the following:

1. See if your instructor believes that you are ready for a postassessment evaluation on human development and the curriculum. Most students will need further work on this curriculum base.
2. Read the articles on human development in this section, and try to determine

how the theories and research being discussed in each article should be considered in curriculum planning and teaching.

3.  Choose additional activities and readings or films from those listed at the end of this section under Additional Learning Activities.

4.  Look for other films, books, or articles on human development in your library or media center.

5.  Discuss the reading you have done and the films you have viewed with your fellow students. The key questions: How should the human development theories and research you've studied affect a school's curriculum? How should they be considered in planning for teaching?

6.  When you are ready, ask your instructor for advice on a suitable postassessment for you for this topic. Satisfactory completion of number 1 under Problems and Projects at the end of this section might be one possibility, or written completion of the preassessment for this section, after completing other learning activities, might be a satisfactory postassessment. Consult your instructor about this. You can evaluate your own ability to do these activities before you see the instructor.

# Today's Children Are Different

## GERALD GRANT WITH JOHN BRIGGS

In contrasting ourselves with our children or our grandparents, we tend to exaggerate change. For instance, maturation now occurs earlier—perhaps a year or so—but nothing on the order of magnitude previously assumed.[1] Yet the relationships between young and old have changed, as well as the way we socialize the young. It is these changes, rather than the shift in maturation rates, that are most important.

Socialization strongly influences the kinds of persons we become and the attitudes we have, including our attitude toward biological change. I would like to reflect on those changes by comparing what adolescent life was like for my father

and myself and is now for my son, a 16-year-old high school sophomore.

My son lives only a mile from the house where my father was born in 1899 and two miles from the neighborhood in which I grew up. He attends the public schools of Syracuse, as we did. Of course the Syracuse that my father knew was a small but bustling city less than a fifth its current size. Barges came through town on a canal that has been filled in, paved over, and renamed Erie Boulevard. The center of the city is relatively dead today—the action, especially for adolescents, is in the suburban malls, where they shop for electronic gear, sports equipment,

From *Educational Leadership* 40, No. 6 (March 1983): 4, 6–9. © 1983, Association for Supervision and Curriculum Development. Reprinted with permission of the Association for Supervision and Curriculum Development, Gerald Grant, and John Briggs. All rights reserved.

and designer jeans, and then return home to talk about their forays, possibly on their own telephones.[2]

My grandfather, James Grant, a Scot who was part owner of Master's and Grant Livery, fell on hard times and into hard drinking and died when my father was 13. Mary Duffy Grant moved her five children to a flat over Madigan's butcher shop, where my father went to work after he completed grammar school in 1912. An older brother was "placed out" with relatives in Cleveland, a common practice in the 19th century. He was the only one of the five to complete high school, not far from the average in 1900 when the nation was still three-fifths rural and 10 percent completed high school. My father's work experience typified the shift that was occurring in an urbanizing nation. He had some apprentice-like jobs in the stable and butcher shop, where adult supervision was close but informal. At 18 he went to work in a new steel factory, where relationships were more hierarchical and the work took on the specialized character of the industrial era.

Most males went to work at 14 and learned what they needed to know in face-to-face relationships on the job. One learned by watching and imitating, picking up skills according to one's interest, effort, and opportunities. From the age of 13, my father turned over his earnings to his mother. He took us on tours of his old neighborhood, pointing out the flats in which he had lived and at what rent—he remembered because he had paid it. This, too, was typical throughout the 19th century, when children aged 12–18 supplied a third of the family income. It was a time when the young were expected to do the work of adults but were treated in most respects as children until 18, when those in rural areas might leave home for a boarding house in the city. Although one was not legally an adult until 21, most were emancipated informally by 18.

## "ADOLESCENCE" IS BORN

By the mid-20th century adolescent culture had been born and given a name by G. Stanley Hall. The adolescent was neither expected to do the work of an adult nor treated as an adult. Adolescence was a moratorium from adult responsibilities and privileges with the exception of those "dropouts" (and the term was just then coming into use) who went to work, bought a car, and weren't kids any longer. Sociologists wrote about the overwhelming power of the peer group as the high school became the major socializing institution for most youth.

In *Adolescent Society,* James Coleman described Syracuse Central, the kind of high school from which I graduated in 1955. It was a place in which rating and dating games rivaled the formal academic curriculum. The curriculum was "tracked" and the path to maturity was partly affected by whether one was preparing for real work on graduation or continuation of the dating game in college, which then had such old-fashioned requirements as curfews and separate dormitories for boys and girls.

The adults in the school had more real power: we students could parody the uptight principal but we were careful when we did so because we knew he could throw us out. We generally observed the rules and believed that completing school was important to our occupational futures, but our strongest emotional commitments were to the values of the peer group. We did not feel the need to challenge adult culture as youth were to do in the 60s; we tended to give it superficial compliance while attending to our own pursuits—within bounds allowed by adults. Those bounds included the acceptance of chaperones at school events, and in the lower middle class neighborhood where I grew up, adults on the block felt free to correct a misbehaving child on the street.

Within my peer group culture, coke was

something that went with french fries. Marijuana or any hallucinogenic drugs were unknown. Beer was regularly smuggled to parties after junior year but hard liquor was rarely seen. The fine gradations of petting dominated sexual discussion and "going all the way" was generally forbidden. Pregnancy meant disgrace and automatic marriage; abortion was rare except among the wealthy. The technology of birth control was limited to the male condom and it was more for show than use.

The school was still perceived as a powerful social escalator. For families like ours, it worked. Whereas my father had gone only as far as eighth grade, three of his sons finished college; two of them are professors. But it was a world much less fair to women and blacks. My sister went to business school, not to college (later she became a nurse). Although Syracuse Central abutted what was then a black ghetto, it enrolled few blacks, and most of them left or were pushed out by the end of compulsory schooling at age 16. Those who could not afford to go to college usually didn't. There was no community college and virtually no free public higher education with the exception of state teachers colleges.

## HIGH SCHOOL EVOLVES

By the 1980s school had become a more open institution. On the way into my son's high school you will pass students in wheelchairs taking a last drag on a cigarette before classes begin. The enrollment is about 55 percent black and includes a variety of new immigrants, including some Cambodian refugees. More than 90 percent graduate. Paradoxically, while graduation no longer gives one an advantage in the competition for jobs, those labeled dropouts pay a penalty. Youth are increasingly granted adult rights but few expect them to bear adult responsibilities. Many work part-time but it is a rare parent

who expects any contribution to the family purse. Teen income goes for teen consumer items—one's own stereo has become a birthright.

The adult keepers often feel stripped of most of their former powers. The courts have held that teenage girls can obtain birth control services over their parents' objection, and the children's rights movement has won new due process rights for young teenagers. In Washington, D.C., regulations forbid a teacher from barring a door to a pupil no matter how late he or she arrives, since pupils have a right to an education (presumably on their terms).

Some schools, particularly large urban high schools, have taken an adversarial turn. In the face of elaborate due process procedures, adults shrink from instituting changes because of the demands it would make on their own time or because they fear they lack evidence that would "stand up in court." Instead, they look the other way.

The reasons for these shifts are complex and it is impossible to assign precise weights to them. To a considerable degree, our problems have been a function of our successes. We have laid a great burden on American public schools: namely, to be the principal avenue of creating a more equal and just society. We have attempted to right some great wrongs and have carried-out a social revolution in the schools. Schools have become larger and more diverse. Perhaps there never has been a true consensus on the socializing and moral functions of the schools, but simply an agreement among the elite whom the schools predominantly served in an earlier era.

Now nearly everyone is in the school tent and feels he or she has an equal voice in deciding what kind of show should go on. Specific court decisions, especially on the Supreme Court decision re Gault, were interpreted as placing strong limits on the discretionary power of principals and teachers, and subject any disciplinary decision to quasi-appellate review. The children's rights movement has exploited these decisions, and concern about genuine child abuse has created the machinery for children to challenge parents in the much more doubtful area of "emotional abuse." There has been a significant shift from the traditional American attitude of independence, absorbed from the cradle, of "ain't nobody the boss of me" to adolescents who have gone a step further. "Don't touch me or I'll have you arrested.[3]

The radical wing of the movement has stressed the oppression of youth, as in this excerpt from the Youth Liberation of Ann Arbor:

> Our lives are considered the property of various adults. We do not recognize their right to control us. We call this control adult chauvinism, and we will fight it. We quickly begin to learn that these schools and families are part of a whole system that is sick.[4]

In addition to the pull of children's rights from below, so to speak, some parents appear to be giving a push from above by relieving themselves of the burdens of parenthood. In recent decades there have been increases in divorce rates, in children living with one parent, in two-career families as well as shifts in attitudes about the responsibilities of parents. Survey data indicate parents are now less altruistic, for example, with 66 percent feeling they "should be free to live their own lives even if it means spending less time with their children." And 63 percent say they have a right to live well now "even if it means leaving less to the children."[5]

There is also evidence that parents have withdrawn from efforts to supervise children, taking a more passive role in relation to their children's curriculum choices (math, science, and foreign language enrollment have fallen markedly), and a 1978 poll showed that nearly three-fourths of all parents had no regular rules limiting television watching.[6] When the students themselves were asked whether teachers demanded enough

of them, 57 percent said they were not asked to work hard enough.[7]

## INCREASED AFFLUENCE

In part, the shifts I am describing reflect the increased affluence of the nation as a whole. My father spent his youth in the working class, whereas my son enjoys upper middle class status. Similarly, some of the privileges that were once extended to a few youth in the 19th century now are enjoyed by a broad middle and upper class. But there has been a shift in the nature of those privileges and in the kinds of relationships that exist between adolescents and adults. At least five significant trends differentiate my father's world from my son's.[8]

1. *From being known to being on one's own:* In the world my father knew, children came into fairly intimate contact with a variety of adults in work and apprenticeship relations. Today, the separate culture of the adolescent has been accentuated by the extension of many formal rights to adolescents. The young act on their own with respect to many fundamental decisions, which they make in isolation from adults and adult responsibilities.

2. *From obvious necessity to seemingly arbitrary authority:* The necessity for doing the task was self-evident in an apprentice-like world. Now reasons are more obscure—learn calculus this term so that you'll be able to do advanced economics later and thus get a good job someday. Adult roles cannot be readily discerned, and the connections between what you are required to do now and might do ten years from now are often difficult to understand.

3. *From a world of likely success to one of possible failure:* In a society in which schooling played a less dominant role, you were seldom asked to do

much beyond your evident abilities. If you could not repair the roof, you could clean the barn. This matching of person to task was less harsh than the sorting and grading that occurs in school where one is tested frequently and faced with the possibility of being stamped a failure. Compulsory schooling requires some to continue at frustrating tasks. Grade inflation and a general reduction in academic standards have been unsatisfactory solutions to this problem.

4. *From shared parenting to teenagers in opposition to parents:* In large families with children aged five to 19, older siblings shared parenting tasks and responsibility for discipline was more diffuse. With the advent of modern family planning techniques and the tendency to have fewer and more closely spaced children, the modern teenager is more likely to feel a member of a cadre in opposition to adults.

5. *From early contributors to long-term borrowers:* Until the end of the 19th century and part way into the 20th, the period of dependency was short and children became significant contributors to the family purse by age 14. Financial dependency now is longer (even to the late 20s for many graduate students) and increases during the late teenage years when many parents must take out a second mortgage to cover college costs.

From the adolescent side of the relation, then, adults seem more distant and less intimately knowledgeable about the talents and capabilities of the young. Adults appear more arbitrary about what they expect the young to do, and they are more inclined to administer tests and to exercise social control through bureaucratic arrangements. In the family, us-them feelings are stronger and adolescents may resent rather than feel grateful for the long-term dependency that the costs of extended formal education usually require.

From the adult side, there are fewer opportunities for the rewards of nurturance that occur in mentoring relationships. Like the young, adults struggle with the lengthened drain on the family purse and the tension that often produces.

## ADULTS IN TRANSITION

Contemporary adults are confused and less certain of their own authority.[9] Many who lived through the cultural revolutions of the 1960s took drugs themselves, participated in the sexual revolution, and experimented with the new "lifestyles." Guilt and pain over increased divorce rates and family breakup is widespread. Those who are internally divided sometimes mask their tension by adopting an authoritarian posture (and both authoritarian sects and schools are on the increase). But the more likely response is to withdraw from the responsibility of enforcing a standard or to let someone else do it. In many cases, that someone else is the adolescent, operating under a new system of rules and rights. The adolescent experiences this not as true freedom—for they yearn for the presence of strong adults who care enough to hold them to worthwhile standards—but as the withdrawal of adults from responsibilities that are properly theirs. I agree with B. C. Hafen that the indiscriminate growth of the children's rights movement could have disastrous consequences: "It would be an irony of tragic proportions if, in our egalitarian zeal, we abandoned our children to their 'rights' in a way that seriously undermined their claim to protection and developmental opportunity."[10]

Daniel Offer and his colleagues have argued persuasively in a recent study[11] that psychologists have overemphasized the supposed turmoil that characterizes relationships between healthy adolescents and adults. Yet his data also show that teenagers have grown much less trusting in the last two decades. Comparing responses by teenagers in the early 1960s with those in the late 1970s, he concluded that "with respect to almost every self-image dimension teenagers in the 1970s felt worse about themselves than did teenagers in the 1960s." Teenagers describe themselves as less able to take criticism without resentment (dropping from 70 to 57 percent), and more likely to "get violent if I don't get my way" (5 percent then, 17 percent now). Increases in teenage worries about their health and feeling "empty emotionally most of the time" corroborate other data showing increased drug use and suicide rates among adolescents.

The loss of trust is quite marked. Nearly twice as many (13 vs. 25 percent) say, "If you confide in others, you ask for trouble." The share of those who believe, "An eye for an eye and a tooth for a tooth does not apply to our society" has fallen from 67 to 40 percent. More now "Blame others even when I know I was at fault." Sidetaking and an adversarial posture are more evident in their views of their own families as well, with a doubling of those who believe, "My parents are almost always on the side of someone else" (14 to 32 percent).

## NO IDEAL PAST

That loss of trust is related more to withdrawal on the part of adult socializers than to changes in children or in their basic needs. The proper response to our contemporary dilemma is neither to seek the restoration of some supposedly ideal past nor to "liberate" children from supposedly oppressive adults. It is rather to accept our responsibilities for having brought children into the world, to counter the current trends toward withdrawal from those responsibilities, to pursue an honest dialogue about the nature of those responsibilities, and to come to some agreement about what share of the responsibility the school should bear. Adults need to summon courage,

conviction, and compassion in order to connect with adolescents even at the cost of painful confrontations and temporary rejections.

We also need to share socializing tasks with young adults as they begin to exercise more responsibility. We should give serious attention to mandating a year or at least a semester of voluntary service for all high school students. They could help feed the elderly in nursing homes, improve parks and public lands, care for the young in pre-school centers, tutor poor readers in elementary schools, assist disabled students and those teachers who are trying to make mainstreaming work, improve food service operations in school cafeterias, paint and repair schools (including the teachers' lounge), coach grade school soccer teams, and minister to the needs of the terminally ill, to suggest a short list.

The young would have an opportunity to learn more by giving more, to develop other sides and aspects of themselves in a noncompetitive environment, to gain dignity and a heightened sense of self-worth by being useful to others, and to build a wider network of mentoring relationships with adults. A volunteer year would help to create a world in which adolescents would have more opportunities to be contributors and not just borrowers, to be known in relationships where authority is less arbitrary, and to feel less a cadre in opposition.

## ENDNOTES

1. See V. L. Bullough, "Age at Menarche: A Misunderstanding," *Science* 213 (July 17, 1981): 365–366. It appears that the alleged steep decline in the average age of menarche from 17 to 12.5 years was based on an atypical sample of Norwegian girls. We are grateful to Christine Murray for pointing out this article to us.

2. A poll of its high school readers by *Highwire* magazine shows 37 percent own their own phones, 71 percent have a stereo system, and

84 percent a radio/cassette. "Students and Their Money," *Highwire* 2, 5 (Fall 1982): 20–23.

3. For a more extensive analysis of these influences, see Gerald Grant, "Children's Rights and Adult Confusions," *The Public Interest* 69 (Fall 1982): 83–99.

4. Youth Liberation of Ann Arbor, "We Do Not Recognize Their Right to Control Us," in *The Children's Rights Movement: Overcoming the Oppression of Young People,* ed. Beatrice Gross and Ronald Gross (New York: Anchor Press/Doubleday, 1977), p. 128. In the introduction to the volume, the authors write: "A good case can be made for the fact that young people are the most oppressed of all minorities. They are discriminated against on the basis of age in everything from movie admissions to sex. They are traditionally the subjects of ridicule, humiliation, and mental torture by adults. Their civil rights are routinely violated in homes, schools, and institutions," p. 1.

5. Daniel Yankelovich, "New Rules in American Life," *Psychology Today* 15, 4 (April 1981): 35–91.

6. National Center for Educational Statistics, *The Condition of Education,* Washington, D.C.: Government Printing Office, 1979, p. 18.

7. Ibid, p. 72.

8. We are indebted to Joseph Kett's *Rites of Passage: Adolescence in America 1790 to the Present* (New York: Basic Books, 1977).

9. Although contemporary parental confusion may be particularly acute, it is certainly not new, as Bernard Wishy notes in *The Child and the Republic* (Philadelphia: University of Pennsylvania Press, 1968) quoting Charlotte Perkins Gilman in 1903 on the timidity and confusion of parents: "Our own personal lives, rich as they are today . . . are not happy. We are confused, bewildered," p. 121.

10. B. C. Hafen, "Puberty, Privacy, and Protection: The Risks of Children's Rights," *American Bar Association Journal* 63 (1977): 1383–1388, quoted in Bettye M. Caldwell, "Balancing Children's Rights and Parents' Rights," in *Care and Education of Young Children in America* ed. R. Haskins and S. Gallagher (Norwood, New Jersey: Ablex, 1980) p. 35.

11. Daniel Offer, Erick Ostrow, and Kenneth I. Howard, *Adolescence: A Psychological Self-Portrait* (New York: Basic Books, 1981).

*Gerald Grant* is a sociologist and *John Briggs* is a historian in the Department of Cultural Foundations of Education and Curriculum, Syracuse University.

# My Idea of Education

## ASHLEY MONTAGU

As an anthropologist who has been studying the six-million-year course of human evolution for nearly sixty years, I have become convinced that the characteristic that distinguishes humans from all other creatures is educability and that the most important of all basic human psychological needs is the need for love. Both of these findings have profound implications for schools and teachers.

The human is capable of learning anything, under the appropriate environmental conditions.

From *Today's Education,* Journal of the National Education Association, 69, no. 1 (February-March 1980) (General Edition): 48–49. Used by the permission of the author and the publisher.

The human brain is an organ for the assimilation of diverse kinds of experiences and for turning accidents into opportunities. It is the most flexible, the most malleable, and the most educable of all the brains in the world.

It is capable of making the most of the improbable. Some people use their brains to arrive at truth and conclusions that others might conceive as utterly impossible. For example, at the very time the flying machine was invented, leading experts of the world said it was a physical impossibility.

We must recognize the educability of the human brain, particularly in dealing with children, who are the most educable of all human beings.

One thing most of us don't understand is the nature of the child and his or her extraordinary educability. Furthermore, we don't understand that we need to grow up into children and not adults. By this I mean that we should preserve some of the traits that the child so conspicuously exhibits.

What are these traits? Besides educability, they are the need to love, sensitivity, the need to think soundly, the need to learn, the need to work, the need to organize, curiosity and wonder, open-mindedness, experimental-mindedness, imagination, creativity, playfulness, sense of humor, joyfulness, laughter, optimism, honesty, trust, compassionate intelligence, and the desire to grow and develop in all these traits.

Frequently, we feel we ought to limit this desire to grow to certain stages that we arbitrarily designate as infancy, childhood, and adolescence or to this one stage or another. Then we treat children of the same chronological age as if they were developmentally of the same age, too.

This is a damaging idea, and it has done an enormous amount of harm to children. Every child has his or her own developmental rate. To treat children, even children the same age, as if they were all equal is to commit a biological and social absurdity. The equal treatment of unequals is the most unequal way of dealing with

human beings ever devised. We're all very different, and because we're all very different, we require individual attention. We should not be treated as if we were an agglutinated mass affixed to one another on the basis of our particular age level.

Even though many teachers recognize the great differences among children, they are not in a position to do anything about them because of the way school systems are organized and the inadequacy of those who are presiding at their top levels. These top level officials are usually unequipped to understand what the child is, what the teacher's needs are, and what education is all about.

What education is all about is being human, in other words, developing those traits that are uniquely human for the benefit of the individual, the family, the community, the society, and the world. Eventually what teachers do in the classroom is going to determine what the world is going to be like; for it is there that children learn all about being human if they have not learned it in the home.

Unfortunately, the probabilities are that children have not learned this in the home, because most parents are not equipped to do the job of parenting. Why? Simply because they have lived in a society that has not recognized the nature of the child, the nature of the human being, and the nature of what the child ought to be.

We now know what human beings ought to be because we understand for the first time in the history of our species that the most important of all human basic psychological needs is the need for love. It stands at the center of all human needs just as our sun stands at the center of our solar system with the planets orbiting around it. So the basic needs, the need for oxygen, food, liquid, rest, for activity, and so on, these revolve around the need for love—the sun of the human being.

It is this need for love that nature designates the mother to satisfy and that we have interfered

with for a very long time by having mothers give birth to babies in hospitals, by taking babies away from their mothers in hospitals, by bottle-feeding babies, and by committing many other frightful offenses against babies at the very beginnings of their lives. These are offenses not only against the baby but against the mother and the family. The family should be involved in the ceremony and the celebration of welcoming a new member into the family. It is the family's job to turn this educable creature into the kind of human being that he or she is striving to be from the moment of birth.

Now that's quite a statement for a scientist to make. How do I know what this baby is striving to be? Well, I have discussed this with hundreds of babies. I've observed them, and I've talked with them. So have a good many other people. What they and I have observed is that the baby wants more than anything else to learn to love. Not only to be loved, but to love, because if the baby fails in this, then he or she fails to grow up as a warm, loving human being.

It's as simple as that. Nothing very complicated, but it's taken a long time for us to understand this.

The child who has not been loved is biochemically, physiologically, and psychologically very different from the one who has been loved. The former even grows differently from the latter. What we now know is that the human being is born to live as if to live and love were one.

This is not, of course, new. This is a validation of the Sermon on the Mount. I who am not a Christian and who am not a member of any religious affiliation say this.

The only religion I believe in is goodness and love. This is what we should be teaching in our schools. The greatest gift a teacher has to give a student is his or her love.

A teacher can recognize that the biggest behavior problems in the classroom are the ones who have been failed in their need for love and that what their need is is not to be sent to the principal but to be loved by the teacher. They will try the teacher again and again because they have been failed so many times and they don't trust anyone.

Every time the teacher offers them love, they may not improve their behavior, but if the teacher persists, then the teacher will win the children over. I speak from experience as an old teacher. I know very well how this works, because I've frequently done it myself.

I know this is very difficult in many cases—and it's extremely difficult in certain parts of America where teachers face behavior problems of the worst kind and where violence and vandalism are increasing at an accelerating rate in the schools. Even in those places, however, I think each teacher can make a difference by doing what he or she ought to do: behaving as a warm, loving human being.

How do we become warm, loving human beings? We act *as if* we were warm, loving human beings. If we act as if we were, someday we may find we've become what we've been trying to be, because what we are is not what we say but what we do.

I have been discussing love, but I have not defined it yet for the simple reason that a definition isn't meaningful at the beginning of an inquiry. It can be so only at the end of one.

Love is the ability to communicate by demonstrative acts to others our profound involvement in their welfare. We communicate our deep interest in them because we are aware that to be born human is to be born in danger, and therefore we will never commit the supreme treason against others of not helping them when they are most in need of us. We will minister to their needs and give them all the supports, all the stimulation, all the succor that they need or want.

That's love, and that's what we should be teaching in the schools, and everything else should be secondary to that. Reading, writing, and arithmetic, yes—but not of primary importance, of secondary importance in the development of a warm, loving human being.

This is my idea of education. If we put this idea into action, we stand a chance of solving most of the problems that bedevil the world at the present time, for teachers are the unacknowledged legislators of the world.

*Ashley Montagu* is an anthropologist. Among many other books he has authored *Growing Young* (1981), *The Human Connection* (1979), *Touching* (2nd ed., 1978), *Life Before Birth* (2nd ed., 1978), *The Direction of Human Development* (2nd ed., 1970), and *On Being Human* (2nd ed., 1966).

# The Biology of Behavior
## ROGER J. WILLIAMS

Biologically, each member of the human family possesses inborn differences based on his brain structure and on his vast mosaic of endocrine glands—in fact, on every aspect of his physical being. Each of us has a distinctive set of drives—for physical activity, for food, for sexual expression, for power. Each one has his own mind qualities: abilities, ways of thinking, and patterns of mental conditions. Each one has his own emotional setup and his leanings toward music and art in its various forms, including literature. All these leanings are subject to change and development, but there is certainly no mass movement toward uniformity. No one ever "recovers" from the fact that he was born an individual.

When a husband and wife disagree on the temperature of the soup or on the amount of bed coverings, or if their sleep patterns do not jibe, this is evidence of inborn differences in physiology. If one child loves to read or is interested in science and another has strong likings for sports or for art, this is probably due to inborn differences in makeup. If two people disagree about food or drink, they should not disregard the fact that taste and smell reactions often widely differ and are inherited. If we see a person wearing loud clothing without apparent taste, we need to remember, in line with the investigations of Pickford in England, that each individual has a color vision all his own; some may deviate markedly from the pack.

The inborn leanings of Mozart were evident by age three, and he began composing when he was four. Capablanca was already a good chess player—good enough to beat his father—when at age five he played his first game. For many centuries, Indian philosophers have recognized innate individuality, which they explain on the basis of experience in previous incarnations.

Biology has always recognized inborn individuality. If this inborn distinctiveness had not always been the rule in biology, evolution could never have happened. It is a commonplace fact in biology that every living organism needs a heredity and a suitable environment. Unfortunately, in the minds of most intellectuals biological considerations have been pushed aside.

From *Saturday Review* 54, no. 5 (January 30, 1971): 17–19, 61 © 1971, Saturday Review, Inc. Used by permission of the publisher.

Professor Jerry Hirsch, a psychologist at the University of Illinois, has protested in *Science* that "the opinion makers of two generations have literally excommunicated heredity from the behavioral sciences." This neglect of the study of heredity has effectively produced a wide gap between biology and psychology. Biology deals with living things, and psychology is logically an important phase of biology.

Bernard Rimland, director of the Institute for Child Behavior Research in San Diego, in reviewing my book *You Are Extraordinary* in *American Psychologist*, wrote

Since between-group differences are commonly a small fraction of the enormous, important, and very interesting within-group (individual) difference, psychology's focus on average values for heterogeneous groups represents, as Williams indicates, a chronic case of throwing out the babies with the bath water. "Throwing out the babies" is bad enough, but we psychologists have the dubious distinction of making this error not only repeatedly but *on purpose*.

Social solidarity exists and social problems are pressing, but we cannot hope to deal with these successfully by considering only generic man, that is, average values for heterogeneous groups. We need a better understanding of *men*. The basic problem of generic man is how to achieve "life, liberty, and the pursuit of happiness." The writers of our Declaration of Independence were on solid ground, biologically speaking, when they took the position that each human being has inalienable rights and that no one has, by virtue of his imagined "royal blood," the right to rule over another. In their emphasis on mankind as individuals, Jefferson and his co-authors were closer to biological reality than are those of our time who divorce psychology from biology and center their attention on that statistical artifact, the average man.

Because each of us is distinctive, we lean in different directions in achieving life, liberty, and the pursuit of happiness. Happiness may come

to individual people in vastly different ways, and so the human problem of achieving life and the pursuit of happiness resolves itself, more than it is comfortable to admit, into a series of highly individual human problems. We need to take this consideration into account in attempting to build an advanced society.

In understanding the scope of human desires, it is worthwhile to consider briefly the problems that real—as opposed to theoretical—people face. These may be grouped under four headings: (1) making a livelihood; (2) maintaining health; (3) getting along with others; and (4) getting along with one's self. These four categories, singly or in combination, cover most of the familiar human problems—marriage and divorce, crime, disease, war, housing, and water pollution, urban congestion, race relations, poverty, the population explosion, the all-pervading problem of education, and the building of an abundant life.

The importance of approaching the problem of making a livelihood from the individual's standpoint lies in the fact that in our complex society a multitude of ways exist—an estimated 23,000—in which people can make a living. People are not by any means interchangeable parts in society. While some might function well in any one of a large number of capacities, many others might be highly restricted in their capabilities and yet be extremely valuable members of society. The idea that it is all a matter of education and training cannot possibly be squared with the hard biological facts in inborn individuality. This perversion of education perpetuates the banishment of heredity—an ever-present biological fact—from our thinking. Fitting together people and jobs is just as real and compelling as fitting shoes to people. People sometimes suffer from ill-fitting shoes; they suffer more often from ill-fitting jobs.

The maintenance of health—both physical and mental—involves individual problems to such a degree that it is difficult to exaggerate their role. Even since the days of Hippocrates it has been known in a vague way that "different sorts of people have different maladies," but we are only beginning to learn how to sort people on the basis of their inborn individual characteristics. When we have become expert in this area, vast progress will result, particularly in the prevention of metabolic and psychosomatic diseases, i.e., those not resulting from infection. As long as we dodge the biological fact of inborn individuality, we remain relatively impotent in the handling of diseases that arise from within individual constitutions.

The problem of getting along with others is a very broad one, in which individual problems are basic. If husbands and wives and members of the same family always get along well together, we would have some reason to be surprised when squabbles break out within business, religious, or political groups. If all these kinds of squabbles were non-existent, we would have a basis for being surprised at the phenomenon of war.

While self-interest and differences in training are vital factors in these common conflicts, another factor should not be overlooked: the inborn individuality of the participants. There is a mass of evidence to support the thesis that every individual, by virtue of his or her unique brain structure and peripheral nervous system, is psychologically conditionable in a distinctive manner. Thus, a person's unique nervous system picks up distinctive sets of impulses, and because his interpretive apparatus is also unique he learns different things and interprets the world in a distinctive manner. Even if two individuals were to have exactly the same learning opportunities, each would think differently and not quite like anyone else. This is the basis for the observation of Santayana: "Friendship is almost always the union of a part of one mind with another; people are friends in spots."

In spite of our attempts to do so, individual minds cannot be compared on a quantitative basis. The minds of Shakespeare and Einstein cannot be weighed one against the other; there were many facets to the minds of each. At birth the two minds were equally blank, but as they matured, each saw, perceived, and paid attention to different aspects of the world around it. Each was conditionable in a unique way.

The recognition of the uniqueness of human minds is essential to human understanding. By developing expertness in this area, psychology will eventually become far more valuable. In an advanced society with a growing population and closer associations, it is obviously essential that we learn better how to get along with each other. When we are unaware of the innate differences that reside within each of us, it becomes very easy to think of one who disagrees with us as a "nitwit" or a "jerk," or perhaps as belonging to the "lunatic fringe." When we appreciate the existence of innate differences, we are far more likely to be understanding and charitable. Strife will not be automatically eliminated, but tensions can be decreased immeasurably.

Individual problems are at the root of the problem of crime. Many years ago, James Devon placed his finger on the crucial point. "There is only one principle in penology that is worth any consideration: It is to find out why a man does wrong and make it not worth his while." The question "Why does a particular man commit crime?" is a cogent one; the question "Why does man turn to crime?" is relatively nonsensical.

Since all human beings are individual by nature, they do not tick in a uniform way nor for the same reasons. Broadly speaking, however, many doubtless turn to crime because society has not provided other outlets for their energies. If we could find a suitable job for every individual, the problem of crime would largely vanish. The problem of crime is thoroughly permeated with individual problems; it cannot be blamed solely on social conditions, because as the studies of Sheldon and Eleanor Glueck have shown, highly respected citizens may come from areas where these conditions are the worst.

Racial relations would ease tremendously if we faced squarely the biological facts of individuality. If we were all educated to *know* that all whites are not the same, that all Negroes do not fit in the same pattern, that all Latins are not identical, that all American Indians are individuals, and that all Jews do not fit a stereotype, it would help us to treat every member of the human race as an individual.

It is no denial of the existence of racial problems to assert that individual problems need to be stressed more than they are. For individual Negroes and individual whites, the pursuit of happiness is by no means a uniform pursuit. Doubtlessly, although there are whites and Negroes who would think they had reached Utopia if they had a decent shelter and were assured three meals a day, this would not satisfy millions of others for whom striving and a sense of accomplishment are paramount. "The Negro problem" or "the white problem"—depending on one's point of view—is shot through with a host of individual problems.

Learning to live with one's self is certainly an individual problem, and will be greatly eased by recognition of inborn individuality. Much unhappiness and many suicides can be traced to misguided desire to be something other than one's self. Each of us as an individual has the problem of finding his way through life as best he can. Knowing one's self as a distinctive individual should be an important goal of education; it will help pave the road each of us travels in his pursuit of happiness.

Why have these facts of individuality not been generally accepted as a backdrop in every consideration of human problems? For one thing, many people, including scholars, like being grandiose and self-inflationary. To make sweeping pronouncements about "man" sounds more impressive than to express more limited concerns. Simplicity, too, has an attractiveness; if life could be made to fit a simple formula, this might be regarded as a happy outcome.

One excuse for excommunicating inheritance from the behavioral sciences for two generations has been the fact that inheritance in mammals is recognized by careful students as being exceedingly complex and difficult to interpret. It is true that some few characteristics may be inherited through the operation of single genes or a few recognizable ones. But other characteristics—those that differ in quantity—are considered to be inherited in obscure and indefinable ways commonly ascribed to multiple genes of indefinite number and character. These multiple-gene characteristics include, to quote the geneticists Snyder and David, "the more deep-seated characters of a race, such as form, yield, intelligence, speed, fertility, strength, development of parts, and so on." To say that a particular characteristic is inherited through the mediation of multiple genes is to admit that we are largely ignorant of how this inheritance comes about.

Recently, some light has been thrown on this problem by experiments carried out in our laboratories. These experiments involved armadillos, which are unusual mammals in that they commonly produce litters of four monozygous ("identical") quadruplets that are necessarily all males or all females.

By making measurements and studying sixteen sets of these animals at birth, it became evident that although they develop from identical genes, they are not identical at all. Organ weights may differ by as much as twofold, the free amino acids in the brain may vary fivefold, and certain hormone levels may vary as much as seven-, sixteen-, or even thirty-twofold. These findings clearly suggest that inheritance comes not by genes alone but by cytoplasmic factors that help govern the size of organs (including endocrine glands) and the cellular makeup of the central nervous system. "Identical" twins are not identical except with respect to the genes in the nucleus of the egg cell from which they developed.

One of the most interesting suggestions arising out of this study is the probability that individual brain structures, which have been known to have "enormous" differences since the investigations of Lashley more than twenty years ago, are made distinctive by the same mechanisms that make for differences in organ weights. The size, number, and distributions of neurons in normal brains vary greatly; this is biologically in line with the uniqueness of human minds. The further elucidation of this type of inheritance should help to focus more attention on heredity.

If this line of thought is valid it makes even more ridiculous the invitation issued by the Ford Foundation to the biological sciences to stay out of the precinct of human behavior. The expression "behavioral science" came into being many years ago as a result of the formulation of the Ford Foundation-supported programs. Biochemistry and genetics, for example, were kept apart from the "scientific activities designed to increase knowledge of factors which influence or determine human conduct."

What can be done to bridge the gap between psychology and biology? More importantly, how can we develop expertise in dealing with the human problems that plague us but at present go unsolved?

A broad, long-range, and practical strategy for learning how to deal more effectively with human problems is to explore, problem by problem, the inborn human characteristics that are pertinent to each one. Differential psychology, for example, needs to be intensified and greatly expanded; this can probably be done most effectively in connection with a series of problem-centered explorations.

Some of the specific problem-areas that require study from the standpoint of how inborn characteristics come into play are: delinquency and crime, alcoholism, drug addiction, unemployability, accident proneness, cancer, heart disease, arthritic disease, mental disease, and, broadest of all, education. Each of these problems could be vastly better understood as the result of interdisciplinary study of the influences of inborn characteristics. Such study would in-

clude differential psychology when applicable, combined with extensive and intensive biochemical and physiological examinations, for example, of blood, saliva, urine, and biopsy materials. To expedite these investigations, automated equipment and computer techniques would be used extensively to help interpret the complex data.

It is not likely that these explorations will find that some individuals are born criminals, others alcoholics, etc. Once we recognize the unique leanings that are a part of each of us, we will see how, by adjusting the environment, these leanings can be turned toward ends that are socially constructive. Every inherited factor can be influenced by an appropriate adjustment of the environment. All this should not be made to sound too easy; it may be more difficult than going to the moon, but it will be far more worthwhile.

One of these specific problems—alcoholism—has been of special interest to me. After about twenty-five years of study, I am convinced that inborn biochemical characteristics are basic to this disease, but that expert application of knowledge about cellular nutrition (which is not far off) will make it scientifically possible to prevent the disease completely and to correct the condition if the application of corrective measures is not too long delayed.

Inborn inherited characteristics have a direct bearing on the current revolt against the Establishment. If biology had not been banished from behavioral science, and if students and other intellectuals were well aware of the biological roots of their existence, it would be taken for granted that conformity is not a rule of life.

If all that we human beings inherit is our humanity, then we all should be reaching for the same uniform goal: becoming a thoroughly representative and respectable specimen of Homo sapiens. There is rebellion against this idea. Revolters want to do "their thing." The revolt takes on many forms because many unique individuals are involved.

If nonconformity had a better status in the

eyes of the Establishment (and it would have if our thinking were more biologically oriented), exhibitionism would be diminished and the desire of each individual to live his own life could be fostered in a natural way.

Human beings are not carbon copies of one another. Students and others who are in revolt have found this out. Perhaps without fully rec-

ognizing it, they are pleading for a recognition of inborn individuality. This is essentially a legitimate plea, but it can take the form of disastrous anarchy. A peaceful means of helping resolve the ideological mess we are in is to recognize heredity by having a happy marriage of biology and behavioral science.

*Roger J. Williams* is Professor of Biochemistry, Clayton Foundation Biochemical Institute, University of Texas, Austin.

# Developmental Tasks
## ROBERT J. HAVIGHURST

I. Outline for Analysis of a Developmental Task (pp. 17–18): *Title of Task*

  1. The Nature of the Task
  2. Biological Basis
  3. Psychological Basis
  4. Cultural Basis
  5. Educational Implications

II. Definition—Developmental Task: A developmental task is a task which arises at or about a certain period in the life of the individual, successful achievement of which leads to his happiness and to success with later tasks, while failure leads to unhappiness in the individual, disapproval by the society, and difficulty with later tasks (p. 2)

III. Developmental Tasks: Infancy to Old Age

  A. Developmental Tasks of Infancy and Early Childhood
  1. Learning to Walk

  2. Learning to Take Solid Food
  3. Learning to Talk
  4. Learning to Control the Elimination of Body Wastes
  5. Learning Sex Differences and Sexual Modesty
  6. Achieving Physiological Stability
  7. Forming Simple Concepts of Social and Physical Reality
  8. Learning to Relate Oneself Emotionally to Parents, Siblings, and other People
  9. Learning to Distinguish Right and Wrong and Developing a Conscience (pp. 9–16)

  B. Developmental Tasks of Middle Childhood
  1. Learning Physical Skills Necessary for Ordinary Games
  2. Building Wholesome Attitudes Toward Oneself as a Growing Organism

From *Developmental Tasks and Education*, 3rd ed. by Robert J. Havighurst. Copyright © 1972 by Longman Inc. Reprinted by permission of Longman (sections I, II, and III in the article are from this book). Also from *Human Development and Education* by Robert J. Havighurst. Copyright © 1953 by Longman Inc. First published by Longmans, Green and Co., Inc. Reprinted by permission of Longman (sections IV, V, VI, and VII in the article are from this book).

3. Learning to Get Along with Age-Mates
4. Learning an Appropriate Masculine or Feminine Social Role
5. Developing Fundamental Skills in Reading, Writing, and Calculating
6. Developing Concepts Necessary for Everyday Living
7. Developing Conscience, Morality, and a Scale of Values
8. Achieving Personal Independence
9. Developing Attitudes Toward Social Groups and Institutions (pp. 19–33)

C. Developmental Tasks of Adolescence (pp. 45–75)
1. Achieving New and More Mature Relations with Age-Mates of Both Sexes
2. Achieving a Masculine or Feminine Social Role
3. Accepting One's Physique and Using the Body Effectively
4. Achieving Emotional Independence of Parents and Other Adults
5. Achieving Assurance of Economic Independence
6. Selecting and Preparing for an Occupation
7. Preparing for Marriage and Family Life
8. Developing Intellectual Skills and Concepts Necessary for Civic Competence
9. Desiring and Achieving Socially Responsible Behavior
10. Acquiring a Set of Values and an Ethical System as a Guide to Behavior

D. Developmental Tasks of Early Adulthood (pp. 83–94)
1. Selecting a Mate
2. Learning to Live with a Marriage Partner
3. Starting a Family
4. Rearing Children
5. Managing a Home
6. Getting Started in an Occupation
7. Taking on Civic Responsibility
8. Finding a Congenial Social Group

E. Developmental Tasks of Middle Age (pp. 96–104)
1. Assisting Teen-Age Children to Become Responsible and Happy Adults
2. Achieving Adult Social and Civic Responsibility
3. Reaching and Maintaining Satisfactory Performance in One's Occupational Career
4. Developing Adult Leisure-Time Activities
5. Relating Oneself to One's Spouse as a Person
6. To Accept and Adjust to the Physiological Changes of Middle Age
7. Adjusting to Aging Parents

F. Developmental Tasks of Later Maturity (pp. 108–113)
1. Adjusting to Decreasing Physical Strength and Health
2. Adjustment to Retirement and Reduced Income
3. Adjusting to Death of Spouse
4. Establishing an Explicit Affiliation with One's Age Group
5. Adopting and Adapting Social Roles in a Flexible Way
6. Establishing Satisfactory Physical Living Arrangements

IV. The "Teachable Moment" (p. 5)

There are two reasons why the concept of developmental tasks is useful to educators. First, it helps in discovering and stating the purposes of education in the schools. Education may be conceived as the effort of the society, through the school, to help the individual achieve certain of his developmental tasks.

The second use of the concept is in the timing of educational efforts. When the body is ripe, and society requires, and the self is ready to achieve a certain task, the teachable moment has come. Efforts at teaching, which would have been largely wasted if they had come earlier, give gratifying results when they come at the teachable moment, when the task should be learned. For example, the best times to teach reading, the care of children, and adjustment to retire from one's job can be discovered by studying human development, and finding out when conditions are most favorable for learning these tasks.

V. Developmental Tasks as Objectives of Elementary Education (p. 92)

The elementary school program contributes in one way or another to the child's achievement of every one of his developmental tasks. Whether consciously designed for the purpose or not, the school curriculum helps or hinders the accomplishment of every task, and every school is a laboratory for the working-out of these tasks.

Consequently, it seems useful to regard the developmental tasks as objectives or goals of elementary education, some more important in the school program than others, of course. Successful achievement of these tasks can be described in terms of observable behavior, and these descriptions may be used in evaluating the progress of a child.

VI. Developmental Tasks and the School Curriculum (pp. 175–176)

  A. Evaluating the School Program
    A good school program is one that makes a maximum contribution to the performance by children of their developmental tasks. In a good school program the staff will know which developmental tasks they wish to emphasize. There will be general agreement that the family and other institutions do a good job helping children with certain tasks, and that the school should specialize with certain other tasks.

The questions we might ask in evaluating the program of a particular school are:

1. Does the school know where each child stands in his achievement of his developmental tasks? And does the school assist each child where his need is greater?
2. Does the school have a clear policy and program for assisting children especially with certain developmental tasks, based on discussions with parents, churches, and youth-serving organizations, while these institutions take more responsibility for assisting with other tasks?
3. Does the school understand the strengths and weaknesses of other community institutions in assisting children with their developmental tasks, and does it aim to help where help is most needed?
4. Do the teachers and other school personnel exert an effective informal influence by their examples as people and through their relations with children so as to help children with their developmental tasks?
5. Does the school definitely and systematically teach reflective thinking in the performance of developmental tasks?

*Robert J. Havighurst* is Professor of Education and Human Development, University of Chicago, Illinois.

# Erik Erikson's Developmental Stages: A Healthy Personality for Every Child

## MIDCENTURY WHITE HOUSE CONFERENCE ON CHILDREN AND YOUTH

Many attempts have been made to describe the attributes of healthy personality. They have been put succinctly as the ability to love and the ability to work. A recent review of the literature suggests that the individual with a healthy personality is one who actively masters his environment, shows a unity of personality, and is able to perceive the world and himself correctly. Clearly, none of these criteria applies to a child. It seemed to us best, then, to present for the Conference's consideration an outline that has the merit of indicating at one and the same time the main course of personality development and the attributes of a healthy personality.

This developmental outline was worked out by Erik H. Erikson, a psychologist and practicing psychoanalyst who has made anthropological field studies and has had much experience with children. It is an analysis that derives from psychological theory, to which is added knowledge from the fields of child development and cultural anthropology. The whole is infused with the author's insight and personal philosophy.

In each stage of child development, the author says, there is a central problem that has to be solved, temporarily at least, if the child is to proceed with vigor and confidence to the next stage. These problems, these conflicts of feeling and desire, are never solved in entirety. Each shift in experience and environment presents them in a new form. It is held, however, that each type of conflict appears in its purest, most unequivocal form at a particular stage of child development, and that if the problem is well solved at that time the basis for progress to the next stage is well laid.

In a sense personality development follows biological principles. Biologists have found that everything that grows has a groundplan that is laid out at its start. Out of this groundplan the parts arise, each part having its time of special ascendancy. Together these parts form a functioning whole. If a part does not arise at its appointed time, it will never be able to form fully, since the moment for the rapid outgrowth of some other part will have arrived. Moreover, a part that misses its time of ascendancy or is severely damaged during its formative period is apt to doom, in turn, the whole hierarchy of organs. Proper rate and normal sequence is necessary if functional harmony is to be secured.

Personality represents the most complicated functioning of the human organism and does not consist of parts in the organic sense. Instead of the development of organs, there is the development of locomotor, sensory, and social capacities and the development of individual modes of dealing with experience. Nevertheless, proper rate and proper sequence are as important here as in physical growth, and functional harmony is achieved only if development proceeds according to the groundplan.

In all this it is encouraging for parents and others who have children in charge to realize that in the sequence of his most personal experi-

From a digest of the Fact Finding Report to the Midcentury White House Conference on Children and Youth, 1951, 6–25.

ences, just as in the sequence of organ formation, the child can be trusted to follow inner laws of development, and needs from adults chiefly love, encouragement, and guidance.

The operation of biological laws is seen, also, in the fact that there is constant interplay between organism and environment and that problems of personality functioning are never solved once and for all. Each of the components of the healthy personality to be described below is present in some form from the beginning, and the struggle to maintain it continues throughout life.

For example, a baby may show something like "autonomy" or a will of his own in the way he angrily tries to free his head when he is tightly held. Nevertheless, it is not until the second year of life that he begins to experience the whole conflict between being an autonomous creature and a dependent one. It is not until then that he is ready for a decisive encounter with the people around him, and it is not until then that they feel called upon to train him or otherwise curb his free-questing spirit. The struggle goes on for months and finally, under favorable circumstances, some compromise between dependence and independence is reached that gives the child a sense of well-being.

The sense of autonomy thus achieved is not a permanent possession, however. There will be other challenges to that sense and other solutions more in keeping with later stages of development. Nevertheless, once established at two or three years of age, this early sense of autonomy will be a bulwark against later frustrations and will permit the emergence of the next developmental problem at a time that is most favorable for its solution.

So it is with all the personality components to be described. They appear in miniature early in life. The struggle to secure them against tendencies to act otherwise comes to a climax at a time determined by emergence of the necessary physical and mental abilities. There are, throughout life, other challenges and other responses but they are seldom so serious and seldom so decisive as those of the critical years.

In all this, it must be noted in addition, there is not the strict dichotomy that the analysis given below suggests. With each of the personality components to be described, it is not all or nothing: trust *or* mistrust, autonomy *or* doubt, and so on. Instead, each individual has some of each. His health of personality is determined by the preponderance of the favorable over the unfavorable, as well as by what manner of compensations he develops to cope with his disabilities.

## THE SENSE OF TRUST

The component of the healthy personality that is the first to develop is the sense of trust. The crucial time for its emergence is the first year of life. As with the other personality components to be described, the sense of trust is not something that develops independent of other manifestations of growth. It is not that the infant learns how to use his body for purposeful movement, learns to recognize people and objects around him, and also develops a sense of trust. Rather the concept "sense of trust" is a shortcut expression intended to convey the characteristic flavor of all the child's satisfying experiences at this early age. Or, to say it another way, this psychological formulation serves to condense, summarize, and synthesize the most important underlying changes that give meaning to the infant's concrete and diversified experience.

Trust can exist only in relation to something. Consequently a sense of trust cannot develop until the infant is old enough to be aware of objects and persons and to have some feeling that he is a separate individual. At about three months of age a baby is likely to smile if somebody comes close and talks to him. This shows that he is aware of the approach of the other person, that pleasurable sensations are aroused.

If, however, the person moves too quickly or speaks too sharply the baby may look apprehensive or cry. He will not "trust" the unusual situation but will have a feeling of uneasiness, of mistrust, instead.

Experiences connected with feeding are a prime source for the development of trust. At around four months of age a hungry baby will grow quiet and show signs of pleasure at the sound of an approaching footstep, anticipating (trusting) that he will be held and fed. This repeated experience of being hungry, seeing food, receiving food, and feeling relieved and comforted assures the baby that the world is a dependable place.

Later experiences, starting at around five months of age, add another dimension to the sense of trust. Through endless repetitions of attempts to grasp for and hold objects, the baby is finally successful in controlling and adapting his movements in such a way as to reach his goal. Through these and other feats of muscular coordination the baby is gradually able to trust his own body to do his bidding.

The baby's trust-mistrust problem is symbolized in the game of peek-a-boo. In this game, which babies begin to like at about four months of age, an object disappears and then reappears. There is a slightly tense expression on the baby's face when the object goes away; its reappearance is greeted by wriggles and smiles. Only gradually does the baby learn that things continue to exist even though he does not see them, that there is order and stability in his universe. Peek-a-boo proves the point by playful repetition.

Studies of mentally ill individuals and observations of infants who have been grossly deprived of affection suggest that trust is an early-formed and important element in the healthy personality. Psychiatrists find again and again that the most serious illnesses occur in patients who have been sorely neglected or abused or otherwise deprived of love in infancy. Similarly, it is a common finding of psychological and so-cial investigators that individuals diagnosed as a "psychopathic personality" were so unloved in infancy that they have no reason to trust the human race and, therefore, no sense of responsibility toward their fellow men.

Observations of infants brought up in emotionally unfavorable institutions or removed to hospitals with inadequate facilities for psychological care support these findings. A recent report says: "Infants under six months of age who have been in an institution for some time present a well-defined picture. The outstanding features are listlessness, emaciation and pallor, relative immobility, quietness, unresponsiveness to stimuli like a smile or a coo, indifferent appetite, failure to gain weight properly despite ingestion of diets which are entirely adequate, frequent stools, poor sleep, an appearance of unhappiness, proneness to febrile episodes, absence of sucking habits."[1]

Another investigation of children separated from their mothers at six to twelve months and not provided with an adequate substitute comes to much the same conclusion: "The emotional tone is one of apprehension and sadness, there is withdrawal from the environment amounting to rejection of it, there is no attempt to contact a stranger and no brightening if a stranger contacts him. Activities are retarded and the child often sits or lies inert in a dazed stupor. Insomnia is common and lack of appetite universal. Weight is lost, and the child becomes prone to current infections."[2]

Most significant for our present point, these reactions are most likely to occur in children who up to the time of separation at six to nine months of age had a happy relation with their mothers, while those whose relations were unhappy are relatively unaffected. It is at about this age that the struggle between trusting and mistrusting the world comes to a climax, for it is then that the child first perceives clearly that he and his environment are things apart. That at this time formerly happy infants should react so badly to separation suggests, indeed, that they had a faith which now was shattered. Happily, there is usually spectacular change for the better when the maternal presence and love are restored.

It is probably unnecessary to describe the numerous ways in which stimuli from without and from within may cause an infant distress. Birth is believed by some experts to be a painful experience for the baby. Until fairly recently doctors were likely to advise that babies be fed on schedule and that little attention be paid to their cries of hunger at other times. Many infants spent many of the waking hours of the first four months doubled up with colic. All of them had to be bathed and dressed at stated times, whether they liked it or not. Add to these usual discomforts the fact that some infants are handled rather roughly by their parents, that others hear angry words and loud voices, and that a few are really mistreated, and it will not be difficult to understand why some infants may feel the world is a place that cannot be trusted.

In most primitive societies and in some sections of our own society the attention accorded infants is more in line with natural processes. In such societies separation from the mother is less abrupt, in that for some time after birth the baby is kept close to the warmth and comfort of its mother's body and at its least cry the breast is produced. Throughout infancy the baby is surrounded by people who are ready to feed it, fondle it, otherwise comfort it at a moment's notice. Moreover, these ministrations are given spontaneously, wholeheartedly, and without that element of nervous concern that may characterize the efforts of young mothers made self-conscious and insecure by our scientific age.

We must not exaggerate, however. Most infants in our society, too, find smiles and the comfort of mother's soft, warm body accompanying their intake of food, whether from breast or bottle. Coldness, wetness, pain, and boredom—for each misfortune there is prompt and comforting relief. As their own bodies come to be more dependable, there is added to the pleasures of increasing sensory response and motor control the pleasure of the mother's encouragement.

Moreover, babies are rather hardy creatures and are not to be discouraged by inexperienced mothers' mistakes. Even a mother cat has to learn, and the kittens endure gracefully her first clumsy efforts to carry them away from danger. Then, too, psychologists tell us that mothers create a sense of trust in their children not by the particular techniques they employ but by the sensitiveness with which they respond to the children's needs and by their over-all attitude.

For most infants, then, a sense of trust is not difficult to come by. It is the most important element in the personality. It emerges at the most vulnerable period of a child's life. Yet it is the least likely to suffer harm, perhaps because both nature and culture work toward making mothers most maternal at that time.

## THE SENSE OF AUTONOMY

The sense of trust once firmly established, the struggle for the next component of the healthy personality begins. The child is now twelve to fifteen months old. Much of his energy for the next two years will center around asserting that he is a human being with a mind and will of his own. A list of some of the items discussed by Spock under the heading, "The One Year Old," will serve to remind us of the characteristics of that age and the problems they create for parents. "Feeling his oats." "The passion to explore." "He gets more dependent and more independent at the same time." "Arranging the house for the wandering baby." "Avoiding accidents." "How do you make him leave certain things alone?" "Dropping and throwing things."

"Biting humans." "The small child who won't stay in bed at night."

What is at stake throughout the struggle of these years is the child's sense of autonomy, the sense that he is an independent human being and yet one who is able to use the help and guidance of others in important matters. This stage of development becomes decisive for the ratio between love and hate, between cooperation and willfulness, for freedom of self-expression and its renunciation in the make-up of the individual. The favorable outcome is self-control without loss of self-esteem. The unfavorable outcome is doubt and shame.

Before a sense of autonomy can develop, the sense of trust must be reasonably well established and must continue to pervade the child's feeling about himself and his world. Only so dare he respond with confidence to his new-felt desire to assert himself boldly, to appropriate demandingly, and to hurl away without let or hindrance.

As with the previous stage, there is a physiological basis for this characteristic behavior. This is the period of muscle-system maturation and the consequent ability (and doubly felt inability) to coordinate a number of highly conflicting action patterns, such as those of holding on and letting go, walking, talking, and manipulating objects in ever more complicated ways. With these abilities come pressing needs to use them: to handle, to explore, to seize and to drop, to withhold and to expel. And, with all, there is the dominant will, the insistent "Me do" that defies help and yet is so easily frustrated by the inabilities of the hands and feet.

For a child to develop this sense of self-reliance and adequacy that Erikson calls autonomy, it is necessary that he experience over and over again that he is a person who is permitted to make choices. He has to have the right to choose, for example, whether to sit or whether to stand, whether to approach a visitor or to lean against his mother's knee, whether to accept offered food or reject it, whether to use the toilet

or to wet his pants. At the same time he must learn some of the boundaries of self-determination. He inevitably finds that there are walls he cannot climb, that there are objects out of reach, that, above all, there are innumerable commands enforced by powerful adults. His experience is much too small to enable him to know what he can and cannot do with respect to the physical environment, and it will take him years to discover the boundaries that mark off what is approved, what is tolerated, and what is forbidden by his elders whom he finds so hard to understand.

As problems of this period, some psychologists have concentrated particularly on bladder and bowel control. Emphasis is put upon the need for care in both timing and mode of training children in the performance of these functions. If parental control is too rigid or if training is started too early, the child is robbed of his opportunity to develop, by his own free choice, gradual control of the contradictory impulses of retention and elimination.

To others who study child development, this matter of toilet training is but a prototype of all the problems of this age-range. The sphincters are only part of the whole muscle system, with its general ambiguity of rigidity and relaxation, of flexion and extension. To hold and to relinquish refer to much more than the bowels. As the child acquires the ability to stand on his two feet and move around, he delineates his world as me and you. He can be astonishingly pliable once he has decided that he wants to do what he is supposed to do, but there is no reliable formula for assuring that he will relinquish when he wants to hold on.

The matter of mutual regulation between parent and child (for fathers have now entered the picture to an extent that was rare in the earlier state) now faces its severest task. The task is indeed one to challenge the most resourceful and the most calm adult. Firmness is necessary, for the child must be protected against the potential anarchy of his as yet untrained sense of discrimination. Yet the adult must back him up in his wish to "stand on his own feet," lest he be overcome by shame that he has exposed himself foolishly and by doubt in his self-worth. Perhaps the most constructive rule a parent can follow is to forbid only what "really matters" and, in such forbidding, to be clear and consistent.

Shame and doubt are emotions that many primitive peoples and some of the less sophisticated individuals in our own society utilize in training children. Shaming exploits the child's sense of being small. Used to excess it misses its objective and may result in open shamelessness, or, at least, in the child's secret determination to do as he pleases when not observed. Such defiance is a normal, even healthy response to demands that a child consider himself, his body, his needs, or his wishes evil and dirty and that he regard those who pass judgment as infallible. Young delinquents may be produced by this means, and others who are oblivious to the opinion of society.

Those who would guide the growing child wisely, then, will avoid shaming him and avoid causing him to doubt that he is a person of worth. They will be firm and tolerant with him so that he can rejoice in being a person of independence and can grant independence to others. As to detailed procedures, it is impossible to prescribe, not only because we do not know and because every situation is different, but also because the kind and degree of autonomy that parents are able to grant their small children depends on feelings about themselves that they derive from society. Just as the child's sense of trust is a reflection of the mother's sturdy and realistic faith, so the child's sense of autonomy is a reflection of the parents' personal dignity. Such appears to be the teaching of the comparative study of cultures.

Personal autonomy, independence of the individual, is an especially outstanding feature of the American way of life. American parents, accordingly, are in a particularly favorable position to transmit the sense of autonomy to their chil-

dren. They themselves resent being bossed, being pushed around; they maintain that everybody has the right to express his opinion and to be in control of his affairs. More easily than people who live according to an authoritarian pattern, they can appreciate a little child's vigorous desire to assert his independence and they can give him the leeway he needs in order to grow up into the upstanding, look-you-in-the-eye kind of individual that Americans admire.

It is not only in early childhood, however, that this attitude toward growing children must be maintained. As was said at the outset, these components of the healthy personality cannot be established once and for all. The period of life in which they first come into being is the most crucial, it is true. But threats to their maintenance occur throughout life. Not only parents, then, but everybody who has significant contact with children and young people must respect their desire for self-assertion, help them hold it within bounds, and avoid treating them in ways that arouse shame or doubt.

This attitude toward children, toward all people, must be maintained in institutional arrangements as well. Great differences in educational and economic opportunity and in access to the law, discrimination of all kinds are threats to this ingredient of mental health. So, too, may be the overmechanization of our society, the depersonalization of human relations that is likely to accompany large-scale endeavor of all kinds.

Parents, as well as children, are affected by these matters. In fact, parents' ability to grant children the kind of autonomy Americans think desirable depends in part on the way they are treated as employees and citizens. Throughout, the relation must be such as affirms personal dignity. Much of the shame and doubt aroused in children result from the indignity and uncertainty that are an expression of parents' frustration in love and work. Special attention must be paid to all these matters, then, if we are to avoid destroying the autonomy that Americans have always set store by.

## THE SENSE OF INITIATIVE

Having become sure, for the time being, that he is a person in his own right and having enjoyed that feeling for a year or so, the child of four or five wants to find out what kind of person he can be. To be any particular kind of person, he sees clearly, involves being able to do particular kinds of things. So he observes with keen attention what all manner of interesting adults do (his parents, the milkman, the truck driver, and so on), tries to imitate their behavior, and yearns for a share in their activities.

This is the period of enterprise and imagination, an ebullient, creative period when fantasy substitutes for literal execution of desires and the meagerest equipment provides material for high imaginings. It is a period of intrusive, vigorous learning, learning that leads away from the child's own limitations into future possibilities. There is intrusion into other people's bodies by physical attack, into other people's ears and minds by loud and aggressive talking. There is intrusion into space by vigorous locomotion and intrusion into the unknown by consuming curiosity.

By this age, too, conscience has developed. The child is no longer guided only by outsiders; there is installed within him a voice that comments on his deeds, and warns and threatens. Close attention to the remarks of any child of this age will confirm this statement. Less obvious, however, are experts' observations that children now begin to feel guilty for mere thoughts, for deeds that have been imagined but never executed. This, they say, is the explanation for the characteristic nightmares of this age period and for the over-reaction to slight punishment.

The problem to be worked out in this stage of development, accordingly, is how to will without too great a sense of guilt. The fortunate outcome of the struggle is a sense of initiative. Failure to win through to that outcome leaves the personality overburdened, and possibly overrestricted by guilt.

It is easy to see how the child's developing sense of initiative may be discouraged. So many of the projects dreamed up at this age are of a kind which cannot be permitted that the child may come to feel he is faced by a universal "No." In addition he finds that many of the projects are impossible of execution and others, even if not forbidden, fail to win the approval of the adults whom he has come to love. Moreover, since he does not always distinguish clearly between actuality and fantasy, his over-zealous conscience may disapprove of even imaginary deeds.

It is very important, therefore, for healthy personality development that much leeway and encouragement be given to the child's show of enterprise and imagination and that punishment be kept at a minimum. Boys and girls at this stage are extraordinarily appreciative of any convincing promise that someday they will be able to do things as well as, or maybe better than, father and mother. They enjoy competition (especially if they can win) and insistence on goal; they get great pleasure from conquest. They need numerous examples of the kinds of roles adults assume, and they need a chance to try them out in play.

The ability that is in the making is that of selecting social goals and persevering in the attempt to reach them.

If enterprise and imagination are too greatly curbed, if severe rebukes accompany the frequently necessary denial of permission to carry out desires, a personality may result that is overconstricted. Such a personality cannot live up to its inner capacities for imagination, feelings, or performance, though it may overcompensate by immense activity and find relaxation impossible.

Constriction of personality is a self-imposed constriction, an act of the child's over-zealous conscience. "If I may not do this, I will not even think it," says conscience, "for even thinking it is dangerous." Resentment and bitterness and a vindictive attitude toward the world that forces the restriction may accompany this decision, however, and become unconscious but functioning parts of the personality. Such, at least, is the warning of psychiatrists who have learned to know the inmost feelings of emotionally handicapped children and adults.

This developmental stage has great assets as well as great dangers. At no time in life is the individual more ready to learn avidly and quickly, to become big in the sense of sharing obligation and performance. If during this preschool period the child can get some sense of the various roles and functions that he can perform as an adult, he will be ready to progress joyfully to the next stage, in which he will find pleasurable accomplishment in activities less fraught with fantasy and fear.

There is a lesson in this for later periods of personality development as well. As has been said before, these conflicts that come to a head at particular periods of a child's life are not settled once and for all. The sense of initiative, then, is one that must be continually fostered, and great care must be taken that youngsters and young people do not have to feel guilty for having dared to dream.

Just as we Americans prize autonomy, so too do we prize initiative; in fact, we regard it as the cornerstone of our economic system. There is much in the present industrial and political mode of life that may discourage initiative, that may make a young person think he had best pull in his horns. What these tendencies are and what they may do to youngsters and to their parents, who too must feel free if they are to cultivate the sense of initiative in their children, is a subject that warrants much serious discussion.

## THE SENSE OF ACCOMPLISHMENT

The three stages so far described probably are the most important for personality develop-

ment. With a sense of trust, a sense of autonomy, and a sense of initiative achieved, progress through the later stages is pretty well assured. Whether this is because children who have a good environment in their early years are likely to continue to be so favored, or whether it is because they have attained such strength of personality that they can successfully handle later difficulties, research has not yet made clear. We do know that nearly all children who get a good start continue to develop very well, and we know that some of those who start off poorly continue to be handicapped. Observations of this sort seem to support psychological theory in the conclusion that personality is pretty well set by about six years of age. Since, however, some children develop into psychologically healthy adults in spite of a bad start, and since some who start well run into difficulties later, it is clear that much research is needed before this conclusion can be accepted as wholly correct.

To return to the developmental analysis, the fourth stage, which begins somewhere around six years of age and extends over five or six years, has as its achievement what Erikson calls the sense of industry. Perhaps "sense of accomplishment" would make the meaning clearer. At any rate, this is the period in which preoccupation with fantasy subsides, and the child wants to be engaged in real tasks that he can carry through to completion. As with other developmental stages, there are foreshadowings of this kind of interest long before six years of age. Moreover, in some societies and in some parts of our own society children are trained very early to perform socially useful tasks. The exact age is not the point at issue. What is to be pointed out is that children, after a period characterized by exuberant imagination, want to settle down to learning exactly how to do things and how to do them well.

In contrast to the preceding stages and to the succeeding ones, this stage does not consist of a swing from a violent inner upheaval to a new mastery. Under reasonably favorable circumstances this is a period of calm, steady growth, especially if the problems of the previous stages have been well worked through. Despite its unspectacular character, this is a very important period, for in it is laid a firm basis for responsible citizenship. It is during this period that children acquire not only knowledge and skills that make for good workmanship but also the ability to cooperate and play fair and otherwise follow the rules of the larger social game.

The chief danger of this period is the presence of conditions that may lead to the development of a sense of inadequacy and inferiority. This may be the outcome if the child has not yet achieved a sense of initiative, or if his experiences at home have not prepared him for entering school happily, or if he finds school a place where his previous accomplishments are disregarded or his latent abilities are not challenged. Even with a good start the child may later lapse into discouragement and lack of interest if at home or school his individual needs are overlooked—if too much is expected of him, or if he is made to feel that achievement is beyond his ability.

It is most important for health of personality, therefore, that schools be conducted well, that methods and courses of instruction be such as will give every child the feeling of successful accomplishment. Autobiographies of juvenile delinquents show time and again a boy who hated school—hated the fact that he was marked out as stupid or awkward, as one who was not as good as the rest. Some such boys find in jobs the sense of accomplishment they miss at school and consequently give up their delinquent ways. Others, however, are handicapped in job finding and keeping by the very fact that in school they did not develop the sense of industry; hence they have work failure added to their other insecurities. Nor is delinquency the only or the most likely outcome of lack of success in school. Many children respond in a quieter way, by passive

acceptance of their inferiority. Psychologically they are perhaps even more harmed.

Our Puritan tradition maintains that children will not work except under the spur of competition, so we tend to fear the suggestion that all should succeed. To help children develop a sense of accomplishment does not mean, however, merely giving all of them good marks and passing them on to the next grade. Children need and want real achievement. How to help them secure it, despite differences in native capacity and differences in emotional development, is one of the school's most serious challenges.

School, of course, is not the only place in which children at this stage of development can secure the sense of industry. In work at home there are many opportunities for a child to get a feeling of mastery and worthwhile endeavor. Rural youth groups and their urban counterparts cater to this need, and many recreation programs put as much emphasis on work as on play. School, however, is the legally constituted arrangement for giving instruction to the young, so it is upon teachers that the professional responsibility for helping all children achieve a sense of industry and accomplishment rests.

In addition to aiding personality development in this way, teachers have many opportunities for reconfirming their pupils' sense of trust, autonomy, and initiative or for encouraging its growth in children who have been somewhat hampered by previous life experiences. Teachers cannot work alone, of course, either in aiding a child in the development of new capacities or in strengthening old ones. Jointly with parents and others they can do much, not only for children of already healthy personality but also for many whose development has been handicapped.

## THE SENSE OF IDENTITY

With the onset of adolescence another period of personality development begins. As is well known, adolescence is a period of storm and stress for many young people, a period in which previous certainties are questioned and previous continuities no longer relied upon. Physiological changes and rapid physical growth provide the somatic base for the turmoil and indecision. It may be that cultural factors also play a part, for it has been observed that adolescence is less upsetting in some societies than in others.

The central problem of the period is the establishment of a sense of identity. The identity the adolescent seeks to clarify is who he is, what his role in society is to be. Is he a child or is he an adult? Does he have it in him to be someday a husband and father? What is he to be as a worker and an earner of money? Can he feel self-confident in spite of the fact that his race or religion or national background makes him a person some people look down upon? Over all, will he be a success or a failure? By reason of these questions adolescents are sometimes morbidly preoccupied with how they appear in the eyes of others as compared with their own conception of themselves, and with how they can make the roles and skills learned earlier jibe with what is currently in style.

In primitive societies adolescents are perhaps spared these doubts and indecisions. Through initiation rites, often seemingly cruel in character, young people are tested out (and test themselves out) and are then welcomed into a socially recognized age category in which rights and duties and mode of living are clearly defined. In our society there are few rituals or ceremonies that mark the change in status from childhood to youth. For those who have religious affiliations, confirmation, joining the church, may serve this purpose in part, since the young people are thereby admitted in this one segment of their lives at least, to the company of adults. Such ceremonies serve, in addition, to reaffirm to youth that the universe is trustworthy and stable and that a way of life is clearly laid out.

Graduation ceremonies might play a part in marking a new status were it not that, in present-day America, status is so ill defined. What rules of law and custom exist are too diverse to be of much help. For example, legal regulations governing age of "consent," age at which marriage is permitted, age for leaving school, for driving a car, for joining (or being required to join) the Army or Navy mark no logical progressions in rights and duties. As to custom, there is so much variation in what even families who live next door to each other expect or permit that adolescents, eager to be on their way, are practically forced into standardizing themselves in their search for status. In this they are ably abetted by advertisers and entertainers who seek their patronage, as well as by well-meaning magazine writers who describe in great detail the means by which uniformity can be achieved.

In this urge to find comfort through similarity, adolescents are likely to become stereotyped in behavior and ideals. They tend to form cliques for self-protection and fasten on petty similarities of dress and gesture to assure themselves that they are really somebody. In these cliques they may be intolerant and even cruel toward those they label as different. Unfortunate as such behavior is and not to be condoned, intolerance serves the important purpose of giving the group members at least the negative assurance that there is something they are not.

The danger of this developmental period is self-diffusion. As Biff puts it in *The Death of a Salesman,* "I just can't take hold, Mom, I can't take hold of some kind of a life." A boy or girl can scarcely help feeling somewhat diffuse when the body changes in size and shape so rapidly, when genital maturity floods body and imagination with forbidden desires, when adult life lies ahead with such a diversity of conflicting possibilities and choices.

Whether this feeling of self-diffusion is fairly easily mastered or whether, in extreme, it leads to delinquency, neurosis or outright psychosis, depends to a considerable extent on what has gone before. If the course of personality development has been a healthy one, a feeling of self-esteem has accrued from the numerous experiences of succeeding in a task and sensing its cultural meaning. Along with this, the child has come to the conviction that he is moving toward an understandable future in which he will have a definite role to play. Adolescence may upset this assurance for a time or to a degree but fairly soon a new integration is achieved, and the boy or girl sees again (and with clearer vision) that he belongs and that he is on his way.

The course is not so easy for adolescents who have not had so fortunate a part or for those whose earlier security is broken by a sudden awareness that as members of minority groups their way of life sets them apart. The former, already unsure of themselves, find their earlier doubt and mistrust reactivated by the physiological and social changes that adolescence brings. The latter, once secure, may feel that they must disavow their past and try to develop an "American" personality.

Much has been learned and written about the adolescent problems of the boys and girls whose early personality development has been impaired. How they can be helped, if their disorders are not too severe, is also fairly well known. The full implications of these findings for parents, teachers, and others who would guide youth are still to be worked out but, even so, there is considerable information.

Less well understood are the difficulties and the ways of helping adolescents who grew up in cultures that are not of the usual run. These boys and girls may have been privileged in having had a childhood in which there was little inhibition of sensual pleasures, and in which development proceeded by easy, unselfconscious stages. For them, difficulties arise if their parents lose trust in themselves or if their teachers apply sudden correctives, or if they themselves reject their past and try to act like others. The new role of middle-class adolescent is often too hard to play.

Delinquency or bizarre behavior marks the failure.

How to reach these boys and girls, how to help them attain their desire, is a matter not well understood. It is clear, however, that they should not be typed by pat diagnoses and social judgments, for they are ever ready to become the "bums" that they are called. Those who would guide them must understand both the psychology of adolescence and the cultural realities of the day. There is trust to be restored and doubt and guilt and feelings of inferiority to be overcome. The science of how to do this is still pretty much lacking, though here and there teachers, clergymen, probation officers and the like are highly successful in the task.

Hard though it be to achieve, the sense of identity is the individual's only safeguard against the lawlessness of his biological drives and the authority of an over-weening conscience. Loss of identity, loss of the sense that there is some continuity, sameness, and meaning to life, exposes the individual to his childhood conflicts and leads to emotional upsets. This outcome was observed time and again among men hard pressed by the dangers of war. It is clear, then, that if health of personality is to be preserved much attention must be given to assuring that America makes good on its promises to youth.

## THE SENSE OF INTIMACY

After the sense of identity, to a greater or less extent, is achieved it becomes possible for the next component of the healthy personality to develop. This is the sense of intimacy, intimacy with persons of the same sex or of the opposite sex or with one's self. The youth who is not fairly sure of his identity shies away from interpersonal relations and is afraid of close communion with himself. The surer he becomes of himself, the more he seeks intimacy, in the form of friendship, love and inspiration.

In view of the early age at which boy and girl attachments are encouraged today, it may seem strange to put the critical period for the development of the sense of intimacy late in adolescence. The explanation is that, on the one hand, sexual intimacy is only one part of what is involved, and, on the other, boy-girl attachments of earlier age periods are likely to be of a somewhat different order. Regarding the latter point, it has been observed by those who know young people well that high-school age boys and girls often use each other's company for an endless verbal examination of what the other thinks, feels, and wants to do. In other words, these attachments are one means of defining one's identity.

In contrast to this use of friendship and companionship, boys and girls late in adolescence usually have need for a kind of fusion with the essence of other people and for a communion with their own inner resources. If, by reason of inadequacies in previous personality development, this sense of intimacy cannot be achieved, the youth may retire into psychological isolation and keep his relations with people on a formal stereotyped level that is lacking in spontaneity and warmth or he may keep trying again and again to get close to others, only to meet with repeated failure. Under this compulsion he may even marry, but the role of mate is one he can rarely sustain, for the condition of true two-ness is that each individual must first become himself.

In this area of personality development as in the others, cultural factors play a part in sustaining or in discouraging the individual in his development. American culture is unusually successful in encouraging the development of the feelings of independence, initiative, industry, and identity. It is somewhat less successful in the area of intimacy, for the culture's ideal is the subordination of sexuality and sensuality to a life of work, duty, and worship.

Consequently, American adolescents are likely to be unsupported by their parents and to find little confirmation in story or song for their desire to sense intimately the full flavor of the personality of others. In many of them, then, the sense of intimacy does not develop highly and they have difficulty in finding in close personal relations the outlet for tension that they need.

There is some evidence that a change in conventions and customs in this respect is in the making, however. Too abrupt change in any such cultural matter is not to be urged, but it is to be hoped that gradual, frank discussion can bring about gradual alteration in attitude and overcome the dangers inherent in the traditional rigidity.

## THE PARENTAL SENSE

"Parental sense" designates somewhat the same capacity as that implied in the words, creativity or productivity. The individual has normally come to adulthood before this sense can develop fully.

The parental sense is indicated most clearly by interest in producing and caring for children of one's own. It may also be exhibited in relation to other people's children or by a parental kind of responsibility toward the products of creative activity of other sorts. The mere desire for or possession of children does not indicate that this component of the healthy personality has developed. In fact, many parents who bring their children to child guidance clinics are found not to have reached this stage of personality development.

The essential element is the desire to nourish and nurture what has been produced. It is the ability to regard one's children as a trust of the community, rather than as extensions of one's own personality or merely as beings that one happens to live with.

Failure to develop this component of the healthy personality often results in a condition which has not been adequately categorized clinically. Although a true sense of intimacy has not developed, the individual may obsessively seek companionship. There is something of egotism in this as in his other activities, a kind of self-absorption. The individual is inclined to treat himself as a child and to be rivalrous with his children, if he has any. He indulges himself, expects to be indulged, and in general behaves in an infantile or immature manner.

There are both individual and social explanations of the failure to develop an adequate parental sense. Individually, the explanation may be found in the inadequate development of the personality components previously described. In some people this failure goes far back. Because of unfortunate experiences in childhood they did not arrive at a firm sense of trust, autonomy, and the rest. In others it is only inadequacies in later stages, especially in the development of the sense of intimacy, that are at fault.

Socially, as has been suggested throughout this analysis, healthy personality development depends upon the culture's ideals and upon the economic arrangements of the society. In order that most people may develop fully the sense of being a parent, the role of parent, both mother and father, must be a respected one in the society. Giving must rank higher than getting, and loving than being loved. The economy must be such that the future can be depended upon and each person can feel assured that he has a meaningful and respected part to play. Only so can most individuals afford to renounce selfish aims and derive much of their satisfaction from rearing children.

## THE SENSE OF INTEGRITY

The final component of the healthy personality is the sense of integrity. In every culture the dominant ideals, honor, courage, faith, purity, grace, fairness, self-discipline, become at this stage the core of the healthy personality's integration. The individual, in Erikson's words, "becomes able to accept his individual life cycle and the people who have become significant to it as meaningful within the segment of history in which he lives."

To continue Erikson's description, "Integrity thus means a new and different love of one's parents, free of the wish that they should have been different, and an acceptance of the fact that one's life is one's own responsibility. It is a sense of comradeship with men and women of distant times and of different pursuits, who have created orders and objects and sayings conveying human dignity and love. Although aware of the relativity of all the various life styles that have given meaning to human striving, the possessor of integrity is ready to defend the dignity of his own life style against all physical and economic threats. For he knows that, for him, all human dignity stands or falls with the one style of integrity of which he partakes."

The adult who lacks integrity in this sense may wish that he could live again. He feels that if at one time he had made a different decision he could have been a different person and his ventures would have been successful. He fears death and cannot accept his one and only life cycle as the ultimate of life. In the extreme, he experiences disgust and despair. Despair expresses the feeling that time is too short to try out new roads to integrity. Disgust is a means of hiding the despair, a chronic, contemptuous displeasure with the way life is run. As with the dangers and the solutions of previous periods, doubt and despair are not difficulties that are overcome once and for all, nor is integrity so achieved. Most people fluctuate between the two extremes. Most, also, at no point, either attain to the heights of unalloyed integrity or fall to the depths of complete disgust and despair.

Even in adulthood a reasonably healthy personality is sometimes secured in spite of previous misfortunes in the developmental sequence. New sources of trust may be found. Fortunate events and circumstances may aid the individual in his struggle to feel autonomous. Imagination and initiative may be spurred by new responsibilities, and feelings of inferiority be overcome by successful achievement. Even late in life an individual may arrive at a true sense of who he is and what he has to do and may be able to win through to a feeling of intimacy with others and to joy in producing and giving.

Evidence of such changes is found in the case records of psychiatrists and social workers. Common sense observation attests that similar changes in health of personality are sometimes accomplished without benefit of any form of psychotherapy. Much remains to be learned about this, however, especially about how life itself may serve as therapeusis.

For the healthy personality development of children and youth it is necessary that a large proportion of adults attain a sense of integrity to a considerable degree. Not only parents but all who deal with children have need of this quality if they are to help children maintain the feeling that the universe is dependable and trustworthy. Integrity is relatively easily attained and sustained when the culture itself gives support, when a meaning to life is clearly spelled out in tradition and ceremony, and roles are clearly defined. Our culture, with its rapidly changing technology and its diversity of value standards, leaves much for the individual to work out for himself. In the American dream, however, and the Judaeo-Christian tradition on which it is based there are values and ideals aplenty. In the interest of the welfare of children and youth, in order that a generation of happy individuals and responsible citizens be reared, it is highly important that these values and ideals be brought into prominence and that the promise of American life be kept.

## ENDNOTES

1. Harry Bakwin, "Emotional Deprivation in Infants," *Journal of Pediatrics* (October, 1949): 35, 512–529.

2. John Bowlby, M.D., Summary of Dr. Rene Spitz's observations, unpublished manuscript.

*Erik H. Erikson* is a psychoanalyst and Professor of Human Development, Emeritus, Harvard University. His stages of development, presented in this article, are also discussed in his book *Identity, Youth, and Crisis* (New York: W. W. Norton and Company, Inc., 1968).

# The Development of Intelligent Behavior: Jean Piaget

## THOMAS ROWLAND AND CARSON McGUIRE

For many years, Piaget's work was almost unknown to American psychologists, primarily it seems because of the lack of adequate translations into English of his elegant but difficult French. D. E. Berlyne was one of the earliest to recognize this inadequacy and to take positive action. Berlyne with Percy (1950) translated Piaget's *Psychology of Intelligence.* Later, he spent the year 1958–59 with Piaget in Geneva. Berlyne's book *Structure and Direction in Thinking* (1965) introduces a system of neobehavioristic concepts to permit an integrative conceptualization of thinking. In this recent volume, Berlyne discusses curiosity as a motive and learning through discovery, as well as the Geneva research and recent developments in Russian psychology.

As a result of such work as Berlyne's and others', the current influence of Piaget's research and writing can be discerned in the ideas of a host of important psychologists, including such diverse figures as D. P. Ausubel (1963) and J. S. Bruner (1965). Today most of his works are available to students, many in inexpensive paperback editions. One such edition, *Psychology of Intelligence,* has been reviewed by Carson McGuire (1967). The review is a highly condensed form of much of the essence of Piaget's work, written in technical terms. This paper, however, further amplifies what is said below:

> Piaget views intelligence as a mental *adaptation* to new circumstances, both *"accommodation"* to stimuli from the environment and modification of environment by imposing upon it a structure of its own, i.e., *"assimilation."* Thus intelligence as adaptation involves an *equilibrium* toward which the cognitive processes tend (the act of "equilibration"). The equilibration is between the action of the organism on the environment and vice versa. Remember that language is a partial substitute for action. Symbols, particularly those of mathematics (which are free of the deception of imagery), refer to an action which could be realized. Where such symbols take the form of internalized actions, they may be interpreted as operations of thought, i.e., an internal action translatable into behavior. Piaget relates affect and cognition—all behavior "implies an energizer or an 'economy' forming its affective aspect." The interaction with the environment which behavior instigates requires a form or structure to determine the possible circuits between subject and object—the cognitive aspect of behavior (schemata). *Similarly, a perception . . . , sensory, motor learning (i.e., habit . . .), insight, and judgment all amount, in one way or another to a structuring of the relations between the environment and the organism* [p. 29].

Hunt (1961) identifies five main themes which he says dominate Piaget's theoretical formulations, namely: (a) the continual and progressive change in the structure of behavior and thought in the developing child; (b) the fixed nature of the order of the stages; (c) the invariant functions of *accommodation* (adaptive change to outer circumstances) and of *assimilation* (incorporation of the external into the inner organization with transfer or generalization to new circumstances) that operate in the child's continuous interaction with the environment; (d) the

From *Psychology in the Schools* 5, no. 1 (January 1968): 47–51. Used by permission of the authors and the publisher.

relation of thought to action; and (e) the logical properties of thought processes.

Roger Brown (1965) attributes to Piaget some twenty-five books and 160 articles, identifying the goal of the Geneva program as the discovery of *the successive stages* in the development of intelligence. Much current American research, such as that at the University of Chicago, reported by Fowler (1966) and Kohlberg (1966), lends strong support to the goals of Piaget's approach to the development of intelligence, while making an important clarification with their insistence that while the stages of Piaget are real and the sequence is constant, the "American misinterpretation" which attributes to *time per se* the status of a significant variable is to be denied. The prospective teacher should grasp this concept of sequence without the chains of time boundaries, especially in view of the longstanding force in American psychology: the Gesellian interpretation of stages with firm upper and lower time limits. *This maturationist view of fixed intelligence and predetermined development is no longer considered valid.* Stages, as identified by Piaget, appear to occur in a constant, invariant sequence, but there are no time boundaries. To support this viewpoint, Smedslund (1961) and Wallach (1963) independently designed a program with the specific intention of accelerating a child's development. Both discovered that acceleration appeared to be successful only if the child was approaching readiness at the time of intensive intervention; otherwise it had no significant effect. Piaget (1953) indicated that this would be the case, saying: "When adults try to impose mathematical concepts on a child prematurely, his learning is merely verbal; true understanding of them comes only with his mental growth." Because many of the conceptions studied by Piaget seem resistant to change by training, there would seem to be a substantial readiness factor involved. Probably readiness is at least partially a matter of varied sensory stimulation (Bruner, 1959; and/or Brown, 1965).

Readiness, like "stage," should not be linked to time per se.[1]

Piaget has hypothesized four distinct but chronologically *successive* models of intelligence; namely, (a) sensory motor, (b) preoperational, (c) concretely operational, and (d) formally operational. Imaginal thought, Piaget (1947, trans. 1950) believes, begins at the end of sensory motor and facilitates a transition into the preoperational stage. Bruner (1964), in what seems to be a related concept concerning the development of intelligence, identifies three stages in cognitive representation of experience; namely: (a) enactive, (b) iconic, and (c) symbolic.

The Geneva research begins with some aspect of common *adult* knowledge. The method of inquiry is to ask questions; and data are the responses of the children. An example of this first method of research is reported in many of Piaget's early works such as *Judgment and Reasoning in the Child* (1924). A different approach was used primarily with his own children, when Piaget employed as the starting point a *set of performances*. His method was *naturalistic observation of infant behavior with experimental interventions*. This second approach is demonstrated most effectively in *The Origins of Intelligence in Children* (1936).

Later Geneva studies began with *systematic adult knowledge,* asked questions and provided materials for manipulation. The resultant data included the *manipulations* and *verbal responses* of the children. In America there is an increasing tendency to set up contrived experiences which parallel Piaget's research. For example, Bruner and his associates (Bruner, Oliver, Greenfield, Hornsby, Kenney, Maccoby, Modiano, Mosher, Olson, Potter, Reich and Sonstroem, 1966) in their book, dedicated to Piaget, report many experiences designed for children which are directly related to the Geneva program, such as Olson's (Bruner, et al., 1966, pp. 135–153) experiment on the development of conceptual strategies with ninety-five children. Of striking similarity is the experiment on multiple ordering conducted by Bruner and Kenney (Bruner, et al., pp. 154–167).

An important understanding brought out in the research and writings of Piaget and others (Kohlberg, 1966; Fowler, 1966; and Brown, 1965) is that typically the child's intelligence turns out to be qualitatively different from adult intelligence. As a result the child simply does not see nor understand things as an adult would.

Answers of children, which appear to be "incorrect" from an adult point of view, are not viewed as ignorance. They are regarded as imperfect understandings of various intellectual matters. Much importance is attached to the observation that the imperfect responses often are alike across a sample of children. Nevertheless, the *order* in which the stages succeed one another usually is *constant*. The word "usually" should be stressed since a range of crosscultural research has not yet been carried out. A beginning has been made by Goodnow (1962, p. 1), who worked with children in Hong Kong. She began her research with the stated intention of determining if children from other milieus would produce results similar to those obtained by Piaget and his associates in Geneva. Combinatorial reasoning, conservation of space, weight and volume tasks of the Geneva program were administered to approximately 500 European and Chinese boys between the ages of 10–13. Ravens Progressive Matrices also were administered. Chinese boys had almost no formal education. Goodnow (1962) summarizes:

> Similarities across milieus were more striking than differences: there was an odd difference between the combinatorial task . . . and the conservation tasks . . . ; replication of the Geneva results was fair to good; the differences occurring suggest a need for a closer look at the concept "stability of reasoning" and at the expected interrelationships among various tasks [p. 21].

Piaget believes the child in the period of sensory-motor intelligence does not have internal representations of the world, even though he acts and perceives. With the development of *imagery*, the most primitive form of *central representation* (the beginning of the second stage), the sensory-motor period ends.

For the adult, an object has an identity which is preserved through various transformations by perceptual constancies, namely: size constancy, shape constancy, and color constancy. Other aspects of the object's invariant identity, regardless of changes of appearance, are dependent on knowledge of certain reversible operations, e.g., the adult does not suppose that a car is a different car because the rear does not have the appearance of the front. For adults, disappearance from sight does not imply the cessation of existence, and objects are continuous in time and space. To an adult, an object retains its identity through changes of position and illumination, and exists outside the domain of personal experience, as Viet Nam exists even though we may not have been there.

Piaget holds that the adult's aspects of identity and perceptual constancies are learned, e.g., one of the most difficult things to understand about the infant's conception of an object is that he does not realize that it exists independently of himself. For example, during the period of sensory-motor intelligence, where the child is governed by his perceptions (what he touches, hears, particularly what he traces), he begins to develop the fundamental categories of experience and a conception of causality begins.

The first signs of imagery are a particular kind of imitation and play. *Deferred imitation* is imitation of an absent model, and Piaget postulates the existence of a *central representation* that guides the performance of the child. *Imagery* is also suggested by representational play; and it is imagery, according to Piaget, which makes the development of highly symbolic language possible.

Preoperational and concretely operational levels of intelligence are essentially two levels of response to a common array of tasks; the pre-operational being (from an adult point of view) less adequate. Though the preoperational child uses language to identify things, ask questions, issue commands, and assert propositions, he does not distinguish between mental, physical, and social reality. He may believe that anything that moves is alive, such as a cloud, and will likely believe that a plant will feel a pin prick. He may expect to command the inanimate and have it obey. To the preoperational child everything is originally made or created—all things are *artifacts*. The parents, as sources for everything, may serve as *models* who make and create things. Close-tied parental figures also may become models for the child's spontaneous conception of a deity. He sees the parents as infinitely knowing and powerful as well as eternal. The pre-operational child is enslaved to his own viewpoint, completely unaware of other perspectives and thereby unaware of himself as a viewer. Things are just the way they are. They are unquestioned. The *egocentrism* is reflected in the child's difficulty in explaining verbally anything to another person. The egocentric child assumes his listener understands everything in advance. It appears that the egocentric child is moving out of his egocentrism in the later developments of the preoperational stage. As the onset of imagery begins this period, so the movement from egocentrism seems to end the preoperational stage and the child begins to function intellectually in the concretely operational stage.

The intelligence of the older child, who has accumulated learning experiences, is more adultlike in its separation of the mental and physical world. He grasps the points-of-view of others as well as relational concepts which tie objects and ideas together. The preoperational child has begun to develop the constancies (space, time, size, shape, color) necessary for

survival. For example, the child who cannot tell the difference perceptually between an oncoming auto a block away and one ten feet away is not likely to survive. To survive in a world of moving vehicles, he has to learn to understand some of the underlying invariance behind the world of shifting appearances. Yet, to a large degree, he is still controlled by perception. Piaget believes that the preoperational child, despite his limitations from an adult viewpoint, operates with an intelligence that is of a different order from that of the concretely operational child, who depends less on perception. This dependence on perception often leads the pre-operational child to focus upon a single dimension of a problem. He is unable to *decenter,* i.e., he is able to recognize a view which he has just experienced, but not able to pick out views he might experience from different positions. The preoperational child cannot treat relations as left or right, before or behind. Compared to his elders, he is lacking in operations—the central events which do not imitate perception as does the image. Piaget believes that *operations are derived from overt operations*—interaction between the organism and environments (see McGuire review, Piaget, 1967). Piaget is convinced that *intelligence develops out of motor activity,* not just out of possible observation—the wider the range of the activity, the more diversified will be the intellectual operations of the developing child.

The *concretely operational child* can deal to a degree with potentiality as well as actuality to which the preoperational child is limited. The *formally operational* child approaches what is to Piaget the highest level of intelligence: the ability to represent, in advance of the actual problem, a full set of possibilities. The consequences of formally operational intelligence are identified as "characteristics of adolescence" by Brown (1965), who attributes to Piaget and Inhelder the belief that the reformism of the adolescent is a temporary return to egocentrism. Inhelder and

Piaget (1958), and Brown (1965, p. 236), identify as "cultural variation" the phenomenon of primitive societies in which *no one attains formally operational intelligence.*

Piaget finds evidence for his theories in the study of the games and the rules for games as children play them, since the understanding of rules appears to reflect the level of intelligence. The child who plays egocentrically holds the rules to be inviolable, and may feel that they have always existed. In a transitional stage (late concrete operations) boys begin to play elaborately articulated social games. His observations of this stage caused Piaget to poke fun at educators who think children of this age are not capable of learning abstract subject matter. For this level of intelligence, a rule can be changed if consensus of the participants is obtained.

Another aspect of the Geneva studies (Piaget, 1948), the *development of moral conceptions,* begins with the understanding that adults judge naughtiness or wickedness on a *basis of intentions,* and can make independent judgments of seriousness as opposed or related to wickedness. In the preoperational child, however, most often naughtiness was judged in terms of perceived *objective damage;* on the other hand, older children judged naughtiness by the intentions of the offender. Similarly, studies of the child's conception of a lie seem to reflect the level of intellectual development. Young children said a lie was "naughty words" while older children believed a lie to be a statement not in accord with fact; for them reprehensibility is proportional to the variance between the falsehood and truth. Too great a departure became a joke instead of a lie, because no one would believe it. Much older children simply saw a lie as an untruth with the intent to deceive. Piaget asserts that in these developmental sequences a child's morality becomes increasingly inward, a process which Brown calls "enculturation" (1965, p. 241).

## ENDNOTE

1. At the University of Texas we prefer to use the term "development" instead of "growth," which is felt to be redundant. Development is understood to include: (a) increase in mass; (b) differentiation of parts; and (c) coordination of parts. Rosenzweig (1966) in his research with brains of rats suggests that feedback from learning experiences influences development.

## REFERENCES

Ausubel, D. P. "A Teaching Strategy for Culturally Deprived Pupils: Cognitive and Motivational Considerations." *School Review,* 1963, 71, 454–463.

Berlyne, D. E. *Structure and Direction of Thinking.* New York: Wiley, 1965.

Brown, R. *Social Psychology.* New York: Free Press, 1965.

Bruner, J. S. "The Course of Cognitive Growth." *American Psychologist,* 1964, 1, 1–15.

———. "The Growth of Mind." President's address to the Seventy-Third Annual Convention of the American Psychological Association, Chicago, September 1965.

———. *Toward a Theory of Instruction.* Cambridge: Belknap, 1966.

Bruner, J. S., Goodnow, Jacqueline J., & Austin, G. A. *A Study of Thinking.* New York: Science Editions (Wiley), 1959.

Bruner, J. S., Oliver, Rose R., Greenfield, Patricia M., Hornsby, Joan R., Kenney, Helen J., Maccoby, M., Modiano, Nancy, Mosher, F. A., Olson, D. R., Potter, Mary C., Reich, L. C., & Sonstroem, Anne Mck. *Studies in Cognitive Growth.* New York: Wiley, 1966.

Fowler, W. "Dimensions and Directions in the Development of Affecto-Cognitive Systems." *Human Development,* 1966, 9, 18–29.

Goodnow, Jacqueline J. "A Test of Milieu Effects with Some of Piaget's Tasks." *Psychological Monographs,* 1962, 76, No. 36 (Whole No. 555).

Hunt, J. McV. *Intelligence and Experience.* New York: Ronald Press, 1961.

Inhelder, B., & Piaget, J. *The Growth of Logical Thinking.* New York: Basic books, 1958.

Kohlberg, L. "Cognitive Stages and Preschool Education." *Human Development,* 1966, 9, 5–17.

McGuire, C. "Commentaries." In Mary Jane Aschner & C. E. Bish (Eds.), *Productive Thinking in Education,* Part II:

*Motivation, Personality, Productive Thinking.* Washington, D.C.: N.E A., 1965, pp. 180–190.

———. Behavioral Science Memorandum #13, Part B, of the Research and Development Center for Teacher Education at the University of Texas. Mimeograph. Austin, Texas, 1967.

Piaget, J. *Judgment and Reasoning in the Child.* (1st ed., 1924) New York: Humanities Press, 1952.

———. *The Moral Judgment of the Child.* (1st ed., 1932) New York: Free Press, 1948.

———. *The Origins of Intelligence in Children.* (1st ed., 1936) New York: International University Press, 1952.

———. *Psychology of Intelligence.* (Paris: Alcan, 1947; trans. by M. Piercy & D. E. Berlyne. London: Routledge & Kegan Paul, 1950). Totowa, N.J.: Littlefield, Adams, 1966 (ILP Paperback #222, $1.75).

———. "How Children Form Mathematical Concepts." *Scientific American,* November 1953. (Reprinted in P. H.

Mussen, J. J. Conger, & J. Kagan (Eds.), *Readings in Child Development and Personality.* New York: Harper & Row, 1965.)

Rosenzweig, M. R. "Environmental Complexity, Cerebral Change and Behavior." *American Psychologist,* 1966, 21, 321–332.

Smedslund, J. "The Acquisition of Conservation of Substance and Weight in Children. III. Extinction of Conservation of Weight Acquired 'Normally' and by Means of Empirical Controls on a Balance Scale." *Scandinavian Journal of Psychology,* 1961, 2, 85–87. (Reprinted in R. C. Anderson & D. P. Ausubel [Eds.], *Readings in the Psychology of Cognition.* New York: Holt, 1966, pp. 602–605.)

Wallach, M. A. "Research on Children's Thinking." In National Society for the Study of Education 62nd Yearbook, *Child Psychology.* Chicago: University of Chicago Press, 1963.

*Thomas Rowland* is Chancellor, The Institute for Epistemic Studies, Fort Worth, Texas.

*Carson McGuire* was Professor of Educational Psychology, University of Texas, Austin.

# Viewpoints from Related Disciplines: Human Growth and Development

## DAVID P. AUSUBEL

What light can the field of human growth and development throw on the issue "What shall the schools teach?" I only wish it were possible for me to list and discuss a dozen or more instances in which developmental principles have been validly utilized in providing definitive answers to questions dealing with the content and organization of the curriculum. Unfortunately, however, it must be admitted that at present our discipline can offer only a limited number of very crude generalizations and highly tentative

suggestions bearing on this issue. In a very general sense, of course, it is undeniable that concern with child development has had a salutary effect on the educational enterprise. It alerted school administrators to the fact that certain minimal levels of intellectual maturity were necessary before various subjects could be taught with a reasonable degree of efficiency and hope of success; and it encouraged teachers in presenting their subject matter to make use of the existing interests of pupils, to consider their

From *Teachers College Record* 60, no. 5 (February 1959): 245–254. Used by permission of the author and the publisher.

point of view, and to take into account prevailing limitations in command of language and grasp of concepts. On the other hand, premature and wholesale extension of developmental principles to educational theory and practice has caused incalculable harm. It will take at least a generation for teachers to unlearn some of the more fallacious and dangerous of these overgeneralized and unwarranted applications.

Much of the aforementioned difficulty proceeds from failure to appreciate that human growth and development is a pure rather than an applied science. As a pure science it is concerned with the discovery of general laws about the nature and regulation of human development as *an end in itself*. Ultimately, of course, these laws have self-evident implications for the realization of practical goals in such fields as education, child rearing, and guidance. In a very general sense they indicate the effects of different interpersonal and social climates on personality development and the kinds of methods and subject-matter content that are most compatible with developmental capacity and mode of functioning at a given stage of growth. Thus, because it offers important insights about the changing intellectual and emotional capacities of children as developing human beings, child development may legitimately be considered one of the basic sciences underlying education and guidance and as part of the necessary professional preparation of teachers—in much the same sense that anatomy and bacteriology are basic sciences for medicine and surgery.

Actual application to practical problems of teaching and curriculum, however, is quite another matter. Before the educational implications of developmental findings can become explicitly useful in everyday school situations, much *additional* research at the engineering level of operations is necessary. Knowledge about nuclear fission, for example, does not tell us how to make an atomic bomb or an atomic-powered submarine, antibiotic reactions that take place in

petri dishes do not necessarily take place in living systems, and methods of learning employed by animals in mazes do not necessarily correspond to methods of learning that children use in grappling with verbal materials in classrooms. Many of the better-known generalizations in child development—the principle of readiness, the cephalocaudal trend, the abstract to concrete trend in conceptualizing the environment, and others—fit these analogies perfectly. They are interesting and potentially useful ideas to curriculum specialists but will have little practical utility in designing a social studies or physical education curriculum unless they are rendered more specific in terms of the actual operations involved in teaching these subjects. This lack of fruitful particularization, although unfortunate and regrettable, does not in itself give rise to damaging consequences except insofar as many beginning teachers tend to nurture vague illusions about the current usefulness of these principles, and subsequently, after undergoing acute disillusionment, lose the confidence they may have left in the value of a developmental approach to educational problems.

Much more detrimental in their effects on pupils and teachers have been the consequences of far-fetched and uncritical application to educational practice of developmental generalizations that either have not been adequately validated or only apply to a very restricted age segment of the total span of children's development. Two illustrations of the latter category of highly limited generalizations—the "internal ripening" theory of maturation and the principle of self-selection—will be given later in this discussion. A widely accepted but inadequately validated developmental principle frequently cited to justify general or overall ability grouping of pupils is that a child's growth and achievement show a "going-togetherness." Actually, except for a spuriously high correlation during infancy, the relationship between physical status and motor ability on the one hand and intelligence and intellectual achievement on the other is negligible and declines consistently with increasing age. Even among the different subtests of intelligence and among the different areas of intellectual achievement, the weight of the evidence indicates that as a child grows older his component rates of growth in these various functions tend increasingly to diverge.

Keeping these qualifications about the relevance of child development for educational practice in mind, I propose briefly to consider from the standpoint of developmental psychology the following aspects of the issue under discussion: (1) readiness as a criterion for curricular placement; (2) developmental factors affecting breadth of the curriculum; (3) the child's voice in determining the curriculum; and (4) the content and goals of instruction in relation to the organization and growth of the intellect.

## READINESS AND GRADE PLACEMENT

There is little disagreement about the fact that readiness always crucially influences the efficiency of the learning process and often determines whether a given intellectual skill or type of school material is learnable at all at a particular stage of development. Most educators implicitly accept also the proposition that an *optimal* age exists for every kind of learning. Postponement of learning experience beyond the age of optimal readiness wastes valuable and often unsuspected learning opportunities, thereby unnecessarily reducing the amount and complexity of subject-matter content that can be mastered in a designated period of schooling. It is also conceivable that beyond a certain critical age the learning of various intellectual skills becomes more difficult for an older than for a younger child. On the other hand, when a pupil is prematurely exposed to a learning task before he is ready for it, he not only fails to learn the task in question but even

learns from the experience of failure to fear, dislike, and avoid it.

Up to this point, the principle of readiness—the idea that attained capacity limits and influences an individual's ability to profit from current experience or practice—is empirically demonstrable and conceptually unambiguous. Difficulty first arises when it is confused with the concept of *maturation* and when the latter concept in turn is equated with a process of "internal ripening." The concept of readiness simply refers to the adequacy of existing capacity in relation to the demands of a given learning task. No specification is made as to *how* this capacity is achieved—whether through prior practice of a specific nature (learning), through incidental experience, through genically regulated structural and functional changes occurring independently of environmental influences, or through various combinations of these factors. Maturation, on the other hand, has a different and much more restricted meaning. It encompasses those increments in capacity that take place in the demonstrable absence of specific practice experience—those that are attributable to genic influences and/or incidental experience. Maturation, therefore, is not the same as readiness but is merely one of the two principal factors (the other being learning) that contribute to or determine the organism's readiness to cope with new experience. Whether or not readiness exists, in other words, does not necessarily depend on maturation alone but in many instances is solely a function of prior learning experience and most typically depends on varying proportions of maturation and learning.

To equate the principles of readiness and maturation not only muddies the conceptual waters but also makes it difficult for the school to appreciate that insufficient readiness may reflect inadequate prior learning on the part of pupils because of inappropriate or inefficient instructional methods. Lack of maturation can thus become a convenient scapegoat when children manifest insufficient readiness to learn, and the school, which is thereby automatically absolved of all responsibility in the matter, consequently fails to subject its instructional practices to the degree of self-critical scrutiny necessary for continued educational progress. In short, while it is important to appreciate that the current readiness of pupils determines the school's current choice of instructional methods and materials, it is equally important to bear in mind that this readiness itself is partly determined by the appropriateness and efficiency of the previous instructional practices to which they have been subjected.

The conceptual confusion is further compounded when maturation is interpreted as a process of "internal ripening" essentially independent of *all* environmental influences, that is, of both specific practice and incidental experience. Readiness then becomes a matter of simple genic regulation unfolding in accordance with a predetermined and immutable time-table; and the school, by definition, becomes powerless to influence readiness either through its particular way of arranging specific learning experiences or through a more general program of providing incidental or nonspecific background experience preparatory to the introduction of more formal academic activities.

Actually, the embryological model of development implicit in the "internal ripening" thesis fits quite well when applied to human sensorimotor and neuromuscular sequences taking place during the prenatal period and early infancy. In the acquisition of simple behavioral functions (for example, locomotion, prehension) that characterize all members of the human species irrespective of cultural or other environmental differences, it is reasonable to suppose that for all practical purposes genic factors alone determine the direction of development. Environmental factors only enter the picture if they are extremely deviant, and then serve more to disrupt or arrest the ongoing course of develop-

ment than to generate distinctive developmental progressions of their own. Thus, the only truly objectionable aspect of this point of view is its unwarranted extrapolation to those more complex and variable components of later cognitive and behavioral development where unique factors of individual experience and cultural environment make important contributions to the direction, patterning, and sequential order of all developmental changes.

It is hardly surprising, therefore, in view of the tremendous influence on professional and lay opinion wielded by Gesell and his colleagues, that many people conceive of readiness in absolute and immutable terms, and thus fail to appreciate that except for such traits as walking and grasping, the mean ages of readiness can never be specified apart from relevant environmental conditions. Although the model child in contemporary America may first be ready to read at the age of six and one-half, the age of reading readiness is always influenced by cultural, subcultural, and individual differences in background experience, and in any case varies with the method of instruction employed and the child's IQ. Middle-class children, for example, are ready to read at an earlier age than lower-class children because of the greater availability of books in the home and because they are read to and taken places more frequently.

The need for particularizing developmental generalizations before they can become useful in educational practice is nowhere more glaringly evident than in the field of readiness. At present we can only speculate what curricular sequences might conceivably be if they took into account precise and detailed (but currently unavailable) research findings on the emergence of readiness for different subject-matter areas, for different sub-areas and levels of difficulty within an area, and for different techniques of teaching the same material. Because of the unpredictable specificity of readiness as shown, for example, by the fact that four- and five-year-olds can profit from training in pitch but not in rhythm, valid answers to such questions cannot be derived from logical extrapolation but require meticulous empirical research in a school setting. The next step would involve the development of appropriate teaching methods and materials to take optimal advantage of existing degrees of readiness and to increase readiness wherever necessary and desirable. But since we generally do not have this type of research data available, except perhaps in the field of reading, we can only pay lip service to the principle of readiness in curriculum planning.

## BREADTH OF CURRICULUM

One of the chief complaints of the critics of public education, both in the United States and in New Zealand, is that modern children fail to learn the fundamentals because of the broadening of the elementary school curriculum to include such subjects as social studies, art, science, music, and manual arts in addition to the traditional three R's. This, of course, would be a very serious charge if it were true, because the wisdom of expanding a child's intellectual horizons at the expense of making him a cripple in the basic intellectual skills is highly questionable to say the least. Fortunately, however, the benefits of an expanded curriculum have thus far not been accompanied by a corresponding deterioration in the standard of the three R's. Evidently the decreased amount of time spent on the latter subjects has been more than compensated for by the development of more efficient methods of teaching and by the incidental learning of the fundamentals in the course of studying these other subjects. Nevertheless, the issue of breadth versus depth still remains because there *is* obviously a point beyond which increased breadth could only be attained by sacrificing mastery of the fundamental skills; and even if we agreed to maintain or improve the present standard of the three R's, we would still have to choose between breadth and depth in relation to other components of the curriculum, particularly at the junior and senior high school levels. It is at these points of choice that developmental criteria can be profitably applied.

Generally speaking, maximal breadth of the curriculum consistent with adequate mastery of its constituent parts is developmentally desirable at all ages because of the tremendously wide scope of human abilities. The wider the range of intellectual stimulation to which pupils are exposed, the greater are the chances that all of the diverse potentialities both within a group of children and within a single child will be brought to fruition. By the same token, a broad curriculum makes it possible for more pupils to experience success in the performance of school activities and thus to develop the necessary self-confidence and motivation for continued academic striving and achievement. The very fact that elementary school children are able to make significant progress in science and social studies also indicates that myopic concentration on the three R's would waste much available readiness for these types of learnings and thus compel junior and senior high schools to devote much of their instructional time to materials that are easily learnable in the lower grades. In fact, one of the major failings of the secondary school curriculum today is that because it still has not adequately adjusted to the expansion of the elementary school syllabus, entering pupils are subjected to much stultifying repetition and fail to break the new ground for which they are obviously ready.

The relationship between breadth and depth must also take into account the progressive differentiation of intelligence, interests, and personality structure with increasing age. The elementary school child is a "generalist" because both his intellect and his personality are still relatively unstable and uncrystallized and lack impressive internal consistency. Thus, many different varieties of subject matter are equally compatible with his interest and ability patterns. Furthermore, unless he has experience with many different fields of knowledge and gives each a provisional try, he is in no position to judge which kinds of intellectual pursuits are most congruent with his major ability and value systems. Hence, quite apart from the future life adjustment values of a broad educational background, it is appropriate on developmental grounds for elementary and early high school curricula to stress breadth rather than depth.

Toward the latter portion of the high school period, however, precisely the opposite kind of situation begins to emerge. Interests have crystallized and abilities have undergone differentiation to the point where greater depth and specialization are possible and desirable. Many students at this stage of intellectual development are ready to sink their teeth into more serious and solid academic fare, but unfortunately suitable instructional programs geared at an advanced level of critical and independent thinking are rarely available. The changes that have taken place in secondary school curricula since the academy days have been primarily characterized by the belated and half-hearted addition of more up-to-date and topical information. Very little has been done in the way of providing the student with a meaningful, integrated, systematic view of the major ideas in a given field of knowledge.

## THE CHILD'S VOICE IN CURRICULUM PLANNING

One extreme point of view associated with the child-centered approach to education is the notion that children are innately equipped in some mysterious fashion for knowing precisely what is best for them. This idea is obviously an outgrowth of predeterministic theories (for example, those of Rousseau and Gesell) that conceive

of development as a series of internally regulated sequential steps that unfold in accordance with a prearranged design. According to these theorists, the environment facilitates development best by providing a maximally permissive field that does not interfere with the predetermined processes of spontaneous maturation. From these assumptions it is but a short step to the claim that the child himself must be in the most strategic position to *know* and *select* those components of the environment that correspond most closely with his current developmental needs and hence are most conducive to optimal growth. Empirical "proof" of this proposition is adduced from the fact that nutrition is adequately maintained and existing deficiency conditions are spontaneously corrected when infants are permitted to select their own diets. If the child can successfully choose his diet, he must certainly know what is best for him in all areas of growth and should therefore be permitted to select everything, including his curriculum.

In the first place, and refuting this theory, even if development were primarily a matter of internal ripening, there would still be no good reason for supposing that the child is therefore implicitly conversant with the current direction and facilitating conditions of development and hence axiomatically equipped to make the most appropriate choices. Because the individual is sensitive in early childhood to internal cues of physiological need we cannot conclude that he is similarly sensitive to cues reflective of psychological and other developmental needs; even in the area of nutrition, selection is a reliable criterion of need only during early infancy.

Second, unless one assigns a sacrosanct status to endogenous motivations, there is little warrant for believing either that they alone are truly reflective of the child's *genuine* developmental requirements or that environmentally derived needs are "imposed," authoritarian in spirit, and inevitably fated to thwart the actualization of his developmental potentialities. Actually, most needs originate from without and are internalized in the course of the child's interaction and identification with significant persons in his family and cultural environments.

Third, one can never assume that the child's *spontaneously* expressed interests and activities are completely reflective of *all* of his important needs and capacities. Just because capacities can potentially provide their own motivation does not mean that they always or necessarily do so. It is not the possession of capacities that is motivating, but the anticipation of future satisfactions once they have been successfully exercised. But because of such factors as inertia, lack of opportunity, lack of appreciation, and preoccupation with other activites, many capacities may never be exercised in the first place. Thus, children typically develop only *some* of their potential capacities, and their expressed interests cannot be considered coextensive with the potential range of interests they are capable of developing with appropriate stimulation.

In conclusion, therefore, the current interests and spontaneous desires of immature pupils can hardly be considered reliable guideposts and adequate substitutes for specialized knowledge and seasoned judgment in designing a curriculum. Recognition of the role of pupil needs in school learning does not mean that the scope of the syllabus should be restricted to the existing concerns and spontaneously expressed interests that happen to be present in a group of children growing up under particular conditions of intellectual and social class stimulation. In fact, one of the primary functions of education should be to stimulate the development of motivations that are currently nonexistent. It is true that academic achievement is greatest when pupils manifest felt needs to acquire knowledge as an end in itself. Such needs, however, are not endogenous but acquired—and largely through exposure to provocative, meaningful, developmental, appropriate instruction. Hence, while it is reasonable

to consider the views of pupils and even, under certain circumstances, to solicit their participation in the planning of the curriculum, it makes little developmental or administrative sense to entrust them with responsibility for significant policy or operational decisions.

## ORGANIZATION AND COGNITIVE DEVELOPMENT

The curriculum specialist is concerned with more than the appropriate grade placement of different subjects and subject-matter content in accordance with such criteria as readiness and relative significance for intellectual, vocational, or current adjustment purposes. More important than what pupils know at the end of the sixth, eighth, and twelfth grades is the extent of their knowledge at the ages of twenty-five, forty, and sixty as well as their ability and desire both to learn more and to apply their knowledge fruitfully in adult life. In light of these latter criteria, in comparing, for example, the quantity and quality of our national research output in the pure and applied sciences with those of European countries, the American educational system stands up relatively well even though our school children apparently absorb less academic material. We are dealing here with the ultimate intellectual objectives of schooling, namely, with the long-term acquisition of stable and usable bodies of knowledge and intellectual skills and with the development of ability to think creatively, systematically, independently, and with depth in particular fields of inquiry. Instruction obviously influences the outcome of these objectives—not so much in the substantive content of subject matter but in the organization, sequence, and manner of presenting learning experiences, their degree of meaningfulness, and the relative balance between conceptual and factual materials.

But obviously, before we could ever hope to

structure effectively such instructional variables for the optimal realization of these designated objectives, we would have to know a great deal more about the organizational and developmental principles whereby human beings acquire and retain stable bodies of knowledge and develop the power of critical and productive thinking. This type of knowledge, however, will forever elude us unless we abandon the untenable assumption that there is no real distinction either between the logic of a proposition and how the mind apprehends it or between the logical structure of subject-matter organization and the actual series of cognitive processes through which an immature and developing individual incorporates facts and concepts into a stable body of knowledge. It is perfectly logical from the standpoint of a mature scholar, for example, to write a textbook in which topically homogeneous materials are segregated into discrete chapters and treated throughout at a uniform level of conceptualization. But how closely does this approach correspond with highly suggestive findings that one of the major cognitive processes involved in the learning of any new subject is progressive differentiation of an originally undifferentiated field? Once we learn more about cognitive development than the crude generalizations that developmental psychology can currently offer, it will be possible to employ organizational and sequential principles in the presentation of subject matter that actually parallel developmental changes in the growth and organization of the intellect. In the meantime let us examine briefly how such generalizations as the concrete-to-abstract trend, the importance of meaningfulness, and the principle of retroactive inhibition have been used and abused in educational practice.

Many features of the activity program are based on the premise that the elementary school child perceives the world in relatively specific and concrete terms and requires considerable firsthand experience with diverse concrete instances of a given set of relationships before he can abstract genuinely meaningful concepts.

Thus, an attempt is made to teach factual information and intellectual skills in the real-life functional contexts in which they are customarily encountered rather than through the medium of verbal exposition supplemented by artificially contrived drills and exercises. This approach has real merit, if a fetish is not made of naturalism and incidental learning, if drills and exercises are provided in instances where opportunities for acquiring skills do not occur frequently and repetitively enough in more natural settings, and if deliberate or guided effort is not regarded as incompatible with incidental learning. Even more important, however, is the realization that in older children, once a sufficient number of basic concepts are consolidated, new concepts are primarily abstracted from verbal rather than from concrete experience. Hence in secondary school it may be desirable to reverse both the sequence and the relative balance between abstract concepts and supportive data. There is good reason for believing, therefore, that much of the time presently spent in cookbook laboratory exercises in the sciences could be much more advantageously employed in formulating precise definitions, making explicit verbal distinctions between concepts, generalizing from hypothetical situations, and in other ways.

Another underlying assumption of activity and project methods is that concepts and factual data are retained much longer when they are meaningful, genuinely understood, and taught as larger units of interrelated materials than when they are presented as fragmented bits of isolated information and committed to rote memory. This, of course, does not preclude the advisability of rote learning for certain kinds of learning (for example, multiplication tables) *after* a functional understanding of the underlying concepts has been acquired. Unfortunately, however, these principles have made relatively few inroads on the high school instructional program, where they are still applicable. The teaching of mathematics and science, for example, still relies heavily on rote learning of formu-

las and procedural steps, on recognition of traditional "type problems," and on mechanical
manipulation of symbols. In the absence of clear
and stable concepts which serve as anchoring
points and organizing foci for the assimilation of
new material, secondary school students are
trapped in a morass of confusion and seldom
retain rotely memorized materials much beyond
final exam time.

This brings us finally to a consideration of the
mechanisms of accretion and long-term retention of large bodies of ideational material. Why
do high school and university students tend to
forget so readily previous day-to-day learnings
as they are exposed to new lessons? The traditional answer of educational pscyhology, based
upon studies of short-term rote learning in animal and human subjects, has been that subsequent learning experiences which are similar to
but not identical with previously learned materials exert a retroactively inhibitory effect on the
retention of the latter. But wouldn't it be reasonable to suppose that all of the existing, cumulatively established ideational systems which an
individual brings with him to any learning
situation have more of an interfering effect on
the retention of new learning material (proactive
inhibition) than brief exposure to subsequently
introduced materials of a similar nature (retroactive inhibition)? Because it is cognitively most
economical and least burdensome for an individual to subsume as much new experience as possible under existing concepts that are inclusive and
stable, the import of many specific illustrative
items in later experience is assimilated by the
generalized meaning of these more firmly established and highly conceptualized subsuming
foci. When this happens the latter items lose
their identity and are said to be "forgotten."
Hence, if proactive rather than retroactive inhibition turned out to be the principal mechanism
affecting the longevity with which school materials were retained, it would behoove us to identify those factors that counteract it and to
employ such measures in our instructional
procedures.

*David P. Ausubel* is Professor of Education, City University of New York.

# The Cognitive-Developmental Approach to Moral Education

## LAWRENCE KOHLBERG

In this article, I present an overview of the cognitive-developmental approach to moral education and its research foundations, compare it
with other approaches, and report the experimental work my colleagues and I are doing to
apply the approach.

### I. MORAL STAGES

The cognitive-developmental approach was fully
stated for the first time by John Dewey. The
approach is called *cognitive* because it recognizes
that moral education, like intellectual education,

From *Phi Delta Kappan* 56, no. 10 (June 1975): 670–677. Used by permission of the author and the publisher.

has its basis in stimulating the *active thinking* of the child about moral issues and decisions. It is called developmental because it sees the aims of moral education as movement through moral stages. According to Dewey:

> The aim of education is growth or *development,* both intellectual and moral. Ethical and psychological principles can aid the school in the *greatest of all constructions–the building of a free and powerful character.* Only knowledge of the *order and connection of the stages in psychological development can insure this.* Education is the work of *supplying the conditions* which will enable the psychological functions to mature in the freest and fullest manner.[1]

Dewey postulated three levels of moral development: (1) the *pre-moral* or *preconventional* level "of behavior motivated by biological and social impulses with results for morals," (2) the *conventional* level of behavior "in which the individual accepts with little critical reflection the standards of his group," and (3) the *autonomous* level of behavior in which "conduct is guided by the individual thinking and judging for himself whether a purpose is good, and does not accept the standard of his group without reflection."[2]

Dewey's thinking about moral stages was theoretical. Building upon his prior studies of cognitive stages, Jean Piaget made the first effort to define stages of moral reasoning in children through actual interviews and through observations of children (in games with rules).[3] Using this interview material, Piaget defined the premoral, the conventional, and the autonomous levels as follows: (1) the *pre-moral stage,* where there was no sense of obligation to rules; (2) the *heteronomous stage,* where the right was literal obedience to rules and an equation of obligation with submission to power and punishment (roughly ages four to eight); and (3) the *autonomous stage,* where the purpose and consequences of following rules are considered and obligation is based on reciprocity and exchange (roughly ages eight to twelve).[4]

In 1955 I started to redefine and validate (through longitudinal and cross-cultural study) the Dewey-Piaget levels and stages. The resulting stages are presented in Table 1.

We claim to have validated the stages defined in Table 1. The notion that stages can be *validated* by longitudinal study implies that stages have definite empirical characteristics.[5] The concept of stages (as used by Piaget and myself) implies the following characteristics:

1. Stages are "structured wholes," or organized systems of thought. Individuals are *consistent* in level of moral judgment.
2. Stages form an *invariant sequence.* Under all conditions except extreme trauma, movement is always forward, never backward. Individuals never skip stages; movement is always to the next stage up.
3. Stages are "hierarchical integrations." Thinking at a higher stage includes or comprehends within it lower-stage thinking. There is a tendency to function at or prefer the highest stage available.

Each of these characteristics has been demonstrated for moral stages. Stages are defined by responses to a set of verbal moral dilemmas classified according to an elaborate scoring scheme. Validating studies include:

1. A twenty-year study of fifty Chicago-area boys, middle- and working-class. Initially interviewed at ages ten to sixteen, they have been reinterviewed at three-year intervals thereafter.
2. A small, six-year longitudinal study of Turkish village and city boys of the same age.
3. A variety of other cross-sectional studies in Canada, Britain, Israel, Taiwan, Yucatan, Honduras, and India.

With regard to the structured whole or consistency criterion, we have found that more than 50 percent of an individual's thinking is always

**TABLE 1**
**Definition of Moral Stages**

**I. Preconventional level**

At this level, the child is responsive to cultural rules and labels of good and bad, right or wrong, but interprets these labels either in terms of the physical or the hedonistic consequences of action (punishment, reward, exchange of favors) or in terms of the physical power of those who enunciate the rules and labels. The level is divided into the following two stages:

Stage 1: *The punishment-and-obedience orientation.* The physical consequences of action determine its goodness or badness, regardless of the human meaning or value of these consequences. Avoidance of punishment and unquestioning deference to power are valued in their own right, not in terms of respect for an underlying moral order supported by punishment and authority (the latter being Stage 4).

Stage 2: *The instrumental-relativist orientation.* Right action consists of that which instrumentally satisfies one's own needs and occasionally the needs of others. Human relations are viewed in terms like those of the marketplace. Elements of fairness, of reciprocity, and of equal sharing are present, but they are always interpreted in a physical, pragmatic way. Reciprocity is a matter of "you scratch my back and I'll scratch yours," not of loyalty, gratitude, or justice.

**II. Conventional level**

At this level, maintaining the expectations of the individual's family, group, or nation is perceived as valuable in its own right, regardless of immediate and obvious consequences. The attitude is not only one of *conformity* to personal expectations and social order, but of loyalty to it, of actively *maintaining,* supporting, and justifying the order, and of identifying with the persons or group involved in it. At this level, there are the following two stages:

Stage 3: *The interpersonal concordance or "good boy-nice girl" orientation.* Good behavior is that which pleases or helps others and is approved by them. There is much conformity to stereotypical images of what is majority or "natural" behavior. Behavior is frequently judged by intention—"he means well" becomes important for the first time. One earns approval by being "nice."

Stage 4: *The "law and order" orientation.* There is orientation toward authority, fixed rules, and the maintenance of the social order. Right behavior consists of doing one's duty, showing respect for authority, and maintaining the given social order for its own sake.

**III. Postconventional, autonomous, or principled level**

At this level, there is a clear effort to define moral values and principles that have validity and application apart from the authority of the groups or persons holding these principles and apart from the individual's own identification with these groups. This level also has two stages:

Stage 5: *The social-contract, legalistic orientation,* generally with utilitarian overtones. Right action tends to be defined in terms of general individual rights and standards which have been critically examined and agreed upon by the whole society. There is a clear awareness of the relativism of personal values and opinions and a corresponding emphasis upon procedural rules for reaching consensus. Aside from what is constitutionally and democratically agreed upon, the right is a matter of personal "values" and "opinion." The result is an emphasis upon the "legal point of view," but with an emphasis upon the possibility of changing law in terms of rational considerations of social utility (rather than freezing it in terms of Stage 4 "law and order"). Outside the legal realm, free agreement and contract is the binding element of obligation. This is the "official" morality of the American government and constitution.

Stage 6: *The universal-ethical-principle orientation.* Right is defined by the decision of conscience in accord with self-chosen *ethical principles* appealing to logical comprehensiveness, universality, and consistency. These principles are abstract and ethical (the Golden Rule, the categorical imperative); they are not concrete moral rules like the Ten Commandments. At heart, these are universal principles of *justice,* of the *reciprocity* and *equality* of human *rights,* and of respect for the dignity of human beings as *individual persons* ("From Is to Ought," pp. 164,165).

From *Journal of Philosophy* 70, no. 18 (October 25, 1973): 631–632. Reprinted by permission.

at one stage, with the remainder at the next adjacent stage (which he is leaving or which he is moving into).

With regard to invariant sequence, our longitudinal results have been presented in the *American Journal of Orthopsychiatry* (see endnote 12), and indicate that on every retest individuals were either at the same stage as three years earlier or had moved up. This was true in Turkey as well as in the United States.

With regard to the hierarchical integration criterion, it has been demonstrated that adolescents exposed to written statements at each of the six stages comprehend or correctly put in their own words all statements at or below their own stage but fail to comprehend any statements more than one stage above their own.[6] Some individuals comprehend the next stage above their own; some do not. Adolescents prefer (or rank as best) the highest stage they can comprehend.

To understand moral stages, it is important to clarify their relations to stage of logic or intelligence, on the one hand, and to moral behavior on the other. Maturity of moral judgment is not highly correlated with IQ or verbal intelligence (correlations are only in the 30s, accounting for 10 percent of the variance). Cognitive development, in the stage sense, however, is more important for moral development than such correlations suggest. Piaget has found that after the child learns to speak there are three major stages of reasoning: the intuitive, the concrete operational, and the formal operational. At around age seven, the child enters the stage of concrete logical thought: He can make logical inferences, classify, and handle quantitative relations about concrete things. In adolescence individuals usually enter the stage of formal operations. At this stage they can reason abstractly, i.e., consider all possibilities, form hypotheses, deduce implications from hypotheses, and test them against reality.[7]

Since moral reasoning clearly is reasoning,

advanced moral reasoning depends upon advanced logical reasoning; a person's logical stage puts a certain ceiling on the moral stage he can attain. A person whose logical stage is only concrete operational is limited to the preconventional moral stages (Stages 1 and 2). A person whose logical stage is only partially formal operational is limited to the conventional moral stages (Stages 3 and 4). While logical development is necessary for moral development and sets limits to it, most individuals are higher in logical stage than they are in moral stage. As an example, over 50 percent of late adolescents and adults are capable of full formal reasoning, but only 10 percent of these adults (all formal operational) display principled (Stages 5 and 6) moral reasoning.

The moral stages are *structures of moral judgment* or *moral reasoning*. *Structures* of moral judgment must be distinguished from the *content* of moral judgment. As an example, we cite responses to a dilemma used in our various studies to identify moral stage. The dilemma raises the issue of stealing a drug to save a dying woman. The inventor of the drug is selling it for ten times what it costs him to make it. The woman's husband cannot raise the money, and the seller refuses to lower the price or wait for payment. What should the husband do?

The choice endorsed by a subject (steal, don't steal) is called the *content* of his moral judgment in the situation. His reasoning about the choice defines the structure of his moral judgment. This reasoning centers on the following ten universal moral values or issues of concern to persons in these moral dilemmas:

1. Punishment
2. Property
3. Roles and concerns of affection
4. Roles and concerns of authority
5. Law
6. Life
7. Liberty

8. Distributive justice
9. Truth
10. Sex

A moral choice involves choosing between two (or more) of these values as they *conflict* in concrete situations of choice.

The stage or structure of a person's moral judgment defines: (1) *what* he finds valuable in each of these moral issues (life, law), i.e., how he defines the value, and (2) *why* he finds it valuable, i.e., the reasons he gives for valuing it. As an example, at Stage 1 life is valued in terms of the power or possessions of the person involved; at Stage 2, for its usefulness in satisfying the needs of the individual in question or others; at Stage 3, in terms of the individual's relations with others and their valuation of him; at Stage 4, in terms of social or religious law. Only at Stages 5 and 6 is each life seen as inherently worthwhile, aside from other considerations.

## Moral Judgment vs. Moral Action

Having clarified the nature of stages of moral *judgment,* we must consider the relation of moral judgment to moral *action.* If logical reasoning is a necessary but not sufficient condition for mature moral judgment, mature moral judgment is a necessary but not sufficient condition for mature moral action. One cannot follow moral principles if one does not understand (or believe in) moral principles. However, one can reason in terms of principles and not live up to these principles. As an example, Richard Krebs and I found that only 15 percent of students showing some principled thinking cheated as compared to 55 percent of conventional subjects and 70 percent of preconventional subjects.[8] Nevertheless, 15 percent of the principled subjects did cheat, suggesting that factors additional to moral judgment are necessary for principled moral reasoning to be translated into "moral

action." Partly, these factors include the situation and its pressures. Partly, what happens depends upon the individual's motives and emotions. Partly, what the individual does depends upon a general sense of will, purpose, or "ego strength." As an example of the role of will or ego strength in moral behavior, we may cite the study by Krebs: Slightly more than half of his conventional subjects cheated. These subjects were also divided by a measure of attention/will. Only 26 percent of the "strong-willed" conventional subjects cheated; however, 74 percent of the "weak-willed" subjects cheated.

If maturity of moral reasoning is only one factor in moral behavior, why does the cognitive-developmental approach to moral education focus so heavily upon moral reasoning? For the following reasons:

1. Moral judgment, while only one factor in moral behavior, is the single most important or influential factor yet discovered in moral behavior.
2. While other factors influence moral behavior, moral judgment is the only distinctively *moral* factor in moral behavior. To illustrate, we noted that the Krebs study indicated that "strong-willed" conventional stage subjects resisted cheating more than "weak-willed" subjects. For those at a preconventional level of moral reasoning, however, "will" had an opposite effect. "Strong-willed" Stages 1 and 2 subjects cheated more, not less, than "weak-willed" subjects, i.e., they had the "courage of their (amoral) convictions" that it was worthwhile to cheat. "Will," then, is an important factor in moral behavior, but it is not distinctively moral; it becomes moral only when informed by mature moral judgment.
3. Moral judgment change is long-range or irreversible; a higher stage is never lost. Moral behavior as such is largely situational and reversible or "losable" in new situations.

## II. AIMS OF MORAL AND CIVIC EDUCATION

Moral psychology describes what moral development is, as studied empirically. Moral education must also consider moral philosophy, which strives to tell us what moral development ideally *ought to be.* Psychology finds an invariant sequence of moral stages; moral philosophy must be invoked to answer whether a later stage is a better stage. The "stage" of senescence and death follows the "stage" of adulthood, but that does not mean that senescence and death are better. Our claim that the latest or principled stages of moral reasoning are morally better stages, then, must rest on considerations of moral philosophy.

The tradition of moral philosophy to which we appeal is the liberal or rational tradition, in particular the "formalistic" or "deontological" tradition running from Immanuel Kant to John Rawls.[9] Central to this tradition is the claim that an adequate morality is *principled,* i.e., that it makes judgments in terms of *universal* principles applicable to all mankind. *Principles* are to be distinguished from *rules.* Conventional morality is grounded on rules, primarily "thou shalt nots" such as are represented by the Ten Commandments, prescriptions of kinds of actions. Principles are, rather, universal guides to making a moral decision. An example is Kant's "categorical imperative," formulated in two ways. The first is the maxim of respect for human personality, "Act always toward the other as an end, not as a means." The second is the maxim of universalization, "Choose only as you would be willing to have everyone choose in your situation." Principles like that of Kant's state the formal conditions of a moral choice or action. In the dilemma in which a woman is dying because a druggist refuses to release his drug for less than the stated price, the druggist is not acting morally, though he is not violating the ordinary moral rules (he is not actually stealing or murdering). But he is violating principles: He is treating the woman simply as a means to his ends of profit, and he is not choosing as he would wish anyone to choose (if the druggist were in the dying woman's place, he would not want a druggist to choose as he is choosing). Under most circumstances, choice in terms of conventional moral rules and choice in terms of principles coincide. Ordinarily, principles dictate not stealing (avoiding stealing is implied by acting in terms of a regard for others as ends and in terms of what one would want everyone to do). In a situation where stealing is the only means to save a life, however, principles contradict the ordinary rules and would dictate stealing. Unlike rules which are supported by social authority, principles are freely chosen by the individual because of their intrinsic moral validity.[10]

The conception that a moral choice is a choice made in terms of moral principles is related to the claim of liberal moral philosophy that moral principles are ultimately principles of justice. In essence, moral conflicts are conflicts between the claims of persons, and principles for resolving these claims are principles of justice, "for giving each his due." Central to justice are the demands of *liberty, equality,* and *reciprocity.* At every moral stage, there is a concern for justice. The most damning statement a school child can make about a teacher is that "he's not fair." At each higher stage, however, the conception of justice is reorganized. At Stage 1, justice is punishing the bad in terms of "an eye for an eye and a tooth for a tooth." At Stage 2, it is exchanging favors and goods in an equal manner. At Stages 3 and 4, it is treating people as they desire in terms of the conventional rules. At Stage 5, it is recognized that all rules and laws flow from justice, from a social contract between the governors and the governed designed to protect the equal rights of all. At Stage 6, personally chosen moral principles are also principles of justice, the principles any member of a society would choose for that society if he did not know what his position was to be in the society and in which he might be the least advantaged.[11] Principles chosen from this point of view are, first, the maximum liberty compatible with the like liberty of others and, second, no inequalities of goods and respect which are not to the benefit of all, including the least advantaged.

As an example of stage progression in the orientation to justice, we may take judgments about capital punishment.[12] Capital punishment is only firmly rejected at the two principled stages, when the notion of justice as vengeance or retribution is abandoned. At the sixth stage, capital punishment is not condoned even if it may have some useful deterrent effect in promoting law and order. This is because it is not a punishment we would choose for a society if we assumed we had as much chance of being born into the position of a criminal or murderer as being born into the position of a law abider.

Why are decisions based on universal principles of justice better decisions? Because they are decisions on which all moral men could agree. When decisions are based on conventional moral rules, men will disagree, since they adhere to conflicting systems of rules dependent on culture and social position. Throughout history men have killed one another in the name of conflicting moral rules and values, most recently in Vietnam and the Middle East. Truly moral or just resolutions of conflicts require principles which are, or can be, universalizable.

## Alternative Approaches

We have given a philosophic rationale for stage advance as the aim of moral education. Given this rationale, the developmental approach to moral education can avoid the problems inherent in the other two major approaches to moral education. The first alternative approach is that of indoctrinative moral education, the preaching and imposition of the rules and values of the teacher and his culture on the child. In America, when this indoctrinative approach has been developed in a systematic manner, it has usually been termed "character education."

Moral values, in the character education approach, are preached or taught in terms of what may be called the "bag of virtues." In the classic studies of character by Hugh Hartshorne and Mark May, the virtues chosen were honesty, service, and self-control.[13] It is easy to get superficial consensus on such a bag of virtues—until one examines in detail the list of virtues involved and the details of their definition. Is the Hartshorne and May bag more adequate than the Boy Scout bag (a Scout should be honest, loyal, reverent, clean, brave, etc.)? When one turns to the details of defining each virtue, one finds equal uncertainty or difficulty in reaching consensus. Does honesty mean one should not steal to save a life? Does it mean that a student should not help another student with his homework?

Character education and other forms of indoctrinative moral education have aimed at teaching universal values (it is assumed that honesty or service is a desirable trait for all men in all societies), but the detailed definitions used are relative; they are defined by the opinions of the teacher and the conventional culture and rest on the authority of the teacher for their justification. In this sense character education is close to the unreflective valuings by teachers which constitute the hidden curriculum of the school.[14] Because of the current unpopularity of indoctrinative approaches to moral education, a family of approaches called "values clarification" has become appealing to teachers. Values clarification takes the first step implied by a rational approach to moral education: the eliciting of the child's own judgment or opinion about issues or situations in which values conflict, rather than imposing the teacher's opinion on him. Values clarification, however, does not attempt to go further than eliciting awareness of values; it is assumed that becoming more self-aware about one's values is an end in itself. Fundamentally, the definition of the end of values education as self-awareness derives from a belief in ethical relativity held by many value-clarifiers. As stated by Peter Engel, "One must contrast value clarification and value inculcation. Value clarification implies the principle that in the consideration of values there is no single correct answer." Within these premises of "no correct answer," children are to discuss moral dilemmas in such a way as to reveal different values and discuss their value differences with each other. The teacher is to stress that "our values are different," not that one value is more adequate than others. If this program is systematically followed, students will themselves become relativists, believing there is no "right" moral answer. For instance, a student caught cheating might argue that he did nothing wrong, since his own hierarchy of values, which may be different from that of the teacher, made it right for him to cheat.

Like values clarification, the cognitive-developmental approach to moral education stresses open or Socratic peer discussion of value dilemmas. Such discussion, however, has an aim: stimulation of movement to the next stage of moral reasoning. Like values clarification, the developmental approach opposes indoctrination. Stimulation of movement to the next stage of reasoning is not indoctrinative, for the following reasons:

1. Change is in the way of reasoning rather than in the particular beliefs involved.
2. Students in a class are at different stages; the aim is to aid movement of each to the next stage, not convergence on a common pattern.
3. The teacher's own opinion is neither stressed nor invoked as authoritative. It enters in only as one of many opinions, hopefully one of those at a next higher stage.
4. The notion that some judgments are more adequate than others is communicated. Fundamentally, however, this means that the stu-

dent is encouraged to articulate a position which seems most adequate to him and to judge the adequacy of the reasoning of others.

In addition to having more definite aims than values clarification, the moral development approach restricts value education to that which is moral or, more specifically, to justice. This is for two reasons. First, it is not clear that the whole realm of personal, political, and religious values is a realm which is nonrelative, i.e., in which there are universals and a direction of development. Second, it is not clear that the public school has a right or mandate to develop values in general.[15] In our view, value education in the public schools should be restricted to that which the school has the right and mandate to develop: an awareness of justice, or of the rights of others in our Constitutional system. While the Bill of Rights prohibits the teaching of religious beliefs, or of specific value systems, it does not prohibit the teaching of the awareness of rights and principles of justice fundamental to the Constitution itself.

When moral education is recognized as centered in justice and differentiated from value education or affective education, it becomes apparent that moral and civic education are much the same thing. This equation, taken for granted by the classic philosophers of education from Plato and Aristotle to Dewey, is basic to our claim that a concern for moral education is central to the educational objectives of social studies.

The term *civic education* is used to refer to social studies as more than the study of the facts and concepts of social science, history, and civics. It is education for the analytic understanding, value principles, and motivation necessary for a citizen in a democracy if democracy is to be an effective process. It is political education. Civic or political education means the stimulation of development of more advanced patterns of reasoning about political and social decisions and their implementation directly derivative of broader patterns of moral reasoning. Our studies show that reasoning and decision making about political decisions are directly derivative of broader patterns of moral reasoning and decision making. We have interviewed high school and college students about concrete political situations involving laws to govern open housing, civil disobedience for peace in Vietnam, free press rights to publish what might disturb national order, and distribution of income through taxation. We find that reasoning on these political decisions can be classified according to moral stage and that an individual's stage on political dilemmas is at the same level as on nonpolitical moral dilemmas (euthanasia, violating authority to maintain trust in a family, stealing a drug to save one's dying wife). Turning from reasoning to action, similar findings are obtained. In 1963 a study was made of those who sat in at the University of California, Berkeley, administration building and those who did not in the Free Speech Movement crisis. Of those at Stage 6, 80 percent sat in, believing that principles of free speech were being compromised, and that all efforts to compromise and negotiate with the administration had failed. In contrast, only 15 percent of the conventional (Stage 3 or Stage 4) subjects sat in. (Stage 5 subjects were in between.)[16]

From a psychological side, then, political development is part of moral development. The same is true from the philosophic side. In the *Republic,* Plato sees political education as part of a broader education for moral justice and finds a rationale for such education in terms of universal philosophic principles rather than the demands of a particular society. More recently, Dewey claims the same.

In historical perspective, America was the first nation whose government was publicly founded on postconventional principles of justice, rather than upon the authority central to conventional moral reasoning. At the time of our founding,

postconventional or principled moral and political reasoning was the possession of the minority, as it still is. Today, as in the time of our founding, the majority of our adults are at the conventional level, particularly the "law and order" (fourth) moral stage. (Every few years the Gallup Poll circulates the Bill of Rights unidentified, and every year it is turned down.) The Founding Fathers intuitively understood this without benefit of our elaborate social science research; they constructed a document designing a government which would maintain principles of justice and the rights of man even though principled men were not the men in power. The machinery included checks and balances, the independent judiciary, and freedom of the press. Most recently, this machinery found its use at Watergate. The tragedy of Richard Nixon, as Harry Truman said long ago, was that he never understood the Constitution (a Stage 5 document), but the Constitution understood Richard Nixon.[17]

Watergate, then, is not some sign of moral decay of the nation, but rather of the fact that understanding and action in support of justice principles are still the possession of a minority of our society. Insofar as there is moral decay, it represents the weakening of conventional morality in the face of social and value conflict today. This can lead the less fortunate adolescent to fixation at the preconventional level, the more fortunate to movement to principles. We find a larger proportion of youths at the principled level today than was the case in their fathers' day, but also a larger proportion at the preconventional level.

Given this state, moral and civic education in the schools becomes a more urgent task. In the high school today, one often hears both preconventional adolescents and those beginning to move beyond convention sounding the same note of disaffection for the school. While our political institutions are in principle Stage 5 (i.e., vehicles for maintaining universal rights through the democratic process), our schools have traditionally been Stage 4 institutions of convention and authority. Today more than ever, democratic schools systematically engaged in civic education are required.

Our approach to moral and civic education relates the study of law and government to the actual creation of a democratic school in which moral dilemmas are discussed and resolved in a manner which will stimulate moral development.

## Planned Moral Education

For many years, moral development was held by psychologists to be primarily a result of family upbringing and family conditions. In particular, conditions of affection and authority in the home were believed to be critical, some balance of warmth and firmness being optimal for moral development. This view arises if morality is conceived as an internalization of the arbitrary rules of parents and culture, since such acceptance must be based on affection and respect for parents as authorities rather than on the rational nature of the rules involved.

Studies of family correlates of moral stage development do not support this internalization view of the conditions for moral development. Instead, they suggest that the conditions for moral development in homes and schools are similar and that the conditions are consistent with cognitive-developmental theory. In the cognitive-developmental view, morality is a natural product of a universal human tendency toward empathy or role taking, toward putting oneself in the shoes of other conscious beings. It is also a product of a universal human concern for justice, for reciprocity or equality in the relation of one person to another. As an example, when my son was four, he became a morally principled vegetarian and refused to eat meat, resisting all parental persuasion to increase his

protein intake. His reason was, "It's bad to kill animals." His moral commitment to vegetarianism was not taught or acquired from parental authority; it was the result of the universal tendency of the young self to project its consciousness and values into other living things, other selves. My son's vegetarianism also involved a sense of justice, revealed when I read him a book about Eskimos in which a real hunting expedition was described. His response was to say, "Daddy, there is one kind of meat I would eat— Eskimo meat. It's all right to eat Eskimos because they eat animals." This natural sense of justice or reciprocity was Stage 1—an eye for an eye, a tooth for a tooth. My son's sense of the value of life was also Stage 1 and involved no differentiation between human personality and physical life. His morality, though Stage 1, was, however, natural and internal. Moral development past Stage 1, then, is not an internalization but the reconstruction of role taking and conceptions of justice toward greater adequacy. These reconstructions occur in order to achieve a better match between the child's own moral structures and the structures of the social and moral situations he confronts. We divide these conditions of match into two kinds: those dealing with moral discussions and communication and those dealing with the total moral environment or atmosphere in which the child lives.

In terms of moral discussion, the important conditions appear to be:

1. Exposure to the next higher stage of reasoning
2. Exposure to situations posing problems and contradictions for the child's current moral structure, leading to dissatisfaction with his current level
3. An atmosphere of interchange and dialogue combining the first two conditions, in which conflicting moral views are compared in an open manner.

Studies of families in India and America suggest that morally advanced children have parents at higher stages. Parents expose children to the next higher stage, raising moral issues and engaging in open dialogue or interchange about such issues.[18]

Drawing on this notion of the discussion conditions stimulating advance, Moshe Blatt conducted classroom discussions of conflict-laden hypothetical moral dilemmas with four classes of junior high and high school students for a semester.[19] In each of these classes, students were to be found at three stages. Since the children were not all responding at the same stage, the arguments they used with each other were at different levels. In the course of these discussions among the students, the teacher first supported and clarified those arguments that were one stage above the lowest stage among the children; for example, the teacher supported Stage 3 rather than Stage 2. When it seemed that these arguments were understood by the students, the teacher then challenged that stage, using new situations, and clarified the arguments one stage above the previous one: Stage 4 rather than Stage 3. At the end of the semester, all the students were retested; they showed significant upward change when compared to the controls, and they maintained the change one year later. In the experimental classrooms, from one-fourth to one-half of the students moved up a stage, while there was essentially no change during the course of the experiment in the control group.

Given the Blatt studies showing that moral discussion could raise moral stage, we undertook the next step: to see if teachers could conduct moral discussions in the course of teaching high school social studies with the same results. This step we took in cooperation with Edwin Fenton, who introduced moral dilemmas in his ninth- and eleventh-grade social studies texts. Twenty-four teachers in the Boston and Pittsburgh areas were given some instruction in conducting moral discussions around the dilemmas in the text. About half of the teachers stimulated significant developmental change in their classrooms—upward stage movement of one-quarter to one-half a stage. In control classes using the text but no moral dilemma discussions, the same teachers failed to stimulate any moral change in the students. Moral discussion, then, can be a usable and effective part of the curriculum at any grade level. Working with filmstrip dilemmas produced in cooperation with Guidance Associates, second-grade teachers conducted moral discussions yielding a similar amount of moral stage movement.

Moral discussion and curriculum, however, constitute only one portion of the conditions stimulating moral growth. When we turn to analyzing the broader life environment, we turn to a consideration of the *moral atmosphere* of the home, the school, and the broader society. The first basic dimension of social atmosphere is the role-taking opportunities it provides, the extent to which it encourages the child to take the point of view of others. Role taking is related to the amount of social interaction and social communication in which the child engages, as well as to his sense of efficacy in influencing attitudes of others. The second dimension of social atmosphere, more strictly moral, is the level of justice of the environment or institution. The justice structure of an institution refers to the perceived rules or principles for distributing rewards, punishments, responsibilities, and privileges among institutional members. This structure may exist or be perceived at any of our moral stages. As an example, a study of a traditional prison revealed that inmates perceived it as Stage 1, regardless of their own level.[20] Obedience to arbitrary command by power figures and punishment for disobedience were seen as the governing justice norms of the prison. A behavior-modification prison using point rewards for conformity was perceived as a Stage 2 system of instrumental exchange. Inmates at Stage 3 or 4 perceived this institution as more fair than the traditional prison, but not as fair in their own terms.

These and other studies suggest that a higher level of institutional justice is a condition for individual development of a higher sense of justice. Working on these premises, Joseph Hickey, Peter Scharf, and I worked with guards and inmates in a women's prison to create a more just community.[21] A social contract was set up in which guards and inmates each had a vote of one and in which rules were made and conflicts resolved through discussions of fairness and a democratic vote in a community meeting. The program has been operating four years and has stimulated moral stage advance in inmates, though it is still too early to draw conclusions as to its overall long-range effectiveness for rehabilitation.

One year ago, Fenton, Ralph Mosher, and I received a grant from the Danforth Foundation (with additional support from the Kennedy Foundation) to make moral education a living matter in two high schools in the Boston area (Cambridge and Brookline) and two in Pittsburgh. The plan had two components. The first was training counselors and social studies and English teachers in conducting moral discussions and making moral discussion an integral part of the curriculum. The second was establishing a just community school within a public high school.

We have stated the theory of the just community high school, postulating that discussing real-life moral situations and actions as issues of fairness and as matters for democratic decision would stimulate advance in both moral reasoning and moral action. A participatory democracy provides more extensive opportunities for role taking and a higher level of perceived institutional justice than does any other social arrangement. Most alternative schools strive to establish a democratic governance, but none we have observed has achieved a vital or viable participatory democracy. Our theory suggested reasons why

we might succeed where others failed. First, we felt that democracy had to be a central commitment of a school, rather than a humanitarian frill. Democracy as moral education provides that commitment. Second, democracy in alternative schools often fails because it bores the students. Students prefer to let teachers make decisions about staff, courses, and schedules, rather than to attend lengthy, complicated meetings. Our theory said that the issues a democracy should focus on are issues of morality and fairness. Real issues concerning drugs, stealing, disruptions, and grading are never boring if handled as issues of fairness. Third, our theory told us that if large democratic community meetings were preceded by small-group moral discussion, higher-stage thinking by students would win out in later decisions, avoiding the disasters of mob rule.[22]

Currently, we can report that the school based on our theory makes democracy work or function where other schools have failed. It is too early to make any claims for its effectiveness in causing moral development, however.

Our Cambridge just community school within the public high school was started after a small summer planning session of volunteer teachers, students, and parents. At the time the school opened in the fall, only a commitment to democracy and a skeleton program of English and social studies had been decided on. The school started with six teachers from the regular school and sixty students, twenty from academic professional homes and twenty from working-class homes. The other twenty were dropouts and trouble-makers or petty delinquents in terms of previous record. The usual mistakes and usual chaos of a beginning alternative school ensued. Within a few weeks, however, a successful democratic community process had been established. Rules were made around pressing issues: disturbances, drugs, hooking. A student discipline committee or jury was formed. The resulting rules and enforcement have been relatively effective and reasonable. We do not see reasonable rules as ends in themselves, however, but as vehicles for moral discussion and an emerging sense of community. This sense of community and a resulting morale are perhaps the most immediate signs of success. This sense of community seems to lead to behavior change of a positive sort. An example is a fifteen-year-old student who started as one of the greatest combinations of humor, aggression, light-fingeredness, and hyperactivity I have ever known. From being the principal disturber of all community meetings, he has become an excellent community meeting participant and occasional chairman. He is still more ready to enforce rules for others than to observe them himself, yet his commitment to the school has led to a steady decrease in exotic behavior. In addition, he has become more involved in classes and projects and has begun to listen and ask questions in order to pursue a line of interest.

We attribute such behavior change not only to peer pressure and moral discussion but to the sense of community which has emerged from the democratic process in which angry conflicts are resolved through fairness and community decision. This sense of community is reflected in statements of the students to us that there are no cliques—that the blacks and the whites, the professors' sons and the project students, are friends. These statements are supported by observation. Such a sense of community is needed where students in a given classroom range in reading level from fifth-grade to college.

Fenton, Mosher, the Cambridge and Brookline teachers, and I are now planning a four-year curriculum in English and social studies centering on moral discussion, on role taking and communication, and on relating the government, laws, and justice system of the school to that of the American society and other world societies. This will integrate an intellectual curriculum for a higher level of understanding of society with the experiential components of school democracy and moral decision.

There is very little new in this—or in anything else we are doing. Dewey wanted democratic experimental schools for moral and intellectual development seventy years ago. Perhaps Dewey's time has come.

## ENDNOTES

1. John Dewey, "What Psychology Can do for the Teacher," in Reginald Archambault, ed., *John Dewey on Education: Selected Writings* (New York: Random House, 1964).
2. These levels correspond roughly to our three major levels: the preconventional, the conventional, and the principled. Similar levels were propounded by William McDougall, Leonard Hobhouse, and James Mark Baldwin.
3. Jean Piaget, *The Moral Judgment of the Child*, 2nd ed. (Glencoe, Ill.: Free Press, 1948).
4. Piaget's stages correspond to our first three stages: Stage 0 (pre-moral), Stage 1 (heteronomous), and Stage 2 (instrumental reciprocity).
5. Lawrence Kohlberg, "Moral Stages and Moralization: The Cognitive-Developmental Approach," in Thomas Lickona, ed., *Man, Morality, and Society* (New York: Holt, Rinehart and Winston, in press).
6. James Rest, Elliott Turiel, and Lawrence Kohlberg, "Relations Between Level of Moral Judgment and Preference and Comprehension of the Moral Judgment of Others," *Journal of Personality*, vol. 37, 1969, pp. 225–52, and James Rest, "Comprehension, Preference, and Spontaneous Usage in Moral Judgment," in Lawrence Kohlberg, ed., *Recent Research in Moral Development* (New York: Holt, Rinehart and Winston, in preparation).
7. Many adolescents and adults only partially attain the stage of formal operations. They do consider all the actual relations of one thing to another at the same time, but they do not consider all possibilities and form abstract hypotheses. A few do not advance this far, remaining "concrete operational."

8. Richard Krebs and Lawrence Kohlberg, "Moral Judgment and Ego Controls as Determinants of Resistance to Cheating," in Lawrence Kohlberg, ed., *Recent Research*.

9. John Rawls, *A Theory of Justice* (Cambridge, Mass.: Harvard University Press, 1971).

10. Not all freely chosen values or rules are principles, however. Hitler chose the "rule," "exterminate the enemies of the Aryan race," but such a rule is not a universalizable principle.

11. Rawls, *A Theory of Justice.*

12. Lawrence Kohlberg and Donald Elfenbein, "Development of Moral Reasoning and Attitudes Toward Capital Punishment," *American Journal of Orthopsychiatry,* Summer, 1975.

13. Hugh Hartshorne and Mark May, *Studies in the Nature of Character: Studies in Deceit,* vol. 1; *Studies in Service and Self-Control,* vol. 2; *Studies in Organization of Character,* vol. 3 (New York: Macmillan, 1928–30).

14. As an example of the "hidden curriculum," we may cite a second-grade classroom. My son came home from this classroom one day saying he did not want to be "one of the bad boys." Asked "Who are the bad boys?" he replied, "The ones who don't put their books back and get yelled at."

15. Restriction of deliberate value education to the moral may be clarified by our example of the second-grade teacher who made tidying up of books a matter of moral indoctrination. Tidiness is a value, but it is not a moral value. Cheating is a moral issue, intrinsically one of fairness. It involves issues of violation of trust and taking advantage. Failing to tidy the room may under certain conditions be an issue of fairness, when it puts an undue burden on others. If it is handled by the teacher as a matter of cooperation among the group in this sense, it is a legitimate focus of deliberate moral education. If it is not, it simply represents the arbitrary imposition of the teacher's values on the child.

16. The differential action of the principled subjects was determined by two things. First, they were more likely to judge it right to violate authority by sitting in. But second, they were also in general more consistent in engaging in political action according to their judgment. Ninety percent of all Stage 6 subjects thought it right to sit in, and all 90 percent lived up to this belief. Among the Stage 4 subjects, 45 percent thought it right to sit in, but only 33 percent lived up to this belief by acting.

17. No public or private word or deed of Nixon ever rose above Stage 4, the "law and order" stage. His last comments in the White House were of wonderment that the Republican Congress could turn on him after so many Stage 2 exchanges of favors in getting them elected.

18. Bindu Parilch, "A Cross-Cultural Study of Parent-child Moral Judgment," unpublished doctoral dissertation, Harvard University, 1975.

19. Moshe Blatt and Lawrence Kohlberg, "Effects of Classroom Discussions upon Children's Level of Moral Judgment," in Lawrence Kohlberg, ed., *Recent Research*.

20. Lawrence Kohlberg, Peter Scharf, and Joseph Hickey, "The Justice Structure of the Prison: A Theory and an Intervention," *The Prison Journal,* Autumn–Winter, 1972.

21. Lawrence Kohlberg, Kelsey Kauffman, Peter Scharf, and Joseph Hickey, *The Just Community Approach to Corrections: A Manual, Part I* (Cambridge, Mass.: Education Research Foundation, 1973).

22. An example of the need for small-group discussion comes from an alternative school community meeting called because a pair of the students had stolen the school's video-recorder. The resulting majority decision was that the school should buy back the recorder from the culprits through a fence. The teachers could not accept this decision and returned to a more authoritative approach. I believe if the moral reasoning of students urging this solution had been confronted by students at a higher stage, a different decision would have emerged.

*Lawrence Kohlberg* is Professor of Education and Psychology and Director, Center for Moral Education, Graduate School of Education, Harvard University, Cambridge, Massachusetts.

# Now Then, Mr. Kohlberg, About Moral Development in Women . . .

## GERALD W. BRACEY

Carol Gilligan of Harvard University stirred up no small amount of controversy with her book, *In a Different Voice*, which attacked the account of moral development advanced by psychologists from Freud to Lawrence Kohlberg. The June 1984 issue of *Child Development* contains one empirical study and one critical review on the topic.

The empirical study is by John Gibbs, Kevin Arnold, and Jennifer Burkhardt of Ohio State University. They administered the Sociomoral Reflection Measure—a group-administered instrument based on Kohlberg's theories that places people at one of four stages of moral development—to 66 males and 11 females and found no differences. But they did find that women justify their actions more often than men by means of "empathic role taking." Over one-half of the women and about one-fourth of the men used such justifications. The authors argue that these results support Gilligan, not Kohlberg. In their justifications women give greater weight to caring, but, since the instrument used places women at the same level of maturity as the men, this difference is not a sign of inferiority in moral reasoning.

The critical review of sex differences in the development of moral reasoning is by Lawrence Walker of the University of British Columbia. Walker found few differences in the studies he reviewed. He points out that Kohlberg's is "a cognitive theory that deals with the adequacy of justifications for solutions to moral conflicts. It does not speak directly to issues of moral emotions or behaviors, although Kohlberg has admitted the necessity and desirability of going beyond 'cognition.'" The critics of Kohlberg's theory fail to consider its self-imposed limitations.

Rather than argue about the extent to which sex bias is inherent in Kohlberg's theory of moral development, Walker says, it might be "more appropriate to ask why the myth that males are more advanced in moral reasoning than females persists in the light of so little evidence. Perhaps it is time to focus our attention on other concerns, such as questions of the . . . relationship of moral reasoning to moral emotions and behaviors."

Although I find it satisfying that the studies show that women are the moral equals of men, I think the studies miss the point. Gilligan has proposed that ethical judgments in males and females issue from different *premises:* "While an ethic of justice [the male ethic] proceeds from the premise of equality—that everyone should be treated the same—an ethic of care [the female ethic] rests on the premise of nonviolence—that no one should be hurt."

If this be true, it is not possible to discuss the "bias" and "inferiority" of the moral reasoning of either sex, because the judgments cannot be placed on the same scale, cannot be measured by the same instruments. We are talking about different realities. As Gilligan notes, "The failure to see the different reality of

From *Phi Delta Kappan* 66, No. 1 (September 1984): 69. Used by permission of the author and the publisher.

women's lives and to hear the differences in their voices stems in part from the assumption that there is a single mode of experience and interpretation."

*Gerald W. Bracey* is Special Assistant for Policy and Planning, Virginia Department of Education, Richmond.

## ADDITIONAL LEARNING ACTIVITIES

### Problems and Projects

1. Continue to develop a "case problem" about one school you know well. Describe the curriculum and teaching in that school as it may be related to human development. Consider the human development theories presented in this section, and ask whether they are being used or ought to be used in curriculum planning in that school. You can add to your study of this school as you work on each of the bases of the curriculum and the criteria.

2. Visit a program and classrooms in a nursery school, an elementary school, a middle school, and a high school. Note differences in learners that are due to their stages of human development, and determine how the differences affect learning.

3. Visit any classroom in an elementary school, middle school, or high school. Note the differences in development among learners in any one class. How should the differences affect the curriculum and teaching? Differences are most noticeable in groups ranging in age from ten, when the first girl may attain puberty, to sixteen, when the last boy may attain it.

4. Try the preassessment again, examining a different school or curriculum plan in the light of human development theories and research (such as the theories of Havighurst, Erikson, Piaget, or Kohlberg).

5. Review the "five significant trends that differentiate my father's world from my son's" that are presented in "Today's Children Are Different" in this section. Do you agree with the changes in school programs that the authors suggest? Can you suggest other changes based on human development theories that might be helpful with these trends?

6. Several school programs described in later sections of this book have been developed substantially in terms of human development concepts. Read one of the following articles at this time and then list and explain the aspects of the program described which you believe are the result of using human development as a basis for curriculum planning: "The Young Reach Out to the Old in Shaker Heights" (Section 7); "Developing Coeducational Vocational Education Courses" (Section 8); "Problem Solving: Encouraging Active Learning" (Section 7); or "James Madison High: A School for Winners" (Section 9).

7. If a child has been unsuccessful in his or her first three stages of development, according to Erik Erikson's stages of development, what are some of the prob-

lems that the child will have requiring the help of his or her elementary school teachers?

8. According to many leaders in human development, including Erik Erikson, developing a "sense of identity" is the major developmental problem of adolescence. Primitive societies helped the young person with this problem through *rites of passage*—rituals and ceremonies that gave the individual cultural identity. To learn about this read *The Rites of Passage* by Arnold van Gennep (Chicago: University of Chicago Press, 1960). Should schools or other institutions provide more rites of passage for students?

9. Dr. Margaret Mead believed that the lack of a close relationship between grandparents and grandchildren in today's society is a serious loss to society and the child. She expresses these views in her autobiography, *Blackberry Winter* (New York: William Morrow & Co., 1973). She said that children need to grow up with three generations. Do you agree? Why? Will the "adopt a grandparent" program help? (See "The Young Reach Out to the Old in Shaker Heights" in Section 7.)

10. In the January 1982 issue of *Psychology Today* (pp. 58–59), Jerome Bruner comments on a study of London, England, high schools in low socioeconomic areas. The study was conducted by Michael Rutter, a British child psychiatrist who found that "where a school shows that it cares, the students care. They respond with regular attendance, better behavior, and higher academic achievement. Caring and demanding school environments make kids work hard and learn." Compare these statements with Ashley Montagu's statement in this section that the "greatest gift a teacher has to give a student is his or her love." How can a teacher give love to his or her students?

11. Review the article by Bracey in this section and then read Carol Gilligan's "In A Different Voice: Women's Conceptions of Self and Morality," *Harvard Educational Review* 47 (November 1977): 481–517. How would the inclusion of Gilligan's views modify the definition of moral stages as they are described in Kohlberg's article?

12. In his article in this section, Kohlberg briefly describes the Cambridge High School "just community school" and states that the sense of community developed in this alternative school leads to behavior change of a positive sort. For a more adequate description of this school, read "Implementing Kohlberg's 'Just Community Concept' in an Alternative High School" by Elsa R. Wasserman in *Social Education* 40 (April 1976): 203–207. What does Wasserman mean when she refers to the "hidden curriculum"? What does the hidden curriculum have to do with moral development?

13. Bruce Joyce and Marsha Weil describe two developmental models of teaching, one based on Piaget and the other based on Kohlberg. Read pages 105–130 in *Models of Teaching*, second edition, by Joyce and Weil (Prentice-Hall, 1980), reread the articles by Rowland and McGuire and Kohlberg in this section, and then try to develop a plan for a lesson based either on Piaget or Kohlberg.

14. The Appendix of this book includes a list of books, each describing a school or

school program. Select one that interests you and determine whether human development has been adequately considered in planning the curriculum and teaching that is described in the book. You can add to your study of this school's program as you work on each of the bases of the curriculum and the criteria.

15. *Facing Life: Youth and the Family in American History* by Oscar and Mary F. Handlin (Boston: Little, Brown and Co., 1971) traces the patterns of relationship within the American family, spanning three hundred years, and concludes that the continually advancing age at which young people leave home has unfortunate consequences for everyone involved. Look through this book to learn the reasons for this conclusion and decide whether you agree. Share your conclusions with other members of your class.

16. Have your personal beliefs or values changed as a result of your experience with this section? If so, state what change has taken place, and relate it to one or more of the activities in this section (an article, the rationale, a postassessment activity, etc.).

## Films, Cassettes and Filmstrips

*Lawrence Kohlberg on "Education for a Society in Moral Transition."* Audiocassette, 1975. Association for Supervision and Curriculum Development, 225 North Washington Street, Alexandria, Virginia 22314.

*Piaget on Piaget: The Epistemology of Jean Piaget.* 16 mm, color, 42 min., 1977. The only film by Piaget about his own ideas incorporates visual documentation and interpretation of some of his experiments with children. Available in English with subtitles or in French. Yale University Media Design Studio, 305 Crown Street, New Haven, Connecticut 06520.

*Everybody Rides the Carousel* (Parts I, II, and III). 16 mm, color. Each part is 24 min., 1976. A view of the psychological stages of life from the works of Erik H. Erikson. Part I includes stages 1, 2, 3. Part II includes stages 4, 5, 6. Part III includes stages 7 and 8. Everyone rides the carousel and each ride has its brass ring. There are eight rides for the eight stages of life. Pyramid Films, Box 1048, Santa Monica, California 90406.

*Interview with Professor Erik Erikson.* (Part I). (Notable Contributors Series). 16 mm, black and white, 50 min., 1964. Professor Erikson explains his theory of the eight stages of psycho-social development. Crowell, Collier, and Macmillan, 866 Third Avenue, New York, New York 10020.

*Cognition.* 16 mm, color, 30 min., 1975. Examines the development of perception, memory, evaluation, and reasoning from infancy through adolescence. Relates this development to Piaget's four chronologically successive models of intelligence. Harper & Row Media, 10 East 53rd Street, New York, New York 10022.

*Language Development.* 16 mm, color, 24 min., 1975. Shows the remarkable, orderly, and exciting process of language development in the first four years of life. Details the ways in which language is acquired, and how it may be influenced. Harper & Row Media, 10 East 53rd Street, New York, New York 10022.

*Teacher Training in Values Education: A Workshop.* Four filmstrips and four cassettes, 65 min., 1976. Part 1 presents sample moral dilemmas based on Lawrence Kohlberg's theory. In Part 2, Kohlberg explains his theory of moral development and describes his research. In Part 3, Ted Fenton demonstrates how to lead moral discussions. Part 4 presents students and teachers recalling their experiences in leading and participating in group moral discussions. Guidance Associates, 757 Third Avenue, New York, New York 10017.

## Books and Articles to Review

Adams, James F. *Understanding Adolescence: Current Developments in Adolescent Psychology,* 3rd ed. Boston: Allyn and Bacon, 1976.

Arlin, Patricia K. "Cognitive Development in Adulthood: A Fifth Stage?" *Developmental Psychology* 11, no. 5 (September 1975): 602–606.

Casement, William. "Moral Education: Form Without Content?" *Educational Forum* 48, no. 2 (Winter 1984): 177–189.

Clabaugh, Gary K.; Feden, Preston D.; and Vogel, Robert. "Revolutionizing Teacher Education: Training Developmentally Oriented Teachers." *Phi Delta Kappan* 65, no. 9 (May 1984): 615–616.

Conroy, Ann R.; and Burton, John K. "The Trouble With Kohlberg: A Critique." *Educational Forum* 65, no. 1 (November 1980): 43–55.

Elkind, David. *Child Development and Education: A Piagetian Perspective.* New York: Oxford University Press, 1976.

Fuller, Robert G. (ed.) *Piagetian Programs in Higher Education.* Lincoln: 213 Ferguson Hall, University of Nebraska, 1980.

Gilligan, Carol. *Carrying A Feminine Approach to Ethics and Moral Education.* Berkeley: University of California Press, 1984.

——— *In A Different Voice: Psychological Theory and Women's Development.* Cambridge: Harvard University Press, 1982.

Gruber, H. E.; and Voneche, J. J. (eds.) *The Essential Piaget: An Interpretative Reference and Guide.* New York: Basic Books, Inc., Publishers, 1977.

Havighurst, Robert J. *Human Development and Education.* New York: Longmans, Green and Co., 1953. (See also paperback edition published in 1972 by Longman Inc.)

Hersh, R. H.; Paolitto, D. P.; and Reimer, J. *Promoting Moral Growth from Piaget to Kohlberg.* New York: Longman, 1979.

Ilg, Frances L.; Ames, Louise B.; and others. *School Readiness.* New York: Harper and Row, 1978.

Joyce, Bruce R. "Dynamic Disequilibrium: The Intelligence of Growth." *Theory Into Practice* 23, no. 1 (Winter 1984): 26–34.

Kamii, Constance. "Autonomy: The Aim of Education Envisioned by Piaget." *Phi Delta Kappan* 65, no. 6 (February 1984): 410–415.

Kaluger, George; and Kaluger, Meriem Fair. *Human Development: The Span of Life,* 3rd ed. St. Louis: Times Mirror/Mosby College Publishing, 1984.

Kohlberg, Lawrence. *The Philosophy of Moral Development.* New York: Harper and Row, 1981.

Levinson, Daniel J. *The Seasons of a Man's Life.* New York: Alfred A. Knopf, 1978.

Lickona, Thomas (ed.) *Moral Development and Behavior: Theory, Research, and Social Issues.* New York: Holt, Rinehart and Winston, 1976.

Montagu, Ashley. *Growing Young.* New York: McGraw-Hill, 1981.

Overvold, Mark C.; and Konrad, A. Richard. "Moral Reasoning and the Public Schools." *Educational Forum* 47, no. 4 (Summer 1983): 393–409.

Podeschi, Ronald L.; and Podeschi, Phyllis J. "Abraham Maslow: On the Potential of Women." *Educational Horizons* 52, no. 2 (Winter 1973–1974): 61–64.

Postman, Neil. "The Disappearing Child." *Educational Leadership* 40, no. 6 (March 1983): 10–18.

Sheehy, Gail. *Passages.* New York: E. P. Dutton, Inc., 1976.

# 4

# *Learning and Learning Styles*

## PREREQUISITE

Reading Sections 1 through 3.

## RATIONALE

The third and fourth curriculum bases, learning and cognition and knowledge, are closely related. However, because of the extensive nature of the theories and research involved and the ways in which they have influenced curriculum planning, the major learning theories are presented in this section; knowledge and cognition theories and research are presented in Section 5. The major learning theories were, for the most part, all defined in the first half of this century and all exerted influence on the work of curriculum planners at that time. Knowledge and cognition theories have developed further as a result of research in the last twenty-five years and have been acknowledged as the fourth basis for curriculum planning during that time.

The third basis of the curriculum is the nature of learning. An understanding of how learning occurs in human beings is obviously of central importance for planning the curriculum and for teaching.

Today, there are four major families of learning theory. Many subgroupings exist within these families, but curriculum workers or teachers who are seeking to clarify their thinking in this area should be aware of the four major families of theory and base further generalizations on them. Understanding of each of the four families is important for the curriculum planner and teacher, because each group defines the curriculum differently, and each leads to or supports different teaching practices. Thus, curriculum content and organization and teaching practices may be based on *S-R conditioning, the field theories, Freudian theory,* or *social learning theory.* Teaching and curriculum practices may include ideas from each of these families of theories because of the needs of different learners, because there are different kinds of learning, or because there are different kinds of knowledge to be learned.

## The Four Families of Learning Theory

1. *The first learning-theory position stresses stimulus-response association.* It includes all the reinforcement and conditioning theories of learning. The key word in these theories is *experience.* Thinking is a part of an S-R sequence that begins and ends outside the individual learner. Learning is a conditioning process by which a person acquires a new response. Motivation is the urge to act, which results from a stimulus. Behavior is directed by stimuli from the environment. A person selects one response instead of another because of the particular combination of prior conditioning and physiological drives operating at the moment of action. A person does not have to want to learn something in order to learn it. People can learn anything of which they are capable if they will allow themselves to be put through the pattern of activity necessary for conditioning to take place.

The S-R learning theories include theories identified by the following names: stimulus-response; behaviorism; associationist; connectionist; conditioning; reward; pleasure or pain. These theories state that learning takes place through *transfer.* Transfer is defined as "a general term for change in ability to perform a general act as a direct consequence of having performed another act relevant or related to it." It is essential that the *learner* see the relevance. Another definition of transfer is "the gain in mastery of other activities after having obtained mastery in one particular task." Transfer is thought to be brought about by emphasizing *identical elements* in different situations. A major construct of S-R theory is that learning is *rewarded responses.* Another major construct is that teaching should emphasize particular *elements* of the learning tasks.

Each learning theory seeks "basic units" of learning. The basic unit in S-R theories is *rewarded response.* You must reward the response to have learning take place. What is a reward? It is different from instance to instance and from learner to learner. It has to be important to the learner. Reward is often especially useful for certain types of learners: slow-learners, those less prepared for the learning task, and those in need of step-by-step learning.

In "Freedom and the Control of Men," B. F. Skinner describes some of the advantages and possibilities of the S-R approach to learning, as he sees them.* He states that science insists that human actions are initiated by forces impinging upon people from the outside. In turning to external conditions that shape and maintain human behavior, while questioning the reality of inner qualities and faculties, we turn

* See *The American Scholar* 25, no. 1 (Winter 1955–56): 47–65.

from the ill-defined and remote to the observable and manipulable. Science can serve humanitarian aims and can play an important role in making a better world for everyone. Notions about human freedom based on an eighteenth-century political philosophy should not be allowed to interfere with the application of the methods of science to human affairs. In "What Is Behavior Modification?" Madsen and Madsen describe specific teaching practices based on S-R theory. The usefulness and applications of behaviorist theory in curriculum planning and teaching are also discussed in the articles by Avila and Purkey, Gregorc, and McDaniel.

2. *The second of the four learning-theory families important in curriculum planning is "field" theory—the Gestalt-field, cognitive-field, and perceptual-field group of learning theories.* In these theories "wholeness" is primary: one should start with the total aspects of a learning situation and then move to particulars in the light of the whole. Obtaining an "overview" is often important in learning. Without this, frequently we cannot see the forest for the trees.

Another major idea in these theories is that the whole is always greater than the sum of its parts. Experiencing a beautiful musical selection is more than hearing the separate notes; seeing a moving picture is more than the thousands of still pictures that make up the movie. The nature of the whole determines the meaning of the components. These statements imply that individual perceptions determine meaning.

Basic units of learning in the cognitive-perceptual-Gestalt-field learning theories are the *meaningfulness of the whole;* the *importance of generalizations, principles, and organization in learning;* and the *significance of self-concept and personal meaning.* Learning should result in cognitive structures, "anchoring ideas," and "subsumers." A teaching plan should provide "advance organizers" (see the final section of the article by Ausubel in Section 3 on "Organization and Cognitive Development" as well as the article by McDaniel in this section). Cognitive-field learning theory emphasizes personal meaning, generalizations, principles, advance organizers, discovery learning, coding, and superordinate categories. In this section Gregorc emphasizes many of these factors in learning. Important applications of cognitive-field learning theory are found in the next section, The Nature of Knowledge and Cognition. In that section Jerome Bruner, a leading cognitive-field learning theorist, applies generalizations concerning structure, organization, discovery learning, the "connectedness" of knowledge, meaningfulness, and the "problems approach" to curriculum planning (see "Structures in Learning" in Section 5).

Another important field learning theory is the one known as perceptual psychology, phenomenological theory, or self-concept learning theory. In this theory the *self-concept* is central. Behavior and learning are functions of *perception.* What most affects learning are the *meanings* that exist for the individual as a result of his unique perceptions. *Self-concept and personal meaning* are the basic units of learning in this perceptual-field learning theory. This learning theory is represented in this section by Combs, "Some Basic Concepts in Perceptual Psychology." Its importance in guiding curriculum planning and teaching is emphasized in the articles by Gregorc, Avila and Purkey, and McDaniel.

The cognitive-field and perceptual-field learning theories emphasize different factors or basic units in learning, but there is much overlapping between them. In all of the field theories, the individual acts, originates, and thinks, and this is the important source of learning. In the S-R conditioning theory, the individual learns by reacting to external forces.

Gestalt-field is another name for the field learning theories. Gestalt is a term that emphasizes wholeness and means that field theories reject elemental analysis in terms of stimuli and responses as the most significant factors in learning. The meaning of learning cannot be derived from its parts in summation. The whole is greater than the sum of its parts.

3. The third family of learning theories consists of those views of learning that have grown out of the work and ideas of Sigmund Freud as well as his numerous present-day followers. Freudian learning theories are utilized freely and compatibly by the exponents of the S-R associationist, the perceptual-field, and cognitive-field learning positions. It would be a major step forward if a more abstract viewpoint might be found that could successfully incorporate the associationist, the perceptual-field, and the cognitive-field viewpoints, as well as the Freudian.

Basic units of learning in Freudian learning theory include *awareness, which is freedom or self-understanding; identification; and imitation.* The other learning theories make use of these Freudian learning concepts. It is generally recognized that much of what people learn in life they learn by imitating examples they see about them. We all learn to talk, eat, and walk, for example, by imitating other people.

Teachers do not often consciously try to serve as examples or models for learners. But children need the teacher partly to serve as a model for their own behavior. Unfortunately often the actions and aims of the teacher may be inconsistent.

The importance of *self-knowledge* is a basic premise of Freudian psychology. Students should be helped to become aware of their own thoughts and feelings if effective learning is to take place.

4. The three families of learning theories described thus far have been developed by psychologists. *Another way of viewing learning is social learning, which is emphasized by sociologists, anthropologists, and social psychologists.* According to social learning theorists, human beings have unlimited capacity to learn. The actual capacity to learn, however, is confined by social expectations and by limitations in behavior patterns that the immediate social environment considers appropriate. In this vew of learning, *the learning process is primarily social, and learning occurs through socialization.* Socialization is carried on by a variety of social agents including the family, the peer group, the school, the job, and religion. Learning through socialization continues throughout life. *The basic unit of learning is the dyadic relationship,* which refers to a relationship between two people. But it takes a group to make an individual; there is no such thing as a self-made man or woman. Socialization as a way of learning is emphasized by Gerald Grant with John Briggs in Section 3.

In describing how learning occurs, social learning theorists make use of the basic units of learning found in the other families of learning theory: rewarded responses, transfer, self-concept, personal meaning, meaningfulness of the whole, the importance of generalizations and organization, self-understanding, imitation, and identification.

### Using Learning Theories in Curriculum Planning

A number of theorists assist us in seeking ways to use these learning theories together in curriculum planning or as the basis for alternative teaching strategies.

If the learning of a body of knowledge or information is the chief objective of a curriculum plan, then *mastery learning* may provide an excellent set of classroom practices for achieving this goal. Mastery learning is described in this section by James H. Block, one of its leading exponents. As he states in his article, this approach to teaching and learning has created much controversy and excitement. It is a set of individualized instructional practices including group-based/teacher-paced and individually-based/student-paced approaches. The focus is on a body of knowledge, and the purpose is to help virtually all students to "learn excellently." The teaching practices seem to be derived largely from the S-R learning theories. Block and others report a body of evidence to show that mastery learning strategies "work very well indeed."

Avila and Purkey emphasize that the learning theories should be used together in planning. McDaniel asserts that they should be used in "eclectic combination," and he offers five principles that can be used to provide better motivation to learn.

Much of the recent research regarding learning focuses on learning styles and teaching styles. *Learning style* refers to individual typical ways of processing information and seeking meaning. Knowledge of learning style differences among learners opens the possibility of developing teaching approaches compatible with these differences and thus individualizing the teaching-learning process. Teachers also have preferred teaching-learning styles and they are more likely to develop teaching strategies which are congruent with their own learning styles rather than those of their students. Implications and applications of the teaching-learning style research are presented in articles by Gregorc, Friedman and Alley, and Hyman and Rosoff.

Curriculum planners and teachers need many ways to encourage learning. Each learning theory position appears to describe a different kind of learning. There are many individual differences among learners, and the various learning theories support different approaches to curriculum planning to provide for the differences in learners. For instance, slow learners learn differently from gifted learners.

There are different kinds of knowledge and human activities. One learning-theory approach is probably best for teaching mathematics and another for teaching the humanities or the social sciences.

There is active and passive, meaningful and rote, part and whole, individual and social learning. Some learning occurs as a result of outside forces; other learning is the result of inner meaning. Curriculum planners need to know how to encourage each of these kinds of learning in individuals by basing instruction on individual learning styles and needs.

Concepts from each of these learning theories are in use in curriculum planning and teaching today. They include the following:

1. Identification. Children learn by and through identification with others, including their parents, peers, and teachers. Thus, it is important that they have good models.
2. Discovery. Obtaining knowledge for oneself by the use of one's own mind frequently has advantages for motivation, organization of what is learned, retention, and meaningfulness.
3. Empathy. Openness, trust, and security in human relationships provide freedom to intelligence, enabling students as well as teachers to learn more and to be successful in activities in which they are jointly engaged.
4. Culture Potential. Anthropological studies have emphasized that different societies and cultures cultivate different qualities and capacities. Learning experiences that build on the cultural capacities of individuals and groups are particularly successful.
5. Knowledge about Learners. Research has shown that students learn more when teachers know them as individuals.
6. Methods of Increasing Transfer. When the teacher points out the possibility of transfer and develops and applies generalizations with the learner, transfer is more likely to occur.
7. Zeal for Learning and Knowledge. Students learn to like learning from teachers who love knowledge, from communities that provide resources for learning, and from a home environment that supports the search for knowledge by example and by providing materials.

## Curriculum Criteria

Curriculum criteria are guidelines or standards by which decisions can be made in curriculum planning or teaching. What guidelines for planning can be derived from the learning theories and research discussed in this rationale, and in the articles and additional activities in this section? *Individual differences, flexibility,* and *systematic planning* are criteria that depend in part on knowledge of the different approaches to learning. The criterion questions are as follows:

1. Does the curriculum or teaching plan include alternative approaches and alternative activities for learning?
2. Have the different learning theories been considered in planning alternative learning approaches and activities?
3. Has the significance of rewarded responses, transfer, generalization, advance organizers, self-concept, meaningfulness of the whole, personal meaning, imitation, identification, and socialization been considered in planning?
4. Has the significance of individual learning approaches and styles been considered in the planning?

## OBJECTIVES

Your objectives in studying learning theories as one of the bases of curriculum planning should be the following:

1.  To be able to analyze curricula or teaching practices with reference to the learning theories involved.
2.  To be able to suggest changes and improvements in a curriculum or in the planning of teaching based on an understanding of the kinds of learning that are developed most successfully by each of the learning theories.

## PREASSESSMENT

The purpose of the preassessment is to determine whether you already possess the performance competencies in curriculum planning listed under the objectives just mentioned. The following activities will aid you in your evaluation:

1.  Explain how S-R learning theory might be applied to curriculum planning or the planning of teaching to the advantage of the learners involved or the knowledge being taught.
2.  Do the same for cognitive-field, perceptual-field, and social learning theories.
3.  Explain how you might combine these learning theories in planning a curriculum or in teaching.
4.  Select any curriculum plan, at any school level, and examine curriculum or teaching practices in different subjects or by different teachers in the light of learning theories. You could do this by visiting a school and studying curriculum plans and teaching practices or by analyzing a written statement regarding a school's program or the instruction in one classroom.
5.  Suggest improvements or changes in the curriculum plan as a result of your analysis in number 4.

Do not be surprised if learning theories do not appear to be considered in the curriculum planning at the school or in the classroom that you study for number 4. Often they are not. Suggest improvements in the planning of curriculum or instruction at that school in the light of the various learning theories. Knowledge and use of the learning theories in planning offer important guidelines in providing for individual differences and instructional alternatives. Remember that there are different kinds of learners, different kinds of learning, and different kinds of knowledge. Each can be the basis of significant decisions or alternatives provided for in curriculum and instruction planning.

In answering number 4, you might choose to analyze either one of two articles in Section 7 in terms of the learning theories presented in this section: "Research,

Reading Instruction, and Children's Learning of the First R" or "Problem Solving: Encouraging Active Learning."

## LEARNING ACTIVITIES

The articles in this section will assist you in identifying and understanding the various learning theories and how they may be applied to advantage in curriculum planning and in teaching. Other learning activities are suggested at the end of this section.

## POSTASSESSMENT

After attempting the preassessment you may do *one or more* of the following:

1. See if your instructor believes that you are ready for a postassessment evaluation on learning theories and the curriculum. Most students will need further work on this curriculum base.
2. Read articles on learning in this section, and try to determine how theories and research discussed in each article should be considered in curriculum planning and teaching.
3. Choose additional activities and readings or films and videotapes from those listed at the end of this section.
4. Look for other films, books, or articles on learning in your library or media center.
5. Discuss the reading you have done and the films you have viewed with your fellow students. The key questions: How should the learning theories you've studied affect a school's curriculum? How should they be considered in planning for teaching?
6. When you are ready, ask your instructor for advice on a suitable postassessment for you for this topic. Satisfactory completion of number 1 under Problems and Projects at the end of this section might be one possibility, or satisfactory written completion of the preassessment for this section, after completing other learning activities, might be a satisfactory postassessement. Consult your instructor about this.

# A Primer on Motivation: Principles Old and New

## THOMAS R. McDANIEL

What does a teacher need to do to motivate today's students to learn? Fifty years ago the topic of motivation was virtually ignored in teacher education programs. Teachers of that day were told to "have a good lesson plan," "be enthusiastic," and "use grades and prizes" to stimulate interest.

Later, the behaviorists developed and promoted some techniques of "extrinsic motivation" that were derived from reinforcement theory. Many of these techniques found their way into schools in the form of behavior modification programs, most notably in special education classrooms. Later still, humanistic educators and psychologists—Carl Rogers, Abraham Maslow, Rudolf Dreikurs, and others—told teachers to focus on "intrinsic motivation": developing self-concept, meeting individual needs, and encouraging student progress.

Today we are asked to improve classroom climate, mediate transactions, and invite school success. The contemporary teacher is likely to be confused and not a little daunted by the number of motivational techniques recommended for the classroom.

And it is not just that we have more theories now, either; we also ascribe more importance to them. The newfound interest in teacher and school effectiveness, the public concern for higher achievement test scores, and the social problems—discipline, drugs, dropouts—of both the community and the school all contribute to new demands that teachers and their classrooms be more motivating. How can schools expect higher productivity and achievement un-

less students *somehow* become more interested in and committed to their own educational improvement? This is the essential challenge of instructional motivation, and the challenge is one that confronts the overburdened classroom teacher daily. So what's a teacher to do?

Motivation is complex and controversial, but it is also a crucial element in instructional success. Why a student will "move" toward instructional goals and how to maximize that movement are questions that arise in every classroom in every school and are resolved—for good or ill—by individual teachers. Nonetheless, there appears to be an emerging set of principles to guide teacher behaviors related to effective instructional motivation. Of course, principles are no better than the teachers who put them into practice, but I present the following five principles as an eclectic combination of techniques—traditional and modern, practical and theoretical, pedagogical and psychological—that teachers *can* use to produce better motivation. Although in reality these principles are closely connected, even interrelated, each focuses on a given aspect of the teacher's role as motivator.

**1.** *Inviting success.* This motivational principle, named by William Purkey, expresses a humanistic notion that students behave in accordance with a teacher's *perception* of their ability. An invitation, says Purkey in *Inviting School Success,* "is a summary description of messages—verbal and nonverbal, formal and informal—continuously transmitted to students with the intention of informing them that they are responsible, able, and valuable."[1] A major premise

From *Phi Delta Kappan* 66, No. 1 (September 1984): 46–49. Used by permission of the author and the publisher.

from which this view of motivation is derived is that positive self-concept is the key to student motivation to learn.

The principle of inviting success is a foundational for several of the other principles of motivation listed below, but it is of special value as the expression of an attitude that effective motivators demonstrate in their relationships with children—an attitude that says in word and deed, "I care about you, I trust you, I know you are somebody, I know you can learn." How much faith do you have in your students? Can you develop and demonstrate more?

More specifically, a teacher should examine words and actions that might be obstacles to motivation. Do you let previous records, horror stories from other teachers, or ability grouping influence your confidence in your students' capacity to learn? Do you slip into sarcasm or ridicule? Do you find yourself continually using such negative terms as "no," "stop," and "don't"? The principle of inviting success asks you to change your perceptions and attitude so that you can bid students to become the trustworthy, capable human beings you *know* they can be.

Invitational techniques include being explicit in sending invitations, talking directly to students and using their names frequently, giving all students your attention and time, reserving time for one-on-one contact with students, listening with care and respect, providing more opportunities for students to talk and participate in class, developing class spirit, letting students know they are missed, using student experts whenever possible, and promoting cooperation.

**2.** *Cooperative learning.* Competition has long been honored and practiced as a means of motivating learning by way of games, contests, incentives, and rewards. But teachers can also motivate students by cooperative strategies. Cooperation can often reach those youngsters who lose in competitions. Indeed, our public schools may have inadvertantly created a large number of "losers" by overemphasizing competition. Students who make no teams, win no prizes, and earn no rewards for superior performance may conclude that they have few reasons for continued effort in the classroom. At the very least, schools should consider ways of balancing the competitive ethos—which the "excellence movement" is likely to exacerbate—with cooperative activities designed to enhance the motivation of noncompetitive students.

At the Cooperative Learning Center at the University of Minnesota, David Johnson, Roger Johnson, and their colleagues have developed a variety of cooperative learning strategies described in such books as *Learning Together and Alone, Joining Together,* and *Circles of Learning.*[2] These researchers contend that "teachers must be prepared to teach needed collaborative skills in order for cooperative learning to be productive."[3] Cooperative learning requires that teachers group students heterogeneously and structure goals to promote positive interdependence of members; teachers must promote shared responsibility for leadership *and* learning; they must directly teach such social skills as leadership behavior, communication, and conflict management; and they must analyze and evaluate for the groups of students the process being used to solve problems and share work.

This motivational principle works because it promotes higher levels of self-esteem while also promoting "belongingness." The teacher needs to set clear goals, explain the criteria for success, structure the group for individual (as well as group) accountability, monitor the process and intervene when necessary, and provide directions for the task. In addition to the product of the group's work, the teacher must pay attention to the process, especially by allowing groups to evaluate their own effectiveness. When students learn the joy of working productively together toward common goals, motivation inevitably improves.

**3.** *High expectations.* Much of the research on

school effectiveness points to the importance of high expectations for students. The principle of inviting success depends on high expectations, and the cooperative learning principle suggests that teachers should expect students to accomplish important affective learning while meeting academic goals. But the principle of high expectations is more far-reaching. It addresses the importance of self-fulfilling prophecies and of teacher behaviors that communicate high expectations.

Sad to say, negative expectations abound in classrooms, especially in classrooms filled with low-achieving students. Current research shows that teachers generally seat low-ability students farther away from themselves, call on low-ability students less often, pay less attention to low-ability students, give low-ability students less time and fewer clues for answering questions, criticize wrong answers from low-ability students more often and praise their correct responses less often, and interrupt the performance of low-ability students more often. Such behaviors communicate lower expectations, less tolerance, and even less affection for low-ability students than for their high-ability classmates. Consequently, the students create negative self-fulfilling prophecies that lead them to become less confident, more passive or more disruptive, and less motivated to work up to their capacity.

The first step in helping *all* students to meet high expectations is to analyze seating assignments, interaction patterns, and teaching practices to identify and correct any negative behaviors. Next, a teacher might examine classroom rules. Do they include long lists (more than five) of negative behaviors that are not allowed? Or do they focus on positive behaviors that are expected? Negative rules convey implicitly the teacher's assumption that, say, fighting, cheating, talking, destroying property, and cursing *will* occur if not prohibited. Positive rules— "walk quietly in the halls," "keep your work space clean," and so on—convey *positive* expectations.

In the academic area teachers can direct students toward future success. Instead of criticizing mistakes, look for what is good in a student's work. To help students see the potential for growth, use positive suggestions, such as, "I expect that, with practice, your multiplication will improve each day."

Teachers must also set clear and explicit goals for student learning each day. These goals should be challenging but not *too* difficult. Teachers should communicate these goals as expectations and let students know that—though the work ahead may be difficult—they *can* achieve.

**4.** *Set induction.* This principle relates to teacher behaviors designed to induce "readiness to learn" in students. Instructional motivation depends on a teacher's skill in getting students to attend to the objectives, skills, knowledge, and values that constitute any given lesson. The old saying goes, "You can lead a horse to water, but you can't make him drink." Motivation by set induction says, "Yes, but you can put salt in the oats!" Set induction can be accomplished by a variety of "focusing events" or "advance organizers" (to borrow David Ausubel's term). The idea is to prepare students for learning by grabbing their attention with an activity that is arresting and relevant (to the lesson *and* to the students' experience).

Consider a few specific techniques. A teacher can begin a lesson with a perplexing question that leaves students intrigued. For example, "If rain falls out of clouds, why don't clouds fall too?" Or (to set up a lesson in grammar), "What would happen if we eliminated all verbs from the English language?" Such questions can establish a state of disequilibrium, a state of tension that motivates students to resolve a problem or dilemma. Whenever we confront students with questions or problems that depart from their experience, we motivate them to relieve the disequilibrium.

Another application of this principle can be found in special objects and activities that focus students on the concepts to be studied. For example, a teacher might hold up a knotted rope before beginning a lesson on the umbilical cord or a faded rose before discussing the theme of "lost beauty." Such objects can be stimuli for questions or brainstorming. Or a teacher could ask students to speculate on why a mechanical bird balanced on the edge of a glass of water magically dips to "drink" from the glass from time to time; all hypotheses could be recorded on the board.

More elaborate applications of set induction could include longer activities that start where the students are but connect to the lesson content. To motivate students for a lesson on slavery before the Civil War, a teacher might begin to discriminate against the blue-eyed (or short or left-handed) children in the class, requiring them to do extra homework, sit in the back of the room, be dismissed last, and so on. Or, in preparation for a lesson on the Plains Indians, a teacher might show a slide depicting an Indian and give students one minute to observe everything they can. Afterward, the teacher could ask whether the Indian had a weapon or what markings were on the Indian's left arm. Inference questions could follow, such as "Was the Indian angry? How do you know? What caused him to be angry?" This in turn could lead to reading a chapter in a history book for the purpose of generating additional answers to these questions. Set induction provides structure, direction, and relevance that together pique curiosity and promote motivation to learn.

**5.** *Interaction.* How can a teacher ask questions and handle responses in ways that increase involvement, participation, interest, and thinking? Teachers who are good motivators know that their interactions and transactions with students are central to a successful lesson. Such teachers enjoy classroom discussion, use humor, draw on personal experiences (theirs and the students'), keep open minds, invite students to teach the teacher, keep a lively pace, and demonstrate genuine enthusiasm. But beyond

these general behaviors, they also give special attention to the kinds of questions they ask students and the kinds of strategies they employ when students answer (or don't answer) a question.

Consider questioning techniques. For an invitational teacher, the basic purpose of questioning is to give students every opportunity possible to show what they know, think, and value. Students quickly lose interest when they discover that questions are designed to find out what they do *not* know and call for convergent responses that will be immediately judged. Motivating questions usually involve little risk for the responders and allow many acceptable answers. Some questions—such as "Let's see who forgot to read the homework assignment. Joe, can you define a prime number?"—tend to be high risk, convergent, and threatening. On the other hand, a question such as "I know you found the assignment on prime numbers interesting and difficult. I wonder if anyone can give us one example of a prime number—Joe?" has a much better chance of motivating a response.

One key to handling student responses successfully is "wait time." A teacher who thoughtfully waits three to five seconds (the average wait time is about *one* second) can expect more answers, longer answers, and better-reasoned answers. Another valuable technique is to ask some questions that even the teacher cannot answer. (It is ironic that teachers who *know* answers ask questions of students who do not.) When possible, suspend judgment on responses by securing several responses before commenting or by saying, "Tell me more about that." Always judging responses and giving too much praise—especially in higher-ability classes—have negative effects on interaction and the response rate. Using questions as a means of increasing motivation requires teachers to develop the skills of divergent and higher-order questioning and the skills of redirecting and suspending judgment.

There is more to good motivation than most teachers believe. Indeed, these few principles and tricks of the trade are but one part of the art of instructional motivation. Teachers can learn how to personalize instruction (using names more frequently, greeting students as they enter the room, using personal examples as a basis for learning); they can learn how to use small-group instruction more effectively, how to capitalize on what students already know, how to end every lesson on a positive note, how to individualize better and provide greater choice, how to use unfinished activity, and how to build interest in the curriculum itself. All of these principles, strategies, and techniques have a place in the repertoire of a teacher who has learned to motivate students for success. Effective teachers use their motivational skills to develop a positive climate that nurtures the educational growth of children. Are *you* skilled in the basics of instructional motivation?

## ENDNOTES

1. William Purkey, *Inviting School Success: A Self-Concept Approach to Teaching and Learning* (Belmont, Calif.: Wadsworth, 1978), p. 3.
2. David W. Johnson and Roger T. Johnson, *Learning Together and Alone: Cooperation, Competition, and Individualization.* (Englewood Cliffs, N.J.: Prentice-Hall, 1975); idem, *Joining Together: Group Theory and Group Skills* (Englewood Cliffs, N.J.: Prentice-Hall, 1982); and David W. Johnson, Roger T. Johnson, Edith Johnson Holubec, and Patricia Roy, *Circles of Learning: Cooperation in the Classroom* (Alexandria, Va.: Association for Supervision and Curriculum Development, 1984).
3. Johnson et al., p. v.

*Thomas R. McDaniel* is Charles A. Dana Professor of Education and Chair, Department of Education, Converse College, Spartanburg, South Carolina.

# Some Basic Concepts in Perceptual Psychology
## ARTHUR W. COMBS

Perceptual psychology is one expression of the great humanistic movement which seems to me to be going on, not only in psychology, but in all of the social sciences and in human affairs generally. Abe Maslow has called this movement in psychology "Third Force" psychology. Perceptual psychology it seems to me is one of the expressions of that force in operation. It is a humanistic, phenomenological, personalistic, existential view of behavior which sees man engaged in a continuous process of being and becoming.

There are two frames of reference for looking at human behavior available to us. One of these is the external or objective approach familiar to most of us as the traditional view of American psychology. Seen from this frame of reference, behavior is described from the point of view of the outside observer, someone looking on at the process. Its classic expression is to be found in

From an address presented at the American Personnel and Guidance Association, 1965. Used by permission of the author.

the various forms of stimulus-response psychology which seeks the explanation of behavior in the observable forces exerted upon the individual. The perceptual psychologist takes a different view. He seeks to understand the behavior of people from the point of view of the behaver himself. His is a phenomenological understanding of human behavior, emphasizing the meaning of events to the person.

Perceptual psychology is basically a field theory and its primary principle is this: *All behavior, without exception, is a function of the behaver's perceptual field at the instant of behaving.* I am using the term perceptual here in its broadest sense as practically synonymous with meaning. Thus, the individual's behavior is seen as the direct consequence, not of the fact or stimulus with which he is confronted, but the meaning of events in his peculiar economy. That people behave according to how things seem to them seems a simple enough proposition. Each of us as he looks at his own behavior can observe that it is true for him. Self-evident as this proposition seems at first glance, however, its ramifications for human interaction are tremendous and its implications for a theory of behavior calls for an entire new psychology. It provides us with a new frame of reference for dealing with some of our most difficult problems. Perceptual psychology is not a denial of former psychologies, let me hasten to say. Rather, it provides us with an additional explanation of particular value to practitioners and to those of us who are confronted with the practical problems of dealing with people, not as subjects of an experiment but as striving, seeking human beings. It does not deny what we have known before. It extends beyond to give us a new string to our bow.

When the perceptual psychologist speaks of the perceptual field he is referring to all those perceptions existing for the individual at the moment of behaving. This includes all aspects of his awareness, not only those perceptions in clear figure which the person may be able to tell us about but, also, those perceptions he has at lower levels of differentiation which he may be incapable of describing. Freud used the terms "conscious" and "unconscious" to describe these levels of awareness. Such designations, however, seem to give the impression of a clear cut dichotomy so the perceptual psychologist prefers to speak of levels of awareness instead. This is a point often misunderstood by some critics of perceptual psychology who have equated "awareness" with "conscious." They have assumed that the term perception referred only to those events the individual was able to report on demand. Such a point of view should make perceptual psychology extraordinarily naive! To understand the behavior of the individual the perceptual psychologist says, it is necessary for us to understand the field of meaning or perceptions existing for him at the instant of his behavior. This includes *all* perceptions from those in clearest and sharpest figure to those so deeply imbedded in the ground of the field as to be quite unreportable.

If behavior is a function of perception, it follows that to understand behavior it will be necessary to study the factors influencing perception in the individual. Some of the variables affecting perception with which the perceptual psychologist is concerned are familiar to all of us from more orthodox psychologies. Among these are:

1. *The Effect of the Physical Organism.* Perception depends upon the possession of the necessary equipment to make it possible. One must have eyes to see, ears to hear, olfactory organs to smell and so on.
2. *The Effect of Time.* Perception takes time. What is perceived is dependent upon the time of exposure and the length of time one has lived in the world.
3. *The Effect of Opportunity or Environment.* Perceptions are learned. To perceive one must have had the opportunity to experience the

events that make them possible. Eskimos do not normally comprehend bananas, nor Hottentots, snow. What meanings exist for the individual are a consequence of his unique experience in the process of his growing up.

These effects of the physical organism, time and opportunity have long been considered in traditional psychology. They are equally important for the perceptual approach. But perceptual psychology adds some additional variables to the picture among the most important of which is the self-concept.

## THE SELF-CONCEPT

Of all the perceptions existing in the perceptual or phenomenal field those pertaining to the individual's self play a crucial role. How a person behaves at any moment is always a result of two kinds of perceptions; how he sees the situation he is in and how he sees himself. By the self-concept is meant all those aspects of the perceptual field to which we refer when we say "I" or "me." It is that organization of perceptions about self or awareness of self which seems to the individual to be who he is. It is composed of thousands of perceptions about self varying in clarity, precision and importance in the individual's peculiar economy. Taken all together these concepts of self are described by the perceptual psychologist as the self-concept.

The more we study the self-concept, the more it becomes apparent how crucial it is to any understanding of behavior. It is at the very center of the individual's personal organization and the frame of reference for his every act. The self-concept is learned especially from the experience of the individual with the significant people in his world in the course of growing up. It is both product and process.

The self-concept is the product of past experience but, once established, exerts its influence on the behavior of its possessor ever after. It is apparent that we have but barely scratched the surface of the full implications of the self-concept for every aspect of human existence. Educators, for example, have discovered that faulty self-concepts are often responsible for children's failures in basic school subjects, like reading, spelling, arithmetic and language. Modern counseling theory holds that the practice of counseling is primarily a problem in self-exploration. Adjustment and maladjustment turn out on examination to be largely questions of healthy or faulty self-concepts. The role of the self-concept is equally important in social psychology. Recent work with the mentally retarded and the culturally deprived even seems to indicate that the self-concept is basic to intelligence and human capacity.

Since the self-concept is learned as a consequence of experience, it can therefore presumably be taught. The implications of this idea have vast importance for education, counseling, social work, and all of the helping professions. It provides the basis for a belief that programs aimed at the defeat of poverty and human degradation have a chance for success.

In recent years the self-concept has become one of the most popular topics for research even for some psychologists who would rather be caught dead than described as perceptualists. Researches on the self-concept now number in the hundreds. Dozens more are completed every week. Many of these, unfortunately, are mislabeled self-concept studies when they are nothing of the kind. Most of them turn out on closer examination to be studies of the self-report which is not the same thing at all. The self-concept is what a person perceives himself to be, it is what he *believes* about himself. The self-report, on the other hand, is what a person is willing, able, or can be tricked into *saying* about himself when he is asked to do so. The assumption that these two concepts are synonymous is naive and represents a return to introspection, which psychology gave up sixty years ago. The basic research technique of perceptual psychology is inference. Introspection is no more acceptable to perceptual approaches than to more orthodox psychologies.

Despite the confusion currently existing in the research on the self, it is apparent that this concept is an extraordinarily useful device for understanding behavior. It makes it possible for us to deal much more effectively with many problems we have not adequately understood before. Among the most exciting aspects of self-concept theory, for me, are those having to do with self-fulfillment, self-realization or actualization. In these ideas we have new definitions of what it means to be well adjusted. These descriptions are not couched in terms of bell-shaped curves in which the well adjusted turn out to be average. It describes them in terms of what it means to be truly living to the fullest of one's potentialities. Better still, these concepts do not simply tell us what such fortunate people are like, they point the way to what we must do to get about the business of producing more of them! In this respect they set the goals for counseling, teaching, social action, and all of the helping professions, for whatever we decide is what man can become, must automatically become the goal of all our institutions.

For example, one of the things we have been finding out about self-actualizing people is that they tend to see themselves in essentially positive ways. They believe they are basically liked, wanted, acceptable, able, dignified, worthy and the like. Psychologically sick people on the other hand see themselves as unliked, unwanted, unacceptable, unworthy and so on. It follows if this is true that the helping professions must find ways of helping clients, students, patients, or colleagues to feel more positively about themselves. Furthermore, since perceptions are learned from experience, it points the way to what we need to do to help other people to greater health and productivity; clearly, it is necessary to provide

them with experiences which will help them feel more positively about self. And the ways to do this are almost self-evident. They are suggested by the very descriptions of self-actualization:

- How can a person feel liked unless somebody likes him?
- How can a person feel acceptable unless somewhere he is accepted?
- How can a person feel he has dignity unless someone treats him so?
- How can a person feel able unless somewhere he has some success?

In the answers to these simple questions lie the guidelines to the conditions for teaching, therapy, social action, supervision and the encouragement of growth and development everywhere.

## THE PERCEPTUAL VIEW OF MOTIVES

If behavior is seen as a function of the perception of self and the world in perceptual psychology, what, then, provides the motive force? For perceptual psychology this is a given. The characteristic of all things to maintain organization finds its expression in human beings in an insatiable need for the maintenance and enhancement of the self; not the physical self—but the phenomenal self, the self of which the individual is aware, his self-concept.

All human beings are seen as continuously engaged in a search for self-actualization or self-fulfillment, even, sometimes, at the cost of destruction of the physical body itself. The drive for self-fulfillment provides the motive power for behavior. It finds its expression through goals which seem to the individual from time to time, to provide the means for actualization. This basic drive for maintenance expressed physically is the drive on which the physician depends to restore his patient to health. Physiologically it has been called the drive to health, the wisdom of the body, etc. Psychologically, it provides the motive power for human growth and development, recovery from psychological illness and the stretch for human achievement.

In the light of this drive, the problem of motivation disappears for the perceptual psychologist, for people are always motivated. Indeed, they are never unmotivated! The motive is always there in the individual's search for the maintenance and enhancement of self. He always does what it seems to him he needs to from his point of view. The problem of motivation as we have usually conceived it is an external problem concerned with the question of how to get somebody else to do something we would like him to do.

Such a view of motivation as I have been describing leads to quite different approaches to dealing with people than those of traditional S-R psychologies. A stimulus-response psychology calls for methods of changing behavior based upon techniques of force, coercion, reward, punishment, or some form of manipulation. The perceptual view of human need places both helper and helpee on the same team. Both are seeking the optimum development of the helpee and the problem is one of facilitation, encouragement and the freeing of forces already in existence to operate at maximum strength. This is a conception of the nature of man basic to some of the most promising conceptions of human interaction, in counseling, education, social work, medicine, nursing and the practice of the clergy. It lends itself to a hopeful view of man concerned with being and becoming and the basic democratic belief that when men are free they can find their own best ways.

In summary, then, the perceptual psychologist attempts to understand behavior from the point of view of the behaver rather than the outsider. He sees the individual behaving in terms of the peculiar field of personal meanings or perceptions existing for him at the moment of acting and motivated by the person's own need for self-fulfillment. In the light of this interpretation, human failures are mostly understood as problems in faulty perception of self, others, and the world. The reasons for faulty perceptions may lie in the world but far more often lie in the individual himself. This means that persons engaged in human relations activities, whatever their nature, as supervisors, administrators, parents, counselors, teachers, social workers, nurses, or whatever are likely to be successful in the degree to which they understand the perceptual worlds of those they seek to work with and become skillful in helping others to change their perceptions of themselves and their surroundings.

There is even evidence lately to suggest that the essence of successful professional work is itself a matter of the use of the self as an effective instrument rather than a question of methods or information.

But whether or not a worker is able to use himself as an instrument well in the helping professions is also a function of the helper's own perceptions.

In a series of researches we have been carrying on at the University of Florida, we have been finding that the success of various kinds of "helpers" is a function of their perceptual organization. Hundreds of previous researches on good teaching and counseling have been unable to find clear cut differences between good practitioners and poor ones either on the basis of the knowledge they possess or the methods they use. Nevertheless in four studies to date, we have been able to show clear cut differences between "good" helpers and "poor" ones in the ways these workers typically perceive themselves, their clients and their purposes. What is more, this difference obtains in all three groups we have so far investigated: teachers, counselors and episcopal priests!

One of the most exciting contributions of

perceptual psychology, in my experience, is its provision of an immediate frame of reference for understanding behavior to add to the historical one we have lived with so long. Let me clarify what I mean.

Stimulus-response psychology originally taught us that human behavior was a consequence of the stimulus and so we were led to look for the causes of behavior in the force exerted on the individual. Freud and his students added to this concept by expanding the notion of the stimulus to include all those stimuli to which the individual had been subjected in the course of his growing up. This led us to seek for the causes of behavior in the person's past. Accordingly, for several generations now we have been almost exclusively preoccupied with the nature of behavior as seen from this historical frame of reference. Such a point of view about human behavior has been immensely useful to us in providing guidelines for the construction of programs, social action, and a thousand other applications. But a historic point of view about behavior is essentially descriptive. It tells us how an individual got like this, but frequently offers the practitioner very little in the way of clues as to what to do about it. In Freud's own use, of course, it led to a method of psychotherapy which required digging about in the patient's past history in search of an understanding of causes that was often more helpful to the psychologist than to the patient. For several generations we have been so preoccupied with this historical view as to hardly recognize that any other existed. This is particularly true of professional workers charged with the responsibility of helping the adjustment of others. Unhappily, the historic view of causation has often been more useful for diagnosis than for treatment.

In my own practice of psychotherapy, for example, I find that the clients I have who spend long hours exploring their past, are almost exclusively graduate students in psychology! They have thoroughly learned that their behavior is the function of their past so, when they come for help, they engage in its exploration. Sooner or later, however, they arrive at the conclusion "Well now I *know why* I feel like I do" but almost at once this statement is followed by "But darn it all, I still feel that way!"

Perceptual psychology provides us with a much more adequate treatment orientation. In addition to understanding how the individual got the way he is, it provides us with an understanding of the present dynamics from which we may more adequately derive effective methods of teaching, counseling, persuasion, and solutions to human interaction of many sorts. Perceptual psychology provides us with another frame of reference which makes it possible to deal with behavior in the present.

Perceptions exist in the present. If behavior is a function of perception, then it should be possible to modify behavior by changing perceptions in the present. Thus, it may be possible to help an individual to better adjustment even if we do not have any knowledge of his past whatever! For many psychologists this is a startling, shocking, almost irresponsible, idea. For many non-psychologists, however, it is good news and comes as a great refreshing breeze. It means that teachers, administrators, counselors, social workers and parents who have to deal with human behavior because their roles demand it can hope to do so with some chance of success without the necessity for being skilled psychologists. It means that if such people can become sensitive enough to how their charges are perceiving and feeling they can find effective ways of being helpful. A teacher who understands that a child feels unliked, unwanted, unacceptable and unable can do things to help such a child even without a knowledge of how he got to feel this way. If this seems to anyone to lessen the importance of psychologists, it should not. The purpose of psychology is not, after all, to run the world. It is to help provide the understandings so that others whose job it is can learn to do it better.

The immediate frame of reference, of course, is not a new conception in the field of practice, for beginning with Carl Rogers' early work with client-centered therapy and running through all of the new psychotherapies we have seen in the past twenty years, all are predicated on the notion that it is possible to help clients, even without full knowledge of the past. What perceptual psychology does for us is to provide a theoretical framework which explains why this is so, and thus provides us with a valuable new tool for the understanding of behavior to add to those which traditional psychology has provided us in the past.

Many of the principles of perceptual psychology are deceptively simple. They have an "of course" feeling about them and often fit one's own experience so closely as to seem like one has always known them. This is very upsetting to some psychologists who feel it can't be accurate if it is that simple. Yet, it is necessary to remind ourselves that simplicity is the *goal* of science. What could be simpler, for example, than the physical formula $E = mc^2$? Furthermore, the simple, and the "obvious" can have vast implications. Take, for example, the simple fact that reality for each individual lies, not in the outside world, but in his own perceptions. This principle is basic to the problems of communication and human misunderstandings everywhere. People just do not behave according to the "facts" as others see them. They behave in terms of what seems so to them. So we pass each other like ships in the night—not only as individuals but as nations as well.

Perceptual psychology is especially valuable as a practitioner's psychology. It is particularly pertinent to the problems of individual behavior with which the teacher, counselor, social worker, supervisor and therapist must deal. It is particularly appropriate to the helping professions and fits the needs of such workers like hand and glove.

As I indicated at the start of this paper I regard perceptual psychology as a basic expression of the great humanistic, phenomenological, existential movement currently sweeping the social sciences. When Donald Snygg and I stumbled on these concepts twenty years ago, we were certain a perceptual psychology was inevitable. Since then we have attempted to set down in two editions of *Individual Behavior,* a systematic framework for a comprehensive perceptual psychology. The response to that effort has been deeply gratifying and has strengthened the hope we expressed in the preface of the first edition that, "as fallible human beings we can only hope that this is if not the truth, then very like the truth."

*Arthur W. Combs* is Distinguished Professor, University of Northern Colorado, Greeley.

# What Is Behavior Modification?

## CLIFFORD K. MADSEN AND CHARLES H. MADSEN, JR.

Stripped to basics, behavior modification means changing behavior by rewarding the kind you want to encourage and ignoring or disapproving the kind you want to discourage. Used with understanding, it is an effective, caring way to control behavior in school.

When we talk about controlling behavior, most teachers think first of the noisy, disruptive child. Behavior modification is useful for such children, but its use is not limited to them; it is for all behaviors of all children. The story of Paul, however, illustrates most behavior modification principles.

Paul yelled, scuffled, pinched, fidgeted, and drummed his heels all day. He seldom concentrated on anything, much less his schoolwork. Scolding, extra attention, acting disappointed, had short-lived results.

In desperation, his teacher Miss Starr decided to try behavior modification. She first needed to find out how many disturbances Paul made in a day. Ticking them off on a sheet of paper, she counted twenty-three incidents, which averaged about one every fifteen minutes. She did this for several days.

Miss Starr knew Paul liked to use the tape recorder more than anything else. "Paul," she said, "Fifteen minutes shouldn't be too long for you to behave. For every fifteen minutes that you pay attention to what you are doing and don't disturb other children at work, I'll let you use the tape recorder for one minute at the end of the day. You can earn up to fifteen minutes of using the tape recorder all by yourself. If you don't earn any time, you can't use it at all. I'll set the timer every fifteen minutes." She made sure Paul had tasks he could do if he tried and that he understood them. She also checked often to see if he was on the right track, and made sure that he knew his efforts were appreciated.

The next day Paul earned seven minutes with the tape recorder. This meant he'd spent an unprecedented hour and three quarters doing his work! Miss Starr resolutely waited out the other outbursts, saying and doing nothing. Once or twice she sharply reminded him, "Paul, you've just lost another minute!" Her judgments between acceptable and nonacceptable behavior were somewhat lenient at first.

It wasn't long before Paul's disturbances became fewer and less intense. The interval was lengthened first to a half hour, then to an hour. One day Paul said, "I want to use the tape recorder for a project. Do I still need to earn the time?" "*Do you need to?*" asked Miss Starr. Paul grinned and said, "I'll let you know if I do!" Paul remained an excitable child, but his behavior now consistently stayed well within the normal classroom range.

Paul's teacher knew that behavioral scientists believe that all behavior is learned, and that it is learned as a consequence of being associated with a pleasant experience. Paul's behavior was the only way he knew to earn something of value to him, probably simple attention. Where and when he had made this unfortunate association of behavior/reward was not important. His behavior didn't cause the problem; it was the problem. Miss Starr didn't try to change his attitude. She worked with an observable piece of behavior that needed to be changed. She didn't try to change Paul's basic personality. She could and did help Paul learn to control his actions so he and his classmates could settle down to their job of learning.

From *Instructor* 81, no. 2 (October 1971), 47, 49, 53–56. Used by permission of the authors and the publisher.

This teacher went through four steps of behavior modification, which can be boiled down to one word each: (1) pinpoint; (2) record; (3) consequate (set up consequences for); and (4) evaluate. She also made use of the learning steps of experience, discrimination, and association. First she structured the situation so Paul would experience good behavior, then so he would learn to discriminate his behavior, and finally to associate his appropriate behavior with reward. The task was geared to allow him success, and the reward was paired with signs of approval. Soon he could give up the extrinsic reward and function in the regular classroom reward system.

The techniques of behavior modification, also called "reinforcement theory" and other names as well, are highly efficient. Based mainly on the work of B. F. Skinner, they have a simple, scientific cause-and-effect basis that has been used with dramatic results in teaching, overcoming learning disabilities, behavioral research, and clinical psychology.

This dependable relationship of cause and effect makes it possible for a behavioral scientist, given time for observation, to break down and classify any behavior that he can observe, directly or indirectly. Behavior, as he uses the word, means anything a person does, says, or even thinks as long as his thinking is manifested in action. It includes *all* behaviors: emotional responses, attitudes, reading, doing math, looking into a mirror, liking a person, becoming frustrated, staying on task, getting off task, disturbing one's neighbors, and so on, to include all of children's "good" and "bad" behaviors.

These behaviors have all been learned. They can be changed by giving the child a reason for changing. Specifically, children change behaviors for things that bring them pleasure. They work for approval from people they love and/or respect; they work to satisfy the desires they have been taught to value; they avoid behaviors they associate with unpleasantness; they act in

ways that have been reinforced, whether by chance or by design.

Some teachers who have not had experience with this teaching technique feel it smacks of "cold-blooded manipulation." Well, yes, if that phrase means "conscious management," not really of children but of their environment. A teacher (or parent) in charge of children can't help conditioning them, since they make constant associations with the other people or things in their environments. Even in the most open education, a teacher conditions his students by his approval or lack of it, his attention or lack of it, his very presence or absence. So why shirk the job? You chose the responsibility of changing children's behavior when you chose to teach. It's your job to learn to do it well.

When a child does not learn, or demonstrates other inappropriate school behavior, it is because he is suffering an error in association or reinforcement. He has made an inappropriate association or has not made an appropriate one, because the reinforcement was incorrect or lacking. You are already working with associations when you use teaching games (learning=fun), and when, in your own words, you try to "make learning a rewarding experience."

With a knowledge of behavioral techniques, a teacher can make these reinforcements deliberately and effectively instead of just hoping they will happen. He can also learn to recognize the frequent errors of association and reinforcement for the purpose of avoiding them. Sarcasm, for example, is an error. "Why don't you just yell louder, Jimmy?" can at best create confusion in the child's mind; you may also find he has taken you literally. The chance of being taken literally is the price one always pays for sarcasm with children or adults.

Behavior modification is a technique for shaping behavior; teachers use it to help children learn because that is their job. The values that it promotes in children are the values the teacher intends them to learn, because that is another part of his job. . . .

## WHAT IS A "PAYOFF"? THAT WHICH KEEPS ANY BEHAVIOR ALIVE

One of the discoveries of behavioral science is that it doesn't matter how or where an inappropriate behavior association got started. What does matter is that the behavior is being kept alive by a "payoff" in the present.

The principle can be stated, "Behavior that goes unrewarded will be extinguished," and, conversely, behavior that does not become extinguished is in some way being rewarded. Although saying so goes against much present-day thinking, looking back is not only unnecessary, it is almost always unproductive. This is especially true when unearthing the "reason" for the behavior is used as a substitute for action.

When you want to change a specific behavior, you must first find the payoff and eliminate it. The possibilities are good that you will be able to do so. Some reinforcements, such as those from the child's family or from his own idea of himself, you can't control and so can't change. But many you can.

The teacher must watch the child carefully to find the payoff in each specific case. This is often not easy. Once again, many of us try to simplify our problem by grouping behaviors together or by categorizing children as "types." This is no more successful than other simplistic solutions for inappropriate behavior, such as "These children came from a disadvantaged background and just need experiences," or "This class just needs a teacher with a firm hand." There are too many differences in the behavior of individuals for such thinking to be of any real use.

Individual differences among children can even result in the same behaviors being dependent on different payoffs. For example, Jim, Alex, and Pete are all acting up in class on the same day. They finally become so disruptive that the teacher sends them all to the principal's office. Jim is delighted; his payoff is that he caused the teacher to lose his cool. Alex's payoff is that he maintained his reputation among the rest of the class for being a tough guy. Pete doesn't care anything about the teacher or the class; the people he wants to impress are Jim and Alex, and he's happy because their friendship and approval are his payoff. Behaviorally, the teacher's response should have been to ignore them. Consistently ignoring a behavior will go far toward extinguishing it. When the teacher doesn't get angry or disturbed, the problem is focused back where it belongs: on the children, not on the teacher. He has not allowed his students to manipulate him.

In extinguishing behavior by means of this technique, you must be prepared for the next development, which is that the behavior will initially become worse rather than better! Remember that the child desires the payoff very much, and has learned this particular behavior as the way to get it. When the payoff is not forthcoming, he will redouble his efforts to earn it the only way he knows. It is not until the child realizes once and for all that the payoff is not going to happen that he will stop the behavior. This may happen quickly, and it may happen slowly. Many teachers give up at this stage, saying, "I've tried ignoring, but the child misbehaved more." Of course.

For this reason, ignoring is not an easy technique. You have to be sure of what you are doing. Sometimes even colleagues or parents won't understand why you're doing it. Explain your reasons and ask for time to achieve results. Stick to your guns. You are extinguishing inappropriate behavior in the child because you care.

## WHAT CONSTITUTES REWARD? THAT WHICH THE CHILD WILL WORK TOWARD

Rewards form pleasant associations and promote the behavior being rewarded. To change a child's inappropriate behavior, often it is enough to track down the payoff and eliminate the specific unwanted behavior. It can be even more effective to institute at the same time a reward or system of rewards for desirable behavior, to form a new association.

Just as it is necessary to extinguish a behavior, it is necessary to pinpoint the specific behavior to be rewarded. For example, you can't try to reward Lucy for "changing her attitude toward her schoolwork." You must look at the overall picture, assign a hierarchy to Lucy's problems, and decide what behavior you can best work with. You might decide that Lucy's worst problem is the fact that she fiddles around before getting to work, so she gets rushed and never finishes her tasks. The behavior you decide to promote is getting down to work in a reasonable time. You wouldn't at first insist that Lucy start everything immediately, and have her reward contingent on that. You'd allow her five minutes. The five minutes could gradually be cut down until, by buckling quickly down to necessary tasks, Lucy shows that she has learned that it's much better not to procrastinate.

When you have a child with multiple problems, as usually is the case, or when you have many children with problems, your decision about what behaviors to work with first will depend on several factors. You may decide to work with what you judge to be the basic behavior problem. Again, you may choose the problem that is most acute; or you may choose to work on the most accessible problem, considering the time and help you have available.

Extinguishing is best done on an individual basis. A reward system, however, can often be set up for an entire group. This can be helpful if a problem of jealousy develops. This does not happen as often as you might think, once the children recognize that the rewarded child needs help, but the possibility is there.

Any system of rewards, whether individual or group, should be set up so each child knows specifically what he must do to earn the reward. What he must do should be enough like his present behavior to enable him to realize that it is within his power. The reward should be something the child desires, the more strongly the better. The reward should be given consistently for each performance of the desired behavior. At first, the reward should be tangible, occur quickly as well as surely, and be generous even to the point of being overly so.

Do your best to catch the child being good, even for a moment. It is important to get the child winning as soon as possible.

We suggest that you write the rules in a conspicuous place or have them easily available. Explain the rules every day. If the reward involves a toy, game, or piece of equipment, hold it up or point to it. If there's a choice of rewards, ask each of several children which one he is working for.

Rewards can be anything a child desires. Obviously, the rewards you choose must be within your resources of money, time, and freedom from restrictive school policies. A teacher who is setting up a reward system on his own probably won't be able to use the more dramatic types of reward. He can make use of what he has with imagination and ingenuity.

The first tangible, quick reward can be as simple as food. For young children, it may be small candies (M&M's are a popular choice), presweetened cereal, or small glasses of juice. Older children may work for candy bars, ice-cream bars, or soft drinks. Rewards can involve toys, games, or puzzles, either the ownership of small ones or time to play with larger ones. One effective reward is simply time for a child to do what he pleases. Another is listening to music of his choice. Some children will grab the chance just to read. Be sure to have available music and reading material they *want* to hear and read.

Some of these rewards depend for their effect on the fact that you usually can't do them in school. Schools with flexible, individualized programs where all children can move around freely will obviously have to find other types of rewards.

Especially with older children, a token system can be highly effective. Actual tokens can be given out, or points marked down in an appropriate place where the child can see how they are accumulating. Specific numbers of points earn specific awards of varying values. The similarity of a token system to our monetary system makes it familiar; it has the added advantage of giving the child the idea that money is earned as a reward for work. Some schools let children earn enough points to take a trip, or to take off an entire day. There are experimental programs that are using commercial trading stamps and even money itself as contingency rewards. You've probably read about some of these, usually reported as "paying children to go to school."

As a variation, a teacher may sometimes point out a child who is doing a particular task well and say, "You can earn a reward if you concentrate on your work as well as Sheila."

You may also at times make effective use of group approval or disapproval, with a special group bonus reward. "If everyone in the math group can work at least one of these programs in a half hour, we'll have a party!" is a powerful stimulus for individual and cooperative work. Such interaction can develop into group self-discipline, and even eventually into a self-governing class and school.

Once the initial stage of behavior/reward is over, the teacher can begin to pair the tangible rewards with approving behavior such as praise, smiles, and pats. Once more you are making use of the principles of association. The time needed between behavior and the original reward will grow longer, and the need for the reward will become less. Eventually teacher approval will begin to function as a reward. The time before this begins to happen is hard to predict. Sometimes it is surprisingly short, sometimes very long.

Traditional teaching takes it for granted that children can be motivated from the beginning by teacher approval. In many cases it's true. But it doesn't work for the problem children, both the ones you notice and those you don't. You must start with the child where he is. You motivate him by what will work, not by what you think ought to work.

After teacher approval, and combined with it, can come the intrinsic rewards of skill achievement and academic achievement. Finally, the skillful teacher can structure the classroom environment in such a way that the child can use self-approval as a reward. Motivation by this means is the ultimate purpose of any kind of discipline, but it isn't going to just happen. It is a goal to be worked toward, knowingly and steadily.

## CAN BEHAVIOR BE MEASURED? IT CAN BE MEASURED EASILY

As a teacher, you are used to spending a good deal of time in devising and employing tests, both formal and informal, for academic skills. To do the same thing for social skills probably seems a formidable task. Although it takes a little effort, it is not so difficult or time-consuming as it might seem, once the behavior you want to test for has been pinpointed as we have suggested. Any specific behavior is observable and occurs over a period of time.

Unlike academic tasks, in behavior modification we are concerned about measuring the number of times a behavior occurs in a given period. To do so, you must set up your criteria as to the extent or quality of the behavior to be measured. For example, the length of time crying goes on before it is counted might be set at two seconds. A noisy disturbance may be considered one that causes other children's heads to turn; a child's getting out of his seat may be counted only when he has no legitimate reason.

Even to start the process of behavior modification, the pinpointed behavior must be counted and recorded. Knowing exactly how many times the behavior occurs helps you set the consequences. It also, of course, tells you when you record again whether the behavior is happening less, more, or at the same rate.

The time period to be counted across will have to be estimated at first. If the occurrences happen over quite a long period, you may find it necessary to take samplings and average them. An aide, team member, or outside observer can be of great help, especially to check on the results of your interaction with the children. Another observer can also verify your count.

Testing tools consist of pencil, paper, and a watch or clock. Numbers of behaviors can be ticked off and any comments noted. A simple form is adaptable to any behavior you want to record.

Videotaping is another method of recording children's behavior. It enables you to watch the results of your manipulation of the classroom environment. It also often happens that children's behaviors are obvious on tape that you were too busy to notice when you were on the spot. The videotape makes an original record from which the behaviors to be recorded can be counted or rechecked.

We'd like here to stress one of the reasons why it's important to record over a time interval. When you speak to children, they will often do what you say for a short time but only until your eye is somewhere else. You say, "Sit down, Diane," and she does; but about a minute later she is up wandering around the room again. The children are conditioning you by seeming to obey; your handling of the situation is reinforced but you have not done anything to solve the problem.

You don't have time for so much recordkeep-ing? Consider all the time you spend repeating directions, scolding, and nagging. One teacher we know absolutely refused to "waste time with all that book work." Our observer checked her as saying, "Now stop that talking!" 143 times in one morning!

## CAN THE CLASSROOM BE STRUCTURED? IT CAN—AND MUST

Experiments with children have shown that if a child knows specifically what is expected of him, if it is within his power to do it, and he wants to do it, he probably will. As we have discussed, the classroom climate can be structured to make use of this basic premise. You can arrange things so the child will want to do what you want him to.

| Teacher Behavior | Student Behavior Social and Academic | |
|---|---|---|
| | *Appropriate* | *Inappropriate* |
| Approval | Yes | No |
| Withholding of approval | No | Yes |
| Ignoring | No | Yes (unless dangerous) |
| Disapproval | No | Yes (unless "payoff") |
| Threat of disapproval | No | Yes |

As the chart shows in summary, the teacher really has five techniques for behavior shaping. Approval is easy to understand; it is a way of acting that gives the child happiness. Giving rewards, whether as concrete as a piece of candy or as intangible as proximity, demonstrates approval. Withholding of approval is another possible technique; it is effective after the expectation of approval is established—especially so if you hold out hope. The simple act of ignoring, just not paying attention to the child, is a technique much used in behavior modification. Disapproval is generally synonymous with the child's unhappiness; it is punishment. The threat of disapproval or punishment results in the child's changing his behavior through fear.

The chart demonstrates quite clearly that when we talk about being consistent in reinforcing behavior, we don't always mean rewarding. It also shows that fear and punishment are not the only alternatives to giving approval and rewards.

The first three techniques, approval, withholding, and ignoring, are all considered positive methods of reinforcement, even though the last two can be construed as a mild form of punishment. It is this that allows us to refute the objections of those who feel that "praising all the time" is false and saccharine, and that it thus soon loses all its effectiveness. Research indicates, however, that children can benefit from a great deal of praise as long as it is earned. All too many teachers spend most of their time in scolding and punishment by means of words, gestures, bad reports, and depriving students of activities that would benefit them. ("No recess for you today, young man!") This is in fact one of the major reasons so many teachers are shocked to see themselves on videotape. "Can that cross, nagging teacher be *me?*" It can actually come as a great relief to know that you don't have to be that kind of teacher—that there is a better way to control children's behavior.

Disapproval and threats of disapproval are negative methods of behavior reinforcement, and should be used sparingly. The most effective proportion of positive to negative reinforcements seems to be about 80 to 20 percent. The extreme forms of negative techniques, heavy corporal punishment and resulting terror, should be avoided. For one reason, a teacher who uses disapproval techniques alone may discover that the child has made an unfortunate and even perverted association: "I get a kick out of making the teacher mad," "I can take anything they can dish out," "There isn't anybody who is worse than I am!" It is in fact quite difficult to find a punishment that doesn't have some sort of payoff. Fear, or the threat of punishment, can be an even more effective behavior suppressant. Neither of these techniques, however, does anything to establish the joy of living and learning. Children who are motivated entirely by these negative techniques pay a high price in guilt, compulsiveness, generalized anxiety, and even ulcers. They do not become the kind of adults any teacher of good sense and sensitivity is trying to produce.

There is some evidence to indicate that positive approaches are a little more effective than negative ones. Even more important to the teacher who has the welfare of his charges at heart is the fact that positive reinforcements do not damage. This doesn't mean that the teacher is being overly permissive, as the term is so often used. The use of such reinforcement methods means that the teacher has recognized the need to structure the learning environment so that the child can reach his highest potential, not only of achievement but of happiness.

We sometimes hear people express fear of the "wrong kind of teacher" learning to use these efficient methods of structuring the classroom. It is true that an insensitive teacher can make very effective use of behavioral principles in a way that raises some serious questions about the other associations his students acquire. We know of one seventh-grade teacher who controlled her class by having the most deviant children—"if they are very, very bad"—participate in a mock wedding ceremony. When the children involved changed their behavior, they were allowed to "get a divorce." An art teacher teaches children to color within the lines by behavioral techniques, a procedure damaging to children's creativity. Another person working with eight- and nine-year-olds said, "when one of the boys misbehaves, I make him wear a girl's hair ribbon." This same person thought it "terrible" to suggest to parents that they occasionally send a problem child to school without breakfast so he will be hungry for rewards of cereal, milk, and cookies. No matter how many "behavioral recipes" there are, there can be no substitute for taste and sensitivity in a teacher.

## IF AT FIRST YOU DON'T SUCCEED? WELL—YOU KNOW!

Sometimes a teacher who understands behavioral principles and has even successfully applied them will run into trouble. He should first review the way he has carried out the four steps of behavior modification.

1. **Pinpoint.** Is the behavior you are trying to extinguish or promote too general? Have you isolated a single behavior sufficiently? Does the behavior you are working with depend on another which you should deal with first? Have you discovered the real payoff? Does the behavior you are building in the child reflect the idea you are trying to get across?

2. **Record.** Have you chosen the best length of time to record across? Does it indicate the true picture of the frequency of the behavior? If you can't record for the full cycle, have you taken different samplings and averaged them? Have you included all necessary data on your sheet or form? Was your recording technique precise? Did every observer understand and use the criteria correctly?

3. **Consequate.** Have you made sure that what you think of as a reward really is one for the child? Is a punishment really a punishment? Does the child understand clearly what he has to do to earn the reward? Does he remember what the reward is? Does the reward need to be changed to add variety? Have you been imaginative in planning rewards? Are you pairing approval techniques with rewards?

4. **Evaluate.** Have you stayed with your original program long enough to see whether it is actually working or not? Did you remember that behavior you are ignoring will worsen before it disappears, sometimes for a long time? Were the intervals before re-recording long enough? When you became certain one technique wasn't effective, did you go back and try another?

There are a few more behavioral principles that can help when you seem to have come to a dead end. One of these maxims is that *it is impossible to maintain contradictory responses at the same time*. Interrupting a stimulus-response chain by postponing the response can help break the conditioning. For example, the child won't cry if you can make him laugh, or just stop to take three deep breaths. He can't jump out of his seat if he is picking up a pencil, or pretending to. He can't stare out the window if you walk in front of him, pull the shade, or ask him to pass out papers. "Count ten before you get angry" is a famous example of this technique. "Speak softly so we can have a 'soft' argument" and "Let's take a break so we can begin fresh" are effective in class.

Another useful and very important hint is not to try to get the child to agree that his present behavior is wrong or that different behavior would be more desirable. It is much easier for a child *to act his way into a new way of thinking than to think his way into a new way of acting*. That's why we work with present, observable behavior rather than causes or attitudes. Causes and attitudes are not the problem; the behavior is. Causes will be irrelevant when the behavior changes. Attitudes will change when behavior changes.

There's no reason to get discouraged if you make mistakes in behavioral shaping. Remember that behaviors are learned, and so can be unlearned or relearned. Behavioral techniques *do* work; their success with severely handicapped children in school and institutions for the retarded and mentally ill shows that even these

children can learn more and learn faster than we ever believed possible. What shouldn't you be able to do, then, for even the child whom you consider your worst problem?

*Charles H. Madsen, Jr.* is Associate Professor, Department of Psychology, Florida State University, Tallahassee.
*Clifford K. Madsen* is Associate Professor, School of Music, Florida State University, Tallahassee.

# Self-theory and Behaviorism: A Rapprochement

## DONALD AVILA AND WILLIAM PURKEY

From the point of view of these authors a sad state of affairs presently exists in psychology and education. Central to this problem is the notion that to accept either behaviorism or self-theory as one's major psychological orientation automatically excludes acceptance of the other. That this assumption is all too prevalent is evidenced by Hitt's description of a recent symposium on behaviorism *vs.* phenomenology, which included some of the most prominent psychologists in the nation:

> The presentations dealt with two distinct models of man and the scientific methodology associated with each Model. The discussions following each presentation may be described as aggressive, hostile, and rather emotional; they would suggest that there is little likelihood of a reconciliation between the two schools of thought represented at the symposium . . . [1969, p. 651].

We contend that this either-or state of affairs is destructive, self-deluding and, if we read the temper of the younger psychologists and educators correctly, a position held only by those who look to the past rather than to the future.

Both self-theory and behaviorism offer important contributions to psychology and education. To make them mutually exclusive automatically blinds us to the significant contributions that each can make to our understanding of man. To be half blind is bad enough, but when an antagonistic situation develops that is characterized by aggression, hostility and anger, our vision is distorted even more.

We submit that to view self-theory and behaviorism as mutually exclusive and antagonistic is not only fruitless, but also misleading. Modern behaviorists recognize central processes as essential to an understanding of behavior, while self-theorists are fully aware of the documented

From *Psychology in the Schools* 9, no. 2 (April 1972): 124–126. Used by permission of the authors and the publisher.

power of reinforcement to modify human behavior. It is becoming increasingly evident that both approaches are parts of a single continuum in the incredibly complex processes of understanding people and influencing their behavior. The purpose of this paper is to explain how we have been able to include both behaviorism and self-theory in our thinking about the dynamics of human activity.

First, we see self-theory as a valuable working hypothesis about the nature of man—in fact, self-theory could serve as a framework for a basic philosophy of life. Thanks to the writing and research of self-theorists, we have valuable insights about the nature of individuals, their perceptions, their needs, and their goals. Further, emerging evidence (Murphy and Spohn, 1968; Purkey, 1970) supports the commonsense notion that behavior is determined by the individual's subjective perceptions of the situation rather than by the situation itself. Thus, we have the indispensable construct of the phenomenological world.

Central to the phenomenological world is one's self-awareness. All of the beliefs, opinions, and attitudes that an individual holds about himself have come to be called self-concept. This concept of self and its related facets of self-esteem, self-enhancement, self-consistency, and self-actualization provide rich hypotheses for researchers and valuable guides for those in the helping professions (Combs, Avila, and Purkey, 1971).

People who work in helping relationships have pointed out the importance of a warm, accepting environment in which a person is treated with respect, dignity, warmth, and care. Furthermore, they have shown that the individual who is being helped needs to accept mutual responsibility for the helping relationship. Finally, the research of self-theorists has demonstrated that the way a professional helper feels about himself and his client or student has as much to do with the outcome of the interaction as the specific technique used, if not more (Combs, Soper, Gooding, Benton, Dickman, and Usher, 1969).

In sum, self-theory provides heuristic guidelines by which to fulfill our professional responsibilities, be they counseling, therapy, teaching, or research. On the other hand, self-theory does seem to have difficulty when it comes to the question of "how." How does one change a self-concept, a perception, or a particular bit of behavior? How can one set up conditions and provide experiences for one's clients and students that will prove to be self-enhancing? This is the point at which we believe behaviorism enters the scene.

Behaviorism, after all, is not a theory, although a person certainly can develop a theoretical position from the approach. Behaviorism is a process and a method (essentially the scientific method) from which psychologists and educators have developed many useful principles and techniques. These principles and techniques can be used to accomplish the purpose of self-theory: *to convince each individual that he is valuable, responsible, and capable of influencing his own destiny.*

The behaviorist has little trouble with the "how" aspects of a given problem. For example, what better way is there to help a person to have positive experiences than to set up situations full of positive contingencies of reinforcement, i.e., situations in which the individual has an excellent chance of success. If a person who has been a failure begins to experience success, he also will begin to change his feelings about himself and others and his perception of the world. This is exactly what the self-theorists want to accomplish. The point has been clarified by Andrews and Karlin (1971), who demonstrated that behavioristic processes can be used to build autonomy in the individual, faciliate his freedom, and strengthen his self-image. Rice (1970) also has demonstrated that the goals of self-theory can be realized by use of behavior modification.

Thus it seems to these authors that enhancement and reinforcement, changing self-concepts and behavior modification are related closely and may sometimes be the same thing. Furthermore, the authors believe that the future of psychology lies in a unification of these two positions, not in the wasted energy of continued conflict.

## REFERENCES

Andrews, L. M. & Karlin, M. *Requiem for Democracy?* New York: Holt, Rinehart, and Winston, 1971.

Combs, A. W., Avila, D. L. & Purkey, W. W. *Helping Relationships: Basic Concepts for the Helping Professions.* Boston: Allyn and Bacon, 1971.

Combs, A. W., Soper, D. W., Gooding, C. T., Benton, J. A., Jr., Dickman, J. F. & Usher, R. H. *Florida Studies in the Helping Professions.* Univeristy of Florida Social Science Monograph No. 37. Gainesville: University of Florida Press, 1969.

Hitt, W. D. "Two Models of Man." *American Psychologist,* 1969, 24, 651–658.

Murphy, G. & Spohn, H. E. *Encounter with Reality.* Boston: Houghton Mifflin, 1968.

Purkey, W. W. *Self Concept and School Achievement.* Englewood Cliffs, N.J.: Prentice-Hall, 1970.

Rice, D. R. "Educo-therapy: A New Approach to Delinquent Behavior." *Journal of Learning Disabilities,* 1970, 3, 16–23.

*Donald Avila* is Professor of Education, University of Florida, Gainesville.
*William Purkey* is Professor of Educational Psychology, University of North Carolina, Greensboro.

# Learning Style/Brain Research: Harbinger of an Emerging Psychology

## ANTHONY F. GREGORC

Education today is making an insufficient impact on the human potential for learning. A primary contributing factor is our fragmented view of instruction. Twenty-two years of teaching and administrative experience, including 12 years of research into how people learn and teach, have left me with two deep concerns.

First, we, as professional educators, lack an aggregate of agreed-upon facts and principles which serve as a basis for our labors. This concern is captured in John Goodlad's statement:

> In spite of some self-congratulatory rhetoric to the contrary, education is still a relatively weak profession, badly divided within itself and not yet embodying the core of professional values and knowledge required to resist fads, special interest groups, and—perhaps most serious of all—funding influences.[1]

From *Student Learning Styles and Brain Behavior,* pp. 3–10 (Reston, Virginia: NASSP, 1982). Used by permission of the publisher, the National Association of Secondary School Principals.

1. John I. Goodlad, "Can Our Schools Get Better?" *Phi Delta Kappan,* January 1979, p. 342.

Second, we lack a coherent psychology which permits us to investigate, classify, and understand the phenomena of learning and teaching. Instead of a holistic, broadly-based psychology, we, as individuals, appear to subscribe to separate "schools"—behaviorist, psychoanalytic, humanistic, existential, transpersonal, Eastern, esoteric, cognitive, developmental, medical intervention (drugs and electrical), etc. Each of these schools has its founders, disciples, interpreters, truths, facts, and methods of investigation and classification. Each also has its strategies and technologies for normalizing people and for improving learning and teaching. Unfortunately, some of these schools are at odds with one another. As a result, we continue to run in educational circles.

My experience tells me that learning style and brain research has the potential to serve as a framework that could put the various facts and psychologies into a perspective and thereby lead us toward becoming a united profession.

## WHAT STYLE RESEARCH IS TEACHING US

One of the greatest findings emerging from learning style research is a reaffirmation of the theory of relativity. Succinctly expressed by Bentov:

> The theory of relativity emphasizes the notion that no matter what we observe, we always do so relative to a frame of reference that may differ from someone else's, that we must compare our frames of reference in order to get meaningful measurements and results about the events we observe.[2]

This finding is profound! It means that there is not just one view of reality and one school of thought. Empirical, phenomenological, and scientific research have revealed that people perceive both the physical, concrete world and the nonphysical, abstract world. Some individuals, however, are more "at home" with one world than with the other. This predilection affects what they see and don't see and what they experience and don't experience despite equal opportunities to interact with the so-called "same environment."

Researchers have found that people organize their thoughts in a linear, step-by-step order *and* in a nonlinear, leaping, "chunk-like" or holistic manner. Again, some people show decided tendencies toward one or the other. Such partiality affects their use and scheduling of time, the physical arrangements of their environments, their daily planning, their view of change, and their view of the future.

The linear-oriented person sees tomorrow as the direct result of yesterday's and today's careful planning, efficient use of time, and task-related efforts. This individual expects to receive the fruits of his labors—not surprises.

For the nonlinear person, tomorrow contains the past, the present, and it could contain a modifying element which is absent today. This individual develops general plans, lives for surprises (sometimes called miracles), and celebrates each day as "the first day of his life."

Learning style research also teaches us that people think in different ways. This view is highlighted by Hannah Arendt's definition of thinking. She states: "Thinking is an activity of examining whatever happens to pass or to attract attention regardless of results and specific content."[3] Some people think with their sensory apparatus; others think with their hearts. A few think with their intuition; and, of course, some think with their intellect. If these are differentiated forms of thinking, then the plea to develop higher level thinking among students takes on broad and exciting connotations.

2. Itzhak Bentov, *Stalking the Wild Pendulum* (New York: Bantam Books, 1979), p. 4.

3. Hannah Arendt, *The Life of the Mind* (New York: Harcourt Brace Jovanovich, 1978), p. 5.

Learning style research indicates that people's styles reveal how they identify, judge, substantiate, confirm, and validate *truth*. To some people, seeing is believing. To others, truth comes through "feeling it in one's bones," through "chills," or through "gut" reaction. Some know truth through insight, hunches, and intuitive flashes; others only accept truths which fit their intellectual formulae and are backed by statistical studies or are replicable on demand. This multiplicity of truth-testing approaches challenges those of us who want people to accept our truths and believe as we believe.

Learning style research has also shown that we, as human beings, can separate ourselves physically and mentally from our environments. We can also associate with environments in varying ways. Again, however, predilections appear. Some of us demonstrate separative, independent, individual "me-oriented" behaviors and appear to learn and produce best in environments which support such behavior. Others, however, reveal a natural affinity toward collective, interdependent, group "we-oriented" activities. Such natural orientations toward and away from specific environments should prompt an analysis of the types of behaviors which are "programed" into our classroom expectations.

These are but a few of the findings about individual styles that appear in the research. They are, however, representative samples of similarities and differences among people. When we turn our attention away from an individual's style, we are immediately confronted with an environment which consists of people, objects, and processes. And, from style research, we quickly come to realize that each of these has stylistic elements built into them too.

For instance, a teacher may present a lesson by using a style that requires high abstraction ability to decode a lecture, linear organization of thought to follow the teacher's logic, a tacit acceptance of the teacher's truths or the truths of cited authorities, a willingness to learn on one's own without discussion, and the ability to sit quietly on hard chairs in a dimly lit auditorium which has a history of heating problems.

The teacher, as both a medium for the content of the lesson and an environmental engineer, places demands upon the student for adaptation through his or her decisions. Some students will and can adapt. Some, however, won't and can't (to the degree needed) for a variety of reasons.

The teacher is, however, not the only medium in the classroom. When we analyze classroom products, activities, and organizational designs, we find that each of these has built-in stylistic demands. Books, computers, programed instruction, and movies all make particular stylistic demands. The same is true for simulations, guided fantasy activities, brainstorming, and silent reading. And, anyone who has experienced both open-classroom and traditional classroom organization structures has certainly experienced variable stylistic demands. This research strongly supports Marshall McLuhan's position that the "medium is a message and a massage." And it causes me to pause and reflect upon how haphazard, naïve, and selfish some educators are in their selection of instructional means, methods, and environmental conditions.

## WHAT BRAIN RESEARCH IS TEACHING US

As I review the data coming to us from brain research, I sense a serious, scientific approach to understanding how the brain functions. I also sense that the major research is moving in two directions: pure research into how the brain works, and physical experimentation designed to remedy certain neurophysiological problems so that a patient can live a more productive life.

These research motivations are not quite the same as those prompting the efforts of learning style researchers. The pure research and medical application thrusts of the brain researchers can benefit us; however, we must be very careful when adapting tentative brain hypotheses or special case training techniques into our everyday classroom strategies. Brain researchers have much to teach us, but we have much to learn before we run amok with homemade conclusions and consequent activities built on our interpretation of their data.

These are, of course, cautionary words. They should not, however, be construed to mean that brain research is not applicable to learning style research. Indeed the two are compatible in certain ways. When the physical efforts of the brain researchers are combined with the psychological efforts of the learning style researchers, several parallels emerge:

1. The brain is differentiated in function: the two halves process different kinds of information in different ways. The hemispheres appear to "house" specific functions like analytical and synthetic processes, imagery and verbal responses, and simultaneous and successive processes in different sections. This supposition supports empirical evidence about the differences in stylistic responses to stimuli.
2. The two halves of the brain are connected and therefore function holistically. Despite reasonable specialization of the hemispheres, they indeed work together. This, in part, accounts for empirical evidence that people can register at least some information to varying degrees irrespective of the instructional technique. This fact also accounts for the generalized impression that we all learn the same way.
3. Certain environmental stimuli and cultural activities stimulate specific functions more than others. If these functions are well developed in an individual, the responses will be refined and clear. This, however, points to the biases in some of our teaching techniques and raises questions regarding the balancing of our approaches.
4. Brain growth periods may occur in which certain data can be gathered and reinforced better than at other times in human growth and development. This lends credence to the empirical and psychological positions regarding cycles, ages and stages, periods of absorption and reflection, transitions, and crisis periods in human life.

These are only a few findings. They are, however, important core findings which provide physical correlations to empirical, phenomenological, and psychological research discoveries. Such parallels provide strong evidence that individual differences do indeed exist and that some of our instructional approaches are inappropriate for many individuals.

## WHAT POTENTIALS STAND BEFORE US

Marvelous opportunities stand before us. Learning style/brain research can provide the impetus toward a framework built on a sound knowledge base and toward an emerging psychology which will help us promote the development of the holistic human being.

These combined efforts can also serve as a launching pad for more thought-provoking questions such as those now being raised regarding mind/brain differences. Is there a difference between the mind and brain as neurosurgeon Wilder Penfield believes? He states:

. . . one cannot assign to the mind a position in space and yet it is easy to see what it does and where it does it. . . . The brain is the vastly complicated master organ within the body that makes thought and consciousness possible. In its integrative and coordinating action, it resembles, in many ways, an electrical computer.[4]

If there are differences between the mind and the brain, what are they?

We can begin to examine our beliefs and presuppositions about thoughts which limit us. If nonlinear, holistic grasping of information is a natural ability anchored in the brain, can we now expand our view of change which, to date, has been built upon the idea of gradualism? Can we seriously begin to consider concepts like synchronicity, eurekas, and the idea of time/no time

and infinity? Can we open ourselves to appreciate people who "march to a different drummer"?

Can we look with renewed vision and hope at some of the people presently labeled "learning disabled"? Are they all truly disabled in a neurological sense or is their disability, in some cases, symptomatic of their inability to align and adapt to style expectations or the demands of the environment(s)? Could we, as a profession, be creating "learning disabled children" through our own ignorance of how the brain functions and how people learn?

These and many more questions need to be addressed. Style and brain research offer serious responses.

4. Wilder Penfield, *The Mystery of the Mind* (New Jersey: Princeton University Press, 1975), pp. 10–11.

*Anthony F. Gregorc* is President, Gregorc Associates, Columbia, Connecticut.

# Learning/Teaching Styles: Applying the Principles
## PEGGY FRIEDMAN AND ROBERT ALLEY

For many years educational leaders have recognized the need for alternative instructional approaches to meet the needs of the wide variety of students in heterogeneously grouped classrooms. Often teachers share the frustration of knowing they are failing to meet the needs of a portion of the students in their classrooms. One reason is the failure to accommodate the unique learning styles of those students. Recognizing and defining the styles by which a person learns is as important to the learning process as diag-

nostic tests are to the healing process in the field of medicine.

In order for teachers to be able to practice the theory which has been generated by learning styles research and development, it is necessary to translate the enormous volume of literature and the more than 30 different learning styles instruments into a manageable, but at the same time meaningful, body of knowledge. The teacher's needs are primarily those of translation. How can the learning styles theory be used in

From *Theory Into Practice* 23, No. 1 (Winter 1984): 77–81. Used by permission of the authors and the publisher. © 1984, College of Education, The Ohio State University.

classrooms? How can so many ideas and so much material be utilized? Fortunately certain principles emerge from the research. Along with case studies which illustrate practices found useful by other schools/teachers, six principles are described below to assist teachers with the translation process.

## PRINCIPLES

*Both the style by which the teacher prefers to teach and the style by which the student prefers to learn can be identified.* Witkin (1981), Dunn and Dunn (1978), Gregorc and Ward (1977), and others have demonstrated the feasibility of classroom applications of learning style instruments. Most teachers are familiar with one or more of those instruments and thus with the latter half of the principle above. A less well known aspect of the dual principle is that teachers have styles by which they prefer to teach (Gregorc & Ward, 1977; Entwistle, 1981). Instrumentation has been developed by which teachers can identify their own preferred styles for teaching (Gregorc & Ward, 1977). Barbe and Milone (1980) have further suggested that teachers are more likely to develop teaching strategies which are congruent with their own learning styles rather than those of their students if they are unaware of the learning/teaching styles literature. This fact implies the second principle: *Teachers need to guard against over-teaching by their own preferred learning styles.* To teach one's own learning style is a natural tendency because teachers subconsciously operate on the assumption that the way they learn is the most effective way for everyone to learn. Therefore, teachers have an obligation to broaden their teaching styles to support opportunities for students to broaden their learning styles.

A third principle is that *teachers are most helpful when they assist students in identifying and learning through their own style preferences.* Self-scoring inventories are available for classroom use. More complex instruments utilizing computer scoring and analysis are also available from vendors such as Price Systems (Dunn & Dunn, 1978). Teacher guidance and counsel can encourage students to utilize their own style data to determine their learning preferences and to deliberately set learning goals which take advantage of those preferences. This principle is important because it supports the premise that students are capable of guiding their own learning when given the opportunity.

That *students should have the opportunity to learn through their preferred style* is a fourth principle also implicit in the assumptions underlying the learning styles movement. By identifying those specific learning styles, teachers are able to provide the means by which students can experience success in the learning environment. Many students have never had that opportunity.

Yet it is not enough for students to learn only through their preferred styles (Strother, 1982). The fifth principle is that *students should be encouraged to diversify their style preferences.* This "style flex" is essential in a complex society which places increasing value on visual or auditory learning but insists that its youth be able to manipulate the computer keyboard with the same facility with which they read a newspaper or listen to a lecture. Speaking to this point, Barbe and Milone (1980) maintain that 15 percent of elementary school age children are kinesthetically oriented in their learning preferences. Yet, they believe our elementary schools continue to rely almost exclusively on audio or visual modalities as primary teaching styles. Barbe and Milone further assert that those children who learn comfortably through a mixture of the three basic modalities have an advantage in school-based learning. Thus teachers need to utilize classroom activities which will assist students in developing flexible learning styles.

The sixth principle implied throughout the research is that *teachers can develop specific learn-*

*ing activities which reinforce each modality or style.* This final principle is crucial to the ultimate success of the learning styles movement. The degree to which teachers are able to develop teaching activities and materials related to basic styles will largely determine the success of the movement. Further attention and effort must be focused upon this need. Teachers do not have time to juggle classes of 30 or more students while giving attention to 20 or more style preference factors for each individual student. The specific need is to delineate ways whereby teachers can focus upon selected basic style preferences of their students and have materials available at their fingertips to utilize as learning activities in support of those styles.

## A SIMPLIFIED INSTRUMENT

In the late '70s a simplified styles instrument was developed with the Dunn and Dunn (1978) Learning Styles Instrument as its basis. The Student Learning Styles—A Survey (Project CITE, 1976) instrument was intended specifically to meet the need for a mechanism which could be utilized by teachers within their classes. It is quick, simple to score, and easily understood by students, yet it adequately identifies student style preferences in the following dimensions.

1. auditory linguistic: prefers to learn by means of the *spoken word*
2. visual linguistic: prefers to *see words* in books, on the chalkboard, charts, or graphs in order to learn
3. auditory numerical: learns easily from *hearing* numbers and oral explanations
4. visual numerical: prefers to *see numbers* on the board, in the book, or on a paper
5. audio-visual-kinesthetic combination: likes a combination of the three basic modalities
6. individual learner: works best *alone*
7. group learner: likes *learning with others*

8. oral expressive: prefers to share knowledge by *telling others*
9. written expressive: prefers the *written sharing* of knowledge

The dimensions above are measured on a self-scoring instrument; results can then be reported on a bar graph to identify the relative strength of each of the dimensions for each student. Those persons responsible for the development of the Project CITE instrument strongly emphasize that the results of the survey are concerned only with preferred learning situations and are in no way indicative as measures of intellectual ability.

Recently, a computerized version of the instrument has been developed (Brown & Cooper, 1983). It may be useful for students, as well as to generate data for the teacher and/or the student.

## FIVE CASES

The following cases are representative and illustrate practices found useful by individual teachers, special programs, and entire districts in the Wichita, Kansas, area. Each case relied on the Project CITE Student Learning Styles instrument.

### Case No. 1—Individual Teacher

Often it is necessary for teachers to experiment with new educational theories in the isolation of their classrooms with little support from anyone else. But teachers who not only accept the responsibility for what they teach but also for what is learned are eager to use any technique they feel will help them in diagnosis, prescription, and treatment with their students.

One such teacher in Wichita, Kansas, attended a district inservice meeting in 1978 where information was presented regarding learning styles theory and application. This junior high school teacher decided to experiment with the idea and invited a consultant from the teacher center to come to one of his classes and explain the concept to the students. The teacher and consultant spent considerable time in making sure the students understood the implications of learning styles research and the teacher's interest in using it.

The teacher administered the instrument and the students scored the survey, developed their profiles, and shared the results within the class. Students were then encouraged to contribute ideas for classroom organization which would take advantage of the variety of preferred learning modalities within their class. They helped set up auditory areas where students could listen to tapes or form discussion groups. They also arranged visual corners where other students could read or work on written assignments.

Student enthusiasm was soon reflected at home and parents also became interested. The teacher decided to carry his program further and arranged a parent meeting. He explained the learning styles concept and how he was implementing it with his students. he then administered the survey to the parents and helped them interpret the results regarding their own preferences. The teacher then begain to utilize the parents' learning styles in conducting parent/teacher conferences.

The results of this experiment were very positive. In this classroom responsibilities shared between students and teacher in the planning of learning procedures and outcomes increased. Student willingness to accept learning differences in others also increased. In addition, the parent/teacher conferences became increasingly effective and mutually appreciated. As a result of enthusiasm for the process in this particular classroom the teacher then introduced the procedure into his other classes. Other teachers in the school also began experimenting with the concept in their classrooms.

## Case No. 2—School-Wide Individualized Program

In 1974 Cloud Elementary School in Wichita adopted the IGE (Individually Guided Education) program as their basic instructional process. IGE is an approach to schooling that provides a framework for individualized instruction and continuous progress. Instead of being organized into the usual self-contained classes in which all students of a single age are grouped together, students and teachers are organized into learning communities. Within each learning community there are students of several years' age-range and teachers of varying talents and backgrounds.

Within the program of this elementary school there were 35 identified outcomes, one of which was determination of students' learning styles. After experimenting with several assessment techniques, the teachers of the school decided that the locally developed learning styles inventory gave them usable and practical information which the faculty could easily manage. They arranged for the local district's computer department to put student data from the instrument onto a computer program. The computer based analysis was designed to identify those students who fell below a previously defined score. Style data was shared both with the students in the advisement program and with the parents during conferences. A profile for each student was developed and the results were used in determining the best way for each student to reach his/her learning objectives. In addition to developing learning objectives to complement each student's learning preference, the teachers identified those students whose style preference analysis revealed a possible inability to successfully utilize a wide range of styles of learning. These students were then given assistance in expanding their styles. Thus one major learning goal was to increase "style-flex" among students.

Results of the experiment were very encouraging with increased student achievement and parental satisfaction evident. Teachers were pleased with the effort because they then had an additional tool for increased individualization of instruction. Teachers also believed that student attitudes toward the classroom were enhanced.

## Case No. 3—School within a School

As a response to the career education movement many high schools across the country established special programs to provide selected students an opportunity to participate in experience-based learning in the community. This concept provides a less formalized learning environment and more effectively meets the needs of certain students.

The Experience Based Career Education Program at Wichita High School East was one such special program. It was organized as a school within a school. Soon after the program begain in 1976, its director became aware of the increased use and application of the learning styles concept. After appropriate planning the staff of the program decided to include a learning preference assessment, the Student Learning Styles instrument, as one of the diagnostic procedures utilized as part of each student's admission to the program. When a student applied for admittance to the program, the Student Learning Styles Inventory was administered as one of the standard battery of tests. The results were used to quickly determine the preferred basic learning modalities of the applicants.

Faculty served as both teachers and counselors in the program. These teacher/counselors had previously categorized jobs and job skills based on the nine specific characteristics identified in the instrument. The style preferences were strongly considered in the placement procedures and openly shared with prospective employers as an aid to developing individual students' learning programs. (Some employers later requested permission to use and help in administering the survey to other employees. They saw it as potentially useful in developing training programs for full-time employees and in hiring procedures.)

The positive outcomes of the program and student successes indicated that the assessment of learning modalities helped the program more completely meet the needs of the students through a closer match of work experience and learning style preferences. There was also evidence that students' confidence in the success of the program was increased, their self concept was enhanced, and they performed better in other phases of their learning experiences as well.

## Case No. 4—Alternative School

Munger Junior High School (now Alcott Alternative Learning Center) was established in 1978 as an alternative for Wichita youth who had experienced considerable frustration in previous learning environments. Potential students were drug abusers, some were school dropouts, others were family dropouts; all had been discipline problems in school. The staff members for the school were selected because of their special interest in "reluctant learners" and their proven ability to work with them. Each teacher functioned as both teacher and counselor.

The principal and staff decided to administer the locally developed student learning styles survey to determine the learning preferences of the students and to use the information to develop individual learning programs. Many students reported this to be the first time they felt that their own specific needs were being considered. They were very interested in the concept and its outcomes and began to question the teachers regarding their (teacher) learning styles. As a result it was decided to carry the program one step further and to assess the learning styles of the entire staff. Survey results were publicly posted and students and staff became aware of the various learning styles each represented.

One unexpected additional benefit was the increased communication that occurred as a result of increased awareness of cognitive styles. For example, those students who were auditory learners made counseling appointments with staff members with complementary preferences. When teachers had the opportunity to utilize their own cognitive preferences, they found it easier to work effectively with students. Administration of the learning style inventory became a standard procedure for admittance of both students and staff members to this alternative junior high school.

## Case No. 5—District-Wide

Cognitive style awareness embraces the concept that both students and instructors are accountable for learning. The Remington district, a small rural district near Wichita decided to support the concept in tangible fashion by experimenting with learning styles through an expanded application of the process on a district-wide basis. The district took steps to administer the student learning styles survey to every student in the district.

The initial purpose of the district-wide application represented in this case was to confirm the effectiveness of existing classroom management techniques and teaching strategies. To implement the plan a Project CITE consultant was scheduled for a series of sessions designed to acquaint the entire professional staff with the concept of learning styles, techniques for administering the specific survey, analysis of the results, and possible teacher/student applications for the classroom.

The survey was then administered to every student in the district. Teachers analyzed the scores of their own students and used them to confirm the various learning groups they had previously established in their classes. To further expand the use of survey results teachers then met as grade-level committees to develop curriculum goals and instructional processes designed to utilize the styles data available on each student in order to enhance student learning. Where team teaching existed, the results were also employed in assignment of students to team groups which could emphasize certain styles.

District-wide use of the learning styles data was the goal. To date, satisfaction with the process has been very high. School officials reported increased student learning, improved self concept, and better communication within the district. The district also anticipates that continued improvement in student learning will be evident as students are able to move through a school system wherein their learning styles are taken into consideration each year of their education.

## SUMMARY

The preceding cases illustrate a variety of ways learning styles theory has been utilized in educational settings. They also illustrate effective implementation of the principles implied in the research, and the variety of applications demonstrates the usefulness of the learning styles process. Teachers can and do find creative ways to use a learning style instrument which they view as manageable. Such innovative uses of the instrument hold promise for increased student learning through individualization of the learning process. The increased awareness of the learning/teaching styles theory and its practical application can also provide appreciation for others, foster growth experiences, tap hidden talents, and teach the art of flexibility (Butler, 1982) for both students and teachers.

# REFERENCES

Barbe, W. B., & Milone, M. N., Jr. (1980). Modality. *Instructor,* 39 (6), 45–47.

Brown, J. F., & Cooper, R. M. (1983). *Learning styles inventory.* Freeport, NY: Educational Activities, Inc. (Microcomputer program with teacher's guide).

Butler, K. A. (1982). Learning style across content areas. In *Student learning styles and brain behavior.* Reston, VA: National Association of Secondary School Principals.

Dunn, R., & Dunn, K. (1978). *Teaching students through their individual learning styles: A practical approach.* Reston, VA: Reston Publishing.

Entwistle, N. (1981). *Styles of learning and teaching.* New York: John Wiley and Sons.

Gregorc, A. F. (1979). Learning/teaching styles: Their nature and effects. *In Student learning styles: Diagnosing and prescribing programs.* Reston, VA: National Association of Secondary School Principals.

Gregorc, A. F., & Ward, H. B. (1977). Implications for learning and teaching—A new definition of individual. *NASSP Bulletin,* 61 (406), 20–23.

Kolb, D. A. (1981). Learning styles and disciplinary differences. In W. Chickering & Associates (Eds.), *The modern American college.* San Francisco: Jossey-Bass.

Project CITE. (1976). *Student learning styles—A survey.* Unpublished learning style instrument. Wichita, KS: Murdock Teachers Center.

Strother, S. D. (1982). Educational cognitive style mapping. In *Student learning styles and brain behavior.* Reston, VA: National Association of Secondary School Principals.

Witkin, H. A. (1981). *Cognitive styles: Essence and origins.* New York: International Universities Press.

*Peggy Friedman* is a consultant at the Murdock Teachers Center of the Wichita Public Schools, Wichita, Kansas.
*Robert Alley* is Associate Dean, College of Education, Wichita State University, Wichita, Kansas.

# Matching Learning Styles and Teaching Styles
## RONALD HYMAN AND BARBARA ROSOFF

The education literature today often recommends that learning style be matched with teaching style to augment achievement. The paradigm for "learning style based education" (LSBE) is: Examine the student's individual learning style; understand it and classify it according to several large categories; match it with a teaching style of an available teacher or ask that a teacher's teaching style be adjusted to match the student's learning style; and teach teachers to do all this in their preservice and inservice training programs.

Three major issues arising from this paradigm present serious difficulties: The concept of learning style is unclear, even among LSBE advocates; the focus on learning style in determining teaching action is inappropriate theoretically and realistically; and the action strategies and unintended consequences of following this paradigm are undesirable. The following recommendations are not sequential steps but together constitute a reorientation of thinking about matching learning styles and teaching styles.

First, educators who aim to help teachers improve should accept a more inclusive perspective on teaching. Teaching is an act which has three elements—the *teacher,* the *student,* and the *sub*

Excerpted from *Theory Into Practice* 23, No. 1 (Winter, 1984): 35–43. Used by permission of the authors and the publisher. © 1984, College of Education, The Ohio State University.

*ject matter*—interrelating in an *environment* and in a particular *time* period. Where there is teaching going on, all five elements are present. Thus, it is improper to focus on learning style as the sole or even main element influencing teacher action. Teachers must always keep in mind the time and place context, the nature of the subject matter under study, and also their own interests, knowledge, skill, and personality because all these are involved.

Second, teachers should realize that the teaching relationship is constantly changing. They ought not to believe that the student's learning style of today is that of next week. All educators, especially LSBE advocates, must be careful not to veiw scores on learning style preference or description tests as final and unchangeable. Learning style, part of the student element in the teaching relationship, is malleable. The student's learning style is always changing and adapting to the four other elements.

## STUDENT ACTIONS

Third, the teacher looking to diagnose learning style should see it as referring to *actions* of the student rather than ability. We also recommend a multidimensional perspective (cognitive, affective, and physiological) on student action. Therefore, teachers should use an informal approach to determining learning style. This approach, which gets information from student feedback and keen observation, will permit teachers to operationalize a definition of learning style with ease and without waiting for a perfect formal diagnostic instrument.

Fourth, teachers should accept a concept of learning broader than cognitive achievement as determined by a numerical score on a paper-and-pencil test. The task of teachers is complex and diverse. Students learn humanness as they blend the knowledge, the skills, and the values taught by teachers, explicitly or implicitly. What stu-

dents learn does not remain separated into neat cubbyholes but becomes an integrated whole. Students learn as they experience, reflect individually and with teacher help, and reconstruct experience. Therefore, it is impossible to identify one bit of learning from the other. This broader concept of learning is not compatible with precise measurement. Yet, teachers are in peril if they neglect it.

Fifth, teachers should recognize and attend to the only actions they can control—their own. No one can make students learn and act in specific ways. By attending to their own actions, teachers will come to accept that there are various teaching models or strategies which they can learn and employ in forms adapted to their particular combination of the five teaching elements. Learning, practicing, and utilizing a variety of teaching strategies will give teachers a sense of efficacy in the classroom. Being knowledgeable and skillful regarding their own actions—what they do, control, and are responsible for—is a requisite for teachers to be able to match learning styles with teaching styles. In this regard, we recommend that teachers attend to the literature on teaching and become students of teaching.

## BILATERALISM

Sixth, teachers should drop their unilateral approach to influencing student action and accept an approach which rests on mutuality, jointness of purpose, and bilateralism. We oppose the unilateral diagnostic procedure and the resulting unilateral action because they serve only to accomplish such negative consequences as lack of trust, low freedom of choice, manipulation, and dependency, while the consequences we want to develop include trust and trustworthiness, high freedom of choice, collaboration, and independence, along with the capacity to make intelligent decisions.

The unilateral LSBE paradigm employs a familiar medical metaphor: Teacher administers the learning style test, diagnoses the test results, prescribes the current teaching style for the "patient," and renders a prognosis for the parents and school officials. A bilateral model leads the teacher to share leadership, encourage students to speak out, and feel successful as a teacher once the students express themselves as individuals. In bilateralism, the students help diagnose their own learning style, help determine the appropriate teaching style, and at times even confront the teacher regarding the teaching situation's five essential elements. The teacher does not act unilaterally, does not define goals unilaterally, and does not impose ideas and values unilaterally.

## ILLUSTRATION

We recognize that the six recommendations made here require a different type of preservice and inservice program. For an illustration of change, we refer to what is already in place in one preservice program as one possible implementation step. In the student teaching seminars at the University of Wisconsin, five themes form the essential core of the discussions:

- Helping students to take a critical approach in the examination of educational issues or classroom problems;

- Helping students to see beyond conventional thought about classroom practice;
- Helping students to develop a sense of the history of their particular classroom and to examine the rationales underlying classroom and school regularities;
- Helping students to examine their own assumptions and biases and how these affect their classroom practice; and
- Helping students to examine critically the processes of their own socialization as teachers.

We believe that treatment of these five themes sensitizes the students to the problems of unilateral decision making in our schools, to the issues surrounding currently used paradigms, and to the need for alternative assumptions, strategies, and consequences. Such a seminar can lead to a solution, at least in part, because it guides the students toward a solid examination of the problems that teachers face. We believe it is a step in the right direction.

The issue of matching teaching styles with learning styles is not as simple as some LSBE advocates would have us believe. However, the LSBE advocates are correct in that the learning style issue is important for all teachers concerned with the proper education of their students. The six recommendations made here will, we believe, yield an acceptable way to match learning styles with teaching styles.

*Ronald Hyman* is Professor, Graduate School of Education, Rutgers University, New Brunswick, New Jersey.
*Barbara Rosoff* is a doctoral student at the Graduate School of Education, Rutgers University, New Brunswick, New Jersey.

# Promoting Excellence Through Mastery Learning

## JAMES H. BLOCK

Mastery learning is a topic currently creating much controversy and excitement in national and international education circles. The controversy centers around mastery learning's views about human potential to learn and teach; the excitement around mastery learning's classroom practices.

This article provides an introduction to mastery learning. [See Anderson and Block (1976), Block (1971, 1974), Block and Anderson (1975), Block and Burns (1976), Bloom (1976), and Torshen (1977) for more detailed treatments.] First, the article defines what mastery learning is. Then it examines how mastery learning works.

## WHAT IS IT?

What is mastery learning? It is two things.

First, mastery learning is an optimistic theory about teaching and learning. Essentially this theory asserts that any teacher can help virtually *all* students to learn excellently; the teacher can help "dumb" students to learn like the "smart" students, "slow" students to learn like the "fast" students, "retarded" students to learn like the "gifted" students. Such teaching, the theory contends, not only improves many students' chances for long term social and personal prosperity, but many teachers' chances as well. In particular, the students acquire those basic intellectual, manual, and emotional competencies which ensure that they can and want to undertake life-long learn-

ing. And the teachers acquire some basic pedagogical skills and career rewards which ensure that they can and want to keep teaching.

Second, mastery learning is an effective set of individualized instructional practices that consistently help *most* students to learn excellently. Some of these practices are of the group-based teacher-paced variety where students learn cooperatively with their classmates and where the teacher controls the delivery and flow of the instruction. The genotype for these practices would be Bloom/Block's "Learning for Mastery" (LFM) strategy (see Block and Anderson, 1975). The remainder of these practices are of the individually-based/student-paced variety where students learn independently of their classmates and where each student controls the delivery and flow of the instruction. The genotype for these practices would be Keller's "Personalized System of Instruction" (PSI) (see Keller and Sherman, 1974).

Like other individualized instructional strategies, such as IPI, IGE, and PLAN (see Talmage, 1975; Gronlund, 1974; Hambleton, 1974), both varieties of mastery learning strategies assume that virtually all students can master a great deal of what they are taught in school if the ". . . instruction is approached systematically, if students are helped when and where they have learning difficulties, if they are given sufficient time to achieve mastery, and if there is some clear criterion of what constitutes mastery" (Bloom 1974, p. 6). Unlike other individualized approaches, however, mastery approaches are

From *Theory Into Practice* 19, no. 1, College of Education, Ohio State University (Winter 1980): 66–74. Used by permission of the author and the publisher.

designed for use in the typical classroom situation where the teacher already possesses a curriculum which s/he must get through in a fixed period of calendar time, where inordinate amounts of instructional time cannot be spent in diagnostic-progress testing, and where student learning must be graded. Moreover, mastery approaches rely primarily on human beings for their success rather than on machines and other technological devices: teachers decide what goes on in the classroom and use their own instructional techniques and materials and students guide their own learning as well as the learning of others. Finally, at least one variety of these mastery approaches, *viz.*, the group-based/teacher-paced variety, can be implemented without major structural changes in school and classroom organization.

## HOW DOES IT WORK?

How do mastery learning strategies work? Let us describe the group-based/teacher-paced "Learning for Mastery" strategy. This strategy reflects all the basic mastery learning concepts and ideas. Moreover, it has proven to be one of the easiest mastery learning strategies to implement. We shall begin by describing the various steps in implementing the strategy. Then we shall examine the basic mastery learning concepts and techniques that underpin these steps.

The "Learning for Mastery" strategy is designed for use in instructional situations where the calendar time allowed for learning is relatively fixed and where students must be taught largely in groups. This strategy attempts to minimize the time a group of students need to learn excellently so that it is within the fixed amount of calendar time available for instruction. This is accomplished through two distinct sets of steps. One set—the Preconditions—occurs outside the classroom and prior to the instruction; the second set—the Operating Procedures—takes

place inside the classroom and during the instruction.

## Preconditions for Mastery Learning

*Defining Mastery.* The teacher who wishes to use a "Learning for Mastery" approach begins by formulating what is meant by "mastery" of the subject. Ideally, the teacher would first define what material all students will be expected to learn. This entails the formulation of course objectives. Next, the teacher would prepare a final or summative examination (Bloom, Hastings and Madaus, 1971) over all these objectives for administration at the course's close. Lastly, the teacher would set a summative examination score indicative of mastery performance. Students who perform better than this predetermined standard would be graded "masters"; those who do not would be graded "nonmasters."

In actual practice, though, teachers have found it useful to use their old course achievement tests as working definitions of the material that each student will be expected to master. They have also found it convenient to administer one or more of these tests throughout the course for grading purposes. Finally, rather than grade the student's performance on a mastery/nonmastery basis, the teachers have found it useful to fix an absolute grading scale wherein mastery corresponds to a grade of A and nonmastery corresponds to a grade of B, C, D, or F. The teacher forms this scale by determining the level of performance that students traditionally had to exhibit on the course examinations in order to earn an A, B, C, D, or F. All students who achieve to a particular level using mastery-learning methods then receive the grade that corresponds to this level.

*Planning for Mastery.* Now the teacher breaks the course to be taught for mastery into a sequence of smaller learning units, each of which typically covers about two weeks' worth of material. In practice, these units correspond roughly to chapters in the course textbook or to a set of topics.

Next, the teacher sequences these units. After all, the teacher has broken the whole course into pieces, s/he must now recast the pieces into a whole. Teachers of mathematics and sciences have tended to sequence their units linearly so that the material in each unit transfers directly to the next unit. Teachers of arts, humanities and social sciences, however, have tended to sequence their units hierarchically so that the material in each unit transfers but not necessarily to the next unit. It may transfer to a subsequent unit.

Then, for each unit the teacher develops perhaps the single most important component of the mastery learning strategy: the unit feedback correction procedures. These procedures will serve to monitor the effectiveness of the group-based instruction and to supplement it where necessary to better suit the learning requirements of certain students.

First, the teacher constructs a brief, ungraded diagnostic progress test or "formative" evaluation instrument (Bloom, Hastings and Madaus, 1971) for each unit. These tests are explicitly designed to be an integral part of each unit's instruction and to provide specific information or feedback to both the teacher and the student about how the student is changing as a result of the group-based instruction.

Next, the teacher specifies a score or performance standard on each formative test which, when met, will be indicative of unit mastery. Usually a score of 80 to 90 percent correct on a formative test indicates that the student is not having learning problems.

Finally, the teacher develops a set of alternative instructional materials and procedures or "correctives" keyed to each item on each unit's formative test. Typically these correctives have consisted of cooperative small group study sessions, individual tutoring by classmates, or alternative learning aids such as different textbooks, workbooks, audiovisual materials, academic games/puzzles, and affective exercises.

Each corrective is designed to reteach the material tested by certain items on the unit formative test, but to do so in ways that will differ from the unit's initial group-based instruction. The correctives may present the material in a different sensory mode or modes or in a different form of the same mode than the group-based instruction. They may involve the student in a different way and/or provide not only different types of encouragements for learning but also different amounts of each type. Hence, should a student encounter difficulty in learning certain material from the group-based instruction unit, he can then use the correctives to explore alternative ways of learning the unmastered material, select those correctives best suited to his particular learning requirements, and overcome his learning problems before they impair subsequent learning.

## Operating Procedures for Mastery Learning

*Orienting for Mastery.* The teacher is now ready to teach. Since students are not accustomed to learning for mastery or to the notion that they all might earn A's, the teacher usually must spend some time at the course's outset orienting them to the procedures to be used—what they are expected to learn, how they are generally expected to learn it, and to what level they are expected to learn. My experience has been that this orientation period—combined with continual encouragement, support, and positive evidence of learning success—is crucial in developing in most students the belief that they can learn and the motivation to learn.

The typical orientation periods have stressed the following:

1. The students are going to learn by a new method of instruction designed to help all of them learn well rather than just a few.
2. Each student will be graded *solely* on the basis of his performance on the final examination(s).
3. Each student will be graded against a predetermined performance standard and not in relation to the performance of his classmates. The standard of A work has been indicated.
4. Each student who attains this standard will receive an A.
5. There will be no fixed number of A's. Accordingly, cooperation with classmates in learning need not hurt a student's chances of earning an A. If a student and his classmates cooperate, and all of them learn well, then all will earn A's.
6. Each student will receive all the help he needs so as to learn. So if a student cannot learn in one way, then alternative ways will be readily available.
7. Throughout the course, each student will be given a series of ungraded diagnostic-progress tests to promote and pace his learning. He should use the information provided by these tests to locate misunderstandings and errors in learning.
8. Each student with learning problems will be given a number of alternative learning procedures or correctives to help him overcome his particular errors and misunderstandings.
9. The student should use his choice of the suggested correctives to "correct" these errors and misunderstandings before they accumulate and impair his subsequent learning.

*Teaching for Mastery.* Following this orientation period, the teacher teaches the first learning unit, using his/her customary group-based teaching methods. When this instruction has been completed, and before moving to the next unit, the teacher then administers the unit's formative test to the entire class. Next, each student usually corrects his/her own test. Finally, using a show of hands to discover the test results, the teacher certifies those students who have achieved the unit mastery standard and identifies those who have not. The former students are free to engage in enrichment activities and/or to serve as tutors for their "slower" classmates; the latter are asked to use the appropriate correctives to complete their unit learning.

The teacher then announces when the group-based instruction for the next unit will commence, and both sets of students are given responsibility for making use of the opportunities provided. If the teacher desires to postpone the start of the next unit, the students are given in-class as well as out-of-class time to discharge their respective responsibilities. If the teacher does not desire to postpone the start of the next unit, then the students must use out-of-class time.

The teacher repeats this cycle of initial instruction, diagnostic-progress testing, and certification or individual correction, unit by unit, until all units have been taught. The cycle is paced so that the teacher covers just as much material as would ordinarily be covered. Two pacing options are possible. If all the student enrichment/tutoring or correction responsibilities are to be discharged outside of class, then the teacher may pace each unit's instruction as in the past. However, if some or all responsibilities are to be discharged in class, the teacher can adjust the pace of the instruction, allowing more time for the early units and less time for the later ones. Essentially, the teacher borrows time that would ordinarily be spent on later units and spends this time on the earlier units. the assumption is that this borrowed time will not be needed later if students learn for mastery earlier.

*Grading for Mastery.* The teacher finally administers the course summative examination and awards A's or their equivalent to all students whose test scores are at or above the predetermined mastery performance standard. Those students who score below this level are awarded grades appropriate to the level they have achieved.

## SOME BASIC CONCEPTS

As noted earlier, some basic concepts about instruction underlie each of the preceding steps. Figure 1 indicates these concepts and the associated mastery techniques.

At the most general level, the conceptual level, mastery learning strategies are *systematic* approaches to instruction. They attempt to build a strong bridge between what the teacher desires to teach and whom s/he wants to teach. First, the instruction is matched to the course outcomes the teacher seeks, i.e., all mastery strategies are outcome-based. Then, the instruction is matched to the learners to be taught, i.e., all mastery strategies provide multiple methods for each student to attain each of these outcomes.

At a more specific level, the extra classroom level, mastery learning strategies are *proactive* approaches to instruction. Much of the teacher's time, effort, and energy is spent in planning outside of class for possible inside of class contingencies. Thus, when these contingencies occur the teacher is ready for them. S/he need not waste valuable time, effort, and energy reactively manufacturing all solutions on the spot.

Proactive teaching, from a mastery learning perspective, entails several stages. One stage is the definition of the learning outcomes the teacher is seeking. Obviously if the teacher has no clear idea of where his/her instruction is headed, then s/he is more likely to be seduced by fruitless pedagogical detours.

Outcome definition is a two step process. First, the practitioner must implicitly define what all students will be expected to attain and at what levels. Second, the practitioner must make his/her implicit definitions more explicit so they communicate clearly to the teacher what

**FIGURE 1**
**Mastery Learning: How Does It Work?**

| Concepts | Techniques |
|---|---|
| **GENERAL** | |
| A. Approach Instruction SYSTEMATICALLY: It Should Provide Bridge Between WHOM and WHAT You Teach | |
|    1. Match Instruction to OUTCOMES | → Base Instruction on Outcomes |
|    2. Match Instruction to LEARNERS | → Provide Multiple Instructional Methods |
| | |
| **SPECIFIC: EXTRA CLASSROOM** | |
| B. Be PROACTIVE, not Reactive | |
|    1. Clarify OUTCOMES | → Pre-Define Mastery and Make it Explicit |
|    2. Provide for APPROPRIATE HELP in Learning | → Pre-Plan Instruction for Mastery |
|    3. Provide for APPROPRIATE LEARNING TIME | → Pre-Plan Instruction for Mastery |
| | |
| **SPECIFIC: INTRA CLASSROOM** | |
| C. Manage LEARNING, not Learners | |
|    1. Provide STUDENT ORIENTATION | → Orient Students to Mastery Learning |
|    2. Vary HOW and HOW LONG Each Student is Taught as Necessary | → Use Pre-Planned Instruction to Teach for Mastery |
|    3. PERSONALIZE GRADING | → Grade for Mastery |

must be taught and to the students what must be learned.

Both of these steps are accomplished in mastery learning strategies in the process of defining mastery. When the mastery practitioner formulates the course instructional objectives and constructs a special course final or "summative" examination based upon them, the practitioner has explicated what all students will be expected to attain. And when s/he sets some mastery grading standards on the summative examination, the practitioner has explicated what levels all students will be expected to attain.

A second stage in proactive teaching is the provision of appropriate help in learning. Oftentimes, student learning problems at one point in the classroom instruction stem from unresolved problems from earlier points. So these earlier problems must be identified and corrected as they occur.

This identification and correction is accomplished in mastery learning strategies through the pre-planning of the classroom instruction. First, the teacher breaks the entire course into smaller learning units. Each unit is long enough to convey a number of skills, ideas, concepts and appreciations but small enough to allow the close monitoring of each student's learning as the units, i.e., the course, unfolds. Second, the teacher sequences these units so that the material in one unit is used over and over in the subsequent units. This procedure helps ensure that if this material is taught well once, then the material will not be forgotten and will be available for later use. Finally, the teacher formulates a plan of mastery instruction for each unit consisting of (a) the *original instruction* whereby the unit's material will be taught initially—typically this instruction will be similar in content and delivery, if not identical, to the teacher's customary group-based instruction; (b) a *feedback* instrument (pencil and paper or otherwise) whereby each student's learning from the original instruction can be described diagnostically and pre-

scriptively; (c) a *mastery standard* whereby sufficient and insufficient learning progress can be judged; and (d) the *correction* whereby the unit's material can be taught in a variety of ways different from the original instruction. This plan enables the teacher to monitor student learning as it unfolds on a unit by unit basis and to exercise a necessary measure of quality control should the learning ever unfold less than excellently.

A third stage in proactive teaching is the provision of appropriate learning time. Clearly, if each student is to be provided with appropriate help in learning, then sufficient time must be found to make use of this help. All students cannot be allowed the same amount of learning time, if this time is insufficient for most students.

The provision of appropriate learning time is also accomplished through the pre-planning of the classroom instruction. This pre-planning helps, first, to increase the quantity of time that each student spends in learning. Essentially, it constrains each student to spend as much time as is necessary to master the material in one unit before attempting the material in the next one. For many students, this means spending far more learning time in class and/or outside of class than is customary. They can no longer passively settle for mediocrity or worse in their learning; they must actively pursue excellence. The pre-planning helps, second, to increase the quality of the time that each student spends in learning. Essentially, it helps to ensure that no student spends unnecessary time learning by methods that are poorly suited to his/her learning requirements. If any student cannot learn excellently from the original instruction, the student can learn excellently from one or more correctives. S/he need not waste time restudying the ineffective original instruction.

And at the most specific level, the intra-classroom level, mastery strategies are *management of learning* approaches to instruction. They propose that inside the classroom ". . . the function of the teacher is to specify what is to be learned, to motivate pupils to learn it, to provide them with instructional materials, to administer these materials at a rate suitable for each pupil, to monitor students' progress, to diagnose difficulties and provide proper remediation for them, to give praise and encouragement for good performance, and to give review and practice that will maintain pupils' learning over long periods of time" (Carroll, 1971, pp. 29–30).

The management of learning is executed in three basic stages by mastery practitioners. In the orientation stage, they indicate in a concrete fashion how and toward what ends students will be taught. Obviously, no instructional technique can succeed if the ground in which it is sown is not properly prepared.

In the teaching stage, they then vary, as necessary, how and how long each student is taught by using their pre-planned instructional units. The original instruction for each unit gives all students a chance to learn excellently from one method of instruction over one period of time. The feedback instrument and mastery standard indicates those students for whom the original instruction and the initial learning time was sufficient and for whom it was not. The unit's correctives provide these latter students with the opportunity to master the material not mastered from the original instruction using additional methods of instruction and additional learning time as necessary.

In the grading stage, the practitioner evaluates the students on a more personal basis. Students are graded for what they actually have learned. In short, they are graded for mastery. Such mastery grading is designed to engage what White (1959) has called "competence motivation," i.e., the intrinsic desire to compete against oneself and the material to be learned, and to disengage what I (Block, 1977) have alluded to as "competition motivation," i.e., the extrinsic desire to compete against others. From

the standpoint of developing the talent of all students, rather than a few, the engagement of the former motivation makes much more sense than the engagement of the latter.

## HOW WELL DOES IT WORK?

How well, then, does mastery learning work? As numerous practitioners have discovered, mastery learning represents a particular commitment about education, i.e., an innovative philosophy and set of practices for its improvement (Dunkin and Biddle, 1974). But is this commitment, like so many others, "attractively argued but unsupported by data" (Dunkin and Biddle, 1974, p. 51) or supported by data that indicates it works 51 percent of the time and fails 49 percent of the other? The answer is No! Mastery learning strategies may not work quite as well as their advocates propose, but they do work very well indeed.

Let us review the mastery learning research according to criteria set out by Dunkin and Biddle (1974) for evaluating any commitment. These are:

1. . . . that a given teaching practice is presently occurring in typical classrooms;
2. . . . that an alternative teaching practice can be encouraged by changes in teacher education programs . . . ;
3. . . . that the alternative teaching practice produces more desirable classroom processes or (preferably) products in pupil growth than the present practice (Dunkin and Biddle, 1974, p. 52).

*Classroom Usage.* There can be no question that mastery learning ideas and practices are presently occurring in many typical classrooms. Indeed, as I (Block, 1979) note in a special issue of *Educational Leadership* on mastery learning, with the help of dedicated practitioners and administrators, of innovative teacher inservice and pre-service programs, of progressive national and international educational organizations (e.g., ASCD, NEA, NASA, UNESCO, IEA), of leading educational publishers (e.g., McGraw-Hill, SRA, Westinghouse Learning Corporation, Random House), and of powerful news media (e.g., New York Times, CBS Television), mastery learning has helped reshape the face of contemporary educational practice. Not only are mastery learning ideas being widely implemented here, they are also being widely implemented abroad.

Two trends in the classroom usage of mastery learning are now obvious. One trend is the growing use of mastery learning ideas and practices on a large scale basis. Mastery learning is being used with a greater *number* of subjects, classes, teachers, and schools than ever before. Whereas in the early part of the 1970s, the typical experiment involved one subject, class, teacher and school, the current experiments often involve many subjects, classes, teachers, and schools. Indeed, in North America it is not uncommon to find entire school districts (e.g., Chicago, Denver, District of Columbia, New Orleans, Philadelphia, Vancouver) actively plumbing the value of mastery learning for their particular educational situation and, especially, for purposes of Competency-Based Education (Spady, 1978). What is true here is even more true abroad. Countries such as South Korea, Indonesia, and Australia already have large-scale tests of mastery learning under way with the South Korean tests involving several million students in all the subjects grades 1–9. About ten to twenty other member nations of the IEA (International Study of Educational Achievement) should have additional large-scale tests off the ground by 1981–82.

The second trend is the growing use of mastery learning ideas and practices on a more adaptive basis. Mastery learning is being used by more variety of subjects, classes, teachers and

schools to meet particular needs. Whereas in the early part of the 1970s, the typical experiment involved:

1. subjects that were basic, required, "closed," and oriented toward convergent thinking;
2. classes that were small and "regular";
3. teachers who were inexperienced, behaviorally or cognitively oriented, and "majority" members; and
4. schools that were suburban, elementary-level, academically-oriented, and public;

The current experiments increasingly involve:

5. subjects that are intermediate or advanced, elective, "open," and oriented toward divergent thinking;
6. classes that are large and "special" (e.g., handicapped, bilingual);
7. teachers who are experienced, humanistically oriented, and "minority" members; and
8. schools that are urban and rural, secondary and tertiary-level, technically professionally oriented, and private.

*Teacher Training.* There also can be no question that mastery learning ideas and practices can be taught to teachers. Teachers both here and abroad have participated in countless local, regional, statewide, and national preservice and inservice teacher training workshops and credentialing courses. Moreover, the experiences gleaned from these workshops and courses have already been packaged in a variety of how to do it manuals perhaps the best known of which are Block and Anderson's (1975) *Mastery Learning in Classroom Instruction,* Keller and Sherman's (1974) *The Keller Plan Handbook,* Okey and Ciesla's (1975) *Mastery Teaching,* and Torshen's (1977) *The Mastery Approach to Competency-Based Education.* More workshops and courses and how to do it manuals are bound to appear.

Nor can there be much question that once teachers are taught for mastery they can use their training in the classroom. Okey (1975), for example, taught twenty inservice teachers and twenty preservice interns how to teach for mastery and then followed them back to their classrooms. He found that students noted a perceptible change in their teachers' and interns' behavior when they taught for mastery. For example, students saw the teachers and interns as telling them what they were expected to learn, allowing them different amounts of learning time, and using diagnostic tests to monitor their progress.

But there is a distinct question as to whether inexperienced preservice teachers use their training as effectively as experienced inservice ones. Okey (1975), for example, found that inservice teachers were far more likely to elicit greater learning from their students under mastery learning conditions than preservice interns. And my own experience, as well as that of others, has been similar. Perhaps this is because learning how to teach for mastery requires less in the way of the acquisition of a whole new set of teaching skills and more in the way of orchestrating and supplementing the skills one already has. Preservice interns would tend to have fewer classroom skills to orchestrate than inservice teachers.

*Student Outcomes.* Lastly, there can be little question that mastery learning ideas and practices promote student growth. Indeed, the impact that mastery learning ideas and practices have had on student cognitive and affective development has been remarkable.

Consider, for example, a recent review by Block and Burns (1976) of some forty rigorous studies of student outcomes under mastery and nonmastery approaches to instruction. This review's findings echoed the general findings of earlier and later reviews. Block and Burns (1976) reported the following:

Learning Effectiveness. Mastery-taught students typically learned more effectively than their nonmastery-taught counterparts. Whether learning was measured in terms of student achievement or in terms of student retention, they almost always learned more, and usually significantly more, and they learned more like one another.

Learning Efficiency. Mastery-taught students also typically learned more efficiently than their nonmastery taught counterparts. Whereas in the nonmastery-taught classrooms some students learned several times as fast as other students, in the mastery-taught classrooms individual differences in learning rate were substantially less. In fact, in these latter classrooms individual differences in learning rate seemed headed toward a vanishing point in which even the "slowest" students would learn roughly as fast as the "fastest" students.

Learner Affect. Lastly, mastery-taught students liked their learning, their teaching and themselves better than their nonmastery-taught counterparts. They virtually always responded more positively than their counterparts, for example, on measures of interest in and attitudes toward the subject matter learned, of self-concept (academic as well as general), of academic self-confidence, of attitudes toward cooperative learning, and of attitudes toward the instruction. Whether their more favorable affective responses were just momentary expressions of enthusiasm or more permanent ones that would carry over into their subsequent work was, however, indeterminable.

## SUMMARY

This article has provided an introduction to the topic of mastery learning. Specifically, the article addressed three questions: what is mastery learning, how does it work, and how well does it work?

We have learned that mastery learning is essentially an optimistic theory about teaching and learning and an effective set of individualized instructional practices for implementing this theory in the ordinary classroom setting. At the heart of this theory is the assertion that any teacher can help virtually all of his/her students to learn excellently.

We have also learned that mastery learning works on the basis of three large assumptions about what constitutes teaching for excellence. The most general of these assumptions is that the teacher must approach his/her instruction more systematically in the sense that the instruction should definitely bridge what is to be taught to who is to be taught. This means that the instruction for mastery learning is outcome-based and provides multiple ways for each student to reach each outcome.

A more specific assumption is that the teacher must become more proactive in his/her instruction in the sense that more time, effort, and energy is spent outside of class readying for possible inside of class contingencies. This means that the teacher predefines and explicates "mastery" in learning so that the classroom outcomes s/he is seeking are clear. And the teacher pre-plans the classroom instruction for mastery learning so that it consistently provides appropriate help and learning time for each student.

The most specific assumption is that the teacher must concentrate more heavily on the management of learning in the classroom. This means the teacher orients students to learning for mastery so that they are clear about how and what they will be taught. The teacher also uses the preplanned classroom instruction for mastery learning so that how and how long each student is taught varies appropriately. And the teacher grades for mastery learning so that each student is graded on a more personal and less competitive basis.

Lastly, we have learned that mastery learning has worked very well indeed. Mastery learning ideas and practices are being widely used in classrooms both here and abroad and their use is on the rise. They are also being widely disseminated to preservice and inservice teachers. When the ideas and practices have been learned and used, they have consistently promoted student growth. Students have not only learned more effectively and efficiently, they have also felt better about their learning, their instruction, and themselves.

Much that we have learned about mastery learning theory, practice and research will, of course, seem "old hat" to some educators. After all, an optimistic faith in all students' capacity for excellent learning, an approach to instruction that is systematic, proactive and learning oriented, and an approach that consistently promotes student cognitive and affective growth have long been the trademarks of the *paragons* of the teaching profession. What should be "new hat," however, is the message that mastery learning theory, practice and research now offer these trademarks of our best teachers to *all* our teachers. Surely, at a time when public confidence in the teaching profession is low, such a message cannot be ignored.

## REFERENCES

Anderson, L. W., and Block, J. H. "Mastery Learning." In Treffinger, D., Davis, J. and Ripple, R. (Eds.), *Handbook on Educational Psychology: Instructional Practice and Research*. New York: Academic Press, 1976.

Block, J. H. (Ed.). *Mastery Learning: Theory and Practice.* New York: Holt, Rinehart and Winston, 1971.

——. *Schools, Society, and Mastery Learning.* New York: Holt, Rinehart and Winston, 1974.

——. "Motivation, Evaluation, and Mastery Learning." UCLA *Educator,* Winter, 1977, vol. 19, no. 2, pp. 31–36.

——. "Mastery Learning: The Current State of the Craft." *Educational Leadership,* vol. 37, no. 2, November 1979, pp. 114–117.

Block, J. H., and Anderson, L. W. *Mastery Learning in Classroom Instruction.* New York: Macmillan, 1975.

Block, J. H., and Burns, R. B. "Mastery Learning." In

Shulman, L. (Ed.), *Review of Research in Education,* vol. 4. Itasca, Ill.: F. E. Peacock, 1976.

Bloom, B. S. "An Introduction to Mastery Learning Theory." In Block, J. H. (Ed.), *Schools, Society, and Mastery Learning.* New York: Holt, Rinehart and Winston, 1974.

———. *Human Characteristics and School Learning.* New York: McGraw-Hill, 1976.

Bloom, B. S., Hastings, J. T., and Madaus, G. F. *Handbook on Formative and Summative Evaluation of Student Learning.* New York: McGraw-Hill, 1971.

Carroll, J. B. "Problems of Measurement Related to the Concept of Learning for Mastery." In Block, J. H. (Ed.), *Mastery Learning: Theory and Practice.* New York: Holt, Rinehart and Winston, 1971.

Dunkin, M. J., and Biddle, B. J. *The Study of Teaching.* New York: Holt, Rinehart and Winston, 1974.

Gronlund, N. *Individualizing Classroom Instruction.* New York: Macmillan Publishing Co., 1974.

Hambleton, R. K. "Testing and Decision-making Procedures for Selected Individualized Instructional Pro-grams." *Review of Educational Research,* 1974, vol. 44, pp. 371–400.

Keller, F. S., and Sherman, J. G. *The Keller Plan Handbook.* Menlo Park, California: W. A. Benjamin, 1974.

Okey, J. R. "Development of Mastery Teaching Materials." (Final Evaluation Rep., USOE G-74-2990), Bloomington: Indiana University, August 1975.

Okey, J., and Ciesla, J. *Mastery Teaching.* Bloomington: National Center for the Development of Training Materials in Teacher Education, Indiana University, 1975.

Spady, W. G. "The Concept and Implications of Competency-based Education." *Educational Leadership,* 1978, vol. 36, pp. 16–22.

Talmage, H. (Ed.). *Systems of Individualized Education.* Berkeley, California: McCutchan, 1975.

Torshen, K. P. *The Mastery Approach to Competency-based Education.* New York: Academic Press, 1977.

White, R. W. "Motivation Reconsidered: The Concept of Competence." *Psychological Review,* 1959, vol. 66, pp. 297–333.

*James H. Block* is Associate Professor, Department of Education, University of California, Santa Barbara.

## ADDITIONAL LEARNING ACTIVITIES

### Problems and Projects

1. Continue to develop a "case problem" about one school you know well. Relate the curriculum and teaching in that school to each of the four learning theory positions. To do this, you may find it necessary to describe the teaching and curriculum in more than one subject field or by more than one teacher. You can add to your study as you work on each of the bases of the curriculum and the criteria.

2. Prepare a lesson plan in your subject which is based on at least three of the learning theory perspectives described in this section. Review the articles by Combs, Madsen and Madsen, Avila and Purkey, McDaniel, and Gregorc in this section; by Grant with John Briggs, and Ausubel (on advance organizers) in Section 3; and by Bruner (Section 5) to assist you in writing this lesson plan.

3. The rationale for this section states that there are different kinds of learners, different kinds of learning, and different kinds of knowledge. Because each of the four families of learning theories offers a different approach to curriculum planning, they supply the planner with alternatives for providing for these differences. Prepare a list of the various areas of the curriculum (such as the humanities, vocational education, etc.) and identify the learning theory ap-

proaches that you consider most appropriate for each. Explain your choices and compare them with those of other members of your class or group.

4. In "A Primer on Motivation," McDaniel presents five principles that curriculum planners and teachers can use to produce better motivation for learning. Examine the five principles and explain the learning theory position from which each principle has been derived.

5. In his article in this section, James H. Block defines mastery learning and examines how it works. He concludes that it works "very well indeed." Another proponent of mastery learning is Benjamin S. Bloom. As a result of his research, he has concluded that "What any person in the world can learn, almost all persons can learn, given the appropriate conditions of learning." To learn what these conditions are, read one or more of the articles by Bloom, Brandt, or Trotter (see Books and Articles to Review at the end of this section). Then analyze mastery learning in terms of the four bases of the curriculum. Compare Bloom's views of mastery learning with those of Block.

6. A psychologist whose views are closely related to those of Combs in this section is Abraham Maslow. In his work on the "self-actualizing personality," Maslow developed a hierarchy of motivational needs that must be satisfied one by one (physiological needs, safety needs, belongingness and love needs, esteem needs, and the need for self-actualization (which includes intellectual and aesthetic needs)). To learn more about Maslow and his work, read Chapter 4 in his book *Motivation and Personality*, second edition, New York: Harper and Row, 1954. Another source: Combs, Arthur, ed., *Perceiving, Behaving, Becoming*, the 1962 ASCD Yearbook.

7. Bruce Joyce and Marsha Weil, in their book *Models of Teaching*, third edition (Prentice-Hall, 1980), have included a model by Carl Rogers (perceptual field learning theorist) called "Non-Directive Teaching" (pages 149–164). Read about this model in that book, and relate what you read to the Combs article in this section. In your opinion, when are these approaches to teaching and learning most appropriate?

8. Joyce and Weil (see problem number 7) have also included a model for teaching called "Behavior Modification" in their book (pages 326–401). Read that section in *Models of Teaching* and relate it to the Madsen and Madsen article in this section. When is it most appropriate for the curriculum planner to use these approaches to teaching? For another description of the "Behavior Control Model," see pages 54–59 in *Second Handbook of Research on Teaching*, Robert M. W. Travers, Ed. (Chicago: Rand McNally & Co., 1973).

9. Examine a recent curriculum guide, of interest to you or in your field of teaching, to determine what learning theory or theories are the basis for the suggested learning activities. Then add some additional learning activities of your own based on a learning theory approach that is not used in the guide.

10. In a discussion of types of teaching strategies, Ronald J. Hyman describes what he calls the "exemplifying strategy" (see chapter 10 in the Yearbook of the National Society for the Study of Education, *Issues in Secondary Education*, Wil-

liam Van Til, ed. [Chicago: University of Chicago Press, 1976]. Hyman states that the exemplifying strategy is the one least used consciously and deliberately by teachers. What are the advantages and disadvantages of this teaching strategy? Which of the learning theory families described in the rationale for this section is the basis for the teaching strategy?

11. Jean Piaget has summarized his views on learning in *To Understand Is to Invent: The Future of Education* (New York: Grossman Publishers, 1973). He states that understanding is a process of discovery or reconstruction by rediscovery, and that the classroom should use an active method of teaching that gives broad scope to the spontaneous research of a child or adolescent. Do you agree? With which of the learning theories do you associate these views? Read this book by Piaget to gain additional knowledge of his views on learning and teaching methods.

12. In chapter 5 of his book, *Two Worlds of Childhood: U.S. and U.S.S.R.* (New York: Russell Sage Foundation, 1970), Urie Bronfenbrenner discusses the potency of models, imitation learning, and social learning and compares the ways that these learning principles are used in teaching children in the United States and the Soviet Union. Read this chapter, and then write a summary about the ways you think these learning principles should be used in curriculum planning or teaching.

13. The Appendix of this book includes a list of books that describe a school or school program. Select one that interests you and determine whether learning theories have been adequately considered in the curriculum planning and teaching described in the book. You can add to your study of this school's program as you work on each of the bases of the curriculum and the criteria.

14. Have your personal beliefs or values about learning changed as a result of your experience with this section? If so, state what change has taken place, and relate it to one or more of the activities in this section (the rationale, an article, an additional learning activity, a postassessment activity, etc.). Compare your ideas with those of the other members of your class.

## Films and Audiocassettes

*James Block on "What Mastery Learning Is All About."* Audiocassette, 31 min., 1980. Philosophy, goals, and outcomes of mastery learning are introduced for effective management of learning. Association for Supervision and Curriculum Development, 225 North Washington St., Alexandria, VA 22314.

*The Process of Teaching.* Six films, 16 mm, black and white, total 50 min., 1976. Modeling (10 min.), shaping (5 min.), negative reinforcement (5 min.), respondent learning (10 min.), operant learning (10 min.), positive reinforcement (10 min.). Instructional Media Center, Michigan State University, East Lansing, Michigan 48824.

*How Children Learn.* 16 mm, color, 23 min., 1972. Various types of schools at all age levels are using new teaching methods that free the creativity of children. National Broadcasting Co., Inc., 30 Rockefeller Plaza, New York, New York 10020.

*Interview with Dr. B. F. Skinner* (Part I). 16 mm, black and white, 50 min., 1964. Dr. Skinner presents his views on motivation, schedules of reinforcement, and teaching machines. Crowell, Collier, and Macmillan, 866 Third Avenue, New York, New York 10022.

*Interview with Dr. B. F. Skinner* (Part II). 16 mm, black and white, 50 min., 1964. Dr. Skinner discusses

*Walden II* and evaluates the American educational system. Crowell, Collier, and Macmillan, 866 Third Avenue, New York, New York 10022.

*Rewards and Reinforcements.* 16 mm, black and white, 26 min., 1968. Economically underprivileged children often must be provided with motives for learning. Behavior may need to be reinforced with extrinsic rewards to gradually shape more difficult tasks. NET Film Service, Indiana University, Audio-Visual Center, Bloomington, Indiana 47401.

## Books and Articles to Review

"An Annotated Bibliography of Selected Learning Styles Instrumentation." Appendix 2 in *Student Learning Styles and Brain Behavior.* Reston, VA.: NASSP, 1982: 228–231.

Ausubel, David. *Educational Psychology,* 2nd ed. New York: Holt, Rinehart and Winston, 1978.

Block, James H., ed. *Schools, Society, and Mastery Learning.* New York: Holt, Rinehart and Winston, 1974.

Bloom, Benjamin S., "The Search for Methods of Instruction as Effective as One-to-One Tutoring." *Educational Leadership* 41, no. 8 (May 1984): 4–17.

Brandt, Ronald S. "On Talent Development: A Conversation with Benjamin S. Bloom." *Educational Leadership* 43, no. 1 (September 1985): 33–35.

Brown, Bertram S. "Behavior Modification, What It Is—and Isn't." *Today's Education* 65, no. 1 (January-February 1976): 67–69.

Combs, Arthur, ed. *Perceiving, Behaving, Becoming.* Washington, D.C.: Association for Supervision and Curriculum Development, 1962.

Combs, A. W., Popham, W. J., and Hosford, P. L. "Behaviorism and Humanism: A Synthesis?" *Educational Leadership* 35, no. 1 (October 1977): 52–63.

Doyle, Walter, and Rutherford, Barry. "Classroom Research on Matching Teaching and Learning Styles." *Theory Into Practice* 23, no. 1 (Winter 1984): 20–25.

Dunn, Rita. "Learning Style: State of the Science." *Theory Into Practice* 23, no. 1 (Winter 1984): 10–19.

Fizzell, Robert L. "The Status of Learning Styles." *Educational Forum* 48, no. 3 (Spring 1984): 303–312.

Gagné, R. M. *The Conditions of Learning,* 3rd ed. New York: Holt, Rinehart and Winston, 1977.

Gregorc, Anthony F. "Style as a Symptom: A Phenomenological Perspective." *Theory Into Practice* 23, no. 1 (Winter 1984): 51–55.

Heiman, Marcia. "Learning to Learn." *Educational Leadership* 43, no. 1 (September 1985): 20–24.

Keefe, James W. "Assessment of Learning Style Variables: The NASSP Task Force Model." *Theory Into Practice* 24, no. 2 (Spring 1985): 138–144.

———— "Student Learning Styles." *Student Learning Styles and Brain Behavior.* Reston, VA.: NASSP, 1982; 227.

Lyons, Carol A., and Languis, Marlin L. "Cognitive Science and Teacher Education." *Theory Into Practice* 24, no. 2 (Spring 1985): 127–130.

"Mastery Learning." (15 Articles) *Educational Leadership* 37, no. 2 (November 1979): 100–161.

NASSP. *Student Learning Styles: Diagnosing and Prescribing Programs.* Reston, VA: National Association of Secondary School Principals, 1979.

———— *Student Learning Styles and Brain Behavior: Programs, Instrumentation, Research.* Reston, VA: National Association of Secondary School Principals, 1982.

Piaget, Jean. *To Understand Is To Invent: The Future of Education.* New York: Grossman Publishers, 1973.

Purkey, William W. *Inviting School Success: A Self Concept Approach to Teaching and Learning.* Belmont, California: Wadsworth Publishing Co., 1978.

Rogers, Carl. *Freedom to Learn for the 80's.* Columbus, OH: Charles E. Merrill, 1982.

Smith, Linda H., and Renzulli, Joseph S. "Learning Style Preferences: A Practical Approach for Classroom Teachers." *Theory Into Practice* 23, no. 1 (Winter 1984): 44–50.

Sylvester, Robert. "Research on Memory: Major Discoveries, Major Educational Challenges." *Educational Leadership* 42, no. 7 (April 1985): 69–75.

Travers, Robert M. W. *Essentials of Learning,* 4th ed. New York: The Macmillan Co., 1977.

Trotter, Robert J. "The Mystery of Mastery." *Psychology Today* 20, no. 7 (July 1986): 32–39.

# 5

# *Knowledge and Cognition*

## PREREQUISITE

Reading Sections 1 through 4.

## RATIONALE

During the 1960s, emphasis was increasingly placed on knowledge as a basis for making curriculum decisions. Before the 1960s, human development, learning, and the society were seen as the bases of curriculum planning.

In *Experience and Education* (1938), John Dewey wrote one of the key ideas regarding knowledge as one of the bases of curriculum planning. He stated that

> finding the material for learning within experience is only the first step. The next step is the progressive development of what is already experienced into a fuller and richer and also more organized form, a form that gradually approximates that in which subjectmatter is presented to the skilled, mature person.

Curriculum theorists and practitioners of that time were so intent on implementing human development or learning or society as the basis for planning that they continued to give little attention to knowledge. Dewey's ideas about knowledge and the curriculum, included in this quotation, are presented in "Progressive Organization of Subject-Matter" in this section.

In 1961, in his presidential address at the Association for Supervision and Curriculum Development, Arthur W. Foshay pointed out that we were trying to plan curricula without considering formal knowledge. He proposed that when curriculum planners make curriculum decisions, they should take directly into account the nature of organized bodies of knowledge in addition to the nature of the growing child and the nature of our society (see *Educational Leadership,* May 1961).

Scholars have organized portions of knowledge into disciplines. A discipline consists of a set of generalizations that explain the relationships among a body of facts and concepts. Also, scholars in each discipline have developed methods of inquiry useful in discovering new knowledge. Each discipline is a human product and is subject to revision if a different organization proves more functional.

*Some think of knowledge as organized bodies of facts and concepts* and believe that all of the knowledge that has been discovered, learned, or invented has been collected, catalogued, and organized into the most useful structures. Further, they often believe that the school's function is to accept the organizations of knowledge that have been made in the past and devise ways of helping each learner acquire as much of it as he or she can. According to this viewpoint, curriculum workers and teachers must examine each subject or discipline and decide upon a sequence in which the facts, concepts, and generalizations should be learned and the pace and procedures by which learners should be brought into contact with them.

Certain problems have arisen for those who follow this logic. The knowledge available to people has accumulated at an extremely rapid rate and will multiply even faster in the years ahead. It is impossible, and will become even more so, to have any one learner learn all the facts, concepts, generalizations, and methods of inquiry— even in one discipline. Moreover new knowledge constantly makes some previous knowledge in each discipline obsolete. What shall be taught? How shall it be taught to enable learners to use their knowledge to greatest advantage and to be able to accommodate additional knowledge?

*Others view knowledge as a much more flexible, fluid product of people's experience.* They say that more often than not the organization of knowledge produced by the scholars is not functional in life experiences and in new situations or problems. They state that the definition and the structure of a discipline are human inventions and may be revised in light of new knowledge, and that new disciplines can be formed as needed. And this is happening today to an ever increasing degree.

Those who believe that knowledge should be more functional say that each individual attempts to understand himself or herself and his or her environment. In the process, individuals invent interpretations of their environment and of their own actions. These interpretations are unique to each person, and constitute the knowledge that is real and of personal value. Through attempts to understand himself or herself and the environment, the individual is brought into contact with facts and concepts that others have discovered and organized. The organization may or may not have meaning for the person. He or she decides. He or she determines how the newly contacted data will be incorporated into his or her system of knowledge. This structure of knowledge—actual structure and not the one the individual may verbalize—is personally invented and constructed. This view of knowledge finds support in the emphasis that perceptual learning theorsts place on *personal meaning.* Each learner determines what information and knowledge means to him or her (see the article by Combs, "Some Basic Concepts in Perceptual Psychology," in Section 4).

Curriculum workers and teachers who hold this second conception of the nature of knowledge approach curriculum construction and teaching in a different manner. They are not sure that the traditional disciplines should be the guides for organizing the curriculum. They want to start with the concerns and needs of the learner, and they want to encourage him or her to use knowledge from any discipline that will help.

If the curriculum is to be related to present social forces, the subject of Section 2, then it is not possible to organize the curriculum just according to the separate disciplines. Problems of race, environment, lawlessness, and social change cannot be understood by anything other than interdisciplinary or multi-disciplinary study. And human development theories and research, as presented in Section 3, suggest the need to organize at least part of what is studied on the basis of the personal-social problems of learners of a particular age level. These personal-social problems are not related to any one discipline but require interdisciplinary or multi-disciplinary study.

*A third position regarding knowledge and its uses in curriculum planning and teaching combines the two positions already described.* Curriculum and instruction planners who adhere to this position believe that interdisciplinary, multi-disciplinary, and problems approaches, *as well as* structured approaches to disciplines, *are all needed* in curriculum planning. As is stated in the Section 4 rationale on "Learning," there are different kinds of knowledge and different human needs for knowledge. Transfer in learning is aided when there is structure, order, and configuration in what is learned. Often the structure of the disciplines can aid in providing order, but frequently the learner needs assistance in providing his or her own structure and order to meet his or her own problems or to understand society's problems.

In "Structures in Learning," Jerome Bruner tells us that knowledge has a structure, an internal connectedness, a meaningfulness, and teachers should strive to assist learners to fit knowledge into that internal meaningful context. He describes a method for doing this which he calls "discovery learning."

Brain research is also now being related to knowledge and cognitive style as one of the bases of curriculum planning. Research studies show that the human brain consists of two parts, or hemispheres, each of which has unique characteristics. According to the research presented in "Children Think With Whole Brains: Myth and Reality" in this section, the two sides of the brain differ in quite important ways. These differences have little to do with the popularized picture of rationality and logic as residing only in the left hemisphere and intuition and creativity as the sole province of the right hemisphere. The left hemisphere leads in such mental activities as analytical, abstract, linear, and sequential thought; the right hemisphere leads in simultaneous, sensory, visual, holistic, and spatial functions. But logic is not confined to the left hemisphere, nor is intuition or creativity confined to the right.

What are the implications of this research for curriculum planning and teaching? Several guidelines are available:

1.  There is ample evidence that the left hemisphere is more active in some learners and the right hemisphere is more active in others.
2.  What is needed is "whole-brain learning" in which the right hemisphere is involved with its emotion and arousal functions.
3.  The gateway to whole-brain learning requires different approaches and methods for different learners (see the articles by Taitt and Taitt and by Brennan in this section, and the one by Bussis on reading instruction in Section 7).
4.  All areas of the curriculum depend equally on both hemispheres and on the synthesis of their specialized abilities.
5.  Challenges are needed in order to engage the whole brain—to generate excitement, interest and attention.
6.  Individual learners need to know about their own special pathways to learning. This knowledge can be the basis for lifelong self-education.

Balance in the curriculum is needed between right and left hemisphere activities and development. Interdisciplinary, holistic, and problem-oriented approaches should be part of the curriculum. Research indicates that courses and experiences in art, music, and physical education should be a significant part of the curriculum for all learners, and should be incorporated into the more linear subjects. Teachers should try to give explanations both visually and verbally.

Restak, in "The Other Difference Between Boys and Girls," describes research on sex differences in brain functioning, and suggests that these differences should be considered in curriculum planning and teaching practices. The findings give added meaning to the criterion of individual differences; they also show that intellectual performance is incompatible with our stereotypes of femininity in girls and masculinity in boys.

Eisner makes a convincing case ("The Role of the Arts in Cognition and Curriculum") for the need to develop "multiple forms of literacy." He asserts that our current views about cognition and intelligence have had disastrous consequences for learners through their focus on mediating ideas through words and numbers. Concepts, he believes, are not linguistic at base; they are sensory. If we wish students to secure deep and diverse meanings, we cannot omit the fine arts from the curriculum.

The articles in this section show how the cognitive and perceptual learning theories (presented as one of the four major learning theory positions in Section 4), through new theory development and research during the past twenty-five years, have established knowledge and cognition as the fourth of the four bases for curriculum planning.

## Curriculum Criteria

Curriculum criteria are guidelines or standards by which decisions can be made in curriculum planning or teaching. What guidelines for planning can be derived from the theories and views of knowledge and cognition described in this rationale and in the articles and additional activities in this section? *Individual differences, balance, flexibility, student-teacher planning, self-understanding, relevance,* and *problem solving* are criteria for curriculum planning that depend in significant ways on the different views about knowledge and cognition described in this section.

In providing for individual differences in curriculum planning and teaching, it is important to understand that each person selects the knowledge that is important to him or her and creates a personal organization and structure of knowledge. Students should be helped in personal belief and value clarification in constructing the guiding ideas and ideals that can assist them in dealing with everyday problems.

Because of the rapid increase in knowledge, balance in the curriculum becomes much more important. Principles, generalizations, and structure must become the constants of academic study, while facts must become the variables, organized to develop understanding of the broader principles. But flexibility and student-teacher planning should be considered in order to better provide for the needs and learning styles of individual learners.

Balance as a criterion also means that the curriculum and many learning activities should include both right and left hemisphere brain functions. Visualization and intuitive, as well as analytical and sequential thinking, should be encouraged.

Self-understanding and problem solving as criteria mean that curriculum planning should help learners understand how a subject-matter can be useful in discovering personal levels of meaning and in problem solving. At least part of what is studied should be organized on the basis of the personal-social problems of learners and the society on an interdisciplinary basis.

As the criterion questions are considered, the curriculum planner and teacher should recognize that there are different kinds of knowledge and different uses for it. However, balance in the curriculum, provision for individual differences, and adequacy in planning are more likely to be achieved when the following questions are considered:

1. Does the planned curriculum assist the learner in identifying key concepts, principles, and the structure of the content to be learned?
2. Does the curriculum provide for learning opportunities that are consistent with individual differences and are related to varying approaches to structuring knowledge (e.g., discovery learning, advance organizers, key concepts, etc.)?
3. Does the planned curriculum recognize that each learner's structure of knowledge is personally invented and constructed, and that the learner may need assistance in identifying the discrepancies between his or her personal constructs and those of organized knowledge?
4. Does the planned curriculum provide for multiple forms of literacy and a balance between, as well as an integration of, the modes of the brain's two hemispheres?
5. Does the planned curriculum include interdisciplinary approaches based on the needs of the learners and their unique personal-social problems?

**6.**   Does the planned curriculum focus on the processes of knowing, including synthesis, wholeness, coherence, and interrelateness?

## Summary of Rationale

The various views of the nature of knowledge and cognition provide another important base for curriculum planning. They help the planner decide (1) what to include in the curriculum and how to teach it; (2) how to plan for the different kinds of knowledge to be taught; and (3) how to provide for the individual differences of learners. How the educator views knowledge and cognition has major significance for his or her planning for teaching and curriculum planning.

## OBJECTIVES

Your objectives in studying knowledge and cognition as one of the bases of curriculum planning should be the following:

**1.**   To be able to analyze a curriculum plan with reference to the theory or position concerning knowledge and cognition that is implicit in the plan.
**2.**   To be able to analyze a curriculum plan or a teaching plan on the basis of the various views concerning knowledge and its nature and uses that are described in the rationale.
**3.**   To be able to suggest changes and improvements in a curriculum plan or a teaching plan that are based on the various approaches to knowledge and cognition.

## PREASSESSMENT

The purpose of the preassessment is to enable you to determine whether you already possess the performance competencies in curriculum planning that are listed under the objectives just mentioned. The following activities will aid you in your evaluation:

**1.**   Name three approaches to deciding what knowledge should be included in the school curriculum and how it should be organized.
**2.**   Taking each of the three approaches to knowledge that you have named, tell how each would affect curriculum planning.
**3.**   Select any curriculum plan of your choice, in any subject or at any school level, and examine it in the light of the approaches to knowledge you have named in number 1. You can do this by visiting a school, or by analyzing a written statement about some part of a school's curriculum or the instruction in one classroom.

4.    Suggest changes or improvements in the curriculum plan as a result of your analysis.

In answering number 3, you might choose to analyze the approach or approaches to the selection and organization of knowledge in the curriculum that are found in one of these articles: "Problem Solving: Encouraging Active Learning"; "Research, Reading Instruction and Children's Learning of the First R." Both articles are in Section 7. Or you might analyze why Joe was in trouble in school (see "It's Joe Again" in this section) in terms of the approaches to knowledge and cognition.

Often, curriculum plans do not give conscious attention to the best approach to selecting and organizing knowledge. If that is true of the plan you selected, suggest improvements on the basis of the nature of knowledge and cognition.

## LEARNING ACTIVITIES

The articles in this section will assist you in identifying and understanding the various approaches to the selection, organization, and uses of knowledge in curriculum and instruction planning. Other learning alternatives are suggested at the end of this section.

## POSTASSESSMENT

After attempting the preassessment you may do *one or more* of the following:

1.    Ask your instructor whether you are ready for a postassessment evaluation on knowledge and the curriculum. Most students will need further work on this curriculum base.
2.    Read the articles on knowledge and cognition in this section, and try to determine how the knowledge theories and research being discussed in each article should be considered in curriculum planning and teaching.
3.    Choose additional activities and readings or films and videotapes from those listed at the end of this section.
4.    Look for other films, books, or articles on knowledge and cognition that are in your library or media center.
5.    Discuss the reading you have done and the films you have viewed with your fellow students. The key questions: How should the knowledge research and theories you've studied affect a school's curriculum? How should they be considered in planning for teaching?
6.    When you are ready, ask your instructor for advice on a suitable postassessment for you for this topic. Satisfactory completion of number 1 under "Problems and Projects" at the end of this section might be one possibility. Or satisfactory

written completion of the preassessment for this section, after completing other learning activities, might be a satisfactory postassessment. Consult your instructor about this. You can evaluate your ability to do either or both of these activities before seeing the instructor.

# Progressive Organization of Subject-Matter

## JOHN DEWEY

One consideration stands out clearly when education is conceived in terms of experience. Anything which can be called a study, whether arithmetic, history, geography, or one of the natural sciences, must be derived from materials which at the outset fall within the scope of ordinary life-experience. In this respect the newer education contrasts sharply with procedures which start with facts and truths that are outside the range of the experience of those taught, and which, therefore, have the problem of discovering ways and means of bringing them within experience. Undoubtedly one chief cause for the great success of newer methods in early elementary education has been its observance of the contrary principle.

But finding the material for learning within experience is only the first step. The next step is the progressive development of what is already experienced into a fuller and richer and also more organized form, a form that gradually approximates that in which subject-matter is presented to the skilled, mature person. That this change is possible without departing from the organic connection of education with experience is shown by the fact that this change takes place outside of the school and apart from formal education. The infant, for example, begins with an environment of objects that is very restricted in space and time. That environment steadily expands by the momentum inherent in experience itself without aid from scholastic instruction. As the infant learns to reach, creep, walk, and talk, the intrinsic subject-matter of its experience widens and deepens. It comes into connection with new objects and events which call out new powers, while the exercise of these powers refines and enlarges the content of its experience. Life-space and life-durations are expanded. The environment, the world of experience, constantly grows larger and, so to speak, thicker. The educator who receives the child at the end of this period has to find ways for doing consciously and deliberately what "nature" accomplishes in the earlier years.

It is hardly necessary to insist upon the first of the two conditions which have been specified. It is a cardinal precept of the newer school of education that the beginning of instruction shall be made with the experience learners already have; that this experience and the capacities that have been developed during its course provide the starting point for all further learning. I am not so sure that the other condition, that of orderly development toward expansion and organization of subject-matter through growth of experience, receives as much attention. Yet the principle of continuity of educative experience

From John Dewey, *Experience and Education*, pp. 86–93 (New York: The Macmillan Co., 1938), a Kappa Delta Pi Lecture. © Kappa Delta Pi. Used by permission.

requires that equal thought and attention be given to solution of this aspect of the educational problem. Undoubtedly this phase of the problem is more difficult than the other. Those who deal with the preschool child, with the kindergarten child, and with the boy and girl of the early primary years do not have much difficulty in determining the range of past experience or in finding activities that connect in vital ways with it. With older children both factors of the problem offer increased difficulties to the educator. It is harder to find out the background of the experience of individuals and harder to find out just how the subject-matters already contained in that experience shall be directed so as to lead out to larger and better organized fields.

It is a mistake to suppose that the principle of the leading on of experience to something different is adequately satisfied simply by giving pupils some new experiences any more than it is by seeing to it that they have greater skill and ease in dealing with things with which they are already familiar. It is also essential that the new objects and events be related intellectually to those of earlier experiences, and this means that there be some advance made in conscious articulation of facts and ideas. It thus becomes the office of the educator to select those things within the range of existing experience that have the promise and potentiality of presenting new problems which by stimulating new ways of observation and judgment will expand the area of further experience. He must constantly regard what is already won not as a fixed possession but as an agency and instrumentality for opening new fields which make new demands upon existing powers of observation and of intelligent use of memory. Connectedness in growth must be his constant watchword.

The educator more than the member of any other profession is concerned to have a long look ahead. The physician may feel his job done when he has restored a patient to health. He has undoubtedly the obligation of advising him how to live so as to avoid similar troubles in the future. But, after all, the conduct of his life is his own affair, not the physician's; and what is more important for the present point is that as far as the physician does occupy himself with instruction and advice as to the future of his patient he takes upon himself the function of an educator. The lawyer is occupied with winning a suit for his client or getting the latter out of some complication into which he has got himself. If it goes beyond the case presented to him he too becomes an educator. The educator by the very nature of his work is obliged to see his present work in terms of what it accomplishes, or fails to accomplish, for a future whose objects are linked with those of the present.

Here, again, the problem for the progressive educator is more difficult than for the teacher in the traditional school. The latter had indeed to look ahead. But unless his personality and enthusiasm took him beyond the limits that hedged in the traditional school, he could content himself with thinking of the next examination period or the promotion to the next class. He could envisage the future in terms of factors that lay within the requirements of the school system as that conventionally existed. There is incumbent upon the teacher who links education and actual experience together a more serious and a harder business. He must be aware of the potentialities for leading students into new fields which belong to experiences already had, and must use this knowledge as his criterion for selection and arrangement of the conditions that influence their present experience.

Because the studies of the traditional school consisted of subject-matter that was selected and arranged on the basis of the judgment of adults as to what would be useful for the young sometime in the future, the material to be learned was settled upon outside the present life-experience of the learner. In consequence, it had to do with the past; it was such as had proved useful to men in past ages. By reaction to an opposite extreme, as unfortunate as it was probably natural under the circumstances, the sound idea that education should derive its materials from present experience and should enable the learner to cope with the problems of the present and future has often been converted into the idea that progressive schools can to a very large extent ignore the past. If the present could be cut off from the past, this conclusion would be sound. But the achievements of the past provide the only means at command for understanding the present. Just as the individual has to draw in memory upon his own past to understand the conditions in which he individually finds himself, so the issues and problems of present *social* life are in such intimate and direct connection with the past that students cannot be prepared to understand either these problems or the best way of dealing with them without delving into their roots in the past. In other words, the sound principle that the objectives of learning are in the future and its immediate materials are in present experience can be carried into effect only in the degree that present experience is stretched, as it were, backward. It can expand into the future only as it is also enlarged to take in the past.

*John Dewey* was Professor of Philosophy, Emeritus, Columbia University, New York.

# Structures in Learning

## JEROME S. BRUNER

Every subject has a structure, a rightness, a beauty. It is this structure that provides the underlying simplicity of things, and it is by learning its nature that we come to appreciate the intrinsic meaning of a subject.

Let me illustrate by reference to geography. Children in the fifth grade of a suburban school were about to study the geography of the Central states as part of a social studies unit. Previous units on the Southeastern states, taught by rote, had proved a bore. Could geography be taught as a rational discipline? Determined to find out, the teachers devised a unit in which students would have to figure out not only where things are located, but why they are there. This involves a sense of the structure of geography.

The children were given a map of the Central states in which only rivers, large bodies of water, agricultural products, and natural resources were shown. They were not allowed to consult their books. Their task was to find Chicago, "the largest city in the North Central states."

The argument got under way immediately. One child came up with the idea that Chicago must be on the junction of the three large lakes. No matter that at this point he did not know the names of the lakes—Huron, Superior, and Michigan—his theory was well reasoned. A big city produced a lot of products, and the easiest and most logical way to ship these products is by water.

But a second child rose immediately to the opposition. A big city needed lots of food, and he placed Chicago where there are corn and hogs—right in the middle of Iowa.

From *Today's Education*, 52, no. 3 (March 1963): 26–27. Used by permission of the author and the publisher, the National Education Association.

A third child saw the issue more broadly—recognizing virtues in both previous arguments. He pointed out that large quantities of food can be grown in river valleys. Whether he had learned this from a previous social studies unit or from raising carrot seeds, we shall never know. If you had a river, he reasoned, you had not only food but transportation. He pointed to a spot on the map not far from St. Louis. "There is where Chicago *ought* to be." Would that graduate students would always do so well!

Not all the answers were so closely reasoned, though even the wild ones had about them a sense of the necessity involved in a city's location.

One argued, for example, that all American cities have skyscrapers, which require steel, so he placed Chicago in the middle of the Mesabi Range. At least he was thinking on his own, with a sense of the constraints imposed on the location of cities.

After forty-five minutes, the children were told they could pull down the "real" wall map (the one with names) and see where Chicago really is. After the map was down, each of the contending parties pointed out how close they had come to being right. Chicago had not been located. But the location of cities was no longer a matter of unthinking chance for this group of children.

What had the children learned? A way of thinking about geography, a way of dealing with its raw data. They had learned that there is some relationship between the requirements of living and man's habitat. If that is all they got out of their geography lesson, that is plenty. Did they remember which is Lake Huron? Lake Superior? Lake Michigan? Do you?

Teachers have asked me about "the new curricula" as though they were some special magic potion. They are nothing of the sort. The new curricula, like our little exercise in geography, are based on the fact that knowledge has an internal connectedness, a meaningfulness, and that for facts to be appreciated and understood and remembered, they must be fitted into that internal meaningful context.

The set of prime numbers is not some arbitrary nonsense. What can be said about quantities that cannot be arranged into multiple columns and rows? Discussing that will get you on to the structure of primes and factorability.

It often takes the deepest minds to discern the simplest structure in knowledge. For this reason if for no other, the great scholar and the great scientist and the greatly compassionate person are needed in the building of new curricula.

There is one other point. Our geographical example made much of discovery. What difference does discovery make in the learning of the young? First, let it be clear what the act of discovery entails. It is only rarely on the frontier of knowledge that new facts are "discovered" in the sense of being encountered, as Newton suggested, as "islands of truth in an uncharted sea of ignorance." Discovery, whether by a schoolboy going it on his own or by a scientist, is most often a matter of rearranging or transforming evidence in such a way that one is not enabled to go beyond the evidence to new insights. Discovery involves the finding of the right structure, the meaningfulness.

Consider now what benefits the child might derive from the experience of learning through his own discoveries. These benefits can be discussed in terms of increased intellectual potency, intrinsic rewards, useful learning techniques, and better memory processes.

For the child to develop *intellectual potency,* he must be encouraged to search out and find regularities and relationships in his environment. To do this, he needs to be armed with the expectancy that there is something for him to find and, once aroused by this expectancy, he must devise his own ways of searching and finding.

Emphasis on discovery in learning has the effect upon the learner of leading him to be a constructionist—to organize what he encounters in such a manner that he not only discovers regularity and relatedness, but also avoids the kind of information drift that fails to keep account of how the information will be used.

In speaking of *intrinsic motives* for learning (as opposed to extrinsic motives), it must be recognized that much of the problem in leading a child to effective cognitive activity is to free him from the immediate control of environmental punishments and rewards.

For example, studies show that children who seem to be early over-achievers in school are likely to be seekers after the "right way to do it" and that their capacity for transforming their learning into useful thought structures tends to be less than that of children merely achieving at levels predicted by intelligence tests.

The hypothesis drawn from these studies is that if a child is able to approach learning as a task of discovering something rather than "learning about it" he will tend to find a more personally meaningful reward in his own competency and self-achievement in the subject than he will find in the approval of others.

There are many ways of coming to the *techniques of inquiry,* or the heuristics of discovery. One of them is by careful study of the formalization of these techniques in logic, statistics, mathematics, and the like. If a child is going to pursue inquiry as an eventual way of life, particularly in the sciences, formal study is essential. Yet, whoever has taught kindergarten and the early primary grades (periods of intense inquiry) knows that an understanding of the formal aspect of inquiry is not sufficient or always possible.

Children appear to have a series of attitudes and activities they associate with inquiry. Rather than a formal approach to the relevance of variables in their search, they depend on their sense of what things among an ensemble of things "smell right" as being of the proper order of magnitude or scope of severity.

It is evident then that if children are to learn the working techniques of discovery, they must be afforded the opportunities of problem solving. The more they practice problem solving, the more likely they are to generalize what they learn into a style of inquiry that serves for any kind of task they may encounter. It is doubtful that anyone ever improves in the art and technique of inquiry by any other means than engaging in inquiry, or problem solving.

The first premise in a theory concerning the *improvement of memory processes* is that the principal problem of human memory is not storage, but retrieval. The premise may be inferred from the fact that recognition (i.e., recall with the aid of maximum prompts) is extraordinarily good in human beings—particularly in comparison to spontaneous recall when information must be recalled without external aids or prompts. The key to retrieval is organization.

There are myriad findings to indicate that any organization of information that reduces the collective complexity of material by imbedding it into a mental structure the child has constructed will make that material more accessible for retrieval. In sum, the child's very attitudes and activities that characterize "figuring out" or "discovering" things for himself also seem to have the effect of making material easier to remember.

If man's intellectual excellence is the most important among his perfections (as Maimonides, the great Hispanic-Judaic philosopher once said), then it is also the case that the most uniquely personal of all that man knows is that which he discovers for himself. What difference does it make when we encourage discovery in the young? It creates, as Maimonides would put it, a special and unique relation between knowledge possessed and the possessor.

After a career as Professor of Psychology and Director, Center for Cognitive Studies, Harvard University, *Jerome Bruner* was Watts Chair of Experimental Psychology, Oxford University, England, 1972–1979.

# Children Think with Whole Brains: Myth and Reality

## JERRE LEVY

I have often been astonished to learn of the ideas about human brain organization that surface in educational journals, teachers' newsletters, the popular press, New Yorker cartoons, and even advertisements for cars. These notions include:

- Rationality and logic are the sole province of the left hemisphere.
- Intuition and creativity are the sole province of the right hemisphere.
- Standard school curricula educate only the left side of the brain.
- Music and art are reflections of right-hemisphere processes.
- Modern technological civilizations depend on left-hemisphere functions and do not engage right-hemisphere functions; therefore, people with potentially high right-hemisphere capacities are the victims of discrimination in modern, advanced cultures.
- When engaged in any particular activity, people think with only one hemisphere at a time, either the left or right, depending on the activity.
- Some people think only with the left hemisphere; others think only with the right hemisphere.
- Scientists who study brain assymmetry now have all the answers regarding how children should be educated.

These assertions are either known to be false by neuropsychologists or are totally lacking in any supportive scientific evidence. Yet they have been accepted by many in the educational community, and inferences derived from them are currently having an impact on educational practice. Further, certain of these myths contain a strong strain of anti-rationalism in their suggestion that: 1. rationality only characterizes half the human brain and, 2. logical reasoning and creativity are polar opposites. Additional implications are that western concepts of intelligence refer solely to left-hemisphere processes, that standard intelligence tests measure only left-hemisphere competencies, and that any real creative insights derive from the right hemisphere.

The realization that the whole brain is actively participating in perception, encoding of information, organization of representations, memory, arousal, planning, thinking, understanding, and all other mental operations whether it be a social interaction, painting a picture, playing the piano, doing mathematics, writing a story, attending a lecture, or seeing a movie, seems to have escaped many, if not most, popular writers.

Only through misapprehension could some endeavors be attributed to left-hemisphere processes, and others to right-hemisphere processes. The two sides of the brain *do* differ, and they differ in quite important ways. The nature of these differences has little connection with the popularized picture, however, and the implications for human cognition and emotion are not what has been propagated.

From *Student Learning Styles and Brain Behavior,* 1982. Reston, Va., NASSP, pages 173–183. Used by permission of the publisher, the National Association of Secondary School Principals.

# INFORMATION ABOUT HEMISPHERIC DIFFERENCES

## Language

Split-brain investigations and studies of patients with damage to one side of the brain demonstrate that speech is almost entirely confined to the left hemisphere in the vast majority of right-handers. There is some evidence that the right hemisphere may occasionally be able to generate spoken words, particularly if these are stimulated by strong emotion, but ordinary language production can be assumed to be almost always under control of the left side of the brain.

Other aspects of language are not nearly so asymmetrically organized as speech. The isolated right hemisphere of split-brain patients understands a great deal of what is said to it, has a comprehension vocabulary equal to that of a normal 12-year-old, and can read at least simple words. Its mechanisms of comprehension almost certainly differ from those of the left hemisphere, since it appears to have little or no comprehension of syntax and grammar, is unable to follow complex verbal instructions if these place too great a burden on short-term verbal memory, and seems to have no capacity for analyzing phonetics and deriving the sound images of words it reads. It knows that the word "cat" refers to a particular creature depicted in a drawing, but it does not know the word "mat" rhymes with the name of the creature shown in the drawing.

Tachistoscopic investigations of brain assymmetry in normal people reveal that the two hemispheres are equally competent at reading concrete nouns and adjectives, but that the left hemisphere controls processing of verbs, abstract nouns, and adjectives. These findings suggest that when word meanings are susceptible to image or representation, there is little difference between the two sides in their abilities to recognize the word. When an imagistic representation is difficult or impossible, however, an assymmetry in favor of the left hemisphere emerges. A full appreciation of the meaning of concepts, of course, includes elaborate sets of verbal associations as well as sensory and experiential associations. When a normal person hears the word "dog," he or she does not merely derive the dictionary definition, but also generates images of dogs in various postures and activities, recalls the sounds of barks and howling, and, probably, recreates the emotions that real dogs elicit. This rich and full meaning of "dog" is derived by an intimate, collaborative integration of the processes of both sides of the brain.

That representations of meaning are incomplete and distorted for each separate hemisphere is apparent from observations of split-brain patients. One of the patients, N. G., asked me one day, "How is Professor Sperry? I haven't seen him for some time." Immediately after being assured that Sperry was well, N. G. passed him in the hallway. Sperry nodded, as did N. G., but neither spoke. When we had returned to the laboratory, she whispered to me, "Who was that man? He looked kind of familiar."

One would think that N. G. possessed a clear representation of who Sperry was, yet her failure to recognize him by visual cues shows that the left hemisphere's representation of the concept "Professor Sperry" did not include how he looked, or at the least, included only a vague and ill-defined image. This image was sufficient for generating a sense of familiarity, but insufficient to permit recognition. Fluent language usage can often mislead the listener into believing that complete and accurate concepts underlie the words and sentences.

Other evidence of the role of the right hemisphere in structuring meaning comes from findings that when patients with right-hemisphere damage are asked to provide a synopsis of stories read to them, they selectively omit emotional and humorous content. Obviously, the left hemisphere's memory structure for verbally presented material is incomplete, and the attentional system is biased to respond to only a subset of the information presented. In speech production, the grammar and vocabulary of these patients is normal, but frequently they are unable to convey emotional intonation. Since, in verbal interactions, tone of voice and speech modulation are important sources of communication, far less meaning is conveyed to the listener than would otherwise be the case. If someone tells us in a completely deadpan tone, "He killed the bear," we do not have the foggiest notion whether the person is elated by this fact, shocked, grieved, angry, proud, or surprised. We know a fact, but we do not know its implications, or how we should respond.

Right-hemisphere processes are very important for the apprehension of full meaning from oral or written communications and for the expression of full meaning.

Both hemispheres not only play critical roles in the purposes of language, but also in organizing the perceptual and cognitive processes that are prerequisite to understanding. Although reading disorders occur more frequently with left-hemisphere than with right-hemisphere damage, complete alexia (inability to read) can also occur when damage is restricted to the right side of the brain. I once examined a right-handed patient with massive damage to the right hemisphere whose speech and speech comprehension were fully intact. This patient had no damage to the left hemisphere, but developed a dense alexia; only after months of training was he able to read single letters, and with great difficulty, single words. He could decode one word at a time if all other words in the sentence were covered with his hands. He could "read" an entire sentence if he moved his hands so as to progressively uncover each subsequent word, but upon completion of the sentence, he was unable to report its meaning.

The patient showed similar difficulties with arithmetic. He could add and subtract single-digit numbers, but made many errors with double-digit numbers as well as with single-digit multiplication. Double-digit multiplication was impossible for him since he was utterly unable to align numbers on the page in a rational manner. When asked to multiply 7 times 8, he said, "Fifty-eight? Thirty seven? I can't get an image of what it is." That he was suffering from a rather severe perceptual organizing disorder was affirmed by the observation that his verbal I.Q. was a normal 110, but his performance I.Q. was a severely retarded 35, yielding a full-scale I.Q. of 77. (This demonstrates quite clerly the fallacy of believing that I.Q. tests assess only left-hemisphere processes.)

Reading and arithmetic are not merely linguistic activities; they depend on perceptual organizing functions and imagistic memory. Research has demonstrated that a normal person's *right* hemisphere actually predominates in initial letter processing or instances when the writing is complex. Longitudinal studies of children reveal that those who prove to be good readers by the time they enter fourth or fifth grade displayed a right-hemisphere superiority at letter and word recognition in first grade that gradually shifted to a left-hemisphere superiority as the recognition process became automatized. These differential superiorities do *not* mean that the other hemisphere plays no role in reading; they merely reflect the relative predominance of one hemisphere or the other at various stages of reading fluency.

This brief review of the roles of the two hemispheres in various aspects of language should be sufficient to demonstrate that in the normal child or adult, both hemispheres contribute important and critical processing operations. The final level of understanding or output cannot be allocated to one hemisphere or the other. As the child learns to read, communicate orally, learn history, or engage in any other so-called "verbal" activity, both sides of his or her brain are learning, being educated, participating in the growth of understanding. The child's appreciation of literature depends on his or her ability to synthesize letters into words, words into sentences, sentences into meaning and thought. It depends on the ability to apprehend and respond to the rhythm of language; to imagine and feel the scenes and moods; to empathize with the characters and understand their emotions, values, and personalities; and to integrate all this into a rich and full meaning with structure, configuration, and detail. Such a process cannot be accomplished by either side of the brain alone, but represents so intimate an integrative activity that, in the end, we cannot say which side of the brain contributed what.

## Art and Music

Disorders of music and artistic production regularly occur with damage to *either* side of the brain. The composer Ravel suffered a left-hemisphere stroke in mid-career and never produced another piece of music for the rest of his life. If music and creativity were the province of the right hemisphere, unfairly suppressed by an uncreative left hemisphere, one might have expected that once Ravel's left hemisphere was destroyed, he would have produced his best and most creative music.

The fact is that the left hemisphere is critically important in discriminating and in producing temporally ordered sequences. Patients with left-hemisphere damage have grave difficulty saying which of two tones occurred earlier in time—an ability unaffected by damage to the right hemisphere. Clearly, an understanding, appreciation, and expression of music depends on an ability to discriminate time relationships. If such discrimination is disrupted by left-hemisphere damage, it is not surprising to find correlated disruptions in musical ability. Studies of normal people have confirmed that it is the left hemisphere that

orders events in time, even when the sensory cues are initially presented to the right hemisphere.

Normative studies show that discrimination and memory for single musical chords is superior in the right hemisphere. This finding is consistent with its general advantage for memorizing sensory experiences that are resistant to verbal, analytical description. Hemispheric asymmetries in the recall of melodies depends on whether temporal, rhythmic elements or chordal tones are of greater importance. Musical training is also a factor. For the musically untrained and unskilled, melodies tend to be perceived as single global configurations—a right-hemisphere predilection—but for the musically trained and skilled, the components of melodies are apparent, a left-hemisphere function.

Music involves sounds, their ordering in time, their loudness and softness, and their form and rhythm. It engages its listeners at the sensory, emotional, and intellectual levels. Neither hemisphere alone possesses all the specializations of music; neither alone can create or appreciate the magnificent compositions of our great composers. No basis exists for believing that music is a speciality of one hemisphere or the other—only overwhelming evidence that both hemispheres are essential for its creation and appreciation.

What of art? Damage to either side of the brain produces disabilities in drawing. With left-side damage, overall configuration continues to be adequate, but detail is radically impoverished. With right-side damage, rich details remain, but overall form is inadequate. We love a Rembrandt painting because of its beauty of color and form, the perfection of a hand, the tiny sparkle in an eye, the fact that every detail is perfectly depicted and part of a whole that is more than itself. It elicits memories, creates imaginations, and has meaning that makes contact with our own experiences. It causes us to think, to reason, to feel.

It is possible to sketch a head, having no eyes, mouth, nose, or ears, yet clearly recognizable as such. Similarly, it is possible to draw features, clearly representative of a human face, but with no unifying outline or form. Real art is neither pure configuration nor pure detail; it is a brilliant synthesis of the two together. A barely discriminable change in the line of a mouth makes a Mona Lisa or not. Art is no more a right-hemisphere process than it is a left-hemisphere process. When it achieves lasting value it is an intimate synthesis of both. It is intellect and feeling; perfection of detail and perfection of form; color that calls up multiple associations and color that calls attention to itself alone.

Studies of perception show that for memory for faces, deciding whether an array of dots is aligned in columns or in rows as defined by relative dot distances, locating a briefly exposed dot in space, discriminating line orientation, or matching arcs with circles of the same diameter, the right hemisphere surpasses the left. This is not true for matching two identical arcs or two identical circles, discriminating depth from binocular cues, mentally folding drawings into their three-dimensional forms, or remembering random shapes that have no verbal labels. These perceptual memory and organizing capacities are obviously important in art, but they certainly do not point to any special "creative" capacity of the right hemisphere. One might as well say that the absolute superiority of the left hemisphere at phonetic analysis, understanding rhymes, and deriving meaning from syntactic construction of sentences is indicative of a special "creative" ability of the left hemisphere!

These and other studies demonstrate that the two hemispheres differ in their perceptual roles, but none supply any evidence that one side is more "creative" than the other, more responsible for music and art, more capable of a truly creative act, more "intuitive."

## Logic and Mathematics

Very little data is available about hemispheric asymmetries in mathematical and logical function, although arithmetical disorders can occur with either right-side or left-side damage. The right hemisphere of split-brain patients can do simple single-digit addition, subtraction, and multiplication and it surpasses the left at discriminating line orientation, orientation of other objects in space, and at discriminating the direction in which a point moves. These capacities, as well as the spatial-perceptual superiorities noted earlier, are of major importance in geometric understanding, which, itself, is necessary for a real understanding of algebraic relationships.

Given the left hemisphere's superiority in extracting meaning from syntactical structure, it might be expected to surpass the right hemisphere in derivation of meaning from algebraic structure and manipulation and reordering of algebraic symbols, but we have no direct evidence of this. The indirect evidence inferred from greatly superior symbol manipulation is so strong that I would be extremely surprised if the prediction were not borne out. Algebraic ability in manipulating symbols is not, of course, the defining characteristic of logic. Logical operations emerge in many endeavors—some involving mathematics, others involving verbal and symbolic manipulation.

In geometric reasoning, the right hemisphere is clearly superior, greatly surpassing the left hemisphere in operations such as viewing an "opened-up" drawing of an unfolded shape and mentally folding the drawing into a three-dimensional object. This mental manipulation of spatial relationships involves not only visualization abilities, but a rule-governed plan of transformation. I would call such rule-governed transformations highly *logical*. An even more striking example of right-hemisphere reasoning comes from split-brain studies showing that the right hemisphere can inspect a set of geometric shapes, extract the defining characteristic property of the set, and identify the shape within the set that does not belong. The right hemisphere does this at a far better level than the left. Given any reasonable definitions, this right-hemisphere ability reflects abstraction, generalization, and logic.

Patients with right-hemisphere damage very often show severe deficits in appreciating their current states, in integrating the various aspects of their lives, and in deriving reasonable expectations for their futures. They often deny that anything is the matter with them, that they are paralyzed, and they confabulate reasons why they are in wheelchairs. In a word, they behave illogically. Former Supreme Court Justice Douglas suffered a right-hemisphere stroke and returned to the Court in a wheelchair. When asked how he was doing, he responded, "Great! I'm just great. Everything's wonderful, and there's nothing the matter with me!" Taken aback, the reporter noted that Douglas was in a wheelchair. Douglas laughed. "The wheelchair? Oh, well, I tripped in the garden this morning and hurt my leg. It'll be well in a few days." If logic were the sole province of the left hemisphere, we would expect *not* to see such disorders with right-hemisphere brain damage.

Lest you think that the mythology is backwards, note that logical disorders also occur with left-hemisphere damage. Even in patients who have not lost speech, verbal reasoning is quite diminished. The ability to interpret proverbs, to recognize verbal analogies, to identify how two things are alike, and to perform other verbal reasoning tasks shows clear disorder. Patients tend to become overly concrete and less capable of drawing abstract generalizations.

The direct implication of these observations is that both hemispheres are involved in thinking, logic, and reasoning, each from its own perspective and in its particular domains of activity.

Thinking and logic in the normal person derive from the specialized processes of both sides. Each hemisphere appears to have a limited and biased perspective and a restricted set of competencies that may allow adequate (but not excellent) performance in a highly restricted cognitive domain, but not a deep grasp of or insight into language, music, mathematics, or any other field of human endeavor. The creations of human culture derive from the fully integrated actions of the whole brain, and any further advances will require an intimate and brilliant collaborative synthesis of the special skills of both sides of the brain. All of the available data point to the validity of this conclusion; none supports the idea that normal people function like split-brain patients, using only one hemisphere at a time.

## INTERHEMISPHERIC INTEGRATION

What is the direct evidence that two hemispheres working together are better than either alone or even the sum of the capacities of the two sides? In contrast to normal people, the two hemispheres of split-brain patients cannot be simultaneously active. Only one hemisphere at a time is capable of attending to the sensory world. With bilateral sensory input, half the sensory world is missed. It is simply not perceived. This implies that the severed *corpus callosum,* the massive bridge of fibers interconnecting the two hemispheres, normally plays a highly important role in facilitating arousal of *both* hemispheres, in making it possible for both hemispheres to process information and to derive perceptions at the same time. Why would the brain be built this way if the *corpus callosum* did not also serve to integrate the cognitive activities of the two simultaneously thinking hemispheres?

Split-brain studies lead to a prediction of normal brain function. If dual tasks require interhemispheric communication, the imposition of a dual task in normal people should increase bilateral hemispheric engagement, even if both tasks are specialized to a single hemisphere. Further, if increased hemispheric engagement promotes optimal functioning of the brain, then subjects should be able to perform the dual task as well as a single task, perhaps even better, if the dual task requirements do not place too great a burden on operating capacities.

Joseph Hellige of the University of Southern California and his associates have shown that as task complexity increases, bilateral hemispheric engagement increases, and performance is, consequently, enhanced. Interestingly, it appears that even split-brain patients attempt to engage both hemispheres as task complexity increases. When two different colors are presented—one to each side of the brain—and patients are asked to match the color they see from among a set of choices in free vision, a single hemisphere controls the match through all trials. For some patients this is the left hemisphere, for others, the right, but the dominating hemisphere retains control of processing throughout all stimulus presentations. If colors are presented in varying geometric shapes, with the shapes irrelevant to the color-match required, unihemispheric dominance decays. It is as if a single hemisphere is unable to retain dominance with the increase in task complexity—a change that, in normal people, might be reflected as an increase in bilateral hemispheric engagement.

These observations suggest that normal brains are built to be challenged, that they only operate at optimal levels when cognitive processing requirements are of sufficient complexity to activate both sides of the brain and provide a mutual facilitation between hemispheres as they integrate their simultaneous activities. When tasks are at a very simple level, bilateral activation may be at a low level, with reliance on a single hemisphere that receives only weak facilitation from the other side. Generalizing from the split-brain findings, this would mean that

attentional capacity would be low. The capacity to sustain attention for more than the briefest periods would be greatly diminished. Psychologically, this would be manifested as boredom and poor attention. Educationally, it would mean that simple, repetitive, and uninteresting problems would be poorly learned, with little benefit for either side of the brain.

Considerable evidence now suggests that the right hemisphere plays a special role in emotion and in general activation and arousal functions. If this is so, if a student can be emotionally engaged, aroused, and alerted, both sides of the brain will participate in the educational process regardless of subject matter. With maximum facilitation of both hemispheres, the result will be an integrative synthesis of the specialized abilities of the left and right into a full, rich, and deep understanding that is different from and more than the biased and limited perspectives of either side of the brain.

## IMPLICATIONS FOR LEARNING STYLES AND EDUCATIONAL PRACTICE

What does all this have to say regarding individual differences in learning styles? The evidence strongly disputes the idea that students learn with only one side of the brain, but, we do have evidence that there are individual differences among people to the extent that one hemisphere is more differentially aroused than the other. Gur and Reivich, for example, have found that people differ in the asymmetry of blood flow to the two sides of the brain, and that those having an asymmetric flow in favor of the right hemisphere perform better on perceptual completion tasks (thought to be right-hemisphere specialized). Individual differences exist in the extent to which people show a biased attention to the left or right side of space. Persons with a leftward bias tend to perform better on face-recognition tasks; those with a rightward bias, on phonetic analysis of nonsense syllables.

These differences suggest that whole-brain learning may be better accomplished for different people with different methods. In other words, the child with a biased arousal of the left hemisphere may gain reading skills more easily through a phonetic, analytic method, while the child with a biased arousal of the right hemisphere may learn to read better by the sight method. I am suggesting only that the *gateway* into whole-brain learning may differ for different children, *not* that one hemisphere or the other should be the object of education. Ultimately, our aim should be to assure that the child who learns to read through phonics will develop a fluent skill in sight reading, and that one who learns through the whole-word method will develop excellent skills at phonetic analysis so that any new word can be decoded.

Similarly, some children may better gain mathematical understanding if they are first taught the structure of algebraic equations and the methods of symbol manipulation. In the end, however, we want these children to appreciate the geometric, spatial functions specified by equations. We want them to understand *why* we say an equation of the form, $X = A + BY$ is called "linear," while one of the form, $X = A + BY + CY^2$ is called "quadratic." We want them to visualize a straight line defining the function between X and Y for the linear equation, and a quadratic curve defining the function between X and Y for the quadratic equation. Other children better understand if they are first taught the visual, geometric relationships, but, ultimately, we also want them to be able to specify these geometric forms in a symbolic equation.

From this perspective, "learning styles" refer to the method of introducing material, not to the type of understanding we ultimately want the child to gain, nor to the hemisphere we seek to educate. Standard school curricula, in contrast to some prevailing mythology, are *not* bi-

ased in favor of the left hemisphere. Reading, writing, grammar, literature, history, science, mathematics, music, and art all equally depend on both hemispheres and on the synthesis of their specialized abilities. Advanced societies and their technological and cultural accomplishments are reflections of brilliant syntheses of the partial perspectives of each hemisphere. Great men and women of history did not merely have superior intellectual capacities within each hemisphere, but phenomenal levels of emotional commitment, motivation, attentional capacities, and abilities for long-sustained interest in their particular areas of endeavor—all of which reflect the highly integrated brain in action.

The research is not yet available to demonstrate conclusively what all this means for educational practice, but at least certain inferences seem to me to follow directly from current research. Since these are merely inferences, without direct data for corroboration, I may be wrong. Educators are cautioned to use their own experiences and wisdom to check the validity of my conjectures. They should also be aware that my interpretations may not be accepted by all researchers, and that future research within a classroom setting may yield a different picture. Nevertheless, I feel some obligation to communicate the educational implications as I see them at the present time.

First, the popular 1960s idea that the educational experience should, under all circumstances be "nonthreatening" to the child often meant that the educational experience should be nonchallenging, that children should not be confronted with material that stretched the limits of their capacities. This viewpoint indicated that the child should be prevented at all costs from gaining any notion of his or her abilities relative to others. To learn of his or her own special weaknesses or special skills supposedly generated either a poor self-concept or produced an unappealing arrogance. Yet challenges are what appear to engage the whole brain, to generate excitement and interest and attention, to provide the substrate for optimal learning.

Indeed, in spite of the best efforts of teachers and parents to hide the truth, children are remarkably adept in discovering where they stand with respect to other children, in understanding their own special skills and recognizing their own special difficulties. Students select fields of endeavor in accordance with their self-recognized abilities, tending to go into areas where their skills are high and avoiding areas where their skills are low. If students are so aware of their differential abilities in different areas, what might be the psychological/emotional consequences of trying to hide their strengths and weaknesses from them? We might unintentionally communicate to them that there is something shameful in being more or less apt than others in certain areas. How much better and healthier it would be to be truthful with children, to let them know that people are highly diverse in their skills and abilities, and that this diversity is what makes societies possible at all. They should be grateful for and appreciate the special skills that others have while acknowledging their own personal skills as gifts to be developed to their highest level.

Even small children can and should understand something about human brains. They can understand that the two hemispheres differ, that within each side there are many different processes, that all children use whole brains but use them in different ways, so that some people understand how cars work, while others find them very confusing. They can understand that some can write stories that everybody loves to hear, while others find writing a difficult chore. The child *needs* to learn how he or she thinks. The child *needs* to learn what constitutes a challenge in each area of endeavor, and *needs* to take comfort in the fact he or she lives in a world where an individual need not be perfect in all things because other people who have different ways of thinking will contribute to his or her life, just as he or she contributes to theirs. The child *needs* to

appreciate people who are different, not resent that they may be better in some things or be ashamed at his or her particular weaknesses. The child *needs* to know where he or she is especially good and can achieve satisfaction and accomplishment, not only for the sake of his or her own emotional well-being, but for the sake of the world.

Formal education is only the beginning; if it is good, it teaches people how to educate themselves throughout their entire lives. And for this continuing self-education, individuals need to learn their own special pathways to learning, the ways they organize their thinking and identify their interests. They need to learn those things that engage their emotions, that are seen as thrilling challenges to understanding, that capture their attention, and that hold through years of effort. They need, in other words, to learn how to engage their whole brains in feeling, thinking, understanding, and achieving satisfaction.

So, in brief, the first of my inferences from current brain research is that challenges are not threats. Recognizing diversities does not leads to shame or arrogance; human brains are built to be challenged and built to understand themselves. In the classroom, I believe that children will learn best if their limits are stretched, if their emotions are engaged, and if they are helped to understand themselves and their own special ways of thinking and seeing the world.

A second inference that I draw is that all subject matters necessarily engage the specialties of both sides of the brain, and that the aim of education is to guide the child toward a deep synthesis of these differing perspectives. Regardless of how the subject matter may be best introduced for a given child, whether through left or right-hemisphere processes, this is only the initial step, a gateway into the whole brain. The synthesis we seek is not merely the sum of understanding of each side. This would yield merely two biased and incomplete representations of reality. We seek something that is more than and different from a simple addition, that is the real power of the human mind. How is such a synthesis to be achieved? We do not yet know. The research has not been done. Yet knowing the goal, perhaps it will be possible for teachers with sensitivity to find a way long before scientists can supply specific recommendations.

**REFERENCES**

Dimond, S. J., and Beaumont, J. G., eds. *Hemispheric Function in the Human Brain.* New York: John Wiley & Sons, 1974.

"Hemispheric Specialization and Interaction." In *The Neurosciences: Third Study Program,* edited by F. O. Schmitt and F. G. Worden. Cambridge, Mass.: The MIT Press, 1974.

Segalowitz, S. J., and Gruber, F. A., eds. *Language Development and Neurological Theory.* New York: Academic Press, 1977.

Vinken, P. J., and Bruyn, G. W., eds. *Disorders of Speech, Perception, and Symbolic Behaviour.* Handbook of Clinical Neurology, vol. 4. Amsterdam: North-Holland Publishing Co.; New York: John Wiley & Sons, 1969.

Wittrock, M. C., ed. *The Brain and Psychology.* New York: Academic Press, 1980.

*Jerre Levy* is Associate Professor of Behavioral Sciences, Department of Biopsychology, University of Chicago, Chicago, Illinois.

# The Other Difference Between Boys and Girls

## RICHARD M. RESTAK

Boys think differently from girls. Recent research on brain behavior makes that conclusion inescapable, and it is unrealistic to keep denying it. I know how offensive that will sound to feminists and others committed to overcoming sexual stereotypes. As the father of three daughters, I am well aware of the discrimination girls suffer. But social equality for men and women really depends on recognizing these differences in brain behavior.

At present, schooling and testing discriminate against both boys and girls in different ways, ignoring differences that have been observed by parents and educators for years. Boys suffer in elementary school classrooms, which are ideally suited to the way girls think. Girls suffer later on, in crucial ways, taking scholarship tests that are geared for male performance.

Anyone who has spent time with children in a playground or school setting is aware of differences in the way boys and girls respond to similar situations. Think of the last time you supervised a birthday party attended by five-year-olds. It's not usually the girls who pull hair, throw punches, or smear each other with food.

Usually such differences are explained on a cultural basis. Boys are expected to be more aggressive and play rough games, while girls are presumably encouraged to be gentle, non-assertive, and passive. After several years of exposure to such expectations, the theory goes, men and women wind up with widely varying behavioral and intellectual repertoires. As a corollary to this, many people believe that if childrearing practices could be equalized and sexual stereotypes eliminated, most of these differences would eventually disappear. As often happens, however, the true state of affairs is not that simple.

Undoubtedly, many of the differences traditionally believed to exist between the sexes are based on stereotypes. But despite this, evidence from recent brain research indicates that many behavioral differences between men and women are based on differences in brain functioning that are biologically inherent and unlikely to be modified by cultural factors alone.

## SOUND SENSITIVITY

The first clue to brain differences between the sexes came from observations of male and female infants. From birth, female infants are more sensitive to sounds, particularly to their mother's voice. In a laboratory, if the sound of the mother's voice is displaced to another part of the room, female babies will react while male babies usually seem oblivious to the displacement. Female babies are also more easily startled by loud noises. In fact, their enhanced hearing performance persists throughout life, with females experiencing a fall-off in hearing much later than males.

Tests involving girls old enough to cooperate show increased skin sensitivity, particularly in the finger-tips, which have a lower threshold for touch identification. Females are also more proficient at fine motor performance. Rapid tapping movements are carried out quickly and more efficiently by girls than by boys.

In addition, there are differences in what attracts a girl's attention. Generally, females are more attentive to social contexts—faces, speech patterns, and subtle vocal cues. By four months of age, a female infant is socially aware enough to distinguish photographs of familiar people, a task rarely performed well by boys of that age. Also at four months, girls will babble to a mother's face, seemingly recognizing her as a person, while boys fail to distinguish between a face and a dangling toy, babbling equally to both.

Female infants also speak sooner, have larger vocabularies, and rarely demonstrate speech defects. Stuttering, for instance, occurs almost exclusively among boys.

Girls can also sing in tune at an earlier age. In fact, if we think of the muscles of the throat as muscles of fine control—those in which girls excel—then it should come as no surprise that girls exceed boys in language abilities. This early linguistic bias often prevails throughout life. Girls read sooner, learn foreign languages more easily, and, as a result, are more likely to enter occupations involving language mastery.

Boys, in contrast, show an early visual superiority. They are also clumsier, performing poorly at something like arranging a row of beads, but excel at other activities calling on total body coordination. Their attentional mechanisms are also different. A boy will react to an inanimate object as quickly as he will to a person. A male baby will often ignore the mother and babble to a blinking light, fixate on a geometric figure and, at a later point, manipulate it and attempt to take it apart.

A study of nursery preschool children carried out by psychologist Diane McGuiness of Stanford University found boys more curious, especially in regard to exploring their environment. McGuiness' studies also confirm that males are better at manipulating three-dimensional space. When boys and girls are asked to mentally rotate or fold an object, boys overwhelmingly outperform the girls. "I folded it in my mind" is a typical male response. Girls, when explaining how they perform the same task, are likely to produce elaborate verbal descriptions which, because they are less appropriate to the task, result in frequent errors.

In an attempt to understand the sex differences in spatial ability, electroencephalogram (EEG) measurements have recently been made of the accompanying electrical events going on within the brain.

Ordinarily, the two brain hemispheres produce a similar electrical background that can be measured by an EEG. When a person is involved in a mental task—say, subtracting 73 from 102—the hemisphere that is activated will demonstrate a change in its electrical background. When boys are involved in tasks employing spatial concepts, such as figuring out mentally which of three folded shapes can be made from a flat, irregular piece of paper, the right hemisphere is activated consistently. Girls, in contrast, are more likely to activate both hemispheres, indicating that spatial ability is more widely dispersed in the female brain.

## SEX BIAS IN TESTS

When it comes to psychological measurements of brain functioning between the sexes, unmistakable differences emerge. In eleven subtests of the most widely used test of general intelligence, only two subtests reveal similar mean scores for males and females. These sex differences have been substantiated across cultures and are so consistent that the standard battery of this intelligence test now contains a masculinity-femininity index.

Further support for sex differences in brain functioning comes from experience with subtests that eventually had to be omitted from the original test battery. A cube-analysis test, for example, was excluded because, after testing thousands of subjects, a large sex bias appeared to favor males. In all, over thirty tests eventually had to be eliminated because they discriminated in favor of one or the other sex. One test, involving mentally working oneself through a maze, favored boys so overwhelmingly that, for a while, some psychologists speculated that girls were totally lacking in a "spatial factor."

Most thought-provoking of all is a series of

findings by Eleanor Maccoby and Carol Nagly Jacklin of Stanford on personality traits and intellectual achievement. They found that girls whose intellectual achievement is greatest tend to be unusually active, independent, competitive, and free of fear or anxiety, while intellectually outstanding boys are often timid, anxious, not overtly aggressive, and less active.

In essence, Maccoby and Jacklin's findings suggest that intellectual performance is incompatible with our stereotype of femininity in girls or masculinity in boys.

Research evidence within the last six months indicates that many of these brain sex differences persist over a person's lifetime. In a study at the University Hospital in Ontario that compared verbal and spatial abilities of men and women after a stroke, the women did better than men in key categories tested. After the stroke, women tended to be less disabled and recovered more quickly.

Research at the National Institute of Mental Health is even uncovering biochemical differences in the brains of men and women. Women's brains, it seems, are more sensitive to experimentally administered lights and sounds. The investigator in charge of this research, Monte Buchsbaum, speculates that the enhanced response of the female brain depends on the effect of sex hormones on the formation of a key brain chemical. This increased sensibility to stimuli by the female brain may explain why women more often than men respond to loss and stress by developing depression.

It's important to remember that we're not talking about one sex being generally superior or inferior to another. Rather, psychobiological research is turning up important functional differences between male and female brains. The discoveries might possibly contribute to further resentments and divisions in our society. But must they? Why are sex differences in brain functioning disturbing to so many people? And, why do women react so vehemently to findings that, if anything, indicate enhanced capabilities in the female brain?

## CHANGING IN THE SCHOOLS

It seems to me that we can make two responses to these findings on brain-sex differences. First, we can use them to help bring about true social equity. One way of doing this might be to change such practices as nationwide competitive examinations. If boys, for instance, truly do excel in right-hemisphere tasks, then tests such as the National Merit Scholarship Examination should be radically redesigned to assure that both sexes have an equal chance. As things now stand, the tests are heavily weighted with items that virtually guarantee superior male performance.

Attitude changes are also needed in our approach to "hyperactive" or "learning disabled" children. The evidence for sex differences here is staggering: More than 95 percent of hyperactives are males. And why should this be surprising in light of the sex differences in brain function that we've just discussed?

The male brain learns by manipulating its environment, yet the typical student is forced to sit still for long hours in the classroom. The male brain is primarily visual, while classroom instruction demands attentive listening. Boys are clumsy in fine hand coordination, yet are forced at an early age to express themselves in writing. Finally, there is little opportunity in most schools, other than during recess, for gross motor movements or rapid muscular responses. In essence, the classrooms in most of our nation's primary grades are geared to skills that come naturally to girls but develop very slowly in boys. The results shouldn't be surprising: a "learning disabled" child who is also frequently "hyperactive."

"He can't sit still, can't write legibly, is always trying to take things apart, won't follow instructions, is loud, and, oh yes, terribly clumsy" is a typical teacher description of male hyperactivity. We now have the opportunity, based on emerging evidence of sex differences in brain functioning, to restructure elementary grades so that boys find their initial educational contacts less stressful.

At more advanced levels of instruction, efforts must be made to develop teaching methods that incorporate verbal and linguistic approaches to physics, engineering, and architecture (to mention only three fields where women are conspicuously underrepresented and, on competitive aptitude tests, score well below males).

The second alternative is, of course, to do nothing about brain differences and perhaps even deny them altogether. Certainly there is something to be said for this approach too. In the recent past, enhanced social benefit has usually resulted from stressing the similarities between people rather than their differences. We ignore brain-sex differences, however, at the risk of confusing biology with sociology, and wishful thinking with scientific facts.

The question is not, "Are there brain-sex differences?" but rather, "What is going to be our response to these differences?" Psychobiological research is slowly but surely inching toward scientific proof of a premise first articulated by the psychologist David Wechsler more than twenty years ago:

> The findings suggest that women seemingly call upon different resources or different degrees of like abilities in exercising whatever it is we call intelligence. For the moment, one need not be concerned as to which approach is better or "superior." But our findings do confirm what poets and novelists have often asserted, and the average layman long believed, namely, that men not only behave, but "think" differently from women.

*Richard M. Restak* is a neurologist in Washington, D.C. and professor of neurology at Georgetown University. He is the author of *The Brain: The Last Frontier* (Doubleday and Co., Inc. 1979), and *The Brain* (Bantam Books, 1985).

# The Role of the Arts in Cognition and Curriculum

## ELLIOT W. EISNER

My thesis is straightforward but not widely accepted. It is that the arts are cognitive activities, guided by human intelligence, that make unique forms of meaning possible. I shall argue further that the meanings secured through the arts require what might best be described as forms of artistic literacy, without which artistic meaning is impeded and the ability to use more conventional forms of expression is hampered.

To talk about the cognitive character of the arts or about the kind of meaning that they convey is not particularly common. The models of mind that have typified U.S. educational psychology (particularly that aspect of psychology concerned with learning and knowing) have made tidy separations between thinking and feeling, feeling and acting, and acting and thinking.[1] The view of thinking that has been most common is rooted in the Platonic belief that mind and body are distinct, and, of the two, body is base while mind is lofty.[2] Feeling is located in *soma*, idea in *psyche*. The literature distinguishes between cognition and affect, and we tend to regard as cognitive those activities of mind that mediate ideas through words and numbers. We consider words more abstract than images, icons less flexible than propositions. We regard words as high in that hierarchy of cognitive achievement we use to describe cognitive growth. Jean Piaget, for example, regarded formal operations, those mental operations that deal with logical relationships, as the apotheosis of cognitive achievement.[3] For some cognitive psychologists, thinking is a kind of inner speech that allows one to reason.[4] Since reason is a condition of rationality, and since reasoning is believed to require the logical treatment of words, operations of the mind that do not employ logic are placed on the margins of rationality.

In this view the arts, if not considered irrational, are thought of as *a-rational*. As for meaning, it is most commonly regarded as an attribute of propositions, the property of assertions for which scientific warrant can be secured. The arts are considered emotive forms that might provide satisfaction—but not understanding.

The consequences of this view of mind have, in my opinion, been disastrous for education. First, this view has created a dubious status hierarchy among subjects taught in schools. Mathematics is the queen of the hill; other subjects, especially those in which students "work with their hands," are assigned lower intellectual status. Simply recall the standard whipping boy of school activities, basket weaving. Basket weaving epitomizes low status and mindlessness. Let me state quickly that I reject mindless forms of basket weaving in school. But let me add just as quickly that I also reject mindless forms of algebra and that I find nothing inherently more intellectually complex in algebra than in basket weaving; it depends upon the nature of the algebra and the nature of the baskets we choose to weave.

Besides making some subjects the targets of verbal abuse, the status hierarchy among subjects that emanates from such an indefensible conception of mind has practical day-to-day consequences in schools. Consider how time is

From *Phi Delta Kappan* 63, no. 1 (September 1981): 48–52. © 1981, Phi Delta Kappan, Inc. Used by permission of the author and the publisher.

allocated in school programs. Time is surely one of the most precious of school resources. As researchers of time on task have told us,[5] the relationship between the amount of time allocated and learning is a significant one. Partly because of our view of intellect, however, some subjects—the fine arts, for example—receive very little attention in school programs. On the average, elementary school teachers devote about 4 percent of school time each week to instruction in the fine arts.[6] And this time is not prime time, such as the so-called cognitive subjects command. For the fine arts, Friday afternoons are very popular.

Space does not permit a lengthy recital of sins that have been committed by schools in the name of cognitive development. Yet it is important to remember that the conception of giftedness used in many states excludes ability in the fine arts, that tax dollars support programs whose criteria discriminate against students whose gifts are in the fine arts, and that colleges and universities do not consider high school grades in the fine arts when making admissions decisions.[7] We legitimate such practices by distinguishing between intelligence and talent, assigning the former to verbal and mathematical forms of reasoning and the latter to performance in activities we deem more concrete: playing a musical instrument, dancing, painting.

I could elaborate at length on each of these points. But I mention them simply to highlight the model of mind that has been so widely accepted and to provide a context for my remarks concerning the role of the arts in cognition and curriculum.

If you were to consult the *Dictionary of Psychology* regarding the meaning of cognition, you would find that cognition is "the process through which the organism becomes aware of the environment."[8] Thus cognition is a process that makes awareness possible. It is, in this sense, a matter of becoming conscious, of noticing, of recognizing, of perceiving. It is a matter of distinguishing one thing from another: a figure from its ground, the various subtleties and nuances that, when perceived, become a part of one's consciousness.

In this process, the functions of the senses are crucial. They bring to awareness the qualitative world we inhabit. To become aware of the world, two conditions must be satisfied. First, the qualities must be available for experiencing by a sentient human being. Second, the individual must be able to "read" their presence. When both of these conditions are met, the human being is capable of forming concepts of the world. These concepts take shape in the information that the senses have provided.

The process of forming concepts is one of construing *general* features from qualitative particulars. The perception of the qualitative world is always fragmented: We never see a particular immediately, in an instant. Time is always involved.[9] General configurations are formed— that is, built up from parts to wholes. Through time they yield structured patterns that constitute a set. The patterns formed in this way are concepts. They are root forms of experience that we are able to recall and to manipulate imaginatively.

The importance of the senses in concept formation is that: (1) no concepts can be formed without sensory information,[10] (2) the degree to which the particular senses are differentiated has a large effect on the kind and subtlety of the concepts that are formed, and (3) without concepts formed as images (whether these images are visual, auditory, or in some other sensory form), image surrogates—words, for example— are meaningless.[11]

It is easy to see how such concrete concepts as dog or chair, red or blue, depend upon sensory information. But what about such abstract concepts as justice, category, nation, infinity? I would argue that these words are nothing more than meaningless noises or marks on paper unless their referents can be imagined. Unless we have a conception of justice, the word is empty. Unless we can imagine infinity, the term is nothing more than a few decibels of sound moving through space. I do not mean to imply that we conjure up an image every time we hear a word. Our automatic response mechanisms make this unnecessary. But when I say, "The man was a feckless mountebank," the statement will have meaning only if you have referents for "feckless" and "mountebank." If you do not, then you turn to a friend or a dictionary for other words whose images allow you to create an analogy. It is through such analogies or through illustrative examples that so-called abstract concepts take on meaning. Concepts, in this view, are not linguistic at base; instead, they are sensory. The forms concepts take are as diverse as our sensory capacities and the abilities we have developed to use them.

The process of concept formation is of particular importance in the development of scientific theory. In the social sciences, for example, theoreticians form concepts by constructing social situations in ways that others have not noticed. Terms such as class, social structure, adaptation, role, status, and reinforcement are meaningful because they bracket aspects of the social world for us to experience.[12] They call to our attention qualities of the world that otherwise would have gone unseen. But the reality is in the flesh and blood of experience, not simply in the words. Put another way, there is an icon—a stylized image of reality—underlying any term that is meaningful. The makers of such icons are people we regard as perceptive or insightful. Indeed, the Latin root of "intuition" is *intueri,* meaning to look upon, to see. In the beginning there was the image, not the word.

One important characteristic of concepts is that they can be not only recalled but imaginatively manipulated. We can combine qualities we have encountered to form entities that never were but that might become: hence unicorns, helixes, ideals of perfection toward which we strive, and new tunes to whistle. We can construct models of the world from which we can derive verbal or numerical propositions or from which we can create visual or auditory images. The point is that, while the sensory system provides us with information about the world in sensory form, our imaginative capacities—when coupled with an inclination toward play—allow us to examine and explore the possibilities of this information.[13] Although our imaginative lives might be played out in solitary fantasy or daydreaming, imagination often provides the springboard for expression. How is experience expressed? What vehicles are used? What skills are employed? And what do the arts have to do with it? It is to that side of the cognitive coin that I now turn.

Thus far I have emphasized the cognitive function of the sensory systems, and I have pointed out that concepts formed from sensory information can be recalled and manipulated through imagination. But thus far, this manipulation of concepts has been private, something occurring within the personal experience of individuals. The other side of the coin deals with the problem of externalization. In some way an individual must acquire and employ a form that can represent to self and to others what has been conceptualized. This task requires what I call a *form of representation.*[14] The problem of representing conceptions is a problem of finding or inventing equivalents for those conceptions. In this task, the form or forms to be employed must themselves appeal to one or more of the senses. A visual concept, for example, might be externalized in a form that is visual, or the form might instead be auditory, verbal, or both. Thus, for example, we could represent an imaginary stream of rolling and flowing blue amoebic shapes either visually or through sound. The stream might be described through words, or it might be represented through movement—perhaps dance. Regardless of the form we select, it must be one that the sensory systems can pick up. Put another way, the form must be empirical.

The kind of information that we are able to convey about what we have conceptualized is both constrained and made possible by the forms of representation that we have access to and are able to use. Some of the things an individual knows are better represented by some forms than others. What one can convey about a river that slowly wends its way to the sea will be significantly influenced by the form of representation one chooses to use. The same holds true for portrayals of classrooms, teaching, love affairs, and memorable cities one has visited.

Consider suspense. Almost all of us are able to invent a way of conveying suspense through music. From old cowboy movies and mystery dramas on radio and television, we already have a repertoire of models to draw upon. But think about how suspense would be represented through painting or sculpture. Here the problem becomes much more difficult. Why? Because suspense is a temporal experience, and painting and sculpture are largely spatial. It is more difficult to use the latter to represent the former than to use music, which itself is temporal.

Some forms of representation can illuminate some aspects of the world that others cannot. What a person can learn about the world through visual form is not likely to be provided through auditory form. What an individual knows takes shape in the empirical world only through a vehicle or vehicles that make knowing public. The vehicles we use for this purpose are the forms of representation.

Although I have described the externalization of concepts as one-directional—that is, as moving from inside out—the process is actually reciprocal. For example, what a person knows how to do affects what he or she conceptualizes. If you walk around the world with black and white film in your camera, you look for contrasts

of light and dark, for texture, for patterns of shadow against buildings and walls. As Ernst Gombrich put it, "Artists don't paint what they can see, they see what they can paint." The ability to use a form of representation skillfully guides our perception. The process flows, as it were, from representation to conception as well as from conception to representation.

Dialectical relationships between conception and representation occur in other ways as well. For example, the externalization of a conception through a form of representation allows the editing process to occur. By stabilizing what is evanescent, the conception can be modified, abbreviated, sharpened, revised, or discarded altogether. Further, in the process of representation new concepts are formed. Indeed, the act of discovery through expression is so important that R. G. Collingwood describes its presence as the difference between art and craft.[15] The craftsman knows how to do a job well, but produces nothing essentially new. The artist not only has the skills of the craftsman but discovers new possibilities as work progresses. The *work* of art is to make expressive form become a source of surprise, a discovery, a form that embodies a conception not held at the outset.

The selection of a form of representation does not adequately resolve the question of how that form, once selected, becomes "equivalent" to the conception. I suggest that we secure equivalence by treating forms of representation in one of three ways. The first of these modes of treatment is *mimetic,* the second is *expressive,* and the third is *conventional.*

Mimetic modes of treatment are efforts to imitate the the surface features of perceived or conceptualized forms, within the constraints of some material. Early examples of mimesis are the running animals found on the walls of the Lascaux Caves. According to Gombrich, the history of art is replete with efforts to create illusions that imitate the visual features of the environment as it was or as it was imagined.[16] But mimesis as a way of treating a form of representation is not limited to what is visual. Mimesis occurs in auditory forms of representation, such as music and voice, and in movement through dance. Mimesis is possible in any of the forms used to provide information that the senses can pick up.

As I have already said, the creation of an equivalent for a conception is always both constrained and made possible by the medium a person employs. Different media appeal to different sensory systems. Thus, when a person transforms visual conceptions into sound or movement, he or she must find what Rudolf Arnheim calls the "structural equivalent" of the conception within the medium he or she elects to use.[17] Such transformation requires the invention of analogies.

In language, analogic functions are performed by metaphor. When we move from the auditory to the visual, however, we must create a structural equivalent between the auditory and the visual. For example, the sounds "ooo loo loo" and "eee pee pee" are represented best by two very different kinds of graphic lines—one waving, the other pointed or jagged. Humans have the capacity to perceive and grasp these structural equivalences even when they take shape in different forms of representation—one visual, the other auditory. Thus mimesis, the business of imitating the surface features of a conceptualization within the limits of some medium, is one way to secure equivalence between a conception and its forms of representation.

The second way to do this is by treating the forms expressively. By expressively, I mean that what is conveyed is what the object, event, or conception expresses—not what it looks like. Thus "sorrow" can be represented mimetically, but it can also be represented expressively. In the arts, this expressive mode of treatment is of particular interest: the tense nervousness of Velasquez's Pope Innocent X, the celebration of color in a Sam Francis, the asceticism of a late Barnett Newman, the ethereal quality of Helen Frankenthaler's work, the symbolic undertones of an Edward Hopper, the crisp architecture of Bach's fugues, the romantic expansiveness of Beethoven's Seventh Symphony, the lighthearted whimsy of the poetry of e e cummings. What these artists have created are expressive images. In general, mimesis is a minor element in their works, used only to complement the dominant intent. Pablo Picasso succinctly stated the importance of the expressive mode of treatment in art when he said, "A painter takes the sun and makes it into a yellow spot, an artist takes a yellow spot and makes it into the sun."

By contrast, the conventional mode of treatment uses an arbitrary sign, on whose meaning society has agreed, to convey that meaning. Thus words and numbers are meaningful, not because they look like their referents but because we have agreed that they shall stand for them. The use of convention is, of course, not limited to words and numbers. Swastikas, crosses, six-pointed stars, the iconography of cultures past and present are all examples of visual conventions. Conventions in music take such forms as anthems, wedding marches, and graduation processionals.

In much of art the three modes of treatment are combined. Erwin Panofsky made his major contribution to the history of art—to the study of iconography—by describing these relationships.[18] The works of Jasper Johns, Marc Chagall, Joseph Cornell, Jack Levine, Robert Rauschenberg, and Andy Warhol demonstrate the ingenious ways in which visual artists have exploited all three modes of treatment in their effort to convey meaning.

I hope that I have made my point clear: Any form of representation one chooses to use—visual, auditory, or discursive—must also be treated in some way. Some forms tend to call forth one particular mode of treatment. The treatment of mathematics, for example, is essentially conventional, even though we may recognize its aesthetic qualities. The visual arts, by contrast, tend to emphasize the mimetic and the expressive. Language tends to be treated conventionally and expressively (save for occasional instances of onomatopoeia, which are obviously mimetic). The forms we choose provide potential options. The options we choose give us opportunities to convey what we know and what we are likely to experience.

Just as any form of representation we elect to use must be treated in a particular way, the elements within that form must also be related to each other. This relationship constitutes a syntax, an arrangement of parts used to construct a whole. Some forms of representation, such as mathematics and propositional discourse, are governed rather rigorously by publicly codified rules, through which the operations applied to such forms are to be performed. To be able to add, one must be able to apply correctly a set of prescribed operations to a set of numerical elements. To be able to punctuate, one must follow certain publicly articulated rules so that the marks placed within a sentence or paragraph are correct. Similarly, in spelling, rules govern the arrangements of elements (letters) that constitute words. There are only two ways to spell most words in English: correctly or incorrectly. Forms of representation that are treated through convention tend to emphasize the rule-governed end of the syntactical continuum. When forms are treated in this way, the scoring of performance can be handled by machines, because the need for judgment is small.

Forms of representation that are treated expressively have no comparable rules. There are, of course, rules of a sort to guide one in making a painting of a particular style or designing a building of a particular architectural period. But

the quality of performance in such forms is not determined by measuring the extent to which the rules were followed (as is done for spelling and arithmetic). Instead, quality is judged by other criteria—in some cases, criteria that don't even exist prior to the creation of the work. Syntactical forms that are open rather than closed, that allow for the idiosyncratic creation of relationships without being regarded as incorrect, are figurative in character. Thus it is possible to array forms of representation not only with respect to their modes of treatment but in relation to the ends of the syntactical continuum toward which they lean. In general, the arts lean toward the figurative. That is why, given the same task, thirty students in music, poetry, or visual art will create thirty different solutions, all of which can be "right," while thirty students in arithmetic will—if the teacher has taught effectively—come up with identical solutions. That is also why the arts are regarded as subjective: One cannot apply a conventionally defined set of rules to determine whether the meanings that are conveyed are accurate. Idiosyncratic arrangements are encouraged when figurative syntaxes are employed.

The importance of this distinction between rule-governed and figurative syntactical emphases becomes apparent when we consider the kinds of cognitive processes that each type of syntax elicits. Learning of rules fosters acquiescence: One learns to *obey* a rule or to *follow* it. Figurative syntaxes, by contrast, encourage invention, personal choice, exploratory activity, and judgment. The use of forms whose syntax is figurative is an uncertain enterprise, since there are no formally codified rules to guide judgments. The student, like the artist, is thrown on his or her own resources. How does one know when the painting is finished, the poem completed, the story ended? There is no predefined standard by which to check a solution. There is no correct answer given in the back of the book, no procedure for determining proof. The necessary cognitive operations are what were known, in earlier psychological jargon, as "higher mental processes." At the least, tasks that emphasize the figurative give people opportunities to form new structures, to make speculative decisions, and to act upon them. Such tasks also enable people to learn to judge—not by applying clear-cut standards, but by appealing to a form of rationality that focuses on the rightness of a form to a function.

It would be well at this point to recall the theme of this article, the role of the arts in cognition and curriculum. I began by describing a commonly held view: Cognition requires that ideas be linguistically mediated, whereas the arts are expressive and affective activities depending more upon talent than intelligence or cognition. I next analyzed the role of the senses in concept formation, arguing that all concepts are basically sensory in character and that concept formation requires the ability to perceive qualitative nuances in the qualitative world and to abstract their structural features for purposes of recall or imaginative manipulation. From there I moved to a discussion of the task of representation. An individual who wishes to externalize a concept must find some way of constructing an equivalent for it in the empirical world. To do this, people invent new forms of representation or borrow from those already available in the culture. Because these forms can be treated in different ways and because they appeal to different sensory systems, the kind of meanings each yields is unique. What we can convey in one form of representation has no literal equivalent in another. I have labeled the modes of treating these forms as mimetic, expressive, and conventional. Because the elements within forms of representation can be ordered according to different rules, I have identified a syntactical continuum, highly rule-governed at one end and figurative at the other. The rule-governed end of the continuum prescribes the rules of operations

that must, by convention, be followed in ordering those elements. The figurative end allows maximum degrees of latitude for idiosyncratic arrangement. The former is more of a code; the latter, more of a metaphor.

But what is the significance of such analysis for education? What bearing does it have on what we do in school? What might it mean for what we teach? There are four implications, I believe, for the conduct of education and for education theory.

First, the view that I have advanced makes it impossible to regard as cognitive any mental activity that is not itself rooted in sensory forms of life. This expands our conceptions of intelligence and literacy. Any conception of intelligence that omits the ordering of qualities through direct experience is neglecting a central feature of intellectual functioning. But no intelligence test that is published today includes such tasks. The models of mind that underlie current tests assign only marginal intellectual status to what is an intellectual activity. One no more plays the violin with one's fingers than one counts with one's toes. In each case, mind must operate, and the kind and number of opportunities a person is given to learn will significantly affect the degree to which his or her ability develops. The concepts of talent and lack of talent have been used too long to cover up weak or nonexistent programs in the arts. To be sure, individual aptitudes in the arts vary, but such differences also exist in other content areas. So-called lack of talent is too often nothing more than an excuse for absent opportunity. It also serves as a self-fulfilling prophecy.

Second, the view that I have advanced recognizes that the realm of meaning has many mansions. Science, for example, despite its enormous usefulness, can never have a monopoly on meaning because the form of representation it employs is only one among the several that are available. It is not possible to represent or to know everything in one form. The way Willy

Loman conveys his inability to cope with a sinking career can only be represented through the expressive treatment of form that Arthur Miller employed in *Death of a Salesman*. The quality of space in the paintings of Georgio de Chirico or Hans Hofmann depends on the artists' arrangements of visual images; it cannot be rendered through number. When Dylan Thomas wrote, "Do not go gentle into that good night,/old age should burn and rage at close of day;/rage, rage against the dying of the light,"[19] he conveyed a message about being in the anteroom of death that cannot be translated fully, even in propositional prose.

What this means for education is that—insofar as we in schools, colleges, and universities are interested in providing the conditions that enable students to secure deep and diverse forms of meaning in their lives—we cannot in good conscience omit the fine arts. Insofar as we seek to develop the skills for securing such meanings, we must develop multiple forms of literacy. Such meanings do not accrue to the unprepared mind. The task of the schools is to provide the conditions that foster the development of such literacy. At present, for the vast majority of students, the schools fail in this task.

Third, educational equity is one consequence for students of the change in education policy that my arguments suggest. As I have already pointed out, the benefits derived from excellence in differing forms of representation are not equal. Students who perform at outstanding levels in the fine arts do not have these grades taken into account when they apply for admission to colleges and universities. The beneficiaries of the funds allocated to education for the gifted often do not include students whose gifts are in the fine arts.[20] The amount of school time devoted to cultivating abilities in the arts is extremely limited; hence, students with abilities and interests in the arts are denied the opportunities that students in science, mathematics, or English receive.

Such policies and practices amount to a form of educational inequity. This inequity would cease if the arguments I have presented were used as grounds for decisions about the allocation of school time, about the criteria used to identify gifted students, and about the aptitudes suitable for college and university study. It is an anomaly of the first order that a university should confer credit in the fine arts for courses taken on its own campus and deny credit to students who have taken such courses in high schools. At present, that's the way it is.

Finally, the view I have presented implies that the cultivation of literacy in, for example, visual and auditory forms of representation can significantly improve a student's ability to use propositional forms of representation. The ability to create or understand sociology, psychology, or economics depends on the ability to perceive qualitative nuances in the social world, the ability to conceptualize patterns from which to share what has been experienced, and the ability to write about them in a form that is compelling. Without such perceptivity, the content of writing will be shallow. Without the ability to manipulate conceptions of the world imaginatively, the work is likely to be uninspired. Without an ear for the melody, cadence, and tempo of language, the tale is likely to be unconvincing. Education in the arts cultivates sensitive perception, develops insight, fosters imagination, and places a premium on well-crafted form.

These skills and dispositions are of central importance in both writing and reading. Without them, children are unlikely to write—not because they cannot spell but because they have nothing to say. The writer starts with vision and ends with words. The reader begins with these words but ends with vision. The reader uses the writer's words in order to see.

The interaction of the senses enriches meaning. The arts are not mere diversions from the important business of education; they are essential resources.

## ENDNOTES

1. These distinctions are reified most clearly in the customary separation between the cognitive and the affective domains, which are typically discussed as if they were independent entities or processes.

2. See especially *The Republic,* Francis M. Cornford, trans. (New York: Oxford University Press, 1951).

3. Bärbel Inhelder and Jean Piaget, *The Growth of Cognitive Thinking from Childhood to Adolescence,* Anne Parsons and Stanley Milgram, trans. (New York: Basic Books, 1958).

4. See, for example, Adam Schaff, *Language and Cognition* (New York: McGraw-Hill, 1973).

5. Barak Rosenshine, "Classroom Instruction," in N. L. Gage, ed., *Psychology of Teaching,* 75th Yearbook of the National Society for the Study of Education, Part I (Chicago: University of Chicago Press, 1976), pp. 335–71.

6. If an elementary teacher provides one hour of instruction in art and one hour of instruction in music each week, the percentage of instructional time devoted to both is about 7 percent. Many teachers provide less time than this.

7. The University of California System, like many other state universities, provides no credit for grades received in the fine arts when computing grade-point averages for students seeking admission.

8. *The Dictionary of Psychology* (Cambridge, Mass.: Riverside Press, 1934).

9. The acquisition of visual information over time is a function of micromovements of the eye and brain called saccades.

10. Insofar as something is conceivable, it must, by definition, be a part of human experience. Experience without sensory content is an impossibility.

11. This view argues that the reception and organization of sensory material require the use of intelligence. Intelligence is not something that one applies after experiencing the empirical world. Rather, it is a central factor in the process of experience.

12. See Morris Weitz, "The Role of Theory in Aesthetics," *Journal of Aesthetics and Art Criticism,* September 1956, pp. 27–35.

13. In a sense, play is the ability to suspend rules in order to explore new arrangements. See Brian Sutton-Smith, ed., *Play and Learning* (New York: Halsted Press, 1979).

14. This concept is elaborated in greater detail in my book, *Cognition and Curriculum, A Basis for Deciding What to Teach* (New York: Longman, Inc., 1982).

15. R. G. Collingwood, *Principles of Art* (New York: Oxford University Press, 1958).

16. Ernst H. Gombrich, "Visual Discovery Through Art," in James Hogg, ed., *Psychology and the Visual Arts* (Middlesex, England: Penguin Books, 1969).

17. Rudolf Arnheim, *Art and Visual Perception* (Berkeley: University of California Press, 1954).

18. Erwin Panofsky, *Meaning in the Visual Arts: Papers in and on Art History* (Garden City, N. Y.: Doubleday, 1955).

19. Dylan Thomas, "Do Not Go Gentle into That Good Night," *The Collected Poems of Dylan Thomas* (New York: New Directions, 1953), p. 128.

20. Until a couple of years ago the Mentally Gifted Minor Program (MGM) in California—now Gifted and Talented Education (GTE)—did not include students who were gifted in the fine arts.

*Elliot W. Eisner* is Professor of Education and Art, Stanford University, Stanford, California.

# Teaching to the Whole Brain

## PATRICIA K. BRENNAN

Preliminary evidence suggests that left-preferenced people learn analytically and right-preferenced people learn globally.

A recent study conducted by Zenhausern, Dunn, Cavanaugh, and Eberle with 353 high school students in Ohio disclosed the following:

| Left-Preferenced Students | Right-Preferenced Students |
|---|---|
| N = 116 | N = 231 |
| • Require formal design | • Require low light |
| • Are teacher motivated | • Need warm environment |
| • Are persistent | • Are relatively less motivated |
| • Are responsible | • Prefer to learn with one peer |
| • Prefer to learn alone | • Have tactile preferences |
| • Do not need mobility | • Need mobility |

The literature on analytic-global learners describes left-preferenced individuals and analytic learners similarly. They both learn sequentially (step-by-step), are inductive (going from the parts to the whole), emphasize the importance of language and verbal ability, and tend to be reflectives. Similarly, the right-brained and global literature describes holistic learners who are deductive (going from the whole to the parts), emphasize spatial relationships and emotions as characteristic, and tend to be impulsive.

I believe that in any given classroom, there are probably an approximately equal number of analytic and global learners. But our school system has traditionally geared education to the left-brained analytic learner. We present all the parts of a given lesson and expect children to be able to piece the puzzle together and "get the picture." Have you ever been asked the question, "Do you get the picture"? Chances are it was a global person who asked the question. Global learners thrive on getting the whole picture and then discovering the elements necessary to make up that picture.

To reach all students in a typical classroom, we must teach in both directions. If you start a lesson by teaching inductively, turn the whole thing around and teach deductively. Mathematics is a useful case in point. When I am teaching the Pythagorean theorem, I start by teaching it inductively, (chiefly because I am a left-preferenced, analytic learner and I am most comfortable teaching in that mode). I could stop there and feel that I had taught a pretty good lesson. I presented logically  and sequentially every step needed to solve the theorem: $a^2 + b^2 = c^2$. If one leg of the right triangle is 3 cm and one leg is 4 cm, $3^2 + 4^2 = c^2$ or $9 + 16 = 25$. Find the square root of $c^2$ and you will know the length of the hypotenuse. We learn to solve for $c$ today, tomorrow for $a$, and the next day for $b$. On Friday we have a test. Sound familiar? If this were the only method for teaching this concept, I can assure you that I would not be the only one frustrated by the results. But, if after teaching inductively you also teach deductively, your joy will be as evident as the other half of your class.

From *Student Learning Styles and Brain Behavior,* 1982, pages 212–213. Reston, Virginia, NASSP. Used by permission of the publisher, the National Association of Secondary School Principals.

One deductive method for teaching the Pythagorean theorem is as follows: Draw a right triangle whose sides are 3 cm and 4 cm and whose hypotenuse is 5 cm. If you draw a square on each side of your triangle, what can you tell from your measurements? Side *a* is 9 sq. cm, side *b* is 16 sq. cm, and side *c* is 25 sq. cm.

Therefore:
$$9 + 16 = 25$$
$$\text{or } 3^2 + 4^2 = 5^2$$
$$a^2 + b^2 = c^2$$

In geometry you *can* "see" the whole picture and then discover how the parts fit to make up the whole. The next time someone says to you, "I hate math, I've always hated math," ask them if they liked geometry. About 75 percent will say that they liked geometry but hated math. The reason? In geometry, you can "get the picture." The sooner we begin to pictorialize other math concepts, the sooner we will have fewer math haters.

Young children are all global learners until about the age of seven and will "get a better picture" of a number concept if it is presented globally. In teaching addition, for example, you might start with a picturesque story of a birthday party to which they are allowed to invite 10 friends. Use actual people; keep it real. They are very excited; the big day is finally here. Who arrived first? *name* Who came second? *name* Now how many people are there? 2 How many presents do you have so far? 2 How do you know you have 2? *Kathy brought one and Maria brought one so now I have two.* Let's open the presents and see what's inside. One doll and one paint set. 1 + 1 = 2. Someone else is coming. And so forth. . . . The typical child will learn far more about the concept of addition from this kind of presentation or a similar life experience than being told 1 + 1 = 2, or shown Δ + Δ = ΔΔ.

Teaching math or any analytical subject can be done globally once the teacher is aware that he or she can and should teach in both directions. Similarly, a very global subject such as social studies can be taught analytically. Take any lesson you have prepared and teach it analytically or globally. About half the class will "see" it. Then turn that lesson around and start from the other perspective. The other half of your class will likely react: "I see what you're saying now. I get the picture!"

*Patricia K. Brennan* is Mathematics Teacher, St. Joseph's Junior High School, Long Island City, New York.

# It's Joe Again
## NANCY TAITT AND HENRY TAITT

In the first grade, Joe sat near the back of the room in a class of 32 students. He was quiet and polite. Joe didn't give the new teacher any trouble; as it was, she had her hands full taking care of the noisy and problem cases. Since Joe didn't create any problems, the teacher didn't have to spend much time with him. When the year ended, he was behind in his reading and math skills.

By the end of the second grade, Joe needed remedial work. To his peers, he was "different."

By the end of the third grade, Joe didn't like school. His reading skills were very poor although his spoken vocabulary was good. He did especially poor with "fill-in-the-blank" type exercises; he always wanted to use a word that wasn't in the answer key.

By the fourth grade, Joe's parents got permission to drive him to a less-crowded school in a nearby town. Here it was hoped he would get more and better attention. This helped . . . some.

In the fifth grade, Joe was required to return to his old school. Near the end of this school year, he took the Iowa Test of Basic Skills and scored poorly. Joe was in trouble.

Joe's older sisters, on the other hand, were both honor roll students. The eldest, a junior in high school, was an outstanding athlete and was constantly getting her picture in the local paper. Joe's other sister was also very athletic and was the top student at her junior high school.

Although Joe was artistic and creative himself, little credit was given for this at school. His "fill-in-the-blank" homework hung over him like a dark cloud, and he would pounce on any ex-cuse to be absent from school; in fact he began planning how to drop out as soon as he could. His sisters overshadowed him with their accomplishments and because he was a late maturer and nonathletic, Joe began to believe that maybe he was adopted and not a real member of his family at all.

That Christmas, Joe got a microcomputer for use at home and started playing around with it. At first, he learned by watching his sisters because his reading skills were not sufficient to comprehend the manuals that came with the computer. But before long, Joe had learned a few commands and was creating programs of his own. By the time summer rolled around, Joe became involved in an out-of-school microcomputer program sponsored by Creative Learning Associates of Charleston, Il. that was researching and developing microcomputer instructional materials for children. Through this program, Joe found he could read and understand the materials, and his programming skills improved rapidly.

At school the next year, it was the same old story. Joe's written assignments were returned with red marks everywhere, yet the ideas he expressed were often very innovative. Joe enjoyed science and was doing well in that class, but he was regularly pulled out of it for his remedial reading. Joe continued to attend the out-of-school microcomputer program where emphasis was placed on individualized progress and learning, self-evaluation, problem-solving skills (not computational skills), guided trial and error and creativity.

When at home, Joe would ignore his "fill-in-

From *Electronic Education* 5, No. 1 (September 1985): 9, 13. ©1985, by Electronic Communications, Inc. Used by permission of the publisher.

the-blank" homework and work on the computer, creating graphic designs and the beginnings of simple games. When one of his teachers gave him permission to use his computer to help in preparing a social studies report, he created an extensive program using PRINT commands and graphics to describe a city of the future. The computer displayed a model of the city, complete with narrative and moving parts, and of course, many misspelled words. But these were easy to correct on the computer.

Joe's skills and maturity level continued to progress. At the out-of-school program, he became a student teacher helping others to learn. This carried over to his school environment. Although he was not often allowed to use the school's computers because he hadn't finished all of his assignments and wasn't in the gifted group, Joe was often called upon to help other students who were having problems with the computers.

Near the end of the sixth grade, Joe took the Iowa Test of Basic Skills again, the results of which wouldn't be known to the school until later. In the meantime, the school had to decide if they should hold Joe back a grade or advance him as a remedial student and put him into the special education classes at the junior high. Joe's parents requested that he be interviewed and tested by a psychologist. Her report was quite surprising! Although she expressed concern about Joe's low self-image and feeling of worth, she stated quite firmly that his I.Q. was in excess of 140 and that he should not be held back. This was a tremendous boost to Joe's ego and self-confidence.

When his sixth grade Iowa Test scores became available, they showed amazing growth. Almost every category was now average or better. His math concepts had jumped from 49th percentile to 88th percentile—his vocabulary from 37th to 56th.

Joe continued to work with the microcomputer—not constantly, but in spurts. Playing computer games was his favorite activity, but he also used it to express his creativity and to help with his own interests. At school the computers were used with software to do drills and computer-instruction. Joe found ways to avoid this form of electronic assisted "fill-in-the-blanks" whenever possible. He often resorted to rather ingenious ways to legitimately be out of the classroom when it was his turn.

By the eighth grade, Joe could program on a dozen different brands of computers. He created a graphic display of the Chicago Museum of Science & Industry which was selected for the cover of the Museum's *Computer & You* booklet. His Iowa Test scores for the eighth grade again showed excellent improvement. His vocabulary concepts increased more than 50 percent over a three year period.

Working freely with a computer had sharpened his attention to detail, allowed him to express his creativity, increased his attention span and improved his problem-solving ability. But most importantly, it had improved his own self-image.

In the ninth grade, Joe wrote a computer program to drill himself in spelling (his worst subject) and soon started getting perfect scores on spelling tests.

In the tenth grade, Joe made the school geometry team which won a regional math contest. By the end of the eleventh grade, Joe was ranked in the top 5% of his class. His ACT scores ranked him with national composite scores of 86%. He had received a 93% in math, 64% in English, 67% in social studies and 95% in natural sciences.

Now a senior, Joe no longer thinks about dropping out of school, but rather of going on to college to major in computer graphics or art. He is an A student in the high school's computer math class. Several of his computer programs have been purchased and published and three of his line drawings have been on exhibit in a local art gallery.

Joe's success story is true and dramatically demonstrates how the computer, used as an out-of-school tool, was able to reconstruct one boy's life. How many other Joe's might it help?

*Nancy Taitt* is Professor of Mathematics and Computer Education at Eastern Illinois University, Charleston, Illinois.
*Henry Taitt* is President, Creative Learning Associates, Charleston, Illinois.

## ADDITIONAL LEARNING ACTIVITIES

### Problems and Projects

1.  Continue to develop a "case problem" about one school you know well. Describe the curriculum and teaching in that school as they are related to knowledge and cognition theories. Do they use discovery learning, the structure of the disciplines, the problems approach? Is the curriculum balanced? Does it provide for individual differences? Does it include learning opportunities in general education, the physical sciences, the social sciences, mathematics, physical and health education, the arts and music for all learners?

2.  Prepare a lesson plan in your field of teaching, in which you use "discovery learning" as the teaching method. Review the articles in this section by Dewey and Bruner for assistance in preparing the plan. For further help, read Jerome Bruner, *The Process of Education* (Cambridge, Massachusetts: Harvard University Press, 1961), pp. 1–34. Try to use your plan in actually teaching a class.

3.  Compare the ideas about teaching and learning that are found in the articles by John Dewey and Jerome Bruner in this section. Does Dewey seem to share Bruner's ideas about the "internal connectedness" and structure of knowledge? Does Bruner share Dewey's ideas concerning the need for finding the materials for learning within experience?

4.  What are the implications for curriculum planning and/or teaching of the research regarding the human brain reported by Levy in this section? How might it affect the curriculum or subject area with which you are involved?

5.  In his article in this section, Eisner asserts that the generally accepted current views about cognition and intelligence have had disastrous consequences for education. What does he mean when he says that it is impossible "to regard as cognitive any mental activity that is not itself rooted in sensory forms of life"? What are the implications of Eisner's views for curriculum planning? Do you see any relation between Eisner's views and Dewey's statement that "Anything that can be called a study . . . must be derived from materials which at the outset fall within the scope of ordinary life experience"?

6.  Both Eisner and Levy stress that the curriculum should focus on visual, spatial, auditory, perceptual, and holistic approaches to knowledge and cognition, as well as verbal, numerical, logical, and linear approaches. Select a curriculum

with which you are familiar and identify which of these approaches it uses. Then try to identify learning experiences that might be developed to make use of some of the other approaches.

7. It is often stated that teaching students how to learn and encouraging lifelong learning are among the most important goals of the curriculum. What does Levy say should be done to accomplish these goals? For another discussion of this topic, read "Teaching Students How to Learn" by Charles M. Letteri, *Theory Into Practice* 24, no. 2 (Spring 1985): 112–122.

8. Why do you think Joe was in trouble in school (see "It's Joe Again")? Analyze his learning problems in terms of the approaches to knowledge presented in this section.

9. Marshall McLuhan was one of the most influential thinkers of the 1960s. When he died in 1981, his insights into the nature of television and the "electronic surround" had become conventional wisdom and people who didn't know his name confidently repeated his most famous statement, "The medium is the message." McLuhan maintained that the individual's modes of cognition and perception are "influenced by the culture he is in, the language he speaks, and the media to which he is exposed." He asserted that we can no longer teach learners all about a subject. We have to introduce them to the "form, structure, gestalt, grammar, and process of the knowledge involved." He also believed that the arts must now play a new role in education because they are "explorations in perception" and provide fresh ways of looking at familiar things. Read "A Schoolman's Guide to Marshall McLuhan" by John M. Culkin, *Saturday Review* 50, no. 11 (March 18, 1967): 51–53, 70–72. Then compare McLuhan's concepts and ideas with those of Eisner in this section. Also select several of McLuhan's ideas and tell how you think they might be applied to curriculum planning.

10. *Individual differences* is a curriculum criterion that is related to the theories and research regarding knowledge and cognition that are presented in this section. How would curriculum planners or teachers make use of the ideas of Levy, Restak, Eisner, or Brennan if they were trying to provide for individual differences?

11. The *Second Handbook of Research on Teaching,* Robert M. W. Travers, ed. (Chicago: Rand McNally & Co., 1973), pp. 59–65, describes the "discovery learning approach to curriculum planning and teaching with the research related to it and criticisms regarding it." Read this description and relate it to the article by Bruner in this section. What are the advantages and disadvantages of this approach to curriculum planning and teaching?

12. In your opinion, are the differences in brain functioning between boys and girls, as described by Restak in this section, due to social stereotypes or are they biologically inherent? Make a list of the ways in which each view might influence curriculum planning. Discuss the items in your two lists and compare them with those of other members of your class or group.

13. In the Yearbook of the National Society for the Study of Education (*Issues in*

*Secondary Education,* chap. 6, William Van Til, ed. [Chicago: University of Chicago Press, 1976]), Arthur W. Foshay states that there are three types of knowledge: knowledge of facts and findings, knowledge of sources and processes, and knowledge of technique. He says that knowledge of sources and processes is the most important, since it incorporates the other two types of knowledge, and that this type of knowledge should therefore be sought in all of the offerings at the secondary school level. Read this chapter and then relate Foshay's three types of knowledge to the other ideas about knowledge found in the articles in this section.

14. The Appendix of this book includes a list of books, each describing a school or school program. Select one that interests you and determine whether curriculum practices growing out of the knowledge and cognition theories described in this section might be used to improve the program.

15. Have your personal beliefs or values about knowledge changed as a result of your experience with this section? If so, state what change has taken place, and relate it to one or more parts of this section (the rationale, an article, a post-assessment activity, etc.). Compare your ideas with those of the other members of your class.


## Films and Audiocassettes

*Maxine Greene on "The Literacy That Liberates."* Audiocassette, 60 min., 1983. Students can be opened to new possibilities through aesthetic education. Association for Supervision and Curriculum Development, 225 North Washington St., Alexandria, VA 22314.

*Leslie Hart on "Student Learning Can Be Enormously Improved, Right Now."* Audiocassette, 1984. Describes a brain-based educational program, already implemented in a New Jersey elementary school. Audiocassette, 1984. Association for Supervision and Curriculum Development, 225 North Washington St., Alexandria, VA 22314.

*Personalizing Educational Programs: Utilizing Cognitive Style Mapping.* 16 mm, color, 20 min., 1975. Students can be helped by determining their personal cognitive style through testing. This film seeks to promote teaching the same course in different ways to accommodate the different cognitive styles of students. Oakland Community College, 2480 Opdyke Road, Bloomfield Hills, Michigan 48013.

*This Is Marshall McLuhan: The Medium Is the Message.* 16 mm, color, 53 min., 1967. Presents Dr. McLuhan's ideas through pictorial techniques, his own comments, and the reactions of others. Examines how the contemporary world is being altered by electronic technology. McGraw-Hill Text Films, 330 West 42nd Street, New York, New York 10036.

*The Secret Life of an Orchestra.* 16 mm, color, 28 min., 1975. The Denver Symphony Orchestra rehearses and performs Wagner's "Meistersinger Overture." The film takes the viewer inside both the music and minds of the musicians to reveal the intimate process of a balanced performance. Pyramid Films, Box 1048, Santa Monica, California 90406.

*The Light of Experience.* 16 mm, color, 52 min., 1971. The stunning canvases of the seventeenth-century Dutch painters dominate this film. The Dutch were the first to grasp the revolutionary changes in thought that replaced divine authority with experience, experiment, and observation. Time-Life Films, Multi-Media Division, Time-Life Building, New York, New York 10020.

*Art from Computers.* 16 mm, color, 8 min., 1972. Mathematics can be used to produce artistic designs by means of computer graphics. National Broadcasting Company, 30 Rockefeller Plaza, New York, New York 10020.

## Books and Articles to Review

Ausubel, D. P. *Educational Psychology: A Cognitive View,* 2nd ed. New York: Holt, Rinehart, and Winston, 1978.

Barger, Robert R.; and Hoover, Randy L. "Psychological Type and the Matching of Cognitive Styles." *Theory Into Practice* 23, no. 1 (Winter 1984): 53–63.

Beyer, Barry K. "Improving Thinking Skills: Practical Approaches." *Phi Delta Kappan* 65, no. 8 (April 1984): 556–560.

Bloom, B. S.; Engelhart, M. D.; Furst, E. J.; Hill, W. H.; and Krathwohl, D. R., eds. *Taxonomy of Educational Objectives: Handbook I: Cognitive Domain.* New York: David McKay Cco., 1956.

Brooks, Martin; Fusco, Esther; and Grennon, Jacqueline. "Cognitive Level Matching." *Educational Leadership* 40, no. 8 (May 1983): 4–8.

Bruner, Jerome. *The Process of Education.* Cambridge, Massachusetts: Harvard University Press, 1961.

Cleveland, Harlan. "Information as a Resource." *Futurist* 16, no. 6 (December 1982): 34–39.

Dewey, John. *Experience and Education.* New York: The Macmillan Co., 1938.

——— *The Sources of a Science of Education.* New York: Horace Liveright, 1929.

Elfand, Arthur D. "Excellence in Education: The Role of the Arts." *Theory Into Practice* 23, no. 4 (Autumn 1984): 267–272.

Eisner, Elliot W. *Cognition and Curriculum: A Basis for Deciding What to Teach.* New York: Longman, Inc., 1982.

Elkind, David. "Teenage Thinking and the Curriculum." *Educational Horizons* 61, no. 4 (Summer 1983): 163–168.

Feldhusen, J. F.; and Treffinger, D. J. *Teaching Creative Thinking and Problem Solving.* Dubuque, IA: Kendall-Hunt, 1977.

Fuller, Jocelyn K.; and Glendening, James G. "The Neuro-Educator: Professional of the Future." *Theory Into Practice* 24, no. 2 (Spring 1985): 135–137.

Gardner, Howard. *Frames of Mind: The Theory of Multiple Intelligences.* New York: Basic Books, 1983.

——— *The Mind's New Science: A History of the Cognitive Revolution.* New York: Basic Books, 1985.

Gazzaniga, Michael S. "The Social Brain." *Psychology Today* 19, no. 11 (November 1985): 28–30, 32–34, 36, 38.

Grady, M. P.; and Luecke, E. A. *Education and the Brain.* (Phi Delta Kappa Fastback 108). Bloomington, Indiana: Phi Delta Kappa Educational Foundation, 1978.

Hald, Alan P. "Toward the Information Rich Society." *The Futurist* 15, no. 4 (August 1981): 20–24.

Hart, Leslie A. *Human Brain and Human Learning.* New York: Longman, 1983.

Kimura, Dureen. "Male Brain, Female Brain: The Hidden Difference." *Psychology Today* 19, no. 11 (November 1985): 50–52, 54, 56–58.

Krathwohl, D. R.; Bloom, B. S.; and Masia, B. B. *Taxonomy of Educational Objectives. Handbook II: Affective Domain.* New York: David McKay Co., 1974.

Letteri, Charles M. "Teaching Students How to Learn." *Theory Into Practice* 24, no. 2 (Spring 1985): 112–122.

Levy, Jerre. "Right Brain, Left Brain: Fact and Fiction." *Psychology Today* 19, no. 5 (May 1985): 38–44.

McLuhan, Marshall. *The Medium Is the Message,* 2nd ed. New York: Random House, 1967.

Restak, Richard M. *The Brain.* New York: Bantam Books, 1985.

——— "The Human Brain: Insights and Puzzles." *Theory Into Practice* 24, no. 2 (Spring 1985): 91–94.

Rossman, Parker. "The Coming Great Electronic Encyclopedia." *Futurist* 16, no. 4 (August 1982): 53–57.

Sadler, William A., Jr. "A Holistic Approach to Improving Thinking Skills." *Phi Delta Kappan* 67, no. 3 (November 1985): 199–203.

Schwab, Joseph J. "The Concept of the Structure of a Discipline." In *Conflicting Conceptions of Curriculum,* edited by Elliot W. Eisner and Elizabeth Vallance. Berkeley: McCutchan Publishing Corp., 1974. 162–175.

# 6

# *Curriculum Criteria*

Reading and studying Sections 1 through 5 of this book.

## RATIONALE

A *criterion* is a standard on which a decision or judgment can be based; it is a basis for discrimination. *Curriculum criteria* are guidelines or standards on which curriculum or instruction decisions can be based.

If you have read this far, you should now understand the significance of values and goals, social forces, human development, learning, learning styles, and knowledge and cognition in planning a curriculum. A major goal of this section is to emphasize that curriculum planners and teachers should consider values and goals and all four of the bases presented in the preceding sections as curriculum criteria. They should be used together as guidelines for curriculum and instruction decisions.

A knowledge of social forces and human development represents two ways of approaching the task of understanding the learner and his or her needs. Learning theories and learning styles suggest that different ways of learning may be superior in different circumstances, for different learning tasks, or for different learners. Knowledge theories indicate that learners have a personal organization of knowledge that may be different from the structure of the disciplines, and that both should be considered by the curriculum planner or teacher.

As you grow in knowledge and understanding of the bases of curriculum decisions studied so far, try to use them together. Theories of human development, of learning, about the individual in society and about the nature of knowledge and cognition each describe only a portion of the learner's setting, nature, and action. But used together they constitute multiple curriculum criteria to aid the teacher and curriculum maker in planning and evaluating.

Other curriculum criteria which are often suggested and used will be described and discussed in this introduction.

## A Multidimensional Approach Is Necessary

John Dewey, in the second article in this section, tells us that the significance of any one factor for educational practice can be determined only as it is balanced with many other factors; various scientific findings should be linked up where possible until they reciprocally confirm and illuminate one another, or until each gives the other added meaning. When the connecting principles are understood, the educational practioner can become more flexible because of a wider range of alternatives to select from in dealing with individual situations.

In his concept of experience as the basis for learning, Dewey combined all of the bases of curriculum planning—values and goals, the learner (human development and learning), the society (social forces), and knowledge. Dewey's article in Section 1 warned against either-or positions in educational planning and practice; his article in this section suggests that the practice of education is an art, but one that should progressively incorporate more of science into it.

My article, "Eighty Years of Curriculum Theory," provides a brief historical treatment regarding the four bases of curriculum planning and links their development to several views of human nature, each of which has been the focus of study during this century: rational-economic man, social man, and self-actualizing man. Curriculum planners committed to one of these views have often tended to neglect or reject the others. Since we know today that all human behavior is a product of complex interacting forces, a "complex person" view is needed. A multidimensional approach to curriculum planning is necessary.

The article by Duke, "What Is the Nature of Educational Excellence and Should We Try to Measure It?" examines the recent push for excellence in education and concludes that the target is educational adequacy rather than excellence. The article makes clear the need for examining values and goals, asking how students learn, and reflecting on the various kinds of knowledge and their significance. In thinking about excellence as a curriculum criterion, it is helpful to remember the two kinds of goals described by Raywid, Tesconi, and Warren in Section 1: goals the attainment of which is demonstrated through performance on standardized tests of academic achievement; and those that have to do not with outcomes but with "circumstances along the way."

Your study of values and goals and the four bases of the curriculum in the first five sections of this book should suggest many different learning strategies and curriculum approaches. Strategies and designs may be selected and used in terms of objectives and differences in learners, learning, and knowledge. Some of these strategies are *person-centered,* some are *group- or social-centered,* and some are *information- or skill-centered.* The strategies are not mutually exclusive; they can be used together or separately to provide for differences in learners, learning, and knowledge to be learned. Competence as a teacher or curriculum planner requires that one be able to use the various planning and learning strategies in order to achieve different objectives and to provide for individual differences. The different models and strategies can also be the basis of *alternative curricula or schools,* where students, parents, and teachers can make choices regarding the type of curriculum or program that a student is to experience. In this section, Klein discusses alternative curriculum designs.

The sources of the *strategies, models,* or *alternative curricula* can be found in the *theories and research* about objectives, social forces, human development, learning, and knowledge and cognition that you have studied in the preceding sections of this book. Included, among others, as the sources of these strategies would be Raywid, Hutchins, Bagley, Kilpatrick, Brameld, Dewey, Shane, Cremin, Tonkin and Edwards, Bohannan, Raffa, Cornish, Cherlin and Furstenberg, Cetron, Montagu, Williams, Grant and Briggs, Erikson, Havighurst, Piaget, Kohlberg, Ausubel, Gregorc, Combs, Madsen and Madsen, Avila and Purkey, McDaniel, Friedman and Alley, Hyman and Rosoff, Block, Bruner, Levy, Restak, Eisner and Brennan.

## Objectives of a Curriculum Plan or Teaching Plan

The purposes of a curriculum or teaching plan are the most important curriculum criteria. They should provide the first guidelines for determining the learning experiences to be included in the curriculum. Unfortunately, schools commonly lack a comprehensive and reasonably consistent set of objectives on which to base curriculum decisions, and teachers often fail to use a set of objectives to guide their planning for teaching.

Without having a set of objectives clearly in view, teachers and curriculum planners cannot make sound professional judgments. They cannot use their knowledge of the curriculum bases to make choices of content, materials, or procedures that will further student learning toward intended ends. To choose among curriculum alternatives or instructional strategies, educators must know the goals they are seeking and the curriculum bases on which they may make their choices. Otherwise, their selections will be little more than random; they cannot be termed professional in the light of today's knowledge of present and future cultural and social forces, human development and learning, and knowledge and cognition.

Learners should be clearly aware of the objectives being sought by teachers and by the curriculum they are experiencing. In the process of instruction, learners should share in defining the objectives. While the objectives the teacher uses to guide his or her planning and those sought by the learners need not be identical, there should be much overlapping. The teacher's and learners' goals for a learning experience certainly must be understood by both the teacher and the learners, and they must be compatible or they are not likely to be achieved. This sharing of objectives by teachers, curriculum planners, and learners can only be achieved by student-teacher planning. In the article, "Who Should Plan the Curriculum?," Hass states that the student is the "major untapped resource in curriculum planning."

Broad, general goals are needed in planning the objectives of a program of education and for teaching it. Such objectives can then be used to define this need for various courses, activities, and experiences in the community. I have found it useful to think of the broad, general goals as necessarily including four areas: education for *citizenship, vocation, self-realization,* and *critical thinking.* These four goals can be placed in two broad areas, both of which should always be considered in curriculum planning: *the goals that relate to the society and its values;* and *the goals that relate to the individual learner and his or her talents, needs, interests, and abilities in a changing society.*

The four bases of the curriculum should be considered in selecting goals and in seeking their attainment.

All teachers should consider the objectives that are pertinent for learners with whom they work. Objectives *in a particular setting* are related to the social forces, values, and needs of that community, the needs for individual development revealed by study of *particular learners,* and the significance of knowledge for interpretive use both in the local and larger society.

In selecting the objectives of a curriculum plan or a teaching plan, planners make choices regarding the relative importance given to society, human development, learning, and knowledge and cognition. As we noted in Section 1, four philosophical positions have influenced curriculum planners during the past fifty years. It may be useful at this time for you to review those philosophical positions in order to determine your views in relation to them and how those views (about which you may not be fully aware) may affect your curriculum and teaching decision making and the emphasis you may place on each of the four bases and various objectives.

## Behavioral Objectives and Performance Goals

A topic which has attracted a great deal of attention in the field of curriculum and instruction since the 1960s is behavioral objectives. The discussion of behavioral objectives has served an important function by calling attention to the need for clearly and publicly stated objectives and by emphasizing the need to use objectives in guiding planning, activities, and evaluation of outcomes of instruction.

Performance goals refer to learning in which performance competencies are the outcomes sought. When performance competencies are the goals of learning, curriculum planning must focus on the development of the knowledge, skills, and experiences that learners need if they are to be able to analyze, organize, implement, and evaluate their performance. Inferences about success in learning are then made from total performance rather than from small specific behaviors.

Performance goals are specified in advance; and to be successful in learning, learners must be able to perform the essential tasks and behaviors related to the goals. As stated in the introduction, the purpose of this book is to help you to achieve skill in many of the performance competencies you need in curriculum planning and teaching.

Behavioral objectives and performance goals are subgoals, and when they are utilized they should be consistent with the broad, general objectives of the curriculum. Because of the general nature of the overall objectives, subgoals are needed to guide planning in the various areas or parts of the curriculum. Behavioral objectives are most useful when they are used to define basic skills and abilities that are needed by all members of our society or that may be needed in some vocation or special activity. In many areas of the curriculum, however, standardization of performance is difficult, impossible, or undesirable. It is these goals that are being emphasized in the calls for excellence in education which are found in the reform reports of the 1980s. Those reports are presented and discussed in detail in Section 9.

## Other Significant Curriculum Criteria

The planned objectives are among the most significant criteria for developing and evaluating any curriculum plan. This is true regardless of what the objectives are or how they are stated. The four bases of the curriculum should also be used as curriculum criteria in curriculum and instruction planning.

Other criteria are often suggested. Among those most frequently suggested are *individual differences, relevance, continuity, balance, flexibility, cooperative planning, student-teacher planning, teaching of values, systematic planning, self-understanding, personalization of instruction,* and *problem solving.* The importance and meaning of all of these criteria can be derived from the bases of the curriculum. For instance, understanding of social forces, human development, learning theories, and knowledge and cognition theories supports the need to provide for individual differences in planning the curriculum.

For a curriculum to be *relevant,* the curriculum planners and the teachers who implement it should consider all four of the curriculum bases. All too often, *individual differences* or *relevance* tend to be used as criteria either by planners who have only one of the curriculum bases in mind, or by planners who are thinking only of making the curriculum relevant for the learners, or relevant to social forces, or relevant to values preferred by the planner. The criteria listed in the preceding paragraph are useful as guidelines when they are used to organize thinking around the ways that each of the bases can contribute to successfully achieving the goals of a curriculum. For example, if *self-understanding* is the criterion being used, then it is necessary to consider how social factors or forces, human development factors, learning approach or style, and knowledge might be involved in contributing to the learner's achievement of self-realization and self-understanding. If *personalization of instruction* is the criterion being used, then the teacher is seeking ways to understand and provide for a particular learner's development in terms of social factors both present and future, developmental stage, learning style, and structure of knowledge and cognition.

A number of the articles in this section assist us in examining these curriculum criteria. Fantini looks at the current view about *individualization* or *personalization of instruction,* which includes matching teaching with learning style and viewing the curriculum as "learning environment."

Sapon-Shevin uses the *individual differences* criterion to examine desirable and undesirable practices in mainstreaming handicapped learners; she emphasizes that *mainstreaming* must be conceived not as changing the special learner to fit back into the unchanged regular classroom, but rather as *changing the nature of the regular classroom* so that is is more accommodating to all children.

Wiles indicates that *balance and continuity* cannot be achieved for everyone in the same way; but they can be achieved by *systematic planning* and the use of procedures that include *parent-teacher-student planning* and evaluation.

In "Who Should Plan the Curriculum," I discuss *cooperative planning* as a curriculum planning criterion and say that scholars in the disciplines, parents, other citizens, students, and professional educators should all be involved in curriculum planning.

## Curriculum Criteria for the 1980s and 1990s

The curriculum criteria examined thus far are those that have been developed and articulated during the past fifty years. But for the 1980s and 1990s I believe that several new or newly focused criteria are needed. These are *anticipation, participation,* and *values.*

As a criterion, *anticipation* is the ability to deal with the future, to engage in future planning, to foresee coming events, and to evaluate both the medium-term and long-range consequences of current decisions. As a curriculum criterion, *anticipation* is needed because of the urgency to educate for a "sustainable society" and to deal with the great strains we are now placing on our planetary resources (see the rationale for Section 2 and the articles by Tonkin and Edwards, Cornish, Shane, Papert, Cetron et al., and Cherlin and Furstenberg in that section).

*Participation* as a curriculum criterion brings into better focus the human character of the problems we face on a local as well as a global basis. It emphasizes the right that each of us should have to influence decisions that shape our environment and our lives. It unites the criteria of *relevance* and *student-teacher planning* and is particularly important at a time when we may be moving toward the extensive use of computers in education. It is useful here to recall Papert's metaphor of "computer as pencil" (see his article in Section 2).

I believe that in the 1980s and 1990s we need more than ever to give attention to *values* in curriculum decisions. Making decisions is based on the capacity to assess preferences, to trade off advantages and disadvantages, and to examine the future consequences of present decisions. *Values* are the borderline between education as an art and education as a science; we need to note with Dewey in this section that there is no opposition between art and science, although there is a distinction. We need to reexamine the *values* in the various philosophical positions presented in Section 1 and to make use of the advantages that each can contribute to better planning and learning.

## CRITERION QUESTIONS

Each of the preceding sections of this book has indicated relationships of objectives and bases to curriculum criteria. In Section 1, we learned that the overall objectives should contribute to balance and systematic planning, and that they should be achieved in part through student-teacher planning. In Section 2, social forces, both present and future, were seen as necessary considerations in planning for individual differences, relevance, the teaching of values, self-understanding, and problem solving. Section 3 expressed the importance of human development in providing for individual differences, relevance, and continuity in learning. The relationship of the nature of learning to flexibility, providing for individual differences, and systematic planning was discussed in Section 4. And Section 5 described the relationship of the nature of knowledge and cognition to balance, flexibility, relevance, providing for individual differences, student-teacher planning, self-understanding, and problem solving.

*Criterion questions* on objectives and the bases of the curriculum were included in each of the preceding sections. Since our present purpose is to develop skill in using all of these criteria on a *multidimensional basis in planning,* it is useful to assemble here all of the criterion questions that have been included in the preceding five sections.

### From Section 1 (Objectives)

1. Have the goals of the curriculum or teaching plan been clearly stated; and are they used by the teachers and students in choosing content, materials, and activities for learning?
2. Have the teachers and students engaged in student-teacher planning in defining the goals and in determining how they will be implemented?
3. Do some of the planned goals relate to the society or the community in which the curriculum will be implemented or the teaching will be done?
4. Do some of the planned goals relate to the needs, purposes, interests, and abilities of the individual learner?
5. Are the planned goals used as criteria in selecting and developing learning activities and materials of instruction?
6. Are the planned goals used as criteria in evaluating learning achievement and in the further planning of learning subgoals and activities?

### From Section 2 (Social Forces—Present and Future)

1. What social or cultural factors contribute to the individual differences of the learners?
2. How can the curriculum and/or teaching provide for these differences?
3. What values *are* we teaching?
4. What values do we *wish* to teach?
5. What can the curriculum do to assist learners in their goals of social self-understanding and self-realization?
6. How can the curriculum and teaching be planned and organized so that learners are assisted in confronting personal and social problems?
7. How can learners be helped to develop the problem-solving skills needed to cope with problems?
8. Is provision made in the curriculum and teaching for the development of the skills of future planning?

### From Section 3 (Human Development)

1. Does the planned curriculum provide for the developmental differences of the learners being taught?
2. Does the planned curriculum include provisions so that learning may start for each learner where he or she is?
3. Has the significance of developmental tasks, stages of growth toward a mature personality, and the four successive models of intelligence been considered in planning?
4. Do the curriculum planners and teachers attempt to provide for earlier tasks inadequately achieved, and for their maintenance when successfully achieved?
5. Has the curriculum planning been adjusted to the biological, social, cultural, and intellectual changes that are occurring and that have occurred in recent years at each stage of human development?
6. Do the curriculum planning and teaching allow for the inborn individuality and innate uniqueness of each learner?

### From Section 4 (Learning)

1. Does the curriculum or teaching plan include alternative approaches and alternative activities for learning?
2. Have the different learning theories been considered in planning alternative learning approaches and activities?
3. Has the significance of rewarded responses, transfer, generalization, advance organizers, self-concept, meaningfulness of the whole, personal meaning, imitation, identification, and socialization been considered in planning?

4. Has the significance of individual learning approaches and styles been considered in the planning?

### From Section 5 (Knowledge and Cognition)

1. Does the planned curriculum assist the learner in identifying key concepts, principles, and the structure of the content to be learned?
2. Does the curriculum provide for learning opportunities that are consistent with individual differences and are related to varying approaches to structuring knowledge (e.g. discovery learning, advance organizers, key concepts, etc.)?
3. Does the planned curriculum recognize that each learner's structure of knowledge is personally invented and constructed, and that the learner may need assistance in identifying the discrepancies between his or her personal constructs and those of organized knowledge?
4. Does the planned curriculum provide for multiple forms of literacy and a balance between, as well as integration of, the modes of the brain's two hemispheres?
5. Does the planned curriculum include interdisciplinary approaches based on the needs of the learners and their unique personal-social problems?
6. Does the planned curriculum focus on the processes of knowing, including synthesis, wholeness, coherence, and interrelatedness?

These thirty criterion questions on objectives and the bases of the curriculum should be viewed as a set of screens, a list of important guidelines, to be considered in planning curricula and teaching.

## STEPS IN CURRICULUM PLANNING AND TEACHING

The curriculum criteria that we have examined so far should be utilized on a multidimensional basis at every step in curriculum planning. The curriculum planner or teacher should be able to identify these various steps in the planning of the curriculum.

The first step is the *identification of the context* in which the curriculum is to be implemented or the teaching is to be done. It is a part of the planning where all our knowledge about present and future social forces and human development should be called into play. Context identification is a process of gathering data about the intended learners and the human, social, and environmental variables with which the learners interact.

The second major step is *determining objectives* or setting goals. The data obtained in step one are utilized in planning the specific nature of the objectives for a unique group of learners. The preplanned curriculum materials should be used by teachers in these two stages, but they should be free to add to or depart from the preplanned curriculum materials in light of the data assembled in step one. Of course, the broad general objectives should be utilized in determining the specific goals for a particular group of learners.

The third step is *selecting, preparing,* and *implementing strategies and alternatives* for achieving the intended changes defined by the goals. Here again the objectives must be kept clearly in mind. The four bases should be used in identifying the available strategies, and in selecting those considered most appropriate for individual learners and the intended learning.

The fourth step is *evaluating.* The purpose of evaluating is to determine what has been accomplished in terms of the intended goals and objectives. This provides information regarding the results of using the preplanned curriculum objectives, strategies, alternatives, and content, as well as the teacher's modifications of that preplanning. The evaluation provides information regarding learner achievement and performance in terms of objectives, but its purpose should also be to provide information that may become the basis for reexamining the personal and social context, setting new or revised objectives, selecting and implementing new strategies or learning processes, and engaging again in evaluation.

One important aspect of evaluation is to inquire whether there were *unintended outcomes or effects,* good or bad, and to try to determine why they occurred. Evaluation actually should take place at each of the steps in a curriculum plan or teaching, as well as at the conclusion of the plan. Evaluation that takes place during the development or operation of a curriculum plan is called *formative evaluation;* the evaluation that takes place at the conclusion of a curriculum plan in operation is called *summative evaluation.*

The four steps described are recurrent and self-renewing. A continuing process of decision making and strategy occurs that should be guided by the objectives, the four bases, and other curriculum criteria. The criterion questions assembled in this section from the preceding five sections, or others like them, might be used to monitor the process. Of course, the process is not very meaningful if the curriculum planner or teacher doesn't have *alternative strategies* available to use. The four curriculum bases can be the source of the data needed to plan and select different strategies. The preplanned curriculum should provide the teacher with strategies and alternatives that he or she can consider. Effort should be made to involve the students in planning during each of the steps in curriculum planning and teaching.

I believe that *teachers are also curriculum planners,* and that they cannot avoid this role. I also believe that *all curriculum planners* should be concerned not so much with answers as with strategies; not so much with product as with process; not so much with things as with persons; not so much with knowledge as with learners and their welfare. But answers, products, things, and knowledge also have an important place in curriculum planning.

This variety of emphases should suggest that you need to develop your own set of criteria for use in planning curricula and teaching. Your criteria should reflect your own thinking, as well as the particular area of the curriculum with which you are concerned.

Another analysis of the steps in curriculum planning and teaching is the focus of "A Systematic Model for Curriculum Development" by Hunkins in this section.

## OBJECTIVES

Your objectives in studying this section on curriculum criteria should be as follows:

1.  To be able to use the four bases of the curriculum together as guidelines for planning and decision making.
2.  To be able to analyze and describe the ways in which some of the contemporary curriculum theorists utilize objectives, social forces, future planning, community factors, student factors, human development, learning theory, and knowledge theory in their curriculum planning.
3.  To be able to develop a set of criteria and strategies appropriate for particular curriculum planning tasks from a knowledge of values and objectives, social forces, future planning, human development, learning and knowledge and cognition theories, and other criteria, such as individual differences, balance, continuity, or flexibility.
4.  To be able to describe and evaluate a curriculum plan in terms of your selected set of curriculum criteria and strategies.
5.  To be able to suggest improvements in a curriculum plan in terms of your selected set of curriculum criteria and strategies.

## PREASSESSMENT

The purpose of the preassessment is to enable you to determine whether you already possess the performance competencies in curriculum planning that are listed under the objectives just mentioned. The following activities will aid you in your evaluation:

1.  Select several objectives, social forces, anticipated future trends and community factors, and at least one theory each from the areas of human development, learning theory, and knowledge theory, and tell how you would use them together in curriculum planning or the planning of teaching.
2.  Prepare a list of curriculum criteria and strategies for the curriculum and instruction planning areas with which you are most concerned. Defend your list for adequacy and appropriateness.
3.  Select any curriculum plan at any school level; describe and analyze it in terms of your list of curriculum criteria and strategies.
4.  Suggest improvements or changes in the curriculum plan as a result of your analysis in number 3.

From your study of earlier sections of this book, you already know that curriculum plans frequently are not based on an adequate set of criteria. Therefore, suggest improvements in the plan on the basis of your curriculum criteria.

You have also undoubtedly noted that often when a curriculum plan makes good use of one of the bases, such as human development, the other curriculum bases are not considered or are not adequately considered. When you recognize this in a curriculum plan, suggest possible improvements derived from the curriculum bases and criteria not utilized in the planning.

In answering numbers 3 and 4 of the preassessment, you might choose to analyze the curriculum plans presented in these articles: "Getting a Headstart on Career Choices" in Section 7 or "James Madison High: A School for Winners" in Section 9.

## LEARNING ACTIVITIES

The articles in this section will assist you in learning to use objectives, the four bases, and other curriculum criteria together or as alternative strategies in curriculum planning and the planning of teaching. The articles will also help you understand the implications of curriculum criteria such as subgoals, balance, continuity, individual differences, relevance, flexibility, systematic planning, cooperative planning, and student-teacher planning.

## POSTASSESSMENT

After attempting the preassessment you may do *one or more* of the following:

1. Ask your instructor if you are ready for a postassessment evaluation on curriculum criteria. Most students will need further work on this topic.
2. Read the articles on curriculum criteria in this section, and try to determine how the criteria discussed in each article should be considered in curriculum planning and teaching.
3. Choose additional activities and readings or films from those listed at the end of this section.
4. Look for other films, books, or articles on curriculum criteria that are in your library or media center.
5. Discuss the reading you have done and the films you have viewed with your fellow students. The key questions: How should the curriculum criteria you've studied affect a planned curriculum? How should they be considered in planning for teaching?
6. When you are ready, ask your instructor for advice on a suitable postassessment for you for this topic. Satisfactory completion of number 1 under Problems and

Projects at the end of this section might be one possibility. Or satisfactory written completion of the preassessment for this section, after completing other learning activities, might be a satisfactory postassessment. Consult your instructor about this. You can evaluate your ability to do either or both of these activities before seeing the instructor.

# What Is the Nature of Educational Excellence And Should We Try to Measure It?

## DANIEL L. DUKE

Hard on the heels of most reform movements in education come the demands to know whether or not the reforms have "made a difference." The current push for excellence in education is not likely to be an exception, so it seems prudent to speculate about how we can evaluate the extent to which excellence has been achieved. To do so we must ask two basic questions: What is the nature of educational excellence? And should we try to measure it?

Before I try to answer these questions, ask yourself which of the following examples most clearly demonstrates educational excellence:

- a class of students, all on-task, listening to a complicated lecture on the Bill of Rights;
- a student whose essay on contemporary challenges to the Bill of Rights wins an American Legion award for patriotism;
- a teacher whose social studies classes achieve a mean score at the 95th percentile on a nationally standardized test covering the Bill of Rights;
- a special education student who spells "Bill of Rights" correctly; or
- a student journalist who speaks out for First Amendment rights to freedom of speech

when the school administration tries to censor an article for the school newspaper.

In some ways, of course, each of these exemplifies educational excellence. I list these illustrations here to dramatize some of the complexity involved in trying to define excellence. It is especially difficult to define excellence without first asking, "Excellence for what purpose?" Excellence for the purpose of establishing social justice might produce a definition quite different from that dictated by excellence for the purpose of sparking an economic resurgence.

Perhaps because of this complexity, few individuals or groups among those calling for reform have gone on record in support of a particular conception of excellence. To its credit, the National Commission on Excellence in Education offered definitions of excellence at three levels—the level of the individual student, the level of the school, and the level of the community. For my purposes here, the definition of excellence at the level of the individual student is the most interesting. According to the National Commission, a student embodies excellence when he or she performs "on the boundary of individual ability in ways that test and push back

From *Phi Delta Kappan* 66, No. 10 (June 1985): 671–674. Used by permission of the author and the publisher.

personal limits, in school and in the workplace."[1]

As appealing as this definition is, it raises a number of practical questions. Consider these, for example. Who determines the boundaries of an individual's ability and by what means? Does the notion of boundaries presume an ideal context, free from constraints, or does it take into account all the competing pressures operating on an individual at a given time? Couldn't each of us push ourselves further if we were not hampered by multiple assignments, conflicting expectations, nonacademic demands, family obligations, and emotional concerns? Are we to conceive of educational excellence in light of or apart from the exigencies of the real world?

In a speech on educational excellence delivered to the Oregon Educational Research Association in November 1983, Walter Doyle suggested that excellence might be defined both in terms of a student's capacity to identify what he or she needs to know and in terms of a student's awareness of when to use what he or she knows. Once again, the definition is appealing; once again, it is fraught with problems. Is a student who knows very little and realizes that he needs to know a great deal more a better example of excellence than a student who knows a great deal but acknowledges that he needs to learn a little more? Does a student who applies his mechanical knowledge to pick the lock on the school safe represent excellence? Or does excellence entail a moral dimension as well? These are questions not often asked and not easily answered.

Probably the most familiar efforts to define excellence are associated with athletic competition, rather than with schooling. Experts in such events as platform diving and gymnastics have reached a working agreement about what a perfect score represents. They have also assumed that such a score will rarely, if ever, be attained. However, as those who watched the recent Olympic games recognize, a perfect score is no longer beyond the grasp of top competitors. As a result, there is speculation that scoring criteria will have to be made more rigorous. Are "excellence" and "perfection" to be kept distinct—the latter denoting, by definition, the unattainable? Would such targets be of value in judging academic performance?

The fact that great confusion surrounds the issue of educational excellence has not deterred thousands of school districts, civic groups, and state agencies from marching off on crusades for excellence. Armed with noble intentions and copious criticisms of current practices—if not with a clear description of their goal—these crusaders have undertaken an unprecedented number of reforms in a very short time. Perhaps we can infer a working definition of excellence by surveying some of these reforms. This approach acknowledges the possibility that the reformers really share a common understanding of excellence, even if they have trouble expressing it.

## INPUTS, THROUGHPUTS, AND OUTPUTS

In reviewing contemporary efforts to achieve educational excellence, it is helpful to borrow some terms used by economists and organization theorists. In theory, the goals of any organization may be achieved by controlling inputs, throughputs, and outputs, or some combination of these factors. If educational excellence is our goal, we can look for 1) efforts to improve the quality of the resources that go into the educational enterprise (inputs), 2) efforts to improve the ongoing allocation and use of resources (throughputs), and 3) efforts to raise the expectations for those who benefit from the resources (outputs).

In the current reform movement, considerable attention has been focused on educational inputs, particularly on the quality of teachers, administrators, and curriculum materials. Funds have been appropriated to provide scholarships for prospective teachers and to retrain experienced teachers. Higher teacher salaries have been urged as a way of keeping up the flow of talented instructors to the schools. Merit pay plans, though they generate controversy, have been implemented in several states. In a number of states, teachers and administrators are now required to demonstrate successful performance on minimum competency tests of basic skills. Several chief state school officers have led attempts to develop new and more rigorous guidelines for textbooks. Although their effort has fallen short of success, publishers are responding to the demand for better materials by creating texts that deal with reasoning, problem solving, and other so-called "higher-order" skills.

Time is another input that has generated a lot of interest among reformers. Though most school systems have refrained from actually lengthening the school day or year, as *A Nation at Risk* recommended, they have nevertheless stepped up efforts to insure that maximum use is made of existing time for schooling.

Reformers have also called for a variety of throughput controls, ranging from standardization of instruction to closer supervision of teachers. In addition, the reformers have placed greater stress on homework, on regular monitoring of student progress, on improved attendance, and on school discipline.

Reforms aimed at controlling educational outputs include such things as increased requirements for high school graduation and college admission, tougher grading policies, and more standardized testing of student performance. High school students must complete more courses in core subjects, which leaves them fewer opportunities to choose electives. Overall, these reforms seem aimed at narrowing the concept of a well-educated high school graduate.

Programs to recognize the performance of outstanding students have been adopted in various locations. These programs include special scholarships and statewide summer institutes. In addition to acknowledging the success of individual students, some states and school systems have adopted schemes for rewarding the performance of entire schools. The criteria for judging a school's performance include such things as the schoolwide dropout rate, the school's average scores on stadardized tests, and the number of students enrolled in advanced courses.

## THE NATURE OF EXCELLENCE

What may we infer about the nature of educational excellence from these recommendations for controlling educational inputs, throughputs, and outputs? First, we must separate the rhetoric of reform from the reality of reform.

When we take a close look at which reforms are actually being implemented, we cannot help but note the preference for output controls, particularly increased course requirements and more testing. This development should come as no surprise to political realists and economists, who recognize that it is usually cheaper to control outputs than to control inputs or throughputs. Simply compare the relatively minor cost of developing and administering a new test or adding graduation requirements to the substantial investment needed to raise teaching salaries, lengthen the school year, provide greater professional development opportunities, or create new curriculum materials.

From the reforms that are actually in place, we can see that our working definition of educational excellence must contain the following elements:

- Excellence is associated more with quantitative than with qualitative factors. The keys to excellence seem to be more credits, more courses of certain kinds, higher test scores, and the like.
- The real target of the reforms seems to be educational adequacy rather than excellence.

So conventional are contemporary reforms that future educational historians are likely to look back on the present not as the birth of a new age of educational excellence, but as the death throes of the back-to-basics movement. The emphasis on adequacy does not represent a marked departure from the decade-long push for minimum competency and accountability. Indeed, the tendency to equate excellence with quantitative change harks back to the Fifties. It is tempting to apply to the current reform movement the words that Alden Dunham, president of the Association for Supervision and Curriculum Development, spoke to the 1959 ASCD convention:

> Dr. Conant talks only of the quantitative point of view. There is nothing about quality, the all-important factor. Administrative machinery—course requirements, number of periods in the day, size of the school—does not determine what goes on in the classroom.[2]

Perhaps the argument can be made that no real harm is done by equating excellence with adequacy or by pursuing adequacy primarily through quantitative reforms. But I believe that there are real dangers associated with such a course of action.

The first danger is disappointment. It is seductive to think that increased testing and more course requirements will raise the level of student performance. A recent study by the staff of the Illinois state board of education gives pause, however.[3] Known as the Decade Study, this research compared the test performance of large, representative samples of 11th-graders from 1970 and 1981. The 1981 group showed an across-the-board decline in scores in four core curriculum areas, despite various efforts to improve performance. In attempting to account for these disappointing findings, analysts concluded that student attitudes played a major role in determining performance. Students were found to

perform close to their own estimates of their ability. One state board staff member noted:

> If you want a child to be good at math and science, that child has to *want* to be good at math and science. If you want to increase achievements in math and science, you should look . . . into how you can increase a kid's interest in becoming an engineer or mathematician or architect.

Is there any dimension of the current reforms that is apt to increase the likelihood that students will want to take more mathematics or other core courses? It could be argued that higher standards for passing courses and meeting graduation requirements provide necessary incentives. But practical experience tells us that this prescription will not work for all students, particularly for reluctant learners. Even those who do not become so frustrated that they give up or drop out may be affected adversely.

The danger of an educational system driven by a single conception of success and monitored by standardized tests is that too much stress will be placed on the "one best way" and the single "right" answer. We must ask whether an overemphasis on conformity during the formative years exacts too great a price in human development and creativity—to be paid over a lifetime. Scientific discovery, for example, is related more closely to making the most of wrong answers and failed experiments than to proving the correctness of what is already known.

In a recent review of research on the conditions that encourage problem solving, Norman Frederiksen failed to find that increased testing was critical.[4] The factors that were important to better problem solving included adequate time for the incubation of ideas and opportunities to practice higher-order cognitive skills in permissive environments in which failure is acceptable. An argument might be made that stressing right answers too much is incompatible with trial-and-error learning. Do we want students whose goal is to pass tests or students whose goal is to apply knowledge? In the worst cases, an obsession with getting right answers could even lead to the devaluation of reasoning and inquiry and to the promotion of cheating, plagiarism, and avoidance.

Meanwhile, conceiving of educational excellence as test performance and credit accumulation has led reformers to think in terms of "standards of excellence"—standards that often resemble minimum competencies. Mauritz Johnson questions whether we should speak of standards of excellence at all. He observes that standards imply standardization, which could be considered the absence of excellence.[5] How can we "standardize" excellence without drastically altering the nature of the term?

If not standards of excellence, then what? Johnson comes to the rescue. He contends that we may have criteria of excellence, models of excellence, even visions of excellence. The school's potential role in promoting excellence, he argues,

> . . . lies in its capacity to make students aware of the criteria for many forms of excellence, to show them models of such excellence, and to encourage them to imagine even higher levels of excellence. We cannot expect people to strive for something that they do not value and that those around them do not respect. But, people will not value and respect excellence if they cannot recognize it.[6]

Johnson's conception of excellence as more of a qualitative than a quantitative phenomenon addresses one of the greatest dangers lurking amid the current reforms. By supporting a single image of excellence—one tied to credit accumulation and test performance—educational reforms threaten the very assumptions on which a pluralistic, egalitarian society is based.

Johnson's work encourages multiple conceptions of excellence. It is a view buttressed by Howard Gardner's recent work on multiple intelligences.[7] Gardner developed criteria for distinguishing among different intelligences and identified seven separate intelligences: linguistic,

musical, logico-mathematical, spatial, bodily-kinesthetic, interpersonal, and intrapersonal. Gardner is highly critical of the heavy—and at times exclusive—emphasis on logico-mathematical intelligence in U.S. schools.

If there are many ways to think about educational excellence, then it makes little sense to try to pin down the term with a single definition. Despite the fact that few reformers have tried to capture the elusive nature of excellence in an operational definition, they have nonetheless relied heavily on standard evaluation techniques as ways of monitoring the pursuit of excellence. We must question the wisdom of stressing the evaluation of something that we have not defined and probably should not try to define. Ironically, it often seems that, the less certain we are about what we want to achieve in schools, the more we depend on evaluation. We must reluctantly agree with Thomas Green, who observes that educational policies are likely to be more successful when they aim at reducing ignorance rather than at achieving excellence.[8] Ignorance, after all, can be defined fairly easily in terms of minimum competencies, whereas excellence, by its nature, defies upper limits.

## PROMOTING EXCELLENCE

In the preceding section, I cautioned against the use of conventional measurement instruments as primary mechanisms for monitoring educational excellence. Testing may be fine for insuring educational adequacy, but it seems less valuable as a way of measuring the push beyond minimum expectations. The temptation to think that everything worthwhile must be evaluated—using formal tests of achievement—should be actively resisted.

Am I saying that schools can do little to promote educational excellence? Hardly. First, schools can see to it that open-ended endeavors that are not subject to standard evaluation procedures are valued. The inclination to think of school success in terms of a single model of student achievement must be reversed, and alternative ways of providing performance feedback must be sought.

One such alternative might be to return without a grade any work that does not seem to represent the best that a student is capable of doing. In this way students would learn what teachers *believe* them to be capable of accomplishing. In addition, they might be less likely to accumulate a large number of low grades simply because they failed to expend sufficient effort. Rather than continue to redo assignments, many students might be motivated to push themselves to do a better job the first time, thereby stretching themselves toward the "boundaries of their abilities."

Another form of useful feedback could be a student's own reconstruction of prior learning experiences. By asking students to express in their own words what they have learned after a lesson, unit, or course, teachers could increase students' ability to take responsibility for organizing, retaining, and making sense of what they are exposed to in classes.[9] Relying too much on conventional evaluation deprives students of opportunities to organize knowledge and encourages them to learn merely for the sake of passing tests.

Educators need to identify situations in which it is desirable to suspend judgment altogether. Certainly conventional evaluation is justified when the goal is mastery of basic or prerequisite skills. However, when we want people to excel, to think creatively, to solve problems in groups, or to tackle challenging material, it might be far more productive to avoid evaluation—at least the kind of evaluation premised on right and wrong answers. Helping students describe what takes place as they confront a problem could be of greater benefit than pointing out their mistakes.

Schools might also make sure that criteria for excellence are developed for a variety of subjects. Students need to understand that excellence in one subject may differ qualitatively from excel-

lence in another. The efforts of the National Science Teachers Association to generate criteria for excellence in various areas of science address this concern well. For example, excellence in programs that foster "science as inquiry" is presumed to include:

- teachers who value inquiry, encourage such an orientation, and possess such skills themselves;
- classrooms in which science objects and events focus on investigation;
- curricula and units of instruction that give attention to science processes;
- teachers who act as role models in debating issues, admitting errors, examining values, and confronting their own ignorance; and
- instruction that focuses on exploration rather than on coverage.[10]

Exposing students to models of excellence could also be helpful. However, in recent years we have witnessed a countervailing trend toward iconoclasm. Demythologizing heroes seems to have replaced the promotion of exemplars as a means of fostering good citizenship. As a result, young people may lack concrete images of outstanding people to help them strive toward personal excellence. Schools could invite role models from the community—people who represent excellence in various walks of life—to visit classrooms and interact with students. Students might be asked to read about and discuss the lives of great scientists, leaders, humanitarians, and the like.

Ultimately, it is the pursuit rather than the achievement of excellence that matters most. By nature, the achievement of true excellence in any area is limited to a relative few. Placing value on the *pursuit* of excellence permits more students to feel good about themselves and to appreciate the accomplishments of others. In the end, such an emphasis may even lead to greater achievement. Teilhard de Chardin has written on this issue with great insight:

Although only a small fraction of those who try to scale the heights of human achievement arrive anywhere close to the summit, it is imperative that there be a multitude of climbers. Otherwise the summit may not be reached by anybody. The individually lost and forgotten multitudes have not lived in vain, provided that they, too, made the efforts to climb.[11]

## ENDNOTES

1. National Commission on Excellence in Education, *A Nation at Risk: The Imperative for Educational Reform* (Washington, D. C.: U.S. Government Printing Office, 1983), p. 12.
2. Robert L. Hampel, "The American High School Today: James Bryant Conant's Reservations and Reconsiderations," *Phi Delta Kappan,* May 1983, p. 611.
3. Don Sevener, "Students Have Lost Their 'Thirst for Knowledge,' Study Indicates," *Education Week,* 17 August 1983, p. 8.
4. Norman Frederiksen, "Implications of Cognitive Theory for Instruction in Problem Solving," *Review of Educational Research,* Fall 1984, pp. 363–408.
5. Mauritz Johnson, "The Continuing Quest for Educational Quality" (School of Education, State University of New York at Albany, 1982), p. 3.
6. Ibid.
7. Howard Gardner, *Frames of Mind: A Theory of Multiple Intelligences* (New York: Basic Books, 1983).
8. Thomas F. Green, "Excellence, Equity, and Equality," in Lee S. Shulman and Gary Sykes, eds., *Handbook of Teaching and Policy* (New York: Longman, 1983), pp. 318–41.
9. Daniel L. Duke, "Debriefing: A Tool for Curriculum Research and Course Improvement," *Journal of Curriculum Studies,* vol. 9, 1977, pp. 157–63.
10. John E. Penick and Robert E. Yager, "The Search for Excellence in Science Education," *Phi Delta Kappan,* May 1983, p. 623.
11. Teilhard de Chardin, cited in Theodosius G. Dobzhansky, *The Biology of Ultimate Concern* (New York: New American Library, 1967), p. 137.

*Daniel L. Duke* is Professor of Educational Administration, Lewis and Clark College, Portland, Oregon.

# The Sources of a Science of Education
## JOHN DEWEY

### EDUCATION AS A SCIENCE

The title may suggest to some minds that it begs a prior question: Is there a science of education? And still more fundamentally, Can there be a science of education? Are the procedures and aims of education such that it is possible to reduce them to anything properly called a science? Similar questions exist in other fields. The issue is not unknown in history; it is raised in medicine and law. As far as education is concerned, I may confess at once that I have put the question in its apparently question-begging form in order to avoid discussion of questions that are impor-

From John Dewey, *The Sources of a Science of Education* (New York: Horace Liveright, 1929), pp. 7–22. © Dewey Center, Southern Illinois University at Carbondale. Used by permission.

tant but that are also full of thorns and attended with controversial divisions.

It is enough for our purposes to note that the word "science" has a wide range.

There are those who would restrict the term to mathematics or to disciplines in which exact results can be determined by rigorous methods of demonstration. Such a conception limits even the claims of physics and chemistry to be sciences, for according to it the only scientific portion of these subjects is the strictly mathematical. The position of what are ordinarily termed the biological sciences is even more dubious, while social subjects and psychology would hardly rank as sciences at all, when measured by this definition. Clearly we must take the idea of science with some latitude. We must take it with sufficient looseness to include all the subjects that are usually regarded as sciences. The important thing is to discover those traits in virtue of which various fields are called scientific. When we raise the question in this way, we are led to put emphasis upon methods of dealing with subject-matter rather than to look for uniform objective traits in subject matter. From this point of view, science signifies, I take it, the existence of systematic methods of inquiry, which, when they are brought to bear on a range of facts, enable us to understand them better and to control them more intelligently, less haphazardly and with less routine.

No one would doubt that our practices in hygiene and medicine are less casual, less results of a mixture of guess work and tradition, than they used to be, nor that this difference has been made by development of methods of investigating and testing. There is an intellectual technique by which discovery and organization of material go on cumulatively, and by means of which one inquirer can repeat the researches of another, confirm or discredit them, and add still more to the capital stock of knowledge. Moreover, the methods when they are used tend to perfect themselves, to suggest new problems, new investigations, which refine old procedures and create new and better ones.

The question as to the sources of a science of education is, then, to be taken in this sense. What are the ways by means of which the function of education in all its branches and phases—selection of material for the curriculum, methods of instruction and discipline, organization and administration of schools—can be conducted with systematic increase of intelligent control and understanding? What are the materials upon which we may—and should—draw in order that educational activities may become in a less degree products of routine, tradition, accident, and transitory accidental influences? From what sources shall we draw so that there shall be steady and cumulative growth of intelligent, communicable insight, and power of direction?

Here is the answer to those who decry pedagogical study on the ground that success in teaching and in moral direction of pupils is often not in any direct ratio to knowledge of educational principles. Here is "A" who is much more successful than "B" in teaching, awakening the enthusiasm of his students for learning, inspiring them morally by personal example and contact, and yet relatively ignorant of educational history, psychology, approved methods, etc., which "B" possesses in abundant measure. The facts are admitted. But what is overlooked by the objector is that the successes of such individuals tend to be born and to die with them: beneficial consequences extend only to those pupils who have personal contact with such gifted teachers. No one can measure the waste and loss that have come from the fact that the contributions of such men and women in the past have been thus confined, and the only way by which we can prevent such waste in the future is by methods which enable us to make an analysis of what the gifted teacher does intuitively, so that something accruing from his work can be communicated to others. Even in the things conventionally recognized as sciences, the insights of unusual persons remain important and there is no levelling down to a uniform procedure. But the existence of science gives common efficacy to the experiences of the genius; it makes it possible for the results of special power to become part of the working equipment of other inquirers, instead of perishing as they arose.

The individual capacities of the Newtons, Boyles, Joules, Darwins, Lyells, Helmholtzes, are not destroyed because of the existence of science; their differences from others and the impossibility of predicting on the basis of past science what discoveries they would make—that is, the impossibility of regulating their activities by antecedent sciences—persist. But science makes it possible for others to benefit systematically by what they achieved.

The existence of scientific method protects us also from a danger that attends the operations of men of unusual power: dangers of slavish imitation, partisanship, and such jealous devotion to them and their work as to get in the way of further progress. Anybody can notice today that the effect of an original and powerful teacher is not all to the good. Those influenced by him often show a one-sided interest; they tend to form schools, and to become impervious to other problems and truths; they incline to swear by the words of their master and to go on repeating his thoughts after him, and often without the spirit and insight that originally made them significant. Observation also shows that these results happen oftenest in those subjects in which scientific method is least developed. Where these methods are of longer standing students adopt methods rather than merely results, and employ them with flexibility rather than in literal reproduction.

This digression seems to be justified not merely because those who object to the idea of a science put personality and its unique gifts in opposition to science, but also because those who recommend science sometimes urge that uniformity of procedure will be its consequence. So it seems worthwhile to dwell on the fact that in the subjects best developed from the scientific point of view, the opposite is the case. Command of scientific methods and systematized subject-matter liberates individuals; it enables them to see new problems, devise new procedures, and, in general, makes for diversification rather than for set uniformity. But at the same time these diversifications have a cumulative effect in an advance shared by all workers in the field.

## EDUCATION AS AN ART

This theme is, I think, closely connected with another point which is often urged, namely, that education is an art rather than a science. That, in concrete operation, education is an art, either a mechanical art or a fine art, is unquestionable. If there were an opposition between science and art, I should be compelled to side with those who assert that education is an art. But there is no opposition, although there is a distinction. We must not be misled by words. Engineering is, in actual practice, an art. But it is an art that progressively incorporates more and more of science into itself, more of mathematics, physics, and chemistry. It is the kind of art it is precisely because of a content of scientific subject-matter which guides it as a practical operation. There is room for the original and daring projects of exceptional individuals. But their distinction lies not in the fact that they turn their backs upon science, but in the fact that they make new integrations of scientific material and turn it to new and previously unfamiliar and unforeseen uses. When, in education, the psychologist or observer and experimentalist in any field reduces his findings to a rule which is to be uniformly adopted, then, only, is there a result which is objectionable and destructive of the free play of education as an art.

But this happens not because of scientific method but because of departure from it. It is not the capable engineer who treats scientific findings as imposing upon him a certain course which is to be rigidly adhered to: it is the third- or fourth-rate man who adopts this course. Even more, it is the unskilled day laborer who follows it. For even if the practice adopted is one that follows from science and could not have been discovered or employed except for science, when it is converted into a uniform rule of procedure it becomes an empirical rule-of-thumb procedure—just as a person may use a table of logarithms mechanically without knowing anything about mathematics.

The danger is great in the degree in which the attempt to develop scientific method is recent. Nobody would deny that education is still in a condition of transition from an empirical to a scientific status. In its empirical form the chief factors determining education are tradition, imitative reproduction, response to various external pressures wherein the strongest force wins out, and the gifts, native and acquired, of individual teachers. In this situation there is a strong tendency to identify teaching ability with the use of procedures that yield immediately successful results, success being measured by such things as order in the classroom, correct recitations by pupils in assigned lessons, passing of examinations, promotion of pupils to a higher grade, etc.

For the most part, these are the standards by which a community judges the worth of a teacher. Prospective teachers come to training schools, whether in normals schools or colleges, with such ideas implicit in their minds. They want very largely to find out how to do things with the maximum prospect of success. Put baldly, they want recipes. Now, to such persons science is of value because it puts a stamp of final approval upon this and that specific procedure. It is very easy for science to be regarded as a guarantee that goes with the sale of goods rather than as a light to the eyes and a lamp to the feet.

It is prized for its prestige value rather than as an organ of personal illumination and liberation. It is prized because it is thought to give unquestionable authenticity and authority to a specific procedure to be carried out in the school room. So conceived, science is antagonistic to education as an art.

## EXPERIENCE AND ABSTRACTION

The history of the more mature sciences shows two characteristics. Their original problems were set by difficulties that offered themselves in the ordinary region of practical affairs. Men obtained fire by rubbing sticks together and noted how things grew warm when they pressed on each other, long before they had any theory of heat. Such everyday experiences in their seeming inconsistency with the phenomena of flame and fire finally led to the conception of heat as a mode of molecular motion. But it led to this conception only when the ordinary phenomena were reflected upon in detachment from the conditions and uses under which they exhibit themselves in practices. There is no science without abstraction, and abstraction means fundamentally that certain occurrences are removed from the dimension of familiar practical experience into that of reflective or theoretical inquiry.

To be able to get away for the time being from entanglement in the urgencies and needs of immediate practical concerns is a condition of the origin of scientific treatment in any field. Preoccupation with attaining some direct end or practical utility, always limits scientific inquiry. For it restricts the field of attention and thought, since we note only those things that are immediately connected with what we want to do or get at the moment. Theory is in the end, as has been well said, the most practical of all things, because this widening of the range of attention beyond nearby purpose and desire eventually results in the creation of wider and farther-reaching purposes and enables us to use a much wider and deeper range of conditions and means than were expressed in the observation of primitive practical purposes. For the time being, however, the formation of theories demands a resolute turning aside from the needs of practical operations previously performed.

This detachment is peculiarly hard to secure in the case of those persons who are concerned with building up the scientific content of educational practices and arts. There is a pressure for immediate results, for demonstration of a quick, short-time span of usefulness in school. There is a tendency to convert the results of statistical inquiries and laboratory experiments into directions and rules for the conduct of school administration and instruction. Results tend to be directly grabbed, as it were, and put into operation by teachers. Then there is the leisure for that slow and gradual independent growth of theories that is a necessary condition of the formation of a true science. This danger is peculiarly imminent in a science of education because its very recentness and novelty arouse skepticism as to its possibility and its value. The human desire to prove that the scientific mode of attack is really of value brings pressure to convert scientific conclusions into rules and standards of schoolroom practice.

It would perhaps be invidious to select examples too near to current situations. Some illustration, however, is needed to give definiteness to what has been said. I select an instance which is remote in time and crude in itself. An investigator found that girls between the ages of eleven and fourteen mature more rapidly than boys of the same age. From this fact, or presumed fact, he drew the inference that during these years boys and girls should be separated for purposes of instruction. He converted an intellectual finding into an immediate rule of school practice.

That the conversion was rash, few would deny. The reason is obvious. School administration and instruction is a much more complex

operation than was the factor contained in the scientific result. The significance of one factor for educational practice can be determined only as it is balanced with many other factors. Taken by itself, this illustration is so crude that to generalize from it might seem to furnish only a caricature. But the principle involved is of universal application. No conclusion of scientific research can be converted into an immediate rule of educational art. For there is no educational practice whatever which is not highly complex; that is to say, which does not contain many other conditions and factors than are included in the scientific finding.

Nevertheless, scientific findings are of practical utility, and the situation is wrongly interpreted when it is used to disparage the value of science in the art of education. What it militates against is the transformation of scientifc findings into rules of action. Suppose for the moment that the finding about the different rates of maturing in boys and girls of a certain age is confirmed by continued investigation, and is to be accepted as fact. While it does not translate into a specific rule of fixed procedure, it is of some worth. The teacher who really knows this fact will have his personal attitude changed. He will be on the alert to make certain observations which would otherwise escape him; he will be enabled to interpret some facts which would otherwise be confused and misunderstood. This knowledge and understanding render his practice more intelligent, more flexible, and better adapted to deal effectively with concrete phenomena of practice.

Nor does this tell the whole story. Continued investigation reveals other relevant facts. Each investigation and conclusion is special, but the tendency of an increasing number and variety of specialized results is to create new points of view and a wider field of observation. Various special findings have a cumulative effect; they reinforce and extend one another, and in time lead to the detection of principles that bind together a number of facts that are diverse and even isolated in their *prima facie* occurrence. These connecting principles which link different phenomena together we call laws.

Facts which are so interrelated form a system, a science. The practitioner who knows the system and its laws is evidently in possession of a powerful instrument for observing and interpreting what goes on before him. This intellectual tool affects his attitudes and modes of response in what he does. Because the range of understanding is deepened and widened, he can take into account remote consequences which were originally hidden from view and hence were ignored in his actions. Greater continuity is introduced; he does not isolate situations and deal with them in separation as he was compelled to do when ignorant of connecting principles. At the same time, his practical dealings become more flexible. Seeing more relations he sees more possibilities, more opportunities. He is emancipated from the need of following tradition and special precedents. His ability to judge

being enriched, he has a wider range of alternatives to select from in dealing with individual situations.

## WHAT SCIENCE MEANS

If we gather up these conclusions in a summary we reach the following results. In the first place, no genuine science is formed by isolated conclusions, no matter how scientifically correct the technique by which these isolated results are reached, and no matter how exact they are. Science does not emerge until these various findings are linked up together to form a relatively coherent system—that is, until they reciprocally confirm and illuminate one another, or until each gives the others added meaning. Now this development requires time, and it requires more time in the degree in which the transition from an empirical condition to a scientific one is recent and hence imperfect.

*John Dewey* was Professor of Philosophy, Emeritus, Columbia University, New York.

# Eighty Years of Curriculum Theory
## GLEN HASS

When the learning of subject-matter was the school's major emphasis near the beginning of this century, it was thought that its chief function was to transmit this knowledge. The curriculum was a body of content to be learned by those who came to school, and its mastery at one grade was usually the basis for moving into the

next grade, for graduation, and for college preparation.

The decades following 1900 saw many important changes influencing the schools. Industrialization and urbanization developed very rapidly, immigration increased, and more and more of the learners in school were the children of the

Article written by Glen Hass for *Curriculum Planning: A New Approach*, Fourth Edition, 1983.

working classes. With these social changes, knowledge from sociology and anthropology seemed more pertinent to the development of the curriculum. A classical content curriculum would no longer do. In the 1930s, with the rise of totalitarianism, arguments urging the use of democratic processes in the classroom gained in relevance and significance. Thus the social forces influencing education were more widely recognized and became a generally accepted basis of curriculum theory even though the school program was not generally affected. Those who emphasized society as the basis of the curriculum saw the needs of the social order as having the highest priority in determining what was to be taught. With this point of view, *Dare the Schools Build A New Social Order?* was written by George Counts and published in 1932.

To the subject-matter to be taught and the society to be served was now added a third emphasis in curriculum development: the learner to be educated. During the 1920s and the 1930s, those who emphasized the learner and his needs had increasing support for their views. The studies of human development at that time showed the uniqueness of childhood and adolescence and the sequential and ordered nature of development. The learner was seen by some as the source of educational means and ends. He or she was not to be sacrificed to the demands of subject matter nor to the needs of the society. Standards which stifled creativity had no place in education. In this approach the curriculum was to serve the learner. During the late 1920s and the 1930s this viewpoint and the resulting curriculum were called the "child-centered curriculum."

## CHANGING VIEWS ABOUT HUMAN NATURE

These concepts about the preferred nature of the curriculum were related to ideas concerning human nature which were developed and which also changed several times during the past eighty years. In the nineteenth century and in the thirty years following 1900, there was the "Rational-Economic Theory of Man" in which people were passive beings to be manipulated. In this view, human beings were considered to be primarily motivated by economic incentives. All human beings were classified in two groups: the untrustworthy mass and the trustworthy, broadly motivated, moral elite. This view was supported by the stimulus-response, conditioning theories of learning then current. These ideas and the S-R learning theories supported the development of a curriculum which was a body of content set forth to be learned.[1]

But scientific evidence accumulated in the 1930s and 1940s showed the importance of social motives in organization life. This, as was illustrated in the Hawthorne studies, showed that people are often motivated by social needs and they are responsive to leadership to the extent that the leader helps to meet their needs for acceptance. This research then led to a new set of assumptions about human nature and to the view known as "Social Man."[2]

In the 1940s and 1950s, a number of psychologists studying human behavior in large organizations came to the conclusion that organizational life, particularly in industry, had removed meaning from work. This group of psychologists, however, believed that this loss of meaning was related not so much to social needs as to the inherent need for people to use their capacities and skills in a mature, productive way. A. H. Maslow developed the assumptions which state that human motives fall into hierarchical classes with the needs of survival, safety, and security near the bottom of the hierarchy and then moving upward by way of social needs to ego and self-esteem needs; needs for autonomy and independence; and finally, to self-actualization needs, in the sense of the maximum use of one's resources.[3] This is the view of human nature which was known as "Self-Actualizing Man." Perceptual and cognitive learning theories have been associated with this position.

## CURRICULUM DIFFICULTIES RELATED TO VARIOUS VIEWS ABOUT LEARNERS

Now the difficulty has been that curriculum workers and teachers have tended to be guided by one or another of these views of the nature of learners and of the bases of curriculum planning. Persons committed to self-actualization and to the child as the focus of the curriculum have often tended to reject or neglect knowledge and society as major guiding foci. But today we know from the behavioral sciences that all human behavior is a product of complex patterns of interacting forces. We know that behavior changes are often produced by psychological elements currently present. On the other hand, there is evidence from research in biology which indicates that powerful physiological and biochemical processes influence learning, behavior, and personality. For each study pointing to a biological or physiological determinant of learning or specific behavior, we can find evidence pointing to sociological and psychological causes. Such variables as level of aspiration, self-concept, and role expectations have effects as significant as enzymes and genes. A "multi-dimensional" approach to curriculum planning and the planning of teaching is necessary.

## ANOTHER VIEW: COMPLEX LEARNERS

Empirical research has consistently found some evidence for each of the conceptions of human nature including the rational-economic, the social, and the self-actualizing views. Human beings are more complex than they are considered to be in any one of these positions. They are complex and are highly variable as well. Learners have many motives arranged in a hierarchy of importance to them—but this hierarchy is subject to change, from time to time, and from situation to situation. Learners are capable of learning new motives through group and organizational experiences. And in any group, the needs and motives of different members will vary—and should be treated differently. Viewed collectively this evidence leads to the view of human nature known as "Complex Person." In this view, we cannot understand human behavior if we look only to knowledge or only to the individual's development or motivations or only to environmental or group or social conditions and practices. These influences interact in complex fashion, requiring a curriculum planning approach which can take account of all of them.

## TEACHERS CAN NOW USE CURRICULUM THEORY BASED ON RESEARCH

The term "theory" has been employed in education in two main senses. A distinction must be made between the two. One usage falls within the area of the philosophy of education. Philosophies of education may include statements about human nature, society, knowledge, as well as statements concerning the proper aims and goals of schooling. Such philosophies are not necessarily consistent with the descriptive findings and theories of the behavioral sciences. They represent value positions that should and do influence curriculum planning.

The second usage of the term "theory" refers to descriptive scientific theory which is based on established empirical data. A scientific theory is an organization of empirical research and data to make them meaningful. There are several sources of descriptive educational theory. They include the analysis and description of peculiarly educational phenomena, and the use of the theories of human behavior from the behavioral sciences.

Now teachers and curriculum makers can make use of many descriptive scientific theories developed in the 1950s, 1960s, and 1970s based on a recognition of the complex nature of learners and learning including the rational-economic, self-actualizing, and social aspects of human nature. One's preferred value position can and should be tested in the light of these several areas of theory which are grounded in empirical research.

## FRAGMENTED CURRICULUM AND INSTRUCTION THEORY LIMITS TEACHING EFFECTIVENESS

Planning for the future requires much more than planning for changes in organization and content of the curriculum. Better planning for

teaching is needed and this can be greatly aided by the understanding and use of research-based instruction theory.

If the teacher uses the concepts of rational-economic, social, self-actualizing, and complex person presented here, he or she will (1) regularly test his or her value assumptions about teaching and seek a better diagnosis of learning goals and problems on this multidimensional basis, and (2) value individual differences and provide alternative routes to learning goals, accordingly.

## ENDNOTES

1. Hoselitz, B. F. *A Reader's Guide To the Social Sciences.* Glencoe, Illinois: Free Press, 1959.
2. Mayo, Elton. *The Social Problems of an Industrial Civilization.* Andover, Massachusetts: The Andover Press, 1945.
3. Maslow, A. H. *Motivation and Personality.* New York: Harper, 1954.

*Glen Hass* is Professor of Education, Emeritus, University of Florida, Gainesville.

# Alternative Curriculum Conceptions and Designs

## M. FRANCES KLEIN

The field of curriculum is not without its critics. Schwab (1978) has called the study of curriculum moribund and Jackson (1981) has even questioned the existence of curriculum as a field of study. Most curriculum scholars, however, are more confident about the existence of the

curriculum field since they have spent their careers in an effort to conceptualize it and study those practices which are called curriculum. Although some scholars may debate whether curriculum studies exist and if so, how to conceptualize them, few practitioners would question the

From *Theory Into Practice* 25, no. 1 (Winter 1986): 31–35. ©1986, College of Education, The Ohio State University. Used by permission of the author and the publisher.

existence or importance of curriculum. Curriculum is the substance of schooling—the primary reason why people attend school.

Many educational resources go to direct and support the curriculum. Countless committee meetings are held to develop it; teachers are hired, trained, and supervised in order to implement it; administrators are exhorted to provide curriculum leadership as their primary role; materials are purchased or created; learning resource centers are built to support the curriculum; and educational researchers seek bases for improving it.

In the comparatively short time since its generally recognized "birth" with the publication of Bobbitt's book, *The Curriculum* (1918), the growth of the field has been slow and difficult. Curriculum scholars have debated significant ideas and proposed changes, but have not always addressed themselves to what difference their ideas make to the practitioner. Little wonder, then, that the practice of curriculum continues along a single strand of development with few alternative ideas considered.

Tyler's syllabus, *Basic Principles of Curriculum and Instruction* (1950), was selected by the leadership group, Professors of Curriculum, as one of two publications which has had the most influence over the field of curriculum (Shane, 1981).[1] In the Tyler syllabus, concepts and procedures are spelled out as a way to view curriculum and they have been applied in diverse situations all over the world in curriculum development efforts. Some curriculum scholars owe their careers to their refinements and modifications of the Tyler rationale.

Tyler identified three data sources which must be used in curriculum development: society, student, and subject matter. These three data sources have historically stimulated alternative conceptions of curriculum and the development of different curriculum designs. Scholars have long recognized the importance of the three data sources, but too often missed Tyler's message—that the use of one of the data sources alone is inadequate in developing curricula. A comprehensive curriculum must use all three.

Current curriculum practice and research focus almost exclusively on just one of these data sources, subject matter. Curricula have been developed using what Eisner and Vallance (1974) call the technological conception. Referred to here as the measured curriculum, it has emerged into dominance over all other alternative conceptions and designs.

## THE MEASURED CURRICULUM

The measured curriculum is familiar to all educators. Behavioral objectives, time on task, sequential learning, positive reinforcement, direct instruction, achievement testing, mastery in skills and content, and teacher accountability are essential concepts used in practice and research. The measured curriculum should neither be condemned nor used exclusively to direct curriculum practice and research. It must be recognized for its strengths and limitations. It is compatible with some of the major educational outcomes valued by society—a store of knowledge about the world, command of the basic processes of communication, and exposure to new content areas. But this conception and design of curriculum cannot accomplish everything students are expected to learn.

Most curriculum scholars have long advocated the use of different designs for a school's curriculum; subject-centered, societal-centered, and individual-centered designs are the most commonly discussed. Unless alternatives to the technological, subject-matter-based curriculum (i.e., the measured curriculum) are used, some of the time-honored and persistently stated educational outcomes will not be accomplished.

## OTHER CONCEPTIONS

Eisner and Vallance (1974) identified four other conceptions of curriculum in addition to the technological process: cognitive processes, self-actualization, social reconstruction, and academic rationalism. These four conceptions propose something the technological process does not—desired outcomes and a focus on the substance of curriculum. Two of the conceptions of curriculum, cognitive processes and academic rationalism, are often planned and implemented through the use of the technological process and a subject matter design. The other two, self-actualization and social reconstruction, require different curriculum designs and different concepts and procedures from the measured curriculum for planning and implementation.

### Cognitive Processes and Academic Rationalism

Most similar to and compatible with the concepts and procedures of the measured curriculum are academic rationalism and cognitive processes. Academic rationalism advocates that the curriculum be based on the storehouse of knowledge which has enabled humankind to advance civilization. This storehouse is defined as organized subject matter in the form of the academic disciplines. The subject-centered curriculum design and the efficient technological process of curriculum building are compatible with this conception. It has been used well in the past and continues to have strong and prestigious advocates—Adler in *The Paideia Proposal* (1982), for example. Classroom practices and research are familiar to all when they are based on this conception. It is a form of the measured curriculum.

Cognitive processes as a conception of curriculum is less tied to specific content than is academic rationalism. Cognitive processes are thought to be "content-free" in the sense that

they are generalizable from one subject area to another. The concept emphasizes the ability to think, reason, and engage in problem-solving activities. The specific content used is somewhat less important than the processes to be learned. This conception, too, has its strong proponents—Bruner (1961) and Bloom (1956), for example. Many curricula include this conception of outcomes as a major part of their intent and substance.

Curriculum development in both of these conceptions occurs in a similar way. The technological approach of the Tyler rationale (1950) is commonly used as a basis for planning and implementing curricula. The subject-centered design also is commonly employed, using concepts such as behavioral objectives, sequential organization of content, time on task, appropriate practice, and achievement tests. However, teachers using the cognitive processes conception might operate more from the information processing models of teaching as conceptualized by Joyce and Weil (1980), while academic rationalists might more often employ behavioristic models.

### Social Reconstruction and Self-Actualization

The last two conceptions of curriculum, social reconstruction and self-actualization, are quite different and require different approaches to their development. The concepts from the measured curriculum are not automatically transferable to research and practice based on these conceptions.

Social reconstructionists look to society as a basis for the substance of curriculum. In their view, the problems and dilemmas of society are what ought to be studied by students with the intent of creating a more just, equitable, and humane society. Students must be involved in studying how obstacles can be overcome so that a more ideal society can be created. This becomes the content of the curriculum. Students are not to learn about them simply through a subject-centered design, however. The traditional textbook coverage in sociology or political science is not what these curriculum advocates favor. They want the students out in the community, using original sources, interviewing people, formulating solutions, testing hypotheses, and solving real problems—not just reading about them.

This design is societal centered rather than subject centered. The disciplines are used only as they relate to the problems being studied. Science is not studied as science nor history as history, but both subjects may be essential to understanding and developing possible resolutions to a local pollution problem. If so, students are expected to draw upon both disciplines. Through this conception and design of curriculum, students learn how to learn. They attack real problems, become meaningfully involved as citizens of the society, and begin to critically examine and help mold a better society.

Traditional concepts and processes from the measured curriculum are not applicable in practice for social reconstruction. No defined body of content can be spelled out in behavioral objectives. Time on task cannot be tracked easily since schooling is extended beyond the classroom. Time may even be "wasted" in tracking down important resources. Efficiency is not inherent to this design. Achievement also takes on a different definition, relating not to a body of prescribed content or skills but rather to how effectively the problem was studied and potentially resolved.

Testing as a form of evaluation is not applicable since each student or group of students may have studied different problems, used different resources, and posed different solutions. Other forms of evaluation emphasizing process more than content must be used. Students must be more involved in the planning, implementation, and evaluation of such a curriculum. In a social reconstructionist approach, curriculum development is not conducted prior to classroom interaction as in the measured curriculum. The curriculum must be developed jointly with the students.

The planning and implementation of a social reconstructionist's curriculum using a societal-based design would be distinctively different from other conceptions and designs. Rather than using behavioral objectives, practice would be guided by goals or general objectives such as those proposed by Zahorik (1976) or by problem-solving objectives as suggested by Eisner (1979). The use of general objectives such as learning how to study a problem or studying about discrimination, or of problem-solving objectives such as investigating the control of pollutants within the community or how the school could be a more democratic institution, allow for greater diversity in what is learned by students. All students are not expected to have the same experience or learn the same content. General objectives or problem-solving objectives open up the parameters for teaching and learning.

Classroom activities and evaluation procedures in social reconstruction would be developed through the use of criteria as proposed by Raths (1971) instead of according to the concepts of appropriate practice and achievement tests. Rather than activities which primarily provide appropriate practice for the behavior and content of the objectives, activities would be planned which permit students to make informed choices and reflect on their consequences; take risks of success or failure; and share the development, implementation, and evaluation of a plan. Evaluation procedures would focus on the provision of such activities and what is learned through them, not on the mastery of content or skills.

Teacher accountability would shift from a focus on how well students learn content to such considerations as processes used, community involvement achieved, and the diversity of relevant resources available to and used by the students. Learning in this design would not be sequential or like a stairstep as in the measured curriculum, but more like Eisner's (1979) spider-web model of learning. Teachers would draw most often from the social interaction family of teacher models as conceptualized by Joyce and Weil (1980).

Curriculum as self-actualization is even further removed from the traditional curriculum practices and research of the measured curriculum. In this conception, students become the curriculum developers, selecting for study what they are interested in, intrigued by, and curious about. The curriculum is not preplanned by adults, but evolves as a student or a group of students and their teacher explore something of interest. Growth is viewed as the process of becoming a self-actualizing person, not learning a body of content, a set of cognitive processes, or studying the problems of society. Content is important to the extent that it is relevant and meaningful to the individual student, not as it is defined by someone else. The design becomes individual centered with the role of the student rather than that of the teacher being dominant.

In this conception and design, traditional concepts guiding practice are incompatible. Objectives are too directing; time on task becomes unmanageable as students pursue different ideas, at different paces, and in different ways; achievement testing is impossible when students learn different things; and appropriate practice becomes idiosyncratically defined based on students' own interests. The classroom becomes an enriched, stimulating environment to challenge and appeal to students, an active, noisy place where students interact with each other as needed, and an extension of a learning resource laboratory with diverse and plentiful materials. Students and teachers become co-learners embarked on a study plan of their own making.

For this conception of curriculum as self-actualization, new concepts and procedures must be developed and legitimatized. Eisner's (1979) concept of expressive outcomes seems uniquely fitted to this conception and design, and educational criticism and connoisseurship are better suited as a mode of evaluation (Eisner, 1979). The personal family of teaching models would be most representative of how teachers and students would interact (Joyce & Weil, 1980).

Macdonald, Wolfson, and Zaret (1973) propose learning organized around a continuous cycle of exploring, integrating, and transcending. They also identify self-evaluation as an important aspect of this conception. Accountability according to them should be social accountability. Is the school exemplifying the values which the society desires to foster within young people? Other compatible concepts will need to be developed through an exploration of this design in practice, an opportunity curriculum workers do not frequently have. From such a curriculum students learn to develop their unique talents and interests, to value learning as a process, to become even more creative, curious, and imaginative, and to become more integrated, humane, caring human beings.

## NEEDED CHANGES IN CURRICULUM RESEARCH

The procedures and concepts used in research help determine what is "seen" in the curriculum. When researchers structure interviews, questionnaires, and observation around behavioral objectives, time on task, appropriate practice, and achievement testing, those are the concepts which are documented. Rather than rely exclusively on those concepts used in the practices of the measured curriculum (upon which much of the current research on curriculum is based), alternative approaches to curriculum research must be applied for different conceptions and designs.

More naturalistic observations in classrooms for the self-actualization conception and individual-based design are needed. New approaches to determining individual perceptions of growth and relating those to classroom practices would be one way to proceed. Eisner's (1979) concepts of educational connoisseurship and criticism seem to have considerable compatibility and already offer an alternative approach to traditional curriculum research. Case studies of classrooms using the social reconstruction conception and societal-centered design may be needed as research documentation.

However the research methodologies and constructs are developed and used in relation to the alternative approaches to curriculum, they must honor and be compatible with the unique expected outcomes of each and the different concepts upon which practice is based. To do otherwise is to destroy the potential any alternative in curriculum conception and design has to enhance the growth of students. This undoubtedly will require the use of ideas other than our traditional research concepts such as validity, reliability, objectivity, and generalizability.

Research methodology and the type of research study conducted must accommodate the alternative shifts in curriculum conceptions and designs which are developed to guide practice. Researchers must learn to operationalize new concepts, to ask different questions, to view curriculum from different conceptions. The new research concepts and procedures must be compatible with the practices and reflective of the differing educational outcomes each design will encourage.

## CONCLUSION

For the purposes of this article, the placement of basic concepts and procedures has been perhaps too narrow and somewhat rigid in order to make the case for using alternative concepts and processes for different conceptions and designs. It may well be that several concepts have applicability in more than one conception and design. Only as they are given rigorous study in research and practice will this become clear, however.

The extent to which schooling can accommodate these designs—and newer ones being developed—is a matter for debate and experimentation. However, much more can be accomplished with alternative conceptions and designs than is even thought about now. Curriculum does not have to be *either* one conception *or* another. With the use of varying conceptions and designs in each classroom, schools might well become much more attractive, challenging, and relevant places for students. And schooling as a process may become more responsive to the needs and desires of both the individual student and society.

The field of study called curriculum is alive, but not as healthy as it might be. Its health could be enhanced by enriching the diet currently restricted to the measured curriculum with more diverse nutrients from the storehouse of alternative conceptions and designs. This enrichment is a fundamental task to which future curriculum workers must address themselves.

## NOTE

1. The other most influential book was Dewey's *Democracy and Education* (1916).

## REFERENCES

Adler, M. J. (1982). *The Paideia proposal: An educational manifesto.* New York: Macmillan.

Bloom, B. S. (Ed.). (1956). *Taxonomy of educational objectives: Cognitive domain.* New York: Longmans, Green.

Bobbitt, F. (1918). *The curriculum.* Boston, MA: Houghton Mifflin.

Bruner, J. (1961). *The process of education*. Cambridge, MA: Harvard University Press.

Dewey, J. (1916). *Democracy and education*. New York: Macmillan.

Eisner, E. W. (1979). *The education imagination*. New York: Macmillan.

Eisner, E. W., & Vallance, E. (1974). *Conflicting conceptions of curriculum*. Berkeley, CA: McCutchan.

Jackson, P. W. (1981). Curriculum and its discontents. In H. A. Giroux, A. N. Penna, & W. F. Pinar (Eds.), *Curriculum and instruction: Alternatives in education* (pp. 367–381). Berkeley, CA: McCutchan.

Joyce, B., & Weil, M. (1980). *Models of teaching*. Englewood Cliffs, NJ: Prentice-Hall.

Macdonald, J. B., Wolfson, B. J., & Zaret, E. (1973). *Re-schooling society; A conceptual model*. Washington, DC:

Association for Supervision and Curriculum Development.

Raths, J. D. (April, 1971). Teaching without specific objectives. *Educational Leadership, 28,* 714–720.

Schwab, J. (1978). The practical: A language for curriculum. In I. Westbury & N. J. Wilkof (Eds.), *Science, curriculum and liberal education* (pp. 287–321). Chicago, IL: University of Chicago Press.

Shane, H. G. (1981, January). Significant writings that have influenced the curriculum: 1906–81. *Phi Delta Kappan, 62* (5), 311–314.

Tyler, R. W. (1950). *Basic principles of curriculum and instruction*. Chicago, IL: University of Chicago Press.

Zahorik, J. A. (1976, April). The virtue of vagueness in instructional objectives. *Elementary School Journal, 76,* 411–419.

*M. Frances Klein* is Professor of Education, University of Southern California, Los Angeles.

# A Contemporary Approach to Individualization

## MARIO D. FANTINI

During this century, the concept *individualization of instruction* has become one of the central tenets of education. Many of our school reforms have been waged in its name. More recently, individualization has also been referred to as "personalized learning," reflecting the influence of humanistic psychology over the past decade. While individualization or personalized learning as conceptions are deep rooted in our history, it is the daily convergence of diverse learners into the schools and classrooms of this nation that has necessitated pedagogical adaptations to human variability. The age-old fact that no two people are alike, that they have different needs, unique interests, talents, aspirations and problems, and learn in different ways has finally begun to penetrate the mainstream of our schools. Consequently, the school front has become the scene of a revolutionary struggle to alter institutional uniformity geared to group norms toward structures in which the individual uniqueness of the learner is given fuller play.

Stated somewhat differently, as the needs of a mass society became expressed, the schools designed a normative structure with primary consideration given to the needs of large groups. As society changed, so did the demands on schools. We are now not only in a period of advanced technology, but in an era of human rights and of consumer awareness. Consequently, whereas in

From *Theory Into Practice* 19, no. 1, College of Education, Ohio State University (Winter 1980): 28–31. Used by permission of the author and the publisher.

the past schooling had been viewed as a *privilege,* today it is more a *right.* Clarifying the right of each citizen, or for that matter each learner, to quality education has become part of our operational procedures.

In the past, delivering services equally meant school operations that were uniform in reflecting group norms. Groups of learners were processed through this standardized structure. In practice, those learners who were more able to adjust advanced; those who could not, withdrew or were placed in "special" tracks. While this scenario is clearly an oversimplification, my main point is that a "normative structure" selects out those who are considered successful from those who are not. In this light, reformers introduced innovations aimed at increasing the number of successes. Individualization was viewed as contributing significantly to this effort.

Part of the reform problem was that each new practice was introduced and initiated as an "across-the-board" solution. Thus, Method A replaced Method B because A was considered better. Further, the same students who were exposed to Method B now were exposed to Method A. The history of American education is characterized by a series of innovations—each with the expressed purpose of replacing a procedure or method which had been established. Studies which set one method against another are of limited value since each method is too complicated to be so simply compared. In fact what research there is (and putting aside any questions concerning the quality of the research itself) supports the conclusion that one teaching method appears to be "as successful" as the previous one. This is extended to such innovative practices as team teaching, nongraded formats, open classrooms, etc. In fact, one of the few research efforts to yield differential data was the longitudinal "eight-year study" of the '30s and the early '40s, but it is questionable whether the result of this study served to guide future practice. Clearly, in the business of schooling, eco-

nomic, political and legal aspects affect the policy and practice of individualization.

In a cumulative sense, however, and as far as general theory and practice are concerned, we appear to be at a stage presently in which the notion of *designing programs to fit learners* is replacing the older notion of *fitting learners to standard programs.* Under the newer orientation, it is not the student who fails but the method or program. Consequently, all methods become a reservoir from which to draw in the quest for a match with learners. Thus, "open classes" may be useful for some learners but not all learners. Similarly, self-contained classes may be helpful for some learners but not all learners; teacher-directed methods may make contact with certain learners; student-directed approaches with others.

As in the past, the newer philosophy is geared toward the hope that more students will learn. Today, the concept of individualization has evolved to a point in which Methods A and B are examined in terms of which method works better with what learners. Clearly, some learners could learn from either. Others might learn in one direction or another. This type of matching and tailoring represents a pedagogical procedure that has found its way into public policy governing, for instance, those considered "handicapped." The so-called "bill of rights" for the handicapped (Public Law 92–142), for example, refers to the right of the handicapped to "a least restrictive environment." The terminology "least restrictive environment" reflects the trend towards greater matching of learner to method and setting. Chapter 766 in Massachusetts and the Alternative Education Legislation in Florida move in this direction.

The advent of individualization through a structural match between learner and instructional environment casts the discussion of methodology, programs, and the role of the professional educator in an entirely different light. Not only is it considered increasingly a *right* to be fully educated, but the design of programs that are compatible with the style of the learner is increasingly the responsibility of the school in conjunction with the major interested parties closest to the learner, including parents and other advisors. Again, the central point is that we are slowly leaving the period in which we were trying to replace one methodological orthodoxy with another, imposing each on all learners. In many quarters, searching for a better match between learner and pedagogical environment is taking the form of "individual learning contracts" in which all interested parties participate; e.g., students, parents, teachers, counselors, administrators, and the like. The result is often a quasi-legal document reflecting a planned and approved team effort, including close contact between home and school.

This trend has meant the institutional conversion of "old" psychologies—"normal, abnormal psych" and the "psychology of adjustment" with the newer ones, the "psychology of individual differences" and the "psychology of becoming"—the latter underscoring the human potential and the search of each unique human organism for the unfolding of one's own distinctiveness.

Moreover, we have been witnessing a period in which increased options and alternatives have been legitimized along with more choices for educational consumers. The need and demand for options and choices has given rise to the so-called "voucher plan" under which families are given the right and the fiscal means to choose a public or a private school for their children. In the last decade, the need for options and choices has led to an increase in public school alternatives, lending further incentive to the design of responsive matches between styles of learning and teaching. The 1970s has been a period of accelerated options: alternative schools, schools within schools, home education, with growing recognition that choice will be a major entitlement in the future—the right of each learner to

an alternative that is compatible with his or her learning style.

Matching teaching/learning styles will also likely raise public expectations concerning results. This contemporary concept of individualization promises to move us beyond equality of *opportunity* and toward equality of *outcomes;* that is to say, more learners will attain higher levels of performance. Under the older model in which diverse learners converged on a singular methodology, there was never the expectation that *every* learner, indeed most learners, could achieve certain minimum levels of competence. In the older system, if Methodology A reached 60 percent, and Methodology B reached 65 or 70 percent, then the latter replaced the former. Attempts to find *one* method that would reach 100 percent is fruitless, especially given economic limitations. The point is that we are now at a stage theoretically and practically in which we should be able to generate the capacity to tailor programs to fit individuals. No one method can be considered superior to the other except as it contributes to the learning of the individual. A methodology that is appropriate for one person may not be for another, and it has taken us a long time to get around to that realization. The emerging strategy for matching learners to programs may be conceptualized as in Figure 1.

Under this approach, a profile for each learner is attained and an individualized prescriptive package is designed accordingly. This individual plan can become quite elaborate, taking into account personality factors such as shyness, self-concept, talents, and the like. It is conceivable that elementary students with special talents in music can take courses at the high school. Other students may take work in social and cultural agencies in the community. Tutorial linkages with talented adults from the arts and community, retired teachers and volunteers are considered, as are mini-sabbaticals, self-instructional technologies, and so forth. All resources

**FIGURE 1**
Diagnostic Prescriptive Matches

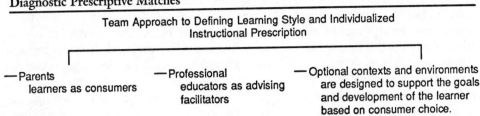

Team Approach to Defining Learning Style and Individualized Instructional Prescription

—Parents learners as consumers

—Professional educators as advising facilitators

—Optional contexts and environments are designed to support the goals and development of the learner based on consumer choice.

within and outside the school are orchestrated into a plan that fits the learner and which the learner and family approve.

Under this model, the teacher does not assume the primary role in delivering services *directly* to the learner but is more a *facilitator* of *services* from a variety of sources. In brief, the learner becomes the consumer, the teacher an advisor and the base of resources from which to orchestrate a tailored program of education extends well into the community.

On another level, the match is more between the learner and teacher than the program. While we have recognized individual differences among students, we have just begun to realize the operational implications of *individual differences among teachers* and other professional personnel. This had led slowly to the notion that it may be useful to attempt to achieve a more synchronized match between style of learning and *style of teaching*. There have been a number of people who have pioneered this effort (Thelen, Tall, Hunt, Dunn and Dunn).

Conceptualizations concerning learning style have outpaced those having to do with teaching styles. The work of cognitive psychologists, Piaget, Bruner, Hunt, and others has helped identify different stages of intellectual development in learners on which a match may be based. More recently, work in the affective realms (Brown, Weinstein, and Alschuler) have integrated cognitive with affective development. However, on the teaching style side, the concep-

tualizations are only now beginning. The methodology used by the teachers (including those inside the school and those outside, such as parents, peers, athletic coaches, etc.) is usually the dimension given most emphasis and is certainly one clear sector in any discussion of teaching style. We do recognize that teachers differ in their basic approach to instruction: for example, some use a more inquiring approach, while others may be more didactic with a whole range in between. However, this is only one aspect of "style" and, if utilized as the sole criterion for matching teaching/learning styles, may yield results not always as promising as expected.

Clearly, in any human interaction as complex as that between teacher and student, *personality and values* must come into full play. Here the *attitudes of the teacher toward the learner* is paramount. If a teacher in the classroom context prefers to interact with certain types of learners, for instance those considered more academically able or those representing a certain lifestyle, then communicating such preferences to learners, either verbally or nonverbally, will doubtlessly affect student/teacher relationships, motivation, and learning. Further, the values of teachers have influenced their relationship as well. For instance, the teacher who begins each semester by explaining to the class, "One third of the students in this class will not pass," is also exhibiting a dimension of style, affecting certain learners negatively. Also, we have been reminded repeatedly that each teacher practices a "psychology of expectations," and the so-called self-fulfilling prophecy becomes yet another important component of style. Suffice it to suggest that how the learner perceives the attitudes of the teacher toward him or her contributes significantly to any match of styles. There are teachers who believe in a closer, more affective relationship with the learner, while others prefer to exercise more detachment. All such ingredients converge on dimensions of style and relate to any serious attempt to connect learner with teacher.

It is interesting that style itself is a conception which has grown out of the arts, especially the performing arts. Viewing the teacher as a "performer" is useful. Just as we can recognize different styles in the world of art, so too can we begin to examine the teacher from that perspective. However, even if we are able to identify the personal factors of both teacher and student that lead to compatibility at this human level, we would still only be touching the surface of personalized instruction.

"Curriculum" is another crucial component of individualization. The evolution of curriculum theory has taken us from a notion of curriculum as *courses of study,* as academic subject matter, toward curriculum as learning *environment.* Contemporary thinking in curriculum circles has begun to shift the conception of curriculum from courses of study such as English, social studies, and language arts, to "learning contexts." Conceptions such as a learning environment, while helpful, must be further delineated to include the physical, social, psychological, and political environments that function within human systems. There are a number of curriculum theorists who are beginning to define curriculum in much broader and more comprehensive terms, such as Robert Sinclair at the University of Massachusetts.

Integrating all these factors into an operational definition of style appears to take us into metaphysical levels of complexity. Nonetheless, the evolution of curriculum from the classroom

and of courses of study to learning environments in and out of school has not only altered the role of teachers but also has begun to affect the whole direction of American education from schooling and the schoolhouse to education and the community. Instead of looking at just the resources inside the school as the chief, if not the only, contributor to legitimate learning, the newer views enhance a more elaborate, integrated view of the total community as educator, with the quality of that community impacting on the growth and potential of the people who interact within its boundaries. The idea surfacing that I believe will be the major learning conceptualization for the next century is "community education"—education by, for, and from the community. Under community education, the basic agents of socialization, those that affect human potential, are once again tied together toward the common goal of promoting the unique development of each human being.

Consequently, we appear to have gone full circle. The nation began by proclaiming the centrality of the person with unalienated rights to full development. This philosophical under-pinning of American society has gone through various stages in the pursuit of that educational promise. More recently, we have begun to realize that education is the process for human and societal renewal. As such, education is a right as basic as any we cherish. The vision of educating every human being and of providing environments that support the unique growth of each and every person is closer at hand. Matching style of teaching with the style of learning is an important step in that direction.

## REFERENCES

Brown, George Isaac. *Human Teaching for Human Learning: An Introduction to Confluent Education.* New York: The Viking Press, 1971.

Dunn, Rita, and Dunn, Kenneth. *Teaching Students Through Their Individual Learning Styles: A Practical Approach.*

Reston, Virginia: Reston Publishing Company, Inc., 1978.

Fantini, Mario D. *Alternative Education: A Source Book for Parents, Teachers, Students, and Administrators.* New York: Doubleday and Company, Inc., 1976.

————. *Public Schools of Choice: A Plan for the Reform of American Education.* New York: Simon and Schuster, 1973.

Hunt, David E.; Greenwood, JoAnn; and Brill, Ronald. "From Psychological Theory to Educational Practice: Implementation of a Matching Model." Paper presented at a symposium, "Models of Teaching and Learning." American Educational Research Association, Chicago, Illinois, 7 April 1972.

Hunt, David E., and Sullivan, Edmund V. *Between Psychology and Education.* Hinsdale, Illinois: Dryden Press, 1974

Sinclair, Robert, and Ghory, Ward. "Curriculum as Environments for Learning: A Practical Meaning and Model." Presented at the Annual Meeting of the American Educational Research Association, San Francisco, California, April 1979.

Weinstein, Gerald, and Alschuler, Alfred. "The Developmental Stages of Self-Knowledge." Unpublished manuscript, 1979.

Weinstein, Gerald, and Fantini, Mario D. *Toward Humanistic Education: A Curriculum of Affect.* New York: Praeger Publishers, 1970.

Mario D. Fantini is Dean, School of Education, University of Massachusetts, Amherst.

# Seeking Balance in the Curriculum

## KIMBALL WILES

In the controversy over education since Sputnik was placed in orbit, many persons have made a plea for balance. Some have asked for more math and science. Some have insisted that we continue to devote the same proportion of school time to the social studies and the humanities that we did before Sputnik. One professional association has designated the study of balance in the curriculum as a major emphasis in its national program.

Demands for balance are not new. Whenever people ask for a new emphasis in the curriculum or argue to maintain the present status, the plea for balance is a typical appeal to reason.

- Some ask for even distribution of time among science, math, art, music, English, and history.

- Some ask that more attention be given to the cultures of the Far East, Africa, and Latin America.
- Some ask for more study which will enable pupils to develop ways of solving social problems.
- Some ask for inclusion of more information about local community.
- Some ask for more attention to problems of social adjustment.
- Some ask that a variety in social points of view be represented in the curriculum and instructional materials.
- Some ask for more time for TV teaching.
- Some ask that pupils be made more anxious and concerned about failure.
- Some ask that pupils be helped to be more secure so that they will be free to venture.

From *Childhood Education* 36, no. 2 (October, 1959), 69–73. Reprinted by permission of the Association for Childhood Education International, 3615 Wisconsin Avenue, N.W., Washington, D.C. 20016.

- Some ask for a greater amount of creative activity.
- Some ask for more teaching of common values.
- Some ask for more stress of the fundamental skills.

What is the balance sought? How can it be attained?

## ATTEMPTS TO ATTAIN BALANCE

Balance in the curriculum has been sought in various ways. Some school systems follow a curriculum pattern designed by scholars, in which all youngsters are brought into contact with the facts, concepts and generalizations it is assumed all students should know.

Some schools attempt to develop balance by assigning portions of days to designated subjects—fifteen minutes for spelling, twenty minutes for reading, twenty minutes for arithmetic, and so on. Certain assumptions are made about desirable balance in amounts of time provided for different activities.

Some schools try to obtain balance by having a classroom teacher plus some special teachers who come in to teach music, art, physical education, and things the administrators think the classroom teacher cannot or does not teach well.

Other schools seek to achieve balance by maintaining self-contained classrooms in which the teacher knows all the activities in which youngsters engage. It is assumed the teacher has some criterion by which he can tell if there is a balance.

Some systems appoint supervisors to guide teachers toward more balance than they are providing. It is assumed the supervisors have a gauge by which they can determine proper balance.

## PROBLEMS IN SECURING BALANCE

From the point of view of recent developments in research, seeking balance through division and allocation of content or administrative procedure has little chance for success. The research on perception (Kelley's report in *Education for What Is Real* or the research of McClellan and others at the University of Chicago) indicates that *people perceive differently, in terms of their purposes, their needs, and their background.* Acceptance of this evidence leads to the proposition that a curriculum provided by a school is not the same for any two people going through it and that a balanced curriculum for the individual cannot be achieved by attempting to give everybody the same thing.

Difference in maturation rates makes it difficult to provide balance for the individual. American education is organized around homogeneous grouping by age. But the evidence being provided about maturation rates reveals that some nine-year-olds are as large as the average seventeen-year-old and some seventeen-year-olds are as small as the average nine-year-old. Willard Olson's studies show that *people grow at different rates and mature at different ages.* When teachers talk about developmental tasks as though they occur for all eleven-year-olds at the same time, they are not supported by research. When balance is sought by establishing a curriculum structure ahead of time, it is gained for one youngster and hindered for another.

Further, *learning rates differ.* If schools do a good job, the longer youngsters are in school, the greater the difference in range of achievement at a given grade level. It seems rather hopeless to look at balance as something that can be prestructured by organizing concepts and activities into scope and sequence for given grades without consideration of a specific individual or class.

Add to differences in rates of maturation and

learning variation in the purpose and the problems that children have, and the prestructuring approach appears even less productive. Statements like Daniel Prescott's "Persistent emotional problems decrease the range of facts that are significant for the individual" illuminate the task of attempting to achieve balance by organizing content.

## BALANCE FOR THE INDIVIDUAL

What alternative is left? How can balance be obtained? *Balance must be sought for the individual.* It is the assumption of the writer that each faculty must decide upon the types of growth it wants to develop and must use the program of activities to promote these growths in each child. Curriculum balance is determined by the extent to which a child's experiences promote *in a satisfactory manner* all of the growths the faculty deems important.

In arriving at the decision concerning desired growth, community groups, such as advisory groups or homeroom parent groups, should be brought in on the thinking. If not, lack of communication or lack of agreement may separate the school and homes, jeopardizing both support for the program and balance in the program.

Continuous evaluation and planning are necessary if balance is to be obtained. Evidence must be collected concerning the amount and kinds of growth being produced and the program for individuals revised in terms of the data secured.

The program that is balanced for one pupil may not be for another. The staff or the individual teacher must revise the schedule, method or activity when the evaluation reveals that classes or individuals are not making some of the growths sought. *Judgments must be made continuously by parents and teachers as to whether the present balance of pupil growth is satisfactory.* The basis for determining satisfactory balance should be the personal and social needs and purposes of the individual.

To maintain balance in the curriculum means that the teacher must be experimental to the extent that he will change his procedures when the evidence indicates he is ineffective. Each school needs a curriculum committee responsible for continuous evaluation of the program and recommendation of needed changes to the faculty.

## THE METHOD IN OPERATION

How does this formula work in a school? Let's examine the operation of one school.

This school, faculty and parents, agreed on the types of growth desired. They said they wanted continuous growth of pupils in eight areas. Note the use of *continuous*. They do not expect all students to achieve given levels at any grade but want *uninterrupted progress* for all pupils in all of the types of growth desired.

*First, they wanted continuous improvement in mental and physical health.* A six-year-old observed students leaving the school at the end of the day. He looked at his mother and said, "This is a happy school, isn't it?" Even a six-year-old could see the youngsters as they came out of the school were happy. If the learning environment is to produce mental health, the people who go there must enjoy it and be happy.

In the kindergarten the five-year-olds go to the teacher when they are troubled, tug on her skirt and say, "lap." She sits down and holds them until they are ready to get down and face the world again. She gives them confidence of their worth. Evidence of her contribution is illustrated in the following incident. Joe, a five-year-old in Miss Jones' class, was being disciplined by his mother. She said, "If you don't behave, people won't like you." The little boy replied, "You know, Mother, no matter what Joe does, two people will like him. God and Miss Jones."

It is hoped all children will develop this sense of worth and acceptance.

*Second, they want continuous growth in the fundamental skills.* The official testing program is designed to sample growth in reading and arithmetic at the end of the second, fourth, and sixth grades, and this is supplemented by each teacher's collecting evidence of progress.

At the beginning of the year the fifth-grade teacher asked each youngster to put into a manila folder samples of all the work during the year of which he was proud. During January she asked each youngster to go through his folder and make a list of the ten most important things on which to work during the second semester. One boy, who read at the eighth-grade level and did arithmetic at the third-grade level, put as Number 1 on his list, "Work on my 8 tables." He did not have to be told to do it. He was using the evidence to make decisions about his status and desirable next steps. In a good intellectual climate, growth in fundamental skills is an individual matter in which pupils move ahead at their own best rate.

*Third, they want continuous growth in the development of a set of values.* The kindergarten teacher has the kind of relationship with children that enables them to discuss their problems with her. Even some youngsters in the first and second grades come back to talk with her. One little girl went to her and crawled upon her knee and said, "What happens if lightning strikes you?" The teacher said, "It may kill you." The little girl said, "What happens if you die?" The teacher said, "Different people believe different things." The little girl said, "Do you go to heaven?" The teacher knew that this little girl's parents did not believe in heaven or hell and she said, "Some people think so." The little girl said, "Is heaven near the sun?" The teacher said, "Some people

think it is." The little girl said, "Is it warm there?" The teacher said, "If it's near the sun, it would be." The little girl said, "Then I want to go there." Each person chooses his own counselor, and the essence of guidance is creating the kind of situation where people can analyze their values with people they trust. The school recognizes this phenomenon and seeks to keep the type of flexible organization which facilitates its operation.

*Fourth, they want continuous growth in creative ability.* Great emphasis is placed on seeking solutions to problems and on expression of feelings and perceptions. When the second-grade teacher asked her class to draw a picture of their family, one girl drew a picture of five fish. In the center was a great big fish and in the corners were four little fish. It would have been very easy to look at this picture and assume that the big fish in the center was the little girl. When the teacher asked her to explain the picture, the little girl said, "The big fish in the center is my big brother and all the rest of us are out on the edges." The picture was drawn at the height of the football season and her brother was the fullback.

When teachers give youngsters a chance to express themselves creatively, not only do they develop a skill that will be important the rest of their lives, they reveal to teachers the learnings that they are doing in such a way that teachers can know how to relate to them. Teachers in this school examine their methods and the activities they provide to see if they are encouraging creativity.

*Fifth, they want continuous growth in skill in making independent and intelligent decisions.* The fifth-grade teacher described previously asked each child as he went back through his folder to decide, "What are the ten most important things for you to do?" Each was asked to analyze himself to determine his strengths and his weaknesses and to say, "These are the important next steps to take." By this process, the staff hopes the school will develop mature, self-directing people.

*Sixth, they want continuous growth in skill in democratic group participation.* From kindergarten to the sixth year, teacher-pupil planning and teacher-pupil evaluation occur daily. Teachers try to foster this growth by the way they work. Group work and committee work are a part of every class. When John Lovell, of Auburn Polytechnic Institute, studied the way teachers develop group participation skill in this school, he found that at every level the way the teacher operated with his class was reflected in the way the committee chairmen behaved with student groups. People learn as much about group participation by the way the teacher operates as by anything they read or hear.

*Seventh, they want continuous growth in individual interests and skill in following individual interests.* When a boy from the north moved to Florida, the thing he became most interested in was poisonous snakes. He went to his third-grade teacher and said, "I want to read about moccasins, rattlers, and coral snakes." She didn't say, "That's not in the third-grade curriculum; that's in tenth-grade biology—you'll get there." She didn't say, "We don't have any instructional materials in the third grade which will permit you to read about poisonous snakes. We didn't buy any last year." She said, "Let's go to the school library and see if the librarian can help us find something." Because this teacher was willing to let this boy follow an individual interest for a portion of the day, his reading ability jumped from the third grade to the sixth grade in one year.

A fourth-grade boy was much interested in writing. He went on Saturday mornings to meet his fourth-grade teacher and began writing a book. It was never published, but the teacher took his time to work with a youngster on the pursuit of an individual interest.

*Eighth, they want continuous growth in acquisition of an understanding of our cultural heritage.* Experiences which acquaint pupils with social studies, language, and literature are a part of the program; and administration of standardized tests at regular intervals throughout the elementary program determines whether or not classes and individual pupils are meeting expectations for pupils of their age and grade. The achievements of others assists in the interpretation of progress but is not a pattern or profile to seek.

Each teacher in this school believes these eight types of growth are important. He uses them as criteria to judge the curriculum of each pupil. He checks each youngster's progress and the things that he does by them. *He brings pupils and parents into decision-making situations at which it is decided if types and amounts of growth are in proper balance.* Teachers cannot make these judgments alone and be assured of validity. The purposes and concerns of those involved must enter the decision as to whether rates of growth in the areas are in balance.

Each teacher attempts to achieve balance by planning with the parents. Both share evidence that they have of growth or lack of growth in any of the eight areas and decide how they can supplement each other to bring a youngster up in an area where he may not be progressing as satisfactorily as they hope.

Not all faculties would establish the same types of growth as important. Differing values and community pressures might lead to the establishment of a different set of desirable outcomes. The formula that looks most promising is:

- clear definition of the types of pupil growth sought
- continuous collection of evidence concerning pupil growth in the specified areas
- revision of the individual student's program

when he is not making satisfactory progress in all areas
- continuous study of the total program to dis-

cover ways of providing flexibility which permits greater adaptation of program to individual needs.

*Kimball Wiles* was Dean, College of Education, University of Florida, Gainesville.

# Another Look at Mainstreaming: Exceptionality, Normality, and the Nature of Difference

## MARA SAPON-SHEVIN

Mainstreaming has been defined in many ways, most of which center on moving handicapped children from their segregated special education classes and integrating them with "normal" children. When mainstreaming is viewed as a technical problem, the concerns identified tend to be technical ones, such as how best to build ramps, enlarge doorways, and provide adequate toilet facilities. When mainstreaming is viewed as another model of service delivery, then concerns focus on administrative issues: to whom the resource teachers should be responsible, how referral and testing can most efficiently be handled, and on whose list the exceptional-needs child's name should be recorded.

Although all the above concerns require attention and solution, the attention to technical and administrative concerns has tended to bypass fundamental ethical and conceptual issues. These issues must be dealt with if mainstreaming is to succeed as more than a symbolic gesture. An analogy may be made with the issue of racial integration: Reducing such a complex issue to the technical concerns of busing and rezoning while ignoring more central elements such as

race relations and economic inequalities has failed to bring about necessary and long-lasting improvements in an intolerable situation.

If mainstreaming is viewed as a conceptual and ethical issue, then the questions raised are very different ones, and not as quickly or easily soluble. Administrative and technical problems may also seem insurmountable, but schools have a better history of dealing with these issues.

One of my concerns with mainstreaming deals with precisely how it is defined and with the implications for implementation of each definition. The frequent use of terms "special children" and "regular" or "normal" children signals an important contradiction. Although the mainstreaming movement may be characterized as a movement to "bring together" groups that have previously been separated, the first step in describing mainstreaming generally involves the dichotomizing of children into two categories: exceptional and normal. This dichotomy reflects current school practices: namely, classes for "special" children and classes for "normal" children. However, by limiting or defining a discussion of mainstreaming to the *integration* of two

From *Phi Delta Kappan* 60, no. 2 (October 1978): 119–121. Used by permission of the author and the publisher.

groups, the focus of the ensuing discussion is often on the discreteness of the groups. Many fundamental questions concerning concepts of normality, deviance, and the labeling of children are bypassed.

Moreover, the very concept of mainstreaming tends to imply that the mainstream is inaccessible and unamenable to change. This orientation puts the burden of change on those being introduced into this environment. The educator's task is seen as that of making children ready to enter the mainstream. My point is that the educational and conceptual implications of mainstreaming extend far beyond some small population of children identified as "special education" students. Many aspects of regular education—that is, of the "mainstream" itself—will need to be reassessed and modified if successful mainstreaming is to occur.

Many philosophical and educational arguments *for* mainstreaming have served functions that may not be in the best interest of all children. One of these conflicts concerns the nature of difference.

Educators trying to increase the acceptance of children formerly categorized and isolated due to their particular disability or handicap have argued that "these children are the same as other children." This argument usually centers on de-emphasizing a child's handicap or disability and emphasizing those aspects of his behavior that are common to all other children. By making such statements, many parents and educators have attempted to increase the probability of these "special" students being treated more like "normal" children, i.e., being invited to birthday parties, included in music and art activities, and having their need for friendship and privacy acknowledged. These efforts, while motivated by a real concern for the "normalization" of the lives of children discriminated against, may have undesirable outcomes.

Perhaps this issue may best be dealt with by identifying a continuum and exploring its posi-

tive and negative implications. On one end is the statement, "Everyone is fundamentally the same"; at the other end lies the statement, "Everyone is fundamentally different."

The broad interpretation of the statement that "all children are really the same" tends to minimize all differences, both superficial and important. Under the canopy of "sameness," then, lie both the acknowledgement of fundamental similarities (a positive interpretation) and the inference that "it is good to be alike and bad to be different" (a negative interpretation). That is, if differences are seen as something to be overlooked in the quest for similarity, then those differences that cannot be overlooked because of their obvious or extensive nature are more apt to be viewed negatively.

At the opposite pole is the statement that "everyone is fundamentally different." It is clear from the previous discussion how such a statement might be interpreted positively. On the other hand, it is possible that pleas for fundamental differences, rather than facilitating smooth social interaction, will *impede* it by blocking the formulation of human universals so necessary in a diverse society. For example, some people's apparent insensitivity to the needs and feelings of handicapped people is excused by statements such as, "I didn't know that they . . . have feelings, . . . would feel that way, . . . would understand," etc.

This is not a matter of hair-splitting semantics. The notions that underlie the use of the words "same" and "different" are important and cannot be overemphasized.

Careful analysis is important in examining statements like this one, made by a special educator: "Exceptional children have the same human needs and wants that you and I have." Such a statement tends to draw the listener into the corner of "normalcy," aligning him against the special child, even though the statement itself purports to stress similarities rather than differences. The introduction to a study of mainstreaming states that "without exceptionality there would be no 'average'," adding that it is normal to vary.[1] Both of these statements, if true, seem incompatible with subsequent discussions, which describe "exceptional children" and how they are different from and similar to "normal children." There is an inherent absurdity in the juxtaposition of the statement "it is normal to vary" with the use of the terms "normal" and "exceptional" unless the real message is, "It is normal to vary as long as you don't vary too much."

A solution to the polarization of concepts surrounding "sameness" and "difference" is some middle ground that both acknowledges and builds upon human differences while recognizing inherent similarities in the general needs of all people—the need to be appreciated, treated with respect, and so on.

Another potentially destructive focus of some discussions of mainstreaming is that statements are sometimes issued with regard to the mainstreamed child that are equally applicable to all children. For instance, Leroy Asserlind states that the mainstream of education is highly competitive, both socially and academically, while special programs are less competitive, geared to the individual needs of the child and designed to accommodate each child's rate of progress.[2] This statement will be interpreted by some to imply that individualized education, lessened competition, and sensitivity to individual differences are important only in special education and that, in fact, these things must and should be abandoned for a child to enter the mainstream successfully. *All* children need appropriate educational planning, success experiences in school, and a positive classroom atmosphere; to imply in any way that these are requirements *only* for special education students is to perpetuate a senseless distinction, in this case at the expense of those students assigned to "regular" education. Some parents of exceptional children are resisting the mainstreaming movement for precisely this rea-

son; they see little reason for their children to be placed in a regular classroom situation that may not offer the same intensive educational planning that their child received in a special education setting. Mainstreaming must be conceived of, not as changing the special child so that he will fit back into the unchanged regular classroom, but rather as changing the nature of the regular classroom so that it is more accommodating to all children.

One central impediment to mainstreaming— competition—is deeply ingrained in our educational system. Many classroom procedures, management programs, and curricular materials emphasize the selection and sorting functions of schools; that is, schools, both officially and tacitly, sort out the able from the less able and rank students according to specific criteria.

However, it seems incongruous for schools to sort and select while purporting to redesign themselves to meet the needs of all children. Although this situation existed long before mainstreaming became an issue, recent attention to those populations previously excluded from public school programs or from regular classrooms serves to reemphasize this incompatibility. Ideally, the concept of mainstreaming should serve as an impetus to examine and redesign not only special education but many other aspects of our system of schooling.

The impact of competition on our philosophy of schooling is enormous. In describing a successful mainstreaming program, one special educator wrote that in this program "exceptional children are successfully competing in regular classrooms."[3] Another, in describing a blind child in the regular classroom, wrote, "Here he functions as a member of the class, competing and participating, learning and interacting."[4] These quotes indicate that we tend to accept competition as a necessary or inevitable component of schooling. Consider this, however: If education is conceived of as a competitive enterprise, then some children are destined for failure regardless of their performance. How can we reconcile this fact with the recent emphasis on individualization and mainstreaming? If we, as educators and as a society, have a responsibility for insuring the success of *all* children in schools, then we cannot also perpetuate a system that creates deviants and failures by its competitive teaching and evaluation system.

The issue of competition is closely related to how differences are viewed. Schools transmit a mixed message with regard to differences: (1) You must all be alike (the value of conformity). (2) You must be better than everyone else (competition). When examined more closely, however, these messages are not at all contradictory, but are indicative of the fact that differences per se are not esteemed and that students are likely to be judged along a single continuum. In school, students are sorted out along that continuum, but *along* that continuum those differences that lead to a better performance are rewarded.

Many of the current schemes of evaluation used in schools (testing, psychological diagnoses, etc.) are norm-referenced, and thus by definition are deviance-creating. Whenever individuals are compared along the same continuum, some must fall at both extremes. When this quantification of differences occurs within an overall framework that does not *value* these differences, then deviants are created. Referral systems tend to focus on (and sometimes even specifically require) comparing the child in question with other children.

In the same way that intelligence testing focuses on those human performances most likely to discriminate among people,[5] competitive schema in classrooms take advantage of the weaknesses of specific children. That is, the classroom teacher does not ask the spelling word she knows everyone can spell but the one that only some children can spell, so as to be able to differentiate the good spellers from the poor.

What, then, is the solution to the competi-

tively organized nature of schooling? The solution touted by many is individualization. The reasoning behind this proposal is that each student will work at his own pace at the work most appropriate to him and thus avoid the undesirable aspects of competition. I propose, however, that the antithesis of competition is not individualization at all, but *cooperation*. Although there are some skills that nearly every individual must have, there are infinitely more skills that, within a social organization that allows and promotes cooperative activity, need not be possessed by everyone. This concept is particularly applicable in the mainstreamed classroom, in which there are children with a wide range of skills and also a specifiable set of behavioral deficits (Billy cannot walk, Susan cannot hear, etc.). Within this framework, a cooperative model would make use of the positive aspects of both shared repertoires (sameness) and individual strengths (differences). Within a cooperative framework, a larger number and greater magnitude of differences could be accommodated because all children in a class would not be required or expected to be functioning at an identical level. Therefore, the teacher could make use of peer tutoring, multi-age grouping, and similar strategies in addition to individualizing those aspects of the curriculum for which cooperation is either not desirable or not feasible.

Many teachers fear mainstreaming because they feel that they will not be able to meet the needs of many different kinds of children. By organizing a classroom that is not solely teacher-centered but, rather, makes use of the shared and combined strengths of classroom members, the burden on the teacher should be eased. Cooperation must be considered a viable alternative to competitively organized classrooms. Without such a shift away from structures that guarantee failure for a portion of the group, regardless of its membership, mainstreaming cannot succeed.

Just as it is inadequate to examine a phenomenon such as mainstreaming in isolation from issues of schooling in general, it is also deceptive to examine schooling and the schooling of "special" children in isolation from other aspects of the world at large. Since school is viewed by many as "preparation for the real world," it is not surprising that schools in many ways mirror people's conceptions of the "outside world." The system of stratification that exists within schools is both a reflection of and preparation for the world outside. Therefore, my critique of the stratification and segregation implied by most definitions of mainstreaming suggests not only that there is something wrong with our schools, it also casts doubt on the highly competitive, comparative nature of our society.

I raise these issues not with the hope of resolving them here but simply with the belief that it is necessary to place the issue of mainstreaming in a broader perspective. To treat mainstreaming as an administrative problem or as merely a reshifting of funding mechanisms is to deny the relationships between mainstreaming and other aspects of our educational system. The implementation of mainstreaming must be accompanied by changes in many areas. It *could* be used as a catalyst for significant change in school and society. Before we can hope for such change, however, we must first acknowledge the broader questions that need to be asked.

## ENDNOTES

1. Leroy Asserlind, *An Overview of the Consortium Project: Module I* (Madison, Wisc.: Wisconsin Consortium for the Preparation of Regular Educators for Participation in the Education of Handicapped Children Series, 1976).
2. Ibid.
3. *Knowledge of Exceptionality, Part II: Module III* (Madison, Wisc.: Wisconsin Consortium for the Preparation of Regular Educators for Participation in the Education of Handicapped Children Series, 1976).
4. Ibid.
5. Herbert Ginsburg, *The Myth of the Deprived Child* (Englewood Cliffs, N.J.: Prentice-Hall, 1972).

*Mara Sapon-Shevin* is Visiting Assistant Professor, Department of Specialized Instructional Programs, Cleveland State University, Ohio.

# A Systematic Model For Curriculum Development

## FRANCIS P. HUNKINS

Curriculum development should be a comprehensive process requiring a broad-based view of the educational system and its place within society. Frequently, however, if curriculum development exists at all, it is a disjointed procedure.

Curriculum development is also a political process. It requires dealing with people and their various power bases and their views of what makes for "good" education.

What follows is a seven-step model that pro-

From *NASSP Bulletin* 69, No. 481 (May 1985): 23–27. Used by permission of the author and the publisher, the National Association of Secondary School Principals.

vides a linear and rational approach to curriculum development. (See figure below.)

In this first major stage of curriculum development, one does what has been called "front-end analysis"—engaging in a series of analytical and decision-making steps that determine the current deficiencies in students' understanding and performance, and noting those that are the legitimate concerns of the school. Here, philosophical questions are raised, the purpose of schooling is debated, potential curriculum designs are considered, and a master management plan is noted for carrying out the other steps of curriculum development.

Unfortunately, educators are often so concerned about getting the program into action that they rush into the formation of objectives and the outlining of instructional strategies. People often resist discussions about philosophical questions, considering them a waste of time.

More time spent on the first step allows us to place the total process of curriculum development in some context. Johnson (1977) has called these contexts *frame factors,* and has labeled them temporal, physical, cultural, organizational, and personal.

The temporal factor of time is critical. How much time do we have to create the program? To teach the program? The physical frame factors refer to the package in which the curriculum is to be experienced by both teacher and students. Just what types of school structures do we have? Also, what is the arrangement of these structures within the community? Is the school design open space or separate classrooms? Considering cultural frame factors forces us to look at the implication of the cultural groups in the environment within which the schools are located. Curriculum content must be built upon the particular society's values, beliefs, knowledge bases, institutions, and artifacts.

Since curriculum activity is a people enterprise, personal frame factors must be considered. Who are our students, teachers, administrators, curriculum specialists, lay citizens? Curriculum development and the manner of its delivery will be affected by the people involved in and affected by education.

## CURRICULUM DIAGNOSIS

The second stage of curriculum development focuses on the reasons for the deficiencies in human performance. Identifying the reasons that students lack certain knowledge, skills, attitudes, or behavior allows one to begin to identify a

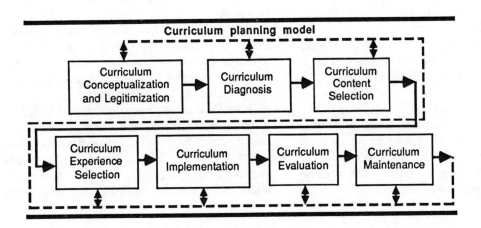

potential direction for correcting such deficiencies.

At this stage of curriculum development, aims, goals, and objectives are created. The exact way in which the learning outcome is to be measured and judged should not be a part of the general curriculum document; such specificity belongs in a lesson plan designed for a particular classroom.

## CURRICULUM CONTENT SELECTION

Content is often assumed or ignored in curriculum development. For example, in far too many schools attention is given to how to teach reading, without attention to what is to be read.

One of the most crucial questions confronting curriculum developers is, "What content shall we select for inclusion in our program?" A second key question is, "How shall we organize the content selected?" Those persons charged with dealing with the first question must have some criteria in mind for selecting content.

Scheffler (1970) argues that the prime criterion is economy—content selected should be such that the learner can attain maximum self-sufficiency in the most economical manner. He identifies three types of economy: economy in terms of teaching effort and educational resources, economy in terms of students' efforts, and finally economy in terms of the generalizability of the subject matter.

Curriculum developers also need to bring to the content selection task the criteria of significance, validity, interest, learnability, and feasibility.

*Significance* refers to the essentialness of the content to be learned. Content is significant only to the degree to which it contributes to basic ideas, concepts, principles, and generalizations, and to the development of particular learning abilities, skills, processes, and attitudes.

*Validity* refers to the authenticity of the content selected and also to the congruence of the content in light of the objectives selected.

*Interest* refers to the degree to which the content either caters to or fosters particular interests in students. It is a criterion that, if carefully considered, will address the motivation factor of content.

*Learnability* refers to the appropriateness of the content in light of the particular students who are to experience the curriculum.

Finally, *feasibility* refers to the question, "Can the content selected be taught in the time allowed, with the current resources, with the current staff and in this particular community?" These criteria, when considered, should allow for the selection of content that is indeed appropriate and in congruence with the general curriculum objectives selected in stage two.

Content must be organized, too. The particular organization rests largely with the view one has of curriculum and the nature of knowledge. Some persons view knowledge as made up of particular disciplines; others view knowledge as a compendium of personal experiences. People in one or the other of these camps will organize content in particular ways—the former frequently favoring the subject-matter or discipline design, the latter favoring a child or student-centered design.

However, the content selection and organization task is still not complete—content must be sequenced—it must be arranged in time. Posner and Rudnitsky (1978) have presented five organizers to determining sequence: world-related, concept-related, learning-related, inquiry-related, and utilization-related.

*World-related* sequences organize content as it seems to or does occur in the world. *Concept-related* sequences draw heavily on the conceptual structures of various disciplines. *Learning-related* sequences take into consideration what we know about how students approach learning—just what sequences do individuals follow when learning something?

*Inquiry-related* sequences organize the curriculum according to the procedures used in inquiring about information—frequently those approaches employed by scholars in the particular field. *Utilization-related* refers to sequencing content in the manner that students will actually use it in the future, or in the manner that persons who need such knowledge will use it in their jobs.

## CURRICULUM EXPERIENCE SELECTION

Once curriculum developers have selected and arranged content, they must decide how students will experience it; how the curriculum content will be delivered. This is the *experience selection* stage in the curriculum development model.

Here educators make instructional decisions, deciding what methods, strategies, activities, incentives, and materials will be used. The nature of the educational environment—where such instruction could take place—is also determined at this stage.

Educational environment is rarely considered in curriculum development. People usually assume that the curriculum will be taught in the classroom with little attention to the arrangement of that classroom.

Instructional approaches should be tied to the curriculum plan. In some cases, teaching methods work against the objectives. For example, curriculum programs noting that students will attain mastery of inquiry strategies often incorporate strategies placing the teacher as main actor—delivering instruction via lecture or demonstration rather than furnishing time for students to formally learn procedures for inquiry and opportunities to try out such procedures.

## CURRICULUM IMPLEMENTATION

The newly defined curriculum guide or unit must be tested to ascertain if all the parts work as planned. Does the content selected get students to address the general program objectives? Are the experiences suggested congruent with the intended direction of the objectives and the content selected?

Piloting, part of the implementation stage, is an attempt to gather data from intensive tryouts with a small number of learners. However, the overall objective is to assess the curriculum and not the students; to fine tune the program. Therefore, designers should not be unduly alarmed if problems with the program become apparent. This is the time for problem identification, so that modifications can be made in the curriculum before total district implementation.

Once piloting has been completed, the curriculum can be implemented district wide. After a designated time period—perhaps a semester or a year—the program should be evaluated.

## CURRICULUM EVALUATION

A key focus of curriculum evaluation is to determine whether the curriculum as recorded in the master plan is indeed being presented. Are the objectives being addressed and presented in the recommended sequence? Are students being involved in the suggested instructional experiences? Are the materials recommended for use being used in the ways recommended? Are students reacting to the contents in the manner anticipated?

If the curriculum checks out—in part due to careful piloting and implementation—and one still finds that students are not doing well, one has good reason to believe that the problem lies within the realm of instructional delivery.

## CURRICULUM MAINTENANCE

Assuming the evaluation process has furnished evidence that the curriculum program is successful, one now enters the final stage of curriculum development—maintenance.

Curriculum maintenance, including the methods and means by which a program is managed, assures that a new curriculum will continue to function effectively. This stage—which serves a program monitoring function—attends to the various effects of the curriculum elements on student and teacher behavior; the various support personnel and services in relation to the ongoing program; the information flow; and those efforts required to assist various staff members in meeting challenges of the program.

## CONCLUSION

Curriculum development is not a simple process. It is not just the selection of the best textbook from among the competition and giving each teacher 30 copies. A systematic curriculum development model increases the likelihood that the fruits of the effort will be on target. It is also likely that the use of such a model will provide those involved with a psychological boost, a sense of ownership of the program: that those involved will have studied the issues, responded to educational demands, and assisted in creating a tangible document that can guide them and their colleagues in furnishing quality education.

## REFERENCES

Johnson, Maurice. *Intentionality in Education*. Albany, N.Y.: Center for Curriculum Research and Services. State University of New York at Albany, 1977.

Posner, George J., and Rudnitsky, Alan M. *Course Design*. New York: Longman, 1978.

Scheffler, I. "Justifying Curriculum Decision." In *Readings in the Philosophy of Education: A Study of Curriculum*, edited by J. Martin. Boston: Allyn and Bacon, 1970.

*Francis P. Hunkins* is Professor of Curriculum, College of Education, University of Washington, Seattle.

# Who Should Plan the Curriculum?

## GLEN HASS

In these times of complex, often insoluble problems and rapid change, it is urgent that professionals in curriculum planning take a new look at the question, "Who Should Plan the Curriculum?" It is apparent that the curriculum planning and teaching that is needed involves many factors that go beyond the scope of any single discipline or profession. In addition, change is now so rapid in our society and world, that today's curriculum is unsuited for tomorrow's world and is as outmoded as the Model T for the world of twenty years from tomorrow—the world whose leaders are now in the classrooms.

Revised, 1979 by Glen Hass. Portions drawn from *Educational Leadership* 19, no. 1 (October 1961): 2–4, 39. Used by permission of the author and the publisher.

## THE CURRICULUM WE NEED

Today's curriculum planners should study conditions and trends in contemporary society and probable conditions and requirements for democratic living in the final years of this century and at least the beginning of the twenty-first century. Education for the future is almost useless unless it prepares learners to meet problems that are new and that neither they nor anyone else has ever encountered before. All professionals in education need an image of tomorrow as curricula are planned. All too often we now see a "good curriculum" as the present one with its problems removed.

In facing toward the future we must find ways to teach innovation, problem solving, a love of learning; students must acquire the tools of analysis, expression, and understanding. We will surely find that learners of all ages must be prepared for work that does not yet exist. We will see that we all will have numerous increasingly complex tasks as buyers, voters, parents, legislators, and cooperative planners.

All interested citizens, parents, learners, and scholars from many of the disciplines should be encouraged to work with teachers, principals, curriculum leaders, state department of education and federal education agency personnel in the planning. This involvement in planning by all interested parties should begin in the local school and school district, but it should also occur regularly on a state, national and international basis. A democratic society cannot permit uniformity and centralization. The undefined, but onrushing future requires many different autonomous, alternative efforts to cope with its challenges and problems.

In the past many curriculum writers have stated that laypersons and scholars should be encouraged to work with professional educators in planning the curriculum. They have also frequently stated that collaborative models for planning are needed. They have, however, often given inadequate attention to the particular role of each type of planner in the planning process. Lacking adequate role definition we have often, as educators, overemphasized our mission to instruct the public, and have been undersensitive to, or intolerant of, suggestion and dissent. Let us try to define the particular role of each group in curriculum planning.

## ROLE OF SCHOLARS

What is the role in curriculum planning of scholars from disciplines other than education? There are at least two ways in which they can help. They can often give crucial advice regarding *what* should be taught; and they can often suggest *means of implementing* curriculum decisions.

For instance, in the 1960s, scholars in biology, mathematics, and physics worked with teachers and other curriculum workers in determining what should be taught. These planners found that the textbooks in use contained almost none of the modern concepts, although greater change in knowledge had occurred in the past fifty years than in the preceding 500. They also learned that greater emphasis was needed on unifying concepts so that the total number of basic ideas to be learned might be reduced. Now the collaboration of scholars is needed to identify the concepts which are most relevant to alternative futures so that they may become the focus of the curriculum.

Sociologists can give particular assistance in determining the means by which goals of education may be achieved and in identifying the essential values and behavior patterns which must be learned as society changes. Of equal importance is the fact that sociologists, as future planners, can aid the educator in understanding some of the characteristics of the society in which his or her students will live in the future.

Together they can devise a better educational program to prepare for it.

Anthropologists can shed light on the reasons for the direction of the development of various aspects of the culture. They can help the school to plan to counterbalance pressures for conformity and to attach greater emphasis to creativity and critical judgment. They can help in planning to develop in each student an understanding of his or her powers and limitations for creating and modifying society. Anthropologists can also help in developing curriculum plans for the future.

Scholars from many disciplines can aid in curriculum planning by identifying the central concepts and rules for discovering the nature of the discipline. In the terms in which they are now represented, many of the disciplines are increasingly unteachable. We need a philosophical synthesis, appropriate to our world, the future, and to the learners, that can be taught—and only the scholars working alongside educators can achieve this synthesis.

## ROLE OF PARENTS AND OTHER CITIZENS

In the long run, we can only build the curriculum and use the teaching methods which the active public will accept. We must work with the public and have orderly patterns for its participation. People need to be involved in the process of planning the curriculum in order to change their beliefs, attitudes, and behavior regarding it.

A fundamental question is, whose values are to be represented in the curricula for the learners of a particular community? Curriculum planners must recognize that a monolithic curriculum is not acceptable to parents and other citizens in a pluralistic society. Curriculum leaders and teachers should work with parents and other active citizens in setting the yearly educational goals for a particular classroom, school, or district.

Within the larger framework of the school system, local communities, teachers, and principals should define *together* what each school community sees as the most important focus for the coming year. Public education transmits values and beliefs as well as knowledge. Since values and beliefs are very much family and community matters, parents and other citizens must be involved in curriculum planning.

From 1960 to the present, the prevailing practice in many school districts has been to curtail opportunities for citizen participation, and, increasingly, to try to confine curriculum decision-making to the professional educators. In the late 1960s this led to the press for community control through decentralization of large, urban school districts—a prime example of our failure to involve citizens in curriculum planning. Such involvement would have helped teachers and other curriculum planners to be sensitive to the realities of life in the school community.

Many parents are concerned today about whether their children seem to be learning the "basics" needed for survival in our society. Some parents are concerned as to whether the content and operation of the school and its curriculum give students pride in their own race and ethnic background. All parents often wonder whether teachers genuinely accept and share their concern about the learning of their children. Without cooperative planning each group often sees the other as insensitive, as having unreasonable expectations, and as making unrealistic demands.

It is a matter of crucial importance that many school systems invent and use structural devices to bring about a sharing of thinking about the curriculum by the lay citizens of the community and professional staff members.

Staff members must learn to work with citizens; citizens must take part but not take over. This should begin at the level of the parents planning with the teacher about their concerns for their children and should move from there to the citizens advisory council and the systemwide curriculum committee. The profession, in each community, and the teacher, in each classroom, is responsible for establishing these channels.

## ROLE OF STUDENTS

The student is the major untapped resource in curriculum planning. Students are in the best position to explain many of the advantages and deficiencies of the present curriculum. Their ideas and reactions are of very great importance. Research has shown many times that learning is significantly improved when students share in planning and evaluating the curriculum.

In the process of instruction, learners should share in setting goals and objectives. In a particular learning experience the initial objectives should be those that the student sees, at that time, as interesting and meaningful. While the objectives the teacher uses to guide his or her planning and those sought by learners need not be identical, there should be much overlapping. The teacher's and learner's goals for a learning experience certainly must be understood by both, and they must be compatible or they are not likely to be achieved.

Too little use is made of teacher-student planning. The understanding and skills of planning are among the most important outcomes of education. Perhaps more teachers would plan with their students if they realized that student-teacher planning has at least seven aspects, and that they might begin to plan with students about any one of them:

1. What is to be studied?
2. Why are we having this learning activity?
3. How shall we go about it?
4. Where might we do what needs to be done?
5. When shall we do it?
6. Who will do each part of the job?
7. How can we evaluate our success in learning?

While student participation in the choice of topics may be possible only in certain subjects, there is no reason why extensive use of the other aspects of teacher-student planning should not be used in all subjects.

## ROLE OF EDUCATORS

The role of professional educators is one that will grow and develop as they work with the scholars, parents, other citizens, and students.

It is the job of the teacher, principal, and curriculum consultant to provide structure for planning with others, to inform, to offer recommendations, to bring together contributions from many sources, and to work out a recommended plan of action. In the analysis of the curriculum that is planned, professional educators must be certain that it takes account of the nature of the learner, of the society of which he or she is a part, and of the future. This part of the educator's role is not new, but it has increasing importance as he plans with others who are not so likely to give adequate attention to the various bases for curriculum decisions.

The professional curriculum planner should be alert to the necessity for relating schools to the surrounding political, economic, and social forces so that the means and goals of the curriculum harmonize with the lives of learners in particular circumstances.

Frequently, educators need to take a stand for what they believe, sharing what they know and feel. The public relies on the vision and courage of educators to present recommendations for curriculum improvement. Such recommendations should be related to a sense of purpose, the ability to think and analyze, and a proper respect for the requirements of human response. The educator, in recommending, must carefully avoid the appearance that the curriculum is solely the professional's business. Experience over time in working together helps to solve this problem.

A most important part of the teacher's role is to communicate to students his or her own valuing of learning. Teachers often motivate learners by their own motivations. Learners learn to like to learn from teachers who exhibit the intellectual accomplishment of regularly acquiring and acting on new knowledge.

Finally, professional educators must evaluate and interrelate the contributions from other planners and evolve a curriculum plan which they implement in their own classrooms or which they submit for the approval of the curriculum council or committee.

## MOVING AHEAD

If it is recognized that all public policy in education is the product of professional-lay interaction, then one of the main roadblocks to progress can be removed. Increasing the communication between scholars in various disciplines and professional educators would be a valuable step forward. A next step is to make greater use of that largely untapped resource—student contributions to curriculum planning. In each community, professional educators should move to establish the structural devices needed so that scholars, citizens, students, and professional educators may share in planning the curriculum needed. Because of the importance of education, each should be enabled to make his or her particular contribution to curriculum planning.

Who should plan the curriculum? Everyone interested in the future; everyone concerned for the quality of education being experienced by the leaders of the future who are now in our classrooms.

*Glen Hass* is Professor of Education, Emeritus, University of Florida, Gainesville.

## ADDITIONAL LEARNING ACTIVITIES

### Problems and Projects

1. Continue to develop a case problem about one school you know well. Relate the curricula and teaching in that school to curriculum criteria such as individual differences, relevance, continuity, student-teacher planning, and teaching of values.

2. The rationale for this section states that broad, general goals are needed to guide curriculum planning and teaching. I have found it useful to consider goals in four areas for such planning: education for citizenship, vocation, self-realization, and critical thinking. Do you agree with this statement of broad goals? Construct your own list of general goals for education. Also, consider your list in terms of the criterion "balance" presented in the article "Seeking Balance in the Curriculum" and in the rationale for this section.

3. Most curriculum leaders consider "cooperative planning" to be a curriculum criterion of major importance. The article "Who Should Plan the Curriculum?" by Glen Hass in this section defines who should be included in cooperative planning and the special role of each group of planners. Who do you think

should be included in the planning of curriculum and teaching? What role do you suggest for each planner? Do you agree or disagree with the statement, "The student is the major untapped resource in curriculum planning"? Why?

4. What do you consider to be the significance of the concept of educational excellence, as discussed by Duke in this section? In answering this question you may find it useful to review the article by Raywid, Tesconi, and Warren in Section 1 and to turn ahead to the section on "Excellence and Standards" in the article by Passow in Section 9.

5. What is a *balanced curriculum*? Do you agree with Kimball Wiles's ideas about balance in his article in this section? What is the relationship of values and goals and the four bases of the curriculum to the concept of a balanced curriculum?

6. Why does John Dewey believe that the effect of an original and powerful teacher is not "all to the good"? What remedy is available to offset the sometimes unfavorable effects of such teachers, according to Dewey? Have you personally known or been taught by this type of teacher? If so, what were the results in your experience?

7. Under what circumstances does Dewey consider science to be antagonistic to education as an art? When, according to Dewey, is "theory the most practical of all things"?

8. Do you share Fantini's views about the individualization of instruction in this section? Allan A. Glatthorn disagrees with Fantini's approach (see "On Finding Some Real Alternatives," *Today's Education* 66, no. 4 [November-December 1977]: 66–71 or *Curriculum Planning: A New Approach,* 4th ed., 1977, 302–306). Try to identify, describe and compare the learning environment that each of these educators would endorse. Which of the philosophical positions presented in Section 1 is closest to Glatthorn's position? Fantini's position?

9. Select ten goals or objectives found in a school's curriculum guide for any grade level or subject area, and outline the procedures and criteria that might be used for determining the extent to which each of them has been achieved.

10. Interview several community leaders who have no connection with the schools. Discuss with them what they think the goals of the schools ought to be. Write up your interview, describing the school envisioned by these community leaders. Compare it with your own ideas and those of Raywid, Tesconi, and Warren in Section 1.

11. In Section 1 it was suggested that each person who engages in curriculum planning or teaching should develop his or her own set of criteria for use in planning. Your criteria should reflect your own thinking and the particular area of the curriculum with which you are concerned, as well as the behavioral science theories and research to which we have given attention in the first six sections of this book. Think about how the criteria presented in this and previous sections may be related to your special area of the curriculum and list those criteria that seem most important from this perspective. Compare your list with that of others who are in your curriculum area, as well as those who are in other areas.

12. Review the summary of the criterion questions from the preceding five sections found in the rationale for this section. Try to decide which of the questions are related to each of the various "Steps in Curriculum Planning and Teaching," also in the rationale for this section.

13. The public schools have been the great equalizer for America's diversity, but, according to Frederick Weintraub, Alan Abeson, and Myron Brenton, this has not been true for handicapped children, who have often been blocked from entering the schoolhouse door. (See "New Education Policies for the Handicapped: The Quiet Revolution," *Phi Delta Kappan* 55, no. 8 (April 1974): 526–529, 569; and *Today's Education* 63, no. 2 (March–April 1974): 20–21, 23–25 for "Mainstreaming the Handicapped.") These authors say that all children should be placed in school in the most normal environment in which they can learn effectively. They are concerned about the "labeling" dilemma in which labels are used to justify isolation of and discrimination against children. Read one or both of these articles and then compare them to "Another Look at Mainstreaming" in this section. Which of the bases and criteria should be used to give support and direction to mainstreaming? Are there any advantages for the other learners when the handicapped are mainstreamed?

14. The Appendix of this book includes a list of books, each describing a school or school program. Select one that interests you and determine which of the curriculum criteria discussed in this section are adequately met by the present program. You might consider such criteria as relevance, individual differences, student-teacher planning, self-understanding, personalization of instruction, systematic planning, or flexibility. Try to suggest improvements in the program on the basis of one or more of these criteria.

15. Have your personal beliefs or values about the criteria that should be used in planning or evaluating a curriculum or teaching changed as a result of your experience with this section? If so, state what change has taken place, and relate it to one or more of the parts of this section (the rationale, an article, a post-assessment activity, etc.). Compare your ideas with those of the other members of your class.

## Films and Audiocassettes

*John I. Goodlad.* Audiocassette, 1984. Asserts that a more human curriculum is needed and that more should be done to create ideas than to evaluate the present educational system. Association for Supervision and Curriculum Development, 225 North Washington Street, Alexandria, Virginia 22314.

*Teachers, Parents, and Children: Growth through Cooperation.* 16 mm, color, 18 min., 1974. Explores the construction of alliances between families and teachers for better learning experiences. Davidson Films, 165 Tunstead Avenue, San Anselmo, California 94960.

*Instructional Development: People, Process, and Results.* 3 films, 16 mm, color, 52 min., 1976. "The People" (17 min.) describes the people orientation of instructional development. "The Process" presents goals, structure, and strategy, and an example is included. "The Results" (7 min.) illustrates applications made at Michigan State University. Instructional Media Center, Michigan State University, East Lansing, Michigan 48824.

# Books and Articles to Review

## General Sources on Curriculum and Instruction

Argyris, Chris; and Schon, Donald A. *Theory in Practice: Increasing Professional Effectiveness*. San Francisco: Jossey-Bass, Publisher, 1974.

ASCD Yearbook. *Considered Action for Curriculum Improvement*. Washington, D.C.: Association for Supervision and Curriculum Development, 1980.

Beauchamp, George A. *Curriculum Theory*, 4th ed. Itasca, IL: Peacock Publishing Co., 1981.

Bogdan, Richard. "A Closer Look at Mainstreaming." *Educational Forum* 47, no. 4 (Summer 1983): 425–434.

Brown, George I.; Phillips, Mark; and Shapiro, S. B. *Getting It All Together: Confluent Education*. Bloomington, IN: Phi Delta Kappa, 1976.

Brubaker, Dale L. *Curriculum Planning: The Dynamics of Theory and Practice*. Glenview, IL: Scott Foresman and Co., 1982.

Caruso, Joseph J. "Toward Shared Educational Policy Decision Making." *Educational Forum* 47, no. 4 (Summer 1983):453–458.

Caswell, Hollis L. "Persistent Curriculum Problems." *Educational Forum* 43, no. 1 (November 1978): 99–110.

Condasco, Francesco. "Bilingual Education: Overview and Inventory." *Educational Forum* 47, no. 3 (Spring 1983): 321–334.

Franklin, Barry. *Building the American Community: The School Curriculum and Social Control*. Philadelphia, PA: The Falmer Press, 1985.

Frymier, Jack. "The Annehurst System: Built on Recognition That People Are Different." *Phi Delta Kappan* 61, no. 10 (June 1980): 682–685.

—— with the assistance of Kathy Bobb. *Annehurst Curriculum Classification System: A Practical Way to Individualize Instruction*. West Lafayette, Indiana: Kappa Delta Pi Press, 1977.

Gage, N. L. *The Scientific Basis of the Art of Teaching*. New York: Teachers College Press, 1978.

Hook, Sidney; Kurtz, Paul; and Todorovich, Miro, eds. *The Philosophy of the Curriculum: The Need for General Education*. Buffalo, New York: Prometheus Books, 1975.

Huenecke, Dorothy. "What IS Curriculum Theorizing." *Educational Leadership* 39, no. 4 (January 1982): 290–294.

Hunkins, Francis P. *Curriculum Development: Program Improvement*. Columbus, OH: Charles E. Merrill Publishing Co., 1980.

Joyce, Bruce R.; Hersh, Richard; and McKibbon, Michael. *The Structure of School Improvement*. New York: Longman, Inc. 1983.

Kliebard, Herbert M. *The Struggle for the American Curriculum, 1893–1958*. Routledge and Kegan Paul/Methuen, Inc., 1986.

Noddings, Nell; and Shore, Paul J. *Awakening the Inner Eye: Intuition in Education*. New York: Teachers College Press, 1984.

Ornstein, Allan C. "Curriculum Contrasts: A Historical Overview." *Phi Delta Kappan* 63, no. 6 (February 1982): 404–408.

Posner, George J.; and Rudnitsky, Alan N. *Course Design: A Guide to Curriculum Development for Teachers*. New York: Longman, Inc., 1978.

Rothrock, Dayton. "The Rise and Decline of Individualized Instruction." *Educational Leadership* 39, no. 7 (April 1982): 528–530.

Sapher, John; and King, Matthew. "Good Seeds Grow in Strong Cultures." *Educational Leadership* 42, no. 6 (March 1985): 62–74.

Schubert, William H. *Curriculum Books: The First Eighty Years*. New York: University Press of America, Inc., 1984.

Schubert, William H. *Curriculum: Perspective, Paradigm, and Possibility*. New York: Macmillan Co., 1986.

Seeley, David S. "Educational Partnership and the Dilemmas of School Reform." *Phi Delta Kappan* 65, no. 6 (February 1984): 383–388.

Taba, Hilda. *Curriculum Development: Theory and Practice*. New York: Harcourt, Brace, and World, 1962.

Tanner, Daniel; and Tanner, Laurel N. *Curriculum Development: Theory Into Practice*. New York: Macmillan Publishing Co., 1975.

Unruh, Glenys; and Unruh, Adolph. *Curriculum Developmental Problems, Processes and Progress*. San Francisco: McCutchan Publishing Co., 1984.

Walker, Decker F. "Reflections on the Educational Potential and Limitations of Microcomputers." *Phi Delta Kappan* 65, no. 2 (October 1983): 103–107.

## On Curriculum Evaluation

Bellack, Arno A., and Kliebard, Herbert M., eds. *Curriculum and Evaluation*. Berkeley, California: McCutchan Publishing Corp., 1977.

Bowers, John J. *Planning A Program Evaluation: An Educator's Handbook*. Philadelphia: Research for Better Schools, 1978.

Gephart, William J.; Ingle, Robert B.; and Marshall, Frederick J. *Evaluation in the Affective Domain*. Bloomington, Indiana: Phi Delta Kappa, 1979.

Guba, Egon, and Lincoln, Yvonne. *Effective Evaluation*. San Francisco, CA: Jossey-Bass, 1981.

Hamilton, David; Jenkins, David; King, Christine; et al. *Beyond the Numbers Game: A Reader in Educational Evaluation*. London: Macmillan Education, Ltd., 1977.

Lewy, Arieh, ed. *Handbook of Curriculum Evaluation*. New York: Longman Inc., 1977.

Nowakowski, Jeri Ridings. "On Educational Evaluation: A Conversation with Ralph Tyler." *Educational Leadership* 40, no. 8 (May 1983): 24–29.

Stake, Robert E. "The Countenance of Educational Evaluation." *Teachers College Record* 68 (April 1967): 523–540.

Stufflebeam, Daniel L. *Educational Evaluation and Decision Making*. Bloomington, Indiana: Phi Delta Kappa, 1971.

Talmadge, Harriet. "Evaluating the Curriculum: What, Why, and How." *NASSP Bulletin* 69, no. 481 (May 1985): 1–8.

Tyler, Ralph W. *Basic Principles of Curriculum and Instruction*. Chicago: The University of Chicago Press, 1949.

Tyler, Ralph W.; Gagné, Robert M.; and Scriven, Michael. *Perspectives of Curriculum Evaluation*. Chicago: Rand McNally & Co., 1967.

Willis, George, ed. *Qualitative Evaluation: Concepts and Cases In Curriculum Criticism*. Berkeley, California: McCutchan Publishing Corporation, 1978.

# II

# *The Curriculum*

# 7

# *Childhood Education*

## PREREQUISITES

1.  Reading Sections 1 through 6 of this book.
2.  The development of, and ability to use, a set of curriculum criteria to describe and evaluate a curriculum plan. You must be able to use this set of criteria in order to analyze critically and make curriculum and teaching decisions regarding programs and trends and teaching practices described in this section.

## RATIONALE

All curriculum planners and teachers should be acquainted with the goals and trends in education at all levels, regardless of the level of the program of education at which they work. For instance, you should know about goals and trends in childhood education whether or not you plan to work at this level. You will be better able to plan a curriculum or teach at one of the other levels if you have this information. This view is based on such curriculum criteria as continuity in learning, balance in the curriculum, and provision for individual differences.

This section is now called Childhood Education rather than Preschool and Elementary School. In keeping with the definition of *curriculum* presented in Section 1, the focus will be on programs of education rather than exclusively on school programs.

The graded elementary school was established in the nineteenth century when there was little knowledge of the nature and extent of individual differences or of the stages of human development. It was developed in conformity with the then prevalent ideas of child development and education. It was conceived in the faith that all men are created equal and that individual differences in education are undesirable.

The elementary school often has the most intense impact of any school in the educational system; the year the child spends in first grade is one-sixth of his or her entire life to that point. Therefore, the lack of adequate provision for individual differences frequently can result in intense feelings of failure and rejection as well as retardation or elimination from school for some children. Failure to achieve in any of the essential functions at the elementary school level can exact a high price at other levels where the resulting deficiency can hardly be overcome. According to Ernest L. Boyer, President of the Carnegie Foundation for the Advancement of Teaching, ". . . the early years are transcendentally the most important, and if this nation wishes ultimately to achieve excellence, we will give greater priority and attention to the early years and start affirming elementary teachers instead of college professors as the centerpiece of learning."

A major problem for the elementary school is to establish effective contact with each child. Provision for *individual differences,* and *flexibility* and *continuity in learning* are thus curriculum criteria of major significance.

A significant thrust toward *early childhood education* will continue to be one of the most significant educational trends of the 1980s. A new study of the United States Census Bureau shows that in 1980 almost 96 percent of all five-year-olds in the United States were attending kindergarten, compared with 65 percent in 1965. To-day there are public kindergartens in every state. More than 2.5 million children nationwide were enrolled in kindergarten in 1980 according to the National Center for Educational Statistics. Throughout the country full-day kindergarten programs are increasing, mainly as a result of studies confirming the value of early childhood education. The New York State Board of Regents is seeking the creation of formal public school programs for four-year-olds throughout that state.

Early childhood education continues to grow despite reductions in federal funding for education at this level. This growth is due in part to the extensive body of research on the importance of early learning experiences. A study based on the results of more than fifty evaluation projects showed that former participants in early childhood programs had improved reading skills, more mature behavior, and lower absenteeism in the elementary school. The growth of early childhood programs is also due to *human development* and *learning theories* that emphasize the need for early stimulation and encouragement of curiosity in infants and young children if their intellectual potential is to be developed. Research indicates that much of a child's intellectual development has taken place by the age of six. Instruction at the preschool level helps increase a child's interest in learning at an age when the impact may be lifelong.

*Follow Through,* which is designed to meet the physical, psychological, and instructional needs of children from low income families, helped hundreds of thousands of children during the 1970s. It uses the *planned variation* approach, which sets up a variety of programs for children and then evaluates those approaches over a number of years. This is, of course, based on the criterion of *individual differences.*

As early childhood education continues to grow, sending better prepared children into the existing elementary schools, the schools will almost certainly come under fierce pressures for change. What is needed now is a focus on (1) the needs of children and how they can be met, and (2) planning for the curriculum changes that must be made at the childhood education level when many children (but not all) bring two, three, or even four years of carefully planned experiences to the primary school.

Traditionally, parents have been told to bring their children to the elementary school door and then to leave. But the increasing emphasis on the importance of parents in early mental development suggests that the parents should have a much more active role in programs of education. This emphasizes the need for our new definition of *curriculum.* It also implies the need for changes in childhood education, in the roles of childhood education teachers, and in teacher education programs for teachers of this age group.

A number of reports urging educational reform were issued between 1982 and 1984. Most of these reports were focused on the high school and gave little attention to childhood education. However, one of them, *A Place Called School,* by John Goodlad, proposed that each child enter school in the month of his or her fourth birthday and finish at age sixteen. Goodlad states that a wait of a year for a child of four is a delay of a quarter of the life lived so far. The proposed practice would create the possibility of a warm welcome for the newcomers since school could begin for each of them with a birthday party. Then they become givers of parties for those who follow. The tumultuous business of socializing twenty-five or more beginners each September would be completely eliminated and schooling could immediately take on a highly individualized character. Teachers could become acquainted with just two or three children and their families at the time of admission and the children would come into a classroom environment already stabilized.

Social changes are putting enormous new pressures on the elementary school. Altered life styles, economic forces, changing immigration patterns, and all of the social forces discussed in Section 2 are having major impact on childhood education. Articles in Section 2 by Fersh, Bohannan, Cremin, Shane, Papert, Cherlin and Furstenberg, and Raffa are particularly pertinent to your study of the social forces now affecting elementary education. In this section, articles by Miklethun, Krogh and Lamme, Comer, and Cole examine social issues regarding the family, moral development, work, culture, and the world community which have particular significance for these learners.

Recent studies of learning style, teaching style, and cognition have major importance for curriculum planning and teaching at the elementary education level. Look again at the articles by McDaniel, Gregorc, Friedman and Alley, Hyman and Rosoff, Levy, and Eisner, in Sections 4 and 5. "Research, Reading Instruction, and Children's Learning of the First R" in this section draws heavily on the research regarding learning style, cognition and knowledge. "Problem Solving: Encouraging Active Learning" is also based on this research.

Human development theories and research are central to the work of the childhood education teacher and curriculum planner; all of the articles in Section 3 should be reconsidered in discussing it. All of the philosophical positions presented in Section 1 continue to influence childhood education. In this section the articles by Katz and Butler focus on values and goals of education for children.

What should be the *objectives* of childhood education programs (ages two through eleven or twelve)? Many goals might be suggested; some are derived from social forces, some from human development and learning theories, and some from theories about knowledge and cognition. The list would surely include many of the following *objectives:*

1. Helping learners to develop feelings of trust.
2. Developing autonomy and initiative.
3. Introducing structure and organization without stopping self-expression and creativity.
4. Developing social skills through large group, small group, and individual activities.
5. Providing adequate and appropriate physical and health education.
6. Teaching the fundamental skills of communication and computation.
7. Establishing a desire to learn and an appreciation for education by teaching under conditions that enhance interest and curiosity.
8. Developing interests in many areas by exposure to many fields of knowledge and experience.
9. Developing feelings of self-worth and security by providing varied experiences on which each child can base and build his or her success.
10. Providing many opportunities for achievement for each child.
11. Developing appreciation for the worth and differences of others.
12. Developing the processes of conceptualizing, problem solving, self-direction, and creating.
13. Developing a concern for the environment, the community, the society, the future, and the welfare of others.
14. Helping learners to examine and develop moral values.

What additions or changes would you propose for this list?

To attain goals like these in programs of childhood education, many innovations are being proposed and tried. The following list of *innovations* and *trends* in childhood education includes references to pertinent articles. The list is arranged alphabetically, and all articles are included in this section unless otherwise noted.

1. *Active learning:* "Early Education Principles and Computer Practices," "Television and Values" (Section 2); "A Primer on Motivation" (Section 4); "Structures in Learning" (Section 5)
2. *Alternative programs:* "Humanistic Early Childhood Education"; "Research, Reading Instruction, and Children's Learning of the First R"

3. *Arts-centered curriculum:* "Television and Values" (Section 2); "The Role of the Arts in Cognition and Curriculum" (Section 5)

4. *Career education:* "Humanistic Early Childhood Education"; "Getting A Headstart on Career Choices"

5. *Cooperative learning:* "Children's Literature and Moral Development"; "Another Look at Mainstreaming" (Section 6); "Who Should Plan the Curriculum" (Section 6)

6. *Experience-focused curricula:* "The Young Reach Out to the Old in Shaker Heights"; "Problem Solving: Encouraging Active Learning"; "Structures in Learning" (Section 5)

7. *Future studies:* "Humanistic Early Childhood Education"; "Why Study the Future" (Section 2); "The American Family in the Year 2000" (Section 2); "Schools of the Future" (Section 2); "Society Will Balk, but the Future May Demand a Computer for Each Child" (Section 2)

8. *Global education:* "Multicultural Education and Global Education"

9. *Interdisciplinary learning:* "Multicultural Education and Global Education"; "Getting a Headstart on Career Choices"

10. *Individualized learning:* "Research, Reading Instruction, and Children's Learning of the First R"; "A Contemporary Approach to Individualization" (Section 6); "Children Think with Whole Brains" (Section 5); "It's Joe Again" (Section 5); "Teaching to the Whole Brain" (Section 5)

11. *Intergenerational learning:* "What is Basic for Young Children"; "The Young Reach Out to the Old in Shaker Heights"

12. *Learning style matching:* "Learning/Teaching Styles: Applying the Principles" (Section 4); "Matching Learning Styles and Teaching Styles" (Section 4)

13. *Mainstreaming:* "Another Look at Mainstreaming" (Section 6)

14. *Microcomputers in the classroom:* "Early Education Principles and Computer Practices"

15. *Moral education:* "What Is Basic for Young Children"; "Children's Literature and Moral Development"; "The Cognitive-Developmental Approach to Moral Education" (Section 3); "Now Then, Mr. Kohlberg, About Moral Development in Women" (Section 3)

16. *Multicultural education:* "Multicultural Education and Global Education"

17. *Parent-teacher-student planning:* "Getting a Headstart on Career Choices"

18. *Peer teaching:* "What Is Basic for Young Children"; "Another Look at Mainstreaming" (Section 6)

19. *Problem solving:* "Problem Solving: Encouraging Active Learning"; "Children's Literature and Moral Development"; "Getting a Headstart on Career Choices"; "Early Education Principles and Computer Practices"; "Television and Values" (Section 2); "Structures in Learning" (Section 5)

20. *Self-realization education:* "Humanistic Early Childhood Education"; "What Is Basic for Young Children"; "Getting a Headstart on Career Choices"; "Multicultural Education and Global Education"; "It's Joe Again" (Section 5)

21. *Student-teacher planning:* "Getting A Headstart on Career Choices"; "Who Should Plan the Curriculum" (Section 6)

22. *Using community resources:* "The Young Reach Out to the Old in Shaker Heights"; "Getting a Headstart on Career Choices"
23. *Using TV in teaching:* "Television and Values" (Section 2)

*Will these innovations and trends, if adopted, provide needed changes in programs of childhood education?* Will they provide improved implementation of the objectives of childhood education? Will they provide the means for new relevance, flexibility, and continuity in these programs, as well as ways to establish effective contact with each child as an individual?

We must evaluate the innovations and trends in comparison with present programs. The consideration of (1) objectives, (2) the four bases of the curriculum, and (3) other curriculum criteria provides professional means for making these decisions.

In the List of Books and Articles to Review at the end of this section, many of the sources listed have one or more of the numbers in the preceding list of trends entered at the end of the citations. These numbers will help you find other recent articles and books on those childhood education trends and innovations which particularly interest you.

## OBJECTIVES

Your objectives in studying childhood education as part of the curriculum should be as follows:

1. To be familiar with the objectives, current innovations, and recent trends in childhood education.
2. To be able to explain the functions and goals of childhood education as part of the total curriculum.
3. To be able to use general objectives, the objectives of childhood education, the curriculum bases, and other criteria in making curriculum and/or instruction decisions regarding present programs, as well as regarding proposed innovations and trends.
4. To be able to suggest improvements in childhood education curriculum plans through the decisions made in number 3.

## PREASSESSMENT

1. Identify each of the childhood education innovations and trends listed in the rationale, and discuss their implications.
2. Evaluate each of the trends in terms of objectives, bases of curriculum, and curriculum criteria, such as individual differences, balance, and continuity.
3. Select any childhood education curriculum plan, and describe and analyze it in terms of general objectives, childhood education objectives, the four curriculum

bases, your list of curriculum criteria, and innovations and trends at this level of education.
4. Suggest improvements or changes in the curriculum plan in number 3 in the light of your analysis.

In answering numbers 3 and 4 of the preassessment, you might choose to analyze the curriculum plans used in "Children's Literature and Moral Development" or "Research, Reading Instruction, and Children's Learning of the First R" in this section or in "Television and Values" in Section 2.

## LEARNING ACTIVITIES

Articles in this section will help you understand the purposes and functions of childhood education as an important part of the curriculum. They will also acquaint you with the problems, as well as the innovations and trends, of programs of childhood education. Other learning alternatives are suggested at the end of this section.

## POSTASSESSMENT

After attempting the preassessment you may do *one or more* of the following:

1. Ask your instructor whether you are ready for a postassessment evaluation on childhood education. Most students will need further work on this topic.
2. Read the articles on childhood education in this section and try to determine how the practices, trends, and innovations discussed in each article should be considered in curriculum planning and teaching at the childhood education level.
3. Choose additional activities and readings or films from those listed at the end of this section.
4. Look for other films, books, or articles on childhood education that are in your library or media center.
5. Discuss the reading you have done and the films you have viewed with your fellow students. The key question: How should the goals, practices, trends, and innovations you've studied affect curriculum planning at the childhood education level? How should they be considered in planning for teaching?
6. When you are ready, ask your instructor for advice on a suitable postassessment for you for this topic. Satisfactory completion of number 1 under Problems and Projects at the end of this section might be a possibility. Or satisfactory written completion of the preassessment for this section, after completing other learning activities, might be a satisfactory postassessment. Consult your instructor about this. You can evaluate your ability to do these postassessment activities before seeing the instructor.

# What Is Basic for Young Children?

## LILIAN G. KATZ

All of us who teach young children often express disappointment over not having had time to do all we had planned to in any given week, or month, or year. We cannot introduce all the topics of potential interest, all the activities that might stimulate learning, all the materials that might help develop skills. Teaching always involves choices. From among the virtually infinite variety of possible topics, ideas, skills and activities, we can only address a few.

On what bases are our choices made? Probably *tradition* accounts for a large proportion of our selections: traditional topics, materials, holidays, games and activities. To some extent the *availability of resources* determines what activities we select. Often choices are made for us by school district mandates or by central office officials, state or federal funding agencies, or boards of directors of day care centers.

Busy teachers have all too little time to examine the bases upon which they select the components of their programs. Most of us do well to cope with the day-to-day demands of our roles. Recently I had an experience with a group of students that caused me to step back and reflect on the underlying assumptions upon which early childhood programming might be based. I hope these reflections will help your own thinking as you look for the bases on which you make the choices in your program.

The occasion that stimulated my thinking was a seminar with a group of young, zealous students who were discussing their reactions and impressions from working in day care centers. One young woman, Susan, spoke of her experience in deeply disappointed tones. Among the complaints against the program she listed was that the director refused to let the children have small animals in the day care center. I listened appreciatively for a while to Susan's righteous indignation, and then asked her as gently as I could: "Let's speculate! What do you think are the chances that a child could develop into a wholesome adult without having had animals to play with in the day care center?"

After a few moments' thought, Susan indicated that the chances were fairly good. "What about finger paint? Block play? Can a child grow into normal adulthood without them in the day care center?" I asked. A lively discussion followed these questions, leading all of us to search for answers to the question, "What does each child have to have for wholesome development?" I want here to share with you my own answers to this question by offering seven interrelated propositions. I hope these propositions will be helpful to you as you consider how you might have responded.

The seven propositions below are built upon an assumed first principle I have discussed elsewhere (Katz, 1975); namely, that whatever is good for children is only good for them in the "right" or optimum proportions. Another way of stating this principle is that just because something is good for children, more of it is not necessarily better for them. This applies to so many influences on children's development that it could be called the "Law of Optimum Effects." Among the many examples of influences that should be experienced in optimum amounts are:

From an address presented at the Australian Pre-school Association 14th National Conference, May 15, 1976. Used by permission of the author and the Australian Pre-school Association, Inc.

attention, affection, stimulation, independence, novelty, choices of activities, etc. All of the latter can be thought to be "good" for children, but only in optimum amounts, frequencies or intensities.

Taking the first principle of optimum effects as fundamental, we can return to the question of what children have to have for wholesome development.

*Proposition One: The young child has to have a deep sense of safety.* I am referring here to psychological safety, which we usually speak of as a sense of "security." Over the last twenty years or so the term "security" has come to be used as a cliché. By psychological safety I refer to the subjective feeling of being connected and attached to one or more others. Experiencing oneself as attached, connected—or safe—comes not just from being loved, but from *feeling* loved, *feeling* wanted, *feeling* significant, etc., to an optimum (not maximum) degree. Note that the emphasis here is more on *feeling* loved and wanted than on *being* loved and wanted.

As I understand early development, feeling strongly bonded or attached comes not just from the warmth and kindness of caretakers. The feelings are a consequence of the child perceiving that what he (or she) does, or does not do, *really matters* to others—matters so much that they will pick him up, comfort him, get angry and even scold him. (After all, we do not become angry with someone we are indifferent to.) Safety, then, grows out of being able to trust people to respond not just warmly but *really*.

This proposition seems to apply to all children, whether they are wealthy or poor, at home or at school; whether they are handicapped or normal, at whatever their ages, until perhaps young adulthood.

*Proposition Two: Every child has to have adequate—not excessive—self-esteem.* At first glance this proposition seems to be quite simple. But a few comments are in order. It is useful to remember that one does not acquire self-esteem at a certain moment in childhood and then have it forever. Self-esteem is nurtured by and responsive to the significant others—adults, siblings and other children—throughout the growing years.

Even more important to keep in mind is that one cannot have self-esteem in a vacuum. Our self-esteem results from evaluation of ourselves against criteria. We evaluate ourselves as having high or low esteem against criteria we acquire very early in life. We acquire them in our families, neighborhoods, ethnic groups and later on from peer groups and the larger community. Early in life these criteria against which we come to evaluate ourselves as acceptable, worthwhile—against which we judge or experience ourselves as lovable—vary from family to family. In some families beauty is a criterion; in others, neatness, or athletic ability, or toughness is a criterion. Consider that such characteristics as being dainty, or quiet, or talkative, or pious, or well-mannered, or academically precocious, etc., might constitute the criteria against which young children are judged lovable, worthy, and acceptable.

Each family has of course the right, if not the duty, to establish what it considers to be the criteria against which esteem is accorded. The process and the patterns by which such criteria are implemented are most likely unself-conscious in formulation as well as expression. One of our responsibilities as educators is to be sensitive to the family's *own* criteria. We may not agree with a family's definition of the "good boy" or the "good girl." But we would be very unwise to downgrade, undermine, or in other ways violate the self-esteem values the children bring with them, even though we must help children acquire criteria that serve to protect the welfare of the whole group in our care. I cannot think of any way it could help a child to have his respect for his family and his family's criteria of the "good person" undermined.

I suggest that children have to have optimum self-esteem wherever they are, whether they are wealthy or poor, handicapped or normal, throughout their growing years.

*Proposition Three: Every child has to feel, or experience his/her life as worth living, reasonably satisfying, interesting and authentic.* I have in mind here the potential hazard inherent in modern industrialized societies of creating environments and experiences for young children that are superficial, phony, shallow and trivial.

This proposition suggests that we involve children in activities, and interactions about activities, that are real to them, significant and intriguing to them. It suggests also that we resist the temptation to settle just for what amuses them. I would suggest as a criterion of appropriateness for children's activities that they give children opportunities to operate on their own experiences, to reconstruct their own environments and give us opportunities to help children to learn what meanings to assign to their experiences.

As I visit early childhood programs in both developed and developing countries, I wonder whether people have taken our longstanding emphasis on warmth and kindness, acceptance and love to mean: "Let's be nice to children!" As I watch adults being "nice" and "kind" and "gentle," I often speculate as to whether if I were a child in such a pleasant environment I would look at the adults and say to myself—everybody is kind and sweet, but inside them is there anybody home (Katz, 1977)?

It seems to me that children should be able to feel that their lives are real, authentic, worth living and satisfying whether they are at home, in schools or day care centers throughout their growing years.

*Proposition Four: Young children need adults or older children who help them to make sense of their own experiences.* By the time we meet the young children in our care, they have already acquired some understandings or constructions of their experiences. Their understandings or constructions may be incorrect or inaccurate although developmentally appropriate. As I see it, our major responsibility is to help the young to improve, extend, refine, develop and deepen their own understandings or constructions of their own worlds. As they grow older and reach primary school age, we may help them with their understandings of other people's worlds. Indeed, increasing refinement and deepening of understandings is a lifelong process.

What do young children need or want to make sense of? Certainly people, what they do, what they will do next, how they feel; how things around them are made and how they work; how they themselves and other living things grow; where people and things come from. The list is endless.

If we are to help young children to improve and develop their understandings of their experiences, we must *uncover* what those understandings are. The uncovering that we do, or that occurs as children engage in the activities we provide, helps us to make good decisions about what to *cover*, or what subsequent activities to plan.

Youngsters need help in making sense of their experiences wherever they are: at home or in programs, whatever their backgrounds, throughout their growing years.

*Proposition Five: Young children have to have adults who accept the authority that is theirs by virtue of their greater experience, knowledge, and wisdom.* This proposition is based on the assumption that neither as parents nor as educators are we caught between the extremes of authoritarianism or permissiveness. Authoritarianism may be defined as the exercise of power without warmth, encouragement or explanation. Permissiveness may be seen as the abdication of power but offering children warmth, encouragement, and support as they seem to need it. I am suggesting that young children have to have, instead of these extremes, adults who are *authoritative;* i.e., adults who exercise their very considerable power over the lives of young children *with* warmth, support, encouragement and adequate explanations. The concept of authoritativeness also includes treating children with respect; i.e., treating their opinions, feelings, wishes and ideas, etc., as valid even when we disagree with them. To respect people we agree with is no great problem; respecting those whose ideas, wishes, and feelings are different from ours may be a mark of wisdom in parents and genuine professionalism in teachers.

The combination of the exercise of optimum power and optimum warmth implied in authoritativeness is helpful for children wherever they are, whatever their background, throughout their youth.

*Proposition Six: Young children need optimum association with adults and older children who exemplify the personal qualities we want them to acquire.* Make your own list of the qualities you want the young children in your care to acquire. There may be some differences among us. But it is likely that there are some qualities we all want all children to have; e.g., the capacity to care for and about others, honesty, kindness, acceptance of those who are different from themselves, the love of learning, and so forth.

This proposition suggests that we look around the children's environments and ask to what extent do our children have contact with people who exhibit these qualities? We might ask also: To what extent do our children observe people who are attractive and glamorous counter-examples of the qualities we want to foster? It seems to me that children need communities or societies that take the necessary steps to protect them from excessive exposure to violence and crime while their characters are still in formation.

The role and significance of adequate adult models seems valid for all children wherever they are, wherever they come from, throughout their developing years.

*Proposition Seven: Children need relationships or experiences with adults who are willing to take a stand on what is worth doing, worth having, worth knowing, and worth caring about.* This proposition seems to belabor the obvious. But in an age of increasing emphasis on pluralism, multiculturalism, and community participation, professionals are increasingly hesitant and apologetic about their own values. Such hesitancy in taking a stand on what is worthwhile causes us to give our children unclear signals about what is expected, and what is worth knowing and doing. When we do take a stand, we cannot guarantee that our children will accept or agree with our version of the good life. Nor do we imply that we reject others' versions of the good life. We must, in fact, cultivate our capacities to respect alternative definitions of the worthwhile life. But when we take a stand, with quiet courage and conviction, we help the young in that they can more easily see us as thinking and caring individuals who have enough self-respect to respect our own values as well as others'. Such thinking and caring adults seem to be important to children wherever they are, wherever they come from, throughout development.

In summary, all seven propositions hang together on the central question of our responsibilities for the quality of the daily lives of all our children—wherever they spend those days, throughout the long years of growth and development.

**REFERENCES**

Katz, Lilian G. "Psychological Development and Education in Early Childhood." In *Second Collection of Papers for*

*Teachers,* L. G. Katz. Urbana, IL: ERIC Clearinghouse on Early Childhood Education, 1975.

———. "Teachers in Preschools: Problems and Prospects." *International Journal of Early Childhood* 9,1 (1977): 111–23.

*Lilian G. Katz* is Professor of Early Childhood Education and Director ERIC/ECE, University of Illinois, Urbana.

# Humanistic Early Childhood Education—A Challenge Now and in the Future

## ANNIE L. BUTLER

Children who are currently enrolled in early childhood programs will be the young adults of the twenty-first century. They will then be moving into positions of leadership and much of the responsibility for the kind of world that will exist in the first quarter of the twenty-first century will rest on their shoulders.

In one sense this is not different from the past. Responsibilities have always been passed downward from the older generation to the younger generation. What is different is that young people of today will face a more rapidly changing and demanding world than any generation in the past. They will have a greater need to understand the nature of change in the modern world. They also will have to acquire greater humanistic skills, greater adaptability, and greater creativity as they will face a future which is so unknown that it cannot be handled as in the past.

## IMPACT OF SOCIAL AND TECHNOLOGICAL CHANGES

In the future, parents and teachers will continue to be guides but no elders know what the children of today know about the world in which they were born. Margaret Mead (1970) indicated that we are developing a new cultural form called "prefiguration" which will depend on a different relationship between adults and children from that which existed in the past. According to Mead there must be a continuing dialogue between the old and the young in which the young, free to act on their own initiative, can lead their elders in the direction of the unknown. Direct participation of the young with their experiential knowledge is required to build a viable future. This prefigurative culture differs from the society of our pioneer forefathers in which culture remained largely unchanged as it was

From *Viewpoints in Teaching and Learning* 55, no. 3 (Summer 1979): 83–90. Used by permission of the publisher, School of Education, Indiana University.

passed from one generation to another. It also differs from the society of the early twentieth century in which the nuclear family was established. In this new unit close relationship between three generations was no longer possible and generation breaks became gradually accepted along with the expectation that each generation would experience a different technological world.

During the past decade, futurists have been warning us that unless we believe that events of the future are inevitable we must consider what kinds of persons are needed to help us obtain not merely possible and probable futures but also preferable futures. We now have the capacity to interfere on a large scale with natural environmental processes. Science and technology permit us to create new realities, yet our understanding of the new dimensions of change and of their immediate and long-range implications have not kept pace with the changes themselves. Brown (1978) has warned that the world stands on the threshold of a basic social transformation. This "revolution," like earlier ones, could raise us to a higher level of humanity. But unlike others it must be reckoned with in advance. Brown further warns that the forthcoming changes will permeate every dimension of human existence: lifestyles, land ownership patterns, economic structures, family size, international relations, and the educational system. The accommodations, which must be made by the beginning of the twenty-first century, will present an enormous challenge to all of us. They will put great stress on individuals and institutions to create new social structures and an economic system different from any we know today. These changes present a problem for early childhood education, and for all education, that forces us to examine our practices and to plan ahead for the kind of education that will be needed to enable us to make the needed accommodations and to plan the required transformations so that we will indeed have a preferable future.

## HUMANISTIC CHARACTERISTICS NEEDED IN THE FUTURE

It is important for us to understand how change affects our lives so we can successfully search out ways to respond to it creatively and to become more adaptable than ever before. A careful analysis of the kind of person futurists say will be needed to create a preferable future reveals the following list of characteristics:

1. *Ability to cope with change.* Has a high level of adaptability, can adapt to constant and rapid change.
2. *A strong positive self-concept.* Has a sense of confidence and trust in one's ability.
3. *A sense of purpose.* Can live purposefully, and compassionately with others.
4. *Future-focused role-image.* Sees oneself in a future role, has a satisfying personal professional self-image.
5. *Autonomous.* Is an inner directed individual, has strength to bear the unknown and peculiar, able to deal with strangeness, can be self-pacing in maintaining oneself within the adaptive range.
6. *Clarity of values.* Has a basis for pursuing one direction instead of another; recognizes when things have greater value, makes difficult value choices.
7. *Interpersonal skills.* Has ability to reach agreement through interaction and reasonable compromise, can work with others in cooperation and friendship, can be a part of a unified effort, can engage in supportive and relevant interpersonal transactions, has skills necessary to supply honest and perceptive emotional support.
8. *Sense of mastery.* Has a sense of control over one's destiny, a feeling of confidence, self-realization.
9. *Acceptant of responsibility.* Can make up one's mind and assume responsibility, courage to do what needs to be done.

10. *Learning abilities.* Has skill in "learning how to learn" more than ability to learn a specific subject.
11. *Capacity for innovation.* Uses imagination creatively; uses creative strategies for shaping, deflecting, accelerating, or decelerating change selectively.
12. *Openness.* Has a quality of being receptive to different points of view, ability to express feelings constructively.

Educators cannot simply go on doing the same things that have been done for generations. From now on learning must assume the presence of a time perspective geared to the future. Learning must be intimately bound up with the future. It must help structure and give meaning to the future. Education must be more experimental and open ended.

Planning future-oriented educational programs may be even more complex than it may seem considering the characteristics of young children. The question that has to be answered is: What are the characteristics of young children that, if encouraged, will help them be better able to cope with the world of tomorrow? What emphases in early childhood education can we plan now that will not violate the present orientation of young children?

## EARLY CHILDHOOD EDUCATION IN THE FUTURE

In building a world that meets human needs, we must start with the needs of infants. Beginning in infancy we can build for contact with other human beings, with the physical environment, with the living world and with the experiences through which the individual's full humanity can be realized. Parents and educators have to ensure that children's lives have a very strong security base from the very beginning and that their experiences include contacts with persons of differ-

ent ages, both within and outside the family, who may look different and speak differently from members of the family, and with materials, both raw and manufactured, that their world comprises. This may mean that for some children educators will assume some roles and responsibilities that have traditionally been assumed by the family; for other children the family will assume some responsibilities that have traditionally been assumed by educators. With changes in family size and lifestyles and as personal computers come into general use both in homes and at school, we will have to examine the appropriateness of roles that until now have been generally accepted.

## Processing of Information

In a rapidly changing world the processing of large amounts of information will become a prerequisite for both planning and decision making. Young children of the future must acquire and process far more information than ever before, and they must do this at high rates of speed.

It has been predicted (Banet, 1979) that the factor that will change teaching and learning most by the end of the twentieth century will be the technology of microelectronics as applied to the design of computers and related information-processing devices. Already microelectronic technology has made possible the $5 hand calculator and the $8 watch. Every current use of paper in education can be enhanced by electronic systems. Tiny, cheap computers and related electronic devices, all "talking" to each other will have more uses in education than paper and ink, blackboard and chalk (Banet, 1979).

From the viewpoint of early childhood education, the feature of computers that holds the most promise in the preschool and elementary years is their use to present gamelike situations with immediate feedback. Computer games can be used to individualize learning goals and content in open learning settings relieving the teacher of some of the uncreative tasks associated with the mastery of basic skills. Interactive electronic systems can be used to invite children to explore many domains of knowledge. They also can be used to support the human values that allow for children to achieve broad competence in a developmentally appropriate manner. From a humanistic point of view, what is important is that we avoid the typical programmed instruction approach to computer assisted instruction and look for ways of inventing games that will stimulate learning of basic concepts and the application of creative problem-solving techniques.

## Development of Motivation to Learn

We need to consider how to encourage the child to want to learn more and more. The responsibility extends beyond the actual facts or skills learned to the development of a joy of learning and the motivation to move on to new and more stimulating tasks. It is important that we create an atmosphere in which children have many opportunities to explore, touch, taste, and experiment. Further, we must help them want to communicate the results of their exploration and find answers to questions that arise from it. Already the world of young children has expanded so that understanding of society in our country is not enough as children's lives are influenced by our interdependence with other nations. What they can do and where they can go are dependent on energy obtainable from other nations. They also may have classmates of different nationalities who speak different languages. Coping with rapid changes requires that learning continue throughout the individual's lifetime. Young children cannot learn all there is to be known but they can acquire a zest for learning that will continue into adulthood.

## Development of a Positive Self-Concept

The emphasis on development of a strong, positive self-concept is not new to early childhood educators. What is new are the circumstances under which it is to be done. The difficulty arises because in the midst of change a young child must be provided with a continuous and familiar and trustworthy environment. This stability is necessary for the child to learn that things will be here tomorrow that are here today, and that a hand reaching out will find what it is seeking, not only in the physical aspects of the environment but also in relationships. A fundamental principle to be put into effect will be the recognition that human beings are not all the same and that children of different psychological temperaments will need to receive different educations. Children must experience acceptance of different cultural backgrounds whatever the backgrounds happen to be and the subtle differences in the treatment of boys and girls must be examined to eliminate those that may cause one sex to feel less valued than the other.

## Development of Feelings of Confidence

School experiences should enable children to see themselves as competent to do the things that are expected of them. The classroom, therefore, must provide for a variety of abilities and must aid children in selecting activities that are challenging but that at the same time allow them to be successful. A gradual building of successes on successes should enable the child to move with confidence toward new ideas and approaches. Experiences with other people also must be positive. Children must like others and feel liked;

their behavior must be reasonably acceptable to other children and adults.

## Focus on the Development of Coping Skills

Concern over coping skills is only a new slant on an old emphasis. The young child's interest and involvement in the process of learning provides the basis for helping the child to identify multiple ways to find out about things and to solve problems. It is important to provide children with varied real situations in which a variety of coping skills can be used, and to facilitate their use of such skills by asking questions such as, "How could you find out . . . ?" or "What would happen if . . . ?" We should try to create within the child's responses a kind of flexibility and power to adapt quickly, rather than seeking a response in terms of rules and carefully transmitted conduct codes (Butler, 1976). Real choices beginning with such simple things as whether to work a puzzle or read a book can be extended to include the performances of real tasks such as cultivating a garden or preparing food for lunch.

Children should be helped to feel comfortable in situations where answers are not all known. They should be encouraged to experiment with a wide variety of materials and develop a creative approach to problems to which the solution is unknown.

## Acquisition of a Future-Focused Role-Image

Teachers can extend what they usually do to help children become aware of occupational options that might be possible for them. In addition to taking the children into the neighborhood to learn about some occupations people engage in, teachers can greatly extend the kinds of materials they provide to help children role-play their ob-

servations of different occupations. A further step can be taken to introduce into children's discussions other occupational roles, those that might come into existence, and what the children might be when they grow up.

Schools will need to tap the information now stored in brains of many non-teachers. Greater awareness of future roles can be created without violating the child's more prominent present orientation.

In their early educational years, children should have the opportunity to meet a person engaged in any occupation in which the child might be interested. To deprive the child of this is to deprive him of an important step in the formation of his future-focused role-image (Shane & Shane, 1974).

## Emphasis on Cooperation

To live in the twenty-first century in sustained peace, it will be preferable for people to see themselves as relatively more cooperative than competitive. This means that the children's thought will need to depart from those of their twentieth century ancestors who placed greater stress on individually-oriented competition than on group-oriented collaboration. Fortunately, young children have not yet become competitive and small group projects can be provided to help them work together to achieve their purposes (Butler, 1976).

## Development of Interpersonal Skills

Children also need to become aware of their interpersonal interactions with other children and adults. Perhaps of all the things that a teacher of young children can appropriately do, it is most important to help children understand how other people respond to their behavior, and how they themselves respond to the behavior of other people. At a time when children are first becoming interested in doing things with other children, they will learn the human relationships skills that form the basis for the way they will interact with people (Butler, 1976). To do this, children must be able to relate freely to other children but they must have adult guidance for meeting a variety of situations. Adults also must have a self-awareness that enables them to provide the needed guidance.

## CONCLUSION

The degree to which success can be attained in developing the characteristics described in the previous section will depend on the insight of adults into the kinds of skills that will be needed and by their abilities to guide children's learning. This interchange requires an openness between adults and children as well as abilities of both children and adults to communicate. These requirements may present greater problems for the adults than for the children. Creative adults who can help children cope with situations in creative ways will do much to provide hope for the future.

## REFERENCES

Banet, B. "Computers and Early Learning." *The High/Scope Report*, #4, 1979.

Brown, L. *The Twenty-ninth Day*. New York: Norton, 1978.

Buchen, I. H. "Humanism and Futurism: Enemies or Allies?" In A. Toffler (Ed.), *Learning for Tomorrow*. New York: Vintage Books, 1974.

Butler, A. L. "Today's Child—Tomorrow's World." *Young Children*, 1976, 32, 4–11.

Cornish, E. *The Study of the Future*. Washington, D.C.: World Future Society, 1977.

Kauffman, D. L., Jr. *Futurism and Future Studies*. Washington, D.C.: National Education Association, 1976.

Kirschenbaum, H., & Simon, S. "Values and the Futures Movement in Education." In A. Toffler (Ed.), *Learning for Tomorrow*. New York: Vintage Books, 1974.

Markley, O. W., et al. *Changing Images of Man*. Menlo Park, Calif.: Center for the Study of Social Policy, Stanford Research Institute, 1974.

Maslow, A. H. "Some Fundamental Questions that Face the Normative Social Psychologist." In R. Theobold (Ed.), *Futures Conditional*. Indianapolis: Bobbs-Merrill, 1972.

McHale, J. *The Future of the Future*. New York: Braxiller, 1969.

Mead, M. *Culture and Commitment*. Garden City, New York: Doubleday, 1970.

———. *Twentieth Century Faith, Hope and Survival*. New York: Harper & Row, 1972.

Michael, D. N. *On Learning to Plan—And Planning to Learn*. San Francisco: Jossey-Bass, 1973.

———. *The Unprepared Society*. New York: Basic Books, 1968.

Pierce, C. M. "The Preschooler and the Future." *The Futurist*, 1972, 6, 13–15.

Toffler, A. *Future Shock*. New York: Random House, 1970.

Shane, H. G. "Education for Tomorrow's World." *The Futurist*, 1973, 7, 103–106.

Shane, J. G., & Shane, H. G. "The Role of the Future in Education." *Today's Education*, 1974, 63, 72–76.

Singer, B. D. "The Future-focused Role-image." In A. Toffler (Ed.), *Learning for Tomorrow*. New York: Vintage Books, 1974.

Theobold, R. *Futures Conditional*. Indianapolis: Bobbs-Merrill, 1972.

Weiss, G. H. "Education for the Future." *Social and Community*, 1973, 59, 19+.

*Annie L. Butler* was Professor of Early Childhood Education and Chairperson, Elementary/Early Childhood Education, Indiana University, Bloomington.

# Problem Solving: Encouraging Active Learning

## STACIE G. GOFFIN WITH CLAUDIA Q. TULL

When Piaget's ideas are applied to early childhood education, the teaching strategies recommended generally focus on ways to encourage children to construct more adequate conceptual frameworks. This focus emphasizes the *process* of cognitive development rather than its results (Duckworth 1972; 1979; Forman 1983; Kamii and DeVries 1978). Problem-solving possibilities can encourage this constructive process.

Problem solving is distinctly different from academic learning. Academic skills represent external knowledge that must be taught; problem-solving opportunities during early childhood encourage the child to create new mental relationships by interacting with the environment. Meaningful problems stimulate children's mental activity as they relate new understandings to previous ones.

### IMPORTANCE OF PROBLEM SOLVING POSSIBILITIES

Cognitive development, from a Piagetian perspective, involves children's creation of increasingly complex relationships that result in a more complete framework for understanding reality. Logical operations are constructed through children's autonomous activites that permit opportunities to discover relationships and ideas (Piaget 1973). Cognitive development is not the accumulation of isolated pieces of information. True cognitive growth takes place when children construct an integrated framework by interacting with their environment. Teachers can support the "child's own struggle to make sense of . . . the data" (Duckworth 1979, p. 302) by introducing problem-solving activites which enable children to actively investigate the causes and effects of their actions on the people and objects in their environment. Problem-solving possibilities also encourage children to elaborate and refine their knowledge, which will provide a deeper foundation for them to use in responding to later experiences (Duckworth 1979; 1981; Goldhaber 1979; Kamii and DeVries 1978).

As children solve problems they make decisions and evaluate their effectiveness individually and with others. Problem-solving situations can promote initiative, cooperation, independence, and curiosity. Children's sense of competence is enhanced by challenging tasks and a responsive environment (Gottfried 1983). A sense of mastery over the environment is encouraged when children can see the impact of their actions.

Finally, problem-solving possibilities avoid the dilemma of readiness by allowing children to respond to materials at their own level and ask their own questions. Readiness becomes an issue only when teachers determine children's source of knowledge (Forman and Fosnot 1982). Children determine their own learning needs during problem solving.

### CHARACTERISTICS OF GOOD PROBLEMS

Good problems necessitate a child's conscious search for a solution. The problem solver must

From *Young Children* 40, No. 3 (March 1985): 28–32. Copyright 1985, NAEYC. All rights reserved. Used by permission of the publisher, The National Association for the Education of Young Children.

have a clear understanding of the goal in order to make decisions about appropriate actions. Problems that are interesting and meaningful allow children to apply their practical knowledge in new ways. Good problems, therefore, are understandable and challenging.

Problems must also be appropriate for children's developmental levels and must take into account their experiences and abilities. Good problems should be solvable at various levels of complexity and in various ways with the possibility of different solutions. One child might solve a problem by trial and error while another child would solve it using deductive reasoning. Problems with multiple levels of difficulty permit both children to experiment with different strategies and solutions.

An example of a good problem is a game that gives two children the opportunity to take either one or two objects from a group of ten (Cruikshank, Fitzgerald, and Jensen 1980). The goal is to be the player who removes the last object. Four-year-olds observed solving this problem made random decisions (trial and error) and were surprised when they won, while six-year-olds quickly realized that the number of objects removed determined the outcome of the game (strategy). This problem also allowed children to increase their understanding of number.

Good problems for young children also use concrete means to gather information and contain few, if any, abstract components. Immediate feedback and observable consequences provide children with information to make further decisions. This is especially pertinent when the search for a solution involves several steps. In the above example, children can observe the number of remaining objects to evaluate their decisions and successfully solve the problem.

Solutions, therefore, should be immediate, observable, and increasingly obvious to the child. To effectively evaluate their decisions, children must be able to recognize their success. Children who evaluate their own solutions are less dependent upon a teacher's affirmation of their success, and this encourages independence and autonomy. The teacher can then facilitate and counsel children rather than serve as a solution expert. When solving problems with others, children become aware of different points of view. This process encourages decentration and decreases egocentricity.

Based on these criteria and characteristics of young children, teachers can ask these questions when creating and evaluating problem-solving strategies for children:

- Is the problem meaningful and interesting to young children? Does it allow children to make use of their knowledge in a new situation?
- Is the problem easily understood?
- Are children required to make decisions?
- Can the problem be solved at various levels of complexity?
- Can children use concrete actions to gather information and solve the problem?
- Can children observe feedback to their actions?
- Can children evaluate their solution?
- Are there opportunities to cooperate and become aware of different points of view?

These eight questions emphasize the primary characteristics of good problems: their possibilities for thinking and their interest to children. Children have to feel the problem is worth thinking about (Duckworth 1981).

Early childhood educators will recognize the possibilities for problem solving in typical classroom activities such as creative dramatics and puppetry, cooking, blockbuilding, carpentry, and art. Teachers can also apply these questions to evaluate or create problem-solving activities in the classroom.

# CREATING PROBLEM-SOLVING POSSIBILITIES

Teachers can expand everyday activities into problem-solving possibilities by encouraging children to plan, predict possible outcomes, make decisions, and observe the results of their actions. By providing open-ended materials, adding complexity to classroom activities, and encouraging children's efforts at problem solving, teachers can offer problem-solving activities that have multiple levels of entry and enough room for failure and self-correction (Forman 1981). Open-ended materials such as blocks, water, sand, wood, and art materials respond immediately to children's actions. They encourage problem solving by allowing children to test ideas (Duckworth 1972).

For example, four-year-old Sadao wanted to make a hill "that comes up, off the paper." Her solutions included using a clay ball or wad of paper, and attaching a separate piece of paper. Sadao decided the clay would be too heavy and the wad of paper too ugly. After several attempts she propped up a piece of paper on her base sheet and clearly explained her solution to other children.

Materials and activities are more likely to suggest ideas when teachers add to their complexity. By adding parts of varieties of materials, teachers add to possibilities for action and increase the range of responses children can generate. For example, teachers can offer paint brushes of various widths and types (e.g., basting brush, toothbrush, hair brush, surgical sponge) at an easel with paints of differing thickness. Children's comments such as "When I want to paint a large space, I use a large brush, and when I want to paint something small, I use a little brush," indicate that children have used these opportunities to experiment and create new understandings.

Adding fulcrums, cylinders, inclined planes, balls, and pulleys to the block area can stimulate the building of more intricate structures. Chil-

dren will have even greater opportunities to understand relationships of gravity, slopes, and movement.

Forman (1981) suggests that complexity be achieved by providing opportunities for children to *transform* objects and events rather than searching for different objects to solve a problem. Children are given hollow balls, for example, and add metal weights to achieve different consequences. Forman (Forman 1981; Forman and Fosnot 1982) argues that the opportunity to transform objects encourages children's understandings of change.

Peer interactions can provide opportunities for interpersonal problem solving. When two preschool children fought over one fire hat, the teacher encouraged the children to find a way they both could use the hat. Their solutions included timed use, flipping a coin, and one wearing the hat to the fire while the other wore it for the return trip. The children chose the latter solution, and immediately resumed their dramatic play.

Interpersonal problem solving encourages children to consider others' points of view, to develop understandings about social interactions, and to assume more responsibility in their relationships with peers. Other ways to encourage social problem solving are described by Edwards, Logue, and Russell (1983).

Teachers can also plan specific problem-solving activities for the classroom. These activities can be organized by the type of response they encourage: movement, discussion, skills, and strategy. These four types of problems are a convenient way to organize, identify, and create problem-solving activities.

*Movement problems* are of two types. Children may move their own bodies in space and generate as many solutions as possible to achieve a particular objective. For example, "How many different ways can you carry beanbags without using your hands?

Children can also act upon objects to see what happens. Actions upon objects can include such movements as pushing, pulling, sliding, and rolling. Kamii and DeVries (1978) emphasize that this type of feedback, called physical knowledge, is a critical source of knowledge during the preschool years. A physical knowledge problem involving experimentation with inclinded planes and small balls, for example, challenges children to construct relationships between the height of a plane and its influence upon distance.

*Discussion problems* facilitate language development. Discussion problems encourage children to verbally formulate their hypotheses and to express themselves so they can be understood by others. Problem-solving discussions differ from other language activities because they offer children the opportunity to identify problems and to generate and evaluate potential solutions. Using open-ended questions such as "What would happen if . . . ?," recording possible solutions, and encouraging children to try out their recommendations can enhance discussion problems.

*Skill problems* emphasize the application of thinking skills such as observation, classification, pattern generalization, estimation, hypothesizing, counting, and ordering. Typical classifying activities, for instance, can become problem-solving possibilities when children are asked to group materials in as many different ways as possible rather than in predetermined categories. Other skill problems include asking children to design a quilt of shapes so that all touching shapes are different, or to complete a matrix of shapes from a set of clues.

*Strategy problems* require the solver to determine the most efficient method of solving a problem. Counting board games can become effective strategy problems when teachers include an element of decision making that results in

observable consequences. For instance, in a teacher-made board game called "Catch a Turkey", a board is divided into a trial of spaces randomly marked by pictures of turkeys. Players throw two dice and must decide which of the dice will be used for their move. The game's objective is to collect as many turkeys as possible.

During the first few times they play, four-year-olds seem unaware of the main objective of the game and focus instead on the die with the greatest number. This seems to reflect the preoperational assumption that more is better. With repeated opportunities to play this game, children construct a relationship between their choice of dice, i.e., number, and the number of turkeys they collect. Because children construct this relationship for themselves, their understanding is a more meaningful solution than one dictated by the teacher.

After experience with strategy problems, teachers can help children become aware of their use of strategy by asking "How did you know to do that?" or "What did you need to know to solve this problem?" (for further discussion of organized problem-solving possibilities see Goffin and Tull 1984).

## TEACHER STRATEGIES

Piaget describes the teacher's role as "a mentor stimulating initiative and research" (1973, p. 16). Teachers can serve as models when they solve problems with children, when they verbalize reflective and probing questions while involved in problem-solving situations, and when they ask children similiar questions to encourage understanding of the relationships between their actions and outcomes.

Children often resolve a problem without understanding how the outcome was achieved (Forman 1981; Forman and Fosnot 1982). Teachers' questions, however, can challenge children to reflect on the thinking process they used to encourage the reorganization of their ideas into more adequate frameworks (Duckworth 1979; 1981; Forman and Kuschner 1983; Kamii 1981; Kamii and DeVries 1978; Piaget 1973). Mental reflection can be encouraged by asking children to justify an answer, explain an outcome, or predict the consequences of an action.

To be effective, questions should be phrased simply and asked only after children have had sufficient opportunity to repeat their solutions several times. Children should be given enough time to respond to questions and to express their thinking. Predicting is more difficult for children than explaining an effect after it has occurred (Copple, Sigel, and Saunders 1979; Forman and Kuschner 1983; Kamii and DeVries 1978). Children are more likely to demonstrate their competence when questions probe their practical knowledge (Black 1981; Donaldson 1978; Gelman 1979; Pines 1983). Questions, therefore, need to be directly related to children's activities.

Children's actions reflect their guesses about the anticipated results of responding to a problem in a particular way (Forman and Fosnot 1982; Karmiloff-Smith and Inhelder 1975). The results, in turn, provide evidence of the adequacy of their reasoning (Duckworth 1979). According to Forman (1981; Forman and Kuschner 1983), learning takes place when children recognize a discrepancy between expected and observed results. Teachers can even prepare activities that conflict with children's experiences. For example, a teacher can divert an inclined plane so that a rolling vehicle goes in the opposite direction from a nearby underpass. The teachers can then encourage the child to solve the problem.

Awareness of a discrepancy allows children to construct new relationships. If the discrepancy is not recognized, however, then the problem does not exist for the child (Duckworth 1979; 1981;

Forman 1981; Forman and Fosnot 1982; Forman and Kuschner 1983). This is an important clue to the teacher to observe in determining whether to pursue an activity.

Problem-solving possibilities challenge teachers to understand children's thinking and to act upon the knowledge that children learn by making new connections and systems of relationships. Children's solutions to problems may not be consistent with teacher interpretations, but the developmental validity of problem solving is negated if teachers seek correct answers. Teachers should be available as resources and probers, but not as authorities. Since good problems provide opportunities for many successful solutions and for children to judge their own success, corrections and evaluative comments are inappropriate. Support and encouragement, however, should always be available.

Problem-solving activities not only allow children opportunities to make meaningful decisions about how to reach a goal, but also allow educators to learn from children. Observations of children involved in problem solving and careful listening to their questions reveal what children are thinking and their levels of understanding. Errors indicate contradictions in thinking. Children's solutions to problems and their questions reflect their point of view. Sensitive observations can help teachers respond more appropriately to children's developmental perspectives.

## SUMMARY AND CONCLUSIONS

According to Duckworth, a good learning situation "must permit the child to establish plans to reach a distant goal while leaving him wide freedom to follow his own routing" (1979, p. 306). This description summarizes the characteristics of problems that encourage children to construct more adequate conceptualizations of their world. In the process, children are given opportunities to make meaningful decisions and to evaluate their effectiveness either individually or with others. Such situations simultaneously promote curiosity, initiative, cooperation, and independence. These goals coincide with the beliefs of early childhood educators that children should be active participants in their own learning. The major value of problem solving, however, resides in the ability of problems to provoke mental construction which is the most critical aspect of Piaget's theory for educators (Duckworth 1979; Forman and Fosnot 1982; Kamii and DeVries 1978).

Teachers promote problem solving by providing an environment rich in potential for exploration and by encouraging children to reflect on their actions. Observations should focus on what children *do* understand (Gelman, 1979) as well as the understandings they still need to construct. Recognizing the relationship between these two states enables teachers to ask the kind of questions and provide the kind of problems that will stimulate a child's future thinking.

# REFERENCES

Black, J. K. "Are Young Children Really Egocentric?" *Young Children* 36, no. 6 (September 1981): 51–55.

Copple, C.; Siegel, I. E.; and Saunders, R. *Educating the Young Thinker: Classroom Strategies for Cognitive Growth.* New York: Van Nostrand Rheinhold, 1979.

Cruikshank, D. E.; Fitzgerald, D. H.; and Jensen, L. R. *Young Children Learning Mathematics.* Boston: Allyn & Bacon, 1980.

Donaldson, M. *Children's Minds.* New York: Norton, 1978.

Duckworth, E. "The Having of Wonderful Ideas." *Harvard Educational Review* 42, no. 2 (May 1972): 217–231.

Duckworth, E. "Either We're Too Early and They Can't Learn It or We're Late and They Know It Already: The Dilemma of 'Applying Piaget'."*Harvard Educational Review* 49, no. 3 (August 1979): 297–312.

Duckworth, E. "Learning Symposium: A Commentary." In *New Directions in Piagetian Theory and Practice,* ed. I. E. Sigel, D. M. Brodinsky, and R. M. Golenkoff. Hillsdale, N.J.: Erlbaum, 1981.

Edwards, P. E.; Logue, M. E.; and Russell, A. S. "Talking with Young Children about Social Ideas." *Young Children* 39, no. 1 (November 1983): 12–20.

Forman, G. E. "The Power of Negative Thinking: Equilibration in the Preschool." In *New Directions in Piagetian Theory and Practice,* ed. I. E. Sigel, D. M. Brodinsky, and R. M. Golenkoff. Hillsdale, N.J.: Erlbaum, 1981.

Forman, G. E., and Fosnot, C. T. "The Use of Piaget's Constructivism in Early Childhood Education Programs." In *Handbook of Research in Early Childhood Education,* ed. B. Spodek. New York: Free Press, 1982.

Forman, G. E., and Kuschner, D. S. *The Child's Construction of Knowledge: Piaget for Teaching Children.* Washington, D. C.: National Association for the Education of Young Children, 1983.

Gelman, R. "Preschool Thought." *American Psychologist* 34, no. 10 (October 1979): 900–905.

Goffin, S. G., and Tull, C. Q. "Ideas! Creating Problem Solving Possibilities for Young Children." *Dimensions,* no. 2 (January 1984): 15–19.

Goldhaber, D. "Does the Changing View of Early Experience Imply a Changing View of Early Childhood Development?" In *Current Topics in Early Childhood Education.* Vol. 2, ed. L. Katz, Norwood, N.J.: Ablex, 1979.

Gottfried, A. E. "Research in Review: Intrinsic Motivation in Young Children." *Young Children* 39, no. 1 (November 1983): 64–71.

Kamii, C. "Application of Piaget's Theory to Education: The Preoperational Level." In *New Directions in Piagetian Theory and Practice,* ed. I. E. Siegel, D. M. Brodinsky, and R. M. Golenkoff. Hillsdale, N.J.: Erlbaum, 1981.

Kamii, C., and DeVries, R. *Physical Knowledge in Preschool Education.* New York: Prentice-Hall, 1978.

Karmiloff-Smith, A., and Inhelder, B. "If You Want to Get Ahead, Get a Theory." *Cognition* 3, no. 3 (1975): 192–212.

Piaget, J. *To Understand Is To Invent.* New York: Penguin, 1973.

Pines, M. "Can a Rock Walk?" *Psychology Today* (November 1983): 46–54.

*Stacie G. Goffin* is Visiting Assistant Professor of Early Childhood Education, University of Missouri, Kansas City

*Claudia Tull* is Kindergarten Teacher, St. Francis School of Assisi, St. Albans, West Virginia. She is also an adjunct faculty member at West Virginia College of Graduate Studies, Charleston.

# Children's Literature and Moral Development

## SUZANNE LOWELL KROGH AND LINDA LEONARD LAMME

"Well, if the Little Red Hen did all the work, she oughta get all the cake," Heather declared, looking and sounding very sure of herself.

"But what about sharing?" Mark asked. "We just said that it's good to share." He sounded less sure of himself than Heather did.

Gregg spoke up. "Yeah, it's good to share, but only if you do something for it. Like you have to earn stuff."

"Right!" Heather vehemently agreed. "The animals didn't work so they didn't earn any of the hen's cake."

Then the teacher stepped in with a question designed to increase the complexity of the discussion. "Suppose the dog and the cat helped a lot, but the turkey and the pig helped just a little. How will the hen split up the cake?"

Ricky had an answer immediately. "Everybody gets the same if everybody helped. It doesn't matter how much they did. Otherwise everybody will be yelling and fighting."

"I don't think so," responded Heather in self-confidence. "If the dog and cat work more they should get more. That's fairest."

The discussion continued for a few minutes with about half of these second graders arguing Heather's side while the other half took Ricky's position. Through it all Mark seemed unsure, listening quietly to both sides. Finally, a smile came to his face. "I've got an idea! Everybody should get cake depending on how hard they worked, but one thing's different. The pig and the turkey are bigger so they're gonna need more food to stay alive. It wouldn't be fair for them to starve to death! That means they should get a little more than the dog and cat even if they didn't work quite as hard."

Realizing that no consensus would be reached, the teacher soon drew the discussion to a close, allowing each child to reach an independent and personal decision concerning the various sharing issues suggested by the story.

## PARALLELS IN COGNITIVE AND MORAL DEVELOPMENT

This experience was one in a series in which two classes, a first grade and a second grade, used literature to explore the issue of distributive justice—fairness in sharing situations. The study of this topic has its roots in the work of Piaget (1932), who recognized that children's cognitive development is accompanied by similar stages in moral judgment. Kohlberg (1975) expanded the research on moral development, especially after the age of ten, while Selman (1980) and Damon (1977) related this theory and research to younger children.

Damon's research shows that children progress according to developmental levels in their understanding of the fair distribution of resources. Subsequent studies based on Damon's work indicate that adults can stimulate children's growth in reasoning (Krogh, in press; Enright 1981) as they progress through several stages.

Damon describes these stages as "a sequence of unfolding confusions in the mind of the child" (p. 74). These stages are briefly reviewed in Table 1.

**TABLE 1**
Stages of Children's Moral Development
(Damon 1977)

**Level 0-A:** Choices are based on self-interest (ages 3–4).

**Level 0-B:** Choices are made based on external realities such as size, sex, or perceived attractiveness (ages 4–5).

**Level 1-A:** Choices are based on strict equality—everyone gets the same (ages 5–6).

**Level 1-B:** Compromises are made between competing claims (e.g., hardest workers vs. most effective) and special needs (e.g., poverty) are taken into consideration (ages 7–8).

**Level 2-A:** Equality, reciprocity, and competing claims are all taken into account so that each person is given what is due (ages 8–10).

In the discussion of the Little Red Hen, the children reasoned at several of these levels, all of them representative of what might be expected for second graders. Rick's argument that everybody gets the same no matter what the effort places him at level 1-A. Heather's contention that distribution should be based on the work contributed indicates level 1-B reasoning. Although Mark was uncertain during much of the discussion, he finally felt comfortable with a level 2-A argument in which the competing claims of the various animals were considered.

## LEADING GROUP DISCUSSIONS

This discussion is an example of the ways in which children's literature dealing with social issues can help children reason about topics such as distributive justice. Although on this day Heather and Ricky remained firmly convinced at their levels of understanding, Mark was ready to move on and it was the discussion that helped promote his growth.

While unstructured discussion may also lead to growth in moral development, the sessions in our series were intentionally designed to further children's reasoning abilities. Note that the teacher in the Little Red Hen discussion purposely increased the complexity of the discussion by asking a well-timed question. Based on the research on children's cognitive and moral development, we identified several guidelines that assisted us in conducting our series of discussions, and that we recommend to other teachers.

### Limit Group Size

Interaction among peers or between children and the adult is facilitated when the number of participants is limited. We found that in a group of eight children, everyone could participate actively. In larger groups, not everyone can be involved. Interaction among peers or between children and the adult needs to be firsthand and concrete in order for young children to grow in their ability to understand how others feel (Castle and Richards 1979). This role-taking skill is essential if children are to come to understand the decision-making process of a story's protagonist.

### Choose Appropriate Stories

Literary merit and appropriateness to the developmental levels of the children are equal considerations. If the Little Red Hen's reasoning had been based on self-interest or unrelated factors, these second graders would have had no model for advancing in their moral development. If the reasoning had been too advanced, or the topic more removed from children's experience, they would not have been able to relate to it (Kohlberg 1975). *The Little Red Hen*'s enduring popularity may in part be because her reasoning about distributive justice is a good match for young children.

## Keep the Discussion Concrete

Young children are capable of in-depth discussions, but they need accompanying concrete experiences as well (Schuncke and Krogh 1983). Therefore, while the children were discussing *The Little Red Hen* they were also drawing pictures of the story! Although children's pictures might have been unrelated to the issues, children seemed more comfortable and natural in this setting than they would sitting in a circle, for example. When the same discussion was tried in other groups without the opportunity to draw, children were bored and fidgety.

## Build on Diversity

Children's moral, social, and cognitive reasoning is expanded through giving and hearing a variety of viewpoints at different levels of development (Kohlberg 1975). If possible, select discussion groups that include a mixture of cognitive abilities, experiences, and other pertinent qualities.

## Take Unscheduled Detours

Because the intent of reading and discussing stories is to help children deal with real life, reality occasionally intrudes into children's discussions. These unscheduled detours may offer even better opportunities to help children apply their newly acquired reasoning and thinking skills.

The teacher of this same second grade class had just read aloud *One Fine Day,* a cumulative tale in which a fox must ask a succession of characters for various items which will lead to getting an elderly woman to sew his tail back on. After some discussion about the sharing aspects of the story, Mark looked up from the picture he was drawing and announced, "I just put the moral of the story on here."

Everyone was interested to know what the moral was, even those who had never heard of one before, so he read aloud, "Say please." Mark's reason for assigning this moral to the story was that if the fox had said "please" to the woman in the first place, he wouldn't have had to go through a whole story full of frustrations!

Gregg looked over Mark's shoulder at the inscribed moral and suggested that he would put the same moral on his own paper. As he carefully studied the words in order to copy the spelling, Mark pulled his paper away, looking quite annoyed. "But that's *my* idea," he said.

Recognizing an opportunity for firsthand experience, but not wanting to pass judgment either, the teacher asked noncommitally, "And you don't want to share your ideas?"

Two other children heard the frequently discussed word *share* and seized the chance. They chanted in unison, "It's good to share, Mark."

"Well," he agreed reluctantly, "I guess so," and returned the paper to the table. Obviously, Mark had shared only because of peer pressure rather than because of growth in his reasoning. You will recall that his earlier discussion of the Little Red Hen showed his thought processes to be more advanced than those of the other children. Now he was faced with the need to put his ideas into practice—difficult for all of us at times!

The following day, the teacher watched Mark with some concern as he again wrote a moral and others asked to copy it. Sighing almost inaudibly, he held the paper up for all to see. "Thanks, Mark!" one or two children said, and he suddenly smiled. Obviously, there was a reward for his sharing, and each day from then on he agreed to show his story morals without hesitation, occasionally reminding the children to thank him.

In a second experience, both ideas of sharing and saying "please" were made concrete when Charles brought a large box of expensive marking pens from home to use during the discussion time. Magnanimously he spread them on the table before the group. "I'm bringing them because it's good to share," he said, "but it's good for you to say 'please,' too. Then I'll want to share them with you."

That day Heather wrote on her picture, "If you share with others they will share with you." This is another example of her 1-B reasoning. From then on, the group challenged itself to find a moral in every story discussed.

## SELECTING GOOD STORIES

Before choosing books to discuss, you will want to review the variation of reasoning abilities in your class. We asked volunteers and the school librarian to conduct discussion groups so that we could limit the group size, but chose the books for them to read to ensure that children's development and needs were matched with the stories.

Flexibility in selections is desirable. A useful description of books on the topic of sharing, categorized by reasoning levels, is found in an earlier article (Krogh and Lamme 1983). The books and questions relating to them which we used over the course of four weeks are listed in Table 2.

These questions made it possible for the group to discuss a book in about 15 minutes. Although at times the children reached agreement, more often they retained their disparity of ideas. The discussion leaders made no judgments and did not try to force consensus. In fact, the children showed a nearly unanimous lack of interest in what any adult thought about the issues.

## REWARDS

Our story discussions took place twice a week for a month. The focus each time was on sharing, with the intent that other social and moral issues would be explored at other times. By focusing on one issue, children are encouraged to think more broadly about the topic than they might otherwise.

An example of how deeply involved the children were in the topic of sharing occurred one day when several children had created their own cumulative tale using *One Fine Day* as a model. After Daniel made the last character in their tale find his pot of gold, he turned to the rest of the group and declared, "I found it, but I'm going to share it with all of you because you helped me!"

It is especially rewarding when the evidence of growth through classroom experience is apparent in children's behavior. Using books gives children an opportunity to analyze the role models which literature provides. Not only do children advance in their reasoning, then, but they also grow to appreciate literature and comprehend stories more fully.

". . . Values do not come from injections by persons in authority or by superficially copying society's patterns. They must be searched for, tried out, discussed and analyzed. Alternatives must be scrutinized and weighed" (Riley 1984, p. 17).

How important it is to include moral issues such as sharing in the early primary curriculum! As Riley continues, "If we expect to survive as a people capable of establishing and holding values consistent with a humanitarian philosophy, we must re-examine the ways in which we are educating our children. It is essential that children grow into adults who not only can read and write but who are curious and imaginative and capable of making choices based on ethical values" (p. 39).

**TABLE 2**
**Books and Questions Used to Stimulate Discussion of Sharing**

*Angus and the Cat* (Flack 1931)
A Scotty dog learns to share in order to keep his friend, a cat.
Why was Angus annoyed with the new cat?
Have you ever been jealous and not wanted to share?
Who should have most of the sunlight (or milk)? Why?

*The Little Red Hen* (Galdone 1973)
A hen chooses not to share any cake with the other animals
because they refused to help her bake it.
Should the Little Red Hen have shared? Why?
Should anyone get more than anyone else?

*John Brown, Rose and the Midnight Cat* (Wagner 1977)
A dog refuses to share his owner with an intruding cat, but
must change his mind.
Why did John Brown pretend the cat wasn't there?
Why did John Brown change his mind and let the cat in?
How did he feel about sharing Rose? Why?

*The Mannerly Adventures of Little Mouse* (Keenan 1977)
A young mouse learns that the essence of manners may be will-
ingness to share.
How did Little Mouse feel after he had shared treats with every-
one in the family?
Which family members deserved the most? Why?

*Morris's Disappearing Bag* (Wells 1975)
Older siblings refuse to share with Morris until it is learned that
he has something to share back.
Do you have a toy that you don't like to share? Why is this toy
so special?
What toys do you like to share with others?
Why didn't the brothers and sisters want to share with Morris?

*One Fine Day* (Hogrogrian 1971)
A fox needs to have his tail stitched back on and must find
characters willing to share materials and skills.
Why wouldn't each character give the fox what he needed with-
out getting something in return?
Which character wanted to share and why was he the only one?

*Pet Show* (Keats 1972)
A young boy shares his first-prize ribbon with an elderly lady
even though she didn't earn it.
Why did Peter decide to share the prize?
How did Peter feel after he had let the lady keep the ribbon?

*Peter's Chair* (Keats 1967)
A boy resists sharing his old possessions with a new baby sister.
How did Peter feel when all of his belongings were painted
pink for his sister?
Why did Peter decide to share his chair with her after all?

364

## REFERENCES

Castle, K. and Richards, H. "Adult/Peer Interactions and Role-Taking Ability Among Preschool Children." *Journal of Genetic Psychology* 135 (September 1979): 71–79.

Damon, W. *The Social World of the Child.* San Francisco: Jossey-Bass, 1977.

Enright, R. "A Classroom Discipline Model for Promoting Social Cognitive Development in Early Childhood." *Journal of Moral Education* 11 (October 1981): 47–60.

Flack, M. *Angus and the Cat.* New York: Doubleday, 1931.

Galdone, P. *The Little Red Hen.* New York: Seabury, 1973.

Hogrogrian, N. *One Fine Day.* New York: Collier, 1971.

Keats, E. J. *Peter's Chair.* New York: Harper & Row, 1967.

Keats, E. J. *Pet Show.* New York: Collier, 1972.

Keenan, M. *The Mannerly Adventures of Little Mouse.* New York: Crown, 1977.

Kohlberg, L. "The Cognitive-Developmental Approach to Moral Education." *Phi Delta Kappan* 56, no. 10 (June 1975): 670–678.

Krogh, S. "Encouraging Positive Justice Reasoning and Perspective Taking Skills: Two Educational Interventions." *Journal of Moral Education,* in press.

Krogh, S. and Lamme, L. "Learning to Share: How Literature Can Help." *Childhood Education* 59, no. 3 (January–February 1983): 188–192.

Piaget, J. *The Moral Judgment of the Child.* New York: Free Press, 1965 (first published in 1932).

Riley, S. *How to Generate Values in Young Children.* Washington, D.C.: National Association for the Education of Young Children, 1984.

Schuncke, G. and Krogh, S. *Helping Children Choose.* Glenview, Ill.: Scott, Foresman, 1983.

Selman, R. *The Growth of Interpersonal Understanding.* New York: Academic Press, 1980.

Wagner, J. *John Brown, Rose and the Midnight Cat.* New York: Bradbury, 1977.

Wells, R. *Morris's Disappearing Bag.* New York: Dial, 1975.

*Suzanne Lowell Krogh* is Associate Professor, Early Childhood Education, University of Florida, Gainesville.

*Linda Leonard Lamme* is Professor, Early Childhood Education, University of Florida, Gainesville.

# Multicultural Education and Global Education: A Possible Merger

DONNA J. COLE

No one should make the claim of being educated until he or she has learned to live in harmony with people who are different. (Wilson, 1982)

Curriculum specialists are becoming increasingly aware of the need to promote learning which enables diverse populations to live in harmony. At one point in educational history societal academicians had the luxury to do little more than dream about a world united by common goals and concerns for all people and nations. However, technological advances coupled with cultural value shifts have transformed this dream into a necessity. Our human survival rests on our ability to educate the public about interdependence and about the adaptation necessitated by the new realities which interdependence implies.

Currently, attempts to educate others about interdependence are being made in both the

From *Theory Into Practice* 23, No. 2 (Spring 1984): 151–154. Used by permission of the author and the publisher. Copyright 1984, by the College of Education, The Ohio State University.

global education movement and the multicultural education movement. These are not separated and unconnected movements, but rather they interface similar concerns. Both want to promote harmony within diversity. The merger of these movements is the major theme of this article. Hence we will examine multicultural education and global education, addressing the meanings and assumptions underlying each, the relationships between the two movements, and a possible, much needed merger.

## MULTICULTURAL EDUCATION

The American Association of Colleges for Teacher Education (AACTE) statement on multicultural education, entitled "No One Model American" (AACTE, 1973), supports a cultural pluralistic ideology. Thus the justification of multicultural education is found in the fact that cultural diversity is an integral part of American society, and in the belief that this condition is to be valued (cultural pluralism). Advocates of cultural pluralism cite the need for educational institutions to help prepare students for life in a nation and world characterized by widespread cultural diversity.

At one point in the American national development, cultural pluralism was viewed as detrimental to the new and growing republic, especially after World War I. But after World War II, the United States vaulted into the international ranks, becoming a world power in a culturally diverse world. American internal politics became competitively pluralistic. Today, the efforts of many civil rights groups and associations—opting to participate in governmental policy making—exemplify this pluralism. Recent federal policy and a broadening of consciousness among members of varying minority groups have promoted the participation of these groups in political affairs. Blacks, Native Americans, and Hispanics, for instance, have formed sufficient

group strength to negotiate legal and social changes favorable to a given group.

Cultural pluralism has been more fully realized because of the recognition that the "melting pot" did not happen. The supposedly cohesive Americanized nation with its customs and traditions reflecting a blend of European and African inputs is a great national myth. This myth denies the diverse richness of the American experience and its cultural heritage. The myth is incompatible with multicultural education, which rests on the assumption that cultural pluralism is an integral, valued aspect of American society.

To accept cultural pluralism, persons need to have a sense of their own identity. Thus, multicultural education curricula portray the contributions of all Americans—black Americans, Mexican Americans, Native Americans, and others—positively. Incorporated in the multicultural education goal are curricula that demonstrate how members of minority groups have contributed to American explorations, territorial expansion, cultural and technical innovation, and industrialization. Multiculturalism strives to make cultural differences credible. Psychologically, there is a strong and positive relationship between accepting oneself and accepting others.

## GLOBAL EDUCATION

The meaning of global education is not quite as well-defined as that of multicultural education. As Goodlad (1979) states in his introduction to *Schooling for a Global Age,* "Because concern for global matters is an emerging and not an established goal for educational systems, there are no readily available, comprehensive, self-contained definitions, descriptions, and analyses of what global education is."

Despite a lack of unilateral agreement concerning a meaning for global education, there are commonly stated assumptions underlying a global perspective. One assumption is that we live in an interdependent world. Embedded in this assumption is the belief that this interdependency is to a great extent symmetrical, and that it is enhanced by technology and communication. A second assumption is that no single nation can solve the world's problems alone. Food shortages, limited fossil energy supplies, overpopulation, pollution, and nuclear war transcend national or political boundaries. The final assumption is that gross inequities in the distribution of the world's goods will negate efforts to promote human survival and justice. Poverty, oppression, and starvation must be reduced and then obliterated if humankind is to survive into the 21st century.

From these assumptions, three imperatives for global education evolve. First, there should be an understanding of the earth's inhabitants and their surroundings, with specific attention to the interrelated network of survival. Second, there should be an awareness of future alternative choices that nations must make. These choices will shape the world's future. Third, from the possible future alternative choices, students must realize that others may choose preferences which differ from their own. A critical awareness of these imperatives may enable us to act in our own time with greater insight and dedication to human justice.

Once the assumptions and imperatives are understood, it is the task of educators to formulate global education goals that focus attention on problems and concerns. To assist in the construction of goals, the National Council of the Social Studies (Position Statement, 1982, pp. 37–38) recommends that global education emphasize: (a) that the human experience is an increasingly globalized phenomenon in which people are constantly being influenced by transnational, cross-cultural, multicultural, and multiethnic interactions; (b) that there are a variety of actors on the world stage; (c) that humankind is an integral part of the world environment; (d) that there are linkages between present societal,

political, and ecological realities and alternative futures; and (e) that citizens need to participate in world affairs.

If global education does give a focus to these goals, then international human rights—the concern for all people's rights—will be nourished. Buergenthal and Torney (1978, p. 26) point out that prior to World War II "international law left states free, with some minor exceptions, to treat their nationals as they saw fit." However, since World War II, documents such as the United Nations Charter and the Universal Declaration of Human Rights have established "international human rights standards governing the manner in which states may treat human beings, whether their own nationals or not." Thus, there is a moral obligation on the part of the "have" nations (nations with an abundance of world goods) to work toward a more equitable distribution of wealth and toward the liberation of the "have nots" (Buergenthal & Torney, 1978). As multicultural education strives to develop an understanding of the value of cultural pluralism by promoting human rights for our nation, so does global education strive to develop understanding of human interdependence and to promote human rights for all people on earth.

## THE MERGER

The paths of multicultural education and global education have followed parallel courses. The growing realization of national interdependence has promoted global education; the acceptance of the value of cultural diversity within American society has promoted multicultural education. Global education pointedly addresses the importance for educational institutions to assist students in understanding international realities. Multicultural education cites the necessity for educational institutions to aid students in comprehending a nation as well as a world characterized by cultural diversity (Cortes, 1980, p. 83). In the United States, state departments of education have required educational policies containing aspects of multicultural and/or global education. Publishing companies are producing more international and multicultural materials, and preservice teacher education institutions are mandating the inclusion of multicultural components within their curricula.

Although the overlap between global education and multicultural education might appear manifestly obvious, the actual connectedness is not seen in curriculum design. It would seem that for a curriculum to be totally multicultural, it should incorporate an international or global thrust, enabling a more complete analysis of American cultural diversity. Similarly, global education should incorporate analyses of the relationship of American ethnic groups, to international social-political situations.

Although multicultural education centers on group and individual understanding and global education is more concerned with world survival, the two movements have common linkages. Each has an aim to strengthen human and intergroup relations—there is a shared desire to aid students in understanding human diversity while exploring commonalities. Moreover, both movements strive to solidify cross-cultural communication, and both attempt to reduce stereotypical thinking. Therefore, the two movements propose to educate for the future in an effort to have a more aware world populace moving closer to the attainment of an interdependent life and its management for the betterment of humankind.

Since multicultural and global education are concerned with cross-cultural diversity and interactions, both lend themselves to fostering an interdisciplinary approach to learning. The two movements attempt to assist students in their acceptance and understanding of others, to produce students who are culturally aware, globally-knowledgeable adults. Through a cooperative

endeavor, "multicultural global literates" with knowledge, skills, and attitudes to succeed on our shared planet can work toward a successful world future.

## SHARED GOALS AND OBJECTIVES

Although there appear to be many fundamental commonalities from which goals and objectives for the two movements could be derived, the following are some of the more relevant:

1. To promote student understanding of social living in groups
2. To aid in understanding of "the other," especially ethnic and foreign cultural appreciation
3. To foster the understanding of interrelatedness and interdependence
4. To assist in the development of skills in living with diversity
5. To assist in the adjustment to changes for the future

It is important to address these five commonalities and suggest how multicultural and global education can work together for educational growth. In the attempt to conceptually merge these movements, one could multiculturalize global education or globalize multicultural education. The first method, multiculturalizing global education, will be employed for practical reasons: No global change begins at the global level; it starts with individuals and then expands to ever larger groups.

A multiculturalized global education would address the basic concern of where the individual fits into the mosaic of humanity and where others fit in the same mosaic. This first commonality promotes students' understanding of groups by introducing world factors which affect their lives and the lives of other members of the same or other groups. The individual is a member of several groups simultaneously, i.e., economic, social, regional, religious, national, sex, age, cultural, and ethnic groups. A multiculturalized global education would aid students in understanding that our membership in groups affects our values and attitudes. When individuals have an understanding of groups, they will be more likely to understand global phenomena and how the given groups interpret world group affairs.

The second commonality is the need to assist students in the understanding of "the other." To be cognizant of the other, students must be assisted in the understanding of stereotypes, how images of groups are formed, and the narrowness of group generalizations. K-12 curricula should continuously examine stereotyping. The students should consistently be challenged to evaluate the process and product of stereotyping, to detect it in their lives, and to identify institutional thinking based on stereotyping.

The third commonality is the need to help students understand the concepts of interrelatedness and interdependence. Hourly we receive news of international events, and yet we are unaware of how these events intrude upon and shape our lives. A multiculturalized global education would promote student understanding of the ramifications of these events. Through a coordinated K-12 curriculum, students would be taught to analyze multicultural and international interrelatedness. The curriculum would also promote student study and evaluation of local and global factors—such as environmental devastation—which would include people from varying cross-cultural and global perspectives.

This does not mean that primary school age children will be expected to study economic theory of other nations—multi-national stock market trends or currency exchange rates—but the elementary child can be encouraged to identify and to evaluate various character roles in their textbooks and the character's role in societal and international affairs in order to determine for themselves that there is a great human variability and uniformity, and these are global phenomena.

The fourth commonality is the need to assist students in the development of skills necessary to appreciate a culturally diverse local and global environment. Multiculturalized global education would strive to help students formulate such skills as:

- the ability to act effectively in intercultural environments (promote interdependence)
- the ability to consider an array of multicultural factors in decision making (negate ethnocentrism)
- the ability to promote cooperation and remedy conflict across ethnic, cultural, and national boundaries (promote cross-cultural understanding)
- the ability to communicate globally, within the United States and internationally (promote the view that we are one species on one globe)

The fifth and final commonality of multiculturalized global learning is to assist students in recognizing the need to be flexible and adjustable citizens in a rapidly changing world. It is important that the citizens of today be multiculturally and globally literate, but it will be essential for tomorrow. It is the educator's function to develop students' ability to face up to changing international conditions and act effectively in unfamiliar stituations. In other words, students must have the ability to be problem solvers in new, ever larger intergroup situations.

## IN CONCLUSION

We have considered multicultural education and global education, with an eye to five possible merged commonalities; a multiculturalized global education. It is hoped that the proposed merger defines the possibilities and challenges for multicultural and global cooperation. Essential to the merger is the assumption that all students—not just ethnic or minority students—should be multiculturally and globally educated. Our strategy assumes that all students will be an affected part of the cast on the future's multiethnic national stage, interacting in international relationships within our increasingly interdependent world stage. Thus, the future of our world may depend upon the ability of teachers to successfully educate citizens multiculturally and globally.

## REFERENCES

American Association of Colleges for Teacher Education. (1973). *No one model American*. Washington, DC: Author.

Banks, J. A. (1973). Teaching ethnic literacy: A comparative analysis. *Social Education*, 37 (8), 738–750.

Banks, J. A. (1977). *Multiethnic education: Practices and promises*. Bloomington, IN: Phi Delta Kappa Educational Foundation.

Banks, J. A. (1979). *Teaching strategies for ethnic studies* (2nd Ed.). Boston: Allyn & Bacon.

Buergenthal, T., & Torney, J. V. (1978). *International human rights and international education*. Washington, DC: National Commission for UNESCO, Department of State.

Cortes, C. E. (1980). *Multicultural education and global evaluation: Natural partners for a better world*. Riverside, CA: University of California-Riverside.

Goodlad, J. (1979). Introduction. In J. H. Becker (Ed.), *Schooling for a global age*. New York: McGraw-Hill.

Haipt, M. (1980). *Multicultural and global education: Relationships and possibilities*. World Education Monograph Series Number Three, World Education Project U-32. Storrs, CT: The University of Connecticut.

King, D., Branson, M. S., & Condon, L. E. (1976, November), Education for a world in change: A working handbook for global perspectives. *Intercom*, Nos. 84–85.

Position statement on global education. (1982). *Social Education*, 46 (1), 36–38.

Wilson, A. H. (1982). Cross-cultural experiential learning for teachers. *Theory Into Practice*, 21 (3), 184–192.

*Donna J. Cole* is Assistant Professor of Education, Wittenberg University, Springfield, Ohio.

# Research, Reading Instruction, and Children's Learning of the First R

## ANNE M. BUSSIS

*The King's Shadow* is a book about a little king who was terribly afraid of his own shadow. In the opening lines of the story, the king asks his three wise men what to do about the shadow, and they respond as follows:

"Chop off your shadow's head," said one.

"Boil it in oil," said another.

"Burn it at the stake," said a third. When Tim came to the third line, he quickly read, "Burn it at the casket. . . ."

Tim is one of many children whose classroom learning was documented for a two-year period (grades K-1 or 1-2) by teachers and researchers in the Collaborative Study of Reading of the

From *Phi Delta Kappan* 64 No. 4 (December 1982): 237–241. Used by permission of the author and the publisher.

Educational Testing Service (ETS). This program of research was funded by the National Institute of Education, the Ford Foundation, and ETS.

Substituting *casket* for *stake* is a puzzling error when considered in isolation, but it was fairly typical of other of Tim's renditions that went astray. His substitutions fell into a pattern; they tended to resemble anagrams, containing some or all of the letters of the text but in scrambled order. (With the exception of the first letters, *casket* is an anagram of *stake*.) This pattern was prominent in Tim's reading from May of first grade through November of second grade, and it is illustrated by the following additional examples. He read *want* for *what, blump* for *blurp, off* for *for, white* for *while, places* for *palace, last* for *least, still* for *silly, tried* for *tired, screeching* for *searching, left* for *felt,* and *Green Cold Superpie* for *Green Cloud Supreme* (the name of a dessert).

Aside from this scrambled-letter characteristic, many of Tim's errors also seemed both prompted and constrained by his anticipation of the story line or of the grammar of a sentence. Most of these mistakes occurred when Tim was reading a relatively unfamiliar book that challenged his capabilities; by and large, they did not daunt his efforts. He would continue reading, and he usually grasped the basic meaning of the text quite well.

Errors of a more debilitating nature surfaced when Tim's teacher asked him to stop and sound out words analytically. This was certainly not an unreasonable request, for Tim had been exposed to intensive instruction in letter/sound correspondence during the previous year in kindergarten, and his first-grade teacher had reinforced that instruction throughout the fall. The kindergarten program had emphasized various sounds of individual letters, of digraphs, and of consonant blends. When asked to apply this knowledge, Tim tried to oblige but invariably failed. He would reverse sound sequences or say he couldn't remember the correct sound; he produced whole words rather than a requested blend; and, if he did manage to articulate a sound sequence that closely approximated the text word, he usually did not recognize what he had said well enough to adjust to the proper enunciation.

In short, Tim seemed unable to process words in the letter-by-letter analytic fashion required by phonic decoding. After a particularly painful session of this nature in January of first grade, his teacher abandoned analytic decoding as a viable instructional approach with Tim. She would remind him of letter sounds from time to time or ask him the sound of a letter, but she never again required that he "sound out" a whole word.

Tim's first-grade teacher taught a combined class, so she kept Tim in her classroom for second grade. By the end of second grade, Tim was a competent and comprehending reader of texts that presented complex ideas and approximated adult books in vocabulary, grammar, and format. The following few lines illustrate a scientific text he read rapidly and discussed intelligently during his last tape-recorded oral reading in June of second grade.

> What did prehistoric man look like? That was the question some people had been asking even before the Paris Exhibition of 1867. Now many scientists all over Europe, including those who had once argued against De Perthe's whole theory, were eager to find the answer to that question. But they couldn't find the answer without first studying some of the clues which to this day are very rare— the actual bones of prehistoric man.*

Tim's progress in reading books was never matched by progress in his ability to perform phonic analysis, a fact periodically highlighted by the program of Individualized Criterion-Referenced Testing (ICRT) mandated by the school

* *All About Prehistoric Cavemen* (New York: Random House, 1959), p. 74.

system. The particular ICRT system used in Tim's district breaks reading into 340 discrete "skills" and provides a card of test items for each one. This system is apparently designed to serve as the major instructional program in reading in a given school throughout the primary years, since it supposes that every child will receive instruction in every skill to the point of mastering the test items. But Tim's teacher didn't use the ICRT system for reading instruction—nor did most other teachers in the district. Rather, she tried to fit the system into her own program. She used the skill cards without giving her students specific prior instruction and then discussed with individual children the skills that they had failed to master.

Tim fared well on many skill cards, but he and his teacher nearly always had to talk about the cards that dealt with letter/sound relationships. However, since Tim and most of his classmates were reading books, the teacher wasn't too concerned about failures on the test items. She noted them in her records and, for purposes of the reading study, wrote periodic reports on Tim's performance. In February of second grade, for instance, she reported about ICRT item #165 as follows: "This was the short *i* vowel sound. The exercise shows two pictures of things that have identical vowel sounds, and the child is supposed to pick the one word from four alternatives that has the same vowel sound. It was hard for Tim."

Tim is a normal child in every respect, including the soundness of his sight and hearing. In fact, his reading errors and strategies were quite similar to the learning behaviors of many children in the ETS study, just as they were dissimilar to the behaviors of other children. Tim's case history illustrates nothing particularly unusual about him, his teacher, his school, or his school district. But it illustrates superbly the kind of incongruity that typifies reading instruction in many schools.

The ingredients that combine to produce incongruity have all been presented above:

- a child who is actually reading books but who cannot answer correctly many test items related to "essential skills";
- a teaching/testing program that focuses solely on such skills, on the premise that they are prerequisites to learning to read;
- a school district that mandates the use of these tests and the recording of scores, presumably in the interest of demonstrating accountability for children's progress; and
- a teacher caught in the middle, trying to steer as intelligent a course as possible between satisfying district policy and supporting children's efforts to learn how to read.

The principal fully backed the teacher's instructional approach in this instance, but that is not always the case. Principals may express uneasiness and even disapproval, if they more often observe children reading books than teachers directing concrete, identifiable reading instruction.

It seems bizarre that emphasis on "essential" reading skills displaces actual reading in the classroom, but this is what happens far too often. And research has repeatedly shown that less competent readers receive the lion's share of the drill on skills. The pattern is predictable. Children who are least able to read text when they enter school are given the least exposure to books. Moreover, this approach "works," in the sense that reading programs that focus on skills are often modestly or highly successful in accomplishing what they claim. They enable children to perform better on tests designed to measure what the programs teach.

This circular definition of success becomes quite maddening; it causes teachers, administrators, researchers, and parents to doubt their own rationality. Given enough arguments in favor of such programs and abundant proof of what they can accomplish, we begin to doubt what we *know* about reading and to look instead to the instructional programs to tell us what reading is. In Tim's case, for example, we may begin to wonder whether fluent reading and intelligent discussion of a book really count for much without mastery of the skills. Has Tim somehow fooled us? Is he adequately prepared for work in the upper grades without a firm grasp of short *i*? We are no longer certain of what it means to read.

Let's look at the evidence—or, in this case, lack of evidence. The International Reading Association (IRA) held a special conference of researchers in 1973 to consider tests of early reading, the skills they typically assess, and the relationship of these skills to reading acquisition. The researchers held diverse theories about reading acquisition; many of them, in their own research, focused on specific components of the reading process. Although they disagreed about the merits and drawbacks of different kinds of tests, they agreed on one thing: No available evidence indicated that *any* identifiable group of subskills was essential to reading.

In 1975, as programs emphasizing basic skills continued to proliferate, the National Institute of Education (NIE) issued a call for intensive research on essential skills and skill hierarchies in reading, along with a plan for accomplishing this end. The plan reflected the deliberation of scientists and educators, most of whom were sympathetic to an instructional approach that focused on reading skills. The plan began with a statement of research objectives:

> [to] determine if there are essential skills or processing skills related to reading, what they are, how to identify and validate them, how they are interrelated, and which are causally related to reading.

The research generated by this plan failed to identify essential skills, skill hierarchies, and causal connections—just as all the prior research, considered at the IRA conference in 1973, had failed to do so.

But studies of a very different nature were also being conducted in the 1970s, and they produced promising results. The findings were so promising, in fact, that they shaped a surer rationale and a very different set of objectives for the new research plan that the NIE issued in December 1980. The 1980 plan argued that the reading process is both constructive and interactive (i.e., interpretation and perception influence one another), that it involves many strategies for constructing meaning, and that a reader adapts the process to deal with different kinds of texts.

Moreover, the 1980 plan presented these characteristics of the reading process as sound conclusions derived from reasonable evidence. It also acknowledged the failure of previous efforts to produce a coherent theory to explain reading acquisition. It attributed much of this failure to the fact that "most early research focused on decoding skills and various methods of teaching children to be good decoders." Only after educators began to realize that many children could master decoding skills and still fail to read effectively did "the focus of research begin to expand," according to the 1980 NIE research plan.

A stranger to the world of educational research, policy, and practice might legitimately wonder how we could have allowed the current situation to develop. Instructional programs in U.S. schools focus on "essential" reading skills; yet these skills have no demonstrable relationship to learning how to read books, and they impose definitions of reading and standards of reading progress that are contrary to common sense. The stranger would have a good point.

To develop a more effective approach to reading instruction, we must first understand some of the evidence on which the NIE based its 1980 statement. The most influential research is not all of a kind, nor did it spring full-blown from research efforts of the 1970s. It represents logical extensions of many years of previous investigations of memory, perception, thought, and language—all of which support a particular view of how the brain functions. This view is now so thoroughly documented that it is accepted as a "given" by most social scientists.

- The brain constructs perceptions and thoughts (instead of behaving as a sponge).
- The central function of the brain is to create meaning.
- Meaning arises through the perception and interpretation of patterns (or relationships) in events.
- Anticipation and intention influence brain activity.

Collectively, these characteristics imply that humans neither "soak up" elements in the environment nor respond directly to environmental stimuli (except in instinctive behavior). Instead, humans create symbolic representations of the environment and then act in accordance with the meanings they have constructed. Although meaning is relative in the sense that it may change somewhat from one context or culture to another, from one developmental stage to another, and from one individual to another, there seems to be nothing relative about its function in life. People in every culture and at every age strive to make their experiences as meaningful as possible. When they find themselves in situations that make little sense and that they cannot anticipate effectively, they become confused, anxious, and often hesitant to act at all.

The propensity of humans to construct meaning is one reason why books that convey meaningful information or tell comprehensible stories are so important to children. And because children—like adults—constantly construct meaning, their learning behaviors constitute a continuous source of information from which teachers can infer the meanings that children are (or are not) constructing in the classroom.

To go beyond these general implications in order to clarify the nature of reading, I must first redefine some terms that educators often use interchangeably and without much thought.

*Information* becomes potentially knowable and meaningful only when it stems from events that an individual actually heeds. But heeding alone does not suffice to transform information into knowledge. An individual must discern some unifying pattern in events before information becomes predictable and thus interpretable. Only when a person interprets information—however tentatively—does information qualify as knowledge. The interpretation need not be formulated in words; many experiences are represented in nonarticulate form. But an individual must note and interpret a pattern before he or she can be said to know something. In other words, information exists "out there" in the physical/social/cultural world or in physiological sensations arising from within the body. *Knowledge* exists in the mind.

This distinction between information and knowledge (and the fact that heeding is not equivalent to knowing) calls into question another popular instructional concern: time on task. Those researchers who stress time on task argue that the more time a child spends attending to instructional information (within reasonable bounds), the more he or she will learn. The problem with this logic is that the human brain doesn't always comply. An individual could conceivably attend to a particular kind of information for years without ever discerning a pattern that unifies the information or relates it to other meaningful patterns. Such a dismal outcome is not only theoretically possible but also quite probable, if the information an individual heeds consists primarily of isolated fragments of an event. Sufficient attention to information is an important and rather obvious condition of learning, but it guarantees nothing.

Written language contains information that is crucial to reading, and the beginning reader must figure out what this information means. This task involves separating irrelevant data (the size and style of print, for example) from potentially meaningful data, and then detecting patterns that make the potentially meaningful information predictable and interpretable. Since pattern detection is the crucial task and since patterns involve relationships between both similar and contrasting events, rich data are more useful to the learner than meager data. For this reason, books that present written language in its naturally occurring variations are helpful to children.

The human brain is an exquisitely designed pattern detector, and it works with remarkable ease and efficiency when it receives appropriate information. Perhaps the most impressive testimony to the prowess of the brain is the fact that infants detect and assimilate the underlying sound patterns and grammatical structures of their native language from the rich speech environment that surrounds them. When the brain must try to construct a coherent whole from fragmented data, however, its efficiency plummets to mediocre at best. Presenting children with written language in piecemeal fashion may seem a logical instructional approach to reading, but it actually imposes formidable burdens on the learner.

As children successfully detect the underlying patterns in written language, they acquire more and more knowledge. However, knowledge about writing does not equate with skill in reading, and to assume that it does will lead an instructional program off course. Reading is a singular skill. A curriculum that focuses on reading skills (in the plural) actually attempts to foster instead various kinds of formal knowledge about written language—some of it important for reading, some of it not, and much of it very difficult to learn if one is not already able to read. Such curricula test children's ability to demonstrate this formal knowledge about written language.

A *skill* supposes intention, it is affected by attitudes, and it depends on knowledge. Yet it is none of these. A skill demands the coordination or orchestration of diverse knowledge to achieve a particular result that is characterized by particular constraints or criteria. Were there no constraints or criteria, virtually any action could be called a skill. The skill of reading requires the orchestration of at least five kinds of knowledge in order to construct meaning from a text while maintaining reasonable fluency and reasonable faithfulness to the information that has been encoded in the text. This is the singular skill of reading.

Beginners execute any skill more awkwardly and less proficiently than do experts. The only way to gain the proficiency that comes with experience is to practice a skill in its overall complexity. Orchestration and coordination are brain functions that seem to be learned only through repeated attempts to perform them. Beginning readers may wish to concentrate on different aspects of the skill at times (e.g., the flow or the accuracy), and they must limit their ambitions at first (e.g., reading a few sentences or short books). But practice is what counts.

The paradox of learning a skill is that neophytes can begin to practice before they control all the knowledge that a polished performance requires. In fact, there is no other way to begin learning a skill. Practice can start as soon as an individual possesses some of the necessary knowledge and understands what the skill is intended to accomplish. The brain picks up additional knowledge in the course of practice. This explains why initial stages of practice are always both fumbling and fatiguing. Beginners are operating under the handicap of incomplete knowledge, they are still learning the crucial act of orchestration, and they are detecting and interpreting relevant patterns of information along the way. Fortunately, the human brain can handle such a complex task quite well. But the effort is tiring, and a beginner needs encouragement from others and the motivation of a desirable end result. If appropriate support is not forthcoming or if the outcomes of early practice sessions continually prove dissatisfying and relatively meaningless, the learner may eventually decide that the reward does not justify the effort.

Children have two strong knowledge resources for reading acquisition. They have a tacit understanding of the grammatical structures and sound patterns of English, and they know a great deal about the everyday world. These resources help them to comprehend and to anticipate the content of books. Children who have attended to such familiar forms of writing as words on signs, on cereal boxes, and on television commercials usually possess implicit knowledge of some letter/sound relationships as well.

The best way to support a beginning reader is to tell him or her what the text says. When children realize that a particular graphic configuration represents "once upon a time" or "Curious George went to the store," they can begin to detect recurring features within the configuration and to relate these to the meaning that the configuration conveys. When they tentatively apply these interpretations to other familiar lines of text, learning to read has begun. As practice proceeds, children acquire more and more knowledge about the two kinds of information encoded in writing: phonetic (i.e., letter/sound) relationships and spelling patterns.

A child who makes any progress in reading at all will, of necessity, interpret many letter/sound relationships. Much of this knowledge may remain implicit, however, and in such form may not lead the beginner much beyond the initial consonant sounds of unknown words. Explicit knowledge of the rules that govern letter/sound relationships is a prerequisite for the kind of phonetic analysis that helps to unlock whole words. Many children can use these formal rules to advantage in learning to read, but many others—like Tim—either cannot or will not.

Tim's classmate, Rita, thrived on instruction in phonics and would try to use what she knew to solve every unknown word she encountered. If she couldn't figure out a word, she would ask her teacher or someone else for help before moving on. In fact, Rita approached text as if every word were a crucial step in a straight and orderly path to meaning. She never skipped a word in her beginning practice efforts, nor would she rest with substituting a good guess for an unknown word. Rita was able to sound out many difficult words by the end of first grade, but by that time her path to meaning had also broadened. She was willing to settle for some intelligent guesses in the interest of getting on with a text, and she was relying heavily on the kind of information on which Tim seemed to focus from the very first.

Tim almost always tackled a new book as if he were eager to get on with the text. He would take a stab at troublesome words, skip them, offer substitute words, or use some combination of these strategies. He tended to read rapidly, and his reading behavior suggested that he was dealing with relatively broad spans of print. These facts alone suggest that Tim was attending to the visual configurations of whole words (i.e., their spellings), rather than to the sounds of the individual letters in each word (i.e., phonetics). And the nature of his errors bears out this hypothesis. Although only a few of Tim's errors seemed to represent faulty interpretations of the sound structures of words, many of his errors reflected faulty interpretations of the spelling structures of words.

Tim was actually attending to the dominant information encoded in writing. Phonetic information may receive more publicity, but linguistic analysis has shown that written English emphasizes consistent spellings more than it emphasizes consistent letter/sound relationships. When the letter *s* is applied at the end of a word, for example, it becomes a meaningful word part—a suffix that always signals the same meaning (i.e., plurality) but that can have any one of three pronunciations (as in *cats, cars,* or *houses*). Written English does not indicate the particular sound of the letter *s* in a given word, because native speakers intuitively predict and accommodate to shifts in the sound of this letter. If the sound rather than the meaning, of *s* were the more important information to convey, then the writing system would indicate plurality by three different spellings.

The spelling principle is especially useful when root words are combined with suffixes. *National* retains the root word *nation;* the suffix *-al* simultaneously signals that the word is an adjective. Although the suffix changes the sound of the first vowel (from the long *a* of *nation* to the short *a* of *national*), English speakers make this shift quite unconsciously. The more important information that the writing system has emphasized is the intimate bond of meaning between the two words. Thus we can predictably transform nouns into adjectives or verbs adjectives into adverbs, and verbs into nouns by tacking on such endings as *-al, -able, -ive, -ful, -less, -ize, -ate, -ly, -ship, -tion, -ity,* and so on.

The semantic information encoded in writing suggests that a learner must eventually attend to the visual organization of spelling patterns if he or she is ever to become a proficient reader. Tim's history suggests that he focused on such organizational features very early in his learning. And Tim's history in this respect duplicates the histories of many other children in the ETS reading study, just as Rita's general learning progress duplicates the progress of many of her peers.

I have emphasized learning, because good teaching begins with an understanding of learning—particularly when it comes to skills. Teachers and curriculum developers cannot crawl inside children's minds and manipulate the orchestration of knowledge that is necessary for reading. But teachers can make this task easy or hard, rewarding or painful, worthwhile or not worthwhile

for students by the provisions they make in the classroom and the help that they offer.

Specific provisions and kinds of help will depend on the child. But let me suggest five general practices.

1. Provide a range of reading materials in the classroom. For the young learner, these materials might include alphabet and counting books, picture books, informational and reference books, classics of children's literature, easy-to-read trade books, and a variety of beginning reading series.
2. Provide time each day for children to read books of their own choosing or—in the case of youngsters who are not yet reading—to look at pictures in self-selected books.
3. Provide time for children to write, preferably every day but at least two or three times each week. Young children can begin by dictating sentences or words to their teachers or to classroom aides and then copying what these adults write for them.
4. Read to the class each day, varying the selections between well-written imaginative literature and interesting informational books.
5. Work individually with children at least some of the time. Listen to each child read or discuss what he or she has read.

The first four practices give children several perspectives on the written word and encourage them to exercise intelligence in choosing, deciphering, and making sense of books and other writing. These practices do not add up to a full instructional program. But they do lend coherence and direction to otherwise diverse instructional approaches (whether phonic, basal, or language experience) in diverse instructional settings (whether large groups, small groups, or one-to-one). The practices are not my idea; rather, they are the key similarities that characterize the classrooms of the most successful teachers I know.

The fifth practice allows teachers to observe

their students. If a general understanding of learning is the first principle of effective teaching, then careful observation of learners must rank a close second. In fact, the first principle presupposes the second. But observation must be of a special kind. The teacher who monitors only students' correct responses will derive relatively little data to inform his or her instructional decisions. Merely counting up errors will add nothing more. It is the nature of children's errors and their general approach to text that reveal what is happening in the orchestration and comprehension process.

"Burn it at the casket" and "Green Cold Superpie" may never be uttered again. Nor will other children manifest a desire to get on with the story or to read every word of text in precisely the same ways as Tim and Rita did. But other children will manifest intentions, strategies, struggles, and errors that are just as revealing—if they have opportunities to read interesting books. And knowledgeable, observant teachers will be informed by children's reading behaviors—if they are freed from paperwork long enough to observe.

## SELECTED BIBLIOGRAPHY

Allington, Richard. "Poor Readers Don't Get Much in Reading Groups." *Language Arts,* vol. 57, 1980, pp. 872–76.

Bartlett, Elsa. "Curriculum, Concepts of Literacy, and Social Class," in Lauren Resnick and Phyllis Weaver, eds., *Theory and Practice of Early Reading,* Vol. 2. Hillsdale, N. J.: Erlbaum, 1979, pp. 229–42.

Bissex, Glenda. *Gnys at Wrk: A Child Learns to Write and Read.* Cambridge, Mass.: Harvard University Press, 1980.

Bobrow, Daniel and Allan Collins, eds. *Representation and Understanding: Studies in Cognitive Science.* New York: Academic Press, 1975.

Bussis, Anne M. with Edward A. Chittenden, Marianne Amarel, and Edith Klausner. *Inquiry into Meaning: An Investigation of Learning to Read.* Hillsdale, N.J.: Erlbaum, forthcoming.

Chomsky, Carol. "Reading, Writing, and Phonology." *Harvard Educational Review,* May 1970, pp. 287–309.

———. "Stages in Language Development and Language Exposure." *Harvard Educational Review,* February 1972, pp. 1–33.

Clay, Marie M. *Reading: The Patterning of Complex Behaviour.* New Zealand: Heinemann Educational Books, 1972.

Conference on Studies in Reading. Panel 10 Report. *Essential Skills and Skill Hierarchies in Reading.* Washington, D.C.: National Institute of Education, June 1975.

Fader, Daniel. *The Naked Children.* New York: Macmillan, 1971.

Freedle, Roy, ed. *New Directions in Discourse Processing, Vol. 2.* Norwood, N.J.: Ablex. 1979.

Goodman, Kenneth S. and Yetta M. Goodman. "Learning About Psycholinguistic Processes by Analyzing Oral Reading." *Harvard Educational Review,* August 1977, pp. 317–33.

Henderson, Edmund H. *Learning to Read and Spell.* DeKalb, Ill.: Northern Illinois University Press, 1981.

Center for the Study of Reading. *RFP Notification.* Washington, D.C.: National Institute of Education, December 1980.

Scheffler, Israel. *Conditions of Knowledge.* Chicago: Scott, Foresman, 1965.

Smith, Frank. *Understanding Reading.* New York: Holt, Rinehart & Winston, 1971.

———. *Comprehension and Learning: A Conceptual Framework for Teachers.* New York: Holt, Rinehart & Winston, 1975.

Spiro, Rand, Bertram Bruce, and William Brewer, eds. *Theoretical Issues in Reading Comprehension.* Hillsdale, N.J.: Erlbaum, 1980.

Weber, Rose M. "First-Graders' Use of Grammatical Context in Reading." in Harry Levin and Joanna Williams, eds., *Basic Studies on Reading.* New York: Basic Books, 1970.

*Anne M. Bussis* is Research Psychologist, Educational Testing Service, Hopewell, New Jersey.

# Getting a Headstart on Career Choices

## JUDY COMER

Few questions are more frequently posed to a youngster and doubtless few are more baffling. "What," ask parents, teachers, relatives, and just about everyone else the child encounters, "do you want to be when you grow up?" Most boys and girls haven't the faintest idea how to reply to that question, since they have no information or experiences on which to base a sensible response. Many graduate from high school still uncertain about what career path to follow. Typically people seem either to drift into their life's work or to find a career on the basis of trial and error, testing the market-place here and there, moving from one job to another until they happen on one they want to stick with.

Which provokes another question: When is the "right time" for a young person to begin seriously charting a future course? Many educators believe that the answer to both questions— what and when—lies in the earliest application, in the earliest grades, of the career education concept: a concept hinging on the proposition that career choice is too important to be left to chance, whim, or the vicissitudes of the job market.

Career education, they say, offers the student a sound, logical approach to selecting a field of work. Equally important, it offers the schools a method of making the overall learning experience more rewarding and more effective by presenting aspects of the curriculum in terms the individual boy and girl find of immediate use and interest.

A good place to see this approach in action is Cobb County, Georgia, just north and a shade west of Atlanta. Here boys and girls have the chance to start thinking about jobs and work and things they want to do with their hands, minds, and lives as soon as they enter kindergarten and the first year of school.

In Cobb County's forty-two elementary schools, youngsters may start "trying on" careers to see what it's like to be a police officer or a dancer or doctor. They are encouraged to examine jobs in all their aspects, considering such characteristics as whether the work is indoors or outdoors, mental or manual or both, demanding creativity or alternatively patience, team work or individual effort. Youngsters query people in particular jobs about whether they think of their jobs as tedious or exciting, stressful or evenly paced, quiet or noisy, stimulating or depressing. And all through their school careers the students are urged to move toward the Socratic principle; Know thyself. Experiences are planned to help them find out who they are, what they are becoming, what kind of things excite them, what kind of things turn them off. Equally important is the practice of involving students in certain decisions affecting the class: decisions about what speakers to invite, field trips to take, topics to discuss, work projects to undertake. From participation in these small decisions, a student develops confidence and a sense of awareness along with the feeling of being part of the action.

Thus, through a three-pronged approach— exposure to a variety of career fields, introspective investigation, and experience making decisions—the goal is to make students better

Article written by Judy Comer for *Curriculum Planning: A New Approach,* Fourth Edition, 1983. Revised by Judy Comer for Fifth Edition, 1986. Portions drawn from "Getting a Jump on Career Choices" by Mary Kay Murphy, *American Education* 9, no. 5 (June 1973): 18–24. Used by permission of the author.

prepared for that future time when they will need to make a career choice. They will know the kinds of careers open to them; they will have some reasonably realistic idea of life goals and their ability to attain them; and they will understand the factors their decisions will entail and how to weigh these factors in selecting the kind of work they are likely to find truly satisfying.

The preliminary groundwork for much that is happening in career education in Cobb County today was laid in the early 1970s. Staff members worked to establish a curriculum plan that could be implemented in most any setting with a minimum of special financial support even though Cobb County had a federal grant at that time to develop a model program. The staff succeeded so well that the career education program is now conducted by the local school system with minimal budgetary support and only an investment in a system wide K-12 coordinator for Cobb County's sixty-eight elementary schools, middle schools, and high schools. In a smaller school system, this role could be carried part-time by a regular staff member with other responsibilities.

One of the reasons career education works so well in Cobb County is because teachers in the program are able to bring about significant student change with little formal change in the teaching process. Teachers and other program participants avoid saying, "It's career education time," and thus treating career awareness as a separate, add-on kind of emphasis. Instead, the focus is on linking career education with math, language arts, science, music, art, and social studies.

Educators in Cobb County have found that the career education concept encourages a large measure of flexibility, in that it is compatible with traditional school settings, open space areas, heterogeneous grouping, affective education, ungraded organizations, and other educational innovations.

Interestingly enough, it is this very flexibility of program organization that has helped contribute to its longevity and success. Originally, at the elementary level, the teaching unit was the instruction strategy most frequently used. Teachers planned unit activities that focused on different career areas tied into the fifteen Occupational Clusters identified by the then United States Office of Education. The instructional organization of the elementary school at that time permitted and even supported the unit approach; changes in organization since the early 1970s have necessitated some rethinking of the original instructional plan. In the early 1970s, elementary teachers operated in primarily self-contained classrooms and taught all subjects to the same group of students. Today Cobb County elementary teachers have differentiated groups for language arts and math, teaching their "own" students for social studies, science, and other disciplines.

Proceeding along these lines of thought, the original unit approach enriched the elementary school curriculum through the inclusion of several standard components. Over time the approach came to include six elements or methods: a "hands-on" activity to provide concrete experiences that illustrate a particular job, tie-ins with academic subjects, a field trip, resource persons, role-playing, and occupational awareness. These elements were mixed into the unit activities as creatively as the imaginations and resources of teachers and students permitted.

Career educators acknowledge that there is absolutely nothing new or innovative about these six elements or strategies. They have been used by teachers for years to present subject-matter ranging from the study of dinosaurs to weather to nutrition. What is innovative about their application to career education is the way they give a creative thread to career-related activities and the regular elementary curriculum.

Teachers involved in various activities state that career education at the elementary level is not intended to help youngsters know exactly what they want to be when they grow up. Instead, the teachers emphasize that career awareness activities are meant to give students the chance to find out whether they like to work standing up or sitting down, to make things with their hands or to use their minds, work outdoors or inside, etc. These classroom and community experiences help point out to children that all jobs are important and that all work fills some social need. Through career education, students get to see the importance of the group and the contribution of each member in that group.

Using a set of systemwide career education goals as their organizing focus, Cobb County teachers have implemented a variety of activities aimed at enhancing the self-awareness and career identities of elementary students. A booklet of suggested activities tied to various goal areas has been developed for teachers as an aid in planning. Learning centers, bulletin boards, enrichment programs, career fairs, modified units, resource speakers—all these and more examples of strategies are used by teachers to link career concepts with classroom learning. Hands-on activities continue in the form of a classroom newspaper in a communications study; model cities in a public services unit investigation; or a videotape production of school and community news in a broadcasting simulation.

Cobb County's success in this instructional program can perhaps be seen in the schools' performance on Georgia's annually administered criterion-referenced tests. Fourth-year students are tested on their understanding of items related to twenty career development objectives in the areas of self-understanding, work and occupations, education, and decision making. Since the first administration of the test in 1976, Cobb students' achievement has exceeded the state average and that of other school systems in the metro-Atlanta area. System instructional planners and local school personnel use their test data as one gauge of program effectiveness and

as information for structuring and modifying activities.

Some educators might question the importance of beginning the career development process with elementary learners. Joel Smith, original career development project director, replied, "It's too late to start thinking about jobs and careers for the first time in high school. All the research in this field tells us that decision making requires time and students should be encouraged to explore career opportunities at an early age. The later we wait to suggest options to students, the weaker their decisions will be and the less likely their long-term satisfaction and happiness with the careers they select."

In Cobb County career education is viewed as an approach to learning that is useful from the elementary years through high school and beyond. While education is not synonymous with guidance, it does include guidance. Neither does the career education concept hinge on either college preparation or vocational education. Cobb educators see career development as much broader than either of these and as being designed to provide students all the experiences possible to help them make sound decisions.

Efforts are made to avoid linking career education activities to one sex more readily than another. Students are encouraged to participate in activities according to their interests and not their sex. In selecting resource persons and other adult role models, teachers and other staff members seek to include a broad range of workers, both those traditional and non-traditional for their sex.

The basic goal, all along the career development path, is to instill confidence in one's individual worth and a feeling of mastery over one's environment and destiny. Research evidence suggests, Cobb educators point out, that there is a high correlation between student positive self-concept and academic success, greater even than that between IQ and academic success. Career development as it is seen in Cobb County seeks to reinforce this self-concept at every opportunity and in every conceivable way, daily if possible, to insure that students keep open their options for academic and emotional growth, and for understanding themselves and their motives and values.

Parents are also another crucial factor in the Cobb County program. Again, educational research strongly indicates that parents are the single most important factor in their children's movement toward academic success from the earliest grades. Only slowly as the years pass are parents replaced in this role by their children's peers. In Cobb County, parents have become actively involved in what the program is attempting to achieve. Parents participate as resource speakers, as enrichment activity leaders, as classroom aides and as field trip helpers. In this way, parents can contribute to their own as well as to others' children.

Educators in Cobb County don't think they've done anything revolutionary. They feel they have found a way to help students try on careers and to think good thoughts about themselves. Their philosophy is probably best expressed in the document that gave birth to the renowned and widely emulated British Infant School movement. "The best preparation for life," it reads, "is to live fully as a child."

*Judy Comer* is Career/Economic Education Supervisor, Cobb County Schools, Marietta, Georgia

# The Young Reach Out to the Old in Shaker Heights

## BETSEY A. MIKLETHUN

Ageism, the invidious stereotyping of elderly persons, often begins with people when they are young. To help stop perpetuating this pattern, staff at Ludlow Elementary School in Shaker Heights, Ohio, developed an Adopt-a-Grandparent program, in which participating students meet and get to know elderly persons. By so doing, the students—and sometimes their families as well—form more positive attitudes toward older persons than they otherwise would.

The idea for Adopt-a-Grandparent came in the spring of 1977. That year my daughter was a second grader at Ludlow School and I was a staff member at Judson Park, a nearby retirement community. I helped arrange a visit by her class to the community.

During the visit, the children had a variety of experiences that fascinated them: They met a woman who was writing her autobiography, visited a copper-enamelling class, saw a blind person using braille and another doing an interpretive dance, and joined in the performance of a rhythm band. They didn't want to leave.

Afterward, their teacher, Janice Wong Shear, and I decided to explore the possibility of pair-

From *Today's Education,* Journal of the National Education Association 70, no. 2 (April–May 1981) (Elementary Edition): 34–35. Used by permission of the author and the publisher.

ing the children one-to-one with people in the retirement community for regular visits that would, we hoped, lead to friendship. Thus the Adopt-a-Grandparent program was born.

The program officially began the following fall when twelve second graders, each with parental permission to participate, toured the retirement community. The children learned that Judson Park has several types of living arrangements: a high-rise for people who can get along by themselves, another unit for those who need some assistance, and a unit that offers nursing care.

During the first year of the program, the children brought things to share with their grandparents—a book, a game, or just a treasured possession. Sometimes activities were structured, other times purposely unstructured.

In the second year, which also involved twelve second graders, two special events—a Saturday morning choral ensemble concert and an end-of-the-year potluck picnic—were added in order to include the children's families.

After the second year, Ms. Wong moved to the fourth grade. Since she wanted to continue working with the program, it moved to the fourth grade with her.

The change in grade level meant there would be some program changes. (It also meant that some children would be involved for a second year.) The program became more structured and activity-centered, with activities designed around a particular theme or event.

On one occasion, for example, the program spotlighted books and authors. The children interviewed three residents who had written books. Another time, children and grandparents shared an exercise day that emphasized the need for both groups to keep physically fit. On a craft day, everyone worked with clay, which was a new experience for several of the grandparents. It was, of course, important to have some time left unstructured in each visit as well as some

entire visits left to grandparents and grandchildren to plan and use as they wished.

Friendships did take hold during the first three years of the program. All but one of the families involved had at least one contact—perhaps for dinner or a session at the bowling alley—with their child's adopted grandparent, and most had two or more. Three relationships spanned two continents. One family spent a year in Great Britain but kept alive the relationship with a grandfather by mail. Another, a British family that had lived in the United States for a few years but moved back to England, continued to correspond with their adopted grandmother. One adopted grandmother started up a correspondence with her adopted grandchild's real grandmother who lives in New Zealand.

We have used a variety of means to evaluate the children's and their families' experiences. We have given attitude surveys to participating students and taped interviews with them and with their parents. We have also had the parents reply to a questionnaire and asked the fourth graders to keep diaries.

The attitude surveys—which were given to a control group as well as to participating students—consisted of several statements about older people (e.g., "As people age, they tend to become more demanding, complaining. . . ." "Achievement and being successful are not important to older people.") The children had to say whether they thought the statements were true or false. On most items, the children in the program were far more likely than the control group students to choose the nonstereotyped response to the statements.

When asked in the interviews what they thought they would be like when they got older, some of the children demonstrated that the program had given them the chance to project their own futures. Several said they would be the same, only older, or pointed to the fact that they wouldn't have to go to school. Some said they thought they would be similar in some way to their adopted grandparent. One girl thought she would be grumpy. When asked why she thought that, she replied, "Because when you're young and grumpy, when you get older you'll still be grumpy."

In their diaries, the fourth graders showed great insight when they made statements about, for example, the similarity between them and the grandparents: "I'm learning more about older people, that they can do the same things we can do." Other statements indicated the breakdown of stereotypes: "Older people are fun even though they are old." Still others showed an acceptance of the frailties of the elderly: "She forgets a lot but that's OK." And, finally, from one youngster came the single statement: "I'm beginning to love her."

On their questionnaires, the parents mentioned such benefits as the fact that their children had developed an awareness of the aging process, an understanding that people slow down as they become older. Some children, again according to the parents, also developed a greater interest in their own grandparents and showed more patience with them than they had before entering the program.

Parents felt that the program built understanding, friendship, appreciation, respect, affection, and love for older people. Important to many was the fact that their children had learned to share—not only tangible items but love and time.

Additionally, some valued the realization on the part of their children that worth and ability to contribute don't go away because someone changes physically. As one parent said, "My child learned that no matter how old you get, you're still the same inside."

A program like Adopt-a-Grandparent is not for every child any more than it is for every older adult. The children who chose to participate in this program felt it was for them, however. There is no doubt that their parents were enthusiastic about it, too. And they should be, for in the long run, they may be the ones who will profit most from it.

*Betsey A. Miklethun* is a student, School of Applied Social Sciences, Case Western Reserve University.

# Early Education Principles and Computer Practices

## DOUGLAS H. CLEMENTS

Computers are rapidly becoming as common as blackboards, crayons and pencils in classrooms, including kindergarten and primary grade classrooms. In a flurry of activity, various producers of software are generating numerous computer programs for the young child. These programs are becoming increasingly easy to use and graphically sophisticated. But will they benefit children?

The numerous computer program evaluation checklists that are available can provide assistance in organizing evaluation efforts around

From *Children Today* 14, No. 3 (May–June 1985): 21–24. Used by permission of the author.

such questions as technical quality; use of sound, graphics and animation; ease of use; user control of pacing; and educational content.[1] However, their concentration on the computer as a medium, and their intended use with materials designed for all grade levels, may place limits on their use as evaluative instruments for computer programs designed for young children. Perhaps the most basic question should be: Do the computer programs reflect the principles of the *educational* program?

Many features of educational computer programs—interactivity, for example—are consonant with educational principles. Not all programs are equally so, however. Does the novelty of the medium and the "flashiness" of computer graphics blind many of us to practices that conflict with these principles?

This article will illustrate how computer practices can be evaluated in terms of accepted principles of early and primary education. However, this type of evaluation could and should be used for all grade levels.

## PRINCIPLES OF EARLY AND PRIMARY EDUCATION

Although there is no one list of accepted principles of early and primary education, there is a great deal of agreement. The following four general categories include those principles most often cited, expressed as guidelines for educational practices.

- **The child as a learner of social and emotional competencies.** The importance of social and emotional development is emphasized in these principles:
  1. Provide opportunities for social interaction and growth and the development of a positive self-image.
  2. Provide many opportunities for learning without pressure for mastery.

- **The child as an active learner.** Often based on Piagetian and/or information-processing theory, these principles state that the child should not be seen as a "vessel to be filled".[2]
  3. Emphasize the child's active participation rather than passive reception in planning and executing the activity.
  4. Provide many opportunities for children to express themselves freely and creatively and to develop aesthetic interests, skills and values.

- **The child as an independent learner.** A corollary of the previous two principles, these five are based on the belief that children should learn how to take responsibilities for their own continuing education:
  5. Provide a minimally restrictive environment that encourages autonomy and exploration and is responsive to the child.
  6. Encourage transfer by allowing children to discover relationships by themselves and by providing them the experience during learning of applying principles within a variety of tasks.
  7. Encourage multiple solutions and alternate routes to any solution.
  8. Provide practice in setting realistic goals and in predicting and confirming events.
  9. Use techniques to ease the learning of complex material; teach general rules about regularities instead of collections of unrelated facts.

- **The child as a learner in the real world.** These principles emphasize that education should involve children in meaningful activities directly tied to their out-of-school life:
  10. Provide for exploration of problems involving real situations and concrete materials.
  11. Provide for feedback which is a natural consequence of child's activity.
  12. Provide for intrinsic, rather than extrinsic, motivation. The curriculum grows out of the personal interests of the child; play is an important vehicle for learning.

As we examine the following examples of computer programs designed for young children, we can consider how well these programs follow the principles listed here.

## COMPUTER PRACTICES

One technically sophisticated package designed for young children teaches several mathematics concepts. A seriation lesson graphically presents five unordered bars of different heights. The child must place a marker under each and type in a number (1 to 5) corresponding to that bar's place in the series; that is, the shortest bar is number 1, the next taller is number 2, and so on. If the child succeeds, a face smiles and a point is added to a running total of the number correct. If the child makes an error, the face frowns and a point is added to a total of the number incorrect. Another lesson deals with weight. A balance scale is shown locked into horizontal position; a number of blocks are drawn on each side. The child must identify the "heavier" side. Feedback is given in the same manner.

Another set of programs presents a pair of shapes, colors or letters on the screen. The child waits until they match and, when they do, presses a key. If the child is correct, a smile face appears; if not, descending tones are heard.

In what ways are these lessons in harmony or in conflict with early education principles?

Several principles are evident in these programs. The child receives feedback concerning the correctness of the response and self-discovery may take place (principles 6 and 11). However, in our initial appreciation of the cleverness of the programming, we may overlook other principles that are not upheld and may even be violated.

For instance, consider the nature of the tasks. The child is not actually actively manipulating concrete materials to solve a problem (principle 10). In the second set of activities, the child is not active at all for considerable periods of time (principle 3). The many possible solution strategies that children use in ordering objects are not only not encouraged, they are not possible (principle 7). When a child orders blocks or uses a balance scale, the feedback he or she receives is real and meaningful—the blocks either form "steps" or they do not; the balance pan tips to one side or balances; the results can be seen *and* felt. In the computer program, the frowning face feedback is not a natural consequence of the child's activity (principle 11). This type of feedback emphasizes extrinsic, rather than intrinsic, motivation (principle 12). The score-keeping may place undesirable pressure for mastery on the child (principle 2). Finally, the programs do not encourage self-expression or aesthetic interests (principles 4 and 5).

## MID-RANGE COMPATIBILITY

Other programs tend to be compatible with more, but still not all, of the principles. With *Story Machine,* a program designed to allow children to compose stories, a child types in sentences and watches as they are graphically portrayed. For example, after a child typed "a girl walks to the store," a small figure and then a store appeared on the screen, and the girl walked over to the store. Feeling silly, the child then typed "the tree runs to the boy." Obligingly, a tree entered the picture, turned to the side and, on its newly discovered legs, ran to a boy who had appeared on the other side of the screen.

How is this program compatible with early education principles?

This program may encourage social and emotional development, for it provides many opportunities to learn without pressuring children to achieve a pre-set standard (principles 1 and 2). Children are actively involved (principle 3). However, if syntactic forms are used that are not recognized by the program, words are crossed out, which could negatively affect the child's self-image. In addition, the limitations in vocabulary and syntax might hinder self-expression (principle 4). Children may discover relationships on their own, and multiple solutions are allowed. However, they are allowed only within this constrained environment (principles 6 and 7).

## TOWARD HARMONY

Other software packages tend to be compatible with more of the stated principles. Young children can "teach the computer," rather than being taught by it, if they use one of the several computer languages that allows them to program the computer to draw pictures using simple commands.

With Logo, children use such commands as "forward 50" or "right 90" to direct a "turtle," a small triangular pointer around the display screen, leaving traces of its path. Logo is procedural—problems can be divided into small pieces, and a separate procedure (list of commands) written for each piece. For example, one popular early project is drawing a house. Children might first "teach" the computer to draw an outline, possibly naming the procedure "sides-and-roof" (or any other word they might choose). Then they construct another set of commands to draw a rectangle for the door. Finally, they assemble these procedures into one procedure that they might name "house," which uses the "sides-and-roof" procedure to draw the outline and move it into position and then uses the "door" procedure to finish the drawing. Two girls used similar techniques to add a rainbow (written in color) and a bird to their program, "outside."

The *Early Childhood Learning Program* contains several different activities. Some allow children to select, color, move and rotate shapes to create designs and drawings. Others permit them to control the color, heading and speed of boats and planes. One invites them to construct small "Worlds" by typing the name of an object, such as "girl" or "house" (which is then pictured on the screen), and moving it to a desired location. The movement and color commands can be used to transform objects into abstract designs or new shapes. In addition, several Logo-like drawing programs are included.

As a final brief example, several programs such as *Songwriter* are being written which allow children to compose and edit simple songs.

How can these programs be evaluated in light of the principles?

I believe that these programs, although quite different, share many educational attributes that are consistent with early education principles. They encourage social (and emotional) growth and the development of positive self-concepts (principle 1). Opportunities for free expression and aesthetic appreciation are provided without pressure for immediate mastery (principles 2, 3 and 4). The open nature of these activities encourages active exploration and multiple solutions, provides practice in setting goals and predicting and confirming events, and encourages transfer by requiring the child to discover relationships and concepts (principles 5, 6, 7 and 8). Powerful, generalizable ideas are taught: directionality, breaking a problem into manageable pieces, spatial and tonal relationships, and so forth (principle 9).

In addition, the problems that are explored are real and concrete to the child (principle 10). (While some may question the latter term, the creation of a drawing is indeed concrete to the child. In fact, Papert maintains that Logo can "concretize" thinking processes and lead children to "think about their thinking."[3] The child receives feedback based on his or her own activity—the triangle is drawn on top of the square, instead of above it, or the song does not sound the way the child intended (principle 11). The motivation is intrinsic; children have scenes to create, pictures to draw, and songs to compose (principle 12).

## EYES OF THE REVIEWER

As with any evaluation of curricular materials, especially those based on educational principles, these are at least partially subjective. To one teacher, the motivation to work with *Story Machine* might be intrinsic, based on children's desire to write stories and animate figures. To another, it might be extrinsic, based on the reinforcement of seeing the figures "perform." Some might not agree that the story writing, or even the Logo drawing, is real or concrete. Differences stemming from subjective evaluations should engender research and professional discussion. Especially because differences will exist in educational principles, differences in evaluations will probably never be totally resolved. However, the point is not that everyone agree but that teachers examine computer programs to be used with young children in light of the particular principles they hold.

I do not intend to give the impression that any program represents a computing panacea. The *World* program, for example, is limited in the number of objects it can create. Overuse may restrict, rather than enhance, creativity and lead to frustration. Also, it is the responsibility of the teacher to create a balanced Logo environment. Without guidance, children could fiddle with trivial tasks or become frustrated by their lack of ability. However, if the individual project approach degenerates into the imposition of a required curriculum, the activity will violate the principles and become one more area in which children may feel anxious and pressured.

Therefore, teachers are still the most important factor. Nevertheless, these programs do represent educational software that, used wisely, is consistent with most of the principles listed earlier.

## WHAT CAN TEACHERS DO?

First, teachers should use the principles on which their program is based to evaluate any computer programs that are being considered for use in their classrooms. Programs should be evaluated directly—catalog descriptions cannot be relied upon. This will ensure that the computer programs selected will be pedagogically consistent with the overall program and of benefit to the students. Other evaluation checklists should also be used, but consistency with educational principles should be the first consideration.

Second, teachers can ameliorate possible ill effects when programs do not match every principle. Most programs will not match perfectly, and in such cases it must be determined how any possible ill effects can be minimized. For example, when children reach the "ceiling" of the *Story Machine* or *Worlds,* teachers could encourage them to attempt other modes of expression, either on (a word processing program) or off (paper and pencil) the computer. As another example, it was noted that *teachers* need to create a worthwhile educational environment, especially for open-ended programs like Logo. On one hand, children need to be guided and challenged, and teachers should provide a framework for children's efforts. On the other hand, children also need to learn how to learn and discover things by themselves. Teachers must teach, but just enough to get children over a hurdle and on the path again.

Third, concerned educators should note the shortcomings of programs and bring them to the attention of the producers. And finally, teachers can avoid using computer programs whenever real-world experiences would be more valuable.

## CONCLUSION

Classroom use of the microcomputer and the number of software programs earmarked for young children will continue to increase. Accepted early and primary educational principles should be used to guide any and all modifications to the educational program. Educators must look beyond the "bells and whistles" and examine to what extent the goals and methodology of software programs are congruent with these principles.

## ENDNOTES

1. See, for example, M. T. Grady, "Software Evaluation Criteria," in M. T. Grady and J. D. Gawronski (eds.), *Computers in Curriculum and Instruction,* Alexandria, Va., Association for Supervision and Curriculum Development, 1983; W. P. Heck, J. Johnson and R. J. Kansky, *Guidelines for Evaluating Computerized Instructional Materials,* Reston, Va., National Council of Teachers of Mathematics, 1981; D. H. Clements, *Evaluator's Guide for Microcomputer-based Instructional Packages,* Eugene Ore., International Council for Computers in Education, 1982; and "The Software Lineup," *Electronic Learning,* Oct. 1982.
2. C. Copple, I. Sigel and R. Saunders, *Educating the Young Thinker: Classroom Strategies for Cognitive Growth,* New York, D. Van Nostrand, 1979.
3. S. Papert, *Mindstorms: Children, Computers, and Powerful Ideas,* New York, Basic Books, 1980.

*Douglas H. Clements* is Assistant Professor, Department of Early Childhood Education, Kent State University, Kent, Ohio.

## ADDITIONAL LEARNING ACTIVITIES

### Problems and Projects

1. If you have been developing a "case problem" regarding an elementary school in relation to Sections 1 through 6, continue to work on that case, examining the curriculum and teaching in the school in terms of the trends in childhood education presented in this section. How can the school's curriculum and teaching be improved by incorporating one or more of the trends? Justify incorporating one or more of them in terms of objectives, curriculum bases, and curriculum criteria.
2. Should future studies be a major part of childhood education? (See "Humanistic Early Childhood Education: A Challenge Now and in the Future" and the articles by Shane, Cornish, Cherlin and Furstenberg, and Papert in Section 2.) Discuss the reasons for your position with other members of your class or group.
3. In the article, "Problem Solving: Encouraging Active Learning" in this section, the authors say that teachers can promote problem solving by providing an environment rich in potential for exploration and by permitting the learner wide

freedom to establish plans to reach a goal. Select a topic in your teaching area and plan a lesson based on problem-solving as it is described in this article. It might be helpful to review the articles by Levy and by Bruner in Section 5. Compare your plan with those of other members of your class or group.

4. Should career education ("Getting a Headstart on Career Choices" in this section) be a part of the childhood education curriculum? Defend your position in terms of objectives, bases, and curriculum criteria.

5. Fourteen objectives for the childhood curriculum are presented in the rationale for this section. Examine each of the objectives in terms of the four educational philosophy or curriculum options positions presented in Section 1. Then try to identify for each objective the philosophical position it might represent.

6. According to "Television and Values" in Section 2, television viewing is a significant factor in value erosion in our society. According to that article, numerous provisions should be made in the childhood education curriculum to counter the impact of television on learners. Make a list of the curriculum practices that are suggested. Do you agree with them? What does the author mean when she says, "the medium of television and the institution of education are both outgrowths of the same values in society?"

7. Do you see a relationship between "Problem Solving: Encouraging Active Learning" and "Children's Literature and Moral Development" in this section? If so, what is that relationship? Do you agree with Krogh and Lamme that moral issues should be included in the childhood education curriculum? In dealing with this question you might review the articles by Kohlberg and Bracey in Section 3.

8. According to the article by Cole in this section, multicultural education and global education should be a part of the childhood education curriculum. What reasons does she give for this view? Relate this article to "A World of Interconnections," "Through the Cultural Looking Glass," and "Our Two-Story Culture" (all in Section 2). How does Cole suggest that multicultural education and global education may be interconnected?

9. In "Early Education Principles and Computer Practices," the author maintains that computer programs should be evaluated in the light of accepted principles of childhood education. Do you agree with the principles that he has identified? Based on objectives, bases and criteria, are there other principles that you would include?

10. According to "Research, Reading Instruction, and Children's Learning of the First R" in this section, "reading is a singular skill" that "requires the orchestration of at least five kinds of knowledge." What general classroom practices does the article recommend? Relate the discussion in this article of how children learn to read to the articles by Levy and Eisner in Section 5.

11. Twenty-three innovations and trends are listed in the rationale for this section along with examples in articles in this book. Decide which eight of these trends are most significant for children aged four to ten. Make a list of your eight trends and tell why you selected them.

**12.** In the rationale for Section 6, several curriculum criteria were presented that are particularly appropriate for planners in the 1980s and 1990s. Prepare a statement or discuss with others the ways you might use *anticipation* as a criterion for planning for a group of elementary school children. Try to do the same for *values* or *participation* as criteria. References in this book related to all three criteria are given in the rationale for Section 6.

**13.** The chronological age period during which most children pass through the concrete operations model of intelligence coincides with the years when they are enrolled in an elementary school (see "The Development of Intelligent Behavior: Jean Piaget" in Section 3). What implications does this have for curriculum planning and teaching at this level?

**14.** Summerhill is one of the world's best-known schools. Read *Summerhill,* by A. S. Neil (New York: Hart Publishing Co., 1964). Which of the curriculum bases— human development, learning, knowledge, social forces—figures most prominently in the curriculum of this school? What are the school's objectives? Based on your knowledge of curriculum planning and teaching, what improvements would you suggest in the school's program of education? Another book about Summerhill is *Inside Summerhill,* by Joshua Popenoe (New York: Hart Publishing Co., 1970).

An abbreviated description of the Summerhill program may be found in *Radical School Reform,* by Ronald and Beatrice Gross, published by Simon and Schuster, 1971 (pp. 247–257). A recent report on Summerhill is available in "Summerhill: It's Alive and Well" by Daniel R. Bock in *Educational Leadership* 35, no. 5 (February 1978): 380–383.

**15.** Jane Elliott, a teacher at the Community Elementary School, Riceville, Iowa, made outstanding use of social forces in planning the curriculum for her class. She conducted an "unforgettable experiment in prejudice and self-delusion." To learn about what she did read one of the following:

"Brown Eyes—Blue Eyes," *Reader's Digest* (April 1971), pp. 61–65.

William Peters, *A Class Divided* (New York: Doubleday & Co., 1971).

What creative suggestions can you make for relating current social forces and needs to the planning of the curriculum and teaching in an elementary school classroom?

**16.** "Students learn best how to be good citizens by practicing good citizenship, i.e., by combining classroom study with efforts to improve their school, community, society, or world." The opening paragraph of an article entitled "Can Kids Improve Their Community? You Bet" includes this statement (see *Learning* 3, no. 5 [January 1975]: 60–61, 64–66). The article describes community service programs involving elementary school children and indicates the ways that children can improve and have improved their communities. Read this article and identify the objectives of the programs described. Which of the curriculum bases figures most prominently in these programs? Many helpful sources for ideas on community improvement projects for children are provided in a "Resource List" at the end of this article in *Learning* magazine.

17. The Appendix of this book includes a list of books, each describing an elementary school program. Select one that interests you and determine whether the curriculum or teaching might be improved by incorporating one or more of the innovations or trends in childhood education discussed in this section. Justify using one or more of these trends in this school in terms of objectives, curriculum bases, and curriculum criteria.

18. Have your personal views about the objectives of curriculum or desirable teaching practices for childhood education changed as a result of your experience with this section? If so, state what change has taken place and relate it to one or more of the activities in the section (the rationale, an article, a postassessment activity, a film, etc.). Compare your ideas with those of the other members of your class.

## Films, Filmstrips and Audiocassettes

*Building Curriculum for the Gifted Student.* Audiocassette, 72 min., 1980. Sandra Kaplan gives suggestions for modifying the curriculum for gifted and talented students, with instructional strategies for the elementary teacher. Association for Supervision and Curriculum Development, 225 North Washington Street, Alexandria, Virginia 22314.

*Theory into Practice.* 16 mm, color, 29 min., 1975. A look at individualized instruction as practiced at University Elementary School at the University of California at Los Angeles, with commentary by Dr. Madeline Hunter, principal of the school. Also included are sequences at an inner-city school where the theory and techniques are being field-tested. Media Five, 1011 North Cole Avenue, Hollywood, California 90038.

*The Open Classroom.* 16 mm, color, 29 min., 1975. Shows various forms of open education in operation in several public schools in New York, Washington, and California. Features Professor Lillian Weber, a leading proponent of the open classroom concept and Director of CCNY's Workshop Center for Open Education. Media Five, 1011 North Cole Avenue, Hollywood, California 90038.

*Building on What Children Know.* 16 mm, color, 29 min., 1975. Presents the ways teachers can take advantage of the rich language background virtually every beginning reader brings to the classroom. Features Herbert Kohl, Jerry Schmidt, and Dorothy Strickland. Media Five, 1011 North Cole Avenue, Hollywood, California 90038.

*Using Human Resources.* 16 mm, color, 29 min., 1975. Explores the ways that parent volunteers, teacher aides, community people with expertise, older students, and other teachers can be used effectively in the classroom. Media Five, 1011 North Cole Avenue, Hollywood, California 90038.

*Children Are People.* 16 mm, color, 35 min., 1975. The curriculum of the British Infant and Junior Schools is examined and demonstrated. Agathon Press, 150 Fifth Avenue, New York 10011.

*A Child's Right to Read: Personalizing Reading for Children.* 16 mm, color, 20 min., 1976. Presents ways of teaching reading in an open classroom setting. Also shows how to develop good relationships with children through frequent discussions. Agency for Instructional Television, Box A, Bloomington, Indiana 47401.

*TV: The Anonymous Teacher.* 16 mm, color, 15 min., 1976. Gives a good view of how TV watching affects children. Shows children's faces while they are viewing various programs and discusses with children what they have seen. Mass Media Ministries, 2116 North Charles Street, Baltimore, Maryland 21218.

*Invention Convention.* 16 mm, color, 11 min., 1976. A resourceful art instructor fills an auditorium with "miscellaneous junk." Children are invited to participate in this celebration of creativity. Paramount Communications, 5451 Marathon Street, Hollywood, California 90038.

*A Strategy for Teaching Social Development.* Two filmstrips and one cassette, 20 min., 1976. Helpful to teachers in making use of the *First Things: Social Development Series*. Shows children discussing one of the Social Development filmstrips. The *Social Development Series* has four parts and is for grades two to five. Guidance Associates, 757 Third Avenue, New York, New York 10017.

*A Strategy for Teaching Values*. Three filmstrips and two cassettes, 26 min., 1976. Demonstrates how to teach values in elementary classrooms using Dr. Lawrence Kohlberg's approach. Shows how to use the *First Things: Values Series,* which has five parts and is for grades two to five. Each of the parts presents moral dilemmas planned to stimulate discussion of truth, fairness, promises. Guidance Associates, 757 Third Avenue, New York, New York 10017.

## Books and Articles to Review

The numbers in parentheses following these books or articles refer to the numbered list of innovations and trends in childhood education listed in the rationale for this section. They will assist you in identifying additional sources regarding those trends and innovations.

"Back to the Beginning-Rethinking the Elementary Years: A Special Report." *Education Week* 5, no. 30 (April 16, 1986): 15–38.

Bartolome, P. I. "Changing Family and Early Childhood Education." *Childhood Education* 57, no. 5 (May/June 1981): 262–266.

Bates, John. "Educational Policies That Support Language Development." *Theory Into Practice* 23, no. 3, (Summer 1984): 255–260.

Berman, Louise M. "Educating Children for Lifelong Learning and a Learning Society." *Childhood Education* 61, no. 2 (November/December 1984): 99–106. (6)

Brown, Bernard. "Headstart: How Research Changed Public Policy." *Young Children* 40, no. 5 (July 1985): 4–13.

Burg, Karen. "The Microcomputer in the Kindergarten," *Young Children* 39, no. 3 (March 1984): 28–33. (14)

Cardenas, Jose and First, Joan McCarty. "Children At Risk," *Educational Leadership* 43, No. 1 (September 1985): 4–8.

Clements, Douglas H. *Computers in Early and Primary Education,* Englewood Cliffs, NJ: Prentice Hall, Inc., 1985. (14)

Cole, Ann; Haas, Carolyn; et al. *Children Are Children Are Children,* Boston: Little, Brown and Co., 1978. (10)

DeCosta, Sandra B. "Not All Children Are Anglo and Middle Class: A Practical Beginning for the Elementary Teacher." *Theory Into Practice* 23, no. 2 (Spring 1984): 155–162. (10)

Elkind, David. *The Child and Society*. New York: Oxford University Press, 1979.

———. "Montessori Education: Abiding Contributions and Contemporary Challenges." *Young Children* 38, no. 2 (January 1983): 3–10. (10)

Gilstrap, Robert, ed. *Toward Self-Discipline: A Guide for Parents and Teachers*. Washington, D.C.: Association for Childhood Education, International, 1981.

Goodlad, John I. *A Place Called School*. New York: McGraw Hill, 1984. (1) (3) (10) (19)

Goodlad, John I. "What Some Schools and Classrooms Teach." *Educational Leadership* 40, no. 7 (April 1983): 8–19 (4) (5) (6) (10) (19)

Hallinger, Philip; and Murphy, Joseph. "Characteristics of Highly Effective Elementary Reading Programs." *Educational Leadership* 42, no. 5 (February 1985): 39–42.

Hunter, Beverly; Dearborn, Donald; and Snyder, Bruce. "Computer Literacy in the K–8 Curriculum." *Phi Delta Kappan* 65, no. 2 (October 1983): 115–118. (14)

Johnson, Tony W. "Philosophy for Children: An Antidote for Declining Literacy." *Educational Forum* 48, no. 2 (Winter 1984): 235–241.

Katz, Lillian G. *Current Topics in Early Childhood Education,* Vol. II. Norwood, NJ: Ablex Publishing Company, 1979.

———. "The Professional Early Childhood Teacher." *Young Children* 39, no. 5 (July 1984): 3–10.

Languis, Martin; and Wilcox, Jean. "A Life Span Human Development Model of Learning for Early Education." *Theory Into Practice* 20, no. 2 (Spring 1981): 79–85.

McClendon, Judith. "Developing Writers in an Intermediate Classroom." *Theory Into Practice* 25, no. 2 (Spring, 1986): 117–123. (19)

Melle, Marge; and Wilson, Fern. "Balanced Instruction Through an Integrated Curriculum." *Educational Leadership* 41, no. 7. (April 1984): 59–63. (1) (5) (9) (19)

Melvin, Mary P. "How Do They Learn? John Dewey Was Right." *Phi Delta Kappan* 67, no. 4 (December 1985): 306–307. (1) (6)

Michaelis, John U. *Social Studies for Children: A Guide to Basic Instruction.* Eighth Edition. Englewood Cliffs, NJ: Prentice Hall, Inc., 1985. (8) (9) (16)

National Society for the Study of Education. *Becoming Readers in a Complex Society.* Eighty-Third Yearbook, Part I. Chicago: University of Chicago Press, 1984.

Platt, Nancy Gaines. "How One Classroom Gives Access to Meaning." *Theory Into Practice* 23, no. 3 (Summer 1984): 239–245.

Postman, Neil. *The Disappearance of Childhood.* New York: Delacorte Press, 1982.

———. "The Disappearing Child." *Educational Leadership* 40, no. 6 (March 1983): 10–17.

Reece, Carolyn. "Headstart at 20." *Children Today* 14, no. 2 (March/April 1985): 6–9.

Sanacore, Joseph. "Six Reading Comprehension Myths." *Educational Leadership* 42, no. 5 (February 1985): 43–47.

Sapon-Shevin, Mara. "Teaching Children About Differences: Resources for Teaching." *Young Children* 38, no. 2 (January 1983): 24–32. (13)

Sesow, F. William. "The Many Learning Environments of Children." *The Social Studies* 75, no. 6 (November/December 1984): 81–90. (6) (10) (23)

Shuy, Roger W. "Language as a Foundation for Education: The School Context." *Theory Into Practice* 23, no. 3 (Summer 1984): 167–174.

Spillman, C., and Lutz, J. P. "Readiness for Kindergarten." *Educational Forum* 47, no. 3 (Spring 1983): 345–352. (10)

Spodek, Bernard. "Early Childhood Education's Past as Prologue: Roots of Contemporary Concerns." *Young Children* 40, no. 5 (July 1985): 3–7.

———. *Teaching in the Early Years,* Third Edition. Englewood Cliffs, NJ: Prentice Hall, Inc., 1985.

Strom, Robert D. "Expectations for Educating the Gifted and Talented." *Educational Forum* 47, no. 3 (Spring 1983): 279–303. (12)

Willoughby, Stephen S. "Will Calculators Rot Our Minds?" *Educational Leadership* 43, no. 2 (October 1985): 90–91. (14)

Wishon, Phillip M. "Serving Handicapped Young Children: Six Imperatives." *Young Children* 38, no. 1 (November 1982): 28–32. (13)

# 8

# *Education for Transescents and Early Adolescents*

## PREREQUISITES

1. Reading and studying Sections 1 through 6 of this book.
2. The development of, and ability to use, a set of curriculum criteria to describe and evaluate a curriculum plan. You must be able to use this set of criteria in order to critically analyze and make curriculum decisions regarding programs and trends and teaching practices described in this section.

## RATIONALE

All curriculum planners and teachers should be acquainted with the goals and trends in education at all levels, regardless of the level of the program of education at which they plan to work. You should know about goals and trends in education for transescents and early adolescents whether you plan to work at this level or not. You will be better able to plan a curriculum or teach at one of the other levels if you have this information. This view is based on such curriculum criteria as continuity in learning, balance in the curriculum, and provision for individual differences.

Simply defined, a transescent is a person passing from childhood to early adolescence. There is a four-year range within each sex group from the time that the first significant fraction of the group attains puberty to the time that the last member of that sex reaches it. Generally, by the time they are twenty, both boys and girls have reached full physical growth and biological maturity. But social, psychological, and cognitive maturation are usually not in step with physical maturation. Pressures in modern industrial society tend to force the social, psychological, and cognitive changes of this period on the young person ahead of the biological. In any event, individual differences among students are greater during adolescence than at other stages of life. In our society, transescence and early adolescence is a period from about age ten to age fifteen.

It is necessary to consider the human development, social forces, learning, and knowledge and cognition bases of the curriculum for guidance in planning teaching and programs of education that are appropriate for persons age ten to fifteen. It is especially appropriate to turn to the research and theories of human development (in Section 3) by Robert Havighurst and by Erik Erikson (in the article "A Healthy Personality for Every Child") and Jean Piaget (in the article "The Development of Intelligent Behavior: Jean Piaget") to see how each of them describes the transescent and early adolescent stage. From them we can identify cultural, psychological, cognitive, social, and sex aspects of this period.

Transescence and early adolescence are characterized by rapid physical growth, which is frequently uneven, with some parts of the body growing faster than others; thus, both boys and girls may frequently be clumsy and awkward. Rapid growth uses up much physical energy, and early adolescents need plenty of food and sleep to maintain good health. On many occasions they may have excess energy that needs to be worked off in lively physical activity. Self-concepts must be adjusted as new physical characteristics appear. These topics are the focus of "Growth Characteristics of Middle School Children: Curriculum Implications" and "Self-Concept and Esteem in the Middle Level School."

The physical changes that take place during this period are only part of the process of change that is occurring. The child who has looked to his or her family for care, affection, and guidance must begin to find independence in order to meet the emotional problems of this period and of adulthood. The early adolescent must learn to make his or her own decisions and to accept their consequences. Parents and teachers are needed who try to overlook shortcomings and praise accomplishments; encourage independence without pushing too far; and give affection without seeking too much in return. The article by Brough examines the special role of teachers as counselors at this level.

What should be the *objectives* of programs of education for transescents and early adolescents? Many goals might be suggested; some are derived from social forces, some from human development and learning theories, and some from theories of knowledge and cognition. The list would surely include many of the following objectives:

1. Helping the learners to seek solutions to experiences and problems of physical change.
    a. Provide help and guidance in finding suitable solutions.
    b. Aid in meeting developmental tasks.
    c. Provide a teacher-centered guidance program.
2. Helping the learners to learn to deal with wider social experiences and new social arrangements.

a. Provide experiences with a more varied group of peers.
b. Provide experiences with new learning arrangements.
c. Provide opportunity for the early adolescent peer culture to develop its supportive functions for its members.
d. Develop a concern for the environment, the community, the society, the future, and the welfare of others.
3. Providing opportunities to explore many areas of knowledge and skill to help determine potential interests.
a. Provide experiences that create broad interests as a basis for considering personal, social, and vocational goals.
b. Provide learners with opportunities to explore their own potentialities.
4. Providing for a transition between childhood education and education for middle adolescents.
a. Help elementary school students to prepare for high school by combining features of both elementary school and senior high school.
5. Providing an atmosphere adjusted to the developmental level of learners.
a. Study each learner carefully and modify crude classifications based on age and grade.
b. Provide a setting where a psychologically mixed group can develop in a framework not dominated by any one subgroup.
6. Helping the learners to deal with value questions that arise because of their developing cognitive competence, their growing need for independence, and rapid changes in society.

A major issue for transescents and early adolescents is whether their education is best provided in a junior high school, a middle school, or some other form of school organization. McEwin ("Schools for Early Adolescents") discusses the social forces that led to the development of the junior high school in the early part of this century, as well as the social influences that led to the development of the middle school in the 1960s.

A 1980–1983 study of "schools in the middle" (grades 5–9) is reported in the August, 1985 (Volume 16, no. 4) issue of the *Middle School Journal*. Part of the study focused on the "effective schools" at this level and the majority of those so selected were organized in patterns of grades 6–7–8 or 5–6–7–8. "Effective principals" in the study were knowledgeable about middle level programs and research, evidenced familiarity with block scheduling, interdisciplinary teaming, co-curricular programs, learning styles, teacher/advisor programs, and developmental age grouping. Principals and parents saw the 6–7–8 middle school configuration as the ideal grade organization structure for middle level learners. But as McEwin tells us, "future research in middle level education should focus on how current practices measure up to quality criteria for early adolescent education rather than focusing on differences in middle and junior high school programs and practices."

Recent research regarding brain growth periodization during early adolescence has particular significance for curriculum planning at this level. The vast majority of the students at this level are pre-formal thinkers (see "The Development of Intelligent

Behavior: Jean Piaget" in Section 3). Instruction in middle schools and junior high schools is often done with little regard for cognitive development. Concrete thinkers must be allowed to approach novel situations in familiar ways. However, brain periodization research does not suggest that learners should be placed on "hold" during plateau periods of slower brain growth. This research is discussed in the article by Brazee in this section. It concludes that we need models of instruction which "assist natural development."

The wide range of differences among learners at this age level suggests that developmental age grouping or nongraded programs are needed. These programs are discussed in "Guidelines for the Middle Schools We Need Now" and "The Middle School Movement: From Emergent to Exemplary."

Because of the particular significance of human development as a base for curriculum planning for this age group, planners often overlook *social forces* and *future planning* as necessary ingredients for adequate planning and balance in the curriculum. Farris and Adams focus on social forces as a factor in curriculum planning for transescents when they assert that coeducational home economics and industrial arts courses offer a major opportunity to change sex role stereotyping. In Section 9, "Developing Responsible Youth Through Youth Participation" reports many types of community activites for high school students that might also have significance for early adolescents. Future planning and social forces should be examined regularly for their implications for transescent learners. "A Computer Literate Middle School" in this section accepts the premise that functioning effectively in the future will require a new basic skill—knowledge of the computer.

The following list of *innovations* and *trends* in education for transescents and early adolescents includes references to pertinent articles in this Section, unless otherwise noted. The list is arranged alphabetically.

1. *Affective education:* "Growth Characteristics of Middle School Children"; "The Teacher as Counselor"
2. *Block time schedule:* "Guidelines for the Middle Schools We Need Now"; "The Middle School Movement"; "Self-Concept and Esteem in the Middle Level School"
3. *Career education:* "The Middle School Movement"
4. *Community service:* "Self-Concept and Esteem in the Middle Level School"
5. *Computer literacy:* "A Computer Literate Middle School"; "Early Education Principles and Computer Practices" (Section 7); "It's Joe Again" (Section 5)
6. *Continuous learner progress:* "Guidelines for the Middle Schools We Need Now"; "Schools for Early Adolescents"
7. *Cooperative learning and rewards in the classroom:* "Self-Concept and Esteem in the Middle Level School"
8. *Critical thinking and learning skills instruction:* "Guidelines for the Middle Schools We Need Now"
9. *Developmental age grouping:* "The Middle School Movement"
10. *Environmental education:* "Guidelines for the Middle Schools We Need Now"

11. *Exploratory program:* "Guidelines for the Middle Schools We Need Now"; "The Middle School Movement"; "Schools for Early Adolescents"
12. *Field trips:* "Guidelines for the Middle Schools We Need Now"
13. *Flexible grouping:* "Guidelines for the Middle Schools We Need Now"
14. *Flexible scheduling:* "The Middle School Movement"; "Guidelines for the Middle Schools We Need Now"; "Schools for Early Adolescents"
15. *Focus on principles, generalizations, and concepts of organized knowledge:* "Guidelines for the Middle Schools We Need Now"
16. *Health instruction:* "Growth Characteristics of Middle School Children"; "Schools for Early Adolescents"
17. *Independent study:* "Guidelines for the Middle Schools We Need Now"
18. *Individualized instruction:* "Growth Characteristics of Middle School Children"; "Guidelines for the Middle Schools We Need Now"; "Self-Concept and Esteem in the Middle Level School"
19. *Interdisciplinary curriculum:* "Guidelines for the Middle Schools We Need Now"; "The Middle School Movement"
20. *Laboratory approach to learning:* "Guidelines for the Middle Schools We Need Now"
21. *Learning resources center:* "Guidelines for the Middle Schools We Need Now"
22. *Middle school organization:* "Guidelines for the Middle Schools We Need Now"; "Schools for Early Adolescents"
23. *Mini-courses:* "Guidelines for the Middle Schools We Need Now"
24. *Multi-age grouping:* "Growth Characteristics of Middle School Children"; "The Middle School Movement"; "Guidelines for the Middle Schools We Need Now"
25. *Nongraded curricula:* "Guidelines for the Middle Schools We Need Now"
26. *Open education:* "Guidelines for the Middle Schools We Need Now"
27. *Out of school and co-curricular activities:* "Growth Characteristics of Middle School Children"; "Guidelines for the Middle Schools We Need Now"; "Self-Concept and Esteem in the Middle Level School"
28. *Parent-teacher-student planning:* "Guidelines for the Middle Schools We Need Now"
29. *Personal approach to instruction:* "The Middle School Movement"; "Guidelines for the Middle Schools We Need Now"; "The Teacher as Counselor"
30. *Problems approach:* "Growth Characteristics of Middle School Children"; "Guidelines for the Middle Schools We Need Now"
31. *Self-esteem curricula:* "Growth Characteristics of Middle School Children"
32. *Special interest courses:* "Guidelines for the Middle Schools We Need Now"
33. *Student self-evaluation:* "Growth Characteristics of Middle School Children"; "Guidelines for the Middle Schools We Need Now"
34. *Student-teacher planning:* "The Teacher As Counselor"; "Who Should Plan the Curriculum?" (Section 6)
35. *Teacher as counselor:* "Growth Characteristics of Middle School Children"; "The Middle School Movement"; "The Teacher As Counselor"

36. *Team teaching:* "The Middle School Movement"
37. *Town meeting:* "Growth Characteristics of Middle School Children"; "Self-Concept and Esteem in the Middle Level School"
38. *Use of community resources in the curriculum:* "Guidelines for the Middle Schools We Need Now"; "Self-Concept and Esteem in the Middle Level School"
39. *Value education:* "Growth Characteristics of Middle School Children"; "The Cognitive-Developmental Approach to Moral Education" (Section 3); "Now Then, Mr. Kohlberg, About Moral Development in Women" (Section 3)

*Will these trends, if adopted, provide needed changes in programs of education for learners of this age group?*

We must evaluate innovations and trends in comparison with present programs. The consideration of (1) objectives, (2) the four bases of the curriculum, and (3) other curriculum criteria provide professional means for making these decisions.

In the List of Books and Articles to Review at the end of this section, many of the sources listed include, at the end of the citations, one or more of the numbers from the preceding list of trends. These numbers will help you find other recent articles and books on the transescent and early adolescent trends and innovations that particularly interest you.

## OBJECTIVES

Your objectives in studying education for transescents and early adolescents as part of the curriculum should be as follows:

1. To be familiar with the objectives, current innovations, and recent trends in education at this level.
2. To be able to explain the functions and goals of education at this level as part of the total curriculum.
3. To be able to use objectives of education at this level, the curriculum bases, and other criteria in making curriculum or instruction decisions regarding present as well as future programs.
4. To be able to suggest improvements in curriculum plans and instruction at this level through the decisions in number 3.

## PREASSESSMENT

1. Identify the innovations and trends listed in the rationale, and discuss their implications for this level of education.
2. Evaluate the trends in terms of objectives, bases of curriculum, and curriculum criteria such as balance, individual differences, relevance, and continuity.
3. Select any curriculum plan for education at this level and describe and analyze it

in terms of objectives, the four curriculum bases, your own list of curriculum criteria, and innovations and trends at this level of education.

4.  Suggest improvements or changes in the curriculum plan in number 3 in the light of your analysis.

You might choose to analyze the curriculum plans described in "The Middle School Movement: From Emergent to Exemplary" in this section in answering numbers 3 and 4 of the preassessment.

## LEARNING ACTIVITES

Articles in this section will help you to understand the purposes and functions of education for transescents and early adolescents as an important part of the curriculum. They will also acquaint you with the problems, as well as the innovations and trends, of programs of education at this level. Other learning alternatives are suggested at the end of this section.

## POSTASSESSMENT

After attempting the preassessment you may do *one or more* of the following:

1.  Ask your instructor whether you are ready for a postassessment evaluation on education for transescents and early adolescents. Most students will need further work on this topic.
2.  Read the articles on education for transescents and early adolescents in this section, and try to determine how the goals, practices, trends, and innovations discussed in each article should be considered in curriculum planning and teaching at this level.
3.  Choose additional activities and readings or films from those listed at the end of this section.
4.  Look in your library or media center for other films, books, or articles on transescent and early adolescent education.
5.  Discuss the reading you have done and the films you have viewed with your fellow students. The key questions: How should the goals, practices, trends, and innovations you have studied affect a school's curriculum? How should they be considered in planning for teaching?
6.  When you are ready, ask your instructor for advice on a suitable postassessment for you for this topic. Satisfactory completion of number 1 under Problems and Projects at the end of this section might be one possibility, or satisfactory written completion of the preassessment for this section, after completing other learning activities, might be a satisfactory postassessment. Consult your instructor about this. You can evaluate your ability to do these postassessment activites before seeing the instructor.

# Schools for Early Adolescents

## C. KENNETH McEWIN

Special schools for early adolescents have become a significant component of American education. These schools have their roots in the later years of the 19th century and the early years of the 20th century. A wide variety of forces have converged to bring about two major approaches to middle level education—the junior high school and then the middle school. This article briefly traces the development of these schools, partially compares them, and suggests characteristics needed in middle level schools, whatever their grade organization.

### THE JUNIOR HIGH SCHOOL MOVEMENT

The junior high school movement evolved from a multiplicity of causes which combined at an opportune time to allow rapid and widespread acceptance of the concept. Although American education had never adopted a universal plan regarding which grade levels should be included in what schools, the 8–4 plan had become very popular following the Civil War. The move to change this pattern had its beginnings in the influence of Charles Eliot, who proposed that courses be shortened and enriched to enable students to enter universities at an earlier age. His proposal quickly gained support and initiated much debate concerning the proper roles and responsibilities of secondary education.

Additional factors influencing the acceptance of the junior high school included: reports of national committees recommending this reorganization; the drop-out problem; the dawning

recognition of individual differences; changing societal needs; and the desire to implement innovative educational reforms. A growing realization of the extent of individual differences gained major support for the movement. The child study and mental testing movements drew attention to the vast differences existing in people. Previous to this time, persons not achieving in schools were considered lazy or lacking in mental or moral fiber, and the general belief was that anyone who tried could learn. The junior high school was viewed as an opportunity to create more suitable learning environments that took these new findings into account.

Support was also received from educators who believed that needed reforms could be more easily accomplished in a new educational unit. It was considered difficult, if not impossible, to effect significant changes in the more traditional eight-year elementary school and four-year high school. Beginning in a new environment with a clean slate was considered a preferable alternative to attempting reform in schools with established traditions and practices (Van Denburg, 1922). Ironically, the same contention was employed in later years as a rationale for moving from the junior high school to the middle school plan.

Chronological coincidences also played a part in the rapid acceptance of the junior high school. The nation was undergoing vast changes when the movement began: the West was growing; urbanization and industrialization were increasing; and there was a growing demand for secondary education. There were pressures from industrialist and business leaders to better relate

From *Theory Into Practice* 22, No. 2 (Spring 1983): 119–124. Used by permission of the author and the publisher.

education to the realistic needs of a growing, changing society. Other factors included the needs of an increasing school population after the rise in the birth rate following World War I, the need for a place to "Americanize" immigrants, and the desire to create schools that could effectively promote the societal reforms of the period.

The growth of the junior high school as an administrative unit (grades 7–9) was rapid, with the number increasing from fewer than 400 in 1920 to more than 2000 in 1940 (Johnson, 1962). The number reached 5000 by 1950 and 6006 by 1964 (Lounsbury, 1960; Van Til, Vars, & Lounsbury, 1961). After the mid-1960s, the growth is more difficult to determine since nation-wide studies after that time focused on the emerging middle school movement. A comprehensive study sponsored by the National Institute of Education in 1980 reported that only 4004 junior high schools (grades 7–9) remained in the nation. Clearly, many 7–9 junior high schools have been replaced by middle schools without grade nine.

## DISENCHANTMENT WITH THE JUNIOR HIGH SCHOOL

Discontent with the junior high school grew by the middle of this century. A gap between theory and practice was evident, and critics were quick to point out shortcomings and weaknesses. The problem did not lie in the inappropriateness of identified goals of the junior high school, but in the failure to fulfill these goals to a significant degree. A major criticism centered around the belief that the junior high school tended to be a scaled-down version of the senior high, with complex departmentalization, interscholastic sports, rigid scheduling, and inappropriate social events. As a result of this mimicking, one of the major purposes of the junior high school—that of providing a transitional pro-

gram—had been impeded if not blocked in many schools.

A second criticism questioned the placement of the ninth grade in the junior high school. It was widely believed that the rationale for placing it there had been overshadowed by the evidence that these youth were maturing physically and socially at earlier ages. It was also noted that these youth were more informed, sophisticated, and knowledgeable than those of previous generations. There were corresponding questions regarding the retention of sixth, even fifth grade, as well as grades seven and eight in the elementary school. Designers of the junior high school were charged with having failed to take these developments and concerns into account.

The decline of the junior high school was also undoubtedly influenced by factors growing out of the times. One such factor was the need for reorganization to introduce desegregation earlier. An additional problem may have been that the early planners of junior high schools in their newfound enthusiasm promised far more than could be accomplished in so short a time. The failure to achieve these goals was due in part to a lack of knowledge about early adolescents and their educational and developmental needs; to the post-Sputnik pressures on secondary education, including ninth grade, which produced almost intolerable scheduling and academic requirements in junior highs; and to the lack of personnel trained for and committed to working at the middle level.

The junior high school movement achieved many important goals while making significant and lasting impressions on American education. For the first time in history, early adolescents were attending schools designed especially for them. However, seeds of discontent and disillusionment surfaced and in conjunction with other forces, gave birth to a second reform movement in middle level education—the middle school movement.

## THE MIDDLE SCHOOL MOVEMENT

A combination of forces converged in the early 1960s to produce the middle school movement. Like its predecessor, the junior high school movement, the middle school movement experienced rapid growth and wide acceptance. Although many persons influenced the development of this new movement, it was William M. Alexander who proposed changing to a new organization and program at a national conference at Cornell University in 1963. He proposed that the positive characteristics of the junior high school be retained and that improvements be initiated in the new middle school. Changes included moving the ninth grade to the senior high school; including grades 5–8 in the middle school; providing programs based on the needs of 10 to 14-year-olds; and developing transitional programs that promote continuity in the total educational ladder (Alexander, 1964).

Disillusionment with the junior high school is often noted as one of the reasons for the success of the middle school movement. Evidence of this disenchantment was widespread by the 1960s (Alexander & Williams, 1965) and has continued until today. As noted, a major criticism is the fact that the junior high school too often became a reflection of the senior high school. In recent years middle schools have been the target of the same accusation, especially criticized as "junior junior high schools." National studies by Alexander (1968), Kealy (1971), Brooks and Edwards (1978), and McEwin and Clay (1982) confirm that this charge has some basis.

Problems of extreme departmentalization, teacher dissatisfaction, poor articulation with schools at other levels, and lack of emphasis on exploratory activities are not unique to the junior high school, but by the 1960s a major change in this institution was inevitable. The middle school movement offered a second chance for the development of schools based on the characteristics of 10 to 14-year-olds.

## Growth of the Middle School Movement

The middle school movement has expanded at a rapid rate since its inception in the 1960s. A survey by Alexander revealed a total of 1101 middle schools in 1967–68 with middle schools defined as having at least three grades, no more than five grades, and including grades six and seven (Alexander, 1968). A survey by Kealy identified 2298 middle schools using the same definition (1971). The number of middle schools increased to 3723 in 1974 (Compton, 1976) and 4060 in 1977 (Brooks & Edwards, 1978). A national study sponsored by the National Institute of Education identified 4094 grades 5-8 and 6-8 middle schools in 1980 (NIE, 1981). This total did not count other grade organizations included in previous studies and thus does not represent the total number of middle schools without grade nine in the nation. The same study reported a total of 2623 middle level schools with grades 7-8. Clearly, the middle school movement has enjoyed great success in numbers while the 7–9 junior high school has decreased in numbers in recent years.

## Which Grade Levels?

The question of which grades should be included in the middle level school continues to be one on which there is divided opinion. However, it has become evident that the majority of educators believe the ninth grade should be housed at the senior high school. Schools are being reorganized into some combinations of grades 5, 6, or 7 through 8 with 6–8 being the most popular pattern. Middle schools without grade 9 have increased from less than 200 in 1960 to an estimated total of over 10,000 today.

A 1980 survey sponsored by the National Association of Secondary School Principals (Valentine, Clark, Nickerson, & Keefe, 1981) found that the majority of over 1400 middle level principals at both junior high and middle schools considered 6-8 the ideal grade organizational pattern regardless of the grade organization of their own schools. This finding reflects a dramatic change of opinion among middle level principals regarding the ideal grade pattern. In 1966, a comparable survey found that 65 percent of middle level principals considered 7-9 to be the ideal plan (Valentine et al., 1981).

## Reasons for Establishment

It is widely recognized that many middle level schools were established for reasons other than the opportunity to better serve early adolescents. Alexander's 1968 survey reported that the reason most often given for moving to the middle school was to eliminate crowded conditions in other schools. Later studies by Brooks and Edwards (1978) and Valentine and his associates (1981) found that the most often quoted reason was to provide programs better suited to the middle level student.

An additional reason for the growth of middle level schools is the new knowledge now available about early adolescents. Factors such as earlier physical and intellectual development indicate that the majority of students enrolled in ninth grade today are fully adolescent, more like older students than those below them, and more precocious and complex than those of previous generations. Even if the junior high school movement had been highly successful in obtaining its goals, the ninth grade population of today would likely need to be moved to the senior high school.

## WHICH IS BEST: MIDDLE OR JUNIOR HIGH SCHOOL?

There is no categorical answer to the question, which is best, although there is a great deal of opinion among educators. When the original components of the junior high school and middle school concepts are compared, a great deal of commonality is found. These commonalities in no way negate the significance of the gains made in the middle school movement nor justify inappropriate practices in either organization. Rather, the middle school movement offers a rallying point for the maintenance and improvement of the many gains made by the junior high school movement, without its losses.

Much attention has been focused on the lack of significant differences found in actual practice in junior high and middle schools. Studies by Alexander (1968), Brooks and Edwards (1978), and McEwin and Clay (1982) have revealed a great number of similarities in programs and practices in middle and junior high schools. One difficulty in conducting comparative research on the two units is the fact that the comparative effectiveness of the junior high school over the organizational patterns it displaced was never determined (Toepfer & Marani, 1980). Therefore, there are little or no data to provide a standard by which the middle school can be compared. The McEwin and Clay study (1982), which compared over 400 middle and junior high schools selected from a random sample, found many commonalities in course offerings, student activities, organizational design, and pupil progress reporting systems. However, middle schools were characterized by more flexible scheduling, more team teaching, less ability grouping, fewer interscholastic sports programs, and more uniform requirements of the basic subjects of mathematics, language arts, science, social studies, and reading, especially at the seventh and eighth grade levels.

Many junior high schools are now adopting practices advocated by the middle school concept and therefore differences between the two units are declining. Future research in middle level education should focus on how current practices measure up to quality criteria for early adolescent education rather than focusing on differences in middle and junior high school programs and practices.

An additional problem related to research on the effectiveness of middle schools versus junior high schools is that most studies reflect only easy to measure objective data related to organizational patterns, evaluation practices, and other such factors. As noted by Lounsbury, Marani, and Compton (1980), the real question is whether the educational experiences being provided early adolescents today are more attuned to the needs of early adolescents than they were a decade or more ago. According to the findings of their shadow study of seventh graders, the answer is "yes." When they compared results with a comparable 1964 study of eighth graders, they stated that the overall picture was ". . . not excellent, perhaps not even very good, but noticeably better" (p. 65). They also pointed out that the major differences were probably more related to school climate than to curriculum. Their study presents important observational data lacking in most studies.

Despite the lack of a large research base categorically showing that middle or junior high schools are "best," increased knowledge regarding the developmental and educational needs of early adolescents has shed light on the essential components of effective educational programs. Additionally, after more than 70 years of experience with middle level schools, a consensus among educators has emerged which largely supports rather than opposes these components. Though these components have not all become a reality in the majority of schools, there is general agreement regarding the direction middle level education should follow.

Accompanying these trends is the fact that the developmental stage of early adolescence (ages 10 to 14 or 15) has gained the attention of educators, researchers, youth-serving agencies, and others responsible for the education and welfare of these youth. This attention is likely to continue as early adolescence becomes better conceptualized with more research better disseminated (Thornburg, 1983).

## ESSENTIAL COMPONENTS OF EFFECTIVE MIDDLE LEVEL SCHOOLS

More important than titles, movements, or organizational plans is the quality of learning experiences provided. The following components are representative of those widely accepted as essential to effective early adolescent schooling. Not included in this discussion are the elements which are essential to *all* schools, such as adequate facilities and budgets, comprehensive curriculum plans, extensive planning and evaluation systems, and clearly defined goals.

### A Developmental Guidance Program

A developmental guidance program including a sound teacher-based guidance (advisor-advisee) plan is essential. Early adolescents are undergoing many traumatic changes and need help from both guidance specialists and teacher advisors who know them well. While the importance of having the classroom teacher provide guidance has been recognized for many years, in practice this role has been left to the counselor and largely neglected by the remainder of the faculty. The concept of teacher-based guidance, which had its beginnings in the junior high school, remains an important part of effective schooling and is implemented in approximately one-third of middle level schools today (McEwin & Clay, 1982). These programs, in conjunction with other sound guidance activities, provide the assistance needed by early adolescents as they move from the protective atmosphere of the elementary school to new, more impersonal learning environments.

### Flexible Scheduling and Grouping

Flexible schedules allow teachers to make important decisions regarding use of time, group size, and other variables. Effective schools utilize schedules which encourage the investment of time based on the educational needs and interests of students rather than on rigid predetermined segments of time. Flexible scheduling allows the diverse needs of middle level students to be recognized and dealt with and returns the primary responsibility for daily scheduling and grouping to the persons who know students best—the teachers.

## Provision for Continuous Progress

Continuous progress is a long sought after and much discussed goal that is seldom fully achieved in most schools. Given the great diversity of learning and developmental needs of early adolescents, such provisions for continuous progress as individualized instruction and progress reporting are essential. Middle level schools should make every effort to implement curricular plans which provide opportunities for students to progress at their own rates.

## The Exploratory Component

The exploratory component is an important part of middle level programs. Typical experiences include: the more traditional elective courses such as home economics, industrial arts, art, and music; special interest activities including interest clubs, and classes; independent study opportunities; and other enrichment options. Variety, considerable student participation in design and selection, and informality of instruction are attributes common to many exploratory activities. These programs expand the scope of the curriculum and allow students to explore many areas of interest. The development of worthwhile interests is an additional result of quality exploratory activities.

## Appropriate Social Experiences

Social experiences at the middle level school should be carefully planned and not simply emulate those practiced at the senior high school. Early adolescents are at various stages of social development, and maturity factors should be considered when designing social activities for them. They are experiencing dramatic and sometimes traumatic needs to adjust to new and little understood social roles. Emphasizing overly sophisticated and highly competitive activities such as interscholastic sports, marching bands, and proms adds to the difficulties experienced by many early adolescents. More fitting activities which promote the acquisition of social skills and minimize elitism are crucial to the healthy social development of 10 to 14-year-olds.

## A Comprehensive Health and Physical Education Program

The tremendous physical changes experienced by the majority of early adolescents make the health and physical education programs crucial to effective schooling. Programs and activities which help them understand the nature of physical maturation and its implications are essential. A broad range of intramural activities should supplement regular physical education classes, and interscholastic sports should be eliminated or de-emphasized. The wide range of physical, emotional, and social characteristics of this age group suggests that emphasis be placed on wide involvement of all students in physical education and sports activities. Emphasis at the middle level should be placed on lifelong sports and leisure time activities. Instruction relating to personal hygiene, regular participation in fitness activities, heterosexual group games, and sports with carry-over value should also be emphasized.

## Personnel Preparation

Middle level education has from its inception been plagued by the fact that virtually no teachers have been prepared specifically for teaching early adolescents. The majority of junior high and middle schools are staffed with personnel with either elementary or secondary preparation. A survey of over 500 teacher education institutions by Alexander and McEwin (1982) found that only 30 percent of those institutions had middle/junior high school teacher preparation programs at any degree level, with only 16 percent of those without programs planning them for the future. Special middle level training for principals and other personnel was almost nonexistent. These results point out the importance of and need for comprehensive inservice programs in middle level schools. Only when those responsible for the education and welfare of this age group are knowledgeable about and dedicated to middle level education will the full potential of middle level education be reached.

## CONCLUSION

Although the movement to create specialized schools and improved programs for early adolescents has experienced some difficulties and disappointments in its relatively brief history, many encouraging signs have emerged that indicate the gap between well intentioned theory and actual practice is narrowing. Approximately 12,000 middle grade schools exist today and the national movement to establish middle grades schools shows no signs of abating. Teacher education institutions have begun to establish specialized training for middle level personnel; the National Middle School Association and over 25 state middle/junior high school associations have been established; prestigious organizations such as the National Association of Elementary School Principals, the National Association of Secondary School Principals, and the Association for Supervision and Curriculum Development have begun to emphasize middle level education interests; research efforts on early adolescents and their schooling have increased; a wide variety of materials concerning the age group and their educational needs has emerged; and a number of states have adopted special middle level certification standards.

However, much remains to be accomplished if quality learning experiences are to be available for all early adolescents. Unless many more teacher education institutions and certification agencies move more rapidly to provide trained and committed personnel, still another approach may have to be found in order for early adolescent schooling to survive and succeed.

## REFERENCES

Alexander, W. M. The junior high school: A changing view. *Bulletin of the National Association of Secondary School Principals,* 1964, *48,* 15–24.

Alexander, W. M. *A survey of organizational patterns of reorganized middle schools.* Washington, D.C.: United States Department of Health, Education, and Welfare, 1968.

Alexander, W. M., & McEwin, C. K. *Middle/junior high school teacher preparation: A national status report,* 1982. (Available from authors: College of Learning and Human Development, Appalachian State University, Boone, N.C.).

Alexander, W. M., & Williams, E. L. Schools for the middle years. *Educational Leadership,* 1965, *23,* 217–223.

Brooks, K., & Edwards, F. *The middle school in transition: A research report on the status of the middle school movement.* Lexington, KY.: The Center for Professional Development, University of Kentucky, 1978.

Compton, M. F. The middle schools: A status report. *Middle School Journal,* 1976, *7,* 3–5.

Johnson, M. School in the middle, junior high school: Education's problem child. *Saturday Review,* 1962, 40–42.

Kealy, R. P. The middle school movement: 1960–1970. *National Elementary School Principal,* 1971, *51,* 20–25.

Lounsbury, J. H. How the junior high school came to be. *Educational Leadership,* 1960, *18,* 145–147.

Lounsbury, J. H., Marani, J. V., & Compton, M. F. *The middle school in profile: A day in the seventh grade.* Columbus, Ohio: National Middle School Association, 1980.

McEwin, C. K., & Clay, R. *A comparative national study of middle and junior high school programs and practices.* 1982. (Available from authors: College of Learning and Human Development, Appalachian State University, Boone, N.C.).

National Institute of Education. Untitled manuscript. Washington, D. C., 1981. (Draft)

Thornburg, H. D. Is early adolescence really a stage of development? *Theory Into Practice,* Spring, 1983, *22*(2).

Toepfer, C. F., & Marani, J. V. School-based research. In Johnson, M. (Ed.), *Toward adolescence: The middle school years.* Chicago: National Society for the Study of Education, 1980.

Valentine, J., Clark, D. C., Nickerson, N. C., & Keefe, J. W. *The middle level principalship: A survey of principals and programs.* Reston, Va.: National Association of Secondary School Principals, 1981.

Van Denburg, J. K. *The junior high school idea.* New York: Henry Holt and Co., 1922.

Van Til, W., Vars, G. F., & Lounsbury, J. H. *Modern education for the junior high school years.* Indianapolis: Bobbs Merrill, 1961.

*C. Kenneth McEwin* is Chair, Department of Curriculum and Instruction, Appalachian State University, Boone, North Carolina.

# Growth Characteristics of Middle School Children: Curriculum Implications

## NICHOLAS P. GEORGIADY AND LOUIS G. ROMANO

The period known as preadolescence has been described by one writer as a stretch of no man's land in child study,[1] while another writer states that during this period the child goes through almost as great a transformation as that seen when a tadpole changes into a frog.[2] The effects of these vast changes are further compounded by educational programs which do not meet the growing needs of this group.

"Transescence is defined as that period in an individual's development beginning prior to the onset of puberty and continuing through early adolescence. It is characterized by changes in physical development, social interaction, and intellectual functions."[3]

As one observes the way in which children grow and develop, the accelerated rate of the physical maturation, particularly in the years from 11 to 14, is evident. Improved diet and upgraded health care have contributed to this earlier maturation. Children are larger, stronger and, in many ways, more mature physically than children of the same ages in previous generations. Along with these physical changes, and perhaps more significant for educators, we also note sociopsychological differences between transescent children of today and those of previous generations. Children today travel a great deal more and benefit from viewing life in widely varied geographic locations. Certainly, one can appreciate the educational value that such widespread travel has on providing them with first-hand information about many different places in this country and, in many instances, in other countries as well.

Another factor in their earlier sophistication is the effect of far more numerous resources provided by the mass media of today. Books are

From *Middle School Journal* 8, no. 1 (February 1977): 12–15, 22–23. Used by permission of the authors and the publisher.

available in quantities never present before. The paperback revolution is a vivid characteristic of this age. Reading material and the information, ideas, and stimulation that these provide contribute to their intellectual development to a considerable degree. The paperback wedged into a trouser hip pocket and the well-worn paperback carried with other possessions of girls are a commonplace sight with today's transescents. Popular magazines, colorful and informative on a wide range of topics, and often designed for the teen reader, inundate the home and school. Even the daily newspaper cannot ignore this growingly significant portion of the population. Columns and entire sections dealing with topics relevant to the interests of young readers have become commonplace in the press.

The tremendous impact of widespread television viewing on the transescent cannot be ignored. Studies by Witty[4] and others conducted over a period of years have yielded ample data which indicate that the time spent by children and youth in TV viewing is a factor of major scope in their environment. Many young individuals spend as much and more often more time viewing television than is spent in school.

A basic principle of education stresses the importance of providing differentiated educational treatment for varied maturity levels. Acceptance of this principle leads to a consideration of the differences inherent in transescents as against younger and older children and follows with an examination of the kinds of educational programs called for by such identified developmental characteristics. In this very essential task lie the reasons for the failure of the traditional junior high school. It did not recognize the unique nature of the students it sought to serve and having failed in this, continued to offer a program that was both irrelevant and inadequate.

The task of the middle school becomes quite apparent in light of the above. It is to be an educational unit with a philosophy, structure, and program which will realistically and appropriately deal with 11- to 14-year-olds as they indeed are and behave. The transescent is an extremely complex and ambivalent individual, still very much a child in many respects. His interests and behavior are much like those of students in the elementary grades. He requires direction and security. Yet he is not always so. His ambivalence is manifested by frequent spells of self-assertion, independence, and a surprising show of maturity, though none of these is displayed consistently. The child in him comes through when he expresses exuberance and enthusiasm about something which captures his interest. In this mood, motivation is easily accomplished. However, in his transitional state of development, he often lapses into a passive mood more characteristic of older children.

Such wide ranges of behavior and performance present problems for the traditional school structure. Transescents cannot be accommodated by outmoded educational patterns. To truly provide for youth possessing these widely ranging and varying characteristics, a school organization must possess certain elements. The middle school as it is conceived by its advocates, seeks to do just this. For one, its commitment is primarily to the youth it seeks to serve. Since these youths show such wide variations of behavior and mood, the key element in the middle school is flexibility. It is designed to respond readily to changes in the nature of its student population as well as to other circumstances which may become altered. By operating in this manner it retains a human-centered approach and recognizes the intrinsic value and importance of individuality among students. Stated somewhat more specifically, the middle school recognizes that its students require the security and stability of a home base to which they can turn when necessary to bolster their feelings. At the same time, it provides more freedom of opportunity and movement which their growing independence calls for. Activities which meet these widely separated and differing demands are an essential characteristic of the middle school program.

Group involvement increases in importance as the growing transescent seeks the company of his peers. The middle school program recognizes this by providing for group activities wherein varying group structures are utilized. Even the pupil-teacher relationship undergoes change in these years. While the elementary child finds comfort in associating with a single teacher, the transescent expresses a frequent interest in and need for varied teacher contacts. The program, ideally, provides both elements in an arrangement of teaching patterns which embody the security of a single teacher assigned to each group for a part of the school program and with other teacher assignments to vary this but not reaching the strict departmentalization so characteristic of later years in the high school.

The transescent is a highly sensitive individual. He often responds to negative circumstances with his whole being. Failures and rebuffs can have crushing effects on him. He desperately requires reinforcement and encouragement. He wants to be liked, to belong, and to contribute in whatever way he is capable. Therefore, the atmosphere of the middle school must be an essentially congenial one with opportunities for each student to find satisfaction for these basic psychological needs. The often serious competitions of the older high school years are something for which he is unprepared and he experiences frequent frustration and defeat when he is forced into this kind of climate. Although he is becoming more socially conscious, he is still developing in this regard and the sophisticated social functions of the older adolescent are not appropriate to his needs.

Since the transescent is still very much in the process of growing and developing intellectually and academically, he requires experiences which will permit him to strengthen his ability to perform in learning activities. In light of this, a basic skills program would be an important part of the middle school curriculum. Far from having completed this kind of development in the elementary school years, these children continue to require additional attention to these important learning skills. Attention would also be needed in the middle school program in providing expert diagnostic services as an aid to the classroom teacher working with her students.

While there is a great deal more to be said with regard to the above and to other aspects of the nature of the transescent and the school program most appropriate for him, it is important to note that generally, the middle school should reflect the transitional nature of the child at this age and to provide a truly transitional program to fit the situation. It is transitional both from the standpoint of bridging the gap from the elementary school to the secondary school and from the transitional or altering nature of the developing transescent.

An examination of the literature related to the preadolescent showed these growth characteristics to fall within the normal range for these children, but the reader should keep in mind that each boy or girl at a given age grows at his or her own rate, which may differ from the rest of the group.

## I. PHYSICAL GROWTH CHARACTERISTICS

### A. Body Growth

The growth pattern is the same for all boys and girls, but there are wide variations in the timing and degree of changes. The sequential order in which

**Implication for the Curriculum**

Emphasize self-understanding throughout the curriculum. This can be done by:

a. Providing health and science experiences that will develop an understanding of growth they occur is relatively consistent in both sexes.

Each person rapidly accelerates before pubescence and decelerates after pubescence.

During the transition between childhood and adolescence (six months after puberty), the greatest amount of physical (as well as psychological and social) change in an individual will occur.

a. growth hormone (anterior lobe of pituitary gland) stimulates overall growth of bones and tissue. This hormone is largely responsible for the growth rate.

b. gonad-stimulating hormone causes gonads (testes and ovaries) to grow, which produce hormones of their own. When gonads reach maturity they seem to dry up the growth hormone.

c. changes in thymus, thyroid, and possibly adrenal glands result in changes in rate of energy production (metabolism), blood pressure, and pulse rate.

d. bones grow fast, muscles slower; legs and arms grow proportionately faster than trunk. Hands and feet mature before arms and legs. This split growth is called *asynchrony*.

**B. Health**

Continues to enjoy comparative freedom from diseases; however, eyes, ears, and especially teeth may require medical attention. Minor illnesses of short duration are fairly common during early preadolescence.

Poor posture and awkwardness become increasingly evident.

**C. Body Management**

Endurance is usually not high, perhaps because of the rapid growth spurt.

such as: (1) weighing and measuring at regular intervals and charting gains or losses; (2) observing growth of plants and animals; (3) learning about individual differences in growth.

b. Providing guidance at the classroom level and by utilizing school counselor(s) as a resource person.

c. During physical education classes, providing for individual differences by having several groups of differing abilities.

Provide opportunities for interaction among students of multi-ages.

Physical education classes should provide health instruction as well as exercise. Periods should be long enough to allow adequate time for showers—which should be required.

Formulate school policy regarding homework assignments to insure adequate play time.

Preadolescents can overtire themselves in exciting competition.

For many, this is a period of listlessness, possibly of an emotional or physical cause.

Pimples and excessive perspiration become problems as glands produce oily secretion.

Discuss good health habits such as to bathe regularly. Discuss sales propaganda for beauty aids.

## II. EMOTIONAL AND SOCIAL CHARACTERISTICS

### A. Emotional Status (Stability)

The comparative serenity of later childhood is left behind and emotions begin to play a more obvious part in their lives. They frequently appear unable to control them and lose themselves in anger, fear, love. Often no relationship between the importance of situation and violence of reaction. Extreme variance in moods.

Uncertainty may begin and a strict self-criticism. Also strict criticism of others. Tend to suppress feelings later in age and to keep things to themselves in contrast to early part of age when they immediately express all feelings.

Strong positive feelings toward ideals that are effectively presented. Frustrations grow out of conflicts with parents or peers, and awareness of lack of social skills, or in failure to mature as rapidly as others. Anger is common and may grow out of feelings of inadequacy, fatigue, rejections, uncertainty.

### B. Feelings of Self and Others

Feelings about parents and peers change. View them more realistically. May be quick and vociferous to younger sibling, which may cause younger sibling to tease to get a rise out of older child. Later in period, he gets along quite well and may in fact be nice to have around.

**Implication for the Curriculum**

Discuss values, morality, and what's important. Get children's feelings on these. If consideration emerges, stress this for children to remember in relationships.

Help child find activities at which he excels.

Provide for an ample variety of outlets to emotions and for educational learning.

Provide dramatic experiences which allow the child to release tension, to take different roles, and to achieve satisfactions in the eyes of peers.

Encourage youngsters to be critical of their work but in a way that will help them not to feel inferior.

Learn to accept others for what they are.
Learn behavior necessary to add to the group.
Develop appreciation for individual company as well as group.

Group is all important. Compulsion to dress conformity, language, possessions, and behavior. Tend to look down on less mature. Failure to achieve status or belonging may lead to self-pity. Often fights in group but may make up quickly. By end of stage the gang changes to the crowd.

Begins by boys loathing girls but girls liking boys. Each stays with own sex. Boys later tend to tease girls and to "steal" loose articles of clothing. Late in period both prefer mixed parties.

**C. Tendency to Have Fears**

Tends to pooh-pooh fears but is apprehensive in dark. Likes flashlight near by or light shining into room from without. Not comfortable on dark streets. Will reject baby sitter but is afraid at home alone. Unexplainable noises or objects stir a wild imagination.

Fears are more in form of worries. Worry over non-acceptance primary. Can imagine that report grades and peer criticism are cues of non-acceptance. Worry over school work, exams, promotion. Boys may worry over money, physical ability, facial blemishes. Girls worry about development (too fast or too slow), belonging, and, later acceptance by opposite sex.

Worries because of increasing demands of self as well as of school and home.

**D. Personal Ideals and Values**

Conscience becomes more apparent at this stage. Exhibits strong feelings about fairness, honesty and values in adults but may "relax" their own. Example: boys cheating in school; girls shoplifting.

This may grow out of greater need for wide variety of articles, greater

Be aware that criticism can be constructive and see the merits of accepting some of it.

Punish the act when necessary. Be firm and fair.

Develop an understanding of the opposite sex through readings, discussions, role playing, etc.

Discuss worries and fears in class. Encourage freedom of expression of feelings and in communicating problems. Show examples of people who have had problems and have learned to overcome them. Show by illustration peers and adults who have learned to overcome them.

Explain that many adults strive to help this group. Attempt to build faith in home, church, school, with emphasis on parent, clergy, teachers and counselors and whom to consult when necessary.

Find ways to release tensions.

Show how to accept disappointment because there is always another way to seek rewards.

Let the children help develop a method for establishment of some classroom rules. Show the need for rules in a simple society and for a complex society.

Attempt to instill a respect for rules, for law, for school, for all authority.

Discuss that there are pressures on every person of every age and understand what forces chance of success in not getting caught, pressure of gang, general emotional instability of age.

Sense of simple justice strong. Want fair teacher and are quick to challenge anyone unfair. May become martyr to include peer left out of crowd. Expect high levels from teachers and parents. Accept drinking and swearing in moderation. Want independence but may feel anxiety when parents' expectations are not met. Want to do what's right. Pressure of crowd strong.

### E. Independence

Begins to cut loose from parents. May look for an adult other than parent for help in understanding complexities of life. Wants to cut loose from authority and to figure things out for self. Protests he is no longer baby. Gripes when restricted.

Much behavior is role playing and cannot be taken at face value. He must respond as the group would expect. May say "The rest of the kids are doing it." Could show lack of concern for family but look out if one is in bad health or needs help. He shows much concern.

Parents often misunderstand and can cause problems by demanding level of performance far beyond child's ability.

During early stage may need help and rules at parties. Later is able to work along quite independently. True in school as well. Often when class is left alone teachers may find them creatively employed when returning.

Wishes to preserve a self-identity. Often wishes to be alone. Often goes to room to read alone or to be alone. Spends time in reflective thinking toward end of age.

these pressures are—parent, gang, friend, etc. Learn that each person is accountable for his own actions and behavior and pays his own price.

Learn to develop a respect for others' feelings, others' rights, others' property.

Develop sense of responsibility, that each of us is responsible to someone or something every minute of our lives.

Expect that they respect each other in everyday courtesies and politeness. Discuss the role of authority in a society.

Understand that it is normal at this age to want to be independent. Provide learning activities which include independent study.

Analyze the behavior of the group and attempt to sort out desirable and undesirable characteristics.

Provide role playing activities to understand personal and family problems.

Provide opportunity for group to plan such as use of time, group activity, independent activity, projects, other.

Provide opportunity for students to work independently when they desire to do so.

Provide a quiet corner for independent study both in the classroom and in the Learning Center.

## F. Responsibility and Sensitiveness

Home hostilities are expanded but if channeled right by giving choice, they are more apt to select an activity to do. Generally hate to work early in period. Especially at home.

Beginning to accept views of others and to live in harmony with those with whom they disagree.

Able to wash car, dishes, babysit, and other home responsibilities. The acceptance of work responsibility seems natural at first. Enthusiasm is great then may slack off toward end of period.

Provide opportunities to discuss feelings displayed at home and how to cope with them.

Provide many situations where he grows in his ability to work with the group or other individuals.

Provide activities which help him to work well, complete jobs, and to be increasingly responsible.

## G. Play

At early stages the competitive spirit and the will to excel are primary. One boy in desire to win may ridicule another who makes an error.

Provide opportunities for a variety of activities so that a student may excel in one.

Provide opportunity for all-girl, all-boy games; for mixed activity; and for activity where the best in it compete against one another to exclusion of poorer-ability students.

Provide activity for increasingly difficult coordination in both boys' and girls' interests.

Team play is understood and practiced. They can work reasonably well together but ground rules should have first been established and a supervisor should be in attendance, especially at the earliest stage.

Girls lose interest in dolls and become increasingly more aware of their appearance and of boys. Boys detest girls at earliest age, later tease them, push them in water, steal little articles of clothing, and run expecting to be chased. Much chasing of one another in halls of school, on street, or wherever with "wait 'til I get you." Toward end of period boys and girls prefer mixed parties.

Some may collect, others write in diaries. Most prefer to play with others. Those alone may need much individual consideration. An especially good time is summer camp as all enjoy swimming, group activity, and running.

Participate in vigorous exercise but also in the quiet and spectator games.

Learn that on a team, all must contribute.

Learn that criticizing each other on a team can cause internal decay. Building each member is a way to win.

Know that there are many kinds of activities to enjoy throughout life, some active and others more passive. That a truly rounded person will participate and appreciate to some extent all of them or at least to appreciate and understand another's participation.

Roller skating, baseball, swimming, jumping rope are favorite activities. Also just chasing one another.

Near end of period, group play is still appreciated, but not for winning. Participants are more concerned about how well each did. Rules not needed as much. Group more able to make up rules as needed.

Provide active and quiet team activities in curricular and noncurricular learnings.

## III. MENTAL GROWTH CHARACTERISTICS

### General Statement

As the child matures physically, increasing in body size and developing more and more motor skills, there is a concurrent growth in mental skills. His world widens with each succeeding experience, and he can cope more readily with abstract ideas. He develops his ability to generalize and to discover relationships. Because of the great differences in mental and physical characteristics, a single, preconceived standard for all may cause extreme pressure on many.

### A. Intellectual Development

Have already learned to make comparisons and to recognize likenesses and differences. Can meet failure and disappointment and accept criticism. Can face reality as well as admit strength and weaknesses.

Is capable of making judgments. Can make generalization reflective thinking.

Can carry out concrete operations (7–11 years) dealing with the properties of the present world.

Develops ability to use hypothetical reasoning, formal operations, using objects (12–15 years). This is the final childhood stage preparatory to adult thinking.

Develops concepts of volume (11 or 12 years).

### Implication for the Curriculum

Provide opportunities for critical reasoning and problem solving.

Use hypothetical situations occasionally in language arts and social studies situations.

Provide experiences such as in science and social studies where the student must look at the data and arrive at suitable conclusions.

Provide for the full range of intellectual development through the provision of activities to meet the needs of the student.

Provide activities in both the formal and informal situations to improve his reasoning powers.

Some will be satisfied in learning the characteristics of electric bell circuits, as one example; others will go on to discover the basic laws of work and apply them to new situations.

While brain and other neural developments are almost complete, experience is lacking to solve adult problems.

Charts, maps, and diagrams are now useful means of communication.

Attention span continues to increase with all activities, with the most striking gains being in problem solving.

Reading rates may become adult.

## B. Interests

Interests are related to accelerating growth, increasingly strong emotional reactions, and the awareness of new roles awaiting them in society. Problems of human relations become increasingly important.

There is a wide variety of interests and individual differences become greater.

Reading and collecting equal or exceed the high rates of later childhood.

This is the period of excessive daydreaming.

Girls become more preoccupied with themselves and their appearance.

## C. Creative Ability and Appreciations

Individual differences in creative ability are pronounced. Exceptional talent, if given opportunity and training, develops rapidly. Some students are self-conscious and highly critical of themselves.

Writing, dramatizing, and painting are particularly appealing for self-expression and creative expression.

Diaries, poetry, and letters are used for expressing thoughts.

Provide experiences to challenge each youngster's thinking abilities in the instructional program.

Provide opportunities for a variety of experiences in curricular and co-curricular activities.

Provide experiences which will help the student learn how to read charts, maps, and diagrams effectively.

Recognize that students have varying attention spans and make provisions for this variation in the instructional program, homework, etc.

Keep an adequate number of books at all levels of reading ability.

Provide reading materials which contain examples of emotional problem solving, various occupations, and problems of human relations.

Provide reading instruction which is individualized. This is more effective than level grouping.

Provide opportunities for reading individually and in organizing clubs in various interest areas.

Provide a program of learnings which is exciting and meaningful.

Provide experiences in clothing and textiles, food and nutrition.

Provide experiences for individuals to express themselves by writing and participating in dramatic productions.

Provide experiences in the various arts for all transescents.

Middle school administrators and teachers need to gain a thorough understanding of the growth characteristics of the preadolescent, and to provide learning experiences which are consistent with these needs. Without this knowledge, teachers do not have an adequate basis for defining the types of teaching-learning experiences needed. This lack of knowledge made the junior high school a pale carbon copy of the senior high school. The middle school movement provides a golden opportunity to develop schools truly designed for preadolescents. Without a full knowledge of the growth characteristics of the preadolescent the dream of a true middle school just cannot be realized.

**ENDNOTES**

1. Redl, Fritz. "Pre-Adolescents—What Makes Them Tick?" *Child Study*, Winter 1943–44, p.44.
2. Murphy, Lois Barclay. "Enjoying Pre-Adolescence," *Childhood Education*, Jan. 1970, p. 179.
3. Eichhorn, Donald. *The Middle School* (New York: The Center for Applied Research in Ed., Inc., 1966), p. 3.
4. Witty, Paul A. "What Children Watch on T.V.," *The Pocket*, XIV, Boston: D.C. Heath & Co., 1960.

*Nicholas P. Georgiady* is Professor of Education, Miami University, Oxford, Ohio.
*Louis G. Romano* is Professor of Education, Michigan State University, East Lansing.

# Brain Periodization—Challenge, Not Justification

## EDWARD N. BRAZEE

Herman Epstein's first presentation to middle school educators, at the 1977 National Middle School Association conference in Denver, was enthusiastically received and hailed by some as the signal of a new direction for middle school education. Yet four years later at the 1981 NMSA conference in Miami, Conrad Toepfer could point to very few schools—the most notable exception being the Shoreham–Wading River School in New York—which have made any serious attempt at using brain periodization theory as rationale for curriculum development. If Epstein's information on brain growth spurts and plateaus is of major importance to educators, why aren't more middle schools using this information?

Before dealing with this question a brief review of some of the work done on brain periodization is in order. Much of the literature since 1977 in the area of brain periodization has been limited to discussions of possible implications for curriculum. With the exception of Shayer's (1981) work in England, brain periodization research is scarce and is little known outside of colleges and universities. Toepfer (1979) reported the effects of "turn-off" on middle school students as a side effect of inappropriately timed instruction. Strahan (1980) and Brazee (1981) outlined characteristics of early adolescents' thinking, based on brain periodization theory. Many more have written about the importance of this theory, but without suggesting specific

From *Middle School Journal* 15, No. 1 (November 1983): 8–9, 30. Used by permission of the author and the publisher.

possibilities for its use. Arnold (1981), in a critique, suggested a different interpretation of the Epstein data.

The point is this: after four years, a large number of people say that the Epstein information is intriguing, fascinating, and very interesting. But it is obvious that few have translated it into curricular implications. In addition, much of brain periodization theory has been misused as individuals have taken statements out of context. Some have used this theory to advance questionable ideas about middle school education. Although there is much to be learned about and from brain periodization theory, it has had a relatively minor impact on schools— too minor when one considers its potential implications for teaching and learning with middle school students.

The minor impact of brain periodization theory is not just unfortunate, it may be indicative of an unwillingness or inability of middle school educators to conceptualize and use some potentially powerful information. I am certainly not suggesting that we begin to implement "programs" which use the brain periodization data without thinking, but, I am suggesting that we look at the data to see what they do suggest.

## WHAT ARE THE ISSUES?

Epstein (1978) says that there are five distinct *brain growth spurts;* these are 3–10 months, 2–4 years, 6–8 years, 10–12 years and 14–16 years. The years in between the brain growth spurts are called *plateaus* or periods of slower brain growth. These five brain growth spurts match up fairly closely with the predicted onset ages of the four Piagetian stages, plus a fifth state of "problem finding" proposed by Arlin (1975). Epstein says that the data he has compiled are the biological evidence of Piagetian theory. Arnold (1981) has raised some questions about the interpretation of data which indicate spurts

and plateaus. Even though he questions the ages at which brain spurts and plateaus occur, Arnold agrees that the important question remains: what do the brain periodization data suggest for curriculum planning in the middle school?

The major questions to be examined are:

1. What kinds of learning can students "handle" during plateaus and spurts?
2. What are the qualitative differences in students' thinking between spurts and plateaus?
3. How do you determine whether a student is in a spurt or plateau?
4. How should a teacher's methods and expectations change from spurt to plateau?

Obviously, there is much to be done with the Epstein data. Perhaps it is too much to expect realistic and logical implications from such a theory this soon. We can expect, however, a responsible approach from those who are attempting to interpret brain periodization theory. With the notable exception of Toepfer little in-depth effort is evident.

## WHAT DOES THE THEORY SUGGEST?

Brain periodization theory *does not* suggest that we should put seventh and eighth graders on "hold" for 18 months to 2 years, merely because the majority of them are in a plateau period. But what should we do during this time? What about students who are in transition from one Piagetian stage to the next?

Epstein's suggestion that memorization be used extensively as a learning tool during plateau periods is disturbing. In a recent publication concerning Epstein's work, Cramer states, "In fact, Epstein's advice for teachers with children at plateau stages should warm the hearts of education's traditionalists . . ." (1981). Epstein then explains, "I think we underestimate the ability of a developed memory. During plateau periods, I think it's important that kids memorize lots of songs and poems and parts of great literature. The Bible remains with me because I memorized long passages during my plateau periods, and what I memorized enriches my life constantly. If I had my way, I'd have teachers start a program of memorization of stories and poems and information that kids find useful and interesting" (Cramer, 1981).

I have no quarrel with the intent of these statements. I am concerned about their interpretation by teachers and administrators who may not understand that Epstein is *not* calling for a return to "traditional" methods. Middle schools are trying to escape the traditional classroom with its heavy use of rote learning and meaningless drills. Epstein *seems* to be calling for a return to this. We should be challenged to use his suggestions as a beginning for learning which is appropriate to the child's cognitive development. What we are seeing, however, are people justifying their programs with isolated and misused statements from Epstein and others.

Within a few years, the cognitive level of a set of materials may be advertised next to the readability of those materials. Materials may ostensibly be written for students in brain spurts or plateaus. And because of this, teachers and administrators could buy these materials thinking that they will meet students' cognitive needs, just by using the materials. The fallacy in such thinking seems clear; the nature of cognitive development is too complex to be solved with simple teacher-proof materials.

## WHAT DO WE KNOW?

The major implications of brain periodization theory for middle schools are:

1. The vast majority of middle school students are pre-formal thinkers.

2. Many of the materials used in middle schools require *formal* thinking strategies.
3. In spite of the rhetoric about "teaching the individual child," instruction in middle schools is often done with little regard for the most important consideration—cognitive development.

These three statements show the need for a considerably different view of teaching and learning from that which exists in many middle schools. Most middle school students are pre-formal. Shayer (1981), in a remarkably comprehensive study in England, found that even fewer pre- and early-adolescents use formal operations than anticipated. He found that at 14 years old, only 20 percent used even early formal operations. This is very important as we consider the next two implications—methods and materials.

Most middle level commercial materials require students to use formal thinking strategies. The teaching methodology assumed consists of three steps: (1) the concept or skill is presented by an explanation or definition; (2) the student uses the concept or skill in several examples, and; (3) finally, the student is tested on the concept or skill.

One benefit from this traditional type of instruction is that it is fairly efficient. A large quantity of material may be "covered" in a short time. The biggest disadvantage is that it requires formal thinking by the student. The student is expected to understand the explanation, see the applicability, and use his background knowledge all before he has a chance to "try out" the concept/skill. Even if the concept is a simple one, this method does not allow the student any opportunity to adjust his thinking to a new situation. The student is expected to grasp the idea and use it successfully, often in an artificial practice exercise.

Although this traditional method of instruction may be efficient, it is not necessarily effective. The majority of middle school students think concretely. For them to understand a concept, it must be presented to them correctly, by referring to the here and now. Concrete thinkers can memorize rules and definitions and use them in practice situations. This system breaks down, however, when students are asked to *apply* rules and definitions to new situations. If learning is defined as memorizing rules to complete practice exercises in textbooks, then the concrete thinker can "learn" using the traditional method. If learning means applying rules and concepts to new situations, then learning does not take place.

Grammar instruction is an excellent example of this dilemma. For years, traditional grammar instruction has taken up an inordinate amount of time in language arts classes. Year after year, students "learn" the same rules and do similar practice exercises. If students were really learning grammar they would not need the repetition. Obviously, they are not learning; they memorize rules long enough to do practice exercises, and their writing does not improve. The reason is deceptively simple. To study traditional grammar is to study a *formal system* with its own vocabulary, rules and interrelationships (Fraser, 1978). Concrete thinkers, because of the nature of their thinking abilities, cannot apply the rules of such a system.

Concrete thinkers are dependent on experiences which allow them to use previously developed thought patterns. They need to deal with the literal, not the abstract. Concrete thinkers must be allowed to approach novel situations in familiar ways. They must be given opportunities to use the familiar to solve the unknown. More importantly, they must be encouraged to formulate questions about a problem as well as being given opportunities to try out alternative ways to solve problems. This type of instruction takes more time because of the built-in "messing around time." Piaget called this necessary component of learning, self-regulation. It is the time when students grapple, mentally and physically,

with problems they are not quite sure how to solve.

## NOTHING NEW

The suggestion that teachers plan activities which allow students to manipulate objects and ideas concretely is not new. The reasons for doing so, which are explained in Piagetian theory and supported by the Epstein data, are just now being recognized. Although middle school teachers have given lip-service to the importance of instruction which forces the pre- and early-adolescent to become active in the classroom, the predominant mode of instruction continues to be telling. The lecture method, like the traditional method of instruction used in texts, often calls for formal thinking on the part of the student. It does not allow concrete thinkers to use what they already know.

In spite of inappropriate instructional strategies in textbooks which require students to think formally, teachers can do a great deal to involve students in concrete thinking. An instructional model called the Learning Cycle (Fuller, 1980) forces teachers to consider the thinking levels of their students. The process includes the steps of *exploration, invention* and *application*. The exploration step is the "messing around" step where students are introduced to a concept, presented in a concrete manner. Students must "try out" different solutions as well as formulate questions which can't be answered at that point. Now that students are involved in the learning, the second step, invention, commences. Here the teacher assists students in naming the concept and identifying its use. Both students and teachers are actively involved in this step. The application step is crucial, because it is here that concrete thinkers receive extra practice in using the concept and early formal thinkers can use the concept in a more abstract and sophisticated way.

An example from language arts will illustrate the differences between the traditional instructional model and the Learning Cycle. In composition, the five paragraph essay, presented traditionally, requires formal thinking because of the understanding needed to comprehend the structure and relationship of ideas in the five paragraphs. It is very difficult for the concrete thinker to understand and use this concept when presented in the usual manner; the concepts must be presented in such a way that the concrete thinker can understand. The Learning Cycle gives such a model. During the *exploration* step, students are asked to order five paragraphs which are presented out of sequence. They are then asked to give reasons for the order of the five paragraphs. In this way students can begin the activity using concrete thinking. Some explanations will be very simple and some will be rather sophisticated; all will give possible reasons. The exploration step is the time consuming step, but it can be worthwhile in student understanding. Instead of listening to the teacher's explanations of the concepts, the student is forced to think on his own to develop an explanation. During the exploration phase, students try out what they know about the concept, in this case, five paragraph essays. Equally important, all students are able to respond to the concept on a concrete level and this builds the base for further learning of the concept.

During *invention*, students and teacher use prior knowledge and generated questions from exploration to formulate general principles about the concept. In this example, students, using teacher help, would develop guidelines for writing five paragraph essays: a five paragraph essay has an introduction and a conclusion; the three paragraphs in-between contain the three major ideas developed in the essay.

The *application* step allows for further practice of the concept in a meaningful setting. Continued practice in writing five paragraph essays would be the application step.

## WHAT NOW?

Middle school educators have been translating physical and social/emotional data into classroom practice. Unfortunately, we have not also used cognitive data to structure curriculum and instruction.

We must avoid a blind, head-long rush into methods and materials which we have now, merely because of brain periodization data. So too, must we guard against brain periodization "shock." Too many misinterpretations of these data are being made. If most students from 12–14 years are in a brain growth plateau, we can't wait until they grow out of it, as some have actually suggested. Shayer (1981) points out the importance of appropriate instruction for all students when he says, "Here it is not so much a matter of waiting until the pupil is ready, but rather, with insight, assisting natural development."

We need models of instruction which "assist natural development." We need teachers who are willing to "try out" ideas. We all must be challenged to determine what the brain growth information means in terms of classroom practices.

## REFERENCES

Arlin, Patricia. Cognitive development in adulthood: a fifth stage? *Developmental Psychology*, 1975, 2, 602–606.

Arnold, John, Presentation at the National Middle School Conference, Miami, Florida, November 1981.

Brazee, Edward N. Student responses to a language arts test of cognitive functioning. *Middle School Research Annual—Selected Studies 1981*, 1981, 75–87.

Cramer, Jerome. The latest research on brain growth might spark more learning in your schools. *The American School Board Journal*, August 1981, 168(8), 17–20.

Epstein, Herman. Growth spurts during brain development: implications for educational policy and practice. In J. Chall and A. F. Mirsky (Eds.). *Education and the Brain—N.S.S.E. Yearbook*. Univeristy of Chicago Press, 1978, 343–370.

Fraser, Jan S. and Hodson, Lynda M. Twenty-one kicks at the grammar horse. *English Journal* December 1978, 49–54.

Fuller, Robert G. et al. *Piagetian programs in higher education.* Lincoln, Nebraska: Project ADAPT, 1980.

Shayer, Michael and Adey, Philip. *Towards a science of science teaching: cognitive development and curriculum demand.* London: Heinemann Educational Books, 1981.

Strahan, David. An observational analysis of problem solving strategies used by transitional early adolescents. *Middle School Research Studies*—1980, 1980.

Toepfer, Conrad F., Jr. Areas for further investigation suggested by brain growth periodization findings. *Transescence,* 1979, 8, 17–20.

*Edward N. Brazee* is Associate Professor, College of Education, University of Maine, Orono, Maine.

# Guidelines for the Middle Schools We Need Now

## WILLIAM M. ALEXANDER AND A SEMINAR

This article presents some guidelines for middle school development. They represent, in the seminar's judgment, twelve essential components of a plan for middle school development. Closely interrelated as they are, each component needs specific attention in an educational plan that aims to achieve the organizational goals described in the introduction to this issue: (1) to provide a good program of schooling for children passing from childhood to adolescence; (2) to offer a significant alternative to past organizations that too frequently crystallized as hard-to-change, at times incompatible, elementary and secondary units; (3) to facilitate the continuous progress of learners from school entrance in early childhood to school exit in adolescence.

Several considerations have influenced the development of these guidelines. For one, we are anxious that the middle schools represent genuine efforts to provide a demonstrably better school program for children of the in-between years. Further, this program should bring about greater continuity in the entire system of schooling. Hence the guidelines tend to present best, rather than average, practice. At the same time, we are also anxious that such guidelines be as fully implemented and thoroughly tested as possible. Accordingly, each section of the guidelines describes the goals of its components and suggests several characteristic features of plans for implementing these goals. To give readers further sources on both the goals and plans for their possible implementation, a brief, selected bibliography is included.

Revised 1982 by William M. Alexander. From *National Elementary Principal* 51, no. 3 (November 1971): 79–89. Copyright © 1971, National Association of Elementary School Principals, National Education Association. Used by permission of the authors and the publisher. The members of the graduate seminar (ED 731) on curriculum change responsible for preparing these guidelines were William M. Alexander, seminar professor, Crystal Compton, Jorge Descamps, Nancy Weber, and Jon Wiles. Assistance was also given by Joyce Lawrence, graduate student, and Emmett L. Williams, faculty consultant.

## FOCUSING ON THE BETWEEN-AGER

### Goals

The middle school program is focused on education of children during the transition from childhood to adolescence. The entire program is based on the study of the physical, intellectual, social, and emotional development of the "between-ager." Thus it facilitates frequent physical activity and helps students relearn to manage their bodies skillfully during a period of rapid change in body dimensions and general awkwardness.

The academic program is oriented to help transescents move away from dealing primarily with concrete operations into levels of abstraction and hypothesizing as well. The transescent is also helped in his social development by interacting constructively with both peers and adults. A change in the individual's perception of himself and, consequently, a quest for a satisfying concept of self require many opportunities for self-direction and self-evaluation. The school as a whole is permeated by an open and democratic atmosphere in order to help students achieve appropriate patterns of independence and develop workable valuing processes. The school bridges, rather than duplicates, the elementary and high schools.

### Plans

1. The entire school program offers many opportunities for movement, treating learners as preadolescents who need frequent change in physical activity, not as "little adults" who are to sit still all day.
2. Through a variety of approaches to learning—including problem solving, laboratory experiences, and independent study—each learner has the opportunity to deal with abstractions, develop and test ideas, and bring personal meaning into the world of concrete experiences.
3. Many social activities, such as school clubs, trips, get togethers, and picnics, are encouraged. Students help to work out their own rules and plans for these activities.
4. Learning tasks are individualized and academic competition deemphasized to provide maximum success experiences.
5. Cooperative planning between students and faculty and student participation in the routine tasks of the school help establish an atmosphere of togetherness, making adults closer and more approachable for the transescents.
6. Out-of-school activities, such as working, camping, scouting, and games, are considered to be curriculum related and are freely discussed and planned at school.
7. Community resources—people, institutions, organizations—of interest to the between-agers are utilized as fully as possible to break down walls between schools and community and to make the curriculum personal and real.
8. Gaming, role playing, and "what if?" activities are frequently used in discussions of school and community problems of interest to the students to sharpen issues, reveal alternatives, and assess value choices. Small groups created from home base, advisory, block of time, or other organizations are used for these learner-oriented discussions.

## PLANNING FOR STUDENTS' INDIVIDUAL DEVELOPMENT

### Goals

All of a middle schooler's experiences in school and out of school contribute to his development as a person. However, a cluster of essential experiences and arrangements to this end can be identified as having a primary, almost exclusive focus on individual development. The learner in transition from childhood to adolescence needs quite particular, direct attention to his personal development. In the middle school planned to meet these needs, each learner is encouraged and helped to achieve self-confidence and self-direction. His counseling and instruction are personalized rather than merely individualized, so that some group norm can be achieved.

## Plans

1. Through a home base, advisory, block of time, or other arrangement, each learner spends a substantial amount of time with one adult to whom he can and does turn, daily if possible, for information and assistance regarding his objectives, program, and progress in school; the advisor frequently works more than one year with the same advisees.
2. The advisor is enabled to refer each advisee as needed to a variety of special services: counseling, psychological, medical, social work, and academic, including other teachers.
3. The health and physical education program provides for each learner opportunities appropriate to his own physical development with regard to: (a) understanding the physiological and related aspects of puberty; (b) personal hygiene, physical exercise, diet, rest, and related health practices; (c) recreation through intramural sports programs, individual and team games, social and folk dancing, and such carry-over activities as swimming, tennis, bowling, and golf; (d) health services for systematic identification and follow-up of visual, hearing, dental, nutritional, and other difficulties.
4. Through exploratory courses, mini-courses, activities and other arrangements, each learner has the opportunity to explore a wide range of possible interests in the arts, in occu-

pations in the community and elsewhere, in leisure-time group and individual activities, and in discussions of current developments and events. Each student participates daily in at least one, and usually more, of these activities.
5. Independent study arrangements include seminars growing out of the major knowledge areas; in-school and out-of-school investigations of an individual nature planned by the student and his advisor or any other teacher; substitutions for, or extensions of, regular group work in a knowledge area; and special courses taken at a nearby high school. Each advisor helps his advisees schedule these arrangements as their interests and learning skills indicate.
6. Special group instruction and individual instruction are arranged for students who have explored and wish extended study in the arts, foreign languages, prevocational areas, or other fields. This instruction is available in either the middle school or a nearby high school, using instructors from other levels as needed and available.
7. Teacher education and staff development programs include specific training that is relevant to the foregoing guidelines. Specifically, provisions are currently lacking and needed in the preparation of most teachers for tasks relating to advisement, exploratory activities, and independent study.

## PROGRAMMING THE SKILLS FOR CONTINUED LEARNING

### Goals

Learning skills introduced in the early grades require further instruction in the middle grades, and additional skills are required. The further career of the child as a learner—a career that needs to be lifelong—may be virtually settled in the middle school years. If he enjoys learning, if he becomes skilled in its processes, then a lifelong pursuit may be assured. At this level of schooling, independent study may be one way of focusing on the development of self-directing learners who will be able to achieve their potential in an ever-changing society.

Skills for continued learning include communications skills, such as listening, viewing, and reading; thinking skills, such as questioning, remembering, comparing, contrasting, inferring, generalizing, hypothesizing, and predicting; study skills, such as reading directions carefully, locating information, using the dictionary, interpreting graphic materials, outlining, and summarizing; and critical thinking skills, such as recognizing propaganda techniques and separating facts from opinions.

Every instructional situation can be an opportunity to encourage the learner to become more self-directing and to help him to strive continually to develop his potential to the maximum. Programs for developing these skills are a part of the curriculum plan and include responsibilities for each faculty member.

## Plans

1. The middle school faculty determines which skills are to be emphasized in all learning situations and which in only certain situations. Thus it is decided where reading skills will be developed and where and on what bases special reading instruction is to be given. Decisions are reached, too, on the responsibility for direct instruction in such skills as listening, viewing, and using the library—whether the latter is to be done in all language arts classes, for example, or by a librarian in a special series of instruction, or by some combination approach.
2. Any middle school is certain to have a number of students who need special instruction in reading, math, study skills, and writing.

Decisions may be required on the use of a laboratory approach. If such an approach is decided on, who directs it? When and for how long shall students needing specialized instruction go to the laboratory? Can programmed materials be used, and under what conditions?

3. Independent study may take any one of several forms: an in-depth study done in conjunction with, or in addition to, regular classwork in response to a student's own interest or need; unscheduled time to work in an open lab situation to develop a skill or to ferret out facts; or a special project in art, science, or home arts that students have identified as "just something we'd like to do."
4. Whatever their form, the independent study plans include: (a) structuring the independent studies by helping students plan the use of their time and by setting limits; (b) selecting and planning students' independent study according to criteria they have helped to develop; (c) interpreting the program to parents; (d) planning the facilities, materials, and services needed; (e) planning content and activities, including library research, creative efforts, and field experience (such as working or doing research in the community); and (f) planning and participating in the evaluation of the independent study program.
5. Preservice and inservice training of teachers is a prerequisite for the processes involved in developing thinking skills, group participation skills, interviewing techniques, and other learning skills.

## PLANNING THE ORGANIZED KNOWLEDGE AREAS

### Goals

Two important considerations help shape the middle school curriculum in the areas of organized knowledge. First, middle school youngsters are developing a strong sense of need to systematize and organize their physical and social worlds. During childhood, almost any successful learning experience is self-rewarding, but during transescence, it becomes increasingly important for the learner to see that achievements represent real accomplishments—achievements that are recognized and rewarded in a more adult world. Second, the major scholarly disciplines represent man's effort to understand, explain, and control the physical and social environments in which he exists. The goals, then, of this curriculum component include identifying the big ideas and underlying principles of the major disciplines and thereafter providing every student success experiences in organizing and using the data and the methods appropriate to the areas of organized knowledge. The school subject areas of English, language arts, mathematics, science, and social studies can make important contributions to the intellectual development of the middle school pupil if they are approached at the learner's own level and rate and if system and order are emphasized, rather than sequence and coverage of set amounts of content.

## Plans

1. Through use of subject area planning teams, the major themes, concepts, and organizing centers of the subject are identified and articulated in an overview plan.
2. Through use of home base teacher and/or instructional level teams, individual variations are planned around a common concept or major organizing center. A variety of topics, assignments, and materials are used for individualization.
3. In selecting and organizing knowledge, the emphasis is on a small, manageable number of big ideas, rather than on scope, sequence, and numerous details. The aim is to foster an awareness of the system and order inherent in the subject area.
4. Students are given directed practice in the use of the materials and the ways of knowing that are appropriate to the subject. That is, students are taught to observe the raw data of the subject field and then to catalogue, organize, apply, make and check out generalizations, and reflect on the meaning of these activities to the individual and his society. Use of problem-solving approaches, active engagement, independent study, and small group projects is frequent.
5. Through use of interdisciplinary team planning, occasional cross-subject theme units are carried on to foster understanding of the applicability and interrelationships among the several learning areas.
6. A guiding principle for selecting themes, topics, and generalizations in the social studies areas is that the tone be generally one of affirmation. That is, the transescent learner needs a base of those things in his background and his society in which he can believe and have pride before moving into systematic criticism and analysis of those things that need change. Biographies, legends, and experiences that illuminate man's ideals and successes are frequently used.
7. Involvement of the learner in helping to set his own learning goals and practice in evaluating his own and his classmates' progress toward accepted goals are important features of the middle school program.

## ORGANIZING LEARNERS FOR INSTRUCTION

### Goals

In recent years, the emphasis in education has shifted from styles of teaching to styles of learning. The teacher is encouraged to be creative not only with his own part of the interaction process in which students learn but with the setting in which it occurs. At the middle school level, the important goal is the matching of students, teachers, and situations to facilitate the interaction process.

Organization for instruction is an individual school matter governed by goals, students, school personnel, and facilities of each school. Flexibility is a necessity if a learner's progress through the educational process is to be continuous and unbroken. The challenge is to utilize the teacher's intimate knowledge of the interests and needs of the individual transescent student, along with the teacher's abilities, the school spaces, and the time available, to work out effective plans for large and small groups, laboratory groups, tutorial instruction, and independent study.

## Plans

1. Assigning a student to a home base where he may have frequent and sustained advisement and encouragement from a teacher-counselor is a popular way to provide the teacher with a better knowledge of the student and to meet the transescent's needs. The teacher-counselor is usually one of the teachers on the team to which the student is assigned.
2. Organizing the middle school into interdisciplinary teams can promote cooperative planning. The plan for teaming that has four teachers—math, science, social studies, and language arts—working with 100 or so students, is widely used.
3. An analysis of the student population to assess the range of intellectual, social, emotional, and physical development aids the faculty in placing students on teams.
4. Placing students in multiage groups helps to individualize instruction. A student may move quickly in areas for which he shows more aptitude and more slowly in areas in which he encounters difficulty.

5. Teaming students and teachers permits the scheduling of learning experiences into large time blocks based on planned activities, with the team responsible for scheduling within their block. Schedules vary from day to day and from team to team. Activities such as lunch, physical education, and unified arts are scheduled in coordination with the other teams.
6. Team planning time is scheduled during the day. This time block is devoted to planning instructional relationships and to pooling observations that help teachers know their students in greater depth.
7. Care is given in scheduling the school day to allow adequate opportunity for recreation breaks and for special activity groupings through an activity period, a half hour after lunch, or another arrangement.
8. Whether children are classified by grades, years, or teams, no individual is assigned to a groove in which he must inevitably remain from year to year. Exploratory courses and activities are generally open to students without regard to grade or year classification.
9. Access to all learning resource spaces (library, audiovisual area, or laboratory) is as immediate and open as the rights of all learners permit, with special provisions possible for after-hours use.

## STAFFING THE MIDDLE SCHOOL

### Goals

The functions that the middle school aims to serve determine the qualifications and categories of the personnel to be employed. Since the middle school focuses on the developmental tasks of the between-ager, the staff is expected to have personal attributes that facilitate this growth. Teachers who have a positive view of themselves, who are not overly protective of their dignity, and who have the emotional strength to live with the ups and downs of transescents are likely to be more successful in their work with this age group. These teachers are flexible and open to change; they can live with and admit their errors and get involved with student concerns; and they have a great deal of patience and a readiness to listen. They have respect for the dignity and worth of the individual and a personal commitment to a value system supportive of a democratic society. They also have the ability to interact constructively with others and can easily relate to transescents. They are approachable, responsive, and supportive as youngsters struggle with the problems peculiar to their stage of development. Most of all, these teachers are personally committed to the education of transescents.

## Plans

1. Several categories of personnel are necessary to accomplish the functions of the middle school.

   a. *Subject specialists and team members* who, in addition to giving instruction in their specialty, can serve as resource persons for other staff members and can lead disciplinary and interdisciplinary teams. These persons also serve as home base teacher-counselors.

   b. *Special areas specialists,* including competent reading specialists and professionally qualified art, music, foreign language, home arts, and physical education resource teachers. These specialists belong on the staff of a good middle school; they cooperate with the teaching teams and may work as home base teachers.

   c. *Specialized staff,* including learning resources personnel who help faculty and students retrieve information and provide ample resources for learning; guidance people who help staff members in their

teacher-counselor role and in working with students; measurement and evaluation specialists who concentrate on the well-rounded development of the child.

   d. *Administrative staff and supportive services* who provide leadership in improving the instructional program by providing services for students and teachers, and who facilitate the work of the instructional staff by managing the business, financial, and housekeeping aspects of the organization.

2. Until preservice programs for middle school teachers are generally available, a realistic approach for most schools is to employ a staff representing both elementary and junior high preparation and experience. Whenever feasible, arrangements are made that combine teachers from elementary and secondary backgrounds for cooperative planning.

3. The newly organized middle school seeks volunteers from all existing schools in the school district rather than automatic transfers from the predecessor schools.

4. Since no one set of teacher characteristics or teaching behaviors can be identified as "best" for all instructional purposes, it is desirable to staff the middle school with a variety of personality types who possess different teaching styles and different experiential backgrounds.

5. The use of student teachers, teaching interns, and paraprofessionals (including teacher aides, clerical aides, and technicians) enhances the instructional program.

## PLANNING AND USING SCHOOL FACILITIES

### Goals

Whether middle school youngsters are to be blessed with a brand new school or housed in a traditional building, a major goal of the plant is to provide for maximum flexibility whereby space is adaptable to the multidimensional, interdisciplinary program of learning. The ideal is a stimulating environment that challenges transescents to develop and fully use their five senses as they set about establishing a system of interrelationships with one another and with their environment. A contrast of colors, textures, and light, as well as a balance in spatial dimensions, relief and solid structures, and auditory effects, can make the school aesthetically satisfying. That middle schoolers like their school and find it a pleasant place to work and play in is a goal worthy of carefully planned efforts.

## Plans

1. Through representative and cooperative planning, teachers and students can contribute ideas for a new building or for renovations of the old. A teacher who has experienced, along with students, the frustration of insufficient storage space for an important but unfinished project can be persuasive when priorities are established.

2. Each aspect of the facility is evaluated for congruence with middle school beliefs. For instance, it would be difficult to justify enough seating space for interschool athletics in a school that professed to deemphasize competitive sports.

3. In recognition of middle schoolers' need for personal development, large open spaces conducive to social interaction are provided, as well as small private areas for pupil-teacher conferences and counseling. Furniture is arranged to encourage small group interaction.

4. Anticipating a team approach to instruction, multiaged groups of transescents are housed in a quad or pod arrangement in order for the students to identify with a smaller group.

5. Staff members have ample storage, work,

and meeting space within their pod, quad, or designated area. The interdisciplinary team approach encourages frequent cooperative planning, and members want to be in close proximity to one another.

6. Students have access to systematized storage areas for learning resources, independent and paired work projects, and in-process endeavors of small and large groups. Opportunities abound in these areas for shared responsibilities in organizing, categorizing, and maintaining materials.

7. Multipurpose areas invite and encourage student participation in creative enterprise, as well as in the world of work. Easy access to these areas encourages experimentation while allowing for depth.

8. Extensive use of the out-of-doors can be an exciting way to implement middle school beliefs and values. Awareness of, and concern for, ecology take on a new meaning for the active transescent as he interacts with the environment beyond the walls of the school.

9. As students and staff spend time in the middle school, they become sensitized to the strengths and weaknesses of their school plant. A periodic charting and recording by a student-faculty committee might look carefully at the use of space within the building: How many students use this area in a week? Has this arrangement ever been changed? How might this area better serve our needs? What really goes on in that space? In addition to learning techniques of data collection, students are involved in important decision-making processes and designing creative alternatives.

10. A school plant is developed to serve society's learners. In that spirit, middle schoolers can use their school many more hours each day than is the current practice. Resource people from the community and parents

who work are often available at night. They provide an excellent opportunity for middle school students to experience authentic relationships with a variety of people—peers and adults!

## SECURING COMMUNITY COOPERATION

### Goals

Four groups with important abilities and responsibilities play significant roles in the process of developing and implementing a good middle school program: (a) students, (b) parents, (c) citizens of the community at large, and (d) the professional staff. The only way to ensure the participation of all concerned groups is to develop an informative community relations program. Involvement, consultation, and continuing dialogue are the necessary components of this program.

### Plans

1. Prior to the opening of the middle school, the professional staff, parents, and selected laymen from the community undertake long-term study of the concepts important to the development of a good middle school program.

2. During the long-term study, the participants develop relevant documents or gather pertinent data, such as a philosophy, guidelines for selecting the staff, data obtained from an analysis of population, and feedback information from pupils who have gone through other schools in previous years. Participants in this phase of the study might be students presently and previously enrolled, parents, selected laymen, and the professional staff.

3. The planning groups arrive at basic commitments about staffing, organizing the school, and curriculum. The superintendent and members of the school board are especially important in this phase of the planning, as well as those people who participate in the previous two study activities.

4. A strong information and involvement plan for readying the community for the change can be undertaken by the professional staff, selected laymen, and parents. Members of the press, radio, and television are included. Besides PTA meetings, coffee klatches and continental breakfasts are scheduled occasionally. Every opportunity is capitalized on to appear before civic clubs or other groups to explain the concepts of the middle school.

5. A continual orientation plan is maintained after the school opens. Newcomers to the community, instructional personnel from other schools within the system, or visitors from other systems will want to know about the program. A slide-tape presentation may be developed that orients visitors to the program before they are taken on a tour.

6. A plan for involving resource people is a very important component of a community relations program. A questionnaire or survey identifies interests among the students or members of the community, and workshops are scheduled during the school day or in the evenings. Parents and teachers or older students conduct these workshops in, for example, flower arranging, arts and crafts, or bowling.

7. A planned community relations program continues year after year to keep the community informed about the progress of the program and to seek continuing community participation in program development.

## PLANNING FOR CONTINUOUS PROGRESS

### Goals

Continuous progress plans are built on learning activities that are determined only after data on all phases of growth are considered. These activities are provided on the basis of individual needs, interests, and abilities and are paced at the individual's own rate of learning. Flexibility is a necessity.

### Plans

1. The first step in the process is the preparation of a statement of goals for each curriculum area and for the skills of continued learning.
2. After the overall goals are written, a list of learning objectives is formulated. If learning objectives are already available in some areas, the faculty or team may wish to adapt and adopt them.
3. After objectives are written or selected, teachers find out which objectives pupils have achieved by administering tests keyed to the objectives. Alternatives to tests might be work samples or activities designed to check specific objectives.
4. Appropriate activities for accomplishing the objectives are then planned, involving the use of media, space, equipment, and personnel.
5. Reassessment or postassessment can take the form of a completed project, a teacher-pupil conference, a written test, work samples, or teacher observation as the students are working on activities.
6. A system of multidirectional communication among the teacher, the learner, and the parents for reporting the learner's progress is a task for the faculty, with parental and student help. It may take the form of some type of written report or a parent-student-teacher conference, or both.
7. Adequate record-keeping systems that describe where a student is on a continuum of skills facilitate the reporting to students, parents, and other staff members.
8. Organizing the school into teams facilitates planning. Each team of teachers can zero in on a specific population, and with common planning time scheduled, they can discuss the students' performance in all areas and develop instructional units that meet the needs and interests of the students on their team and capitalize on each others' strengths.
9. Assigning students by age, with a range of two to four years, is a promising alternative to a graded system. After securing parental consent, put some ten-, eleven-, and twelve-year-olds together; and some eleven-, twelve-, and thirteen-year-olds together; and some twelve-, thirteen-, and fourteen-year-olds together. At the end of the year, compare this procedure for assigning students with the traditional grade level assignment procedure. If steps 1–7 have been followed in the curriculum planning process and if a good teaming relationship has been established, the result is a plan for continuous progress that parents and teachers will like and accept.

## EVALUATING LEARNING AND SCHOOLING

### Goals

Evaluation in the middle school is a continual process by which information is gathered to find out how well the goals of the organization are being achieved. Some questions to be answered in the evaluation process are: (a) How well are the developmental needs of the betweenagers being filled? (b) How much individualization of curriculum and instruction is being achieved? (c) How well is the curriculum providing a planned sequence of concepts in the basic knowledge areas, a major emphasis on interests and skills for continued learning, a balanced program of exploratory experiences, and services for personal development? (d) How much continuous progress and smooth articulation is there between the several phases and levels of the total educational program? (e) How well are the personnel and facilities available for continued improvement of schooling being used?

## Plans

1. Periodic testing, individual student self-report files, and teachers' and parents' reports provide data to evaluate how well the program is helping the personal development of the transescents.

2. An evaluation team randomly selects student cases throughout the year, determining how much the program is being individualized and adjusted to these students' needs and how much articulation between the different phases of the program is being achieved for each student. Student schedules are checked periodically to discover imbalance.

3. The curriculum coordinator and a curriculum committee maintain a continuing evaluation of the total program, based on the school's stated objectives and utilizing data from the previously mentioned evaluation procedures, plus polls of students, parents, and faculty on specific issues.

4. A personnel and space utilization study is periodically conducted to identify unused, overused, and poorly used resources and facilities.

5. Until teacher preparation programs provide adequate skills in measurement and evaluation, an inservice education program helps teachers acquire the knowledge and skills they

need to participate effectively in the planning and evaluation process.

6. Follow-up data are secured from the high school on the continued learning skills of former middle schoolers and on their high school interests, successes, and difficulties. This information is used as basic data for the continuing evaluation outlined in item 3.

## RENEWING THE PROGRAM AND STAFF

### Goals

Renewal of the program and staff takes two common forms: conversion of a faculty from another, more traditional type of program to a middle school program; and the year-by-year renewal of a regular middle school program and staff. In either case, this period of renewal can be greatly affected by the degree of advance planning that has taken place.

The very nature of the middle school calls for continual planning, whether it takes the form of an annual updating of an established school or a basic change to a continuous progress middle school program. Middle school programs are not fixed but are continually evolving. The changing nature of the learner at this age is paralleled by continual faculty planning.

Basic to changes that involve new staff and programs is planned preparation that allows time for the acceptance of the middle school concept, for teachers' input into the planning and implementation stages, and for an overall emphasis on change at the classroom level.

### Plans

1. Any successful program of renewal spells out in concise language the regular procedures for curriculum development. The role of each

contributing part, such as advisory groups and curriculum councils, is detailed.

2. Teachers who will be affected by the change are given sufficient lead time to understand the proposed program and to prepare themselves to become active participants in the change process.

3. Sufficient time and resources are provided so that curricular planning and teacher input are of value to the effort. Resources can take such forms as teacher aides, consultant help, the provision of space and materials, a professional library at the school level, and easy access to duplication services.

4. The scheduling of teacher planning time, if effective, includes the provision of daily team planning periods and some provision for long-range planning.

5. The timing of the transition period is aided by consideration of the change process as a whole, rather than from the perspective of many unrelated parts. For there to be effective coordination of the change effort, a minimum of one year of advance planning is called for.

6. Included in any planning for conversion to the middle school concept is visiting existing middle schools; visits are usually planned to see particular programs and features, and time is provided for interaction with the personnel of the school visited.

7. An effective change effort builds in a regular and organized method of evaluation. Vital to the evaluation program and process is the possibility that the program will reverse itself if it does not seem to be working as planned.

8. Special summer workshops are used to renew existing middle school faculties and for the pilot study of programs envisioned by new middle schools. To be effective, such summer workshops have direct access to children attending regular classroom sessions.

9. Before middle schools are adopted on a systemwide basis, a pilot study utilizing one middle school is conducted. Such pilot studies can prevent large-scale mistakes. Furthermore, within the individual middle school, many new programs, such as activity periods, exploratory courses, team teaching, multiaged grouping, and problem-solving laboratories, are piloted in individual situations before being adapted for schoolwide use.

## SEARCHING FOR MIDDLE SCHOOL IDENTITY

### Goals

The middle school is a distinct unit in the educational system, bridging the elementary and high schools. As a bridging unit, it has some characteristics of both schools; yet it cannot, and must not, be merely an upward or downward extension of either. Its program must provide for the immature learner, who needs the close guidance of a single teacher, and for the mature learner, who needs the challenge of many specialists; thus the learning opportunities, organization, and schedule must be as flexible as these guidelines have proposed in order to accommodate all the differences in its students. Such a school cannot be classified, accredited, and evaluated by standards designed for the upper or lower schools. Instead, the standards must also accommodate the variety of provisions essential in the bridging school. Its personnel require special training and certification related to the goals of the middle school. But despite the necessary accommodations for its unique goals and programs, the middle school cannot rightly stand as a wholly separate organization. As a bridge that promotes continuity of education, the middle school must be carefully planned and interrelated with both elementary and high schools so as to maintain a single system of continuous schooling.

## Plans

1. The state department of education officially recognizes the middle school, and accreditation programs have been specifically designed for middle schools.
2. Teacher education programs provide special preparation for teachers at the middle school level. These programs include such unique features as a study of theory and research and case studies of transescent children, an extended experience in a good middle school through practicums and internship, competence in more than one subject area, and basic training in the teaching of reading and other learning skills.
3. Where regional accreditation is required of the middle schools, the plan for accreditation is based on unique criteria related to middle school objectives.
4. Middle school planning groups include personnel representing the elementary and high schools, so as to advance continuous schooling aims and maintain the unique characteristics and objectives of the middle school.
5. Personnel in the middle school continually clarify the definition and program of middle schools and work to eliminate all activities and practices not consistent with the concepts and objectives of the program.
6. Parents and laymen are involved in middle school programs, because their recognition of the concept will eventually legitimize the identity the middle school seeks.
7. Budgetary priorities for the middle school program reflect the objectives of the middle school.
8. The programs of professional organizations provide specific sections for middle school personnel.

## USING THE GUIDELINES

The middle schools still lack adequate accrediting standards and other fixtures of the established elementary and high schools. This fact should encourage experimentation and flexibility, although it also leaves the middle school with less identity and sanction. To guide experimentation and aid professional organizations and other sanctioning groups to understand and assist the new school organizations, an orderly process of continuing preparation, review, and modification of such guidelines as these seems essential.

This set of guidelines is intended as a possible aid to middle school faculties and other planning groups seeking bases for planning and evaluating their middle schools. They are not intended to be prescriptive or authoritative, but illustrative of the thinking of one planning group about the goals and plans of middle schools. It is hoped that many such guidelines will be developed and shared as a means of moving the middle school program toward identity and sanction.

## REFERENCES

Alexander, William M., and George, Paul S. *The Exemplary Middle School.* New York: Holt, Rinehart and Winston, 1981.

Eichhorn, Donald H. *The Middle School.* New York: The Center for Applied Research in Education, 1966.

Johnson, Mauritz, ed. *Toward Adolescence: The Middle School Years.* Seventy-Ninth Yearbook of the National Society for the Study of Education, Part I. Chicago: University of Chicago Press, 1980.

Lounsbury, John, and Vars, Gordon F. *A Curriculum for the Middle School Years.* New York: Harper & Row, 1978.

Moss, Theodore C. *Middle School.* Boston: Houghton Mifflin Co., 1969.

*William M. Alexander* is Professor Emeritus of Education, University of Florida, Gainesville.

# Self-Concept and Esteem in the Middle Level School

## JAMES A. BEANE

The more we can know about young people, the better our chances to be sensitive to their needs and characteristics. To do this we find ourselves testing the waters of biophysics, biochemistry, and new frontier-psychology, often learning new vocabularies and wrestling with complex concepts. For middle level educators this difficult task has been met with enthusiasm. After all, increased understanding of transescents has been at the top of their agenda for almost two decades, and the result has been the appearance of many exciting and effective new middle level programs.

### SELF-CONCEPT AND ESTEEM IN EARLY ADOLESCENCE

Self-concept and self-esteem have been the subject of substantial study in recent years. While most of that work has been of a general nature, some theory and research has focused on the transescent stage of development. As a result we can now make some fairly strong statements about the power of self-perceptions in the lives of transescents.

As a stage in human development, transescence is virtually without parallel. These young people undergo dramatic change and re-orientation in all areas of development: physical, cognitive, and social. Consequently, the content of their self-thoughts (self-concept), and their self-satisfaction (self-esteem), are subject to a constant state of flux. Self-concepts must be adjusted as new physical characteristics appear, as

the beginnings of logic unfold, and as orientation shifts from egocentrism to peer approval. (See figure on page 439.) At each step in this process the question of self-esteem reopens: "Do I like my new self?" and "Do my friends still accept me?"

It is no wonder that these young people so frequently seem confused, unclear, and even desperate about how they look, who likes them, and how they should act. Their lives seem to be ruled by two great myths, "the personal fable" (this doesn't happen to anyone else) and "the imaginary audience" (everyone is watching me). One has to wonder how so many youngsters make it through transescence with their psyches intact. On the other hand, we also know that many do not; they become victims to one degree or another of unhappiness with themselves.

The issues of self-concept and self-esteem are compounded for this group by the ambiguous place of transescence in our culture. Neither children nor adolescents, they are often torn by expectations that they act like one or the other. Some adults, exasperated by their volatile behavior, beg them to act like the stable children they so recently were. Other adults, impatient or fooled by physical stature, demand that they behave like the more stable and self-assured adolescents they have yet to become.

In the peer group, transescents find both comfort and conflict: they are accepted, but on the basis of narrow standards and often at the risk of conflict with adults. Being a transescent is something like being an educator; demands

From *NASSP Bulletin* 67, No. 463 (May 1983): 63–71. Used by permission of the author and the publisher, the National Association of Secondary School Principals.

come from all sides and the delicate balance must be kept of pleasing as many as possible without completely alienating the rest.

Transescent self-concept and esteem are also subject to influence by other forces in our society. Television, the "parent" of the '80s, suggests values, behavior, dress, and other aspects of an ideal self that are often far-removed from the economic means and social realities of real life. An abundant array of lifestyles present an unsure picture of what is right or wrong. Easy access to drugs, including alcohol, and sexual activity offer convenient means of momentary escape with the chance of dire consequences.

Meanwhile, these youngsters come to school, carrying with them their self-concepts and self-esteem, already complicated by their stage of development and the world around them. But the school offers yet another arena for self-thinking. This is where the peer group congregates on a daily basis.

Here is a new set of adults with their own set of expectations. Here is where one publicly displays the self in academic exercises, gang showers, and the fine line between pleasing teachers and pleasing peers. Research on the relationship between self-perceptions and school-related variables indicates that the former correlate with academic achievement, participation in group activities, behavior, acceptance, and school completion.

Transescents who feel good about themselves also seem to have more success in each of those areas. Furthermore, in school-related feedback in each area, transescents learn about academics.

This is the hidden curriculum. For this reason, middle level educators must seriously consider the place and power of self-perceptions in school. The school-related variables that correlate to self-perceptions represent much of the essence of life and purpose in the school.

Beyond that, the middle level school has a responsibility to help transescents be as good as possible at being transescents. Given the central place of self-perceptions in the transescent personality, the school must do whatever it can to enhance those self-perceptions so that growth and development through this stage is as positive and constructive as possible.

## PLANS AND PROGRAMS

In the current mood of academic efficiency the kinds of curriculum plans and programs that are necessary to enhance self-perception are often criticized. This may be partially due to the fact that misguided advocates of the affective curriculum portray self-enhancement as simply being "nice" to learners. But the criticism also arises from a misunderstanding of the importance of self-perceptions and the hard work that is involved in formulating self-views that are clear, positive, and based upon worthwhile values.

To begin with, if self-perceptions are to be enhanced in the middle grades, they must serve as a central feature of curriculum plans. Unit topics or themes must be drawn from those aspects of the transescent's environment that may influence the self. As shown in the figure there is a wide variety of sources for organizing centers. These include influential others, growth and development, social problems, and personal interest areas. In any of these cases, as well as others like them, transescents have opportunities to directly explore issues in ways that may lead to understanding of self in relation to the environment.

For example, a careful study of television can reveal how that medium attempts to influence values, consumer habits, views of others, and self-satisfaction. Studying the peer group can help transescents to clarify their beliefs about age-mates and how the latter contribute to self-perceptions.

With all of these organizing centers, ample opportunities are available to integrate cognitive

## Sources of Organizing Centers

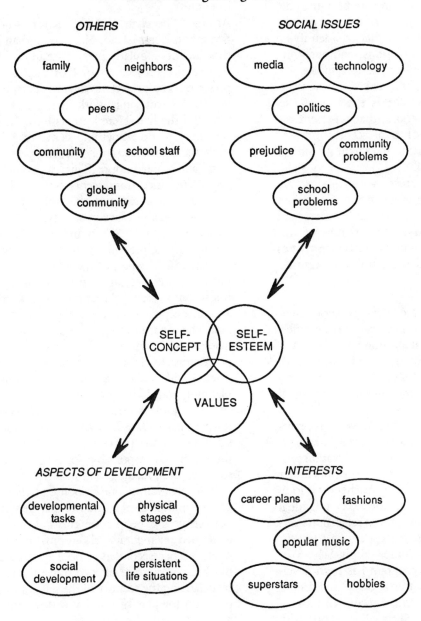

From James A. Beane and Richard P. Lipka, *Self-Concept, Self-Esteem and the Curriculum,* Boston: Allyn and Bacon, 1984.

and psychomotor objectives as well as functional use of learning skills. Reading about human development, tabulating results of a survey on television viewing, writing in diaries, identifying historical bases of superstitions, and analyzing media commercials are but a few examples.

The idea that affective curriculum plans exclude cognitive knowledge is sheer nonsense. More likely, affective topics that represent the compelling interests of transescents offer the best chance for enhancing the cognitive side of the curriculum as well.

Activities that deal directly with self-views are the key element in self-enhancing curriculum plans and programs. Individual teachers and teams have developed many activities of this type. The following examples illustrate activities that have been found successful with transescents.

1. Many transescents are unhappy about their physical appearance; they wish it were different. When this dissatisfaction with the physical self involves traits that can be controlled, many middle level schools have instituted activities which allow transescents to do something about their appearance.

   In some cases this involves programs aimed at weight loss, such as aerobic exercise classes. In other cases, physical education programs focus on fitness and nutrition rather than sports. In a few cases, teachers and local pediatricians work together on individual cases. Others have introduced relaxation exercises to help transescents cope with stress.

2. At the Greenacres Junior High School in Spokane, Wash., a program has been developed that involves transescents in learning about self-concept and esteem. Groups of learners are introduced to self-perceptions in terms of what they are, how they are influenced, and so on. This kind of activity should be part of overall learning about the self so that misperceptions such as the "personal fa-

ble" and the "imaginary audience" can be put in context.

3. At the Shoreham-Wading River Middle School on Long Island, N.Y., more than half the students regularly participate in community service projects as part of their school program. The projects involve visits to nursing homes, tutoring, work in day-care centers, and the like. Here learners have the opportunity to do something concrete, which helps them to feel a sense of worth, participation, and contribution. This is particularly important since transescents often feel that they are unwanted and that they have no really responsible place in society.

4. At the Noe Middle School in Louisville, Ky., learners participate in town meetings within their teams as part of the school's governing structure. We know from research that transescents often feel that they are powerless and incompetent in controlling their own fate. The town meetings, where decisions are made about conflicts and rules, provide opportunities to develop a sense of place and power in the school as well as the skills of planning and decision making.

5. In the middle schools in Olympia, Wash., learners participate in a daily, single-teacher block-time (two period) program in which the teacher is responsible for language arts, social studies, reading, and health.

   This program is one response to the concern of middle level educators that these vulnerable young people are thrust from self-contained elementary classrooms into the multi-teacher secondary school format. The block-time program offers a transition mode by balancing the security of the self-contained program for part of the day with the multi-teacher format of the rest.

6. At the McFarland (Wis.) Junior High School, a learning disabilities teacher carries out a unit yearly in which each student is responsible for teaching others about a personal

hobby or interest. Many transescents, particularly those who experience prolonged failure, come to believe that they are unskilled and that others find nothing worthwhile about them. A program in which each teaches others provides opportunities to demonstrate personal skill or talent. Each student has some unique skill and should be given an opportunity to earn status in the group by sharing it.

7. Middle level students in Blacksburg, Va., participated in a play about what it is like to be a transescent. The play became the NASSP-sponsored film "Coming of Age." This drama and others like it are particularly effective devices for studying personal and social development at this age. The in's and out's of status among peers, dawning sexuality, the "imaginary audience," and other topics may defy personal discussion or disclosure. Drama offers a safe avenue for examining those topics.

8. At the Galvin Middle School in Canton, Mass., a sixth grade teacher has developed two units that offer opportunities for self-enhancement. In one, "Colonial Living," students actually build a log cabin while in the other, "African Life," students build huts representative of several different tribes. These activities contribute to two critical aspects of self-esteem.

The first involves the feeling of satisfaction that may arise from producing something which can be viewed with pride. The second involves the chance to work cooperatively with peers.

These eight program activities illustrate the kind of action involved in the self-enhancing middle level school. Other examples include adviser-advisee programs, parent education meetings, interest-centered activity programs, and so on. These activities involve commitment to self-perceptions as an important issue, peer cooperation, concrete activity, and action in addition to talk. Other features of the self-enhancing school include avoiding stereotyping of transescent learners, developing cooperative reward structures, peer tutoring, and self-evaluation as part of the reporting process.

None of us questions the fact that we are becoming an information or knowledge society. However, we are also a society of people, and self-concept and esteem are central features in the human personality. This is particularly important for middle level schools. Transescents are not only involved in the search for self, but must do so in the context of enormous personal changes and increasingly complex social pressures. Furthermore, for many transescents, the school is a last resort for help in dealing with personal and social issues.

The self-enhancing programs described in this article are the result of hard work. But, as rough as the going may be, middle level educators cannot afford to abandon the affective dimension. Programs directed toward enhancing self-concept and esteem emerge and survive because of principals and teachers who care about transescents.

We need such middle level educators today more than ever before. We need to keep the appeal of technology and academics in perspective (at bay, if necessary) and renew our commitment to personal and social development of transescents.

## REFERENCES

Beane, James A., and Lipka, Richard P. "Enhancing Self-Concept/Esteem in the Middle School." *Middle School Journal,* August 1979.
———. "The Peer Group and the Transescent Self in the School." *Transescence,* 1982.
———; ———; and Ludwig, Joan W. "Synthesis of Research on Self-Concept." *Educational Leadership,* October 1980.
Eisenman, Thomas. "Olympia School District: School in the Middle." *Dissemination Services on the Middle Grades,* May 1981.

Elkind, David. "Egocentrism in Adolescence." *Child Development,* December 1967.

Guerriero, Carl, and Coldiron, Robert. "Assessment of Affective Education: The Pennsylvania Approach." *Impact on Instructional Improvement,* July 1975.

Hyman, Irwin J. *Corporal Punishment in American Schools.* Philadelphia, Pa.: Temple University Press, 1979.

Ludwig, Joan W., and Beane, James A. "When Transescents Talk About Themselves in School." *Dissemination Services on the Middle Grades,* May 1982.

Purkey, Stewart C., and Smith, Marshall S. "Too Soon To Cheer? Synthesis of Research on Effective Schools." *Educational Leadership,* December 1982.

Stromberg, Robert. "Social Studies Simulations in the Middle School Classroom." *Dissemination Services on the Middle Grades,* April 1981.

*James A. Beane* is Professor, School of Education, St. Bonaventure University, St. Bonaventure, New York.

# The Teacher as Counselor: Some Practical Considerations

## JUDITH A. BROUGH

Guidance has been widely recognized as a function of middle level education. But what is the role of the classroom teacher in this guidance function? It is certainly not to replace or even substitute for the trained guidance counselor. Instead, it is to assist transescents in their daily decision-making and in their relationships.

This function may be approached through a formal advisor-advisee program or even, to some extent, through values clarification type activities. But, there remains a general guidance-counseling perspective in classroom teaching which calls for some practical counseling skills. In addition, the effective teacher-counselor must possess knowledge about their needs and characteristics and have a genuine liking for transescents. With this attitude and knowledge of transescents in hand, the following considerations and activities may be developed and used by the effective teacher-counselor.

**Get to know each child as an individual.** Middle school teachers all talk with students as individuals; greet them at the door; show genuine concern; and become familiar with their various countenances. But we need to take it a few steps further. Get involved in informal groups of students; become a club advisor or chaperone. Home visitations can also be extremely enlightening, if you can somehow find the time. If you do not actually want to sit down in the home with parents and child, at least drive or walk by each of their homes. Literally go to see "where they're coming from."

Frequent contacts with parents are invaluable. Call them with good news, not just the bad. Send home a memo about something special which the child has done or accomplished. This dissemination of good news helps to establish trust and a sense of fairness in the child—something of which middle school youngsters are acutely aware.

Observe the students and perhaps jot down some of your observations. Try to note who is not participating in class discussions; is that nor-

From *Middle School Journal* 16, No. 4 (August 1985): 4, 8–9. Used by permission of the author and the publisher.

mal behavior for him/her? Who is monopolizing the conversation(s)? Who is sad? Who is moping? Who seems scared? Who needs some advice in cleanliness habits? Who just needs someone to care?

And finally, ask the kids. Ask them to put in writing anonymously what is troubling them, or what you should know about kids their age. The necessary role of the teacher as counselor becomes apparent when one considers a response I received on such an anonymous questionnaire: "Help us, because we want to grow up more faster than we should."

**Develop a secure and comfortable classroom atmosphere.** Be certain that your students feel free to ask questions. Conrad Toepfer, that stalwart advocate of transcents, has frequently said, "the only dumb question is the question that isn't asked."

**Try a little self-disclosure.** Let the students know that your life has not always been a bed of roses, and that you somehow managed to get through it. Emphasize that people can learn to deal with all sorts of problems. Try to come across as a real person. Let them come to know you as an individual with outside interests and a family.

**Never downplay a student's problem or concern.** Refrain from saying, "Don't worry, it'll get better." The student's problem may seem trivial to you, but it is monumental to them. Remember that they are in the throes of developing a sense of identity—trying to determine who they are and what is important to them. They are cognitively unable to intellectualize emotional situations, but adults commonly expect them to do so. Try to envision crises which you encountered at that age: your diary falling into your brother's hands; not having a boyfriend/girlfriend when *everyone* else did (I made one up); pimples; the inability to do a cartwheel which excluded you from any cheerleading exploits; and the frayed carpet in your living room which precluded anyone from visiting your

house in the daylight. You are talking basic traumas here!

**Organize some units of learning with your students.** These are not to be confused with units of instruction which center on the teacher doing the instruction. Rather, these are units which emphasize the students doing—exploring wants and needs and learning the difference between the two. My co-teacher, students, and I developed one on respect for self, others, animals and the environment. The results were more than gratifying.

**With caution, try some large group "What's Bugging Me" Sessions.** If it bugs one of the kids to be pushed in line, the students can discuss alternative ways of dealing with such a situation (besides pushing back). This is not intended to be a group counseling session to address deep-seated emotional problems; it is meant to help kids learn to deal with various daily situations. Blount and Klausmeier (1968) listed the following emotional needs of emerging adolescents which could be used as guidelines for sessions:

1. Understanding socially approved methods for relieving emotional tensions and substituting those for childish or otherwise disapproved methods.
2. Analyzing emotional situations objectively.
3. Obtaining a broader understanding of situations in which disruptive emotions are produced.
4. Acquiring many social skills to meet new situations.
5. Eliminating fears and emotionalized patterns of response that are already firmly established.

**Plan learning experiences appropriate to transcent developmental stages.** Community service projects work wonders. Students could tutor younger children, meet with and get to know senior citizens, organize food drives for the needy. There seems to be no substitute for community service as a means of building a sense of worth and accomplishment.

**Let the children solve their own problems; do not attempt to solve problems for them.** Most often a shoulder to cry on or a listening post is all that is necessary. Isn't it easier to solve a problem once you have stated it out loud? The voicing of the problem seems to help put it into proper perspective. A few good questions asked at the right time might also be of value. "Why do you think so?" "What else could you have done?" But avoid didactic responses such as, "Why don't you try. . . ." Remember that your objective is to assist the children in solving their own problems.

The following guidelines are recommended:

1. Let the student release his/her emotions and try to tap into real feelings.
2. Encourage that the whole story be told.
3. Ask clarifying questions; try to get the student to identify specific instances and feelings.
4. Remember that silence is fine. It isn't necessary that someone is always talking. Silence gives time for choice making.
5. Look at alternatives to the problem's solution. Reframe it; look at the problem from a different perspective.
6. Remember that people are resilient.

**Refrain from promising confidences which you may not be able to keep.** Be wary if a student starts with "If I tell you something, do you promise not to tell my parents?" You cannot make such a promise, and should tell that to the student. Add that although you will do all in your power to help them with their problem, parental or administrative involvement may be necessary avenues to solution.

**Make and continually update a resource file.** Know to whom or what to refer your students when it seems appropriate. Is there a book or pamphlet which may help them better than

you are able? Is there another teacher about whom a child has expressed confidence?

**Recognize serious problems as such and do not hesitate to seek assistance from counselors, psychologists, parents and administrators.** You are not trained to deal with deep-seated emotional problems; admit that and relinquish them to more qualified others in the particular realm. What you *can* do is help the student to become more willing to see a counselor. Ligon and McDaniel (1970, p. 78) commented:

> It takes counseling skill on the part of the teacher to help some students becoming willing to see a school counselor and be receptive to such counseling. Future counseling or therapy will be most effective if the teacher is able to prepare the student for help from the school counselor or other specialist. Merely asking the counselor to call in a student is asking him to counsel an unwilling student. Doing so without first asking the permission of the student is also breaking confidence with the student.

**Note problems which seem to crop up often and alternative means of getting them out in the open.** The most frequently encountered problems seem to fall into three categories:

1. a death in the family. The student develops a sense of vulnerability and loss. Then, to top it off, the other students do not know what to say to a grieving peer and consequently ignore him/her. Discussing suggestions on how to treat and talk to a grieving friend would help immensely—especially before any such tragic event occurs.
2. problems with parents. These may include separation, divorce, and subsequent parental dating and remarriage. Many transescents feel unaccepted (the myth that "It isn't happening to anyone else"), abused, and/or overprotected. One of my students felt that her parents didn't trust her and weren't very proud of her. Her brothers had been very successful

students and she felt that she wasn't up to par. All she needed was a little bit of my time and attention—reassurance and encouragement from an adult. Other students feel too pressured; their parents are overdemanding, or at least they appear that way to the transescent.
3. problems with peers. This one, of course, is a constant. It includes unpopularity, overpopularity. Who do you choose to sit next to at lunch when everyone wants to sit next to you and someone is bound to get mad? Then there is the age-old problem of being "different"—too smart, too dumb, too underdeveloped, too overdeveloped, just "too. . . ."

**Recognize that as a teacher-counselor your job is not to cure mental illness, but in some small way to help prevent it.** To help children to know themselves is of paramount concern. The following activities may help:

1. "Daily emotional release"—at the end of each day each student fills out a card answering the question, "How do you feel today and why?" The student has the option of then ripping it up.
2. Every day students name at least one thing which they did well and/or something nice which happened to them.
3. Make a list of courtesies each student did for someone else. Build the number slowly. One discourtesy necessitates doing two courtesies.
4. Brainstorm on items which make them feel well mentally and physically.

## WHAT THE COUNSELING ROLE REQUIRES

The teacher who assumes the role of counselor inevitably gives unstintingly of time. Planning periods, lunch periods and alone time before and after school may fall by the wayside. Children cannot talk to you in confidence during class, so it is hard not to devote extra time to pressing situations.

You must be willing to work *with* your students in discovering problems, solutions, and alternatives. The teacher will not know all the problems, and certainly cannot know all of the answers. The counseling aspect, then, logically becomes a joint effort.

Learn to accept failure, as difficult as that may be. You cannot help all of the students all of the time. Some must be referred to others, some must be placed in different situations, and some, as harsh as it may sound, will just plod on as before. The students must recognize that they have a problem and seek help. You cannot hope to convince them that they need assistance. They might be perfectly content as they are.

Beane and Lipka (1984) differentiated between self-concept and self-esteem, which distinction has importance for the guidance oriented teacher. They defined self-concept as "the description of self in terms of roles and attitudes." Self-esteem, however, "refers to the evaluation one makes of the self-concept description and, more specifically, to the degree to which one is satisfied or dissatisfied with it, in whole or in part." (pp. 5–6). They illustrated:

Self-esteem judgments are based on values or value indicators such as attitudes, beliefs, or interests. For example, an adolescent might describe himself as a good student (self-concept), but may wish to change that (self-esteem) because he wants to be accepted by peers who devalue school success (value indicator). . . . a teacher working with the adolescent just described may have difficulty understanding why the student may begin to show a decline in school achievement. The teacher, not knowing the value-base of the student, may further complicate the situation by praising the student's work in front of the peers who devalue school success, in an attempt to bolster self-esteem. The point of understanding the place of values in self-perception is that an individual may not have the same self-esteem judgments others would have under similar circumstances. (p. 6).

And finally, the teacher must be willing, sometimes, to subordinate subject matter to more pressing "guidance" concerns. Some subject matter may relate to transescent concerns, and therefore be "legitimately" covered. However, the middle level teacher must always keep in mind the social and emotional as well as academic objectives of the school. The students will not learn the academics if they are feeling insecure, so the counseling activities must take precedence when deemed a priority by the professional, the teacher-counselor. Both you and your students are able to distinguish among the teacher's various roles and responsibilities. Ligon and McDaniel (1970, p. 81) stated, "Teachers can learn to be counselors but they often have to make some changes. They can learn to shift from one role to another, from the one who must keep order in the classroom to the one who listens and understands. Students understand this dual role. One student approached a teacher who was supervising in the lunchroom. He started to ask her something, and then said, 'You have to be strict now, don't you? I'll see you after school.' "

## CONCLUSION

The activities and suggestions given can be adapted to almost any teacher-counselor situation. Their use will depend upon the characteristics and teaching methods of individual teachers. What is of paramount importance is not the particular activities used, but the spirit in which they are offered. A poem written by a student and quoted by Moss (1969, p. 189) has a message which should be heeded.

### And Gladly Lerne

I trudge through endless halls
and sit in musty cubicles
(only they're labs, most of them)
and gaze through someones
(only they're no ones, most of them)
who look over my head to watch the clock
and scribble important nothings on blackboards
(only they're greenboards, most of them).
and sometimes
i meet a teacher

## REFERENCES

Beane, J. and Lipka, R. *Self-Concept, Self-Esteem and the Curriculum.* Boston: Allyn and Bacon, Inc., 1984.

Blount, N. and Klausmeier, H. *Teaching in the Secondary School.* 3rd ed. New York: Harper & Row, 1968.

Ligon, M. and McDaniel, S. *The Teacher's Role in Counseling.* Englewood Cliffs, NJ: Prentice-Hall, Inc., 1970.

Moss, T. *Middle School.* Boston: Houghton Mifflin Co., 1969.

*Judith A. Brough* is Assistant Professor of Education, Shippensburg State University, Shippensburg, Pennsylvania.

# Developing Coeducational Vocational Education Courses

## CHARLOTTE J. FARRIS AND J. MICHAEL ADAMS

For years educators have designed junior high school industrial arts and home economics courses to encourage career exploration; to develop confidence; to teach basic life skills; and to make young people better consumers, homemakers, and citizens. The home economics courses were for girls; the industrial arts courses, for boys. With rare exceptions, school systems sanctioned—and counselors, teachers, parents, and students encouraged—such sex segregation.

Even today, when educators focus attention on inequitable treatment of the sexes in public schools, they often neglect to consider industrial arts and home economics courses. For example, efforts to establish both male and female varsity athletic teams (which affect a relatively small percentage of a school's population) make headlines, yet efforts to establish coeducational home economics and industrial arts courses (which have the potential to affect every student) draw hardly a footnote.

Many educators, however, are coming to recognize that industrial arts and home economics have much more to offer than sewing and cooking and sawing and hammering. These subjects have the potential to provide the fundamental step in the development of a sense of agency and to lay the foundation for sex equity.

A *sense of agency,* a phrase coined by Frank Fields and David Tiedeman, describes an individual's need for a feeling of control over his or her own life. In *Career Education: New Approaches to Human Development,* Larry Bailey and Ronald Stadt identify a sense of agency as a fundamental building block in an individual's career development. They suggest that one's recognition of responsibility for actions is "prerequisite to later acceptance of responsibilities for career planning." Without a sense of agency, individuals are limited, perhaps without even knowing it, in their understanding of and expectations for their lives.

Junior high school is an especially critical time for a student's development of a sense of agency. It is a period when preadolescents begin testing their own abilities and the world's reaction to those abilities. The ways in which they experiment, the types of tests they are allowed to make, and society's responses to their efforts form patterns that last a lifetime.

Home economics and industrial arts can help students form a sense of agency because these courses provide students with opportunities to work with the materials, equipment, concepts, and processes of our physical world. They enable students to modify, to create, and to develop a feeling of accomplishment.

Equipment and tools, for example, are means of amplifying human abilities. Mixing a batter, sewing a button, pounding a nail, drilling a hole, cooking an egg, cutting a board all involve manipulation of materials that would be impossible without tools or equipment.

As skills increase with practice in use of tools, so does the sense of individual control. Rapidly, the sense of control spills over into other areas of life. Students begin to recognize control of personal space, personal appearance, home life, and family relations. A sense of agency emerges.

From *Today's Education,* Journal of the National Educational Association 70, no. 2 (April–May 1981) (Vocational—Career Education Edition): 40–42. Used by permission of the authors and the publisher.

It is impossible to develop an increased sense of agency for both sexes without awareness of the limits imposed by sex stereotyping and sex bias. Four facts contribute to the importance of coeducational home economics and industrial arts courses for developing sex equity:

- *Home economics and industrial arts are high-interest areas.* Students look forward to coursework where they have hands-on experiences and have the opportunity to create. Students in these areas are typically enthusiastic and open to new experiences. These classes, too, stress cooperation rather than competition. When all students are enrolled in such high-interest courses, they generally do not become involved in social, economic, or sexual hierarchy.
- *Female students have limited backgrounds in industrial arts; male students have limited backgrounds in home economics.* Girls commonly arrive in junior high school with some awareness of and, sometimes, skills in home economics. Boys frequently walk into the industrial arts shop with perceived skills in woodworking. Males and females need to have knowledge in both areas so they will not have restricted views.
- *Boys and girls need to see each other as competent.* Cooperating in carrying out activities is a major step in eliminating sex-stereotyped role expectations. Home economics and industrial arts if taught together can provide a medium for substantive attitude and behavior changes.
- *At the junior high school level, coeducational home economics and industrial arts courses offer a major opportunity to change sex-role stereotyping.* The Training Institute for Sex Desegregation of Public Schools says of junior high schools: "This is a time when attitudes begin to take concrete form, when the teacher can help to shape positive attitudes toward acceptance of a variety of roles for both girls and boys." The

junior high years—when students' ideas are still malleable—offer a major opportunity for schools to intervene. In senior high, peer pressures reach their peak and are almost impossible to combat.

Educators should recognize that coed assignment of students to classes in these two content areas does not, in itself, eliminate sex-role stereotyping. Educators must plan and carry out changes in the curriculum and class activities and projects and work to improve the classroom climate. School districts nationwide are starting to recognize the potential contributions of home economics and industrial arts and therefore to require both classes for both sexes.

Since 1967, the H. B. Thompson Junior High School in Syosset, New York, has had a successful coed home economics and industrial arts program. This "Discovery" program has wide student and community support. Its success is based on cooperative and purposeful team planning by the subject area teachers.

A review of the Syosset program shows five steps that appear common to most successful planning efforts:

- *Awareness.* Teachers first recognize the worth of both industrial arts and home economics for all students.
- *Team Study.* Teacher teams work together to identify common educational goals, program commonalities, and overlapping activities and topics.
- *Support.* After the team builds a sound philosophical base, they make an effort to gain administrative and community support. School boards and parent organizations are target groups.
- *Curriculum design.* With full administrative support, teacher teams review the existing curriculum and redesign it to encourage cooperation between the two subject areas. The

teams select projects that relate to both subjects and reinforce educational goals.

- *Delivery schedule.* In union with the administration, the teacher teams work to design a way to present the courses within the constraints of existing facilities, the calendar year, and other scheduling constraints.

At Babylon Junior and Senior High School in Babylon, New York, the home economics and industrial arts teachers developed a vocational education exploration curriculum for all seventh- and eighth-grade students. The guidance counselor identified the team effort—teachers working together—as the critical element in making the program a success.

At Evans-Brant Central School District's Middle School in Angola, New York, Ed Dempsey, the industrial arts teacher, reported that "girls have expressed a desire to enter industrial arts courses throughout the nineteen years I have been employed at the Middle School," but "pressures from peers and parents often sway their decisions. A problem also arises when only one girl is scheduled for an industrial arts class. The boys tend to help the girl too much. Learning is not as great for either sex with one female in the class."

Over the years at Evans-Brant, teachers and administrators have tried several approaches: single-sex classes for boys and girls, coed groups, and classes with just one or two females. This year, students can select either home economics or industrial arts as their practical arts requirement.

As a result of Dempsey's assertive effort, in cooperation with a supportive home economics staff, next year all students will have industrial arts and home economics as a required course. The administration is scheduling the classes to ensure that the sexes are distributed equally among them.

Perhaps the most important element in the success of coeducational vocational courses is the way students feel about them. The following are comments from students who are enrolled in industrial arts and home economics courses at Newark Junior High School in Newark, New Jersey:

> If you are a boy and don't know how to cook, you'll probably end up eating at a fast-food restaurant. Learning to cook is almost as important as talking or walking.
>
> I like shop a lot. It's the best class in the school. When you get to make stuff by yourself, you feel proud. I think it is a fun and educational class.
>
> I think girls should take shop because it gives everybody a chance to find out what they can do.
>
> Both boys and girls should take home economics so when they grow up they will know how to cook and take care of themselves and others.

*Charlotte J. Farris* is Director, Project Move, State University of New York College of Technology, Utica.

*J. Michael Adams* is Associate Professor, Department of Industrial Arts and Technology, State University of New York, Oswego.

# A Computer Literate Middle School

## CHARLES TERRY

"The bugs are finally gone and it runs really great!" interrupted the thrilled seventh grader, oblivious to the fact that she has just interrupted a math lesson. She moves further into the classroom and asks, "Would you like to come and see it now?" Instantly, twenty-five young faces light up with the anticipation that they might be on the verge of getting a special treat. "We'll continue working on these percentages tomorrow, let's go upstairs to the computer center to see Erika and Serena's program", the teacher announced to a delighted class.

Erika and Serena, both seventh graders, had been working on this program for two weeks. They worked incredibly hard with minimal supervision and assistance. Both are average students that take great pride in their work and accomplishments.

The entire class settled around the demonstration monitor in the front of the computer center. Erika sat at the keyboard and began to run the program while Serena stood beside the monitor to explain details of their product. The program began with a colorful graphics display that explained how the program could be used to keep a daily record of the morning temperature reading taken from the thermometer outside the window. Serena pointed out that they designed the program to be very "User Friendly". Directions appeared on the monitor and remained there until the user pressed a key to signal that he was ready to continue. Next the user was asked to choose from among several options which would permit entering today's temperature reading, converting it to its celsius equivalent, obtain the high low readings of the current month, or report the average of the daily temperature readings.

As students experimented with the program, the girls explained various techniques and the B.A.S.I.C. commands that they employed in program statements. The teacher beamed as Serena explained to several students the intricacies of "Nested For—Next Loops" while Erika showed other students a difficulty she encountered utilizing a counter within one of her "Subroutines." A dozen or so students could be seen taking notes on things they wished to use in their own programs. When the time came to go to the next class, many students left reluctantly while several approached the teacher about staying after school that day.

The scene described might seem idealistic and far removed from the realities of an actual middle school classroom. However, scenes such as these occur with increasing frequency at the Henry H. Wells Middle School.

### THE EVOLUTION OF THE PROGRAM

Two years ago the administration and seven members of the teaching staff decided to develop a program that would make every one of its six hundred students computer literate. They accepted the premise that functioning effectively in the future will require a new basic skill— knowledge of the computer. The group was advised that the amount of funding that could be expected would be very modest. Today, the program at Wells is working. And it could happen at your school.

From *Middle School Journal* 14, No. 3 (May 1983): 25–27. Used by permission of the author and the publisher.

Initially, the task seemed to be very ambitious and somewhat overwhelming. We began by getting everyone together who might be interested in working on such a program. The aim was to brainstorm. A series of steps or stages evolved as follows.

## 1. Arrange Visitations

Visits to school in our area that were using microcomputers in their instructional program were arranged. These visits were very helpful as teachers and administrators shared their concerns, provided a wealth of information, and gave useful suggestions on pitfalls to avoid.

## 2. Evaluate the Marketplace

Next the market place was surveyed to determine which microcomputers would be most suitable for our needs as well as what special purchase arrangements and discounts were available.

## 3. Get the GO AHEAD

Finally, a meeting was arranged with the Superintendent to find out how much money and what type of administrative support there would be for instituting a computer program. The superintendent was delighted with the prospects of having such a contemporary program in the middle school. He promised to go to bat at the monthly school board meeting for approval of our final proposal.

## 4. Equipment and Facility DECISIONS

Decision time had arrived. After much discussion of the pros and cons of the various equipment available, it was decided to purchase six computers (this year two more were added) with disk drives, one 25 inch color monitor, four 19 inch color monitors, one 12 inch green screen monitor and two printers.

The 25 inch color monitor was mounted on a high stand in the front of the computer center. This station can be utilized by teacher and students when demonstrating a program to the entire class. The remaining computers and monitors were located around the perimeter of a large classroom that became the computer center. Six long tables and thirty chairs and casters were placed in the room. This would enable students to work on writing up their program at the work tables and then roll their chairs easily to the computer station when they're ready to type in or run their program.

Color monitors enable students to enjoy creating beautiful color graphics, but green screen monitors could be substituted at substantial savings.

Students learn and develop excellent "Coordinate Graphing Skills" as well as having an opportunity to display their creativity. Even students without much natural artistic ability are able to create stunning graphics displays that give the student a sense of pride. In addition, middle school students seem adept at giving the minute attention to detail required by many graphics creations.

The **disk drive** is an important component of each computer station. Unlike the slow, but less expensive cassette recorder, the disk operating system allows for fast and efficient storage of data on $5\frac{1}{4}$ inch diskettes. This allows students the luxury of not having to complete typing in their program during one sitting. Considering the fact that this equipment is servicing over six hundred students, the flexibility that the disk system provides is really a necessity. Many students carry their own diskette with them, much as they would carry a notebook. The disk system also allows the teacher to review student programs, since making a diskette copy of their work takes a mere few seconds.

Our computer center contains two versatile, reliable, and economical printers. The availability of a printer in the center is important. One on each side of the room is sufficient since students can easily bring their diskette to the appropriate computer station. The printout gives both student and teacher the opportunity to evaluate the work and spot errors or omissions more easily than when viewing the program on the monitor. In addition, their "hard copy" allows the work to be reviewed even away from the center or when others are using the computers. It also enables students to show family and friends what they've done.

## 5. Designing the Curriculum

Equipment is an important part of any program, but it's what you do with it that really matters. The bulk of our planning and thought went into designing the curriculum necessary to implement our goal of a computer literate middle school. Every student would receive a minimum of fifteen forty-five minute lessons in using the computer. These lessons would come during the math period. Most of them would take place in the computer center so that each student would have the opportunity for hands-on practice at the keyboard.

Teaching computer programming in BASIC to middle schoolers may be a worthwhile endeavor in and of itself. However, we felt it was crucial for our students to have an immediate and practical use for these newly acquired skills. To do otherwise might lead to the equipment being relegated to the status of an expensive toy in the minds of our students. Many of us remembered the advent of another technological wonder, the teaching or reading machine. How many schools across the country have these devices collecting dust? Funds are tough enough to

come by without squandering them on expensive technology that is doomed to limited use due to faulty curriculum design. We reasoned that if computers are to meet the challenge of educating children they must elevate thinking skills.

Therefore, it was decided to incorporate an ongoing computer programming component into the 6th, 7th and 8th grade mathematics curriculum. As students are given their regular math instruction they would be given the necessary computer instruction so they could develop computer solutions to math problems. In effect, they utilize the computer as a "tool" to enhance and extend their understanding of mathematics. As the student progresses through the curriculum more sophisticated computer programming techniques are given to enable the student to tackle more complicated problems. Using the computer in this way enables the student to focus on understanding the methods and algorithms of the solution instead of becoming bogged down with complicated calculations. Besides getting extra practice on a math concept presented in class, the student also learns how to generalize on the mathematical solution to a problem when preparing it for a computer solution.

Recognizing that students' mastery occurs at different rates we made allowances in our modification of the mathematics curriculum to provide for individual differences. Activities require the use of various levels of skills and techniques, from simple analysis to complete organization of computer solutions. Students are given the opportunity to:

1. Revise already written programs to produce different outputs.
2. Code programs using a given flowchart.
3. Develop their own algorithms and flowcharts in solving problems.

The modification of the mathematics curriculum was thorough. Charts were developed that coordinated the computer lessons with the regular mathematics curriculum, emphasizing review, reinforcement and enrichment. Nearly ninety detailed lessons were written with instructional objectives to enable teachers with varied computer backgrounds to successfully implement the program.

## PROGRAM IMPACT

Since the program was first implemented in September, 1981, we have observed the tremendous impact it has had on the school environment. Our students have become aware of career opportunities available in the computer field. Each of them has had the opportunity to be a computer operator, programmer and analyst. They all recognize the value of what they are learning and are highly motivated. It seems that mastery of the machine has resulted in a quantum leap in scholastic and emotional achievement.

One of the benefits of not having a "typing room" atmosphere full of computers is that it has fostered team building among the students. Students learn to get along with one another as they work toward a common goal. With a little encouragement, students begin to assist one another in removing "glitches" and "bugs" from each other's programs. As they read and learn about new commands and techniques, they eagerly share them. Many become proficient typists.

As we near the end of our second year of this program we've encouraged our "computer literate" students to begin writing programs that would be useful in other areas of the middle school curriculum. Several classes are learning how to use a word processing program to compose compositions and term papers. Several students are writing and designing software requested by teachers for drill and reinforcement in their subject. For example, Michele is writing a program that helps students identify factors that lead to heart attacks, while Stephen has written a program that quizzes the user on state capitals. The student council treasurer is learning how to use "VISICALC" to keep track of the student activities account, while student office Cadets are busy typing records onto disk files that can be retrieved under several categories. The P.T.A. is sponsoring after school computer classes for students in grades 3–5, as well as a summer computer camp and a Computer Fair. Currently, there is a waiting list to attend the evening adult education computer classes sponsored by the Board of Education. And now our Principal and Librarian want their own computers. Despite all the use this equipment is getting, less than $150 has been spent on equipment repair. That's reliability!

At Wells Middle School we concluded that although facilities and equipment may be limited, given administrative support, faculty cooperation, and a committed team, it is possible to achieve the goal of a computer literate middle school.

*Charles Terry* is Mathematics/Computer Education Administrative Assistant to the Superintendent of Schools, Brewster, New York.

# The Middle School Movement: From Emergent to Exemplary

PAUL S. GEORGE

Phase One (1960–1975) of the comtemporary middle school movement was concerned with the recognition of the uniqueness of the middle school students and with the emergence of general guidelines for school programs based on the characteristic needs of those students. Phase Two (1975–present) of the movement is witnessing the development of greater consensus on the specific components required as a part of the fully functioning, exemplary middle school program.[1] Phase One was dominated by theoretical conceptualization. Phase Two is characterized by an emphasis on effective implementation.

Two criteria seem more important than others in analyzing the essentials of the complete middle school program as it is now being implemented. First, the accumulation of more and more data testifying to the critical significance of early adolescence as a special period of life has led to the acceptance of the need for a middle phase of schooling which is unique; that is, one which is sufficiently different from both the elementary and the high school, a special program for special needs. Second, because of its position in the middle of the public education spectrum, the middle school has an additional obligation. It must be unique, but it must also be transitional, leading in a smooth and continuous way from the elementary school years into the high school experience. It must be different from both, but not so much so that the transitional process is made more difficult. It must weave together the most appropriate elements of elementary and high school so that the educational fabric is of whole cloth.

One way to represent the elements of an exemplary middle school program is contained in Figure 1. In constructing this chart, no attempt is made to imply that the elementary or high school components listed are those that should be; only that, considering both past and present practices, this is what has been and is most frequently found in school programs across the country.[2] Applying the two criteria (the demand for something special in the middle and the requirement that these components comprise a truly transitional program), the essential elements of a fully functioning middle school program are rather easily derived. Fortunately, the logic of this approach has also been confirmed by enlightened practice in various forms of middle level programs (e.g., many junior high schools) throughout the last half century.

## EXEMPLARY MIDDLE SCHOOL PROGRAMS

### The Teacher-Student Relationship

In any school that focuses sharply on the characteristics of the learner one would expect to find the teacher-student relationship high on the list of program priorities, and so it is in exemplary middle schools. The middle school attempts to provide a special variety of this relationship: one which, while qualitatively different from the types of relationship available in the elementary and high schools, does in fact lead from one to

Article written by Paul S. George for *Curriculum Planning: A New Approach,* Fourth Edition 1983. Used by permission of the author.

**FIGURE 1**
**The Exemplary-Middle School: Unique and Transitional**

| Program component | Elementary | Middle | High |
|---|---|---|---|
| Teacher-student relationship | Parental | Advisor | Choice |
| Teacher organization | Self-contained | Interdisciplinary team | Department |
| Curriculum | Skills | Exploration | Depth |
| Schedule | Self-contained | Block | Periods |
| Student grouping | Chronological | Multi-age or developmental | Subject |

the other. The teacher-student relationship in the middle school program is not one of quasi-parental exclusivity so often required by young children, nor is the middle school student given the entire responsibility for choosing adult figures for friendship and guidance from among the faculty. Although there are a number of effective methods for tending to this aspect of the program, exemplary schools do make special efforts to guarantee its success.

In the Advisor-Advisee Program of the four middle schools of the city of Dothan, Alabama, for example, every student has an advisor and every faculty member has a group of advisees. The overall purpose of this program is to develop a sense of community among a group of twenty to twenty-five students and their advisor. Even though a student may interact with over one hundred other students and a half dozen teachers on a daily basis, every day begins with a thirty minute time period when getting to know and care about each other is the major assignment. Social and emotional education, values clarification, moral development, discipline, and guidance are other objectives of this successfully modernized version of the original junior high school homeroom idea.

In all eight middle schools of Marion County, Florida, another type of program has been promoting the development of teacher-student relationships for about ten years. In these schools the schedule is designed so that teachers on the academic teams each have about forty advisees. Each day of the week the advisor sees a different group of about ten of his advisees for a fifty-minute period, while the remainder of the students have physical education. By the end of the week each advisor has had a class hour with each advisee in a quite small group, and each student has also had four days of physical education. Students benefit from a weekly intensive hour with their advisor and a small group of peers, in combination with frequent physical education. Faculty members enjoy this effective opportunity to get to know their students, and the fact that an entire period of every day is limited to interaction with nine or ten students.

The existence of Marion County's "small group guidance" program for over a decade is an important indicator of its significance for teachers, students, and parents alike. In fact, advisor-advisee programs of all kinds and varieties are being implemented more rapidly in the nation's middle schools than almost any other program component, with the exception of the interdisciplinary team organization of teachers.

## Interdisciplinary Team Organization

One of the most common misunderstandings of the middle school concept has been that it required a certain type of team teaching: either master teachers engineered presentations to large groups of pupils, or every teacher on the team had to be in the same room at the same time, or each teacher had to teach from lesson plans drawn up by someone else. None of these situations is mandated by or even very desirable in middle schools.

Interdisciplinary team organization in the middle school refers to the grouping of teachers to facilitate instruction. It differs from both the self-contained classrooms of the primary school years and the departmentalized organization of the high school, but it leads from one to the other. Interdisciplinary organization usually involves a group of from two to five teachers who share: (1) responsibility for planning and, perhaps, teaching from two to five subjects in the academic area of the curriculum; (2) the same group of from 50 to 150 or more students; (3) the same schedule, at least in regard to planning periods, where they exist; and (4) the same part of the school building. Notice that actual shared teaching responsibilities may or may not be a part of the structure.

The self-contained classroom in which one teacher taught the entire curriculum is almost entirely absent in exemplary middle schools. Nor do teachers group themselves in terms of a common subject as in the departmentalized secondary school. There is, however, a considerable array of possibilities which fit the above description of interdisciplinary organization.

Consider the faculty at Spring Hill Middle School. For the past decade the teachers at this school in High Springs, Florida, have been engaged in what they call interdisciplinary team teaching. At S.H.M.S. this means that teachers are organized in groups of four, one teacher as a resource for each of the four standard areas of mathematics, science, social studies, and language arts.

But at Spring Hill every teacher teaches a part of every subject. Not in a self-contained approach where every teacher might cover the same topics, and not in a semi-departmentalized way in which each teacher on the team taught only their specialty. Each group of teachers, following the planning model of Individually Guided Education (I.G.E.), plans each unit together, with teachers choosing which aspects of each unit they want to teach.

In the middle schools of Dothan, Alabama, teachers are organized in groups of three. Teams of three teachers have joint responsibility for the four academic subjects, and each team is free to determine what division of the teaching load they will adopt. The team may decide, for example, that every teacher will teach every subject, much in the manner of Spring Hill Middle School. Or, they may decide that each teacher will teach two subjects, one specialty and one in common. That is, all three teachers might teach math, and then each assumes responsibility for one other subject. There are, of course, several other possibilities.

Most interdisciplinary teams, however, function in approximately the same way as the teams at North Marion Middle School, in Citra, Florida. Here the four-teacher team is the rule, and each teacher is responsible for instruction in only one subject. Teams of this type occasionally combine their strengths and responsibilities to produce truly exciting, thematic interdisciplinary units, in which every subject is represented (e.g., Space, The Westward Movement, The Bicentennial, etc.).

Regardless of the size of the team or the ways in which the division of labor occurs, it is, flatly, impossible to find an exemplary middle school without some form of interdisciplinary organization. It is the keystone of the complete program; without it little else succeeds for long. With a firm commitment to the interdisciplinary grouping of faculty almost everything else is possible.

## The Exploratory Curriculum

Middle schools have sometimes been accused of ignoring the basics, of becoming "muddle" schools where anything goes but little of value is learned. Actually, although it is likely that nothing could be further from the truth, the middle school has attempted to approach the curriculum in a different way from the elementary school or the high school.

Most middle school educators seem convinced that a mindless repetition of the exercises and experiences which teachers used to instill skills in the elementary school child is a fruitless approach with the early adolescent. These same educators are often equally opposed to an earlier and earlier intrusion of the university-cum-high-school curriculum into the middle school years. All of this is not to say, however, that the middle school curriculum ignores skills or avoids difficult content. How does the middle school lead from an emphasis on skills to a focus on depth in subject matter and still do something different with its curriculum?

Middle schools attempt to foster the continued development of skills and to introduce more of the world of knowledge through an emphasis on exploratory experiences in the curriculum. Exploration includes what is often called The Unified Arts (art, music, home arts, industrial arts, etc.), as well as special-interest classes, academic inquiry via mini-courses, and several other avenues.

Typically, The Unified Arts program, by whatever name, carries the major burden of the exploratory program. Most frequently, students spend one period a day in one of six courses offered on a rotating "wheel" every six weeks. Thus a sixth-grade student would be scheduled for six weeks of art, music, home economics, industrial arts, foreign language, and, perhaps, something like "occupational education." It is quite common for this to be modified to allow for longer periods of time (e.g., nine, twelve, or eighteen weeks) and some opportunity for choice for seventh- and eighth-grade students. Having inherited much of this from the junior high schools which preceded them, one might

find this pattern followed in more than half of the middle schools in the country.

Where size and financial support permit, The Unified Arts programs are frequently diversified and expanded. At Griffin Middle School, in Cobb County, Georgia, the exploratory program is divided into two parts, fine arts and unified arts. A complex scheduling process (which, of course, students quickly grasp) allows these options to be combined with physical education so that students go to two of the three every day. At the end of three weeks the student has had ten periods each of unified arts, fine arts, and physical education.

At Tuttle Middle School in Newton County, North Carolina, every teacher is an exploratory teacher. During one of the six time blocks each day, academic team teachers collaborate with Unified Arts specialists to offer a host of exploratory choices for students on the team. A student may actually be able to choose his or her exploratory class from among a dozen options. At Lincoln Middle School, in Gainesville, Florida, where the same basic processes are followed, students have been able to choose one-third of their curriculum fresh and new each six weeks. Teachers get to teach aspects of their specialties or their personal interests which might not otherwise be permitted into the curriculum, and students choose from a wide array of options that interest them and about which teachers are excited. Little wonder that the exploratory times in these schools are often the favorites of both teachers and students.

More often, middle schools have attempted a special-interest program such as the one at Azalea Middle School in St. Petersburg, Florida, where the last period of the day has been used for a schoolwide special-interest exploration time. Special interest, in this case, most often refers to the cultivation of leisure time pursuits. Usually, it replaces or supplements the long term commitments required by the traditional secondary school clubs.

## Student Grouping

Students in elementary schools are most often grouped by chronological age, whereas high schools often group by readiness for subject matter and student choice of program. The middle school, grounded in the knowledge that chronological age is not a reliable indicator of characteristics and needs of early adolescents, and rejecting the subject matter focal point of the high school as inappropriate for its students, seeks other options. Three seem to be gaining increasing acceptance among practitioners in exemplary programs. Since dissimilarity and variability seem more often the case among middle school students, grouping strategies which allow for this phenomenon are more likely to be effective. Such patterns also satisfy the requirements of helping students move from a school based on chronological age grouping to one where subject matter choices are the deciding factor, providing a unique but transitional program.

At Lincoln Middle School, in Gainesville, Florida, multiage (sometimes erroneously referred to as nongraded or ungraded) grouping is a central part of the program. Each of the six teams in the school is composed of approximately fifty sixth-graders, fifty seventh-graders, and fifty eighth-graders, randomly assigned to each team. Each team, is therefore, a microcosm of the school, a school-within-a-school, some might say. The five teachers on each team and the students on the team remain together for three years. Such an arrangement dramatically enhances the opportunities for continuous progress in students, and discipline problems are a fraction of what they might be without the opportunity for the development of really meaningful relationships between teachers and students and among the students themselves.

At Wakulla Middle School, Crawfordville, Florida, the school-within-a-school program is working beautifully. The students are assigned to interdisciplinary level teams, but the building is organized so that three different wings each hold three separate teams, one sixth grade, one seventh, and one eighth. Students stay on the same team for three years, in the same general area of the school, with the same counselor, but each year they have a new group of teachers. This method of grouping offers an excellent combination of continuity and change, of the traditional and the innovative. Hence, its growing popularity.

At Spring Hill Middle School, developmental age grouping, supported so well by theorist-practitioner Donald Eichhorn, works effectively. Spring Hill has grades five through eight, but only three teams. How does a student spend four years in a school where there are only three teams? Team One is composed of the sixty fifth-graders and thirty sixth-graders whose development leads them to be classified as "younger." Team Two is made up of the sixty "older" sixth-graders and sixty younger seventh-graders, and Team Three contains the thirty older seventh-graders and sixty eighth-graders; approximately ninety students in each team. Students who mature early will spend two years in Team Three, those who are late in their development will most often spend their first two years on Team One. Students whose development occurs at more nearly the mean rate will spend two years in Team Two. Because it is a small school (approximately 300), teachers, the counselor, the school principal, and sometimes the parents collaborate on the decisions surrounding student placement.

Just down the road at Mebane Middle School, in Alachua, Florida, the best of both multiage and developmental age grouping are available. Each team in the school has approximately thirty-five fifth, sixth, seventh, and eighth graders, 140 in all. Students and teachers remain together on the same team for four years, allowing continuous progress to occur, and encouraging the development of enrichingly long term teacher-student relationships. Within each team, however, students are grouped according to development into "younger," "average," and "older" students, facilitating instructional planning for teachers.

At Noe Middle School in Louisville, Kentucky, there is a mixture of age-graded teams (i.e., sixth grade, etc.) and multi-age grouping, three age-graded teams and two multi-age teams. Because this arrangement permits some degree of choice for everyone involved, teacher and student morale appears to benefit.

Multi-age grouping is probably the middle school's best kept secret, in the sense of being practiced by a small minority of schools. The schools that have given this program component an adequate trial have, however, unanimously affirmed its significant contributions. The next decade will most likely see a relatively rapid increase in the number of schools adopting multi-age groupings.

## Scheduling

The organization of time in a middle school turns out to be as crucial to the success of the program as any other factor. Neither the self-contained classroom with its individual teacher autonomy or the lock-step periodization necessary in so many high schools is appropriate for the middle school. Teachers working in interdisciplinary groups must have an option beyond one large block of time and the seven period day, yet in order to meet the criterion of being transitional, that option must lead from the elementary school schedule to the high school style.

More and more middle schools, quite possibly a majority at this point, are adopting what is known as the "block" schedule. Teams of teachers share responsibility for time structuring with the principal. With fixed times usually assigned for lunch, physical education, and Unified Arts, each team is more or less free to manipulate the remainder of the day to suit the needs of their plans for instruction.

The block schedule is simple, relatively easy to design, and promotes a greater degree of teacher autonomy, and involvement in professional decision making. It makes continually ringing bells unnecessary. With all these virtues, there is no mystery about its growing popularity. There are, in fact, virtually no exemplary programs without one.

## Synergism

One final comment about the nature of exemplary middle school programs is essential. As might have been predicted by common sense observation, each of these program components is even more successful when accompanied by one or more of the others. The whole actually is greater than the sum of the parts. Interdisciplinary organization of teachers, for example, adds infinite strength to advisor-advisee programs. Multi-age grouping cements the strengths of the interdisciplinary team, and exploratory curricula seem to find their way into schools that are already strong and stable due to the presence of these other factors.

Schools which possess all of these components are, unfortunately, rare. They are, however, immediately recognizable as strong, healthy, productive environments for early adolescents when they are identified. And, there are more of them every year.

## CONCLUSION

The middle school movement is passing from Phase One to Phase Two: from the emergent to the exemplary. Successful middle schools are evolving toward similar programs affirmed by both conceptual logic and effective operation. Should this most fortunate trend continue, confusion about the nature of the middle school should disappear within the next decade.

Phase Three? Yes: When the middle school movement has matured to the point at which differences of emphasis, style, and approach co-exist with the knowledge that effective programs for early adolescents do indeed flow from a common base. Only then will the profession be able to evaluate the wisdom of having separated out a middle phase of education in the first place.

## ENDNOTES

1. In this article *exemplary* is defined as those programs which have: (1) been evaluated positively by parents and educators from their own community; (2) achieved some level of national recognition; and (3) implemented a majority of the "essentials" of the complete middle school program as described in the pertinent literature of the last decade.

2. Space limitations make it impossible to adequately describe the meaning of each of the terms listed as elementary and high school program components. The author apologizes in advance for any misinterpretation caused by such brevity.

*Paul S. George* is Professor of Education, College of Education, University of Florida, Gainesville.


## ADDITIONAL LEARNING ACTIVITIES

### Problems and Projects

1. If you have been developing a "case problem" about a middle school or a junior high, examine practices at the school in the light of the trends and innovations studied in this Section. Should your school incorporate any of these trends in its curriculum and teaching? Your suggestions should be based on: (1) examination of the trend in light of objectives, the curriculum bases, and other criteria, and (2) examination of present practices at the school to determine if the suggested trend would improve what is now done to provide for the learners' needs and social goals.

2. Why is a different program of education needed for transescents and early adolescents? While preparing your answer to this question, refer to the articles "A Healthy Personality for Every Child," "Developmental Tasks," "The Development of Intelligent Behavior: Jean Piaget" (all in Section 3), and "Growth Characteristics of Middle School Children: Curriculum Implications," "Brain Periodization—Challenge, Not Justification," and "Self-Concept and Esteem in the Middle Level School" in this section. Try to list the developmental changes mentioned in several of these articles which you think should influence the planning of curricula and teaching for transescents. Compare your list with those made by others in your group or class.

3. What social and psychological influences led to the development of the junior high school? The middle school? What are some essential components of effective curricula for transescents and early adolescents? Refer to the article by McEwin in this section for a discussion of these questions.

4. Use the bases and criteria of curriculum planning to examine the proposals for the middle school made in the article "Guidelines for the Middle Schools We Need Now," in this section. Which of the four curriculum bases have been used extensively in this proposal? Were any of the four bases not used in planning this proposal? Also examine the proposal in terms of continuity, provision for individual differences, balance, and flexibility. Discuss your ideas about the guidelines with others. Suggest improvements in the guidelines. Have important trends been overlooked in these guidelines?

5. What are the implications, for curriculum planning for and teaching of transcents, of the statement by Brazee that the vast majority of them are pre-formal thinkers? Why does Brazee give the title "Brain Periodization—Challenge, Not Justification" to this article?

6. In Section 7, the article "Early Education Principles and Computer Practices" presented four principles to be used in judging the worth of computer packages and practices for early childhood education. Would the same principles be appropriate for evaluating the computer curricula described in "A Computer Literate Middle School" in this section? Construct your own list of principles for use in evaluating these curriculum and teaching proposals.

7. Which of the physical growth characteristics of transcents listed by Georgiady and Romano in this section do you feel are most significant for curriculum planning at this level? Discuss your choices with other members of your class or group.

8. What influence might coeducational vocational education courses in the middle school or junior high have on sex role stereotyping (see article by Farris and Adams in this section)? What do these authors mean by a "sense of agency"? Besides developing coeducational vocational courses, what other changes might be considered in middle school curricula and instruction to heighten a "sense of agency"?

9. Section 6 presented several curriculum criteria that are particularly appropriate for planners in the 1980s and 1990s. Prepare a statement or discuss with others the ways in which you might use *anticipation* as a criterion for planning for a group of early adolescents. Try to do the same for *values* or *participation* as criteria.

10. Talk with a group of transcents and early adolescents about the social forces of concern to them in the school, in their community, or on the national level. Share your findings with your fellow students.

11. Two reports advocating changes in the junior high school were issued in the early 1960s. One was "The Junior High School Years" by James B. Conant (Los Angeles, California: Educational Testing Service, 1960), and the other was "The Junior High School We Need" (Washington, D.C.: Association for Supervision and Curriculum Development, 1961). Read these two reports and compare their recommendations to those now being made in this section regarding the middle school. In what ways are the recommendations alike? How are they different?

12. Reread Kohlberg's article "The Cognitive-Developmental Approach to Moral Education" in Section 3. Should teachers of early adolescents try to make use of Kohlberg's approach to moral education? You may select additional readings on this subject from the list of resources on moral education in Books and Articles to Review at the end of Section 3. Share the results of your reading and thinking with other members of your class.

13. Some of the pioneering early work in developing curricula that are particularly appropriate for transescents was done by Carleton W. Washburne at the Skokie Junior High School in Winnetka, Illinois. Washburne believed that group and creative activities were essential to the development of children and transescents. He thought that they would motivate them and give meaning to the development of the tool subjects, as well as practical application. Some of these early activities are described in articles by Logan and in Chapter 7 of the book by Washburne and Marland (see Books and Articles to Review at the end of this section). Read one or more of these sources to gain more knowledge of early work in developing curricula for this age group. Would the activities described be appropriate and challenging for learners in middle or junior high schools today? Explain your answer. Which philosophical positions presented in Section 1 do these activities represent?

14. Thirty-nine trends and innovations are listed in the rationale for this section along with the articles describing them. Try to decide which fifteen of these trends are most significant. List your fifteen trends and explain why you selected them in terms of objectives, bases, or criteria that you regard as particularly significant for transescents and early adolescents. Compare your list with the selections made by other members of your class.

15. The Appendix of this book includes a list of books, each describing a junior high school program. Select one that interests you and determine whether the curriculum or teaching might be improved by incorporating one or more of the innovations or trends in early adolescent education discussed in this section. Justify using one or more of these trends in this school in terms of objectives, curriculum bases, and curriculum criteria.

16. Have your personal beliefs or values about programs of education for early adolescents changed as a result of your experience with this section? If so, state what change has taken place and relate it to one or more of the activities in this section (an article, the rationale, a problem or project, etc.). Compare your ideas with those of other members of your class.

## Films, Filmstrips, and Cassettes

*Hopkins West Junior High School, Minnetonka, Minnesota.* 16 mm, color, 30 min., 1981. Presents a rationale for a junior high as a place for learners in transition between childhood and adulthood. Parents are team members, aides, and advisors. The "basics" are emphasized. National Association of Secondary School Principals, 1904 Association Drive, Reston, Virginia 22091.

*Stoughton Middle School, Stoughton, Wisconsin.* 16 mm, color, 22 min., 1981. This former junior high was reorganized as a middle school and was "turned around." Team teaching and mainstreaming are featured. National Association of Secondary School Principals, 1904 Association Drive, Reston, Virginia 22091.

*The Middle School Program in Depth.* A twenty-minute filmstrip-cassette tape, 1980, which explores the central components of the middle school program. Includes an analysis of the interdisciplinary team organization, exploratory programs, student grouping patterns, and instructional strategies. Teacher Education Resources, P.O. Box 206, Gainesville, Florida 32602.

*Theory Into Practice: A Tour of Lincoln Middle School* (in Gainesville, Florida). A thirty-five minute filmstrip-cassette tape, 1980. A tour of a highly praised middle school, including visits to classrooms and with students. Teacher Education Resources, P.O. Box 206, Gainesville, Florida 32602.

*Relationships and Values Series.* Ten filmstrips and five cassettes. Dramatizes a series of open-ended moral dilemmas that point up the daily concerns of junior and senior high school students. Two filmstrips and cassettes on Teaching Relationships and Values are also available. Guidance Associates, 757 Third Avenue, New York, New York 10017.

## Books and Articles to Review

The numbers in parentheses following these books or articles refer to the numbered list of innovations and trends in transescent and early adolescent education listed in the rationale for this section. They will assist you in identifying additional sources regarding those trends and innovations.

Adelson, Joseph. "The Growth of Thought in Adolescence." *Educational Horizons* 61, no. 4 (Summer 1983): 156–162.

Alexander, William M.; and McEwin, C. Kenneth. "Middle Level Schools—Their Status and Their Promise." *NASSP Bulletin* 70, no. 486 (January 1986): 80–85.

Alexander, William M.; and George, Paul S. *The Exemplary Middle School.* New York: Holt, Rinehart and Winston, 1981.

Arnold, John. "Rhetoric and Reform in Middle Schools." *Phi Delta Kappan* 63, no. 7 (March, 1982): 453–456.

Association for Supervision and Curriculum Development. "The Junior High School We Need." Washington, DC: ASCD, 1961.

Clark, Sally N.; and Clark, Donald C. "Continuous Progress: A Curriculum Responsive to the Needs of Early Adolescents." *Contemporary Education* 52, no. 3 (Spring 1981): 142–145.

Compton, Mary F. "The Middle School Curriculum: A New Approach." *NASSP Bulletin* 67, no. 463 (May 1983): 39–44. (18) (19) (36)

Curtis, Thomas E.; and Bidwell, Wilma W. *Curriculum and Instruction for Emerging Adolescents.* Reading, MA: Addison-Wesley Publishing Co., 1977.

Dorman, Gayle; Lipsitz, Joan; and Verner, Pat. "Improving Schools for Young Adolescents." *Educational Leadership* 42, no. 6 (March 1985): 44–49. (6) (11)

Eichhorn, Donald H. "Focus on the Learner Leads to a Clearer Middle Level Picture." *NASSP Bulletin* 67, no. 463 (May 1983): 45–48. (19)

Elkind, David. "Adolescent Thinking and the Curriculum." *New York University Education Quarterly* 12, no. 2 (Winter 1981): 18–24.

Epstein, Herman. "Brain Growth and Cognitive Development." *Educational Leadership* 41, no. 5 (February 1984): 72–75.

George, Paul S.; and Lawrence, Gordon D. *Handbook for Middle School Teaching.* Glenview, Illinois: Scott, Foresman and Co., 1982.

Griggs, Shirley A. "Counseling Middle School Students for Their Individual Learning Styles." Chapter 4, *Student Learning Styles and Brain Behavior.* Reston, VA: National Association of Secondary School Principals, 1982: 19–24.

Hester, Joseph P.; and Hester, Patricia J. "Brain Research and the Middle School Curriculum." *Middle School Journal* 15, no. 1 (November, 1983): 4–7, 30.

Hodges, Helene. "Madison Prep—Alternatives Through Learning Styles." Chapter 6, *Student Learning Styles and Brain Behavior*. Reston, VA: National Association of Secondary School Principals, 1982: 28–32.

Hutson, Barbara A. "Brain Growth Spurts—What's Left by the Middle School Years." *Middle School Journal* 16, no. 2 (February 1985): 8–11.

Johnson, Mauritz, ed. *Toward Adolescence: The Middle School Years*. The 79th Yearbook of the National Society for the Study of Education, Part I. Chicago: University of Chicago Press, 1980.

Kindred, Leslie W.; et. al. *The Middle School Curriculum: A Practitioner's Handbook*. Boston: Allyn and Bacon, 1976.

Lipsitz, Joan Scheff. *Successful Schools for Young Adolescents*. New Brunswick, N.J.: Transaction Book, Inc., 1984.

Logan, S. R. "Adventuring with Little Corporations." *Clearing House* 20, no. 2 (October 1945): 73–81.

———. "More Adventures with Little Corporations." *Clearing House* 21, no. 4 (December 1946): 201–213.

Lounsbury, John H., Ed. *Perspectives: Middle School Education 1964–1984*. Columbus, OH: National Middle School Association, 1984 (22)

Lounsbury, John H.; and Vars, Gordon F. *A Curriculum for the Middle School Years*. New York: Harper and Row, 1978.

Lounsbury, John H.; et al. *The Middle School in Profile*. Fairborn, Ohio: The National Middle School Association, 1980. (22)

McQueen, Richard. "Spurts and Plateaus in Brain Growth: A Critique of the Claims of Herman Epstein." *Educational Leadership* 41, No. 5 (February, 1984): 66–71.

Smith, Ralph M.; and Mauceri, Paul K. "Suicide: The Ultimate Middle School Trauma." *Middle School Journal* 14, no. 1 (November 1982): 21–24.

Strahan, David B. "Brain Growth Spurts and Middle Grades Curriculum: Readiness Remains the Issue." *Middle School Journal* 16, no. 2 (February 1985): 11–13.

———; and Toepfer, Conrad F., Jr. "Transescent Thinking: Renewed Rationale for Exploratory Learning." *Middle School Journal* 15, no. 2 (February 1984): 8–11. (11)

"Surviving Adolescence: Have the Middle Schools Found the Secret?" Theme Issue. *Principal* 60, no. 3 (January 1981): 8–32.

Thornburg, Hershel D. "Early Adolescents: Their Developmental Characteristics." *High School Journal* 63, no. 6 (March 1980): 215–221. (18)

Valentine, Jerry W. "A National Study of Schools in the Middle." *Middle School Journal* 16, no. 4 (August 1985): 12–17. (2) (22)

Withrock, M. C. "Teaching Learners Generative Strategies for Enhancing Reading Comprehension." *Theory Into Practice* 24, no. 2 (Spring 1985): 123–126.

Washburne, Carleton W.; and Marland, Sidney P., Jr. *Winnetka: The History and Significance of an Educational Experiment*. Englewood Cliffs, New Jersey: Prentice-Hall, Inc., 1963.

# 9

# *Education for Middle Adolescents*

## PREREQUISITES

1. Reading and studying Sections 1 through 6.
2. The development of, and ability to utilize, a set of curriculum criteria to describe and evaluate a curriculum plan. You must be able to use this set of criteria in order to analyze critically and make curriculum or teaching decisions regarding programs described in this section.

## RATIONALE

All curriculum planners and teachers should be acquainted with the goals and trends of all educational levels, regardless of the level of the program at which they plan to work. You should know about goals and trends in education for middle adolescents whether or not you plan to work at this level. You will be better able to plan a curriculum or teach at one of the other levels if you have this information. This view is based on such curriculum criteria as continuity in learning, balance in the curriculum, and provision for individual differences.

This section is now called Education for Middle Adolescents rather than The High School. In keeping with the definition of *curriculum* presented in Section 1, the focus will be on programs of education rather than exclusively on school programs. The title is intended to focus attention on a group of learners and their needs rather than on a school program.

In the introduction to Section 8, adolescence in our society was described as the period from approximately age ten to age twenty; transescence and early adolescence were described as spanning approximately ages ten to fifteen. Middle adolescence, then, is the period approximately from ages fifteen to eighteen, the high school years.

Middle adolescents are beginning to seek some assurance of eventual economic independence from parents and other adults. They sense their possession of new intellectual powers and they need to develop cognitive skills. Their dominant motivation most frequently is to achieve social status in the adolescent community, according to their peer world expectations. They often have a dual orientation: engaging in behavior approved by adults versus engaging in behavior approved by peers. Middle adolescents, according to Erikson, seek a "sense of identity" and the development of values to have as their own. According to Bennett Berger, sociologist at the University of California at San Diego, adolescence is one of the ways that culture violates nature by insisting that, for an increasing number of years, young persons postpone their claims to the privileges and responsibilities of common citizenship. It is useful, at this point, to review the theories of Williams, Grant with Briggs, Havighurst, Erikson, Piaget and others by turning to Section 3.

The American High School has been under heavy internal pressure during recent years. It has been plagued by hostility, violence, despair, alienation, and drug abuse. A study in New York stated that these problems, to a substantial extent, result from the high school's *massive size, monolithic structure, and authoritarian lines.* This report stated that students express underlying negativity and tension toward their teachers. Some students find their school experience painful, and many find it unenjoyable. Minority students feel they receive differential treatment. In general, students ask for more openness and mutual respect. Neither students nor teachers see students as influential in school policy. Many students feel they are not learning very much. The high school typically does not use the rich resources of the community. In addition to these internal pressures, the high schools of the nation have been constantly buffeted by many contradictory and conflicting waves of criticism and demands for reform from external sources (see "Tackling the Reform Reports of the 1980s").

To meet the needs of middle adolescents, most American educators advocated the *comprehensive high school* during the 1950s and 1960s. A truly comprehensive high school would provide needed learning opportunities for all the normal adolescents from the slow learner to the gifted and talented. Its purpose would be to enable all learners to develop to the greatest potential for their own success and happiness and to make a maximum contribution to their society. This would necessitate that the school affect positively the behavior of students now, as adolescents and unique human beings, and later, as adult wage earners, citizens, and family members. Such a school must offer a curriculum with *breadth and depth, individualized instruction,* and many *functional learning opportunities.* And it must have teachers who are not overburdened and harassed, who can enjoy working with middle adolescents, and who attempt to see the world from the students' point of view. It is clear that we have a long way to go before most American high school students are participating in programs of education with these characteristics.

The comprehensive high school, even if generally attained, is inadequate for the program of education many middle adolescents need. One significant approach for learners at this level is the development of *alternative curricula* to meet the needs and interests of different learners. Some examples of this kind of program may be found in "James Madison High: A School for Winners" in this section. Sizer suggests that alternatives should not be a spinoff to accommodate a special group of students; instead they should be experiments that affect or replace the central system (see "High School Reform: The Need for Engineering").

Being in high school is the *way of life* for most young people age fifteen through eighteen today, because approximately 75 percent of them now graduate from high school. It is a time in which many of them have little involvement in responsible tasks. This situation is complicated by the fact that, though adolescents mature much earlier today than they did thirty or forty years ago, they experience an *unnatural age segregation* in which high school students are denied significant interaction with children or adults. "Developing Responsible Youth Through Youth Participation" describes programs developed to cope with these factors. A recent report recommends a new Carnegie unit* to be required for graduation that students would fulfill through volunteer activities in the schools or other community institutions, either after school or during summers (see "Carnegie Report Presents Another Plan for Reforming U.S. High Schools").

From 1972 to 1974 five reform reports on the high school were issued as a result of studies by the National Commission on the Reform of Secondary Education, the Carnegie Commission on Higher Education, the President's Science Advisory Committee, the National Panel on High Schools and Adolescent Education, and the Task Force on Secondary Schools of the National Association of Secondary School Principals. All of these reports sought major changes in the high school. Generally they proposed alternatives to the traditional academic curriculum either through alternative curricula or schools, or through responsible social service and public work in the community. Another recommended alternative was specialized high schools in occupational fields. One of the reports recommended lowering the *compulsory* school attendance age to fourteen, while giving each citizen fourteen years of tuition-free education. Another proposed the reduction of time spent in school to two to four hours daily. Generally the reports criticized high schools as being too large and not assisting youth sufficiently in making the transition to the adult world of work and community participation. These reform reports of the 1970s are reviewed and summarized in "Tackling the Reform Reports of the 1980s" in this section. They are reviewed here in order to show how rapidly and mindlessly the external pressures on the schools can change. These 1970s reports are almost completely ignored today.

Since 1982 there have been eight new national reform reports on education, which with few exceptions focus on the high school. Six of these reports are the result of studies by the National Commission on Excellence in Education; the Carnegie Foundation for the Advancement of Teaching; the National Science Board Commis-

---

* Course credit in secondary schools has traditionally been expressed in *Carnegie units*, which are measures of time. One unit represents a *minimum* of 120 clock hours in one school year.

sion on Pre-college Education in Mathematics, Science and Technology; the Education Commission of the States; the National Association of Secondary School Principals with the National Association of Independent Schools; and the Twentieth Century Fund Task Force on Federal Elementary and Secondary Education Policy. The other two reports are *The Paideia Proposal,* prepared under the leadership of Mortimer Adler, a perennialist philosopher; and *A Place Called School,* an eight year study of 38 schools, conducted by John Goodlad, a national curriculum leader. These eight reports are reviewed, summarized, and contrasted by Harry Passow in "Tackling the Reform Reports of the 1980s."

All of the 1980s reports have a number of topics in common, although the recommendations of the reports do not always agree. The general emphases are quite similar: raising standards of achievement, promoting *excellence,* and rebuilding public confidence in the schools. All the reports conclude that American education is experiencing a serious crisis—but this was also true of the 1970s reports (the reasons given then for the crisis were different).

The most media attention has been given to *A Nation at Risk* which recommends raising standards (not clearly defined), requiring "five new basics" for graduation, testing achievement more regularly, and lengthening the school day and the school year (see "A Nation at Risk" in this section. It is excerpted from the report of the same title.)

Another widely discussed report is *High School: A Report on Secondary Education in America* by Ernest Boyer (sponsored by the Carnegie Foundation for the Advancement of Teaching). This report recommends first and foremost a "core of common learnings" and volunteer activities for all, more flexibility in scheduling, a program of electives to develop individual interests, the mastery of language, and a single track for academic and vocational students (see "Carnegie Report Presents Another Plan for Reforming U.S. High Schools").

Theodore Sizer, the author of *Horace's Compromise,* the 1984 reform report of NASSP and NAIS, asserts that higher order thinking skills should be the core of senior high school work and they should be learned through confrontation. According to this report, high schools need better defined goals and must require mastery of subject matter for graduation. Interdisciplinary non-graded curricula are essential, and instruction must be adapted to students' differing learning styles. Sizer calls these changes "revamping the structure" of the high school (see "High School Reform: The Need for Engineering").

The fastest growing curriculum area in American education in recent years has been vocational education. Most of this growth has occurred in comprehensive and vocational high schools and community colleges. In 1963 only four million students were enrolled in vocational courses. By 1978 the National Center for Educational Statistics reported an enrollment of more than 17 million students, with 12.7 million of them in public secondary schools. The curriculum in every vocational education course has been replaced since 1963, and the number of programs offered has increased from fewer than twenty to more than 400. This phenomenal growth has occurred because a high school diploma is no longer a passport to employment. Very few jobs remain today that require no special preparation.

The 1980s reform reports with their emphasis on more academic requirements and more time to be spent on them are of great concern to high school vocational educators. A report representing their point of view was issued in 1984. It argues for a balanced curriculum—one that includes both academic and vocational preparation for high school students (see "The Unfinished Agenda: Report from the National Commission on Secondary Vocational Education").

"Effective High Schools—What Are the Common Characteristics," the first article in this section, reveals the recurring presence of eight general factors in high schools which are identified as the most effective.

What *objectives* should guide programs of education for middle adolescents? At this level, the objectives would include the following:

1. Helping learners in career development, whether through vocational guidance, vocational education, or additional academic development.
2. Offering learners many opportunities to grow in citizenship skills, understanding, and responsibilities.
3. Aiding students to grow in self-direction in study and learning.
4. Assisting learners in many ways toward self-realization and identity.
5. Encouraging the development and practice of critical thinking.
6. Assisting learners in preparing for the transition to the world of work, to community participation, and to the world of the future.

*Continuity of learning* and the great variety of *individual differences* in learners suggest the need for the reader to reexamine the objectives stated for education of early adolescents in the introduction to Section 8. And because some middle adolescents will be advanced in their development socially, emotionally, or cognitively, you may wish to look ahead to Section 10 to consider in that introduction the discussion of objectives of educational programs for late adolescents and young adults.

To better provide for the attainment of objectives at this level, the following innovations are being proposed and tried. This list of *innovations* and *trends* in education for middle adolescents includes references to pertinent articles in this section, unless otherwise noted. The list is arranged alphabetically.

1. *Active learning:* "High School Reform"; "Developing Responsible Youth Through Youth Participation"; "James Madison High"; "The Unfinished Agenda"
2. *Advanced placement courses:* "Effective High Schools"; "James Madison High"
3. *Alternative programs or schools:* "A Nation at Risk"; "High School Reform"; "The Unfinished Agenda"
4. *Basic education (the "new basics"):* "High School Reform"; "A Nation at Risk"
5. *Clear goal statements:* "High School Reform"; "Effective High Schools"
6. *Club activities:* "James Madison High"
7. *Combined English-social studies curricula:* "High School Reform"
8. *Community service curricula:* "Carnegie Report Presents Another Plan"; "Tack-

ling the Reform Reports"; "Developing Responsible Youth Through Youth Participation"; "The Unfinished Agenda"

9. *Computer curricula:* "Tackling the Reform Reports"; "James Madison High"
10. *Co-curricular activities:* "James Madison High"
11. *Continuous learner progress:* "High School Reform"
12. *Critical thinking:* "High School Reform"
13. *Excellence defined:* "Tackling the Reform Reports"; "Effective High Schools"; "James Madison High"
14. *Extensive elective courses:* "Effective High Schools"; "James Madison High"
15. *Flexible scheduling:* "High School Reform"; "Carnegie Report Presents Another Plan"
16. *Foreign language requirement:* "A Nation at Risk"; "Tackling the Reform Reports"; "James Madison High"
17. *General education curricula:* "Effective High Schools"; "Carnegie Report Presents Another Plan"; "James Madison High"
18. *Heterogeneous grouping:* "James Madison High"; "Tackling the Reform Reports"
19. *High expectations:* "Effective High Schools"; "High School Reform"; "Tackling the Reform Reports"; "A Nation at Risk"; "James Madison High"; "The Unfinished Agenda"
20. *Homework required:* "High School Reform"; "James Madison High"
21. *Individualized curricula:* "Effective High Schools";"James Madison High"
22. *Interdisciplinary curricula:* "High School Reform"
23. *Learning style alternatives:* "High School Reform"; "Matching Learning Styles and Teaching Styles" (Section 4); "Learning/Teaching Styles: Applying the Principles" (Section 4)
24. *Longer school day:* "A Nation at Risk"; "Tackling the Reform Reports"
25. *Mastery learning:* "High School Reform"; "James Madison High"; "Promoting Excellence Through Mastery Learning" (Section 4)
26. *Parent participation:* "James Madison High"; "Effective High Schools"; "Who Should Plan the Curriculum?" (Section 6)
27. *Problem solving curricula:* "High School Reform"; "James Madison High"
28. *School within a school:* "James Madison High"
29. *Self-actualization curricula:* "James Madison High"; "Effective High Schools"; "Some Basic Concepts in Perceptual Psychology" (Section 4)
30. *Student-teacher planning:* "James Madison High"; "Who Should Plan the Curriculum?" (Section 6)
31. *Value education:* "James Madison High"
32. *Vocational education curricula:* "Tackling the Reform Reports"; "The Unfinished Agenda"

Will these trends, if adopted, provide the changes needed in programs of education for this age group?

We must evaluate innovations and trends in comparison with present programs. The consideration of (1) objectives, (2) the four bases of the curriculum, and (3) other curriculum criteria provide professional means for making these decisions.

In the List of Books and Articles to Review at the end of this section, many of the sources listed have one or more of the numbers in the preceding list of trends entered at the end of the citations. These numbers will help you find other recent articles and books on those middle adolescent education trends and innovations that particularly interest you.

## OBJECTIVES

Your objectives in studying education at this level as part of the curriculum should be as follows:

1.  To be familiar with the objectives, current innovations, and recent trends in education for middle adolescents.
2.  To be able to explain the functions and goals of education at this level as part of the total curriculum.
3.  To be able to use the objectives of education at this level, the curriculum bases, and other criteria in making curriculum or instruction decisions regarding present as well as proposed programs.
4.  To be able to suggest improvement in middle adolescent curriculum plans through the decisions made in number 3.

## PREASSESSMENT

1.  Identify the innovations and trends listed in the rationale for this section, and discuss their implications for education at this level.
2.  Evaluate each of the trends in terms of objectives, bases of curriculum, and curriculum criteria that you regard as appropriate.
3.  Select any middle adolescence curriculum plan; describe and analyze it in terms of objectives, the four curriculum bases, your list of curriculum criteria, and innovations and trends at this level of education.
4.  Suggest improvements or changes in the curriculum plan in number 3 in the light of your analysis.

In answering number 3 and 4 of the preassessment, you might choose to analyze the curriculum plans described in "James Madison High: A School for Winners" in this section.

## LEARNING ACTIVITIES

Articles in this section will help you understand the purposes and functions of education for middle adolescents. They will also acquaint you with the problems, as well as the innovations and trends, of programs of education for middle adolescents. Other learning alternatives are suggested at the end of this section.

## POSTASSESSMENT

After attempting the preassessment you may do *one or more* of the following:

1.  Ask your instructor whether you are ready for a postassessment evaluation on education for middle adolescents. Most students will need further work on this topic.
2.  Read the articles on education for middle adolescents in this section, and try to determine how the problems, goals, trends, and innovations discussed in each article should be considered in curriculum planning and teaching.
3.  Choose additional activities and readings or films from those listed at the end of this section.
4.  Look in your library or media center for other films, books, or articles on middle adolescent education programs and teaching.
5.  Discuss with your fellow students the reading you have done and the films you have viewed. The key questions: How should the goals, innovations, trends, and suggestions you've studied affect a school's curriculum? How should they be considered in planning for teaching?
6.  When you are ready, ask your instructor for advice on a suitable postassessment for you for this topic. Satisfactory completion of number 1 under Problems and Projects at the end of this section might be one possibility. Or satisfactory written completion of the preassessment for this section, after completing other learning activities, might be a satisfactory postassessment. Consult your instructor about this. You can evaluate your ability to do these postassessment activities before seeing the instructor.

# Effective High Schools—What Are the Common Characteristics

## JOSEPH MURPHY AND PHILIP HALLINGER

What constitutes an effective school? Researchers undertook a study of schools in California that was designed to answer that question.

## CURRICULAR AND CLIMATE VARIABLES

Analysis of questionnaires completed by administrators of schools identified as effective[1] reveals the recurring presence of eight general factors:

- A clear sense of purpose.
- A core set of standards within a rich curriculum
- High expectations
- A commitment to educate each student as completely as possible
- A special reason for each student to go to school
- A safe, orderly learning environment
- A sense of community
- Resiliency and a problem-solving attitude.

## Clear Sense of Purpose

A very clear sense of mission, with a specific emphasis on high academic performance, was

1. Effective schools were identified in a nationwide government-sponsored study. California schools so identified were then screened by the writers to locate the 18 "most effective" high schools in the state.

identifiable in the effective schools. There was total dedication to academic excellence. Unlike many of the effective elementary schools identified in earlier studies, these schools did not often translate their sense of purpose into levels of achievement sought on standardized achievement tests. Rather, there was a prevailing norm that guided decision making and other important activities in the school which can best be described as "academic press"—the sense that all activities combine to create an environment of academic rigor (Murphy, et al., 1982).

## Core Set of Standards Within a Rich Curriculum

One of the most interesting findings had to do with the curriculum content. One the one hand, as would be expected from reviews of effective schools (Levine, 1982; Cooley and Leinhardt, 1980), these schools had a core set of curriculum standards which all students were expected to master. On the other hand, contrary to what has sometimes been suggested, this core program did not limit the scope of course offerings at the schools.

Each of the schools in this study had rich and diverse academic programs with intensive and extended course content available in almost all subject areas. There was also some evidence of schools trying to integrate the common core standards into a wide range of courses.

From *NASSP Bulletin* 69, No. 477 (January 1985): 18–22. Used by permission of the publisher, the National Association of Secondary School Principals.

## High Expectations

Permeating the atmosphere in all of these schools was the expectation of academic achievement and educational excellence. This was obvious in a number of ways. First, administrators and teachers in these schools held high expectations for themselves and took responsibility for what students accomplished. Second, the school mission of academic achievement created a strong press for academic excellence. Third, these schools were characterized by a number of policies and practices which conveyed the importance of high achievement. These included such things as regularly assigned and graded homework, policies that permitted participation in cocurricular activities only if grades were high, and quick and regular notification of parents when expectations were not being met.

Somewhat surprisingly, however, the expectations of these schools in terms of formal graduation requirements were not particularly high. The average number of years of each subject needed for graduation were: math—1.6; English—3.5; social studies—3.2; science—1.3; foreign language—0. It seems that, as with goals or mission, expectations tended to be reflected in a norm of academic press rather than in high targets for performance.

One of the most interesting aspects of high expectations was that they spilled over into almost every activity the schools undertook. That is, these schools not only developed students who won numerous academic awards and honors and scored well on tests, but they also regularly produced award-winning sports, music, and art programs as well.

## Commitment to Educate Each Student as Completely as Possible

One of the most exciting aspects of effective elementary schools is that they see to it that every student in the school progresses. Selected groups of students are not forgotten about or relegated to a second-class academic citizenship. This factor was also abundantly evident in the high schools in this study. In addition to a rich and diverse general curriculum, these schools had excellent remedial and advanced placement courses and programs. They had, on an average, almost 30 percent of their students working in advanced placement courses.

On the other hand, they were leaders in developing a variety of programs and strategies to ensure that no students fell through the cracks because of academic or adjustment problems; and to ensure that students with special needs received programs consistent with mainstream core curriculum standards. The schools developed an especially effective array of methods for monitoring and working with the following groups of students: limited English proficient, special education, remedial, school-age mothers, and potential dropouts.

Very few of the students in these schools failed to graduate because of academic deficiencies and the dropout rates were extremely low. Contrary to popular belief, it may be that high expectations reduce rather than increase dropouts.

## Special Reason for Each Student to Go to School

In addition to ensuring that each student progressed as fully as possible academically, these schools all created rich environments where there were multiple opportunities for student responsibility and meaningful involvement. These schools had a wide variety of sports teams, an array of interest and curriculum clubs, opportunities for students to work in the larger community, and a number of ways for students to take responsibility through student government. These various activities captured a high percentage of the students.

Responses in the questionnaires indicated

that two factors were primarily responsible for both the depth of the cocurricular program and the high level of student involvement. First, there were strong efforts on the part of the entire school community to bring new students into the programs. Second, there was the commitment of dedicated staff pushing for the same levels of excellence in these activities that they required in the classroom.

## Safe, Orderly Learning Environment

In all of the eighteen schools, a great deal of attention was devoted to creating effective learning environments. Attendance rates were generally high and increasing while dropout rates were generally low and decreasing. There were five key elements of the discipline policies and practices in these schools. First, school rules and standards for behavior were clearly specified. Second, the rules and consequences for breaking them were systematically communicated to parents and students.

Third, the consequences were incremental in nature. Fourth, the rules were fairly and consistently enforced everywhere on the school campuses. Fifth, a great deal of thought and energy went into the enforcement of school rules. Specifically, regular telephone contacts with parents, high administrator visibility on campuses, and innovative disciplinary programs in lieu of suspension were common characteristics in these schools.

## Sense of Community

Three factors combined to create a strong sense of community in these schools. First, they enjoyed strong support from the parents and the communities in which they were located. There was a good deal of parent participation in these schools and involvement in advisory and decision-making bodies. Second, these schools maintained an internal atmosphere of professional collegiality.

There were strong indications of groups working together, making decisions, resolving conflicts, etc., in pursuit of a common goal— academic excellence. Third, there was evidence of cohesion and support among professional staff and students. There was a feeling of mutual respect throughout these school communities.

## Resiliency and a Problem-Solving Attitude

Since Proposition 13 was passed in California, the level of financial support for schools has decreased dramatically. While once among the top 10 states in school support, California is now fiftieth in percent of personal income provided for education. This decline has caused serious hardships on many of the schools in the state.

One of the interesting things about the schools in this study was the way they responded to these hardships. There was a sense of resiliency in these schools as they bounced back from such difficulties as mergers, the loss of funds for special programs, and reductions in personnel. The schools did not allow these difficulties to become excuses for failure but, rather, treated them as problem-solving opportunities.

For example, in one school, a merger was translated into new organizational arrangements for greater academic rigor; in another, a loss of funds was offset by the development of a foundation which also helped bind the community and school closer together; in a third, the elimination of counselors meant the development of an administrator-adviser program to ensure that students could still receive needed services.

## CONCLUSION

One of the tentative conclusions that can be drawn from this study is that the suggested differences between effective elementary and effective secondary schools may be more apparent than real. That is, both types of schools share a number of common characteristics such as a clear mission, high expectations, a commitment to fully educate each student, a sense of community, and a safe, orderly learning environment. Where secondary schools seem to move beyond this common definition is in the richness of the curriculum and the complexity of the social system.

Although the effective secondary schools in this study had a core set of standards, these were embedded in a rich and diverse curriculum. These schools also differed from effective elementary schools in relying less on the parenting aspect of teacher-student relations and more on the involvement of students in the social system in which they functioned. In both cases, the differences appear to be due less to a basic difference between effective practices in elementary and secondary schools than to greater organizational complexity at the high school level.

## REFERENCES

Cooley, W., and Leinhardt, G. "The Instructional Dimensions Study." *Educational Evaluation and Policy Analysis* 2 (1980): 7–25.

Levine, D. "Successful Approaches for Improving Academic Achievement in Inner-City Elementary Schools." *Phi Delta Kappan* 63 (1982): 523–526.

Murphy, J.; Weil, M.; Hallinger, P.; and Mitman, A. "Academic Press: Translating Expectations into School Level Policies and Classroom Practices." *Educational Leadership* 40 (1982): 22–26.

*Joseph Murphy* is Associate Professor, Department of Administration, Higher, and Continuing Education, University of Illinois, Champaign.

*Philip Hallinger* is Assistant Professor, Department of Educational Administration, St. Johns University, Scarsdale, New York.

# A Nation at Risk

## NATIONAL COMMISSION ON EXCELLENCE IN EDUCATION

Our nation is at risk. The educational foundations of our society are being eroded by a rising tide of mediocrity that threatens our future as a nation and a people. What was unimaginable a generation ago has begun to occur—others are matching and surpassing our educational attainments. This final report of the National Commission on Excellence in Education is the result of 18 months of study by an 18-member panel appointed by Secretary of Education Terrel H. Bell.

The educational dimensions of the risk before us have been amply documented in testimony to the Commission. Our recommendations promise lasting reform. They are based on the beliefs that everyone can learn, that everyone is born with an *urge* to learn which can be nurtured, that a solid high school education is within the reach of virtually all, and that lifelong learning will equip people with the skills required for new careers and for citizenship.

*Recommendation A: Content.* We recommend

Excerpted from *A Nation at Risk: The Imperative for Educational Reform* (Washington, D.C.: The U.S. Government Printing Office, 1983).

that state and local high school graduation requirements be strengthened and that, *at a minimum, all* students seeking a diploma be required to lay the foundations in the five New Basics by taking in high school four years of English, three years each of mathematics, science and social studies, and one-half year of computer science. For the college-bound, two years of high school foreign language are strongly recommended in addition to those taken earlier. The New Basics are the foundation of success for after-school years and therefore form the core of the modern curriculum. A high level of shared education in these basics, together with work in the fine and performing arts and foreign languages, constitutes the mind and spirit of our culture.

High school *English* should equip graduates to comprehend, interpret, evaluate, and use what they read; write well-organized, effective papers; listen effectively and discuss ideas intelligently; and know our literary heritage and how it enhances imagination and ethical understanding and relates to the customs, ideas, and values of today's life and culture. High school *mathematics* should equip graduates to understand geometric and algebraic concepts; understand elementary probability and statistics; apply mathematics in everyday situations; and estimate, approximate, measure, and test the accuracy of their calculations. Besides traditional studies for the college-bound, new, equally demanding mathematics curricula are needed for those not continuing their formal education immediately.

High school *science* should introduce graduates to the concepts, laws, and processes of the physical and biological sciences; the methods of scientific inquiry and reasoning; the application of scientific knowledge to everyday life; and the social and environmental implications of scientific and technological development. Science courses must be revised and updated for both the college- and the non-college-bound.

High school *social studies* should be designed to enable students to fix their places and possibilities within the larger social and cultural structure; understand the broad sweep of ancient and contemporary ideas that have shaped our world; understand the fundamentals of how our economic and political systems function; and grasp the difference between free and repressive societies. High school *computer science* should equip graduates to understand the computer as an information, computation, and communication device; use the computer in studying other basics and for personal and work-related purposes; and understand the world of computers, electronics, and related technologies.

Other important curriculum matters must also be addressed. Achieving proficiency in a *foreign language* is desirable and should be started in the elementary grades. The high school curriculum should also provide programs requiring rigorous effort in subjects that advance students' personal, educational, and occupational goals, such as the fine and performing arts and vocational education. The pre-high-school curriculum should provide a sound base for study in those and later years in such areas as English-language development and writing, computational and problem-solving skills, science, social studies, foreign language, and the arts. These years should foster enthusiasm for learning and development of the individual's gifts and talents.

We encourage continuation of efforts by groups to revise, update, improve, and make available new and more diverse curricular materials. We applaud the consortia of educators and scientific, industrial, and scholarly societies cooperating to improve the curriculum.

*Recommendation B: Standards and expectations.* We recommend that schools, colleges, and universities adopt more rigorous and measurable standards, and higher expectations, for academic performance and student conduct, and that four-year colleges and universities raise their requirements for admission. This will help students do their best educationally with challenging materials in an environment that supports learning and authentic accomplishment.

Grades should indicate academic achievement and be reliable evidence of readiness for further study. Four-year colleges and universities should raise admission requirements and advise potential applicants of admission standards in terms of courses required, performance in these areas, and achievement levels on standardized tests. Standardized achievement tests should be administered at major transition points from one level of schooling to another, and particularly from high school to college or work, to certify the student's credentials and to identify the need for remedial intervention and the opportunity for advanced or accelerated work. The tests should be part of a nationwide (but not federal) system of state and local standardized tests including other diagnostic procedures to evaluate student progress.

Texts and other learning and teaching tools should be upgraded and updated for more rigorous content. University scientists, scholars, and members of professional societies, in collaboration with master teachers, should assist willing publishers in developing products, or publish their own alternatives where inadequacies persist.

In considering texts for adoption, states and school districts should evaluate for ability to present rigorous, challenging material clearly, and require publishers to furnish evaluation data on the material's effectiveness. Funds should be made available to support text development in "thin market" areas such as those for disadvantaged students, the learning-disabled, and the gifted and talented. All publishers should furnish evidence of text quality and appropriateness based on field trials and credible evaluations. New materials should reflect the most current applications of technology, the best scholarship, and research in learning and teaching.

*Recommendation C: Time.* We recommend that significantly more time be devoted to learning the New Basics. This will require more effective use of the existing school day, a longer school day, or a lengthened school year.

High school students should be assigned far more homework. Instruction in effective study and work skills should be introduced in the early grades and continued throughout schooling. School districts and state legislatures should strongly consider seven-hour school days and a 200- to 220-day year. Learning time should be expanded through better classroom management and organization of the school day. If necessary, additional time should be found to meet special needs of slow learners, the gifted, etc.

The burden on teachers for maintaining discipline should be reduced by developing firm, fair, consistently enforced codes of student conduct, and by considering alternative classrooms, programs, and schools to meet needs of continually disruptive students. Attendance policies with clear incentives and sanctions should be used. Administrative burdens on the teacher and related instrusions into the school day should be reduced. Placement and grouping of students, as well as promotion and graduation policies, should be guided by the academic progress of students and their instructional needs, rather than by rigid adherence to age.

Educators, parents, and public officials at all levels must assist in bringing about the educational reforms proposed here. Citizens must provide the necessary financial support. Excellence costs. But in the long run, mediocrity costs far more.

It is the America of all of us that is at risk; it is to each of us that this imperative is addressed. It is by our willingness to take up the challenge, and our resolve to see it through, that America's place in the world will be either secured or forfeited. Americans have succeeded before, and so we shall again.

# Carnegie Report Presents Another Plan for Reforming U.S. High Schools

## PHI DELTA KAPPAN

American high schools have not failed, but most of them are not doing much more than simply surviving. So concludes a major report and blueprint for reform from the Carnegie Foundation for the Advancement of Teaching.

"The conditions in the schools are mixed," Ernest Boyer, president of the Carnegie Foundation and author of the report, said at a Washington, D.C., news briefing. "For a small percentage of students—10% to 15%, perhaps—the American high school provides an outstanding education, the finest in the world. . . . A larger percentage of students—perhaps 20% to 30%—mark time in school or drop out," Boyer wrote in his book, *High School: A Report on Secondary Education in America.* "The majority of students are in the vast middle ground" he continued, attending schools "where pockets of excellence can be found but where there is little intellectual challenge."

"Most secondary schools in the United States are—like the communities that surround them—surviving but not thriving," Boyer wrote. They are beset by competing goals, serious financial problems, and social change.

Nevertheless, Boyer said that recent actions by states and local schools, as well as scattered increases in student achievement, attest to "a rising tide of school improvement." In addition, the national spotlight thrown on education recently will have an effect. "America has the best opportunity it will have in this century to improve the schools," Boyer wrote. "There is a growing national consensus that our future depends on public education. . . . If we do not seize this special moment, we will fail the coming generation and the nation."

The Carnegie report presents a comprehensive plan for reforming the high school. It calls first and foremost for a "core of common learning" for all high school students. That core would include literature, civics, American history, mathematics, science, foreign languages, Western and non-Western civilization, the arts, technology, and the meaning of work.

The report also proposes a new Carnegie unit—in service—that students would fulfill through volunteer activities in the schools or other community institutions, either after school or during summers. Contributing to the community would make high school students feel more productive, Boyer theorized. "If powerlessness marks the condition of teachers, uselessness marks the condition of students," he said.

In addition to the core courses, the foundation recommends that all students be required to complete for high school graduation a senior essay based on an independent project. Boyer is confident that, "if education is effective, every high school graduate will be able to gather information from a range of sources, organize important ideas, think carefully about an issue, and, with clarity, put his or her thoughts on paper."

"Academic achievement begins with the mastery of language," said Boyer, who called writing "a skill that's scandalously neglected." Language skills should be taught early, and students should be formally tested in English proficiency

From *Phi Delta Kappan* 65, No. 3 (November 1983): 229. Used by permission of the publisher.

before entering high school. High school English should be taught in small classes that emphasize writing and that include the study of the spoken word as well.

The 300-page Carnegie report is based in large part on field studies of the high schools. A group of 25 educators spent at least a month visiting each of the 15 high schools selected for the study, observing and interviewing teachers, students, parents, and administrators. The study includes a wide range of observations, from the amount of class time lost to trivial announcements over the school loudspeaker to students' passionate debate about suicide, called forth by their reading of *Death of a Salesman*.

The recommendations include structural changes and suggestions for greater involvement by parents, colleges and universities, and the private sector. Boyer recommends, for instance, that schools break away from 50-minute units, whenever longer study would be productive. He also suggests that high school study extend to special residential schools in mathematics and science and to other sites of learning, such as science and art museums.

Asserting that the purpose of public education is to produce "an enlightened citizen," Boyer envisions a single track that would supplant separate tracks for academic and vocational students. All students would take core courses in the first two years of high school and then move on to advanced study, the exploration of job options, or both.

Carnegie researchers turned up "miserable conditions for teachers," according to Boyer. "They are being asked to do more and more," he said, "while being given less recognition, less preparation time, and less authority," especially over what they teach. The report concludes that better working conditions for teachers are even more important than higher salaries. It recommends that secondary school teachers teach four classes at most and a two-week professional development "term" should be added to the school year (with appropriate compensation) for professional projects and study.

As a national goal, the report recommends that average salaries for teachers be raised 25% above the rate of inflation over the next three years. It also outlines a rigorous five-year course of teacher training and certification based on exams and faculty recommendations.

Although Boyer thinks that most of the suggested reforms must originate in states and in individual schools, the study also recommends that some costs should be borne by the federal government.

*Ernest L. Boyer* is the author of the Carnegie Report, *High School: A Report on Secondary Education in America* (1983). He is President, Carnegie Foundation for the Advancement of Teaching, and former United States Commissioner of Education.

# High School Reform: The Need for Engineering

## THEODORE R. SIZER

Most of the central problems crippling high schools in the United States are obvious, but none of the remedies seems to stick, and the reason lies in the basic structure of the high school. Its organizing framework dates from the late nineteenth century and persists today with remarkable consistency across all regions of the country and across public and private sectors.

Most adolescents attend high schools with a thousand or more age-mates, under a structure highly fractionated horizontally by age group and vertically by program track. The program revolves around subjects taught by specialists—another element of fragmentation—and the students "cover" a succession of topics each day, seemingly at random. The social rituals of schools are numerous and widely uniform.

Changes in school structure over the last 40 years have been remarkably small relative to those in American living patterns, careers, values, needs, and technologies. High schools are complicated organisms; to be orderly, the pieces must work together smoothly. Not surprisingly, any significant change in structure and procedure that is proposed must usually be vetoed on practical grounds; it disturbs too many things. Or it is spun off as an "alternative" program, in effect a school-within-a-school with its own structure. In these purposeful, pessimistic 1980s, when orderliness is a cardinal virtue, these alternatives are all too rare.

Thus, things remain the same because it is impossible to change very much without changing most of everything. The result is paralysis.

The first step in our search for better schools will be to clear our minds of some well-intentioned traditions that simply don't work very well. There is no serious way to improve high schools without revamping their structure. Politically painful though such a renovation may be, it is inescapable. What might it involve?

**1.** In most high schools, a shorter, simpler, better-defined list of goals is necessary, involving shelving the long-standing claims of certain subject areas. For example, driver education may have to give way to English. Athletic and chorus trips may no longer be allowed to preempt teaching time, which might mean curtailing interscholastic athletic and arts programs. Chemistry may have to be dropped as a separate subject so biology and physics can be taught well. The list is long, and the necessary constrictions painful.

**2.** Students entering high school unable to read, write, and cipher adequately will have to concentrate exclusively on these subjects. These are the foundations of secondary school work, and until they are mastered, studying much else is wasteful. Teachers will need substantial time to work with these youngsters, as the students almost certainly will be demoralized and ready to fail.

**3.** Higher-order thinking skills—reasoning, imagining, analyzing, synthesizing—are the core of senior high school work, and they are learned through confrontation, through dialogue. One isn't *told* how to think; one reasons and has that reasoning critiqued. This requires

Excerpted from *Phi Delta Kappan* 64, No. 10 (June 1983): 679–683. Used by permission of the author and the publisher.

different kinds of teaching formats and lower teaching loads than are now the rule.

**4.** Until mastery of subject matter determines whether or not a diploma is granted, students will see minimal incentives for achieving such mastery. There must be some kind of culminating examination or other exhibition of mastery to place the emphasis of schooling squarely on learning.

**5.** A central goal of schooling is for students to be able to teach themselves and to wish to do so. The way one learns to teach oneself is to practice doing it and to have that practice critiqued. This requires serious independent work (homework) and time available both for teachers to challenge students' efforts and for students to struggle with this process of learning to learn. Any course with such a focus will be able to "cover" fewer facts than is now the case. The world history course will cover fewer centuries; the mathematics sequence will not get to calculus; the biology course will no longer include some phyla. We will have to let go of many cherished sectors of the curriculum in pursuit of "Less is more."

**6.** Sorting out what students require uncovers the inadequacy of traditional interpretations of the subjects of study. Absolutely fundamental skills in thinking and expression cut across the domains of existing departments. Thus, they are given short shrift. The fractionated curriculum high schools inherited from the 1890s serves us poorly. To reconstruct it will infuriate many academic scholars, scare many teachers who have been narrowly trained by those scholars, and send shivers of apprehension down parents' spines.

**7.** The frenetic quality of many high schools needs to be eased, the pace slowed, and larger blocks of time made available for the kind of dialectical teaching that is a necessary part of helping adolescents learn to think clearly and constructively. This will mean that some things will have to go.

**8.** Age-grading must cease, and students must be allowed to progress at their own rates. Adult attitudes about "where a student should be" will have to change; the assumption must always be that mastery is not only possible but expected. We will need to adapt instruction to students' differing learning styles. To adapt our school structures to a more complicated view of learning will be a bureaucrats' nightmare, but adapt they must.

**9.** Lessening segregation and stereotyping by class, race, gender, and ethnicity requires unprejudiced attitudes from those who work in schools and also changes in the structure of schooling. Mastery of the basic core of high school work should be the goal for everybody—a common purpose even if addressed through widely differing means. Diversions from this through early tracking or magnet programs must be resisted. People, especially more affluent people, *like* tracking. Any challenge to their enclaves will be fiercely fought.

**10.** The way to connect the world of school and the world outside of school is to make thoughtful use of the latter bear usefully on the former. Adolescents can and will learn much from the tumble of information and experience that pervades modern life. Schools should seize upon the best of that learning and give incentives to students to use their out-of-school opportunities in ways that help them learn still more.

**11.** Teachers cannot provide the kind of teaching required to help students learn higher-order thinking skills in groups of 30 or more and with overall teaching loads of 130 to 175 students. A practical way to reduce these loads somewhat is for a greater percentage of the school staff to teach and for each teacher to become less specialized. Students will learn more if they are taught English and social studies by the same teacher. A single teacher has to work with about 80 students; two specialists must try to know 160 each. Launching a challenge against specialization in high schools will be difficult.

12. Proper accommodation of individual student differences demands that teachers have control over their own and their students' schedules and programs. Standardized procedures (30 minutes per week of physical education, no fewer than 215 minutes per week of English) fly in the face of common sense—save that of administrators who do not trust their teachers or who run schools so understaffed that such rigid policies are necessary simply to maintain order.

13. Good teachers value their autonomy. They know they need it to do a first-class job. If denied it, they do mediocre work or leave teaching. To attract and hold top professionals in teaching, we will have to give them appropriate autonomy. Trends today are working to weaken the teaching profession. Ever more regulation comes from the top.

14. Top professionals want a career that gradually develops, with more responsibility and compensation following experience and demonstrated excellence. This requires differentiated staffing within teaching and salaries that follow this differentiation. Such schemes require us to redefine the ways of deploying teachers in schools.

The list of conditions that need changing is depressingly long. But the center of the target is the dysfunctional structure of the American high school. Am I being unrealistic? I would protest that I am being realistic in admitting candidly what clearly is not functioning well. It is unrealistic to accept the existing structure of the high school. Trying to reform it within that structure is like trying to push a large square of Jell-O across a plate with the sharpened point of a pencil. You can do it, but you certainly don't get much traction.

The answers all point in the same direction. High school reform will start as an effort in exploratory *engineering*, designing and testing new structures appropriate to the adolescents, teachers, and culture of the 1980s. We need new models of schooling that attempt several new approaches at once—a necessity, given how most of the important aspects of high school structure affect every other aspect.

Such a strategy of "model" schools will bring us back to the "alternative school" approach of the 1960s, but this time the "alternatives" will not be spinoffs to accommodate a special, atypical group of students. Rather, they will be experiments that ultimately should affect the central system—indeed, that should replace it. Both short-range and long-range needs must now be addressed. We must not let our desperation about meeting the former prevent us from tackling the latter.

A sensible rebuttal here would be that there is neither money nor political will for this sort of thing. And it is true. But this is why the burden is on those of us who have been given the privilege of studying and writing about high schools. It is our duty to join with colleagues to persuade the American political system—its public authorities *and* its great private philanthropies—that investment in imaginative educational engineering is absolutely essential if we are to have a secondary school system worthy of the talent and promise of American adolescents.

*Theodore R. Sizer* is Professor of Education, Brown University, Providence, Rhode Island. He previously served as Dean of the Harvard University Graduate School of Education. He is the author of *Horace's Compromise: The Dilemma of the American High School* (1984).

# Tackling the Reform Reports of the 1980s

## A. HARRY PASSOW

The publication last March of *Horace's Compromise: The Dilemma of the American High School* marked the end of a spate of reports urging educational reform that began in November 1982 with *The Paideia Proposal: An Educational Manifesto*. Each of the reports described the ills affecting U.S. schools and made recommendations for change.

The report of the National Commission on Excellence in Education, *A Nation at Risk*, proved to be a major media event; it convinced the public of the need for drastic educational reform if America was once again to become industrially and militarily competitive with other nations. *A Nation at Risk* concluded that the very future of America was threatened by the erosion of its educational foundations: "Our once unchallenged preeminence in commerce, industry, science, and technological innovations is being overtaken by competitors throughout the world."[1] The rhetoric in other reports was not as strident.

At the Wingspread Conference on Studies of the American High School in November 1982, a total of 29 projects were represented. These projects varied in purpose, design, time frame, data base, expectations, and outcomes. All of them were studying aspects of the afflictions and shortcomings of American education, especially in the nation's high schools. While John Goodlad's Study of Schooling extended over a decade and Theodore Sizer's project took five years, other groups issued their reports in a matter of months. Some projects involved extensive data collection from school sites; others relied on discussions of specially prepared position papers.

Common to all the reports is the clear, firm conclusion that American education is experiencing a serious crisis, which, if left unattended, will render the U.S. vulnerable to its industrial, commercial, and even military competitors. As Harold Howe II, former U.S. commissioner of education, observed, "Frustration over the diminishing capacity of the U.S. to compete in worldwide markets has awakened new interest in the old idea that the quality of human resources is a key element in the efficiency of the nation's economy."[2]

This equation of the deterioration of the nation's schools with weakened national security and a failing national economy recalls the widespread condemnation of the schools following the launch of Sputnik in 1957; then the "sorry state of teaching of mathematics and science" in U.S. high schools was made the scapegoat. The Sputnik-initiated criticisms had been preceded in the early 1950s by denunciations of "life adjustment education" and other forms of progressive education and calls for a return to basic subjects and academic disciplines. Indeed, some of the current reports discuss improving teaching and learning in mathematics and science, raising standards and requirements in these areas, and recruiting and training better teachers—all reminiscent of the Sputnik era and the National Defense Education Act of 1958 that followed.

The deplorable state of American education is not a theme that is unique to the current wave of reports. This theme has recurred regularly over

From *Phi Delta Kappan* 65, No. 10 (June 1984): 674–683. Used by permission of the author and the publisher.

the past 90 years or so. Crisis was the theme expressed in the several reports on the high schools in the 1970s, in the literature dealing with disadvantaged youths and urban education in the 1960s, in the attacks on progressive education in the early 1950s and in the post-Sputnik literature toward the end of that decade, in the life adjustment and vocational education literature of the 1940s, and in the education reports issued during the Depression years of the 1930s—to look back just a few decades.

One of the major reasons for the calls of crisis in American education is the shifting expectations of the American public. As Diane Ravitch points out:

> Throughout history, Americans expected much of their educational institutions; sometimes schools have been expected to take on responsibilities for which they were entirely unsuited. When they have failed, it was usually because their leaders and their public alike had forgotten their real limitations as well are their real strengths.[3]

*A Nation at Risk* listed 13 "educational dimensions at risk" that constituted indicators of a crisis. These included reports of poor achievement test scores, declines in both enrollments and achievement in science and mathematics, the high cost incurred by business and the military for remedial and training programs, and unacceptable levels of functional literacy found among American children and adults. Other reports mention many of these same indicators, though they vary in the extent of blame they assign to the schools. Despite the consensus that an educational crisis exists, the data can be read in different ways. For example, Lawrence Stedman and Marshall Smith reviewed four reports and observed:

> [T]hese reports are political documents; the case they make takes the form of a polemic, not a reasoned treatise. Rather than carefully marshaling facts to prove their case, they present a litany of

charges without examining the veracity of their evidence or its sources. By presenting material starkly and eloquently, the commissions hoped to jar the public into action, and to a great extent they have been successful. Caveats and detailed analysis of evidence might have lessened the reports' impact.[4]

Paul Peterson viewed the proclamations of crisis as the most arresting aspect of the six reports he reviewed; he concluded that the data used to support claims of the failure of American schools were "patchy, dated, and not nearly as dramatic as the rhetoric employed."[5] Peterson regards the objectives proclaimed by the various commissions as little more than truisms and faults the reports for failing "to show us how to get the quality and excellence we all desire."

## Reform Reports of the Seventies

Less than a decade ago, eight reports—almost completely ignored today—also proclaimed the shortcomings of U.S. high schools, examined the nature and causes of the problems of educating and socializing youngsters, and proposed policy and program changes that, had they been implemented, would have dramatically affected schools and other institutions serving youths. Although some of the criticisms of the high school in those earlier reports were similar to those found in the present crop, the reports of the Seventies adopted a very different tone. Those reports seemed to focus more on the lack of relevance and humaneness of the high schools rather than on the schools and their students as contributors to industrial productivity and national security. The reports of the Seventies viewed our nation as threatened by what was happening to the personal development of students and to society in general. The Kettering Commission, for instance, focused on sudden and traumatic changes in the missions of the schools:

The American comprehensive high school today must be viewed as an establishment striving to meet the complex demands of society in the throes of social change, at a time when the school system has become too large an institution and is literally overrun with a mix of young people from inconsistent social backgrounds. This is a difficult circumstance. The pressure of these forces exhausts the strength of the high school as an institution.[6]

Similarly, the National Panel on High Schools and Adolescent Education concluded that the U.S. high school was failing to respond to the needs of individual students:

[T]he high school is increasingly ill-matched to many, possibly a growing majority, of its present adolescent population who are either too old or too mature to live under the routine controls and strictures of a large high school without serious disturbances to them and to the school.[7]

Ronald Gross and Paul Osterman, noting widespread student disruptions in high schools by 1970, observed that the three most troublesome issues were racism, authoritarianism, and the irrelevance of curriculum and instruction. They concluded:

The ideas . . . that study involves devoting one-self to boring or uninteresting subjects of the teacher's choosing, that good grades equal good education, and that studying hard to pass an exam is a worthwhile expenditure of energy and spirit—all are typical of the ideas which inform most high school curricula. Equally outdated is the idea that there is a given body of knowledge all students should learn. . . . Students are insisting that the curricula grow out of their own interests and concerns, that they be permitted to choose which path to learning to take.[8]

In contrast to the reports of the 1970s, which faulted schools because they did not provide curricula that evolved from students' needs, interests, and concerns, the reports of the past 18 months fault the schools because they do not have sufficiently rigorous requirements, are mediocre (and worse) in the quality of teachers and teaching, are not educating workers adequately, and are doing an especially poor job of teaching mathematics, science, and computer technology.

The reports of the Seventies recognized that both society and schooling had changed and were continuing to change. The various commissions were much more concerned with the broader context of schooling and of school climate as these affected the quality of life and education in schools. By contrast, the recent reports tend not to discuss societal changes, seeming to argue that a consideration of such factors affecting student behavior and performance is simply an abrogation of the school's responsibility.

Despite differences in focus, methods of inquiry, data bases, and recommendations, the reports of the last year and a half have a number of topics in common. Though the recommendations of the various reports do not always agree, the general emphases are quite similar: raising standards of achievement, promoting excellence, and re-building public confidence in the schools.

## Excellence and Equity

The charge to the National Commission on Excellence in Education included the mandate that it "do all other things needed to define the problems of and the barriers to attaining greater levels of excellence in American education."[9] What the Commission and similar groups have done to operationalize the definition of excellence is to recommend, among other things, raising standards (not always clearly defined); setting high requirements for high school graduation and admission to college; eliminating "soft" subjects and mandating a common core curriculum for all students; increasing requirements in mathematics, science, and foreign languages, testing achievement more regularly; lengthening the school day and the school year; and generally "getting tough" with students, teachers, and even administrators.

Many of the reports of the Eighties assert a strong commitment to excellence and equity, usually by stating that raising standards need not mean lessening the commitment to provide high-quality education to a very diverse student population. As the National Commission on Excellence in Education puts it: "The twin goals of equity and high-quality schooling have profound and practical meaning for our economy and society, and we cannot permit one to yield to the other either in principle or practice."[10]

Understandably, considering the billions of dollars that have been spent in an attempt to raise the levels of verbal and mathematical literacy of *all* students to acceptable minimum standards, many educators are concerned that the new "get tough" approach to excellence will jeopardize the drive for educational equity. The *Paideia Proposal,* for example, recommends that "instruction in mathematics, beginning with simple arithmetic in the first grade, should rise to at least one year of calculus."[11] Teachers who have struggled to instill in their students even the most elementary competence in mathematics may not be inclined to accept the notion that all students can master even one year of calculus. Many would not agree with Dennis Gray that: "When schools fail, the chief missing ingredient—the necessary, but absent wherewithall—is will: the will to set goals, the will to say what is essential, the will to reduce or abandon what is not, the will to do what reform-oriented research dictates."[12] Most reform reports seem to assert that excellence is simply a product of will.

Although reports that treat the issue of excellence versus equity all agree that both goals must be pursued simultaneously, achievement of both goals continues to present a challenge. The New York State Board of Regents' *Action Plan,* for instance, was sharply criticized at 10 regional hearings for ignoring the needs of disadvantaged and underachieving students, as well as academically gifted ones. The *Action Plan* continued the efforts of the Regents to raise standards and levels of expectation while simultaneously trying "to ensure equal access through special assistance to those in need."[13] Critics argued that the Regents-endorsed requirements for the high school diploma were so rigid that only college-bound students could meet them; they feared that the higher standards would increase the dropout rate, as students, unable to meet the stiffer requirements, would withdraw from school. Supporters claimed that all students like a challenge and that all could rise to meet the requirements.

## Goals and Objectives

Most of the reports agree that U.S. schools continue to try to do too much, responding to too many requests from diverse sources. Both John Goodlad and Ernest Boyer use the same phrase—"We want it all!"—to describe what Americans want from their schools. Goodlad recalls that, at the 1965 White House Conference on Education, Vice President Hubert Humphrey said that our country "would go down in history for having used its educational system to overcome problems of illiteracy, unemployment, crime and violence, urban decay, and even war among nations."[14] A few years later, Goodlad notes, some began to doubt whether the schools could even teach children to read, write, and spell.

Several of the reports suggest essential goals for American schools—some as specific as the proposal by the Twentieth Century Fund Task Force that "the federal government clearly state that the most important objective of elementary and secondary education in the United States is the development of literacy in the English language."[15] Goodlad observes that "we are not without goals for schooling. But we are lacking an articulation of them and commitment to them."[16]

A dozen years ago, Charles Silberman criticized the schools for their "mindlessness." The reports of the 1970s called for clarification of goals and objectives and proposed aims that were broader and more encompassing than those suggested in the past year. However, both sets of reports agree that schools are burdened with responsibilities that they cannot fulfill, and both recommend that the goals of schooling be limited. The reports of the Eighties tend to recommend that the schools set more traditional goals—essentially those that dominated the high school curriculum of the first third of this century, those that have continued to be viewed as the college-preparatory program, and those to which schools were called to return in the late 1950s.

## The Curriculum

The reports of the Eighties give very specific attention to matters of curriculum, standards, teaching, and testing, but their specific recommendations tend to equate curriculum with subjects to be studied. Several reports explicitly recommend that all students complete a common core of prescribed subjects; that students be required to take more mathematics and science, as well as more English, social studies, and foreign languages; that fewer electives be allowed; and that students be tested more frequently to assess achievement.

It is in the area of prescribed curricula and more rigorous courses that the current reports differ most from those of the 1970s. The key words in the reports of the Seventies were *electives, options,* and *alternatives.* As the Kettering Commission put it, "The variety of alternative schools in American education will be limited only by the legitimate needs of adolescents and the vivacity of imagination of educational plan-

ners."[17] That Commission argued that "the reform of secondary education will be meaningless unless the focus . . . becomes the needs of students rather than the desires and interests of competing members of high school staffs."[18]

*The Paideia Proposal* offers a single curriculum for all students, K-12. *A Nation at Risk* proposes "five new basics" that specify the number of years of English, mathematics, social studies, science, and computer science to be required through four years of high school. In addition, two years of foreign language study are recommended for the college-bound. Goodlad returns to the " 'five fingers' of human knowledge and experience" of the Harvard Report, *General Education in a Free Society,* and suggests the proportion of total instructional time to be allocated to each area. Boyer details his priorities for the curriculum, giving highest priority to mastery of English followed by a core of common learning that he regards as basic for all students. Sizer would organize the high school into four areas or large departments. The Twentieth Century Fund recommends literacy in the English language as the most important area of study. The College Board report details what college-bound students should know and be able to do. The National Science Board Commission outlines a K-12 curriculum in mathematics, science, and technology. The Education Commission of the States urges that the curriculum be strengthened by eliminating soft, nonessential courses; encouraging mastery of skills beyond the basics; and enlivening and improving instruction in the remaining subjects.

Although his report recommends a common curriculum and the allocation of time to various subjects, Goodlad also describes the current press for curriculum reform as follows:

> The "obvious" and "logical" solutions to the schools' curricular inadequacies being bandied about today are those that were most frequently bandied about yesterday and the day before that.

Essentially, they involve a "get tough" approach combined with a dose of elitism. Course requirements in basic subjects are to be extended; textbooks are to become "harder," with less watering down to the lowest common denominators of student abilities.[19]

In short, most of the new wave of reports propose the standard college-bound program with few or no electives and little curricular differentiation, a common curriculum to be taken by all students. Most of the reports recognize the notion of individual differences but recommend that such differences are to be accommodated pedagogically, not by curricular differentiation.

## Tracking

In his 1959 report on the American high school, James Bryant Conant recommended that tracking be abolished but that students be grouped subject by subject. In the past 18 months, Adler, Boyer, and Goodlad have all attacked the practice of tracking and, in fact, any kind of grouping whatsoever. To Goodlad, tracking precludes equal access to knowledge, especially for poor and minority students, who are usually relegated to lower tracks. Tracking, says Goodlad, divides students into two kinds of people: "head oriented" and "hand oriented." Adler calls tracking "an abominable discrimination." Boyer recommends that tracking be abolished in favor of a single track; students would tackle the core courses in the common curriculum in different ways, though the basic content would be the same for all.

Few of the reports deal with the education of gifted and talented students, other than to note that many schools have used various forms of grouping to offer differentiated curricula for the gifted. Adler would not make any curricular distinctions for the gifted but would have them tutor their fellow students who are not learning as rapidly. While recommending the elimination of tracking, Boyer suggests that "every high school have special arrangements for gifted students—credit by examination, independent study, or special study with universities."[20] Boyer also recommends magnet schools and even a network of residential academies in science, mathematics, or other fields.

## Vocational Education

Development of an effective work-study policy for all students was a consistent theme of the reports of the 1970s. For example, *Youth: Transition to Adulthood* suggested a number of alternatives for mixing education and work. The U.S. Office of Education panel recommended that all youngsters be provided with actual jobs through programs that would emphasize job knowledge, on-the-job training, and occupational citizenship. The National Manpower Institute proposed that actual work or service experience become an integral part of all education. Now, in *High School,* Boyer proposes a "new Carnegie unit" that would require all students to spend 30 hours per year working in the community or school.

Boyer describes vocational education as an unfulfilled promise in America's high schools. Vocational education programs, he says, are limited by a lack of modern, adequate instructional resources and an inability to keep up with shifting patterns of employment in the workplace. Moreover, Boyer fears that vocational education students are being short-changed academically—acquiring job training at the cost of high-quality academic study.

Goodlad criticizes vocational education for the same reasons, as well as for the fact that poor and minority students are overrepresented in vocational training classes. Goodlad found the anachronistic nature of much vocational training depressing; he argues that all students should be involved in a common curriculum that would provide them with equal access to knowledge, as well as "the development of a mature perspective on careers, career choice, and bases of career decision making."[21] Adler sees absolutely no place in the common school for specific job training and believes that a sound general education is the best vocational education.

Implicitly or explicitly, the reports of the Eighties call for major changes in vocational education—in the student populations served, the curriculum and instruction provided, and the sites of such education. By proposing a common core curriculum with few, if any, electives or options, the reformers are asserting that a sound general/liberal education is the best vocational/specialized education, that all students need career orientation but not job-specific training, that career orientation is best undertaken in experience-based internships, and that equity is better achieved through such approaches than through a vocational education that creates a second-class citizenry. On the other hand, though vocational educators accept some elements of these proposals, they regard them as dangerous and prone to inequity; they argue that the vocational experience keeps large numbers of students in school and provides them with meaningful academic experiences.

## Technology

The reports of the Seventies scarcely mentioned the growth in technology, but the concept figures prominently in several of the reports of the past year. Some reports deal with technology as a subject to be studied, some as an instructional aid, others as a teaching resource. The College Board report observes that the "revolution in communications and information technology is making the computer a basic tool for acquiring information, organizing systems, and solving problems."[22] College-bound students should have a basic knowledge of how computers work.

They should also be able to use computers for self-instruction, collecting and retrieving information, word processing, modeling, doing simulations, and problem solving. The National Commission on Excellence in Education proposes a half-year of computer science as one of its "five new basics."

The reports of Goodlad's observers caused him to ask how the schools managed to shield themselves so effectively from the technological revolution. He believes that students must become functionally literate in their understanding and use of computers. The National Science Board Commission linked mathematics, science, and technology as basic study areas. The Education Commission of the States proposed computer literacy as one of the basic skills needed for productive employment. Adler and the Paideia group "embrace" the new technologies; they believe that, since computers will soon be found in many homes and workplaces, they should also be present in schools and classrooms. Boyer discusses learning about, learning with, and learning from computers; he also discusses computers as teaching and learning resources.

Although the reports seem to agree on the need for computer literacy for all, the notion of what constitutes computer literacy differs and, in some reports, is quite vague. The imminence of a high-tech society seems to be generally accepted, but, despite the enthusiastic treatment of computers in several reports, the implications for education and training seem ill-considered.

## Time

In comparing the U.S. with England and other industrialized countries, *A Nation at Risk* noted that those nations have a much longer school day (eight hours as compared with six in the U.S.) and longer school years (220 days as compared with 180). The recommendation of the National Commission is that more time should be devoted to learning the "five new basics" and that this will require more effective use of the existing day or a longer school day or year.

Goodlad recommended a 25-hour instructional week instead of the present 22½-hour week, but he pointed out that establishing a single target for time use probably would be less constructive than initiating a process of improvement in each school. Goodlad would opt for more efficient use of the hours now available rather than poor use of a greater number of hours. Boyer would not make lengthening the school year a high priority for school reform. "The urgent need is not more time but better use of time," he says.[23] Sizer would discourage the use of time as the standard and would give "room to teachers and students to work and learn in their own appropriate ways."[24] In fact, Sizer strongly recommends that mastery of material, not investment of time, be the basis for graduation from high school.

The Education Commission of the States proposes that schools "should *increase both the duration and intensity of academic learning,*" using the existing day more effectively but considering lengthening it as well.[25] Some reports suggest using a longer school year as a means of extending teachers' contracts and enabling both staff development and curriculum development to occur. In some ways, the reports seem to misapprehend the concept of time-on-task, which does not suggest a direct relationship between quantity of time and student engagement or achievement. Instructional time can be used more efficiently and effectively, but simply lengthening the school day or the school year is hardly likely to have the desired results.

## Teachers and Teaching

The reports of the Eighties seem to agree that teachers and teaching are central to the crisis in education. *A Nation at Risk,* for instance, reports that "not enough of the academically able students are being attracted to teaching; that teacher preparation programs need substantial improvement; that the professional working life of teachers is on the whole unacceptable; and that a serious shortage of teachers exists in key fields."[26]

Boyer takes the position that, while teachers are blamed for much of what is wrong with schools, the quality of education cannot be improved without the help of the teachers already in the nation's classrooms. Teachers must be viewed, he says, "as part of the solution, not the problem." Like other authors, Boyer finds that "the teacher's world is often frustrating, frequently demeaning, and sometimes dangerous."[27]

Sizer calls his book, *Horace's Compromise,* a celebration of the work of the classroom teacher; "its primary recommendation," he says, "is that America restore to teachers and to their particular students the largest share of responsibility for the latter's education."[28] Sizer is convinced that there are many good teachers in the classrooms but that too many of them are demoralized and frustrated in their efforts to teach effectively. Goodlad found that the large majority of the teachers in his study "tended to be idealistic and altruistic in their views of why they chose to teach."[29] Once in the schools, however, they encountered many realities not conducive to professional growth. Boyer, Goodlad, and Sizer all suggest that the instructional time of teachers be reduced, that the number of students they teach be reduced sharply, and that school-based programs for curricular and instructional improvement be initiated by the entire staff.

*A Nation at Risk* includes seven recommendations aimed at improving the preparation of teachers and making teaching "a more rewarding and respected profession." These include: raising the standards for admission to teacher education programs; increasing salaries of teachers to make them "professionally competitive, market sensitive, and performance-based"; providing an 11-month contract for teachers for professional and curriculum development; developing career ladders; employing substantial nonschool personnél resources to solve problems of shortages in key fields; providing grants and loans to attract outstanding students into teaching; and involving master teachers in designing teacher preparation programs and supervising new teachers.

Variations of these same recommendations appear in other reports. Adler, for example, would have prospective teachers follow the curriculum of *The Paideia Proposal* at the college level. Boyer would have them take a liberal arts curriculum with a bare minimum of pedagogical training. Several reports would reduce or eliminate much of the professional component of teacher education and focus on liberal arts preparation with a concentration (or major) in one discipline, together with a supervised teaching experience. Although these reports never define "excellence in teaching," they imply that excellent teaching results in high academic achievement by students. Thus the recommendations reopen the debate regarding the balance between the liberal/general education and the technical/professional education of the teacher and the nature and quality of the research base on which teacher education programs are or might be developed. In taking the position that teacher preparation and certification, especially for high school teachers, should focus on subject matter and that persons who are "well prepared" in subject-matter areas should be permitted to teach, even though they have little or no pedagogical training, the reformers are not proposing a new style of teacher preparation and certification but are once again reviving a position that has been advocated many times before. Even the recent attention to "competency-based teacher education" that was so popular among state education departments in the 1970s has apparently been overshadowed by the proposals for teacher education programs and certification based on subject-matter achievement. Whatever approaches are used for teacher preparation and certification, the reports agree that continuing education or inservice education is essential for staff development. Beyond the agreement that continuing education must be an integral part of professional development, however, there is little agreement on the nature of such education, where and how it should take place, under whose auspices, and under what conditions.

The recent studies of schooling have given new life to ideas for merit pay, differentiated pay, career ladders, and master teachers, as well as increased salaries for all teachers. Moreover, the studies indicate that factors which enable teachers to teach and students to learn in a safe, dynamic environment are at least as important as better salaries in making teaching a rewarding and respected profession.

## School Principal

Both Boyer and Goodlad discuss the pivotal role of the principal in effective schools. In Adler's view, the principal differs from other school administrators in that he or she must facilitate the main business of the school; teaching and learning. The ECS Task Force recommends that "the principal should be freed from distractions; encouraged to give priority to improving classroom instruction; given sufficient discretion over personnel and fiscal planning; and put squarely in charge of maintaining the school's morale, discipline, and academic quality."[30]

Boyer and Sizer both feel that schools are top-heavy with administrators; they propose that principals be given greater authority over functions for which they have responsibility. Boyer recommends that in the areas of budget, discretionary funds for school improvement, monitoring and rewarding good teaching, and selection and retention of teachers, the school principal should become "not just the top authority but the key educator, too."

Goodlad suggests that "head teachers" be appointed as instructional leaders because they could serve as role models for teachers, they would have more expertise in the subject area than a generalist principal might have, and they would not have to evaluate teachers and would thus be closer to them. The ECS report recommends that "in many places, the prevailing definition of the principal's role must be changed to put the principal squarely in charge of educational quality in each school."[31]

## Business/School Partnerships

Several of the 1983 reports urge businesses to become more heavily involved in public school education. Boyer observes that corporations have traditionally remained aloof from the schools but have complained about the quality of education in those schools. He suggests that corporations might get involved by adopting schools; helping disadvantaged students; enriching the education of gifted and talented students; helping teachers by providing opportunities for summer employment, inservice education, and mini-grants for innovative projects; helping students connect school and work; and providing management and leadership training for school staffs. The Business-Higher Education Forum focused its entire report on forging new partnerships between business and higher education. The Education Commission of the States called for a new alliance among educators, business, labor, and other groups to set educational goals and assist schools in attaining them.

## REFLECTING ON THE REPORTS

We must ask two kinds of questions about all of these recent reports *as policy documents:* 1) Do they have the situation right; that is, are their descriptions of U.S. education accurate? 2) Are their recommendations sound, and do they derive from data? Responding to these questions is difficult because of the natural tendency of educators to become defensive and to pick apart the analyses as being biased and inaccurate, since the data or descriptions rarely match their own situations and settings. This lack of compatibility with one's own perception of the state of things is quite understandable; obviously, commissions must deal with the generality that is "American education" or "the American high school." In addition, in order to make their case, most committees tend to stress negative points or problem areas. For example, the National Commission on Excellence in Education was "created as a result of the Secretary's concern about 'the widespread public perception that something is seriously remiss in our educational system.' "[32] The Commission identified the dimensions of risk and presumably based its recommendations on its findings. As with most reports, the analysis of the situation and the recommendations proposed tend to be controversial.

As for the recommendations, though they are proposed with conviction and readers are urged to see that they are implemented forthwith, in fact that is neither desirable nor possible. Many of the recommendations simply cannot be implemented but can serve to stimulate thoughtful reflection, study, and planning. It is easy, for instance, to mandate the "five new basics," as the National Commission did, but a school would still be forced to design improved curricula in order for the mandate to make any significant improvement in the quality of instruction. After all, four years of English can range widely in terms of the nature of the content, instructional strategies, and the like. It is not as if English is English is English.

Stedman and Smith criticize the reports for proposing "simplistic" recommendations without considering their ramifications: "[The reports] proposed increasing time without altering pedagogy, instituting merit schemes without describing procedures, and adopting the 'new basics' without changing old definitions."[33] With rare exceptions, a commission cannot provide adequate curricular and instructional specificity and cannot do more than urge staff development and curriculum development that might result in the qualitative changes intended.

## Urban Schools and the Poor

One recurrent criticism of the reports of the Seventies was that they seemed to be based on a high school population that was white, middle class, male, and suburban. Although some of Boyer's and Goodlad's schools were certainly urban, the reports of the Eighties, even more than the earlier ones, fail to attend to the particular problems and needs of schools with large populations of poor and minority children.

For more than two decades, urban schools in particular have been engaged in compensatory education aimed at insuring equality of educational opportunity for disadvantaged students. Though these programs have brought about a discernible improvement, if there is a real crisis in education, it is in the urban schools. The levels of literacy and numeracy among students in urban schools tend, for the most part, to fall below those of the nation's schools in general and probably account for a sizable share of the National Commission's perception of risk. Some urban schools are "effective," of course, but they are far too small in number to justify ignoring the needs of poor and minority students.

The implicit assumption in many of these reports is that disadvantaged youngsters are really no different from other students and to believe otherwise is both anti-intellectual and anti-democratic. However, the basic concept of compensatory education is to design curricula, instructional strategies, educational resources, and

school climates that will stimulate both affective and cognitive development. Simply recommending that school personnel get tougher, stiffen academic demands, and crack down on discipline problems without effecting necessary changes in pedagogy, curriculum, and personnel is an inadequate solution.

A related concern for all U.S. schools—but particularly for urban schools—is the issue of bilingual education. Only one report addresses this topic. The Twentieth Century Fund Task Force recommends that the federal government clearly assert that the development of English literacy is the most important objective for elementary and secondary schools; the Task Force also recommends that bilingual education funds be used instead to teach English to non-English speakers. This recommendation ignores both the problems that bilingual eduation attempts to address and the current policies, which are based on legislation, judicial decisions, and research.

## Excellence and Standards

*A Nation at Risk* defined excellence at three levels: the individual learner, the school, and the society. "Excellence" has become the shibboleth of the day. The term has come to mean "higher standards," which are defined as tougher academic requirements, reduction or elimination of electives (which are viewed as "soft subjects"), more mathematics and science, more homework, more tests, tighter discipline, longer school days and school years. Chester Finn observes that most of the current "efforts to improve educational quality are universalistic, scholiocentric, and cognitive. They unabashedly assume that everyone can and should learn the same things, at least up to a point, and that that point should be the same for everyone in a school, a community, or an entire state."[34]

In fact, the debate over "excellence" simply reopens the ideological schism between those who believe that there is a common culture to be transmitted to all through a common curriculum and those who believe in individualized, differentiated programs focused on students' needs. This grossly oversimplified statement of the issue might also be viewed as the difference between the *Report of the Committee of Ten* in 1893 and the *Cardinal Principles of Secondary Education* in 1918.

The reports force us to raise a number of questions: Are a common curriculum and uniform requirements appropriate in a pluralistic society? Can a common curriculum and uniform standards be implemented effectively with diverse groups of students? Should uniform standards be our goal? Can individual differences be accommodated? Should they be? Adler cites Robert Maynard Hutchins's assertion that "the best education for the best is the best education for all" and proposes common goals and a common curriculum for all. He and other reformers challenge those who believe that differentiated programs and services are necessary if we are to be, in the words of the Educational Policies Commission, "up to the weighty task of giving life to the great ideal of educational opportunity for the varied children of a heterogeneous people."[35]

The concept of excellence being used by current reformers is different from that espoused by John Gardner in "The Pursuit of Excellence: Education and the Future of America" and in his 1961 classic, *Excellence*. Gardner urged that we avoid the adoption of a narrow and constricted view of excellence but that we embrace many kinds of achievement at many levels; that excellence be recognized as a product of ability, motivation, and character, not native ability alone; and that judgments of differences in talent be recognized as not being judgments of differences in human worth. Gardner argued:

> It is possible for us to cultivate the ideal of excellence while retaining the moral values of equality. . . . Our society will have passed an important milestone of maturity when those who are the most enthusiastic proponents of a democratic way of life are also the most vigorous proponents of excellence.[36]

## Teaching and Learning

If we accept the sad diagnoses concerning the sorry state of American education in the 1980s, then many of the recommendations for improvement must be regarded as simplistic, conservative, and unrealistic, even though their tone is one of great earnestness and urgency. With few exceptions, the reports focus on the high schools, paying little or no attention to early childhood and elementary education as they prepare (or fail to prepare) youths for the "five new basics" and the rigorous courses they are to take at the secondary level. *The Paideia Proposal* and the report of the National Science Board Commission are concerned with a K–12 program, and Goodlad studied some elementary and junior high schools. For the most part, however, most of the recommendations are weakened by their failure to attend to the entire spectrum of education.

The curricular recommendations of the reports call to mind the traditional college preparatory program prior to World War II, when colleges began dropping foreign language and other requirements. With the exception of Sizer's report, the studies revive and revise the "old" Carnegie unit, recommending that graduation requirements and admissions standards be based on years of study or numbers of units. Sizer proposes that exhibitions of mastery—not numbers of units or years of study—become the basis for a high school diploma.

Naturally, the reports do not spell out the substance or content of the core curricula they propose. Students may take more mathematics, science, or other subjects without substantially improving their level of achievement. The most difficult part of reforming the schools is developing curricula that are more appropriate for the 21st century, designing instructional strategies for implementing such curricula, and educating and recruiting teachers capable of teaching such curricula. Recommending more of everything is not enough.

The recommendations concerning mathematics and science are not surprising. Students should have more of these subjects, for longer periods of time, taught by better teachers. And extra resources should be provided to upgrade instruction in these areas for *all* students, not only for the gifted and talented.

But having agreed to so much does little to answer the barrage of questions that logically follows. Can more study in mathematics and science be demanded without building the skills required for more advanced study in those areas? Will there be a cost in terms of instruction in the humanities? In the arts? In citizenship? If so, should we be concerned? In short, should we be concerned about curricular balance, and, if so, what is the nature of that balance? Is a balanced curriculum the same for all, as *The Paideia Proposal* asserts? Is Boyer right in advocating the elimination of vocational education courses that seek to teach "marketable skills" but lack intellectual substance? Will career education prove the basis for an effective policy on education for work? A rethinking of vocational/career education is long overdue. But we cannot simply return to the traditional academic subjects—or can we?

Marvin Lazarson believes that critics of what has been called the smorgasbord or cafeteria approach to curriculum have forced us to look more carefully at the purposes of schooling. However, he warns that too often the debates about a core curriculum ask the wrong questions: "Most of all . . . debates about a core curriculum which concentrate on what students are taking rather than how much and how well they are learning will fail to enhance either the commitment to learning or learning itself."[37]

## School Climate and Environment

Much has been written recently about schools as communities and about the quality of life in those communities. Some high schools are depicted as prisons, others as combat zones, and still others as thriving, living communities in which real learning occurs. But schools can be all of these things and much more.

Considerable attention has been given to improving school discipline, so that teaching and learning can proceed without hindrance. School violence and vandalism, absenteeism and truancy, and class cutting were all cited as significant problems more than a decade ago; they were even the focus of congressional investigations and National Institute of Education studies. A decade ago, there were calls for lowering the age of compulsory attendance in order to improve the climate for learning. The Kettering Commission urged that "by the age of 14, a student who has not developed some motivation toward learning is not likely to profit from compulsory schooling. Secondary education must drop its custodial burdens."[38] Several of the recent reports recommend tightening discipline in the schools, and the Reagan Administration is giving this problem high priority—including studying ways of altering civil rights legislation that the Administration believes is hampering school officials' ability to deal with discipline.

Gerald Grant's report focuses on how schools create different kinds of ethos or climates. In his view, the central problem is one of "how we reconstitute the necessary intellectual and moral authority without which schools cannot function while preserving the gains we achieved in fashioning a more equitable and just system. . . ."[39] Grant points out that schools educate emotions as well as intellect. New curricular requirements introduced without attending to the climate of the classroom and the school are hardly likely to bring about significant reform.

## The Changing Nature of Teaching

The reports of the Eighties seldom recognize that teachers and teaching have changed over the past two or three decades. A number of writers have pointed out that the women's movement has recently opened up professional opportunities previously unavailable to women. Thus classroom teaching is no longer the attractive option it once was for educated women. The pool of women candidates for teaching has been reduced as professional choices for women have broadened.

The growth of "teacher militancy," which has led to bargaining and negotiating a wide variety of terms and conditions beyond salary issues, has also changed the nature of the teaching profession. The growth of accountability systems, competency-based teacher education programs, and testing programs aimed at both students and teachers has affected the conditions of teaching and learning. Grant asserts that "the spread of children's rights literature through the secondary schools has been one of the great untold curriculum stories of the last decade," contributing, he believes, to "a collapse of adult authority as representing a standard for all children."[40]

Most of the recommendations regarding teachers and their education have a very familiar ring to them: recruit a greater number of academically able people into teacher education programs, give them a liberal arts education with depth in one discipline, deemphasize pedagogical or professional education, alter the credentialing process so that specialists not trained in education can teach, teach "methods" through supervised internships, institute merit pay, and develop career ladders. Even the recommendations of more time for staff development and curriculum development are not new. Unfortunately, such proposals do not address the central problems involved in making teaching a more respected and more rewarding profession. Nor do they take account of the many sources of the satisfactions derived from teaching. There is

a very real danger that legislators, state education departments, and schools of education will implement these recommendations piecemeal, without coming to grips with the central problems of the profession of teaching.

## Education in and out of School

In 1975 the California RISE Commission rejected what it called the traditional view of schooling, "restricted to a piece of real estate where licensed adults teach and students passively learn during specified times of the day." The RISE Commission projected instead "a school system that takes place at many times and places in which both adults and young people work as teachers and learners . . . [one] that attracts, motivates, and satisfies young people."[41] This proposal recognized that education and socialization take place in a variety of settings other than the place called school. As a way of formalizing the relationships of schools and communities, Boyer proposes a "new" Carnegie unit to consist of 30 hours per year of voluntary service in the school or in the community for four years.

With the exception of the National Science Board Commission, the current reports scarcely take up the implications of education in nonschool settings, except to mention home computers and television. The National Science Board Commission observes: "Much that affects the quality of formal education occurs outside the classroom and beyond the control of the school—a great deal of learning takes place unintentionally and unconsciously through casual reading and experiences."[42] This report suggests that school learnings be reinforced by a wide range of activities: "Youth organizations, museums, broadcasters, and other agents of informal education should cooperate with school districts and each other to provide a rich environment for early and continued learning and motivation outside the schools."[43]

## Intrinsic Value of Education

What seems to be missing from many reports is a meaningful discussion of the intrinsic worth of education—the pleasure of learning, the affective aspects of learning, the building of polity and community. As in the post-Sputnik era, when the primary purpose of schools was seen as helping to meet the nation's needs for specialized manpower and skilled workers, the current emphasis is on producing workers who will enable the U.S. to compete industrially and commercially with other nations. True, the National Commission on Excellence in Education asserted its concern for "the intellectual, moral, and spiritual strengths of our people, which knit together the very fabric of our society."[44] But recommendations dealing with those concerns are hard to find. Goodlad found very little of "anything designed to deliberately cultivate the values and skills of constructive social interaction and group accomplishment," values we extol as characteristic of our people.[45] Goodlad was not hopeful that much moral and ethical learning could come from schooling.

In raising questions about the intrinsic worth of education, one need not denigrate cognitive and academic aims. Rather, asking such questions should remind us that learning that is exciting and satisfying *has* an intrinsic worth. Such learning is more than an accumulation of subjects to be studied and courses to be taken. It also includes the interpersonal relationships, the formal and informal learning opportunities, and the sheer pleasures that can be ours in a "learning society." This notion of learning is missing from the arguments put forth by most of the reports: that excellence means high academic achievement and nothing else.

## REFORMING AMERICA'S SCHOOLS

In summing up the prospects for reform in the mid-Seventies, I observed that "the education professions and general citizenry have never faced such a plethora of commission and panel reports as they do presently. Their number alone might be sufficient basis for immobilizing those individuals who would like to change the high schools."[46] Perhaps I spoke too soon. The reports currently available outnumber those of the 1970s by better than two to one. The National Commission on Excellence in Education noted that it was "not the first or only commission on education, and some of our findings are surely not new, but old business that now at last must be done. For no one can doubt that the United States is now under challenge from many quarters."[47]

The various reports urge a wide variety of persons and institutions to become concerned and involved with education and school reform. The National Commission urges students and parents to join "faculty members and administrators, along with policy makers and the mass media" in an effort to reform the education system. No report is more specific than the National Science Board Commission, which details specific responsibilities of government agencies, private corporations and foundations, the states, and other groups in its plan to improve mathematics, science, and technology education by 1995. For the most part, however, the recommendations are essentially policy concepts that must be implemented at many different levels by many different agents.

Despite the assertions of several reports, American schools remain diverse on all the dimensions of schooling and education—ecology, climate, relationships, nature and quality of instruction, school/community interactions, personnel and material resources, and more. Some schools have already achieved equity and excellence, while others have attained neither. Some schools seem to be constantly engaged in a process of self-renewal, while others have never begun. Some schools would have to do relatively little to implement most of the recommendations of the reports, while others probably could not implement any of the recommendations in full, even with herculean efforts.

Some recommendations, such as mandating a common core curriculum, can be implemented by a single school or school system; others, such as changes in teacher education and certification, would probably require action at the state level. Still other recommendations, such as establishing research and development centers to improve mathematics, science, and technology education, would probably require joint federal, state, foundation, and—possibly—corporate funding.

A quarter of a century ago, in *The American High School Today,* Conant made 21 recommendations that served as a checklist for improving the nation's comprehensive high schools. Gardner called *The American High School Today* a "down-to-earth report" aimed at individuals who were ready to roll up their sleeves and say: "[W]hat can we do tomorrow morning to improve our schools?"[48] Few reform reports have ever been as clearly focused and as specific with recommendations that could be readily implemented by every high school. Few if any of Conant's recommendations were radical proposals.

Paul Peterson has argued that national commissions "do have their functions in American politics, but fact-finding, rigorous analysis, and policy development are usually not among them. Commissions are more appropriate for dramatizing an issue, resolving political differences, and reassuring the public that questions are being thoughtfully considered."[49] As with earlier reports, most of the current reports do not reflect what has been learned in the past two or three decades about how institutions change— or do not change. A good many studies during that time have focused on the processes whereby changes are likely to occur in schools and classrooms, and there is some knowledge base that reformers might use. At a minimum, we know that exhortation, however strongly worded, is not likely to produce change.

Although some common themes and topics recur in the many 1983 reports, the recommendations are not uniform and congruent. Sometimes they conflict with one another or deal with different aspects of education and schooling. How then do the various publics deal with these disparities? Do they attempt to implement only those on which there is consensus?

The reforms that take place in the near future may actually be larger and effected more quickly than those recommended by commissions of the past. A combination of factors, including the current political climate and the fact that the media have already made education a hot item, make such sweeping and rapid change possible. Every state has committees, commissions, and panels at work considering various kinds of educational reform, and policy mandates and legislation implementing at least the simplest of the recommendations will almost certainly follow. Whether these reforms will lead to significant improvements in the quality of education in schools and classrooms is, of course, another question. The era of curriculum innovation that followed the launching of Sputnik ultimately did not result in the radical changes that had been intended and anticipated.

The media and most of the reports themselves call for "radical reform"—massive, not incremental. The current crop of proposals can once again mobilize the various groups, agencies, and institutions to assess their own programs and operations, using the reports as a guide. There are different demands made on leaders at the local, system, state, and federal levels; in the public and private sectors; and in the educational and noneducational components. Leaders at each level must start their self-studies and relate them to other levels. Everyone is in on the act, but everyone's act is different. The National Commission is right when it declares that all of us have a role to play in reforming our schools and our society. Reforming schools, however, is very different from reforming society. Yet both must occur simultaneously if real reform of the education system is to take place. A combination of factors and events have made possible significant change in the processes of education and schooling. Whether those reforms will actually occur and whether they will actually be improvements is difficult to discern. The history of educational reform is not encouraging, but perhaps this time things will be different.

# ENDNOTES

1. National Commission on Excellence in Education, *A Nation at Risk* (Washington, D.C.: U. S. Government Printing Office, 1983), p. 1.
2. Harold Howe II, "Education Moves to Center Stage: An Overview of Recent Studies," *Phi Delta Kappan,* November 1983, p. 168.
3. Diane Ravitch, *The Troubled Crusade: American Education 1945–1980* (New York: Basic Books, 1983), p. xii.
4. Lawrence C. Stedman and Marshall S. Smith, "Recent Reform Proposals for American Education," *Contemporary Education Review,* in press.
5. Paul E. Peterson, "Did the Education Commissions Say Anything?," *Brookings Review,* vol. 2, 1983, p. 4.
6. B. Frank Brown, chairman, National Commission on the Reform of Secondary Education, *The Reform of Secondary Education* (New York: McGraw-Hill, 1973). p. 10.
7. John Henry Martin, chairman, National Panel on High School and Adolescent Education. *The Education of Adolescents* (Washington, D.C.: U.S. Government Printing Office, 1976), p. 37.
8. Ronald Gross and Paul Osterman, *High School* (New York: Simon and Schuster, 1971), p. 13.
9. National Commission on Excellence in Education, p. 40.
10. Ibid., p. 13.
11. Mortimer J. Adler, *The Paideia Proposal* (New York: Macmillan, 1982), p. 24.
12. Dennis Gray, "The 1980s: Season for High School Reform," *Educational Leadership,* May 1982, p. 568.
13. New York State Education Department, *Proposed Action Plan to Improve Elementary and Secondary Education Results in New York* (Albany: New York State Education Department, 1983), p. 2.
14. John I. Goodlad, *A Place Called School: Prospects for the Future* (New York: McGraw-Hill, 1983), p. 33.
15. Twentieth Century Fund Task Force on Federal Elementary and Secondary Education Policy, *Making the Grade* (New York: Twentieth Century Fund, 1983), p. 11.
16. Goodlad, p. 56.
17. Brown, p. 101.
18. Ibid., p. 41.
19. Goodlad, p. 291.
20. Ernest L. Boyer, *High School* (New York: Harper & Row, 1983), p. 238.
21. Goodlad, p. 344.
22. College Board Educational EQuality Project, *Academic Preparation for College: What Students Need to Know and Be Able to Do* (New York: College Board, 1983), p. 11.
23. Boyer, p. 232.
24. Theodore R. Sizer, *Horace's Compromise: The Dilemma of the American High School* (Boston: Houghton Mifflin, 1984), p. 214.
25. Education Commission of the States Task Force on Education for Economic Growth, *Action for Excellence* (Denver: ECS, 1983), p. 38.
26. National Commission on Excellence in Education, p. 22.
27. Boyer, pp. 154–55.
28. Sizer, p. 4.
29. Goodlad, p. 173.
30. Education Commission of the States, p. 40.
31. Ibid.
32. National Commission on Excellence in Education, p. 1.
33. Stedman and Smith, p. 35.
34. Chester E. Finn, Jr., "The Drive for Educational Excellence," *Change,* April, 1983, p. 21.
35. Educational Policies Commission, *Public Education and the Future of America* (Washington D.C.: National Education Association, 1955), p. 24.
36. John Gardner, "The Pursuit of Excellence: Education and the Future of America," *Prospects for America: The Rockefeller Panel Reports* (Garden City, N.Y.: Doubleday, 1961), pp. 356–57.
37. Marvin Lazarson et al., *An Education of Value* (Cambridge, Mass.: unpublished manuscript,

Harvard University Graduate School of Education, 1983), p. 7.4.

**38.** Brown, pp. 41–42.

**39.** Gerald Grant, *Education, Character, and American Schools: Are Effective Schools Good Enough?* (Syracuse, N.Y.: unpublished manuscript, Syracuse University, 1982), p. 13.

**40.** Ibid.

**41.** California Commission for Reform of Intermediate and Secondary Education, *The RISE Report* (Sacramento: California Superintendent of Schools, 1975), p. 2.

**42.** National Science Board Commission on Precollege Education in Mathematics, Science, and Technology, *Educating Americans for the 21st*

*Century* (Washington, D.C.: U.S. Government Printing Office, 1983), p. 59.

**43.** Ibid.

**44.** National Commission on Excellence in Education, p. 7.

**45.** Goodlad, p. 241.

**46.** A. Harry Passow, *Secondary Education Reform: Retrospect and Prospect* (New York: Teachers College, Columbia University, 1976), p. 52.

**47.** National Commission on Excellence in Education, p. 36.

**48.** John Gardner, "Foreward," in James B. Conant, *The American High School Today* (New York: McGraw-Hill, 1959), p. xii.

**49.** Peterson, p. 11.

*A. Harry Passow* is Jacob H. Schiff Professor of Education, Teachers College, Columbia University.

# The Unfinished Agenda: Report from the National Commission on Secondary Vocational Education

## LINDA S. LOTTO

In the wake of numerous studies and commission reports, U.S. secondary education is in the grip of a back-to-basics movement. According to a November 1983 report to Secretary of Education Terrel Bell by the National Commission on Excellence in Education, 44 states have stiffened high school graduation requirements to include more mathematics, science, foreign language, English, social science, and computer education.[1] Forty-two states have initiated reforms in curriculum content, and 20 have moved to extend the school day or year. Secondary educators across the U.S. are striving to inject new rigor and higher standards into their programs.

However, consider the efficacy of these moves in light of some additional data.

- A recent study by the Philadelphia public schools suggests that "nearly two out of five Philadelphia students would be unable to meet a promotion standard that required them to read and compute at grade level."[2]
- Nationally, roughly 28% of youths of high school age never graduate.[3]

Excerpted from *Phi Delta Kappan* 66, No. 8 (April 1985): 568–573. Used by permission of the author and the publisher.

More than 25% of recent college graduates report that they are underemployed in their current jobs,[4] and this situation is likely to get worse instead of better.[5]

Simply put, the situation in U.S. public schools is more complicated than it may appear. Requiring additional and more rigorous courses is only part of the solution, for some of the students. To reflect this situation, the National Commission on Secondary Vocational Education has titled its report *The Unfinished Agenda*.

This Commission was appointed by the National Center for Research in Vocational Education at Ohio State University (and funded by the Office of Vocational and Adult Education of the U.S. Department of Education) to examine the role of secondary vocational education in the high school. The Commission had 14 members, who represented business, labor, and education. Harry Silberman of the Graduate School of Education at the University of California, Los Angeles, chaired the group. The Commission members held hearings and visited schools at 10 sites across the U.S., which put Commission members in contact with hundreds of individuals—parents, teachers, employers, students, and administrators. The Commission's report describes the promise of secondary vocational education and the problems to be addressed in fulfilling that promise; it also contains recommendations for action.

Reactions to *The Unfinished Agenda* will no doubt vary. The vocational education community will probably be gratified by the Commission's endorsement of its programs. Educators who support the view that U.S. education needs to emphasize the basics more strongly may be less supportive. Those who stand somewhere between these two extremes will probably find some brief observations on the report, drawn from research and practice, helpful to them in assessing both the extent of the problems identified by the Commission and the efficacy of its recommendations.

## THE PROMISE OF VOC ED

Unlike many of the earlier commission and task force reports, which painted an ominous picture of the state of secondary schooling in the U.S., the National Commission on Secondary Vocational Education has painted a picture of promise. The Commissioners feel that vocational education has for too long been relegated to the periphery of the high school curriculum, where it has served as a program of occupational skills training for students who plan to enter the labor market immediately after graduation. The commissioners are convinced that secondary vocational education can, and frequently does, offer much more. They see vocational education as capable of functioning coequally with academic education to serve the needs and interests of all high school students.

> Vocational education is both a body of knowledge and an educational process, but the educational process has not received the degree of attention it deserves. Vocational education's potential to respond to diverse learning styles has been underutilized.[6]

The Commission points out that vocational education courses provide opportunities for applied learning and individualized instruction. Most important, perhaps, vocational education is stimulating and relevant for students. Therefore, potential dropouts may find vocational education a powerful incentive to remain in school.

The evidence certainly suggests that high school students like vocational education, because they routinely enroll in vocational education courses. In 1982, for example, 95% of all graduates of public high schools had earned some credit in vocational courses.[7] Moreover, 75% of all 1982 graduates of public high schools had taken at least one vocational course designed to provide intensive preparation for a specific occupation.[8] In his Study of Schooling, John Goodlad found that high school students consistently rate vocational education, physical education, and the arts as their most-liked subjects.[9] They rate vocational education among the top three subjects in importance and near the bottom in level of difficulty.

We can infer from these data that vocational courses provide skills and experiences that students perceive to be valuable and that are not readily accessible elsewhere. Vocational education helps students master avocational and vocational skills; provides an involved, hands-on learning environment; and offers a curriculum that is closely tied to students' everyday lives outside of school.

Whether vocational education keeps potential dropouts in school is more uncertain, since most dropping out occurs in grade 10 and most vocational programs begin in grade 11. However, many effective dropout prevention programs have vocational education and on-the-job experiences as components.

## PERCEPTIONS OF VOC ED

Vocational educators have resigned themselves in some instances to the second-class status that is generally accorded their programs. Whether vocational education programs are viewed as preparation for blue-collar occupations or as dumping grounds for low-ability or disruptive students, they are seldom perceived as prestigious. Yet, in the 1984 Gallup Poll of the Public's Attitudes Toward the Public Schools, 83% of the respondents said that vocational education courses should be required of all students who do not plan to go to college.[10] This is an appreciable increase over 1981, when only 64% of Gallup Poll respondents said that non-college-bound students should be required to take vocational education courses.

To improve the status of vocational education, the Commission recommends that "both general and vocational education leaders must undertake to integrate their curricula and demonstrate the co-equal importance of academic and vocational learning."[11] *The Unfinished Agenda* lists 32 strategies for achieving this curricular integration.

Four things seem clear. First, secondary vocational education courses and programs *are* often used as dumping grounds for less-able or disruptive students who are not succeeding in academic courses. Second, vocational education students score significantly lower on standardized tests of proficiency in basic skills than do students who are enrolled in academic programs.[12] Third, among males, twice as many graduates who have vocational education concentrations (33%) as graduates without vocational coursework (15%) hold jobs in craft occupations.[13] Finally, among females, 61% of graduates who have vocational education concentrations work in clerical occupations, whereas only 37% of graduates without vocational coursework do so.[14]

Despite the existence of some clearly elite vocational high schools and programs (for example, Bronx Aviation High School), secondary vocational education programs generally hold positions of low status within the secondary school. This is the case for at least two reasons. First, vocational education tends to lead to respectable, but scarcely prestigious, occupations. Second, vocational education attracts those students who are either not able or not willing to succeed in traditional academic courses. Thus enrollment in a vocational education program provides a student with a network of peers who have low occupational aspirations, low cognitive ability, and—usually—low socioeconomic status.

It is little wonder then that the benefits of vocational education are overlooked by many potential students. If vocational programs and academic programs could be more closely knit, conceptually, and if movement from one curriculum to the other could be accomplished more easily, then perhaps vocational education would be viewed more positively as yielding benefits for all students.

## ACCESS TO VOC ED

Students' access to vocational education courses and programs has always been a function of counseling and of scheduling compromises. As more and more vocational programs have been consolidated into area schools and skills centers, access has been further constrained; now travel time must also be scheduled. The physical displacement of some vocational programs to facilities away from the "home" high school may tend to reinforce the perception of vocational education as low in status.

But the increased emphasis on academics is what makes the problem of access to vocational education particularly acute right now. As states and local school districts move to increase graduation requirements, the time available for electives—including vocational courses—shrinks.

The National Commission on Secondary Vocational Education feels strongly that student options must be preserved and that the amount and quality of counseling must be increased, so that students can make better-informed choices about their secondary programs. The Commission's most important recommendation in this area is that all students should be able to choose from a comprehensive set of course offerings across academic and vocational areas. To achieve that goal, the commissioners recommend ways of enhancing school guidance and counseling programs and ways of reducing the physical and social segregation of students who are enrolled in vocational courses and programs.

What do we know about student access to vocational education? We know that vocational education is being squeezed out of the secondary school curriculum.[15] We also know that, with an average annual load of nearly 400 students, high school counselors have roughly 15 minutes to spend with each pupil per year.[16] Moreover, in 1978, about 60% of the secondary schools that offered five or more vocational programs were located in areas with populations of less than

100,000—even though only about 27% of the U.S. population lives in such areas.[17]

Vocational educators perceive the current reform movement in secondary education as a threat to their programs. Nearly every state is currently moving to enforce stiffer graduation requirements, which will cause the time available for electives (including vocational courses) to shrink. The greater emphasis on academic subjects will also support a move by many school districts to concentrate their scarce financial resources on the academic areas. Already, roughly 24% of all secondary vocational teachers in the U.S. are hired to teach only part-time. Most of these part-time teachers also hold full-time jobs in private industry.[18]

*All* educators should be concerned about the implications of current curricular reforms for students who do not plan to attend a four-year college or university, for students who have difficulty succeeding in academic courses, and for secondary vocational education courses and programs. We need to carefully consider the unintended consequences of emphasizing "the new basics." We must be certain that we are providing appropriate reinforcement and remediation for those students who need it. Meanwhile, emphasis on the basics ought not to preclude experiences with vocational education and applied learning.

Few individuals would argue that the amount of counseling and guidance now available to high school students is adequate. Students must too often turn to peers, parents, and teachers for advice about courses, career choices, and personal problems. Hiring more counselors for U.S. high schools would be desirable but is probably not financially feasible. Therefore, efforts to extend the expertise of available counselors through the use of computers or group techniques and efforts to train classroom teachers in counseling practices may be realistic ways to improve services to students.

Today, most vocational courses are offered in

comprehensive high schools. But many of the best vocational courses, in terms of equipment and facilities, are taught in schools that offer their students a comprehensive range of vocational programs, i.e., five or more. Many such schools are magnet schools, area skills centers, or regional vocational schools. Access to many of these better programs has become competitive (with admission determined by faculty recommendations and proficiency in the basic skills) and dependent on a student's ability to schedule class and travel time. Access is clearly a problem for students who wish to take part in vocational education.

## EQUITY

Ever since the 1976 Amendments to the Vocational Education Act of 1963, vocational education has been charged with providing opportunities for special groups of students. The new vocational education law, the Carl Perkins Act of 1984, continues and even increases this emphasis. But success has been elusive. Students with handicaps and those who have limited proficiency in English are not represented in high school vocational education courses in proportion to their incidence in the population. Gender-linked enrollment patterns resist most efforts to change them.

The National Commission on Secondary Vocational Education recommends that local and state school officials not only work to improve equity in vocational education, but that they guarantee it. The Commission further recommends that individualized employability plans be established for all students, in order to better coordinate instructional support services and career planning.

The commissioners' concern for equity extends beyond providing equal opportunities for special groups. They are concerned that enrollment in vocational education might keep students from participating fully in general and academic education and thus might deprive them of certain desirable outcomes of such participation, e.g., a baccalaureate degree. Channeling less-able students into vocational courses and programs serves only to reinforce existing socioeconomic distinctions within the high school and may serve to limit the aspirations and academic development of these students. According to the commissioners:

> It is as unfair to limit the vocational education opportunities of academic students as it is to stigmatize those who are in the programs. We need an enriched vocational curriculum that serves all students, regardless of their academic ability or aspirations.[19]

Available evidence suggests that vocational education students do take substantially fewer credits in mathematics and science than students in the academic and general tracks complete.[20] Research also shows that public school graduates from families of lower socioeconomic status and graduates whose scores were lower on cognitive tests tend to earn more vocational credits than their classmates.[21] Hispanic graduates of public high schools earn more credits in vocational education than do their black or white counterparts.[22] Moreover, when cognitive ability is controlled, black students are somewhat more likely than whites to enroll in academic programs.[23] But, as Sue Berryman has observed, vocational education "gives students a niche in the high school and a future direction with which they can identify."[24]

Clearly, there are two ways of looking at the issue of equity in vocational education. Some people see vocational education as a means of providing needed educational services for the disadvantaged, for the less able, and for those students who plan to enter the labor force immediately after high school. But others see vocational education as a means of reinforcing social class distinctions, diminishing students' aspirations, and allowing students to avoid learning essential literacy skills.

The Commission recognizes that both perceptions are valid to some extent. Thus the commissioners recommend that the content of vocational courses be upgraded and made more rigorous *and* that the range of students who take part in such courses be expanded—to include not only youngsters enrolled in the academic track but also those with handicaps or limited proficiency in English. In the Commission's view, an integrated secondary school curriculum that includes complementary academic and applied experiences would properly focus attention on the quality of a student's education and on the appropriateness of each educational experience to his or her individual needs.

## CURRICULUM

In vocational education classes, the smoothly-running engine, the well-fit blouse, the errorless letter too often become the ends of instruction rather than the means. The National Commission on Secondary Vocational Education argues instead for a balanced curriculum that includes both abstract and applied learnings in classroom, laboratory, and work settings. High schools should give students "opportunities to experience the interrelatedness of ideas, the implications and applications of knowledge, and the process of discovery, dissemination, and use of information."[25] The Commission recommends that vocational courses include more instruction in the basics and that students be allowed to use vocational courses to satisfy graduation requirements in academic subject areas.

Research provides scant data on what goes on in vocational classrooms. However, a recent study shows that vocational students spend about 56% of total class time on content-related tasks; moreover, when they work on content-related tasks, they spend 73% of their time on technical (as opposed to basic and employability) skills.[26] Instructional materials for vocational education reflect this emphasis: many focus on occupational tasks (e.g., taking dictation) or on equipment (e.g., operating a lathe).

New York State is now developing an integrated curriculum that will include both academic and applied learning experiences for *all* students in grades 7 through 10.[27] Under the revised system, all students in public schools will be required to take units in Technology and in Introduction to Occupations, beginning in grade 7 and continuing through grade 10. After grade 10, students may choose to specialize in an occupational or an academic area.

The Commission's interest in a unified secondary curriculum clearly coincides with practice, at least in New York State. Elsewhere, the Commission's recommendations will probably run counter to existing practice and long-standing tradition. If secondary vocational education is to achieve its promise, as described by the Commission, attention must be given to changes and improvements in curriculum content and organization. If vocational education is to enjoy an enriched and expanded role in the high school, we must enrich and expand both the secondary curriculum and our expectations for student achievement.

## FIELD-BASED LEARNING

Field-based learning refers to educational experiences that students have in the workplace or in community service. Whether paid or unpaid, these experiences provide relevant, hands-on learning. Unfortunately, too few students have opportunities for field-based learning. Among those students who concentrate their coursework in vocational education (roughly 20% of all secondary students), fewer than 5% participate in cooperative vocational education programs. The National Commission on Secondary

Vocational Education calls for "more help from business, industry, labor, and public agencies to provide training slots and supervision for a greater number of students in a wider variety of occupations."[28]

Evidence suggests that high school students want these kinds of experiences. Two out of every three students hold regular part-time jobs during their high school years.[29] Whether out of economic necessity, to buy luxury items, to save for college, or simply for pin money, teenagers are increasingly likely to be wage earners.

Some researchers have found evidence that unsupervised work experiences may negatively affect school achievement.[30] It may also be that, as teenagers spend more time on jobs, they spend less time on homework.

Nonetheless, the potential benefits of early work experiences for high school students are powerful: the acquisition of practical knowledge about the workplace, the development of desirable work habits and attitudes, and the opportunity to earn money while still in school. The Commission's recommendation with regard to field-based learning reflects a strong faith in the value of early work experience, as well as a desire to shift such experience from part-time jobs to planned learning experiences in the workplace that are related to the high school curriculum.

No one would argue the value of cooperative vocational education programs. The problem is simply the amount of resources that would be necessary to extend the benefits of such programs to greater numbers of students. Cooperative programs require placements for trainees in local industries, enough teachers to supervise the trainees, and curricula that relate to and enhance on-the-job experiences.

The report of the National Commission on Secondary Vocational Education goes beyond merely endorsing vocational education. Repeatedly, it hammers at the theme that vocational education should become coequal and complementary to academic education within the secondary school.

A second focus of the report concerns the nature of school improvement initiatives. Merely increasing the number of courses or credits required for graduation will not suffice. The students who attend public secondary schools are too varied and the communities these schools serve are too diverse for simplistic responses of this kind to be effective. Instead, the Commission urges us to attend more carefully to students' individual needs and interests, to classroom procedures and instructional processes, and to the constraints imposed by the available resources and the specific characteristics of each local setting.

*The Unfinished Agenda* argues for a balanced curriculum—one that includes both academic and vocational preparation—for every high school student. The report supports an expanded and stronger role for vocational education within the secondary school. The potential of vocational education is clear, but the barriers to realizing that potential are not insignificant. Overcoming these barriers will require substantial changes in the attitudes and behaviors of both vocational and academic educators. New York is one state that is trying to effect such changes.

Meanwhile, we must remember that the recommendations of the National Commission on Secondary Vocational Education are "designed to give every young person in America the opportunity and the right to experience the best of academic and vocational education. For some time to come, this is the unfinished agenda."[31]

## ENDNOTES

1. *Meeting the Challenge: Recent Efforts to Improve Education Across the Nation,* report to the Secretary of Education prepared by the staff of the National Commission on Excellence in Educa-

tion (Washington, D.C.: U.S. Department of Education, 15 November 1983).

2. Thomas Toch, "The Dark Side of the Excellence Movement," *Phi Delta Kappan,* November 1984, pp. 173–76.

3. National Center for Education Statistics, *Digest of Education Statistics,* 1982, p. 74.

4. Lois Datta and Corinne Reider, "The Socialization Value of the Workplace: Some Educational Perspectives," *UCLA Educator,* Fall 1979, pp. 52–64.

5. Russell W. Rumberger, "The Growing Imbalance Between Education and Work," *Phi Delta Kappan,* January 1984, pp. 342–46.

6. National Commission on Secondary Vocational Education, *The Unfinished Agenda* (Columbus: National Center for Research in Vocational Education, Ohio State University, 1984), p. 4.

7. Ibid.

8. National Center for Education Statistics, *The Condition of Education* (Washington, D.C.: U.S. Department of Education, 1984).

9. John I. Goodlad, *A Place Called School* (St. Louis: McGraw-Hill, 1984).

10. George H. Gallup, "The 16th Annual Gallup Poll of the Public's Attitudes Toward the Public Schools," *Phi Delta Kappan,* September 1984, pp. 23–38.

11. *The Unfinished Agenda,* p. 8.

12. Linda S. Lotto, *Building Basic Skills: Results from Vocational Education* (Columbus: National Center for Research in Vocational Education, Ohio State University, 1983).

13. Paul Campbell, Molly Orth, and Patricia Seitz, *Patterns of Participation in Secondary Vocational Education: A Report Based on Transcript and Interview Data of the 1980 National Longitudinal Survey New Youth Cohort* (Columbus: National Center for Research in Vocational Education, Ohio State University, 1981).

14. Ibid.

15. *Survey of State High School Graduation Requirements* (Arlington, Va.: American Vocational Association, 1984).

16. Ernest L. Boyer, *High School: A Report on Secondary Education in America* (New York: Harper & Row, 1983).

17. Committee on Vocational Education and Economic Development in Depressed Areas, *Education for Tomorrow's Jobs,* Susan Sherman, ed. (Washington, D.C.: National Academy Press, 1983).

18. National Center for Education Statistics, *The Condition of Education* (Washington, D.C.: U.S. Department of Education, 1981).

19. *The Unfinished Agenda,* p. 12.

20. *The Condition of Education,* 1984.

21. Sue E. Berryman, *Vocational Education and the Work Establishment of Youth* (Santa Monica, Calif.: Rand Corporation, 1980).

22. *The Condition of Education,* 1984.

23. Ibid.

24. Berryman, p. 12.

25. *The Unfinished Agenda,* p. 14.

26. Ida M. Halasz and Karen S. Behm, *Time on Task in Selected Vocational Education Classes* (Columbus: National Center for Research in Vocational Education, Ohio State University, 1983).

27. Willard R. Dagget, *Strategic Vision and Planning: Keys to Educational Improvement.* Occasional Paper No. 100 (Columbus: National Center for Research in Vocational Education, Ohio State University, 1984).

28. *The Unfinished Agenda,* p. 22.

29. Morgan V. Lewis, John A. Gardner, and Patricia Seitz, *High School Work Experience and Its Effects* (Columbus: National Center for Research in Vocational Education, Ohio State University, January 1982).

30. Laurence D. Steinberg, Ellen Greenberger, Laurie Garduque, and Sharon McAuliffe, "High School Students in the Labor Force: Some Costs and Benefits to Schooling and Learning," *Educational Evaluation and Policy Analysis,* Fall 1982, pp. 363–72.

31. *The Unfinished Agenda,* p. 24.

*Linda S. Lotto* is Associate Professor, Educational Administration, University of Illinois, Champaign.

# Developing Responsible Youth through Youth Participation

## MARY CONWAY KOHLER

Maturity is measured by one's ability to accept and follow through on responsibilities for one's self, one's family, one's work, and one's community. To make the transition to adulthood, young people urgently need opportunities to be responsible, caring, participating members of our society. In adolescence young people begin to define self-worth in terms of what they are able to do and the impact they have on their surroundings. Yet this opportunity to discover one's self through action and contribution is missing in our society. We ask young people to prepare for a nebulous future without allowing them to participate here and now. By denying young people an immediate role in our society, we prolong their dependence, undermine their self-esteem, and cripple their capacity to care. No wonder young people feel anxious, alienated, and unwanted.

The problem of empty adolescence is relatively recent. In the past, no one expected young people to go through a lengthy adolescence. Agricultural and early industrial society required immense amounts of labor, and young people were absorbed early into the work force. Families were large, and simple survival of the household depended upon contributions from everyone, including young children. As the children grew, they gradually assumed more and more responsibility until, almost without noticing it, they became adults with jobs and families of their own.

Today the nuclear family is faltering. Parents often attempt to shield their children from responsibility. Instead of being seen as contributing to their families, young people are more often seen as a burden to them. Moreover, automation has reduced the need for unskilled workers so drastically that there are not enough jobs for adults, much less adolescents. Teenagers account for more than 25 percent of the unemployed. In a culture that too often equates personal worth with earning power, joblessness inevitably damages the self-images of young people.

The frustration of youth is compounded by the fact that adolescence has been prolonged. A weary mother once said to me, "I'd like to bury them at fourteen and dig them up at twenty." Today our society tries to bury young people in schools from the time they are six or seven until they are over twenty. This attitude is made more unreasonable by the fact that young people mature earlier today than ever before. By age ten or twelve, most youngsters are physically mature and, through the influence of television and other media, tremendously knowledgeable about the world around them. Social and economic pressures, however, force them to defer their entry into adult roles such as work, parenting, and citizenship until their mid-twenties. Society offers little for them to do in the intervening years, even though this is the time when they most urgently need to examine and explore the alternatives that will be available to them as adults.

Schools have borne the brunt of this problem. The role of other institutions such as church and family has been weakened. Society has assigned to schools the task of occupying

From *Phi Delta Kappan* 62, no. 6 (February 1981): 426–428. © 1981, Phi Delta Kappa, Inc. Used by permission of the author and the publisher.

young people and "preparing" them for adulthood. Schools that were originally organized to meet a student's intellectual needs have been slow to accept the responsibility for meeting the developmental needs of young people. Without debating whether the responsibility is appropriate, we must face the stark fact that schools are probably the only remaining institutions that reach all young people and hence can help them make the transition to adulthood. Because of compulsory attendance, schools have an unmistakable opportunity to teach young people responsibility as well as reading, caring as well as computation, self-esteem as well as science.

Unfortunately, many schools interpret "preparation for adulthood" as narrowly as possible. Too often, preparation has been equated with postponement, and students are asked to master concepts, skills, and information to be used in some vague future. Actually, the best learning usually occurs when students are motivated by present needs, when they see the link between what they study and what they do. The importance of immediacy has been acknowledged by many educators, including John Dewey, who wrote:

> The idea of using the present simply to get ready for the future contradicts itself. It omits, and even shuts off, the very condition by which a person can be prepared for his future. We always live at the time we live and not at some other time, and only by extracting at each present time the full meaning of each present experience are we prepared for doing the same thing in the future. This is the only preparation which in the long run amounts to much.

The same idea was expressed more concretely to me by a regional director of the U.S. Office of Education, who remarked, "I did poorly in math until I worked in a general store and had to make change."

The concept of adolescence as a waiting period reflects our society's failure to understand or respond to the needs of youth. In this respect

some "primitive" societies are more advanced than we are. In Africa, for example, many tribes expect male children to leave home at thirteen or fourteen. The youth receives a plot of land on which he builds his own house and lays out his own garden in preparation for the time when he will marry and start a family. Although friends and family are available to help, the young person is expected to assume responsibility for his life. As he does, he earns a respected place in his tribe. In contrast, our culture puts young people on hold. At a time when they need above all to believe in their own value, they are forced to be passive and dependent, deprived of the chance to make a difference in the world.

The sad consequence is that young people often turn their energies toward activities destructive to themselves and the society that ignores them. We've all seen the recurring headlines about teenage crime, pregnancy, suicide, vandalism, drug abuse, and alcoholism. The Gallup polls of attitudes toward education perennially report that adults consider discipline the number one problem in school. Employers complain that they can't hire young people because they don't have enough personal responsibility to come to work on time. Newspaper accounts tell of teenage girls who have babies because they want something of their own, teenage boys who rob senior citizens, and countless young people who drift through high school chronically "stoned." Clearly, these young people are not taking responsibility for themselves or their actions. Yet how can they be blamed when they have had so little opportunity to learn about responsibility, so few chances to make a positive contribution? Of course society blames them. Instead of seeing such problems as cries for meaningful roles, adults use them as an opportunity to dismiss young people as "no good."

This is doubly sad because small groups of young people around the country are doing remarkable things that few adults hear about. Instead of headlines such as "Teenage Pregnancy Hits New High" or "Vandals Wreck High School," we could be reading that "Students Save Historic Building," "Young People Feed Senior Citizens," or "Teenagers Counsel Each Other." Each of these headlines refers to a youth participation project documented by the National Commission on Resources for Youth.

- Juniors in a Connecticut history class learned that a schoolhouse built in 1799 was to be demolished, so they raised the money and did the work to renovate it and move it to its original location.
- Teenagers in California, including delinquents and the handicapped, cooperate with adults to run a food service that makes inexpensive food available to senior citizens.
- Rap Room is a peer-counseling project in New York where students can talk to, share with, and get advice from other students on topics ranging from sex to parental separation, academic failure to friendship.

These three programs are not isolated examples. Instead, they are the predictable result when young people are given responsibility for work that has meaning to them. In each of these programs young people become important to others through their concern and action. The significance of such an experience is best illustrated by a conversation I once had with a young man in prison. This youngster operated the prison printing press, which he had found and repaired. I watched him ready the press for operation and noticed that, although the people around him were sullen and despondent, his face glowed with satisfaction. Finally I asked why he seemed so happy. He simply pointed to the printing press and said, "But for me, it wouldn't work." In that single sentence the young man summed up the power of youth participation. By challenging young people to do something difficult, we allow them to discover untapped

resources within themselves. By providing settings in which something important depends upon their efforts, we offer them the opportunity to prove themselves responsible. By allowing ourselves to need young people and the contributions they can make, we acknowledge that they deserve a significant place in our society.

That sense of making a difference, of having a significant role, is at the core of what the National Commission on Resources for Youth calls its Youth Participation project. For the past thirteen years the commission has promoted Youth Participation because we believe that young people can assume responsible roles and that they will become better adults if they have the opportunity to care about and contribute to their own communities. Founded by a group of concerned educators, social scientists, and businesspeople, the commission has sought out the good things young people have done, both to counter the negative image of youth and to provide examples for those who serve young people. Our clearinghouse files are now bulging with thousands of projects in which young people have made decisions and taken action resulting in significant improvements for their schools and communities.

The things young people have done are tremendously varied. Teenagers can and do renovate buildings in disadvantaged neighborhoods, tutor younger children, record the oral history of their communities, lobby for pollution controls, run day-care centers, work as apprentices, operate employment or counseling services for their peers, and perform hundreds of other services. Despite this diversity, we have discovered that the most successful Youth Participation programs have several features in common. First, they require decision making by adolescents. Second, they involve young people in working relationships with adults. Third, the activity of the young people satisfies a genuine need in their communities. Fourth, the program provides regular opportunities for students to reflect on their work and learn the skills related to it.

Although schools are not the only setting for Youth Participation, they are often best equipped to provide this component. Teachers know how to communicate the information, concepts, and skills that students need to carry out a Youth Participation project. From an educator's point of view, Youth Participation is an ideal way of motivating students to learn traditional subjects. When students feel responsible for doing something that requires math, English, science, or some other subject, they knuckle down and learn so that they can accomplish their goal. Often teachers can create this effect simply by encouraging students to take responsibility for an experiential component of a course. The following examples illustrate how traditional subjects can be the basis for Youth Participation.

- *Mathematics.* Students in a computer class in Denver, Colorado, designed and executed a program that placed commuters in car pools. Young people in Maine had to master computation skills in order to design and build a boat.
- *Science.* Young people in New York City researched, designed, and built a passive solar wall to help heat a community center. In Illinois young people gathered evidence of pollution in a local river and eventually brought suit against the polluters.
- *Home Economics.* Students in Colorado run their own food service center called Munchies, Inc. In day-care centers all over the U.S. young people learn about parenting by planning activites and caring for younger children.
- *History.* Students in Georgia dug up archeological materials from an area that was about to be bulldozed for construction. Students from many parts of the country have pre-

served the oral history and traditions of their regions in magazines such as *Foxfire*.
- *Physical Education.* In New York State young people helped design and build a fitness course on a local college campus. In Chicago students learn about sports medicine so they can teach the high school's teams and gym classes to avoid injury.
- *English.* Students in St. Paul wrote and distributed a handbook with consumer information for teenagers.
- *Social Studies.* In Philadelphia young people undertake internships in various social agencies. In California teenagers provide therapy and companionship for patients at a state mental hospital.
- *General.* In all subject areas students are motivated to learn when they are responsible for teaching younger students. The commission's highly successful Youth Tutoring Youth program matches students one-to-one with younger schoolmates.

All of these projects motivate young people to learn specific subjects, but they do much more. By giving young people responsibility for doing something that affects other people, these programs also teach them to make decisions and carry them out, to care and then act on that caring. In order for students to benefit fully from this aspect of Youth Participation, teachers must adopt a different role. Instead of being all-knowing authorities, teachers must become facilitators. Instead of organizing projects and assigning roles, teachers must draw out of young people their own talents for leadership and decision making. This role is easier for teachers who remember that, in Youth Participation, the process of choosing goals and figuring out how to accomplish them is as important as the task that is finally accomplished. Teachers involved in Youth Participation must create an environment of trust in which young people are not afraid to exert themselves, to take chances, and even to fail. Obviously, this is possible only when the adults involved have faith that youngsters can make good decisions and carry them out responsibly.

Even well-intentioned adults often find it difficult to give up the notion that they "know what is best" for young people. In many cases the young people themselves are so conditioned to be passive and dependent that they will be suspicious and reluctant to take responsibility when it is offered. The teacher must have the confidence that students can handle responsibility and the patience to wait until the students believe that themselves. Teachers must also restrain personal tendencies to dominate and intervene, so that students can develop their own leadership. The adult role is like that of an advocate who draws out of the students alternative plans of action. When problems surface, adults and students examine potential solutions until the students are ready to choose a course of action.

Obviously, Youth Participation deviates from the traditional school curriculum; yet the benefits outweigh the risks. Often a single successful Youth Participation project has a positive ripple effect on other areas of the curriculum or on the attitude of students. In one school, where service has become a unifying theme for the entire curriculum, teachers and students deliberately look for ways to use the knowledge and skills of each discipline to benefit the wider community.

Youth Participation also provides an opportunity to bridge the gulf that exists between most schools and the communities they serve. Most communities have unexploited resources that can benefit young people and unresolved problems that can be addressed by them. Further, as Youth Participation ends the isolation of young people, more adults see that young people can be a resource rather than a problem.

America must face the fact that we need our young people—not only as the adults they will be tomorrow but as the spirited citizens they are today. Educators can tap that spirit by giving young people opportunities to participate in the world while they learn about it. Teaching responsibility may, indeed, be more challenging than teaching the other R's. There are no textbooks, no visual aids, no achievement tests. There are, however, visible signs of success—the confidence of young people who can take initiative, the self-esteem of young people who have made a recognized contribution, the motivation of young people who believe that their effort matters. Measurable or not, these are the qualities of caring, contributing adults. Youth Participation is a proven way of producing those qualities in young people, thereby helping them with the difficult transition to adulthood. Educators could have no better goal.

*Mary C. Kohler* is Chairperson, Board of Directors, National Commission on Resources for Youth, New York.

# James Madison High: A School for Winners

## NORMAN FISHER

On May 11, 1984, a James Madison High School student was selected to represent the students of New York State at a White House ceremony inaugurating the President's Academic Fitness Awards Program (PAFA). This honor was a fitting culmination to our school theme "James Madison High School: A School for Winners." During the past two years our students have received considerable recognition for their accomplishments in many areas; from chess, football, and soccer championships to a Westinghouse Science Talent Search semi-finalist award and increases in the number of New York State Regents-endorsed diplomas from 39 percent (1981–1982) to 55 percent (1983–1984), and a 33 percent increase in the number of New York State Regents Scholarships awarded.

These accomplishments and our participation at the White House ceremony was in sharp contrast to a racial incident that occurred in May 1982 which marred our school's reputation and changed our school's image in the community. The reality that James Madison High was a school that had served its students and its community well since 1926 was being challenged. During its history of academic excellence—with rigorous training in the traditional subjects, where the great majority of students went on to college—it was consistently a source of pride to its community. Among its graduates were judges, a congressman, nationally-known entertainers, educators, and successful business people. James Madison High School could have served as a model for any study of academic excellence. However, as was the case with many

urban schools, changing demographics, an aging population, and increased attendance at private schools shifted James Madison from a predominantly middle-class school to a high school that reflected the diversity of New York City's population. It appeared that many community residents, as well as students and parents, no longer perceived their school as a solid academic institution, but one in which violent confrontation was commonplace. It was under these circumstances that I was assigned to James Madison High School as principal in September 1982.

It was apparent to me, if not always to all of its constituents, that there were many things right at James Madison High School. It was on the whole a happy place that students found inviting and where teachers enjoyed teaching. A sizable portion of the faculty volunteered to serve as advisors to clubs and activities after the school day. In reality, we were not a school at risk academically, but we were at risk of becoming a school that was complacent with past accomplishments. Although we had many students who were academically fit, there were others who did not feel part of the school and still others who left our school with inadequate preparation for their lives. If not at risk, James Madison High School was certainly being challenged.

In essence, our goal at James Madison High School was to build upon its foundation of excellence while meeting the many challenges. Our efforts took many forms.

The challenges we identified at James Madison High School included:

From *American Education* 20, No. 9 (November 1984): 10–14. Used by permission of the author.

*The challenge to personalize a youngster's education to insure a sense of belonging to the school community*

To support our theme, we developed new programs and expanded on existing ones to build a series of smaller schools within James Madison, a school with 3,200 students. Each school or institute program was made up of 50 to 250 youngsters. These smaller groupings enabled our students to participate in programs based on their interests and to build personal bonds of friendship. Each student in an institute takes a common core of subjects: English, social studies, science, mathematics and a foreign language. But each youngster is also afforded an opportunity to select additional course offerings based on personal interest.

The institute system also allows us to implement co-curricular activities that support the particular institute's theme. (These activities are also available to the entire student body.) Our Law Day Program enabled our Law Institute youngsters and their advisors to provide a series of workshops that featured a Deputy Police Commissioner, the Chief Medical Examiner of New York City, and the Brooklyn District Attorney.

*The challenge to recognize that our youngsters come to us with a different set of needs than previous generations*

The education studies published during the past two years encourage raising standards for all youngsters.

At Madison, we have put into effect many of the suggested reforms, but not without the recognition that youngsters—especially those in an urban environment—come to James Madison High School with a different set of needs and values from those of previous generations of students. We know that a sizable number of students come to us from single-parent homes, and it is the exception rather than the rule to find a parent at home during school hours. The problems of our youngsters can be found in all the headline stories of the media, including child abuse and violence.

Each of our special institutes publishes its own magazine and develops a number of special event programs. In addition to a Law Institute, we have successful programs in the Center for Administration and Management (CAM), the Bio-Medical Institute Program, and the Theatre-Arts Program. The emphasis on specific fields helps secure the support of private sector organizations. They "adopt" our youngsters for both intensified learning sessions and external learning experiences. Our Law Institute youngsters are paired with Cadwalader, Wickersham, and Taft, and have toured their offices as well as witnessed a variety of court proceedings with Cadwalader's legal staff. The youngsters gain insights not only into law careers, but also into the role of high technology in law while working with Lexis, the legal computer. Our Theatre Arts youngsters work with a performing arts troupe from Lincoln Center, and our CAM students have been paired successfully with the Hyatt Hotels for the past two years.

A mini-school has been in operation for the past eight years for students who are over seventeen and have not earned sufficient credits to graduate with their class. A special year-long curriculum was developed in the basic skills and culminates in youngsters sitting for the General Equivalency Diploma. The success rate was 100 percent for the 63 students who were in our mini-school to earn an equivalency diploma. Although the program is a success, still it reflects the school's failure to integrate every student into the mainstream of education. We must resort to a last-ditch effort to save these youngsters. Our success with students who had personal and academic problems in one mini-school has led to a teacher-initiated proposal to personalize the program for all entering 9th grade students beginning September 1984. If successful, our General Equivalency Diploma Program may become obsolete in the years ahead, as we seek a formula for success for all youngsters. The teacher-initiated 9th grade institute program takes into account the need to serve as a model holding-power program. To be successful, the program will ensure that youngsters will not be anonymous and will participate in school programs. Also, their performance and attendance will be monitored on a regular basis, with appropriate feedback to their parents.

Education reform without plans to meet the individual needs of students will be fruitless. At Madison, we have moved to heterogeneous grouping for almost all students. We have identified youngsters who are seriously deficient in basic skills and have provided them with special courses in mathematics and English. We recognize that no two youngsters are alike and that they require alternative strategies of instruction. In addition, we have honors level classes for students who excel in a subject area. We have reduced mathematics remediation from a two-year program to a one-year course in Fundamentals of Mathematics. After the one-year program, 65 percent of our students go on to algebra classes for college-bound students. This program results in greater numbers of students who go on to take courses in geometry and trigonometry.

The use of heterogeneous groupings has been most successful in foreign language instruction. We attribute the success to the fact that, unlike other disciplines, youngsters begin foreign language instruction without the need to have mastered previous concepts, as is true in other disciplines. All youngsters enter foreign language instruction without prerequisites and must go on to complete a three-year sequence. Our success in foreign language instruction is demonstrated by a passing percentage of more than 90 percent in French, Italian, and Spanish on the New York State Regents Examination. Many of

our Level 1 classes are taught with a Mastery Learning Model which enables youngsters to learn the language at their own rates. This program is based on the concept that most students can raise their level of achievement when given corrective feedback and/or enrichment materials during the learning diagnostic test prior to the formal test. Our success in foreign languages has encouraged us to introduce new offerings in Hebrew and Latin. A Foreign Language Apprentice Teacher Program has been implemented at local intermediate schools where our youngsters earn independent study credit while serving as tutors and assisting the lower school teachers.

The guidance staff meets with each student at least twice a term to review appropriate selections for our heterogeneous program. A paraprofessional is assigned to make telephone calls prior to the school day, beginning at 6:30 a.m. when parents are still at home, to arrange a meeting if the youngster is doing poorly or has poor attendance patterns.

An evening conference is held the first Thursday of each month, when the guidance staff invites parents to discuss problems they may be having with their youngsters. Parents are offered opportunities to exchange ideas with guidance staffers and to share common concerns about their youngsters' performances.

The guidance staff includes the deans, and unlike the traditional model of a dean's office in which the primary focus is to deal with disciplinary infractions, it has been a department that tries to be preventive rather than punitive. Our deans have been taught to be sympathetic listeners and to ensure that every youngster receives a similar response for the same infraction. In addition, only one dean remains in the office during any given period, while the other deans and school security officers are highly visible in our corridors, the student lunchroom, and in front of our school building. The number of suspensions has decreased dramatically from 199 in 1980–1981 to 96 in 1983–1984. In a recent incident in which three black junior high school students were harassed at a local video arcade, the youngsters chose to run the few blocks into our school for assistance. Although this is only soft data, it certainly is rewarding to know that a school that had witnessed racial disturbances two years before is now viewed as a sanctuary by some youngsters.

The support services and the recognition that everyone gets a "fair shake" at Madison are the key factors for our decline in the number of discipline problems.

*The challenge to provide every youngster with the opportunity for success*

Although we emphasize the importance of student academic achievement, we understand that youngsters must have practical reasons, as well, for doing well in class. In the Center for Administration and Management, students established their own corporation, called Business Leaders of Madison. (We adapted this program from Community School District 22.) The 120 students participating in the program learn the fundamentals of business by going into business themselves. During the school year, the students sell engraved lucite desk clocks, canvas tote bags, credit card calculators and a variety of other items. The Business Leaders keep their own books, establish their own marketing techniques, earn a profit, and determine which items to reorder. This unusual program was highlighted in the *New York Daily News* of May 9, 1983. Student Sandra Forskin was quoted: "Because of this program, I've taken tons of business classes. I'm learning how to work a word-processor, how to handle balance sheets, and I've developed a good sales pitch. I see myself in ten years sitting behind a big desk giving orders to a male secretary." It is this type of success that schools strive for—where a youngster recognizes the value of her own education.

A program to encourage students graduating

from local feeder schools helps them continue to develop their special talents at James Madison High School. A local elementary school has a devoted teacher who established a chess club and competition at the school. Her husband, a teacher at James Madison, enrolled the students in a club to sharpen their chess skills and to compete in chess matches with other schools. The 1982–1983 school year saw these youngsters win the New York State Chess Championship, the North American Chess Championship, and the U.S.A. Chess Championship. You can be certain their success has led to better performance in the classroom. Since the N.Y.C. Board of Education has implemented stringent requirements for students to play in any competitive sport, they have to shape up and pass all classes or be barred from playing.

Our students have worked harder both on the field and in the classroom. We are proud of our football and soccer teams who have won city-wide recognition. However, we are most proud of the fact that of the 88 seniors on varsity teams, 18 students earned Regents Scholarships, and 79 of the 88 entered college in 1983.

The model of success has encouraged us to develop new programs that—once again—have come about from student interest. Youngsters in our Bio-Medical Program exhibited an interest in sophisticated scientific research. With the support of our superintendent, Mr. Martin Ilivicky, who provided our school and others in his district with additional funding for a research class, as well as with a computer with research and networking capabilities, we encouraged students to select a research project. This enabled four students to enter the National Westinghouse Science Talent Search. These four students were the first applicants in more than a decade from James Madison High School; one student became a National Semi-Finalist with a research project called "The Effects of Ethyl Alcohol on Volvox Carteri (a Bacterium)." Her successful research project could never have been accomplished without the tireless efforts of faculty members and a Brooklyn College advisor.

The laboratory facilities available at nearby Brooklyn College cannot be duplicated at most high schools. Many of those in our Bio-Medical program and research classes plan a career in medicine and seek admission to the special medical program. Four members of the class of 1984 were accepted to the Sophie Davis Medical School Program of the City College of New York. This program offers a BA/MD program in seven years and guarantees acceptance in a participating medical school. In addition, three students were selected into the Downstate Medical School/Brooklyn College Program.

Our concern for raising standards and encouraging all students to take a college-bound program within the heterogeneous classroom has succeeded far beyond our expectations. The most coveted diploma in New York State is the Regents-endorsed diploma. Fifty-five percent of the class of 1984 earned this diploma, as compared to 39 percent two years ago.

Each youngster who finds a "hook"—whether in business, sports, or research—is successful and a winner at James Madison. Our goal is to provide a variety of alternatives and options for making winners out of as many students as possible.

### The challenge of preparing a generation of thinking students

After the release of the national education reports, the buzzword seemed to be the mediocrity of American education. If our high schools were indeed mediocre, I am convinced it is because we expected our classrooms to be mediocre. Theodore Sizer, in his study, *Horace's Compromise: The Dilemma of the American High School,* emphasizes the uniformity of the American high school regardless of size and the diversity of the United States, as well as the politically decentralized character of the schools. Our class-

rooms were fixed by units of time that encouraged passive learning in which the teacher lectured and students listened. The old saying, "Children should be seen but not heard," seemed to apply in the American high school. James Madison was no exception. A school with a 58-year tradition of many successes and a faculty of veteran teachers is not stimulated to change. Most of us will not tamper with a good thing. The result was success for those students who were highly motivated, but mediocrity for those who were not. Fortunately, I inherited a professional faculty willing to improve teaching strategies. Teachers were encouraged to use a variety of relevant media and materials to supplement textbooks.

In social studies, teachers were encouraged to begin in the present and move to the past. The sending of troops to Grenada began an analysis of earlier American foreign policy, rather than beginning in the historical period under discussion. An evaluation of student government accounts became the basis for teaching bookkeeping entries, and an examination of interchangeable parts in automobiles introduced the concept of congruent parts in geometry. The teachers are trained to plan their lessons around a current problem, leading students through a series of questions to understand the problem. In many instances, youngsters are not yet ready for this kind of instruction and feel more comfortable with teacher lectures and a board full of notes. But we keep seeking new and varied strategies to ensure that students learn to think.

In every class, students are expected to write, to do homework and participate in class discussion. At the start of each semester, all youngsters are informed of the key ingredients that comprise their final grades. There are to be no mysteries as to how the final grade is determined.

If I were to tell you we were 100 percent successful, it would be a lie. We certainly are winning student support, as well as increased teacher support, as many teachers recognize that teaching is more fun and "easier" when students become involved.

Perhaps the most significant aspect of our success is the emphasis on staff development. Many teachers were prepared to give up a portion of their summer vacation without compensation to improve their teaching strategies. This past summer approximately 10 percent of the faculty was involved in some institute program to improve teaching strategies. In addition, during the school year teachers are encouraged to participate in conferences and workshops. This program does place a strain on the school, since classes have to be covered without additional substitute teachers, but teacher growth and professionalism makes the effort well worth it. A successful staff development program was instituted by the superintendent. This "lead teacher" program enabled teachers in each discipline to visit another school and observe a lesson. This enables teachers to share insights with colleagues and then lead department conferences at their own schools based on their observations.

Our monthly faculty conferences are devoted to professional topics and not to administrative concerns. The most successful conferences were those that had a workshop format in which teachers participated and shared insights. Topics that cross disciplines enable teachers to meet with other subject area teachers. We have conducted workshops on teaching strategies for dealing with special education students who are mainstreamed, the role of computers in classroom assisted instruction, how to avoid student confrontation, and a host of other topics.

*The challenge to develop an appropriate value structure*

If we accept the assumption that youth enter our schools today with a different set of problems when compared to previous generations, then our challenge must be to develop a value structure that is suitable for all. The first step in the development of such a value structure is to treat high school students as adults and as citizens. The principal has to be a "real" person with whom youngsters can communicate. Students participate as consultants in meetings with faculty and parent representatives, providing input into school decisions that include discipline and dress codes. The student representatives have the responsibility to share the discussions with other students. The principal's visibility is essential so that students recognize the principal as a participant who is interested in every aspect of school life. In the principal's disciplinary conferences with parents and students, the students have the opportunity to express their opinions and describe an alternate behavior pattern which they might have followed. The youngsters are made to understand that their antisocial actions have benefited no one. If the low number of repeat offenders is an indication of success for 99 suspension conferences held during the 1983–1984 school year, only two dealt with the same youngster.

We have also sought to encourage youngsters to demonstrate a value structure that will serve to put our school in the limelight to receive positive press coverage. Once youngsters and a school are presented to the public in a positive manner, every citizen appears to understand the ramifications of negative behavior and the blemish it could be for the community. A positive perception of the school must be promoted through the local press. Our theme, "School for Winners," has instilled a sense of pride in our entire school body. Students wanting to be identified with James Madison High School have increased the sale of James Madison jackets, sweatshirts, and tee shirts.

The results of our efforts have shown us that a school with strong academic traditions and high expectations can demand more of its students, develop new options for youngsters, and bask in the accomplishments resulting from an improvement in student performance. During the past two years, our students have demonstrated a daily attendance rate of 88 percent, far above the city-wide rate: and nearly 90 percent of Madison's graduates continue on to a two-year or four-year college.

I would be naive to believe that our school is problem-free. Our class size still averages 35 students per class. We have insufficient funds for computers, library books, equipment and equipment repair. We have a school building that is in desperate need of renovation. A heavy rain places many rooms out of commission because of roof leaks through gaping holes in the ceilings of classrooms. However, our youngsters have demonstrated that they are "winners" in spite of the condition of our facility. We have demonstrated that we are not a school at risk nor a school that lives in the glory of its past achievements. James Madison High School will provide excellence in education for this generation of students who enter beneath the portal that reads, "Education is the foundation for civil liberty."

*Norman Fisher* is Principal, James Madison High School, Brooklyn, New York.

## ADDITIONAL LEARNING ACTIVITIES

### Problems and Projects

1. If you have been preparing a case study about a high school in connection with your study of Sections 1 through 6, decide which innovations and trends presented in this section should be incorporated in the curriculum of the school you are studying. Use general objectives and the objectives at this level and the four bases of curriculum as well as other criteria to support your decisions.
2. Examine the program described in James Madison High: A School for Winners" in terms of objectives, bases and criteria. Then evaluate it in terms of the eight factors present in effective high schools (see "Effective High Schools— What Are the Common Characteristics?"). What changes would you suggest for the school in the light of your evaluation?
3. What do Murphy and Hallinger mean in "Effective High Schools: What Are the Common Characteristics?" when they say that high expectations should be reflected in a "norm of academic press instead of high targets for performance"? What three factors do they consider essential for "a sense of community"?
4. Are *anticipation, participation,* and *values* appropriate curriculum criteria for use at this school level (see "Curriculum Criteria for the 1980s and the 1990s" in the rationale for Section 6)? How might the curricula in the typical high school be modified if these criteria were utilized in planning?
5. Kohler, in "Developing Responsible Youth Through Youth Participation," deals with a problem she calls "empty adolescence." What sort of activities does she describe that might cause young people to "turn their energies away from activities destructive to themselves and the society that ignores them"? What are

the objectives of curricula of this kind? Which of the four curriculum bases are important to consider in such planning? Could learning experiences of this kind "culminate in organized knowledge" (as discussed by Dewey in "Progressive Organization of Subject-Matter" in Section 5)? What must the teacher do if this is to happen? Projects of this kind for youth development are not new. A distinguished and still significant report of such curriculum activity is *Youth Serves the Community* by Paul R. Hanna (New York: Appleton-Century, 1936). Included are reports of contributions to public safety, civic beauty, community health, agricultural and industrial improvement, civic arts, local history, and protection of resources. You might enjoy reading a portion of this book and comparing the youth activities described to those reported by Kohler.

6. Are a common high school curriculum and uniform requirements appropriate in a pluralistic society? Can a common curriculum and uniform standards be implemented with diverse groups of students? Can individual differences be accommodated? Should they be? Review the sections on "Excellence and Equity" and "Excellence and Standards" in "Tackling the Reform Reports of the 1980s" as preparation for answering these questions.

7. According to "Tackling the Reform Reports of the 1980s," the current reports simply reopen the ideological schism between those who believe the high school should transmit a common culture to all through a common curriculum, and those who believe in individualized, differentiated programs focused on students' needs. Review the articles by Hutchins, Bagley, Kilpatrick, Brameld, Dewey, and Shane in Section 1. You may be surprised how directly pertinent they are to the 1980s reform reports on the high school. It is interesting to take three or four of the 1980s reform reports and to ask which of the philosophical positions (perennialism, essentialism, progressivism, reconstructionism, or eclectic) each of them represents.

8. Read the article "The Unfinished Agenda: Report from the National Commission on Secondary Vocational Education" and the section on "Vocational Education" in "Tackling the Reform Reports of the 1980s." Should vocational education be a major part of the high school curriculum or should it be postponed until later? Should both academic and vocational preparation be part of a balanced curriculum for every high school student, as recommended in "The Unfinished Agenda?"

9. Think through the suggestions for change in the curriculum you would make for middle adolescents in light of the objectives at this level, the four bases of the curriculum, and curriculum criteria. Which recommendations from the 1970s and 1980s reform reports would you like to see implemented? (See "Tackling the Reform Reports of the 1980s.")

10. Should moral education be part of the curriculum for middle adolescents? Values clarification seeks the learner's judgments about issues or situations in which values conflict. Kohlberg, however (see "The Cognitive-Developmental Approach to Moral Education" in Section 3), believes that the teaching of values and morals should go further than this. He has identified six stages of reasoning

and moral judgment and has tested a plan for developing the higher stages with learners. It involves exposing learners to the next higher stage of reasoning, as well as to situations posing problems for each learner's current moral structure. An atmosphere of interchange and dialogue in which conflicting moral views are compared in an open manner is also part of the curriculum plan. Reread the article by Kohlberg (Section 3) and try to decide whether you think this approach should be used in curriculum planning for middle adolescents. Compare your views with those of other members of your class.

11. Some educators were greatly concerned by the recommendations in the 1970s reform reports that the age for compulsory education be lowered. Read the article "Assaults on a Great Idea" by R. Freeman Butts in the *Phi Delta Kappan* 55, no. 4 (December 1973): 240. Why does Butts oppose these recommendations? What sort of curriculum is needed at the middle adolescent level to achieve his stated objective for learners?

12. In 1963, Kimball Wiles recommended that the high school of the future provide opportunity for every learner to develop values to guide his or her behavior. To accomplish this, the curriculum for every learner would include an "Analysis Group" as the basic element of the educational program. In 1969, twenty of Dr. Wiles's professional associates reviewed his ideas in *The High School of the Future: A Memorial to Kimball Wiles* (William M. Alexander, ed. [Columbus, Ohio: Charles E. Merrill Co.]). Read Chapter 1 of this book for a summary of Kimball Wiles's proposals, and at least one of the chapters written by another contributor. Do you believe that "analysis groups" should become part of the high school curriculum? Does the book propose other curriculum changes that you believe should be adopted? Summarize your views and discuss them with others.

13. Thirty-two innovations and trends are listed in the rationale for this section along with the articles describing them. Try to decide which ten of these trends are most significant in terms of objectives, bases or criteria which you regard as particularly significant for middle adolescents. Make a list of your trends and explain why you selected them. Compare your list with the selections made by other students.

14. The Appendix of this book includes a list of books, each describing a high school program. Select one that interests you and determine whether the curriculum or teaching might be improved by incorporating one or more of the innovations or trends in middle adolescent education discussed in this section. Justify using one or more of these trends in this school in terms of objectives, curriculum bases, and curriculum criteria.

15. Have your personal beliefs or values about programs of education for middle adolescents changed as a result of your experience with this section? If so, state what change has taken place and relate it to one or more of the activities in this section (an article, the rationale, a problem or project, etc.). Compare your ideas with those of other students.

## Films, Videocassettes and Audiocassettes

*High Schools.* The prize-winning documentary and PBS special based on the Carnegie Report, *High School: A Report on Secondary Education in America* (see pages 479–480; 489–493 in this section). Videocassette, color, 60 min., 1986. The Carnegie Foundation for the Advancement of Teaching, 5 Ivy Lane, Princeton, New Jersey 08540. (Also available in 16 mm. film).

*Redefining General Education in the American High School.* Ernest Boyer, Harry S. Broudy, and Gordon Cawelti address such issues as curriculum fragmentation and preparation for the 21st century. Videocassette, 24 min. Association for Supervision and Curriculum Development, 225 North Washington St., Alexandria, Virginia 22314.

*Criteria for High School General Education Programs.* Theodore R. Sizer presents five issues to be considered in evaluating existing or proposed common learnings programs. Audiocassette, 1982. Association for Supervision and Curriculum Development, 225 North Washington St., Alexandria, Virginia, 22314.

*The Future of the Comprehensive High School.* Daniel Tanner critiques studies of secondary education and calls for renewed commitment to general education. Audiocassette, 1981. Association for Supervision and Curriculum Development, 225 North Washington St., Alexandria, Virginia 22314.

*What Happens in High School.* 16 mm, color, 29 min., 1976. Mario Fantini and several other educational authorities examine secondary education and look optimistically to its future. A number of innovations and trends are shown, including a visit to a "school within a school" program. Media Five, 1011 North Cole Avenue, Hollywood, California 90038.

*High School.* 16 mm, black and white, 75 min., 1969. A documentary film by Frederick Wiseman. Presents a series of formal and informal encounters between teachers, students, and parents, in classes, sex education lectures, school entertainments, gym, cooking lessons, a simulated space flight, and disciplinary proceedings. The *American Library Association Booklist* for May 15, 1971, stated that "the probing camera reveals bad teachers, stifling student-counselor encounters, and frustrating parent-teacher conferences; it also shows good teachers and excited students . . . but the overwhelming tone is one of dullness, student boredom, teacher boredom, and the futility of individuality." Articles about this film have appeared in *Saturday Review* (April 19, 1969); *Newsweek* (May 19, 1969); *The New Republic* (June 21, 1969); and *The New Yorker* (October 18, 1969). If you cannot see the film you may find it useful to read these articles as a basis for discussion. Zipporals Films, 54 Lewis Wharf, Boston, Massachusetts 02110.

*Black and White Together?* 16 mm, black and white, 58 min., 1969. Interracial understanding between high school students was promoted by two six-week sessions of living and learning together at a local hotel. Dissensions occur and the premise of the experiment is challenged. Audio-Visual Center, Indiana University, Bloomington, Indiana 47401.

## Books and Articles to Review

The numbers in parentheses following these books or articles refer to the numbered list of innovations and trends in middle adolescent education listed in the rationale at the beginning of this section. They will assist you in identifying additional sources regarding those trends and innovations.

Bailey, Adrienne Y. "The Education Equality Project: Focus on Results." *Phi Delta Kappan* 65, no. 1 (September 1983): 22–25. (2) (4) (16) (19)

Ball, Stephen J. *Beachside Comprehensive: A Comprehensive Study of Secondary Schooling.* New York: Cambridge University Press, 1981.

Best, John Hardin. "Reforming America's Schools: The High Risks of Failure." *Teachers College Record* 86, no. 2 (Winter 1984): 265–274.

Boyer, Ernest. "Clarifying the Mission of the American High School." *Educational Leadership* 41, no. 6 (March 1984): 20–22. (1) (4) (5) (19)

Brickell, Henry M. "How Can We Teach Abstractions to Nonintellectual Students?" *Educational Leadership* 41, no. 4 (December 1983): 64–65. (1) (32)

Cavanaugh, David P. "Meeting the Needs of Individuals Through Their Learning Styles." *Student Learning Styles: Diagnosing and Prescribing Programs*. Reston, VA: National Association of Secondary School Principals, 1979: pp. 99–103. (23)

Cross, K. Patricia. "The Rising Tide of School Reform Reports." *Phi Delta Kappan* 66, no. 3 (November 1984): 167–172. (4)

Daniel, Neil; and Cox, Jane. "Providing Options for Superior Students in Secondary Schools." *NASSP Bulletin* 69, no. 482 (September 1985): 25–30. (2) (14) (19)

Decker, Robert; and Krajewski, Robert J. "The Role of Technology in Education: High Schools of the Future." *NASSP Bulletin* 69, No. 484. (November 1985): 2–6.

Eberly, Donald J. "Youth Service Initiatives—A Promise of the Future." *NASSP Bulletin* 69, no. 481 (May 1985): 82–88.

Goldberg, Milton. "The Essential Points of a Nation at Risk." *Educational Leadership* 41, no. 6 (March 1984): 15–16. (4)

Gray, H. D.; and Tindall, Judith A. *Peer Counseling*. Muncie, Indiana: Accelerated Development, Inc., 1978.

Hansen, J. Merrill. "The Accidental Curriculum: The Unplanned Nature of Curriculum Implementation." *NASSP Bulletin* 65, no. 443 (March 1981): 16–21.

Joekel, Ronald G. "Student Activities and Academic Eligibility Requirements." *NASSP Bulletin* 69, no. 483 (October 1985): 3–9 (10)

Lightfoot, Sarah. *Good High Schools: Portraits of Character and Culture*. New York: Basic Books, 1983. (5)

Mackey, James; and Appleman, Deborah. "The Growth of Adolescent Apathy." *Educational Leadership* 40, no. 6 (March 1983): 30–33.

Martin, John Henry. "Reconsidering the Goals of High School Education. *Educational Leadership* 37, no. 4 (January 1980): 278–285. (5)

Menacker, Julius; and Wynne, Edward A. "Helping Students to Serve Society." *Phi Delta Kappan* 63, no. 6 (February 1982): 381–385. (8)

Molander, Roger; and Woodward, Ellis. "How to Teach Nuclear War to High School Students." *Educational Leadership* 42, no. 8 (May 1983): 44–48. (12)

Parkay, Forrest. *White Teacher, Black School*. New York: Praeger Press, 1983.

Powell, Arthur G.; Farrar, Eleanor; and Cohen, David K. *The Shopping Mall High School*. Boston: Houghton Mifflin Co., 1985. (14).

———. "The Shopping Mall High School: Winners and Losers in the Educational Marketplace." *NASSP Bulletin* 69, no. 483 (October 1985): 40–51. (14)

Pfeifer, Jerilyn K. "Teenage Suicide: What Can the Schools Do." Phi Delta Kappa Fastback No. 234. Bloomington, IN: Phi Delta Kappa Educational Foundation, 1986.

Raywid, Mary A. "The First Decade of Public Alternative Schools." *Phi Delta Kappan* 62, no. 8 (April 1981): 551–554. (3)

Reimer, Joseph. "Moral Education: The Just Community Approach." *Phi Delta Kappan* 62, no. 7 (March 1981): 485–487.

Renfro, Jean. "Mission Possible: Adolescents Do Not Have to Self Destruct." *Educational Horizons* 62, no. 4 (Summer 1984): 141–143.

Rush, Jean C. "Should Fine Arts Be Required for High School Graduation?" *NASSP Bulletin* 69, no. 478 (February 1985): 49–53.

Seidel, Robert J. "It's 1980: Do You Know Where Your Computer Is?" *Phi Delta Kappan* 61, no. 7 (March 1980): 481–485. (9)

Sizer, Theodore R. "Rebuilding: First Steps by the Coalition of Essential Schools." *Phi Delta Kappan* 68, no. 1 (September 1986): 38–42.

Tanner, Daniel. "The American High School At the Crossroads." *Educational Leadership* 41, no. 6 (March 1984): 4–13.

Tye, Barbara Benham. *Multiple Realities: A Study of Thirteen American High Schools*. Lanham, MD: University Press of America, 1985. (3)

Weisberg, Alan. "What Research Has to Say About Vocational Education and the High Schools." *Phi Delta Kappan* 64, no. 5 (January 1983): 355–359. (32)

Wigginton, Eliot. *A Shining Moment: The Foxfire Experience*. Garden City, NY: Anchor Doubleday, 1985.

Wilson, Bruce L.; and Rossman, Gretchen B. "Collaborative Links with the Community: Lessons from Exemplary Secondary Schools." *Phi Delta Kappan* 67, no. 10 (June 1986) 708–710.

## Reform Reports of the 1980s

Boyer, Ernest, L. *High School: A Report on Secondary Education in America*. New York: Harper and Row, 1983.

Education Commission of the States Task Force on Education for Economic Growth. *Action for Excellence*. Denver: ECS, 1983.

Goodlad, John I. *A Place Called School: Prospects for the Future*. New York: McGraw Hill, 1983.

Adler, J. Mortimer. *The Paideia Proposal*. New York: Macmillan, 1982.

National Commission on Excellence in Education. *A Nation at Risk*. Washington, D.C.: U.S. Government Printing Office, 1983.

National Commission on Secondary Vocational Education. *The Unfinished Agenda*. Columbus: National Center for Research in Vocational Education, Ohio State University, 1984.

National Science Board Commission on Precollege Education in Mathematics, Science, and Technology. *Educating Americans for the 21st Century*. Washington, D.C.: U.S. Government Printing Office, 1983.

Sizer, Theodore R. *Horace's Compromise: The Dilemma of the American High School*. Boston: Houghton Mifflin, 1984.

Twentieth Century Fund Task Force on Federal Education Policy. *Making the Grade*. New York: Twentieth Century Fund, 1983.

# 10

# *Education for Late Adolescent, Mature, and Senior Learners*

## PREREQUISITES

1. Reading and studying Sections 1 through 6.
2. The development of, and ability to use, a set of curriculum criteria to describe and evaluate a curriculum plan. You must be able to use this set of criteria in order to critically analyze and make curriculum decisions regarding programs described in this section.

## RATIONALE

All curriculum planners and teachers should be acquainted with the goals and trends in education at all levels, regardless of the level of the program of education at which they plan to work. You should know about goals and trends of education for late adolescents, adults, and senior learners whether you plan to work at this level or not. You will be better able to plan a curriculum or teach at one of the other levels if you have this information. This view is based on such curriculum criteria as continuity in learning, balance in the curriculum, and provision for individual differences.

This section is now called Education for Late Adolescent, Mature, and Senior Learners rather than Community College and Higher Education, as in earlier editions. In keeping with the definition of *curriculum* presented in Section 1, the focus is on programs of education rather than exclusively on school programs.

*Late adolescence* in our society is a critical period in the development of self-concept. It is important for psycho-social identity, work- or role-related success in terms of the achievement values of the society, and integration into the life of the local community. According to Havighurst, *late adolescence and early adulthood* is a tumultuous period in our society during which the individual questions values, courtship, and marriage, as well as his or her new status as worker, parent, or citizen. The period may cover five or ten years of highly individualistic life in which the young person may tend to grow into alienation, loneliness, or ruthlessness with little feeling for the values of community life. Havighurst believes early adulthood is the period most full of *teachable moments*, but that in the past it has been "emptiest of efforts to teach." This is one of the challenges to community college and university programs.

In terms of traditional students, higher education is in a period of enrollment decline. The number of eighteen-year-olds will drop nearly 20 percent during the 1980s, from 4.2 million in 1980 to 3.4 million in 1990. The population aged 18 to 25 will decline 13.4 percent between 1980 and 1990. That means there will be 3.8 million fewer persons in the traditional college age group in 1990 than there were in 1980. The community college, a relatively new educational institution, developed in America and has become a major element of the American and Canadian systems of public education. It evolved from the junior college, but it has been designed to serve many more social purposes.

The *community college* serves the community with adult education and senior learner programs in a variety of fields. It provides a college-parallel program for those who wish to transfer to four-year colleges or universities after two years. It offers terminal education in many vocational, technical, and commercial subjects for those who will go no further in formal education programs. A number of states have developed master plans to provide community colleges within commuting distance of all high school graduates.

The community college has grown from one serving a limited number of students to one providing education for all youth not in four-year colleges and for many adults and senior learners. Community colleges also now offer many programs to help meet the needs of communities and society.

Today community colleges often offer five types of programs:

1.  *A Junior College Transfer Program.* This is the equivalent of the first two years of undergraduate college work in a four-year college. It leads to the associate of arts (A.A.) degree. For many students the community college, located near home, may be a better place to take this work than at a larger, often more impersonal, college or state university.

2.  *A Technical and/or Vocational Program.* There are many jobs important in a technological society for which the needed preparation can be completed in two years or less. Such preparation provides outstanding opportunities for many young people. The United States Office of Education, in cooperation with many large corporations, publishes a pamphlet entitled "Twenty-Five Technical Careers You Can Learn in Two Years or Less." It lists technicians in varied fields such as air conditioning, commercial flying, electronic data processing, police science, and oceanography.

3. *An Adult Education Program.* This program serves the whole community. Classes are formed according to interest and demand. The program can be particularly important for our growing number of senior citizens.

4. *Developmental Programs.* These programs serve all students whose previous backgrounds may prevent them from successfully completing academic or technical education. Most public community colleges now have special provisions for students who have not satisfactorily completed traditional academic requirements in high school.

5. *Community Service Programs.* These programs focus on programs of education rather than programs of schooling, in keeping with our definition of curriculum in Section 1. "Multi-Service Outreach Programs," extension centers, in-plant training, and programs for the disadvantaged are examples. The college goes to the community with instruction and programs when and where they are needed.

In the 1970s the number of and enrollment in community colleges continued to increase dramatically, but the functions and relative significance of the five types of programs changed considerably. At the beginning of the decade it was thought that the transfer program would be the most important one because of the expanded opportunity it gave high school graduates to go to college. Later the emphasis shifted to new types of students—women, middle-aged adults, senior learners, new immigrants, and minorities. By the end of the decade fewer than 5 percent of the students in states with thriving community college systems transferred each year as juniors to colleges and universities. The changes in goals and functions of the community colleges during the past ten years are described in the article "Can the Community Colleges Survive Success?" in this section.

One of the major concerns for community colleges today is the large number of students who drop out before completing their programs. Because many students seem unable to succeed, attention to individual learning needs and problems is important as a major part of curriculum planning and teaching. An earlier section of this book examined the ways in which learning style has been made the basis for individualized approaches to teaching and learning.

The community college serves many young people who are late maturers or "late bloomers" who wouldn't be permitted to enter a four-year college or university on the basis of high school grades. Many students who need remedial work in basic skills get such work in "guided studies" noncredit programs. Success in such work enables them to continue in other areas of study.

The *university* today is being challenged and its benefits being questioned in ways that have not happened previously in this century. It is clear that the university cannot continue to do for the next twenty years, only better, what it has done for the last twenty. The demand for *alternatives and alternative programs* is as strong at this level as at the other levels of education that we have studied. Many students have gone to college after high school by default because no one offered them anything else and because middle-class parents have been conditioned to believe that higher education is something they owe their children. Over 50 percent of the high school graduates in the United States now go on to college (in some communities, 70 or 80 percent) expecting to get better jobs as a result of getting a college degree—in spite of the fact that 80 percent of the country's jobs do not require a college degree. The broad general objectives of education at this level are the same as those at the other levels we have studied—*citizenship, self-realization, vocation, and critical thinking*. But alternatives are needed to serve the needs of late adolescents in attaining the goals.

In the past the word "college" meant four uninterrupted years of full-time enrollment in one institution. During the 1970s the alternatives for undergraduate education for late adolescents and adults were increased considerably by the development of the concept of "colleges without walls" and their "external degrees" in many parts of the United States. By 1980 nearly 14,000 bachelor's degrees had been awarded through such programs in New York, New Jersey, Connecticut, and Illinois. One of the most successful *non-campus* undergraduate college programs is that of Empire State College of the State University of New York, which Ernest L. Boyer describes in this section in "College with Connections." The academic community's acceptance of the best of these programs is indicated by the number of the recipients of these external degrees who have been able to use them to gain admission to graduate studies.

A number of national reports regarding current goals and practices in higher education were issued in 1984 and 1985 (see "Some Higher Education Reports of the 1980s" at the end of this section). Excerpts from two of these reports are included in this section. The report of the Carnegie Foundation for the Advancement of Teaching calls for the restoration to higher education of its original purpose of preparing graduates for lives of involved and committed citizenship. It also calls for renewed effort to develop creativity and independence of mind. The increased focus on academic disciplines has resulted in a "gradual retreat from values." Two solutions are proposed: "active learning" and the "ideal of service." This report also expresses great concern regarding minority enrollment in higher education (see "Higher Education and the American Resurgence" in this section).

The recent report of the National Institute of Education also calls for more active modes of learning. It states that college curricula have become excessively vocational in orientation and that curriculum content should be addressed not only to subject-matter but also to the development of analysis, problem-solving and synthesis. Students and faculty should integrate knowledge from various disciplines (see "Involvement in Learning: Realizing the Potential of American Higher Education").

*Adult education* is changing drastically. Before 1945 it was generally believed in this country that adults, once they were past adolescence, had very little learning capacity. When thousands of World War II veterans returned to college campuses, there was great fear that they would not be able to learn and would lower academic standards. Just the reverse happened; they did better academically than their younger colleagues—because they were older, more mature, and often highly motivated. Now we know that adults, regardless of age, can learn almost anything they want to, given time, persistence, and assistance. This is related to another notable change in enrollments in colleges and universities: In 1986 more than one-third of all college students are over age 25 and this percentage will continue to increase for the foreseeable future (see "The Changing University: Survival in the Information Society").

A major educational issue during the next twenty years will undoubtedly be the establishment of an equilibrium between *youth-terminal* and *adult-continuing education*. Two traditionally held ideas about education must now be rejected: (1) the assumption that the need for organized educational opportunities can be met during the first one-fourth of the life span; and (2) the assumption that the need for education during the remaining three-fourths of a lifetime can be adequately met by incidental learning through the daily experiences of living and working. Now the major thrust must be to provide recurring learning opportunities available to everyone throughout life. This need is discussed and described in "Can the Community Colleges Survive Success?" and "College with Connections." A person's education now becomes obsolescent with a rapidity never before known.

A major emphasis in *adult education* now is to provide learning opportunities for people who were previously left out: native American Indians, Blacks, Mexican Americans, Puerto Ricans, and the poor. Community college programs for some of these groups are described in "Can the Community Colleges Survive Success?"

Colleges and universities are beginning to take seriously the challenge posed by the reentry of adult students. "Model Programs for Adult Learners in Higher Education" in this section summarizes the efforts of eighteen universities and community colleges to meet the individual needs and developmental differences of adult learners.

"Give me your tired, your poor, your homebound masses yearning for a degree." This might be the motto of higher education for the 1980s. In the fall of 1981, 500 colleges working with the Public Broadcasting Service (PBS) began offering nine courses for credit via 206 public television stations. These courses reach thousands of students—housewives, full-time workers, handicapped adults, and people who live several hundred miles from the college of their choice—who otherwise could not have such learning experiences. Community colleges and such universities as Iowa, Temple, Wisconsin, and Indiana are giving college credit for them. There are hefty supplemental materials, homework, and mid-term and final exams at campus, at local schools, or by mail.

Another group previously left out has been *senior learners*. Fifteen percent of Americans, thirty-two million individuals, are now classified as senior citizens (over sixty years of age). With today's low birthrate and longer life span, those over sixty-five are increasing twice as fast as the population as a whole. Many colleges are now opening their doors widely to senior citizens; roughly one-fifth of the 3,300 institutions for higher learning offer courses for retirement age students (many offer free or reduced tuition). Courses vary from cultural enrichment, retirement services, and crafts to liberal arts programs and vocational reeducation for those over age fifty-five.

The greatest group participation of older adults in regular college level courses has been through Elderhostel, which began in 1975 and offered people sixty and over the chance to take courses, staying in residence while paying only for living expenses. By 1986 this program for senior learners was offered in all fifty states by more than 400 colleges and universities, for 111,000 students. In describing Elderhostel and its "irresistible momentum" in this section, Kaplan states that more attention should be given to the teaching of senior learners and that the fight against ageism should begin in the minds of the elderly. Elderhostel is based on the idea that retirement does not mean withdrawal, but that the later years of life are an opportunity for new learning and new experiences.

A growing field for the curriculum planner is that of *educational gerontologist*, one who develops educational programs for an aging population. Until now, it has sometimes been true that one of the greatest barriers to education for older adults lies in the minds of some adult educators.

What will be the shape of higher education in the future? According to "The Changing University: Survival in the Information Society," linkages with other institutions will be all-important to the survival and significance of the university of the future. Many different approaches to curriculum presentation will be utilized. Much faculty time will be devoted to diagnosing student needs and prescribing individual courses of study. Exit competency programs will be utilized.

Are higher educational institutions providing young people and adults in our society with the skills and knowledge needed to function in a world community? Millions of jobs depend upon contacts with people in other parts of the globe and the interrelatedness of global and national events is only marginally reflected in what is being taught in our schools and colleges (see "International Education's Expanded Role in Higher Education").

The *human development, learning, and knowledge and cognition* theories discussed in Sections 3, 4, and 5 apply to adult learners and senior learners as at other age levels. Teaching practices which are based on *cognitive learning theory* are especially useful with adults. If adults and senior citizens understand the major features of a topic, they are more able to relate it to what they already know and are thus able to accumulate additional knowledge. *Advance organizers, clear instructions,* and *explanation of concepts* are as useful with adults and senior learners as they are with other learners. Adults and senior citizens usually learn more effectively when they proceed at their own pace. And they learn from many resources including books, films, experts, and peers. Like learners at other age levels, they learn better when they are able to use their preferred resources. The same curriculum criteria as at other ages are important in planning—such as *relevance, individual differences, continuity, self-understanding, and personalization of instruction.*

In January, 1979, a new law covering civil rights of older Americans went into effect; the law prohibits discrimination on the basis of age in any programs funded by the federal government. At the same time, another law became effective pushing the mandatory retirement age from sixty-five to seventy for those in private industry, and setting no limits for those in government. At this age as at others, the criterion of *individual differences* should be a major guideline in curriculum planning and teaching. It is likely that some members of this age group will seek education related to vocation, as well as citizenship, critical thinking or self-realization.

Studies by the U.S. Department of Labor and the National Council on the Aging have found older workers able to produce work which is, in quantity and quality, equal or superior to that of younger workers. Supporting this finding, Havighurst (see "Developmental Tasks" in Section 3) says, "It's speed of reaction that seems to slow down, probably after 40. . . . But this is compensated for in experience, wisdom and endurance." Labouvie-Vief, in a recent article in the *Merrill-Palmer Quarterly* (see Books and Articles to Review at the end of this section), points out at least six major deficiencies in past research about adult cognitive development, and refutes the common notion that advancing years must be accompanied by intellectual deterioration. Bardwick, also in the *Merrill-Palmer Quarterly,* provides evidence that the people who will emerge more mature and stronger from the crisis due to awareness of their aging after forty will be those who have been able to create a "sense of future."

It seems clear that community colleges and universities should be aware of the growing population of the middle-aged and senior learners, and should provide appropriate educational opportunities for them in the areas of instruction for new careers, self-enhancement, self-preservation skills (income tax, insurance, and investment opportunities), development of civic awareness and civic responsibility, and counseling services designed to deal with problems specific to these age groups.

What *goals of education* should be established for late adolescent, mature, and senior learners? As stated previously, the general goals are the same as at other levels—vocation, self-realization, citizenship, and critical thinking. At this level a major goal should be to provide a *great diversity of educational opportunities* for everyone. For late adolescents a major goal is to provide help in making the transition to adult society. There should be more opportunities for family life education and consumer education. At this level as at others, the learners should participate in planning the educational program. Senior learners have many needs for learning and should have curricula available to them in the various types of institutions. The single most pervasive need for many senior citizens is the need for *a sense of positive self,* after retirement, when the "category door" is slammed shut. For many, retirement means that they are so thoroughly stripped of previous evaluators that they feel invisible, anonymous, and ignored.

Curriculum planners and teachers must recognize that within the life span there are *normal but critical transitional periods* that require new adjustments to meet new life situations. Community colleges and universities should be geared to meeting these needs of late adolescent, mature, and senior learners, as well as the needs we all have as a result of changes in society and the world.

To better provide for the attainment of objectives at this level, the following innovations and trends are being proposed and tried. The list of *innovations* and *trends* in education for late adolescents and adults includes references to pertinent articles in this section. The list is arranged alphabetically.

1. *Active learning:* "Higher Education and the American Resurgence"; "Involvement in Learning"; "The Changing University"
2. *Adult education:* "The Changing University"; "College with Connections";

"Can the Community Colleges Survive Success?"; "Model Programs for Adult Learners"

3. *Adult peer counseling:* "Model Programs for Adult Learners"
4. *Alternative curricula:* "College with Connections"; "The Changing University"; "Model Programs for Adult Learners"
5. *Career education:* "College with Connections"; "Can the Community Colleges Survive Success?"; "Model Programs for Adult Learners"
6. *Changing faculty roles:* "Higher Education and the American Resurgence"; "The Changing University"; "Involvement in Learning"
7. *Civic education:* "Higher Education and the American Resurgence"; "College with Connections"
8. *College without walls:* "College with Connections"
9. *Community education:* "Can the Community Colleges Survive Success?"
10. *Continuing access for all:* "The Changing University"; "Can the Community Colleges Survive Success?"; "College with Connections"; "Model Programs for Adult Learners"
11. *Corporate education:* "The Changing University"; "College with Connections"
12. *Developmental (remedial) programs:* "Involvement in Learning"; "Can the Community Colleges Survive Success?"
13. *External degree programs:* "The Changing University"; "College with Connections"; "Model Programs for Adult Learners"
14. *Flexible curricula:* "The Changing University"; "Model Programs for Adult Learners"
15. *High impact courses:* "The Changing University"
16. *Independent study:* "The Changing University"
17. *Individualized instruction:* "The Changing University"; "Involvement in Learning"; "Can the Community Colleges Survive Success?"; "College with Connections"; "Model Programs for Adult Learners"
18. *Information technology curricula:* "The Changing University"; "College with Connections"
19. *Interdisciplinary learning:* "The Changing University"; "International Education's Expanded Role"
20. *International education:* "Higher Education and the American Resurgence"
21. *Learning communities:* "Involvement in Learning"
22. *Linkages with business:* "The Changing University"; "College with Connections"
23. *Lifelong learning:* "College with Connections"; "Can the Community Colleges Survive Success?"; "Model Programs for Adult Learners"; "Elderhostel: Using a Lifetime of Learning and Experience"; "The Changing University"
24. *Minority education:* "Higher Education and the American Resurgence"; "College with Connections"; "Can the Community Colleges Survive Success?"
25. *Output quality assessment:* "The Changing University"
26. *Peer teaching:* "College with Connections"
27. *Self-actualization education:* "College with Connections"; "Elderhostel: Using a Lifetime of Learning and Experience"

28. *Services and instruction for senior learners:* "Model Programs for Adult Learners"; "Elderhostel: Using a Lifetime of Learning and Experience"
29. *Strengthened general education:* "The Changing University"; "Involvement in Learning"; "Higher Education and the American Resurgence"; "International Education's Expanded Role"
30. *Student evaluation of programs:* "Involvement in Learning"
31. *Television, radio, computers, and cassettes as a means of instruction:* "The Changing University"; "College with Connections"
32. *Value education:* "Higher Education and the American Resurgence"
33. *Voluntary youth service:* "Higher Education and the American Resurgence"

Some of these trends are found in the community colleges; others are occurring in the universities. Can these institutions successfully serve the diverse needs of late adolescents, young adults, adults, and senior citizens? Can they successfully provide programs as diverse as college transfer, vocational, community service, and recreational?

In the List of Books and Articles to Review at the end of this section, many of the sources are followed by parentheses containing one or more of the numbers in the preceding list of trends. These numbers will help you find other recent articles and books on those late adolescent and adult trends and innovations that particularly interest you.

## OBJECTIVES

Your objectives in studying education at this level as part of the curriculum should be as follows:

1. To be familiar with the objectives, current innovations, and recent trends in education for late adolescents, adults, and senior citizens.
2. To be able to explain the functions and goals of education at this level as part of the total curriculum.
3. To be able to use the objectives of education at this level, the curriculum bases, and your own list of criteria in making curriculum or instruction decisions regarding present as well as proposed programs.
4. To be able to suggest improvements in community college, university, and lifelong education curriculum plans through the decisions made in number 3.

## PREASSESSMENT

1. Discuss the implications of each of the thirty-three innovations and trends in the rationale.
2. Evaluate each of the trends in terms of objectives, bases of curriculum, and selected curriculum criteria.

3.  Select any curriculum plan at this level and describe and analyze it in terms of objectives, the four curriculum bases, your curriculum criteria, and innovations and trends.
4.  Suggest improvements or changes in the curriculum plan in number 3 in light of your analysis.

In answering numbers 3 and 4 of the preassessment, analyze the curriculum goals and plans described in the articles "College with Connections" or "The Changing University: Survival in the Information Society."

## LEARNING ACTIVITIES

Articles in this section will help you to understand the purposes and functions of education for late adolescent, mature, and senior learners. They will also acquaint you with the problems, as well as the innovations and trends, of programs of education at this level. Other learning alternatives are suggested at the end of this section.

## POSTASSESSMENT

After attempting the preassessment you may do *one or more* of the following:

1.  Ask your instructor whether you are ready for a postassessment evaluation on education for late adolescents, adults, and senior learners. Most students will need further work on this curriculum topic.
2.  Read the articles on education for late adolescents and adults in this section and try to determine how the problems, goals, innovations, and trends being discussed in each article should be considered in curriculum planning and teaching.
3.  Choose additional activites and readings or films from those listed at the end of this section.
4.  Look for other films, books, or articles on educational programs for this age group that are available in your library or media center.
5.  Discuss the reading you have done and the films you have viewed with your fellow students. The key questions: How should the problems, goals, trends and innovations you've studied affect a school's curriculum? How should they be considered in planning for teaching?
6.  When you are ready, ask your instructor for advice on a suitable postassessment for you for this topic. Satisfactory completion of number 1 under Problems and Projects at the end of this section might be one possibility. Or satisfactory written completion of the preassessment for this section, after completing other learning activities, might be a satisfactory postassessment. Consult your instructor about this. You can assess your ability to do these activities before seeing your instructor.

# Higher Education and the American Resurgence

FRANK NEWMAN

## PROLOGUE: A MATTER OF WILL

Higher education in the United States is entering a period of questioning of its purposes and its quality. The searchlight of educational reform, which has been focused on elementary and secondary schools, is now moving to include colleges and universities. My colleagues on the panel and I welcome this challenge, encourage it, believe it will be positive in its effects. This report is intended to extend and deepen that debate.

Our confidence in encouraging public scrutiny stems from a simple yet important observation—the American system of higher education is the best in the world. Our motivation to do so flows from another observation—despite its high quality, American higher education must be even more effective if it is to meet the needs of this country in the decade ahead. New and powerful forces are reshaping American society, increasing and changing the demands placed upon higher education.

The most visible new demand is the need to be more effective in an economy that for the first time is truly international; an economy in which the traditional hierarchical approach to organization is rapidly being displaced by a more decentralized, entrepreneurial approach. The jolt of growing competition, most notably from Japan, has already turned the attention of the nation toward the roles that education plays: the importance of research and new technologies to the growth of jobs; the need for scientific and technical talent; the adequacy of our base of elementary and secondary education. The states have already made plain their determination to focus on these issues.

At stake is more than simply the issue of the health of the American economy. At stake is the fundamental issue of the place of the United States in the world; whether it will define itself as a country moving ahead or as a country drifting into a lesser role. We believe that the United States is gearing up for an economic renewal. Education at all levels is expected to play a major role.

If the need to respond to the new world economy were the only force for change, it would be essential that higher education respond. As important as this is, we do not believe that it is the most urgent issue. The most critical demand is to restore to higher education its original purpose of preparing graduates for a life of involved and committed citizenship. It is a need which arises from the unfolding array of societal issues of enormous complexity and seriousness—issues such as, how to accelerate the integration of growing and diverse minorities, how to control the continuing proliferation of nuclear arms, how to reduce the dangers of toxic wastes. Toxic wastes, to use one example, are now recognized as not merely an annoying issue of pollution confined to certain areas but a widespread problem potentially lethal to society in which the critical issue is not technological but political—the ability to fashion solutions acceptable to the community. Not only are new issues added regularly to an already formidable list, but those issues that have been visible for several decades remain maddeningly intractable, if anything, revealing themselves as even more complex than anticipated.

This growing complexity adds greatly to the tasks of citizenship at the very time that the capacity for citizenship seems to be declining. How, in these circumstances, can the public avoid becoming tired of its civic responsibilities, avoid the temptation to accept simplistic solutions? The need to resolve complex problems intelligently places an ever greater demand on higher education—a demand for graduates who have a profound understanding of what it means to be a citizen; graduates capable of an interest larger than self-interest; graduates capable of helping this country to be not simply a strong competitor but a responsible and effective leader in a complicated world. Yet by every measure that we have been able to find, today's graduates are less interested in and less prepared to exercise their civic responsibilities. Colleges and universities are less willing to recognize the teaching of civic skills as part of their missions. How, then, can higher education transform the experience of going to college so that it fosters a sense of civic responsibility?

Much of the attention of policy makers—and students—focuses on technical expertise necessary for today's careers. Such expertise is essential for the successful functioning of society, but, as we have seen, American higher education will, with continued support, provide that expertise in the depth and diversity required. More problematic is whether graduates will have those capacities beyond technical expertise, or even beyond intellectual skills, that are now critical—the ability to be creative, the willingness to take

risks, and the desire to participate constructively in the civic affairs of the country.

## The Stifling of Creativity

Despite the advantage that American higher education has over other systems of higher education, it far too often stifles the inherent creativity of the student. Students too frequently sit passively in class, take safe courses, are discouraged from risky or interdisciplinary research projects, and are discouraged from challenging the ideas presented to them.

We now know that the development of creativity in the student is discouraged by fear of censure, or distrust, or fear of failure; a stifling atmosphere; attempts to closely control behavior and thinking; restricted communication; the assumption, in the classroom and in texts that there is one right answer to every problem; and a passive role. Creativity and independence of mind are encouraged when students learn to question; select projects or research topics themselves (within whatever framework is necessary); and learn how concepts are related.

The values teachers hold, and their ability to act as role models, also seem to play an important role in producing creative students. There is strong evidence that working closely with teachers who are themselves creative, or who value creativity and the character traits associated with it, tends to reproduce those characteristics in students. Among other things, students are less likely to be stifled by those who encourage questioning and are not threatened by inquiring students.

## Education for Civic Responsibility

Liberal education has always focused on more than the acquisition of knowledge. In ancient

Greece, "liberal education" was for those citizens with the civic responsibility to govern. Its opposite, "servile education," was for those who needed education for their work but who did not share in the responsibility for public affairs.

American higher education, from the first, assumed that all of its graduates would participate fully in public affairs as well as in their own careers. Although higher education's commitment to education for civic responsibility remains undiminished, at least in the rhetoric of college catalogues, there has been an erosion in the practice.

Education for public responsibility includes but goes beyond a knowledge of how the system of governance works. It encompasses the sensitive issue of values and, specifically, the value of moving from self-interest to larger-than-self interest. For the first two centuries of American higher education, the development of the character of the student was seen as the central task of the administration and faculty. For the last half century, it has declined in priority. Despite the decline, the concept, as Ernest Boyer and Fred Hechinger argue, remains integral to the expectations of a college education:

"For all the nagging doubts of the contemporary age, the belief persists that the process most capable of holding the intellectual center of society together, preventing it from disintegrating into unconnected splinters, is education. It may not have lived up to this vision of cohesion, but, at its best, the campus is expected to bring together the views and experiences of all its parts, and create something greater than the sum, offering the prospect that personal values will be clarified, and that the channels of our common life will be deepened and renewed."

The importance of universities and colleges in the development of values has grown for two reasons—the decline in the role of family and church, and the larger share of the population who now obtain higher education.

The college years are ones of special signifi-cance. Students begin their life away from their families. They begin to vote. It is a time of a shift from the narrowly held views of adolescence to the more reasoned views of adulthood. It is a time when students are led into a larger view of moral problems and decisions, and a time when they learn to move from the abstractions of moral theory to the dilemmas of moral action. The values that are developed at this time in their lives will persist throughout life.

Despite the importance of this period in the student's life, and the concomitant urgency for building a sense of community in a society increasingly pressed by difficult problems, there is little evidence to indicate that colleges and universities are interested, let alone effective, in encouraging value development. Students seem less and less interested in the civic life and less and less able to mobilize themselves to get involved in public issues.

Allan Bloom, after examining the university role in the teaching of values, argues:

". . . students in our best universities do not believe in anything and those universities are doing nothing about it. . . . An easy-going American kind of nihilism has descended upon us, a nihilism without the terror of the abyss. The great questions . . . hardly touch the young . . . the universities, which should encourage the quest for the clarification of such questions, are the very source of the doctrine which makes that quest appear futile."

Why have colleges and universities seemed to abdicate such a central responsibility? Some faculty members and administrators argue that it is the inevitable result of the growth in size of campuses. Size does make the task difficult. A recent Carnegie Foundation survey reinforces earlier findings that students at large universities feel the most isolated and the least involved. Other studies suggest that students at such institutions are substantially less involved in extracurricular activities than students at small colleges. Still, size seems to us only a complication, not a root cause for the lack of value education.

Faculty attitudes are a more significant factor. Many described to us a slow shift in the attitudes of faculty (and administrators) that, over time, has come to treat warily at best and often reject outright the role of higher education in treating values. Many argue that higher education must be concerned with absolute truths and not deal in values. It does teach values, of course. To proclaim to students that the campus is neutral toward all ideas is in itself to propose a profound value. Besides, values are inherent in how the college treats the issue of honesty (prohibiting cheating) or merit (not everyone gets A's).

At least one cause of the wariness is the fear that any attempt to address values will gradually slip over into indoctrination. There is a strong fear that an individual faculty member will begin to impose his or her personal ideology.

The most common explanation of the gradual retreat from values is the increased focus on the academic disciplines. As fields become more complex, the temptation rises for faculty to stay within the limits of "factual" knowledge, to see one's task as teaching the methodology of physics, or sociology, and therefore to abdicate responsibility for the whole student. The faculty reward system has come to focus increasingly on publications and research grants. It is expedient to concentrate on what is familiar and real—namely one's research—rather than on the messy, controversial, uncertain, and often unrewarding area of value development. For the last 60 years as well, faculty also have become less involved in extracurricular affairs where values are often transmitted to students. These activities are now the domain of a new breed of professionals, the student affairs officers.

Is the situation hopeless? Probably not. In fact, there seems to be a slowly emerging interest in addressing values once again. A group of universities and colleges has begun an effort to encourage students to undertake public service before, during, or after their college experience. Their assumption is that engagement in service to the community helps develop a fuller understanding of both the nature of American society and each citizen's responsibility. They have found an excellent response. Since 1970, 12,000 courses explicitly designed to explore practical moral questions have come into existence. In light of the evidence available, it is hard to argue that students are turning sharply toward a public interest, but it does seem as if there is now a moment in which the issue can again be addressed. How then can colleges and universities, with due regard for the risks of indoctrination that must be avoided, move toward the restoration of the teaching of civic responsibility to its rightful role?

## Active Learning

As the need has been addressed to encourage each student's creativity and each student's sense of responsibility, the tendency of higher education to think in narrow terms about the process of teaching and learning has repeatedly been confronted. Too often, quality is assumed to be measured only in terms of selectiveness of admission and effectiveness only in terms of knowledge transferred to the student as measured by grades and test scores. Of course, knowledge is an important outcome of education. But the focus of the student's interest cannot be just grades, which in turn lead to academic credit, which in turn leads—when enough credits have been accumulated—to a degree, and finally, as students and parents hope, to a job. Rather, education must be an opening to an exciting experience.

A number of authorities who have studied the growth and development of students were consulted to determine how colleges can encourage both creativity and civic responsibility. There was a wide variety of responses, but one recommendation was universal: the student must become more actively involved in his or her own learning. Far too often, students are treated as the object of learning rather than as colleagues in the learning process.

Ironically, there is a danger that emphasis on a new rigor in American education may cause just the opposite to happen. The pressure to improve test scores may be translated into an emphasis on rote learning. Yet rote learning does not provide a base for higher order integrative thinking. Instead it inhibits creative potential and frustrates the learning of responsibility. Therefore, emphasis must be more on understanding than on memorization of facts.

College education is nowhere near as exciting nor as effective as it could be. In many ways it is boring, particularly the classroom part. The student is expected to sit quietly in class, listen to a lecture, make notes with the purpose of memorizing not only the information about the subject being transmitted but the interpretation that is provided in a predigested form.

Students spend somewhere between 5 and 20 per cent of their time in active participation in class. Discussions with students and observations of undergraduate classes suggest that active classroom participation is probably closer to the 5 per cent figure than the 20 per cent. A new Carnegie Foundation survey shows that more than half of the undergraduates at large universities feel that "most students are treated like numbers in a book." The recent Carnegie Foundation report, *High School*, as well as other recent reports on elementary and secondary education describe a similar pattern of teaching at those levels. Theodore Sizer, in *Horace's Compromise*, argues:

"No more important finding has emerged from the inquiries of our study than that the American high school student, *as student*, is all too often docile, compliant, and without initiative. Their harshest epithet for teacher is 'boring.' There are too few

rewards for being inquisitive; there rarely is extra credit for the ingenious proof. The constructive skeptic can be unsettling to all too many teachers who may find him cheeky and disruptive."

A student cannot learn to reason solely by listening to a description of how a teacher or professor has reasoned. Lectures, at their best, transmit knowledge, but they are rarely inspiring. They seldom transform the experience of learning from the humdrum to a level of excitement that captures the student's attention. Students know that mastering data or a given professor's viewpoint is only peripherally related to the purposes of education but intimately related to the grades necessary for admission to selective programs. So the process breeds cynicism toward the teaching.

Beyond that, the passive process fails to accomplish the most fundamental goals of a liberal education. To become creative, one must practice being creative. To become a risk taker, one must try to take risks. Particularly in a world where constant change has become the norm, students must reject facile answers and pre-digested certainty. They must fashion their own conclusions, tentative as they may be, and their own plans for learning. Perhaps most crucial, if one is to understand the importance of judgment and the importance of responsibility, one must learn by attempting to make such judgments and acting responsibly.

There is no more critical task ahead for American higher education than to transform the undergraduate experience into a more active learning process.

## The Ideal of Service

For all of the cynicism about political life in this country, for all of the worry about the TV-created passiveness and self-interest of young people, there remains deep in the American psyche a belief in the ideal of service to country as a proper step to adulthood. It is like a quietly burning ember, waiting to be fanned into a visible flame.

Repeatedly over the post-war period, and earlier during the 1930's, a variety of federal programs attempted to respond to that belief. They include the Civilian Conservation Corps, the National Youth Administration, the Peace Corps, the Young Adult Conservation Corps, the National Health Service Corps, the Teacher Corps, the University Year for Action, and various forms of student aid linked to military service. Almost all have proven effective at the three tasks expected of these programs—getting something done for society that needs doing, providing opportunities for personal growth for young men and women, and—most important—burnishing the ideal of service in the youth of the country.

All young men and women should be encouraged to serve the country. Because this report is aimed at higher education, we have focused on a concept by which those who aspire to college may gain that opportunity—the concept of a social contract, providing student aid in return for service. College graduates are particularly important in this regard, for it is from among them that the country's leadership emerges. The opportunity to serve, however, should be available to all.

One possible approach to voluntary youth service is the concept of national service for all young Americans, but although service in some form for essentially all young men and women is desirable, a voluntary program would be more effective than any compulsory system. Another approach would be for colleges and universities to prescribe some form of service as a graduation requirement. This has much to recommend it, and colleges and universities should consider how to achieve this objective without trivializing the service performed. Such an approach would be even more effective in the high school. The

school system in Atlanta has already moved to implement such a program.

Both high schools and higher education can move immediately to create more public service opportunities on a volunteer basis. Many institutions such as Berea, Berry, Brown, Cornell, Georgetown, Hampshire, Minnesota, Stanford, Vanderbilt, and Yale have already done so. States and cities can do so as well.

## PARTICIPATION OF MINORITIES IN THE PROFESSIONAL LIFE OF THE COUNTRY

If one considers the forces with which this country must contend over the next decade, it is clear that all segments of society must be drawn into the fullest possible participation. Yet for significant parts of the minority communities, after a short burst of progress in the 1970s, there has been little or no recent progress in entering into programs of higher education that lead to the professional and managerial life of the nation. Whether one addresses this as an issue of social equity or of social efficiency, new and more effective approaches must be found.

### Beyond the Open Door

The term "minorities" encompasses growing diversity. Each group has different rates of growth, geographic areas of concentration, cultural and family customs, and institutional supports. The historically black colleges play a unique role in the black community. Hispanics, on the other hand, have developed close associations with certain community colleges. Even within the term "Hispanic," there are considerable differences between Cubans in Miami, Puerto Ricans in New York, and Chicanos in Los Angeles.

Over the last decade, from 1975 to 1984, the enrollment share of blacks and Hispanics in higher education barely changed at all. The absence of change contrasted sharply with the preceding decade; when the United States belatedly turned its attention to civil rights, their enrollment increase was startling. As the public turned to other issues, minority participation reached a plateau and, despite the growth in minority populations, even declined in some fields. Black enrollment, for example, has fallen despite the rise in the share of all 18-year-olds that are black. The Hispanic share of enrollment grew very slightly, but less than the growth in the share of all Hispanic 14- to 24-year-olds in the population, so Hispanics are proportionally less involved in higher eduation than before. For both blacks and Hispanics, the share of high-school graduates going on to college has fallen.

The number of bachelor's degrees earned by members of black and Hispanic minorities also is falling. Minorities are far more likely to attend two-year public institutions than are their white counterparts. Blacks and Hispanics who enroll at urban community colleges are less likely than white students to transfer to four-year programs. In all programs, save some of the effective programs for minorities noted below, attrition rates for both groups are higher. Native American enrollments, though far smaller, follow similar patterns.

These shares of enrollment overall and at four-year and two-year colleges, and of degrees earned and years completed, contrast strikingly with the steadily increasing share of blacks and Hispanics and particularly of those in the college-age years in the total population. Data on Hispanics are sparse, but the situation with respect to blacks is well documented. In 1970, black youth aged 18-24 comprised 11.9 per cent of all youth in the U.S. This rose to 14 per cent by 1982. Hispanic youth are estimated to constitute 7.5 per cent of all youth in that age group.

The problem this creates is clear. Traditionally, the large majority of the country's leaders, the managers and professionals—engineers, architects, lawyers, teachers, legislators, faculty members, etc.—have come from white middle class families. It is precisely these families that have had the sharpest drop in the number of children over the past 20 years. Over the next decade it is likely that the number of white 18-year-olds—who have historically formed the overwhelming majority of entrants to the professional class—will decline by roughly 35 per cent from the 1980 peak while the number of black and Hispanic 18-year-olds—who tend to enter higher education at lower rates—will be expanding steadily.

Asian Americans are quite separate from other minority groups in their pattern of enrollment. Though they make up only 2 per cent of the population, they receive 3 per cent of M.D. degrees, 4 per cent of engineering bachelor's, 7.5 per cent of Ph.D. degrees in engineering, and 18 per cent of all Doctor of Pharmacy degrees. They are underrepresented, however, in other fields—for example, they receive 1.5 per cent of law degrees, and less than 1 per cent of the degrees in education and the social sciences.

Family structure and cultural norms have an enormous amount to do with who goes on to college to study what. They contribute to differing rates of completion of high school, deficiencies of math and science skills among some groups, language barriers, and add to the concern over the adequacy of counseling, and the disputes over the suitability of standardized tests. What is needed is an array of imaginative programs. No single simple solution is likely to solve the problems of achieving equal opportunity. The diversity among minorities is a reminder as well that the country has a major task ahead to teach not only language skills but civic understanding and responsibility to many for whom American concepts are unfamiliar.

We must all recognize the demands that the

American role of leadership in the world places on higher education—leadership in the best and fullest sense of that word. Economic leadership is involved, as is scientific and technological leadership. But more is involved—cooperative efforts at home and abroad, a willingness to face the difficult social and political problems, and a determination to work toward constructive solutions. In short, what is needed is more than just an economic renewal; what is needed is a true American resurgence.

Within this resurgence, higher education should not take its present status for granted. An American resurgence requires that the country challenge itself to change and improve in many dimensions. While higher education has a unique role in helping to articulate that challenge, it has a special responsibility to question *its own* effectiveness. It is toward the fostering of this spirit of reexamination that our proposals are intended.

*Frank Newman* is President of the Education Commission of the States. He was formerly President of the University of Rhode Island.

# Involvement in Learning: Realizing the Potential of American Higher Education
## NATIONAL INSTITUTE OF EDUCATION

*The October 1984 publication of National Institute of Education's* Involvement in Learning: Realizing the Potential of American Higher Education *served notice to the academic community that its time had come. The spotlight that for two years had shone so brightly on the nation's K–12 classrooms would now shift to the campus. And with the light would come heat–pressure for comprehensive reform throughout U.S. higher education.*

*Excerpts from the NIE report follow.*

The strains of rapid expansion, followed by recent years of constricting resources and leveling enrollments, have taken their toll. The realities of student learning, curricular coherence, the quality of facilities, faculty morale, and academic standards no longer measure up to our expectations. These gaps between the ideal and the ac-

tual are serious warning signals. They point to both current and potential problems that must be recognized and addressed. . . .

- One out of eight highly-able high school seniors does not choose to attend college.
- Only half of the students who start college with the intention of getting a bachelor's degree actually attain this goal.
- Student performance on 11 of 15 major Subject Area Tests of the Graduate Record Examinations declined between 1964 and 1982. The sharpest declines occurred in subjects requiring high verbal skills.

One cannot blame these trends entirely on the decline in the preparation of entering college

Excerpted from *Involvement In Learning: Realizing the Potential of American Higher Education* (Washington, D.C.: The U.S. Government Printing Office, 1984).

students. Part of the problem is what happens to students after they matriculate in college. . . .

- Increasing numbers of undergraduates are majoring in narrow specialities. American colleges, community colleges, and universities now offer more than 1,100 different majors and programs, nearly half of them in occupational fields.
- The proportion of bachelor's degrees awarded in arts and sciences (as opposed to professional and vocational programs) fell from 49 percent in 1971 to 36 percent in 1982. The percentage of arts and sciences (or "general program") degrees awarded by community colleges . . . declined from 57 percent in 1970 to 37 percent in 1981, with a corresponding rise in occupational degrees.
- Students have abandoned some of the traditional arts and sciences fields in large numbers. Just since 1977, the proportion of entering freshmen intending to major in the physical sciences has declined by 13 percent—in the humanities by 17 percent; in the social sciences by 19 percent; and in the biological sciences by fully 21 percent.
- Accreditation standards for undergraduate professional programs often stand as barriers to the broad understanding we associate with liberal learning. . . .

Specialization may be a virtue for some students. But as ever more narrow programs are created, they become isolated from each other, and many students end up with fragmented and limited knowledge . . . [T]he college curriculum has become excessively vocational in its orientation, and the bachelor's degree has lost its potential to foster the shared values and knowledge that bind us together as a society.

To a large extent, our recommendations seek to reverse the trends implied by these indicators and to restore liberal education to its central role in undergraduate education.

The power of the campus as an environment for fostering student involvement is crucial. . . . Administrator's attitudes toward students, the degree of collegiality among faculty, the number and diversity of cultural events, the degree to which the college interacts with its surrounding community—all of these factors, and others, determine the tone of the environment.

If students are reluctant citizens of a campus, the degree and quality of their involvement in learning will suffer. The recommendations we offer below are designed to help administrators, faculty, governing bodies, and students themselves improve their learning environments. . . .

- Faculty should make greater use of active modes of teaching and require that students take greater responsibility for their learning.
- Learning technologies should be designed to increase, and not reduce, the amount of personal contact between students and faculty on intellectual issues.
- All colleges should offer a systematic program of guidance and advisement that involves students from matriculation through graduation. Student affairs personnel, peer counselors, faculty, and administrators should all participate in this system on a continuing basis.
- Every institution of higher education should strive to create learning communities, organized around specific intellectual themes or tasks.
- Academic and student service administrators should provide adequate fiscal support, space, and recognition to existing co-curricular programs and activities for purposes of maximizing student involvement. Every attempt should be made to include part-time and commuter students in these programs and activities.
- Academic administrators should consolidate

as many part-time teaching lines into full-time positions as possible.

- Faculties and chief academic officers in each institution should agree upon and disseminate a statement of knowledge, capacities, and skills that students must develop prior to graduation.

- All bachelor's degree recipients should have at least two full years of liberal education. In most professional fields, this will require extending undergraduate programs beyond the usual four years.

- Liberal education requirements should be expanded and reinvigorated to ensure that (1) curricular content is directly addressed not only to subject matter but also to the development of capacities of analysis, problem solving, communication, and synthesis, and (2) students and faculty integrate knowledge from various disciplines.

- Each institution should examine and adjust the content and delivery of the curriculum to match the knowledge, capacities, and skills it expects students to develop.

- Community colleges, colleges, and universities should supplement the credit system with proficiency assessments both in liberal education and in the student's major as a condition of awarding degrees.

- Institutions should offer remedial courses and programs when necessary but should set standards and employ instructional techniques in those programs that will enable students to perform well subsequently in college-level courses.

- Faculty and academic deans should design and implement a systematic program to assess the knowledge, capacities, and skills developed in students by academic and co-curricular programs.

- In changing current systems of assessment, academic administrators and faculty should ensure that the instruments and methods used are appropriate for (1) the knowledge, capacities, and skills addressed and (2) the stated objectives of undergraduate education at their institutions.

- Faculty should participate in the development, adoption, administration, and scoring of the instruments and procedures used in student assessment and, in the process, be trained in using assessment as a teaching tool.

- Student evaluations of academic programs and the learning environment should be conducted regularly. The results should be widely disseminated as a basis for strengthening the quality of undergraduate baccalaureate education.

# The Changing University: Survival in the Information Society

## SAMUEL L. DUNN

The university of tomorrow will differ considerably from today's university, borrowing from the past and adapting to the future as it evolves new links between students, faculty, and community.

Surprisingly, the role of the professor and the organization of the curriculum will be more similar to that of a medieval university than the university of the last 100 years, with students attending fewer lectures and working more independently. On the other hand, new information and communications technologies will transform the classroom and campus as the university moves toward the twenty-first century. And the student body will include a much higher percentage of older adults.

Universities will form linkages with businesses and industries to provide new kinds of educational programs. More human resource development leaders in business will be recognized as educators as they provide full-scale educational programs in competition with the universities. Many students will obtain degrees without even setting foot on a university campus.

Both exciting opportunities and perplexing uncertainties will accompany the shift to the new university. Many institutions will close over the next 20 years, falling victim to demographic changes, new technologies, funding problems, external degree programs, and competition. But exciting days are ahead for those institutions that can make the transition and realize the unlimited potential of the information society.

## END OF A MONOPOLY

While universities and colleges will continue into the foreseeable future as teaching institutions, the traditional university will not have a monopoly on higher education. High-quality educational programs will be available from many other institutions.

At present, it is customary to divide U.S. post-secondary institutions into three groups (1) the private nonprofit college; (2) the public college; and (3) the private entrepreneurial institution. However, this breakdown ignores the significant educational programs that are carried on in business and industry.

The total budgets for training and development in business and industry now run at about $80–$100 billion per year. American Telephone and Telegraph alone spends approximately $1.3 billion per year on training. There are approximately 700,000 full- and part-time educators in business and industry.

The educational and training programs run by business and industry offer a good deal of diversity in terms of quality, intent, and philosophy. Some courses of study are clearly training programs at a basic level, while others equal or surpass typical college courses in terms of theoretical content, quality of instruction, and demands on the student.

Many organizations offer integrated programs leading to certificates that are recognized by other employers, and a growing number of corporations are granting bachelor's and mas-

From *The Futurist* 17, No. 4 (August 1983): 55–60. Used by permission of the publisher, The World Future Society.

ter's degrees in fields related to management and disciplines of interest to that corporation. Mona Milbrath's book *Credentials: A Guide to Business Designations* (Blue River Publishing Co., P.O. Box 882, Sheboygan, Wisconsin 53081) lists over 100 recognized credentials, many of which are available through corporate training and development programs. Other organizations that provide high-level instruction include the armed services and other governmental organizations, professional societies, unions, and community service groups.

In addition to their formal educational programs, business and industry invest heavily in informal educational programs through on-the-job training of higher-level employees. New managers generally need start-up time before they can become full, producing members of the corporate team.

Job experience will have a greater effect on a worker's formal education, since universities and colleges will increasingly recognize and certify experiential learning. Over 1,000 colleges and universities now have programs that award credit to students for learning obtained through experience. Thus, older adults can get a head start when they return to formal educational programs. These programs, of course, blur the lines between the traditional university and training programs in business and industry.

Universities will be increasingly willing to consider a variety of arrangements as they move to improve services to adults. Many more consortium arrangements will link universities and colleges with businesses and industries. Even now, some universities give credit for courses sponsored and taught by corporations. Universities will contract to provide training and development programs for specific companies and even offer on-site degree and certificate programs to complement the corporations' own human resource development programs.

Universities will make increasing use of businesses for internship and cooperative education programs. Many disciplines—not just teacher education and nursing—now use internship programs to provide significant percentages of the programs for majors. These programs provide experience, learning, access to employers, linkages between professors and potential consulting clients, and a source of inexpensive labor.

The educational preparation of the human resource development personnel in American corporations is steadily improving. There are now over 100 formal academic programs for human resource development personnel in the United States, with at least 40 at the master's and doctoral levels. As human resource development leaders become credentialed as educators, the lines will be further blurred and it will be easier for universities to create linkages.

## ELECTRONIC CONSORTIA

In another kind of consortium, traditional colleges will band together to pool resources for nontraditional educational delivery systems. These arrangements will be important from an economic perspective, particularly when entire degree programs are offered via television, computer, videocassette, videodisc, or combinations of these technologies. Typically, a large student base will be needed to cover the investment costs in terms of the hardware and software needed to deliver the programs, especially since the software will be short-lived due to rapid increases in knowledge.

Public television, public radio, and newspapers will also deliver course programming. This will lead, of course, to situations in which students can exercise an option to earn credits from one of many different colleges. Consequently, universities will more readily accept transfer credits from a student not enrolled at the college from which the transcript comes. External degree programs will be common, with most universities of tomorrow providing access to degrees with no residence requirements at all.

The university of the future will no longer be a stand-alone institution, providing in and of itself all aspects of a student's educational program. Linkages will be all-important to its survival, and significance in the future.

## EDUCATING FOR THE INFORMATION SOCIETY

Tomorrow's university will provide both education and training. The distinction between the two may be somewhat artificial, but it may also be helpful. To paraphrase Robert Theobald's description, the study of a problem whose solutions are known is training; the study of a problem whose solutions are unknown is education. At present, over half of all instruction at the undergraduate level in U.S. colleges simply presents facts and solutions—and hence may rightly be called training. In some disciplines, over 90% of the instruction is at this lower cognitive level. Training *must* occur for education to occur, but on the other hand, it will be a constant challenge to the university to instruct at higher cognitive levels.

The university of tomorrow will provide three categories of educational experiences:

First, it will provide general educational programs that will prepare students to be knowledgeable and useful citizens, family members, and workers. Courses in communication, problem solving, decision-making, societal issues, the arts, and human nature should be taken by younger adults to make their lives more satisfying and productive. This category of educational programming is especially important in a dynamic society such as ours, since students can no longer prepare in advance for a specific lifetime career. The liberal arts or general education ap-

proach is the most practical for individuals in the information society.

Second, the university of tomorrow will provide educational programs—both for young adults and mid-life career switchers—that can be used to gain entry to career opportunities. Universities will find it very important to provide these programs for older, working adults in a manner that does not disrupt their income.

Third, the university will provide educational programs for adults at all levels of instruction. Courses in basic skills, taking into account adult needs and learning theory, will be common. The university of tomorrow will be a place where adults go to learn, regardless of level.

The university will also continue its other tasks of discovering, originating, critiquing, and disseminating information and knowledge, as well as its research and consulting services.

## TOWARD MORE FLEXIBLE PROGRAMS

Today, more than one-third of all full-time and part-time college students are over 25. In the future, most students will be over 25 years of age. Most will be working adults and will not be able or willing to forgo income for long periods of time. These students will want programs that enhance knowledge and skills useful in their present careers or ones that will help them gain entry to new careers. Some will want programs that enrich the quality of their personal, family, and social lives, but most adults will go to school for pragmatic purposes.

These older learners will, on the average, be more highly motivated than the 18- to 22-year olds. They will want to have easy access to courses or programs, to move through the educational experience as rapidly as possible with maximum learning, and to receive certification of their new knowledge and skills.

These students will desire a broader range of offerings in the evenings, early mornings, and weekends, through courses by audiocassette, videocassette, and independent study. They will prefer programs that do not have extended prerequisite structures, and in many cases they will want courses that are shorter and more focused than typical college courses. Total immersion, high-impact courses that meet for about 12 hours per day for a period of two to five days will be popular, as will modules—one or one-half credit segments of a three- to five-credit course.

Many younger students, unable or unwilling to spend four years obtaining the baccalaureate degree, will also desire more flexibility. They will be willing to attend school full time only if they can complete their programs more quickly, in time-compressed programs of two or three years.

Of course, many students will still want a more leisurely approach to their programs while in residence on campus. Thus, while the residential component will be relatively less important, it will continue to include a significant percentage of students.

## REORGANIZING THE CURRICULUM

Over the past 300 years, the curriculum has been organized largely in terms of disciplines, the number of which has grown greatly. This division promotes the tendency to view the world, nature, life, and work as segmented, differentiated into separate parts. Particularly at the secondary level and above, information and learning now come in fairly rigidly defined categories, an approach that will be detrimental to the citizen of the information society, who will need to know much more about the interactions of various bodies of knowledge.

The modern world is complex and interconnected. Problem solving must be considered from a systems perspective, taking into account the total knowledge base. A narrow view of life, discipline, or career is inappropriate in these circumstances.

The need to prepare citizens for the telematic society will lead to new organizations of the curriculum in the future. However, despite some experimentation, the present approaches are still firmly entrenched and it may take 10 to 20 years before other methodologies become widely accepted.

One approach that looks promising is to organize the curriculum around the concept of problem solving. In this system, the student works through a series of problems, researching information as needed. Teams of professors work with certain classes of problems.

For example, a student might tackle the problem of planning a new suburb. In the process of working with this problem, the student would have to work with a great deal of information in the disciplines of sociology, urban planning, statistics, business, the biological or environmental sciences, and law, and would consult with a team of professors from these various fields. Preparing written and oral reports would sharpen communication skills, and accessing information from data banks and interviewing experts would add retrieval skills.

Whether this particular approach will be widespread in the future cannot be predicted, but it does appear clear that different approaches to curricular presentation will be utilized. The telematic society will significantly affect the curriculum.

## EMPHASIS ON RESULTS

The quality of today's university is generally measured in terms of inputs to the learning process. That is, the quality of the program is judged by the number of faculty members, the percentage of faculty holding doctorates, the student/faculty ratio, the admissions requirements, the number of books in the library, etc. In the future, this system of quality assessment will be complemented and then replaced by an emphasis on measurements of outputs. As consumers, students will demand full value for the investment they make. They will be interested in the ability of the university to provide programs that fulfill the claims it makes about its graduates, and many schools will strengthen their general education programs accordingly. The university of the future will certainly require all students to be competent in using information technologies.

Because of the emphasis on outputs rather than inputs, universities will introduce exit competency programs. Before this century, most universities and colleges had significant exit requirements, such as the undergraduate thesis or the undergraduate major examination that students had to successfully complete before receiving a bachelor's degree.

## CHANGING FACULTY ROLES

The heart of the university is the faculty. Faculty members teach, advise, motivate, model, publish, consult, testify, and do research. The reputation and future of the university rest with the faculty—and this dependence will continue in tomorrow's university.

The faculty of tomorrow's university will perform the same tasks as in the past, but in a different way.

Faculty members will need to spend more time keeping up with their disciplines. Direct study of new material being generated, with extended periods of refreshing and retooling, will be mandatory. The professors of tomorrow will also have to spend more time keeping abreast of changing teaching technologies. Considerable

amounts of time will be devoted to collecting, formatting, and presenting information via the new technologies.

Another task that will require more time will be that of diagnosing student needs and prescribing individual courses of study. Diagnostic tests must be located or constructed and updated regularly. This system will permit students to learn in a more individualized manner as they master the materials in a given course.

The model of the professor as the manager of a mini-educational system involving staff support, hardware, and courseware appears to be a promising one for meeting changing academic and economic goals. In a typical situation, the undergraduate professor would have one full-time professional-level support person with a bachelor's degree in the discipline being taught. The helper would be able to program a computer and do word processing. This assistant would also be able to run the typical educational machinery (minicomputers, videotape players, videodisc players, film projectors, etc.) as well as manage a records system and administer and correct objective diagnostic course tests.

Courseware would be available to be checked out by the support helper for the student to use on site. Some courseware—largely audiocassettes and discs—might be available for purchase in the university bookstore.

Most students in tomorrow's university will have their own personal computers and will be able to access information banks with ease and skill. The personal computers will be linked to university-wide networks that will allow students to call up most library materials and view them from their dormitory rooms or homes.

The course support system supplemented by the student-supplied equipment would be used in the following way: The student would enroll for a course or module, then go to an assigned classroom for initial instructions and diagnostic tests covering the course material. On the basis of the diagnostic results, a personalized course of study would be prescribed tht would involve interaction with a collection of courseware materials, submission of papers, attendance at occasional lectures given by the professor, individual consultation with the professor, and examinations to demonstrate mastery.

## THE MEDIEVAL MODEL

In this approach, the professor spends less time preparing and presenting formal lectures to large groups of students and more time keeping abreast of the information in the subject being taught and formatting that information in ways that students can access readily. The professor is then available for more interaction with students who need counsel or assistance. The net result is that the professor spends less time lecturing and more time responding to the individual needs of the students.

In this model, the professor assumes duties that are similar, at least conceptually, to those of professors in the European universities of 500 years ago. In the medieval universities, the typical student came to a professor who, through discussion, analyzed the student's needs, then prescribed a course of readings and study. The student started working through the materials on his own, checking back with the professor if he encountered difficulty or wanted to discuss some aspects of the readings. The student discussed the material with other students on his own initiative. When he thought that he had mastered the material, he returned to the professor for an examination (formal or informal), turned in any required papers or theses, and received approval for or failed the course. The professor might give a small number of lectures, usually announced in advance, to the entire university community.

One can see the similarities between the telematic university of the future and the medieval university. The significant difference is that the professor in tomorrow's university will be able to use more sophisticated procedures to diagnose and track the student's experience more readily, working with more students at a time.

## SURVIVAL STRATEGIES

To help professors make the transition to this kind of teaching, the university will need to provide learning experiences, staff, and equipment. The transition in any given situation must be well planned, with the faculty development staff providing the leadership. There will certainly be resistance, and only if the rewards are adequately described and the experiences of the first professors making the transition are pleasant will the new approach be easily accepted.

The university of tomorrow will be considerably more complex than today's university. Varied approaches to the curriculum, linkages with other organizations, blurred lines between public and private funding, increased quality expectation, severe competition, and teaching/learning from a distance will make the university more difficult to manage. Universities will need professional academic administrators with special skills not directly related to those of the teaching and research faculty to manage the transition. Only those institutions with the ability to adjust to the challenge of the future will survive into the twenty-first century.

*Samuel L. Dunn* is Dean of Professional, Graduate, and Continuing Studies, Seattle Pacific University, Seattle, Washington.

# College with Connections

## ERNEST L. BOYER

Ten years ago, I dreamed a dream. My dream was a college of great excellence. A college where the focus was not on buildings or bureaucracy or on rigid schedules—not on mindless regulations but on students and education: the essence of the enterprise. My dream was a college located all across the state geared to serve the student, not the institution or the process. And one of my first moves as Chancellor of the State University was to propose a new, radical, non-campus institution called Empire State College. Today, ten years later, I am filled with tremendous pride. Empire State College has grown far beyond my fondest expectations. This unique institution has become known as the Cadillac of non-traditional institutions. Empire State has a reputation for excellence all around the world, and, most importantly, thousands of students have been served.

But today, in 1981, I would emphasize some priorities that seemed less urgent ten years ago. Simply stated, I think I would urge upon Empire State College the following motto: I would say let's call this a College With Connections. First I'd suggest that in the decade of the 1980s this college must establish close connections between the nation's colleges and schools. Everyone has heard that America is growing older, and if you check our hairlines you will understand. But we know that in just ten years we have moved from a baby boom to a baby bust, and we have heard that the number of eighteen-year-olds in this country will drop by 25 percent by the year 1990. But I am increasingly impressed that the real story of demography in America is the change that is occurring within the student pool. The simple fact is that the face of young America has taken a dramatic turn. Today, in the United States, 26 percent of all white Americans are eighteen years of age and under. Thirty-three percent of black Americans are under eighteen, and 49 percent of all Hispanics are eighteen years of age and under.

Not all of America is aging. Today the immigration pattern has dramatically tilted away from Europe and toward Latin America and the Pacific. Today America is the fourth largest Spanish-speaking nation in the world. And this fall, 50 percent of all children who enroll in kindergarten in Los Angeles county are Hispanic. The point I make is this: America is changing, and these minorities which are fast becoming the majority of populations in many schools are precisely the students who have not been well served by the educational institutions of the past.

Consider also the failure rate in the academic institutions. Eighteen percent of all whites who enter school will drop out before they graduate—30 percent of all blacks—and over 40 percent of all Hispanics leave before they finish high school. Today it seems to me we confront a situation in this nation not unlike the early immigration periods, times when there were great waves of Irish, Italians, East Europeans who enrolled in the nation's schools. It was interesting to read Larry Cremin's recent summary of American education around the turn of the century, and one of my predecessors as the Commissioner of Education established as his first priority a new bureau of Immigrant Education because in many of our schools 80 percent or more of all children were first generation of Americans, and in some classrooms, 70 percent spoke no En-

Excerpted from *Empire State College News,* State University of New York, September, 1981, pp. 6–8. Reprinted by permission of the publisher.

glish. I do not think that this nation has confronted the urgency of the new immigration pattern which is as great as it was at the turn of the century, and the implications are possibly more awesome because this time there is great resistance to the Melting Pot assumptions of those days gone by.

Now I do not have an easy answer. I merely say that those who are sanguine about education in this country miss, I think, the churnings just below the surface, and the battle-grounds—the frustrations—the tensions that surround the changing face of young America will be the schools themselves, and while I was Commissioner there was no issue that caused more anxiety—no question that caused the White House to call me more frequently—than the code word "bilingual education." And the longer it went, and the more I saw anxieties, the more I understood that we are not talking about bilingual education—we are talking about the cultural tensions of this country about which there is great unease.

I merely suggest that as we begin this marvelous institution called Empire State College I think it important we consider the fact that education is a seamless web. The tensions and the battles and the cultural collisions in the early years of schooling in this country are moving inexorably along, and I would urge this College to think carefully about its obligation to the schools. For example, should Empire State College in the decade just ahead place mentors in selected schools to test the capacity to promote students into college at an early rate? And also should we be more mindful to educate teachers about the changing conditions of this culture?

I am suggesting this be a College With Connections, and the connections of the next decade are the connections that bridge the cultural and the ethnic gaps that perhaps could drive great cleavages in the heart of this united nation.

Second, I suggest as we move into the 1980s that this College make connections with mass communication. Ten years ago, quite frankly, we talked about TV. We thought about the Open University in Great Britain. There was neither the money nor the capacity to link this to the other teachers of our culture. I believe the coming decade will not allow us the distance that 1970 provided. We face, I am convinced, an information revolution which will explode in the decade of the '80s, and this revolution will have enormous impact on our colleges and schools.

Today, in America, students watch television four and a half hours every day—before they ever go to school they will have watched it 6,000 hours. They spend 16,000 hours in front of television, and only 11,000 hours in front of teachers before they graduate from high school.

Christopher Evans in his new book, *The Micromillennium*, talks about the impact of yet another form of language—the computer. He says that during the 1980s the book will begin a slow and steady slide into oblivion. Computers will take over, he declares, because they store more information and because their information can be more easily retrieved. Evans says that, in the future, books will be tiny silicone chips which can be slipped into small projectors, and can be read from viewing screens or against the wall, or even on the ceiling if you like to read in bed. And those who do not understand the power of those satellites, and the dishes in the lawns, do not understand the connections of this world. Last week, in Aspen, I talked to a glassy-eyed enthusiast who says he spends three hours a day at his computer talking to specialists all around the world. He gave me his code name—their code names. He has a love affair network with similar computers that span the globe. Cable television will now bring not three channels but perhaps sixty or more into our homes. The awesomeness of being plugged in with all of the imagination and all the terror that provides will, in my view, have unbelievable influences on those of us who enjoy the coziness of a system of learning that we will control. I do not, in this remembering, worship the machine. I only suggest that the nontraditional teachers in our culture will have an impact on our generation we hardly understand.

A recent survey revealed that twenty years ago in 1960, teenagers were asked, "What influenced you the most?" You will be pleased to know that parents were number one, teachers were number two, and peers rated number three. In 1980, American teenagers were asked, "What influenced you the most?"—parents have now been replaced by peers, parents are number two and television is number three with teachers number four. If you study those shifts, it seems to me, clearly observed, that what has been happening is a shift in influence away from the traditional structures with their formative values, good or bad, parents and teachers, to the much slipperier, more open-ended, more culturally normative teachers of peers and television. And the traditional structures have lost both their authority and prestige.

In my view, then, the traditional and the nontraditional teachers must somehow be combined. I think it is absolute madness and wasteful of energy to rail against the new technologies and the potential that they provide. After all, television can take students to the moon. Television can take students to the bottom of the sea, and we can listen to the burping of the whale. When Sadat and Begin met on a Tel Aviv airstrip, they tell me that 500,000,000 human beings watched those two former enemies embrace. And anyone who misses the potential of that kind of shared experience, I think, lacks dramatic vision. Television can teach. Calculators can solve problems, and computers can retrieve instantly millions of information bits, but, perhaps old-fashioned, I declare television, calculators, and computers cannot and will not make discriminating judgments: they cannot or will not teach the students wisdom.

The challenge of the future is not to fight or imitate the electronic teachers in our midst.

Rather, the challenge of Empire State College is to build a partnership between traditional and nontraditional—letting each do what it can do best. With all of our lamenting of education in this country, we do it in the context of an overload of information. The irony of that is incredible to me, and I feel quite certain that if we could ever get the nontraditional teachers and the traditional teachers to join forces, we could, in one decade, be the smartest, the most informed, and, one would hope, the most humane society on earth. The connection stands to be embraced, and Empire State College, with its great imagination and flexibility, can lead the way.

Third, I believe in the 1980s this College must make connections with corporate education. The harsh truth is that education in industry and business is the fastest growing sector in our culture, and in the 1980s more and more students may be going to school, not on the campus, but at the corporation. Latest data suggests that if you add up all that is being spent for schools and colleges in this country, it's 60 billion dollars. But if you add up all that is being spent for education in business and industry, it's 60 billion dollars.

Ten years ago, or more or less, I stopped at a hotel in Buffalo, New York, on my way to one of the campuses, and I picked up the inhouse magazine on the table which was placed conveniently next to the Gideon Bible. The Holiday Inn magazine, I discovered, had a front page story, in bold letters, announcing Holiday Inn University. I opened the magazine, and there it was: a beautiful campus in the South. It had a board of trustees, and a few of my friends were named on it—I thought they were hedging their bets. That has been, however, taken over now by endless variations. The McDonald Corporation has, and I do not kid you, Big Mac University. Arthur D. Little now offers an accredited master's degree.

Accredited degrees are being provided by several major corporate enterprises, and if you read the literature carefully, it is absolutely true that businesses and industries are offering every educational program, in some form, that colleges, schools, and universities traditionally have claimed. The other evening on television a firm announced its new program to teach the basic skills. Just last week in the *Chronicle of Higher Education,* Harvard and DuPont Corporation have joined in a six million dollar merger so that Harvard does the research, and DuPont Corporation gets the findings. I am convinced that in the next ten to twenty years, higher learning in America faces an interesting prospect, having lost its allegiances to the church, having diminished its connections to the nation state, it will find increasingly its affiliations in the business and corporate world. I see this as an unacceptable trend because business, if left to its own devices, will mix ends and means. I believe connections must be made—not to serve business on its own ends; that will lead us, I think, only to a world of technical sophisticates lacking values and traditions.

Thomas Jefferson was greatly concerned that higher learning serve the nation's interest and, no doubt, business interests too. He urged colleges to offer what he called a practical and useful education, and he listed as practical courses: botany, chemistry, surgery, agriculture, and modern language. But Jefferson also included in the useful arts: ethics, history, art, and moral philosophy. I suggest that vocational and moral education belong together.

As I dream of Empire State College in the 1980s, I see it going into the work place more and more. That connection must be made. However, with the strong caveat not to imitate or be consumed by business, but to bring to business and to labor the perspective, the heritage, and the civility of liberal learning. Empire State is the leavening process as it meets those who need it most.

Finally I would like to suggest the last proposal, and that is that we make connections for public good. A long time ago this College dreamed of the possibility of becoming a public institution with a public agenda, and I believe that that commitment must increase. The idea that I see ahead of us is the possibility of a nation that will become so consumed by the technology of our time that we will not, in any way, be able to keep our moral perspective. Professor Carl Shorsky described nineteenth century Basel, Switzerland as a place where civic life and university life were tightly locked. It is a historical lesson worth our consideration. Carl Shorsky said to understand the special qualities of Basel, it is important to remember that the primary function of a university was to foster a civic culture. The city state, he said, assumes some political obligations, but the broad purpose was the advancement of learning. And I believe that as more and more adults come back to college—for degrees—for new careers—for enrichment, I think the nation's colleges should become more systematically engaged in the civic education of adults.

Now this goal can be achieved in a variety of ways: through weekend seminars, through special public issues institutes, and through alumni colleges that bring alumni together for a day or two. What we need, perhaps, is a network of town meetings all across the country in which the people will meet to deal more carefully with the issues of public conscience and public consequence. After all, the public agenda is getting enormously complex and yet the information that we have to think carefully about such matters seems increasingly beyond our grasp.

I don't know how you felt during the Three Mile Island crisis two years ago, but I was sitting in front of the television and I listened to talk about rems and cold shutdowns, and to me it seemed like a foreign language. It occurred to me that I just didn't know how to make sophisticated judgments. The point is this: as a nation we are becoming civically illiterate, and unless we find a better way to educate ourselves as citizens we run the risk of drifting unwittingly into a new kind of dark age—a kind of pre-Gutenberg time when a small band of specialists will control knowledge. These high priests of technology will understand, or claim to understand, the complicated issues, and they will tell the rest of us what we should or should not believe. In this new age of intellectual darkness, citizens will make critical decisions—not on the basis of what they know, but on the basis of who should be believed.

Now some conclude that our circuits are already hopelessly overloaded, and that representative government is not likely to endure. But I believe for those of us who care about government by the people, this prospect cannot go unchallenged. And so my dream would be that in the future, in the decade of the 1980s when this College moves ahead, Empire State might make connections with the public issues of our time—providing perhaps forums for issues to be examined with great care so that the dream of Thomas Jefferson, which combined democracy and intelligence, could be sustained at a time when the issues of awesome complexity confront us all.

In 1750, Benjamin Franklin wrote to Samuel Johnson as follows, he said: "I think with you that nothing is of more importance for the public good than to form and train up youth in wisdom and in virtue." Franklin went on to say that "Wise and good men are, in my opinion, the strength of the state; much more so than riches or arms which under the management of ignorance and wickedness, often draw destruction instead of providing safety for the people."

Well today in my "What If" game, I am announcing that we are starting a new college. We have decided to call it Empire State. We have given it a slogan, a motto: A College With Connections. This College will go forward because it is flexible, but it is committed to excellence as well. But I also believe that this College will make it in the 1980s as it establishes connections with the new Americans—as it establishes connections with the new technology—as it makes connections with the new corporate classrooms and brings to them civility and guidance, and as it establishes connections with the urgent public agenda which will determine the future of us all. I feel very good about this institution. The flexibilities of the past give me enormous confidence that it will remain flexible and committed in the days ahead.

*Ernest L. Boyer* is President, Carnegie Foundation for the Advancement of Teaching, former Chancellor, State University of New York, and former United States Commissioner of Education.

# Can the Community Colleges Survive Success?

## ARTHUR M. COHEN AND JOHN LOMBARDI

What happened to the community colleges in the 1970s? They swept into the decade on a wave of enthusiasm for their low-cost programs, open admissions policies, and expanded services. Now, although their directors complain of sagging revenues and tight competition, the two-year institutions have nailed down a secure position in American education. The position, however, is not fixed. Some of their leaders and many state and federal legislators are calling for the community colleges to become locally based career and compensatory education centers. Others, especially the chief administrators and the faculty, cling tenaciously to their association with higher education.

As the decade closes it is useful to reflect on community college developments of the past ten years and to speculate on coming events. What new functions were taken on in the 1970s? What happened to the old ones? Should the two-year colleges look forward to expanded support in the 1980s for jobs well done? Or should they fear shrinking public esteem?

First some data. Although the furious building rate of the 1960s slowed, 250 new community colleges opened between 1968 and 1978. Forty-one states showed a net increase, with the greatest expansion occurring both in areas where the community colleges had not been widespread—Arizona, Texas, and Virginia—and in those with mature systems: California, Illinois, and Ohio. Enrollment totals ballooned dramatically. The number of students registered for credit more than doubled—from 1.82 million in 1968 to 4.2 million in 1978. The percentage of freshmen and sophomores 18 to 21 attending public community colleges gained where the colleges were new but remained stable in states with well-developed systems. In California, for example, that figure stayed within a point of 88 percent throughout the decade.

Most striking in the early 1970s was the change in the type of writing done about two-year colleges. In the 1960s they were sketched as "teaching institutions" that "meet the needs of the community" through "specially designed curricula." The notion that the colleges could teach undergraduates better because of their "student-oriented faculty" and "smaller classes" was frequently mentioned. They expanded opportunities to go to college, so the ideology ran, because of their location within commuting distance for most students, their easygoing entrance requirements, and their affordability.

Later the promotional rhetoric, if not the ideology, shifted to an emphasis on access for new types of students: women, middle-aged people, senior citizens, and minorities. These groups signed up in droves, comprising most of the enrollment increase. Now, at decade's end, more than half of blacks attending college are in two-year institutions. The colleges have also become the main entry point to higher education for the new immigrants: Puerto Ricans in the middle Atlantic states, Cubans in Florida, Chicanos in the Southwest, and Asians in California. De facto segregated colleges developed in several large cities: Los Angeles and San Francisco, St. Louis and Kansas City, Chicago, El Paso, New York.

A new mission was born during the 1970s and the term "community-based" was coined to

From *Change* Magazine, Vol. 11, No. 8 (November–December 1979): 24–27. © Council on Learning, 271 North Avenue, New Rochelle, New York. Reprinted by permission of the publisher.

describe it: Short courses and a range of cultural and recreational activities that would serve the community in ways different from the traditional programs were the fare. Several community-based colleges were opened, including Whatcom in Washington, Coastline in California, Pioneer in Missouri, and the Community College of Vermont. They operated without campuses, full-time faculty, or formal curricula. Ad hoc programs were taught by part-time instructors to part-time students. Six years after it opened Coastline claimed it served half the population of its county.

Management, governance, and control of community colleges followed the higher education shift to larger units in the 1970s. State-level agencies had a bigger hand in planning. The trend toward uniform methods of accounting for courses, faculty workloads, and expenditures picked up speed. Among the forces responsible for this change were the facts that local districts found it harder to maintain funding from a local tax base; and that faculty collective bargaining, established in one third of the colleges during the decade, introduced rules that had to be more uniformly applied to larger units.

The new methods of the 1970s were hastened by other factors. For example, federal and state legislators began looking increasingly to the two-year colleges to solve social problems, just as they had once used the K–12 system. The colleges were charged with teaching the three R's to people who had not learned them in the lower schools. They were to ease unemployment by training new and displaced workers and by upgrading and certifying the skills of people seeking to climb career ladders. They became transfer agents, not only for veterans' benefits and tuition grants, but for such quasi-educative programs as the Comprehensive Education and Training Act. Many community college administrators and trustees welcomed the new missions as an answer to dropping enrollments of traditional college-bound students. Most faculty

were less enthusiastic because of the different patterns of curriculum and instruction that were required. Nonetheless, by the end of the decade the changes were firmly rooted.

Nothing is without its price, however, and the community colleges paid for their metamorphosis with an erosion of the university transfer function. The slide occurred imperceptibly since transfer programs remained prominent in the catalogs and sizable numbers of the new part-time students enrolled in them. But when full-time and part-time students are considered together, along with everyone taking credit courses for any reason, less than 5 percent each year in states with thriving community college systems transferred as juniors to colleges and universities. In 1977 transfers totaled 5,100 of 181,000 students in Washington, 10,200 of 357,000 in Illinois, and 41,000 of the more than 1,000,000 California students. On paper the university parallel programs remained intact; but the transfer function was a marked casualty of the 1970s.

Curricular shifts mirror this trend. Half the students are enrolled in occupational programs—significantly more than half when the figures are adjusted only for full-time students or for those in some formal program leading to a degree or certificate. Programs in allied health, business, various human services, and those designed for civic workers—including parole and police officers and firefighters—have been in the forefront. Between 1971 and 1976 occupational degrees doubled—from 108,000 to 216,000—while all other degrees (arts, science, etc.) increased by only 20 percent to 175,000.

Under the dual impact of declining academic standards in the secondary schools and the matriculation of students who formerly did not go to college, the two-year institutions also moved decidedly away from the liberal arts in the direction of remedial studies. One third of all mathematics offered in two-year colleges is general or business math—that is, at a level lower than college algebra. In no area of the curriculum has more effort or experimentation taken place. And despite repeated disappointing results the community colleges doggedly seek more effective ways of teaching mathematics. The same is true in the other liberal arts: Courses in basic reading and writing enroll far more students than do the more traditional higher education offerings. In fact, except for U.S. history, Western civilization, American and state government, introductory literature, and Spanish, little in the humanities remains.

The slipping enrollment in traditional courses is accentuated by another phenomenon: Few students take them in sequence even though the college may recommend sequences and list course prerequisites. They declare a major or enter a formal program if required to do so but they use the community college for their own purposes: attending for one term, dropping out to work, dropping back in, enrolling as part timers, taking classes while attending a nearby university, doing course work for no credit, and so on. A recent Texas study showed that only 57 percent of students *enrolled in transfer programs* listed transferring to a university as their primary educational goal. The transfer courses have become discrete. Many students already have baccalaureate degrees and are taking the "transfer" course in photography to gain access to the darkroom, the "transfer" course in art to have their paintings criticized, the "transfer" course in a language so that they can travel abroad.

University-parallel education survives regardless, largely because of the funding patterns that in most states reimburse the community colleges for students enrolled in degree-credit courses. Moreover, whenever a financial crisis occurred during the 1970s transfer courses fared well, directly and indirectly—in dollar support and through the reestablishment of admissions, retention, probation, and dismissal standards. Thus the two-year colleges try hard to include current-interest courses in the transfer curricu-

lum. If students don't want Geography of World Regions but will sign up for The Living Desert or Tidepools of California, the administrators attempt to make these offerings acceptable for transfer credit and money.

During the 1970s the community colleges' power to attract older students, part timers, and those in need of nontraditional higher education, especially remedial, was not matched by their ability to organize and sustain new programs. Although they increased their short courses, courses off campus, remedial studies laboratories, and instructional resource centers, all of which were highly effective in certain ways, the overall effect was an attempt to build a new type of institution on an old structure. Since entrenched personnel could not be dislodged and few were willing to be reoriented, classroom-based instruction and traditional counseling and library services remained intact. Most of the added services were provided through new staff and programs, which caused tensions in both institutional funding and internal dynamics. There is a certain paradox in an institution seeking to provide basic studies for the masses while its employment policies mean it must attract instructors from traditional graduate school programs and its work load measures remain based on hours spent in the classroom. By the end of the decade new employment criteria and faculty development opportunities were growing but the inertia of the pre-existing staff was still highly evident.

A weighty question for the 1980s seems to be how far the community colleges will go in the direction of the three C's: career, compensatory, and community education. Career education, a favored function throughout the history of the two-year colleges with federal and state largess backing it, is certainly entrenched. The programs are usually characterized by a well-organized faculty interacting with trades advisory committees; sequenced curriculum patterns; separate facilities; and controlled student recruitment, admission, and placement procedures. This affords program heads a power not often seen in the liberal arts curricula.

Yale's Burton Clark has said that no society has figured a way to confer equal status on all occupations nor on the schools that prepare people for them. Institutions that train for the higher-status professions are perceived as higher-status schools regardless of their faculty and curricula. In the 1980s the community colleges will lose some of their career programs as state colleges offer them or as the professions for which they train begin requiring the baccalaureate; by the end of the decade nursing, dental hygiene, and some of the human services programs may move out. They will work vigorously to maintain the highest-status occupational programs possible for a less than baccalaureate college.

How much remedial education will the community colleges do? The proportion has inched steadily higher as more incoming students learn at a slower rate, creating a morale problem among faculty and the other students. Teaching remedial students can be overwhelming for faculty, many of whom are academically and emotionally unprepared (and often unsympathetic). High-aptitude students, discouraged by large numbers of slow learners, gravitate toward other colleges in the same district or out of the community colleges entirely. This is not true of the basic education offered to people who have not graduated from high school. Such students are usually adults attending part time or in the evening. They are taught by instructors prepared for the task who do not expect college-level work, whereas remedial students are often high school graduates who want college subjects for transfer credit.

Properly done, remedial education is expensive. In addition to teachers and courses, remedial students need tutors, counselors, special materials, and other aids. These tend not to be provided in credit courses: A large-scale nation-wide survey of instructors of science, social science, mathematics, humanities, and technologies done by the Center for the Study of Community Colleges in 1977 showed the lecture-discussion mode still used in overwhelming preference to reproducible media, simulations, and other innovative techniques. Even though a hefty percentage of instructors recognized the need for new materials, few systems have been able to afford them.

Community education is another matter. The term is not used consistently; in perhaps half the two-year colleges it is a catchall for community services, continuing education, adult basic education, and all non-credit programs and activities. Its future hangs on how successful the colleges are in obtaining funding for the activities and programs that make up the category. Since many are self-supporting their continuation depends on the directors' vigor in promoting them to the public. Those that operate on tax funds will be in a shakier position. The incentives offered for regular course funding will accelerate attempts to transform as many of the activities as possible to credit course status.

Transfer education will survive because of tradition and because of inertia in staffing and funding patterns, but an increasing percentage of students will be inadequately prepared. Attempts to convert the courses to the students' standards and to increase instructional support services will continue but will not keep pace. Thus the dropout and failure rate will not diminish. If transfer curricula are judged by the number who pass through on their way to senior institutions, they will fall short of success.

The number of traditional college-age students will drop throughout the 1980s; because the senior colleges will work harder to attract them, the proportion attending two-year institutions will drop even lower. Actually, many community college leaders since Walter Eells in the 1930s have said that starting students in higher education is not the most important function of community colleges. Consider this 1978 statement by the chancellor for the California Community Colleges:

> Our success can no longer be measured by our transfer record to the four-year institution. Other criteria are more indicative of our goals and missions: namely, what we can do to improve low-income, racial, and ethnic opportunity; our contribution to the labor force; what community colleges are doing to reduce unemployment, to provide needed skills, and to respond to the manpower needs of a rapidly changing industrial technology; our assistance and service to community human services and how we meet the requirements of the adult learner; how successful we are in promoting the concept of lifelong learning.

Nonetheless the colleges will keep the transfer function rather than give up their hard-won place in the higher education stream.

The sort of liberal or general education that leads to individual freedom and social cohesion will be hard to maintain because traditionally it has been linked with the transfer courses. In order to thrive it will have to be separated into its fundamental components and offered in different patterns. Transfer students will need to be given interdisciplinary courses, a trend that is gaining in the humanities and social science. Liberal education modules will have to be placed into each occupational program. And short courses or forums on contemporary issues should be offered through community services. But this reorganization will be difficult to enact; too few administrators and faculty see its importance.

Funds available to the community colleges will probably change only in tandem with inflation but questions of costs per student will surface because so few go on to senior institutions or complete occupational programs. In what ways do people benefit merely from attendance? How much do students learn even when they do not complete a course or program? Public faith in the value of education has been assaulted by the grade inflation and quasi-educational activities in which all institutions engage. College leaders will be asked continually to defend their expenditures against those who would assess the institutions by the number of students completing their programs.

The community college philosophy of offering something for everyone is a fixture in American education. Henry Steele Commager has noted:

> Schools, and universities too, were called on to prepare the young for everything in general; for the professions, for industry, for farming, for business, for nursing, for the stock market, for marriage, for citizenship, for society, even for life. No other educational system on the globe is required to be quite this eclectic or this ambitious. The wonder is not that American schools so often fail, but that they so often succeed in these miscellaneous aims.

The modern state university, in addition to its degree programs, conducts research for the industrialists, advises the farmer, and offers a potpourri of personal interest courses through its extension division. But the factor that deflects criticism is that the university keeps its regular degree program separate from its community service activities. The community college, because of its infatuation with numbers, tends to group all its enrollments together.

The decade opened with exhortations to break the access barriers, to open the system to the masses. It is closing with calls for new marketing strategies to maintain enrollments in the face of competition from other types of institutions. However, public support will be hard to hold on to for a community college whose leaders suggest that its greatest value lies in providing marginally educative pursuits and in acting as an agency for transfer payments. The question of institutional legitimacy is more than one of educational philosophy; it turns on the public's perception of what a college should be doing.

Fortunately there has been no move to dismantle the system. That seems to suggest success.

The most significant development of the 1980s may be the abandonment of the no-tuition policy. The public will be less disturbed about anything the community college does as long as the students are paying for part of their education. Access for everyone who wants to learn has been achieved. The challenge of teaching them all and limiting institutional claims and growth remains open.

*Arthur M. Cohen* is Director, ERIC Clearinghouse for Junior Colleges at University of California, Los Angeles, and Professor of Higher Education.
*John Lombardi* is Staff Writer, ERIC Clearinghouse for Junior Colleges and former President, Los Angeles City College.

# International Education's Expanded Role in Higher Education

## DOROTHY A. MOORE AND DUCKSOON YU-TULL

Are educational institutions providing the young people of our society with the skills and knowledge needed to function in a world community? Are they able to understand the front pages of our daily newspapers? More important, do they care?

Rapid transportation, instantaneous communication, and the technical sophistication of modern industry have brought about a growing interdependence among nations. Millions of jobs depend upon contacts with people in other parts of the globe. Awareness and understanding of other cultures, their values, their religious beliefs, and their historical and geographical heritage is becoming increasingly important. Therefore, it seems logical that if we can expand the role of international education in our colleges and universities today, the leaders of tomorrow will be better equipped to function, understand, communicate, and make global decisions.

## WHAT IS INTERNATIONAL EDUCATION?

Scholars have begun to see international education as more than just a specialized area of comparative education. In 1969, Gordon I. Swanson, in *Changing Dimension of International Education,* stated:

> The study of international education is of interest to every educator who desires a broader perspective of educational enterprise in general. It is an important area of human inquiry and can lead us to a deeper understanding of the common humanity of man.[1]

Dorothy Moore, co-author of this article and director of The Program of International Education at George Washington University, has developed a useful and operational definition of international education for the 1980s.

From *Educational Horizons* 61, No. 3 (Spring 1983): 144–147. Used by permission of the authors and publisher. Copyright 1983, by Pi Lambda Theta.

International education is related to learning about other peoples and incorporating this knowledge into understanding, acceptance, and enrichment of one's own life. International education is the development of worldmindedness, which is a sensitivity or awareness of other cultures and a willingness to accept the likenesses and differences between them.

To develop worldmindedness, one should:

- Concentrate on likenesses, then differences, relating experiences in a meaningful manner.
- Develop an understanding of how and why the various cultures have evolved.
- Develop an understanding of the interdependence of countries and the awareness of common goals.
- Create the desire in students to seek information about other peoples.
- Try to develop a sensitivity to how others view a situation.

In the Western world, international education had its early beginning in the seventeenth century. Moravian churchman and teacher John Amos Comenius was the first person to envision an organization with a goal to pursue better understanding through international awareness. Later, ideas relating to international education appeared in the writings of philosophers such as Rousseau, Kant, Montaigne, and Fichte.

In the late 1800s and early 1900s, the U.S. was the scene of large immigration of peoples with diverse religions, customs, values, and languages. The newcomers were expected to blend into the great American melting pot, become *American,* and leave behind ethnic customs, values, and even language.

After World War I, the League of Nations pursued the major goals of international education, peace through education and understanding. Recently, the United Nations Educational, Scientific and Cultural Organization has expanded them.

World War II created the need to provide short-term, on-campus international education courses for military personnel, which gave considerable leverage to those interested in introducing international studies into American higher education.[2] International education curricula after World War II reflected the study of other nations and cultures as a means of promoting or preserving our own national institutions or ideologies. The bipolarization of the world around Communist and non-Communist countries, and the threat of nuclear annihilation were major topics of study in world studies curricula.

If we look at the development of international education in the U.S., we find that we have grown from the melting pot philosophy of the early part of this century to a more recent mosaic philosophy, one that appreciates the uniqueness of each individual culture. It is also notable that most legislation involving international education has taken place since the mid-Fifties.

Following Sputnik, considerable concern arose about American schools' preparedness to counteract expanding Soviet development. The National Defense Education Act (NDEA) of 1958 encouraged and assisted in the expansion and improvement of educational programs to meet critical national needs. This Act enabled the government to make grants or contracts that promoted languages and area study centers in institutions of higher learning. In addition, Title VI of the NDEA strengthened language development in the public schools and increased American awareness, particularly of the non-Western world. In 1964, Title XI of the NDEA, the teacher institute program, was passed to include new subject areas such as modern foreign languages and international affairs.

Colleges and universities in the U.S. became more interested in international education in 1966 when Congress passed the International Education Act of 1966, 20 U.S.C. 1172–1177, which declared:

> The Congress hereby finds and declares that a knowledge of other countries is of utmost impor-

tance in promoting mutual understanding and co-operation between nations; that strong American educational resources are a necessary base for strengthening our relations with other countries; that present and future generations of Americans should be given the opportunity to develop to the fullest extent possible their intellectual capacities in all areas of knowledge pertaining to other countries, peoples, and cultures; and the economy of the U.S. and the long-range security of the nation are dependent upon acquiring such knowledge. It was, therefore, deemed both necessary and appropriate for the Federal Government to assist in academic and professional fields, and to coordinate the existing and future programs of the Federal Government in International Education to meet the requirements of world leadership.[3]

The major objectives of this Act were to strengthen American educational resources, correct ethnocentrism, create an international outlook, and encourage education free of national biases.

In the 1980s, the increased interest and need concerning international education is reflected in the International Understanding Program of 1980. Authority for this program is now contained in Title III of the Elementary and Secondary Education Act of 1965 as amended by the Education Amendments of 1980, Public Law 96-374. The purpose of the International Understanding Program is to stimulate, at all levels of U.S. education, programs to increase students' and the public's understanding of other cultures and the interdependence of nations so that they may better evaluate the international and domestic impact of major policies and actions of the U.S. This is a more pluralistic and global approach to international education.

Today, the concerns and activities of international education include:

- The traditional study of other cultures in the curriculum at all levels of education,
- The interdisciplinary approaches to the specialized study of world affairs, international relations, and foreign policy,
- Foreign aid programs to assist in technical and educational development,
- Cooperative and cross-cultural studies,
- Educational exchange of scholars and students,
- Programs concerning the ethnic diversity of America.

## NEED FOR EXPANSION

Young people live daily with international happenings. They are no longer restricted to thinking in terms of single nation-states. According to the Committee on Foreign Students and Institutional Policy, created by the American Council on Education, by 1990 there will be more than a million international students enrolled in U.S. colleges and universities. In addition, there are increasing opportunities in both private business and in government for persons involved in international education. This is true in America, and in other countries as well. Recently, the British Foreign Office revealed that 75% of their everyday business is essentially international. At home, the American government sends official representatives each year to some 700 intergovernmental conferences.[4]

It is incumbent on higher education in America to provide students with knowledge of our own multicultural environment, and give them skills to communicate on a global level. However, in recent years, higher education institutions frequently have been attacked for their allegedly irrelevant curriculum and ineffective teaching. George W. Bonham expresses his concern that traditional organization of scholarly life is ill-suited to deal with global issues that inevitably cross every conceivable area of knowledge.[5]

Former Secretary of Education Shirley M. Hufstedler has written:

It is increasingly difficult to separate domestic from global issues. Our civic concerns can now be rarely seen in purely local or national terms, and few non-American events are any longer in fact extraneous to our lives. Our mass media reflect these new complexities fairly well, but the interrelatedness of global and national events is still only marginally reflected in what young Americans are learning in their schools and colleges.[6]

At present, there are shortages of personnel who are adequately qualified in the area of international, multicultural business. Many American corporations, which previously considered their foreign sales only as a supplement to profits at home, now see greater need for cooperation with international business firms. Consequently, managers with foreign or international education background have enjoyed faster job promotions in many of the key U.S. corporations.

Corporations frequently comment that many Master of Business Administration (MBA) degree holders were not adequately prepared by their institutions to deal with cross-cultural populations. According to a recent article in *Business Week,* the narrowmindedness of many MBA holders is a common complaint of their employers.[7]

It is increasingly apparent that the kind of education and training a new college generation receives will determine our future success in commercial and other national interests abroad. Consequently, our business administration colleges also should be expanding the knowledge and global perspectives of these students. William Voris of the American Graduate School in International Management recently commented: "The manager of the future is going to have to immerse himself in other cultures and other religions."[8]

Business schools are not alone in the need for expansion of curriculum in the area of international education. Unfortunately, teachers also are often as outdated in their world outlook as the textbooks schools provide for students. The teacher education curriculum must be restructured in order that prospective teachers will possess the skills and knowledge to help their students develop global perspectives. Appropriate text materials will help, but as noted educator Leonard S. Kenworthy remarked, "Fine bulletins, excellent equipment, administrative sanction, and community support are important, but nothing happens unless teachers are vitally concerned. The teacher always remains the keystone in the educational arch."[9]

More than any other time in our history, teachers have the responsibility for acquiring tools that will help students who are increasingly affected by cross-cultural issues. Students need to know how to analyze cross-cultural questions of value that require an international point of view. However, at this time, far too many of our teachers are not capable of meeting this challenge.

The May 1980 issue of *Change* contains a very disturbing article revealing that college seniors know very little about the interdependent world in which they live. The article summarizes the results of a national assessment by the Educational Testing Service that measures college students' comprehension of current global complexities. Unfortunately, the average student achieved a score of only 50.5 correct answers out of 101 on the test. Even more alarming, education majors scored lower as a category than students from any other area. The scores are: history majors, 59.3; mathematics, 54.07; engineering, 53.2; social science, 52.77; business, 51.35; foreign languages, 50.22; English 48.84; vocational technical, 45.0; education, 39.83.[10]

In view of the universally dismal scores in the study cited above, there is an obvious need to broaden the world view of all college and university students, especially teachers since they are specifically responsible for the education of others.

## THE WIDER WORLD

The scope and goals of international education have undergone many changes during the course of our country's history and have increased in importance to cause change in our ways of thinking about other parts of the world. Although the characteristics of cultures and peoples of the world are greatly pluralistic, world civilization may be evolving in some unified ways. Although fractionalized, cultures may become one in the sense that they will be based on common knowledge, common assumptions, and the recognition of a common fate.[11] As a recent *Change* editorial warned, America's young face a set of new national and international circumstances about which they have only the faintest of notions. They are, globally speaking, blind, deaf, and dumb; and thus handicapped, it is they who will soon determine the future directions of this nation.[12]

Higher education institutions must provide information to young people about the world in which they are living. Educators must take a hard look at their current curriculum with an eye to its relevance. In order for students to understand present worldwide complexities, educators must broaden their perspectives, help them see beyond individual professions, departments, and even nationalities, to think in terms of a global frame of reference. International awareness must be at the center of the curriculum.

## ENDNOTES

1. Gordon I. Swanson, "International Education: Portents for the Future," *Changing Dimensions in International Education,* ed. Paulsen F. Robert (Tucson: The University of Arizona Press, 1969), p. 1.
2. Ellen M. Gumperz, *Internationalizing American Higher Education* (Berkeley, CA: Center for Research and Development in Higher Education, 1970), p. 2.
3. U.S. Department of Education, *International Understanding Program* CFDA Number: 84.095 (Washington, DC: Office of Postsecondary Education, 1981), p. D2.
4. Harlan Cleveland, "Forward to Basics—Education as Wide as the World," *Change,* May 1980, p. 21.
5. George W. Bonham, "The New Missionaries," *Change,* April 1981, pp. 9, 10.
6. Shirley M. Hufstedler, "A World in Transition," *Change,* May 1980, p. 8.
7. "A Better Crop for B-Schools," *Business Week,* 14 September 1981, p. 111.
8. George W. Bonham, quoting William Voris, "The New Missionaries," *Change,* April 1981, p. 10.
9. Leonard S. Kenworthy, *Introducing Children to the World* (New York: Harper and Row, 1956), p. 23.
10. Barrow, et al., "What Students Know About Their World," *Change,* May 1980, pp. 15, 16.
11. Ibid, p. 13.
12. Hufstedler, "A World in Transition."

*Dorothy A. Moore* is Professor of Education, The George Washington University, Washington, D.C.
*Ducksoon Yu-Tull* is Director, Academic Staffing, The George Washington University, Washington, D.C.

# Model Programs for Adult Learners in Higher Education

ANN Q. LYNCH, RICHARD J. DOYLE, AND
ARTHUR W. CHICKERING

In recent years, the enrollment of adults in higher education has increased significantly. A declining birthrate, an extension of life expectancy, and the influence of the women's movement have combined to shift the demographics of college students.

In 1970, 1.7 million adults made up 22% of college enrollments; by 1975 that figure had grown to 3.7 million and accounted for 34% of college enrollments.[1] The total number of college students between the ages of 25 and 34 increased by 17.7% between 1974 and 1979, and the number of students over age 35 increased by 6.6% during the same period.[2] The Carnegie Council on Policy Studies in Higher Education reported that, within the three-year period from 1975 to 1978, the number of women between the ages of 24 and 34 who were returning to college rose by 187%.[3] According to the U.S. Department of Labor, more than two-thirds of all adult college students in 1979 were women.[4]

In 1980 the Carnegie Council predicted that the enrollments of students in the age group that traditionally attends college would decline by 23% by the year 2000.[5] The National Center for Education Statistics indicates that by the year 2000 the U.S. population will be dominated by people in their middle years; those between the ages of 30 and 44 will make up the largest group, and the group between the ages of 45 and 64 will be steadily increasing.[6] According to Patricia Cross, as the baby boom generation has

grown older, the pressure for educational expansion has shifted to education for adults.[7] In addition, a study by Solomon Arbeiter suggests that at least 40 million adult Americans are in a career transition and that 60% of them plan to seek additional education.[8]

The financial condition of most institutions of higher education, coupled with the growth in demand for educational services for adults, makes it worthwhile for colleges and universities to accept the challenge of the reentry of adult students. "The challenge," according to Joseph Mangano and Thomas Corrado, "is not simply to absorb adult students into extant academic programs, but to recast the total institutional effort to facilitate adults' successful return to, participation in, and completion of formal study."[9]

The growing interest in education of adults returning to college can be seen in the growing number of college programs specifically designed for adults and in the increased attention that the media have given to such programs. Nevertheless, many of these programs are perceived on campus as "poor relations," and they are regarded as academically inferior to programs for 18- to 22-year-olds. Moreover, there is still considerable resistance to such new alternatives as credit for experiential learning, contract learning, credit by examination, alternative scheduling arrangements, and off-campus teaching.

We will summarize here the efforts of 18 in-

From *Phi Delta Kappan* 66, No. 10 (June 1985): 713–716. Used by permission of the authors and the publisher.

stitutions that have taken seriously the individual needs and developmental differences of adult learners. These institutions participated in the Higher Education for Adult Mental Health Project, sponsored by the National Institute of Mental Health and Memphis State University. Participants in the Project created model programs to enhance the quality of their responses to adult students.

Led by the staff of the Center for the Study of Higher Education in the College of Education at Memphis State University, the Project was designed to generate new knowledge about the preparation of college and university administrators, faculty members, and student services professionals for program-development roles in preventive mental health. The model programs served the growing number of older people who are entering or returning to colleges and universities with purposes, orientations, lifestyles, and demands on their time that differ markedly from those of students in the traditional college-age group.

The institutions that participated in the Project included a mix of two- and four-year colleges and universities. Small interdisciplinary teams from each campus were trained by means of a series of problem-solving learning experiences. These learning experiences stimulated the team members to study the theory, research, and applications that related to adult development, preventive mental health, and planned institutional change. Team members learned to assess the needs of adult students at their institutions, to set goals for responding to these needs, to make action plans for developing model programs to meet these goals, to design strategies for implementing the action plans, and to evaluate the impact of the changes.

The Project was rooted in a developmental approach to preventive mental health. Its aims were 1) to increase the knowledge and skills of staff and faculty members at the participating institutions and 2) to develop institutional prac-

tices that are responsive to mental health needs associated with the challenges of various stages of the life cycle; with stages of ego, intellectual, moral, and ethical development; with different learning styles; and with different levels of self-esteem, competence, and coping skills. Through activities in these areas, the Project helped participating institutions to create contexts more conducive to adult learners, to reduce the stress experienced by adult students, and to increase the information available to adult students so that they could better manage their own lives.

Project teams took as their starting points existing institutional policies and structures, services and programs, curricular offerings, and teaching strategies. At each institution, the teams identified the needs of adult learners and developed model programs to meet those needs. Each team developed an action plan that set long-range goals and more specific objectives and activities. Each team identified people responsible for various activities and established target dates for completing them. These action plans were revised annually to meet changing needs and goals.

Because the institutions were as diverse as the adult learners in them, some teams established new structures, courses, or services, while others were content to improve existing services or programs. At every institution, the Project team recognized the need to make administrators, faculty members, and other staff members more aware of the special needs and problems of adult students. Model programs were created in four different areas: 1) administrative structures, policies, and procedures, 2) curriculum and instructional programs, 3) adult student support services, and 4) professional development programs. A description of a number of programs in each of these areas follows.

*Administrative structures, policies, and procedures.* At several institutions, new administrative structures were developed for working with entering adults. Millsaps College adapted the Adult Degree Program of Mary Baldwin College to establish a Bachelor of Liberal Studies degree. As an alternative to mainstreaming adults, the newly established program at Millsaps College featured an introductory seminar, credit for prior learning, independent study, and a stop-out option.

The Project team at Birmingham Southern College introduced "Wednesday College" to provide returning women students with an alternative to the traditional scheduling format. The program allows women to enter (or reenter) the academic world one step at a time by giving them the chance to experience college in a supportive and stimulating atmosphere. Wednesday College appeals to working professionals whose companies value their employee's gains in knowledge and skill but cannot afford to lose their services entirely. But it also is attractive to homemakers who need only make child-care arrangements for one day each week.

Other administrative and structural changes in participating institutions included the expansion by the College of Charleston of evening and off-campus credit-bearing courses. At Judson College, a new program offers adult women the opportunity to study on a full 12-month schedule and to begin individualized learning contracts at any time during the year. In order to meet the needs of working adults, the Adult Degree Program at Sacred Heart College offers courses year-round in eight-week intensive sessions, as well as independent study, proficiency testing, and documentation of prior college-level learning. The External Degree Program at Salem College offers tutorial programs with faculty members or approved off-campus tutors to women with families and/or jobs. Adult women students also receive individual support from two Salem College academic advisors.

The Project team at Saint Mary-of-the-Woods College gained approval for a new mission statement acknowledging adult students and pushed through a policy change requiring that all new faculty members must be willing to do some teaching in the Women's External Degree (WED) Program. Such a policy change means that all new faculty members must participate in professional development seminars that deal with the special components of the WED Program: the introductory orientation and advising sessions, the individualized contract and project system, and the close student/mentor relationships.

A new institutional mission statement was also necessary for acknowledging the place of adults at Ball State University. The Project team at Ball State University gained the provost's approval to amend the mission statement of that institution to include specific references to adult learners and a commitment to provide services to accommodate their needs.

*Curriculum and instructional programs.* Several teams devoted their energies to changing the curriculum and developing instructional programs. The Life, Career, Education Planning Seminars, developed by the Project team at Rockland Community College, incorporate adult developmental theory, learning-style assessment, decision-making strategies, career exploration, educational planning, and life-skills development through a credit-bearing course taught by trained personnel. The seminars were piloted, revised, and delivered in a variety of forms, and the group leaders were trained through active participation in workshops that simulated the seminars. A *Facilitator's Manual for Life, Career, and Educational Planning* was published as a resource guide for leaders of the seminars. Within a year and a half, more than 700 students took part in the program, and their learning has been synthesized in a series of video presentations titled, "Who Am I and Where Am I Going?" This has turned out to be a highly visible adult program that sends a more general message to the rest of the institution, its students, and the surrounding community.

The Project team at the University of Alabama in Birmingham developed a teaching model for the instructors of adult students. This model improved the instructors' understanding of student learning styles by focusing on the assessment of and feedback on their own instructional styles, using the Myers-Briggs Type Indicator (MBTI). The model also provided knowledge about creative problem solving and adult development.

Several other teams introduced new courses for adults as part of their model programs. At East Arkansas Community College, the Project team developed a new orientation course for entering adults, using the MBTI and videotapes of local professionals and workers in different careers. The University of Florida team set up "Challenge of Learning," a course that used the MBTI as a basis for the students' explorations of themselves and their learning styles. This course also encouraged intergenerational sharing.

The Project team at Birmingham Southern College started an adult development course, as well as a new noncredit refresher course for entering adults. The concept of assessment of prior learning was introduced to the faculty members of the RN/BSN program in the College of Nursing at the University of Alabama. A free adult development course for unemployed adults was offered at Sacred Heart College. The College of New Rochelle also began an Adult Learner course using the MBTI and adult development theory.

As part of its new Liberal Studies Program, Millsaps College started an Introduction to Liberal Arts Seminar. The seminar orients adult learners to the academic community, enables them to acquire or sharpen the basic skills required for academic success, and introduces them to the theory of liberal arts education.

The Memphis State University team, through the newly established Adult Student Association, lobbied for a change that would allow the granting of awards and honors to part-time students—80% of whom are adult learners. The External Degree Program of New College at the University of Alabama set a precedent for certification programs. The program administrators negotiated with the American Council of Education and the National Court Reporters Association to develop a procedure for reviewing programs to train court reporters for purposes of nationwide certification.

*Adult student support services.* Student services in most institutions have been primarily geared toward students of traditional college age. The efforts of the Project teams expanded existing services or created new programs to accommodate adults. Several teams worked to improve orientation, advising, and information services for adults. The University of Florida team, through the Students Older Than Average (SOTA) group, instituted a special orientation session for older students. Birmingham Southern College improved its advising by having adult studies advisors and career counselors visit each evening class to tell students about their services. The appointment schedules of the advisors filled immediately thereafter.

East Arkansas Community College moved to a faculty academic advising system and improved its tutorial program to accommodate more adult students. Millsaps College established a new system for advising and recruiting adult students. The Project team at Memphis State University improved services by updating information on cassette tapes to include adult students, by developing an adult peer-counseling program called "Warmline," and by extending the hours during which advising and counseling services were offered. The Adult Student Association at Memphis State produced a brochure titled, *Now That You Have Enrolled.* . . .

Rockland Community College opened a Life Skills Center that included career information, counseling services, and peer assistance programs. The College of Charleston team published an *Adult Student Handbook* that explained the options for admission and the requirements for a degree and listed the names of people to contact for specific services. The Charleston team also established a peer-mentor system for adults, which operated out of the Learning Skills Center. At Saint Mary-of-the-Woods College, the Project team helped establish a telephone counseling service for students in the Women's External Degree Program. The service advises students about such matters as preadmission requirements, special orientation sessions, and the development of learning contracts.

*Networking and linking programs.* Several institutional teams recognized the importance of creating informal networks of faculty and staff members and adult students. The University of Florida team identified people in each college and unit within the university system who could act as advocates for the interests of adult students. Then the team began to publish a *Newsletter for Faculty* to inform faculty members about the unique needs, motivations, and contributions of adult learners. The Webster College team also set up a network among members of its faculty and staff to increase their awareness of adult students.

Mary Baldwin College created a consortium to share expertise and knowledge about adult degree programs at small, southern, liberal arts colleges. The Mary Baldwin College team visited the campuses of the other colleges in the consortium, presented workshops, and worked with the faculty members of each member institution. A grant from the Fund for the Improvement of Post-Secondary Education promoted the dissemination of a model adult degree program and the adaptation of components of the model to fit the needs of each institution in the consortium. Project Adult Learner at Memphis State University involved more than 40 faculty and staff members, who worked in subcommittees to improve services for adult students.

Support groups for adult students have also played an important role in the preventive men-

tal health approach to dealing with the problems of adult students. The Project team at Memphis State University helped create an Adult Student Association that has recruited more than 200 members who have worked at orientation, published a brochure, held social events, and gained recognition for the academic excellence of part-time students. Because Memphis State is largely a commuter campus, the Adult Student Association saw the value of establishing a convenient meeting place for adult students. Through its efforts, a lounge in the University Center was designated for the Adult Student Association and a graduate student coordinator was assigned to it.

At the University of Florida, the Project team strengthened the SOTA group. SOTA members planned activities and became politically organized so that they could be recognized by and receive funds from the Student Government Association.

*Professional development programs.* Fifteen of the Project teams conducted or sponsored professional development programs at their institutions to make the faculty and staff more aware of and more knowledgeable about adult learners. The Project team from Saint Mary-of-the-Woods College conducted an adult development program for the student affairs staff, for the faculty improvement committee, and for the Women's External Degree Program faculty and staff. The University of Florida team held a series of workshops on adult development, learning styles, and liberal education, attended by administrators, faculty members, the student affairs staff, the residence hall staff, and graduate assistants.

At Rockland Community College, the Project team set up an intensive 30-hour training program for facilitators in the Life, Career, Education Planning Seminars. This program involved 49 faculty members, adjunct faculty members, and faculty candidates in learning about adult development, learning styles, life-cycle theory, decision making, group facilitation, and modeling behavior. The training extended over a 30-month period. Even though they may never actually lead one of the seminars, several influential administrators and faculty members became advocates for the seminars after taking part in this training.

The Project team at the College of Charleston sponsored workshops for faculty members and staff that dealt with adult development, life cycles, and learning styles. The team at the University of Alabama in Birmingham sponsored workshops for selected faculty and staff members on creative problem solving, life-cycle issues, and adult learning styles. The Mary Baldwin College Consortium team conducted a conference in Winston-Salem, North Carolina, on serving adult learners. The conference attracted professionals from Columbia, Judson, Millsaps, Sacred Heart, and Salem Colleges. Subsequently, the Millsaps College team held a faculty workship on academic advising and adult development. Teams from Salem, Judson, and Sacred Heart Colleges also sponsored professional development programs for their faculty members.

Birmingham Southern College held an orientation on learning styles for adjunct faculty members. The College of New Rochelle conducted workshops on psychological types, the use of the MBTI, and adult learning styles. The New Rochelle team also conducted professional development programs on alternative assessment models for life experience that attracted 49 administrators and faculty members. The East Arkansas Community College team sponsored a faculty/staff workshop on retention of adult students through understanding personality types; the Webster College team offered faculty workshops on life cycles, learning styles, and personality-type theory.

Three teams went beyond their own institutions to disseminate knowledge and programs to other professionals. The Project team from Rockland Community College conducted a training workshop for professionals from other institutions and plans to disseminate their model program nationally. The School of New Resources of the College of New Rochelle co-sponsored a workshop with another university and a community mental health center on "Understanding the Adult Learner." And the Project team from the University of Florida visited other state universities and plans to participate in state conferences on adult learners. In addition, team members from several institutions have made presentations at local, state, regional, and national conferences of professional associations.

The Higher Education for Adult Mental Health Project has shown that model programs to serve adult learners can be successfully developed by teams trained in the theory of adult development, preventive mental health, and planned change. But the programs must be adapted to fit the needs of a specific constituency of adult learners. Needs assessments and institutional analyses can help teams identify and develop programs and target them where they are most needed. Information gathered in this way also provides a more general perspective for long-range planning.

The range of programs that can be developed by campus-based teams is very broad. Some, such as new adult degree programs, will require entirely new administrative structures, policies, or procedures. Others, such as extended hours for counseling and advising adult students, can be built into existing structures. In either case, linking segments of the college community through newsletters and informal networks is an important step in planning for the growing numbers of adult students.

Campus organizations of adult students offer their members and other adult students a support network, some visibility on campus, and some political power. They can often help provide an on-campus meeting place.

Student services that deal specifically with the needs of adult learners are very helpful in recruiting and retaining adult students. For example, orientation and advising for adult students should take into account the different lifestyles of adult learners, as well as the reasons they have for entering or returning to college. Often adult learners need special tutorial services to refresh skills that have grown rusty over the years. But the most important feature of student services for adult learners is the sensitivity of staff members to the needs of adult students. Thus professional development programs that disseminate information about the lives and psychology of adult students are crucial to the success of any program for adult learners.

## ENDNOTES

1. David J. Graulich, "Graying of Campus: Adult Students Alter Face of U.S. Colleges as Enrollments Falter," *Wall Street Journal,* 24 January 1977, p. 1.

2. Jack Magarrell, "The Enrollment Boom Among Older Americans: 1 in 3 College Students Is Now Over 25 Years Old," *Chronicle of Higher Education,* 4 May 1981, p. 3.

3. Carnegie Council on Policy Studies in Higher Education, *Three Thousand Futures: The Next Twenty Years for Higher Education* (San Francisco: Jossey-Bass, 1980).

4. U.S. Department of Labor, *Monthly Labor Review,* August 1979, p. 53.

5. *Three Thousand Futures . . .,* p. 153.

6. National Center for Education Statistics, *The Condition of Education: A Statistical Report on the Condition of Education in the United States* (Washington, D.C.: U.S. Government Printing Office, 1976), p. 12.

7. K. Patricia Cross, *Adults as Learners* (San Francisco: Jossey-Bass, 1976), p. 5.

8. Solomon Arbeiter et al., *40 Million Americans in Career Transition: The Need for Information* (New York: Future Directions for a Learning Society, College Board, 1978).

9. Joseph A. Mangano and Thomas J. Corrado, "Reentry Adult Students: Needs and Implications," *NASPA Forum,* vol. 1, 1980, p. 5.

*Ann Q. Lynch* is Associate Professor of Counseling and Personnel Services, Memphis State University, Memphis, Tennessee.

*Richard J. Doyle* was formerly Associate Professor of Educational Research, Memphis State University. He is currently Training Director, Input-Output Computer Services, Boston, Massachusetts.

*Arthur W. Chickering* is Distinguished Professor of Higher Education, Memphis State University and Director, Center for the Study of Higher Education.

# Elderhostel: Using a Lifetime of Learning and Experience

## MAX KAPLAN

It is July 1980 and thirty-eight students sit in a large room with long tables and a dozen sewing machines in the Department of Home Economics at Auburn University. They are not college girls, learning to sew. All are over 60; seven are men, and among them are seven couples. They come from Florida, Mississippi, Kentucky, Tennessee, South Carolina, California, Georgia, Texas, Pennsylvania, and Alabama. Among them are former bankers, teachers, government workers, a postmaster, military men, and housewives. About a third are college graduates.

In the classroom, Professor Wayne Flynt discusses "Dixie's Forgotten People" and "Southern Folk Culture." Wayne—everyone uses first names—is head of Auburn's history department. Later Professor John W. Kykendall takes over on "Contemporary Religions." Two afternoon groups meet to learn about drawing from Professor Doug Olson of the art department. Afternoons and evenings also include such options as a tour of the campus, ice-cream making, a movie, a cookout in a nearby state park, and a play presented as part of the theater's summer season.

This is one of the sessions of the Elderhostel program, which offered more than 1600 courses in the summer of 1980, taught at more than 300 colleges and universities in every state as well as in New Brunswick and Ontario. One of the most significant developments in adult education of recent decades, the program began in 1975 with five colleges in New Hampshire. Its founder, Martin Knowlton, described it as an attack on the modern American myth of the "used-up elderly" and the idea that "high age is a time to be endured with dignified sadness and resignation." Recognizing that a college community is a self-contained "world of intense intellectual and social stimulus," the program provides courses taught by professors of the campus to older persons at modest cost and with no credit. (For another look at Elderhostel see *Change,* January 1980).

## CHANGING CIRCUMSTANCES

The Elderhostel program arose from the changing circumstances of our national development. By 1975 those over the age of 65 were as many as one of every ten Americans; at the beginning of this century, they were about one of every twenty-five, in colonial times, as few as one of every fifty. Looking ahead a half-century to 2035, this generation will be one of every five. But beyond numbers, the elderly among us have become a different type in respect to background and aspirations. Whereas the "old old" had been busy building America during their lifetimes, the early years of which, in many cases, had been spent in other countries, the "new old" were the sons and daughters of these immigrants; many were urban residents who had worked for others, rather than on farms; they retired earlier, or had been displaced by machines; their educational backgrounds were higher; they had travelled more, for pleasure or

From *Change* 13, no. 1 (January–February 1981): 38–41. © 1981, Council on Learning. Used by permission of the publisher. *Change* Magazine is a publication of the Helen Dwight Reid Educational Foundation.

out of curiosity; frozen foods, jet airplanes, and television were part of their life; their health was better; the alternatives open to them for leisure, as for all Americans, were larger; and even with rising inflation, Social Security had reduced the numbers of them existing below the official poverty levels from one in four to about one in six within recent decades.

Thus, the concerns for improving the material conditions of the elderly have now been augmented by comparable concern for the less tangible components of personal development. The adult education movement, of course, had always numbered some retirees among its growing body of students under a variety of sponsorships. Such important centers for continuing education as the University of Wisconsin had modelled their philosophies on the famous folk high schools of the Scandinavian countries. In recent years other special programs and schools for the elderly, such as the Institute for Retired Persons in New York's New School and one at Case Western Reserve University in Cleveland, have been created. Official recognition of cultural issues for this population came dramatically on February 7, 1980, when the Select Committee on Aging of the House of Representatives held its hearing on "the arts and older Americans" to establish closer ties between the Administration on Aging and the National Endowment for the Arts. An even more recent and more inclusive case was the award of a grant to the National Council on the Aging by the AOA for creation of a national policy center on education and leisure.

Within this growing movement of intellectual and cultural format opportunities for older persons, the Elderhostel programs are unique in their short schedules of a week, permitting the student to move from one to the other (one of the Auburn couples in the summer of 1980 had in several years attended eleven programs). A second unique characteristic is the diversity of offerings, both those of a national or cultural nature (most popular in 1980 were courses on the presidential election) and those of a distinctly regional character.

## CLASS PARTICIPATION

The uniqueness of these classes, however, is not their content, but the participation arising from lifetimes of experiences of the class members. As a natural part of Dr. Flynt's sessions, Vivian Eady of Montevallo, Alabama, recalls her childhood in North Dakota, confirming the social gatherings that accompanied house raisings. As tapes are played of fa-sol-la singing, several in the class hum or sing along. One lady brings along a lamp she had constructed.

Professor Flynt comments in his reconstruction of the experience, "Being older people and already having established a degree of confidence in their profession or their lives, they're not intimidated like many seventeen- or eighteen-year-olds are when they come to college for the first time." He had considered teaching a course in contemporary China, "but that assumes a lot of knowledge on my part and none on theirs. Hence the format would have been of necessity more lecture, or giving out/receiving rather than participation." Again contrasting this experience with his usual undergraduate teaching, he observes that the people in Elderhostel "come to learn; they are not goal-oriented persons who are trying to manipulate learning into something—a degree, a job, a better salary. I'd say that motivation is the single most important difference."

And how did the students themselves assess their week's experience? About fifteen of the class came together the last Friday afternoon to tape some reactions. One remarked, "I got something out of each course." (She had attended previous Elderhostels.) "When I get home there are things that come to mind, and I say, 'I learned that at college.'" Another, raised in another state, observes, "One thing that fascinated me was that the rural lives in both sections of the country were so similar; many of the things that they did in Alabama was just exactly what was done in North Dakota." Another finds that the course "has given me pride that I did not have in my heritage." Many commented on the experience of renewed youth from being on a campus and interacting with younger students and professors. One described her experience in this way: "We had a young man in a course about the Great Depression. He talked from the books as an economist, and what his father had told him. We told him how it was from our own experience."

## KINDS OF STUDENTS

Data on attendance at Elderhostel programs are now available. They give us a better understanding of the types of people being served by these courses.

The educational backgrounds of 1979 Elderhostel students were: elementary, 1 percent; high school, 12 percent; some college, 27 percent; college degree, 16 percent; some graduate school, 15 percent; and graduate degree, 29 percent. Note, therefore, that whereas only 13 percent of these students had not gone beyond high school, for the country as a whole as many as 46 percent, almost half, of persons over the age of 65 reported in 1978 that they had not finished more than one year of high school. Compared to the 60 percent of Elderhostel students who had college degrees and graduate work, only 8 percent—less than one in ten—of the elderly as a whole had finished college. Indeed, according to a summary of developments in aging for 1978, issued by the U.S. Senate Special Committee on Aging, "about 2.2 million or 10 percent of the older people were 'functionally illiterate,' having had no schooling or less than 5 years." Certainly, Elderhostel was not initiated to teach literacy, and its very setting in the framework of college campuses almost guarantees a skewing of its clientele upwards in terms of past education.

What is the picture as to incomes? In the 1979 classes, students with under $6,000 of family income comprised 15 percent of the total; $6–12,000, 40 percent; $12–20,000, 26 percent; $20–30,000, 14 percent, and over $30,000, 5 percent.

The Senate report on aging tells us that in 1977 in the population as a whole half the families headed by an older person had incomes of less than $9,110. Though the categories are not quite comparable, 45 percent of the Elderhostel students reported incomes over the $12,000 level. This is to be expected, based on the much higher educational responses. On this matter, the planners of Elderhostel's future can move more confidently than on the matter of educational backgrounds and disparities. Even in the central city, there are possibilities of this program tying in with community colleges or other agencies.

These data comparisons prepare us for the high degree of career levels reported by Elderhostel students. As many as 50 percent were professional workers, followed by 14 percent clerical workers, 11 percent managers and administrators; others fall considerably in proportion: technical workers, 5 percent; sales workers, 5 percent; craftsmen, 2 percent; factory workers, farmers, and laborers, each 1 percent.

To insure that the various institutions would not lose money, about one of every three states in 1978 obtained partial funding from Title I of the Higher Education Act. In 1980 about forty-five states met their costs from tuition income. Also, in 1978 and 1979, almost a million dollars was raised from corporations and foundations such as the Pew Memorial Trust, the Rockefeller Brothers Fund and the Atlantic Richfield Foundation.

## OBSERVATIONS

Moving away from official reports, a few personal observations about the program will conclude.

- A major factor in the success of any educational program goes beyond the scholarly qualifications of the instructor; there must be an understanding of the elderly. Therefore, we should anticipate some alignment in the future between Elderhostel, the national adult education movement, and gerontologists. General principles need to be developed for the teaching of retirees, using their accumulated experiences; and special training courses might be considered for retirees who could serve as instructors because of their special knowledge.
- The issue of state and local autonomy is bound to creep into the national picture in the course of time. Undoubtedly, the present policy is that the individual institution (in coordination with the state office) determines what will be offered and by whom. Such decisions are affected on the institutional level by the space that is available, the professors who are there in the summer, their interests, and so on. Nationally, the issue of "guidelines" may emerge around a ratio of regional courses.
- No educator can be happy with a total experience that extends only one week, four class sessions. Since students often come a considerable distance and to a strange place, the program is over before it has really started. The 1980 catalogue acknowledges requests for longer periods of time and other times of the year as well as summer. "We have begun to work with colleges, universities and other educational institutions, to see if we can come up with imaginative solutions that would permit Elderhostel to be extended to a year-round basis." In this exploration, we may

hope that the organization will also see how it may relate, formally or informally, with other educational programs for the elderly, such as the Humanities Program carried on in several hundred senior centers by the National Council on Aging, and the Institute for Lifetime Learning by chapters of the AARP. Each format has its unique advantages; all need to be interrelated and conceptualized in a bold way that has not yet been done. If the university schools of education are not yet sensitive to this need, a comprehensive, unified attempt outside of the usual academic framework is essential. The gerontology profession, preoccupied until recently with bread-and-butter issues of income, health, and shelter for the elderly, has begun to turn more directly to social roles and ongoing development of older persons. We may anticipate that the 1981 White House Conference on Aging, as well as the 1982 sessions in Vienna to be convened by the U.N. General Assembly, will reflect this growing need and interest.

- Elderhostel may not be the group to provide for it, but a program of educational stimulation is needed for the millions of older persons who are limited to their homes, quite literally. We are in an age of miracles of communication, yet even in the university we ignore those opportunities. The Library of Congress now provides machines and records to bring literature to blind and elderly citizens. Could this, or other federal agencies—perhaps the new Office of Education—be brought into the picture on behalf of persons with limited mobility?
- Is it not time for longitudinal research on students of Elderhostel? What can be learned from the ongoing impact of these experiences, short as they are? Studies should be conducted not only by social scientists and students of education (and gerontologists), but by college administrators as well, who

must ask what is the future for a rising proportion of older persons on a "normal" campus.

- We may anticipate, and hope, that the present
format of Elderhostel, no matter how successful it is judged to be by its students and evaluators, will modify itself, adjust to new situations, and adopt a stance of flexibility. This
may turn out to be the major problem for
Elderhostel in the years ahead; and its resolution will depend in good part on how well its
administrative leaders incorporate the views
and skills of the elderly whom they intend to
serve. For our "new old" may wish to be students again, but at their age and level of experience, there is a potential transition from student to sage.
- The most important question to be asked is
what may be the potential meaning of
Elderhostel—indeed, of any mature educational program or demonstration—upon the
elderly themselves? Even the brief excerpts
from several Auburn students quoted earlier
suggests that in both the realms of information and attitudes, older persons can learn
and change in significant ways. That the older
person cannot learn has long been a myth,
dutifully taught in many schools of educa-

tion, starting some decades ago in Teachers
College. The Elderhostel movement, together with a variety of other programs for
the elderly, is now in the process of conducting burial rites to that hallowed myth, spun in
classes of education and woven into the flimsy
cloth of the vernacular literature and mass
media.

## IRREVERSIBLE MOMENTUM

The stereotypical myth that old people are useless, noncreative, sick, sexless, conservative, and
senile has not only served the purpose of profit
planning in our industries, it has penetrated the
universities in the administrative halls as well as
the classrooms. The greater tragedy is that the
mythology has too often been accepted by the
elderly themselves. It is just here that education
for them, and sometimes by them, provides the
juices of confidence. The fight against ageism
must begin first in the minds of the elderly.

The momentum of Elderhostel, after half a
decade, is irreversible. Its impact is ultimately
immeasurable, as all humanistic advance is immeasurable. But it is real all the same, and a
cause for celebration.

*Max Kaplan* was the founder and director of the Leisure Studies Program at the
University of South Florida. He is the author of *Leisure: Lifestyle and Lifespan—
Perspectives for Gerontology* (1979).

## ADDITIONAL LEARNING ACTIVITIES

### Problems and Projects

1. If the "case problem" that you have developed in Sections 1 through 6 is about a
community college or other post-high school institution, develop the case further by relating the trends and innovations described in this section to the
present program. Which trends should be adopted as part of the educational
program?

2. The rationale for this section states that the general goals at this level are the same as at the other levels—vocation, self-realization, citizenship, and critical thinking. Would any difference be needed in the relative emphasis on these goals at the different stages of life covered in this section—late adolescence, adult, or senior citizen? Discuss this with other members of your class or group.

3. What are the functions of community colleges in today's developing system of lifelong learning? How did these functions change between 1973 and 1983? In preparing your answer to this question, review the article by Cohen and Lombardi in this section. Then to get another perspective on these changes read the article by Patricia Cross, "Changing Student Populations and Community Colleges," *Community College Review* 10, No. 3 (Spring 1983): 30–34.

4. What demographic changes are occurring in young Americans, as noted by Ernest L. Boyer in "College with Connections"? How does he believe that these changes will affect our colleges and universities in the 1980s and 1990s?

5. Why does Boyer believe (see "College with Connections") that civic education for adults should be a major function of higher education in the 1980s and 1990s? How does he propose that this might be accomplished?

6. Why does Frank Newman ("Higher Education and the American Resurgence") believe that the importance of universities and colleges in the development of values has grown? Why does he think that universities and colleges have abdicated this central responsibility? Do you agree with Newman? Give your reasons.

7. What reasons does Newman (see preceding question) give for believing that the most important issue facing higher education is to restore its "original purpose of preparing graduates for a life of involved and committed citizenship?" What would you select as the most important issue?

8. Review the recommendations for changes in higher education in "Involvement in Learning: Realizing the Potential of American Higher Education," and compare them to those in "Higher Education and the American Resurgence." Are there recommendations on which both reports agree? How do they differ? Of the proposals in the two reports, which do you regard as most important?

9. What changes are predicted for faculty roles in the university of the future (see "The Changing University: Survival in the Information Society")? What changes are predicted for the curriculum? Are the predicted changes desirable ones?

10. Dr. Carl Eisdorfer, noted gerontological psychiatrist, recently said that older Americans are less like one another than any other segment of the population. What do you think might be the basis for this statement? If this is true, what implications does it have for programs of lifelong education?

11. Eighteen community colleges and universities tried to create learning situations conducive to adult learning by providing for different learning styles and for different levels of self-esteem, competence and coping skills characteristic of adults (see "Model Programs for Adult Learners in Higher Education"). Would any of the programs they developed be useful at an institution with which you

are familiar? What does the article say must be done if the programs are to be successful?

12. According to the rationale for this section, late adolescence is often a period in which the young person may grow into alienation, loneliness, or ruthlessness with little feeling for the values of community life. Do you agree? If the statement is correct, what might the community college do to assist its students in dealing with these problems?

13. What curriculum criteria do you consider to be the most important for community college curriculum planning? Explain how you would like to see them applied.

14. Clark Kerr, President Emeritus of the Unviersity of California, recently visited higher education institutions across the country as chairman of a study for the Association of Governing Boards (see "Higher Education: In Transition Once Again", *Education Digest* 50, No. 9 (May 1985): 14–17). He found that campuses have become divided more and more by interest groups, field versus field, caucus versus caucus: there is much less sense of unity than before. Among students there is new emphasis on economic advancement and vocational subjects rather than on the total advancement of human life by developing new interests, as citizens, in the welfare of American and world society. He also found that there is a sense of lack of mission in American higher education; there is not the same feeling that higher education is serving the nation as in earlier periods. These impressions underscore aspects of the reports of the Carnegie Foundation for the Advancement of Teaching and the National Institute of Education (the first two articles in this Section). In your opinion, what steps should be taken to deal with these problems? Discuss this with other members of your class or group.

15. According to "International Education's Expanded Role in Higher Education," an article in this section, today's university students "are, globally speaking, blind, deaf, and dumb." According to the article, how might this be changed? should international education have a major place in the undergraduate general education curriculum?

16. The rationale for this section includes the statement that a major emphasis in adult education now is to provide learning opportunities for people who were previously left out—Blacks, American Indians, Mexican-Americans, Puerto Ricans, and the poor. What provisions do you think should be made for these groups through continuing and adult education? For help in formulating your answer, reread "Higher Education and the American Resurgence" and "College with Connections" in this section.

17. What do you consider the potential meaning for senior learners of the Elderhostel program (see the rationale and the article by Kaplan in this section)? What should be the goals of the Elderhostel program? Why does Kaplan think that the "fight against ageism must begin in the minds of the elderly"?

18. Will the innovations and trends discussed in the rationale for this section result in the curricular modifications needed in universities and community colleges?

Identify the eight innovations or trends that you regard as most significant and explain why you chose them.

19. Have your personal beliefs or values regarding programs of education for late adolescents, adults, and/or senior citizens changed as a result of your experience with this topic? If so, state what change has taken place and relate it to a class discussion, the rationale, an article, a problem or project, etc. Compare your ideas with those of other members of your class.

## Films

*Universities: Tearing Down the Ivy.* 16 mm, color, 22 min., 1972. Trends toward moving university learning out into the mainstream of society are discussed by Kenneth Keniston and several other professors. Document Associates, Inc., 880 Third Avenue, New York, New York 10022. In Canada, 43 Britain Street, Toronto, Ontario M5A1R7.

*Alternatives for Learning.* 16 mm, color, 52 min., 1974. Depicts seven trends in innovation at the university level: audio-tutorial instruction, computer-assisted instruction, simulation and gaming, junior year abroad, the floating campus, the open university, and the university without walls. University of Michigan Audio-Visual Center, 416 Fourth Street, Ann Arbor, Michigan 48103.

*Four Walls.* 16 mm, color, 11 min., 1977. An eighty-year-old "with so much yet of life to live" finds new meaning in life as a lunchtime assistant in a nursery school. CATEC Consultants, 2754 San Gabriel Street, San Bernardino, California 92404.

*Personalizing Educational Programs: Utilizing Cognitive Style Mapping.* 16 mm, color, 20 min., 1975. Students can be helped by determining their personal cognitive style through testing. This film promotes teaching the same course in different ways to accommodate the different cognitive styles of students. Oakland Community College, 2480 Opdyke Road, Bloomfield Hills, Michigan 48013.

## Books and Articles to Review

The numbers in parentheses following these books or articles refer to the numbered list of innovations and trends in late adolescent, mature and senior learner education listed in the rationale at the beginning of this Section. They will assist you in identifying additional sources regarding some of those trends and innovations.

Allbach, Philip G.; and Berdahl, Robert O., eds. *Higher Education in American Society.* Buffalo, N.Y.: Prometheus Books, 1981.

Bardwick, Judith M. "Middle Age and a Sense of Future." *Merrill-Palmer Quarterly* 24, no. 2 (April 1978): 129–138.

Bloom, Allan. "Our Listless Universities." *Change* 15, no. 3 (Apr¹ ¹983)· 29–35.

Bok, Derek. *Beyond the Ivory Tower: Social Responsibility of the Modern University.* Cambridge, MA: Harvard University Press, 1982.

Burn, Barbara B. *Expanding the International Dimension of Higher Education.* San Francisco, Calif.: Jossey-Bass, 1980. (20)

Carnegie Council on Policy Studies in Higher Education. *Three Thousand Futures: The Next Twenty Years for Higher Education.* San Francisco, Calif.: Jossey-Bass, 1980.

Carnegie Foundation for the Advancement of Teaching. *Higher Education and The American Resurgence.* Lawrenceville, NJ: Princeton University Press, November, 1985. (20) (24) (29)

Covey, Herbert C. "American Higher Education and Older People." *Educational Gerontology* 6, no. 4 (June 1981): 373–383. (23) (28)

Cross, K. Patricia. *Adults As Learners: Increasing Parti. pation and Facilitating Learning.* Washington, D.C.: Jossey-Bass Publishers, 1982. (2) (10)

———— "Changing Student Populations and Community Colleges." *Community College Review* 10, no. 4 (Spring 1983): 30–34. (1) (2) (10) (12) (13) (14).

Darkenwald, Gordon G.; and Merriam, Sharon B. *Adult Education: Foundations of Practice.* New York: Harper and Row, 1982. (2)

Duffy, Karen Louise; and Fendt, Paul F. "Trend in Adult Learning: Implications for Community College Educators." *Community College Review* 12, no. 1 (Summer 1984): 4–47. (1) (2) (4) (5) (6) (9) (10) (14) (17) (27) (28)

Finn, Chester E., Jr. "The Drive for Educational Excellence: Moving Toward a Public Consensus." *Change* 15, no. 3 (April 1983): 14–22.

Forman, Bernard I. "Reconsidering Retirement: Understanding Emerging Trends." *Futurist* 18, no. 3 (June 1984): 43–47.

Goldthwait, John T. "The Sub-Literate College Student." *Educational Forum* 47, no. 2 (Winter 1983): 199–207. (12) (17)

Gulette, Margaret M. "The Heart of Good Teaching." *Change* 16, no. 5 (July/August 1984): 8–11, 48.

Houle, Cyril O. *Patterns of Learning.* San Francisco, CA: Jossey-Bass, 1984.

*Involvement in Learning: Realizing the Potential of American Higher Education.* Final Report of the Study Group on the Conditions of Excellence in American Higher Education. Washington, D.C.: National Institute of Education, U.S. Department of Education, October, 1984. (1) (12) (17) (21) (29) (30)

*Integrity in the College Curriculum: A Report to the Academic Community.* Washington, D.C.: Association of American Colleges, 1985. (29)

Jarvis, Peter. *Adult and Continuing Education Theory and Practice.* New York: Nichols Publishing Co., 1983. (2)

John, Mary Tyler. "Skills for Teaching the Elderly Subculture." *Educational Gerontology* 6, nos. 2–3. (March/April 1981): 151–164. (2)

Kerr, Clark. "Higher Education: In Transition Once Again." *Education Digest* 50, no. 9 (May 1985): 14–17.

Kouri, Mary K. "From Retirement to Re-Engagement: Young Elders Forge New Futures." *Futurist* 18, no. 3 (June 1984): 35–42. (3) (5) (9) (10) (18) (23) (26) (27).

Labouvie-Vief, Gisela. "Adult Cognitive Development: In Search for Alternative Interpretations." *Merrill-Palmer Quarterly* 23, no. 4, (October 1977): 227–263.

Lauter, Paul. "University Reform: Threat or Opportunity." *Thought and Action* 2, no. 1 (Winter, 1986): 5–22. (10) (29).

Levine, Arthur. *The Institutionalization and Termination of Innovation.* Albany, N.Y.: State University of New York, 1980.

Melendez, Winifred A. "Powerless Prof: From Candle Bearer to Burnout." *Thought and Action* 2, No. 1 (Winter 1986): 63–72. (6)

Peterson, David A.; and Eden, Donna Z. "Cognitive Style and the Older Learner." *Educational Gerontology* 7, no. 1 (July 1981): 57–66. (23)

Ravitch, Diane. *The Troubled Crusade: American Education 1945–1980.* New York: Basic Books, 1983.

Roueche, John E.; Baker III, George A.; and Roueche, Suanne D. "Access with Excellence: Toward Academic Success in College." *Community College Review* 12, no. 4 (April 1985): 4–9.

Solomon, Barbara Miller. *In the Company of Educated Women: A History of Women and Higher Education.* New Haven, CN: Yale University Press, 1985.

Stadtman, Verne A. *Academic Adaptation: Higher Education in the 1980s and 1990s.* San Francisco, CA: Jossey-Bass, 1980.

Trachtenberg, Stephen Joel. "What Universities Will Be Like in the Year 2000." *Phi Delta Kappan* 64, no. 5 (January 1983): 327–330. (18)

Weinstock, Ruth. *The Graying of the Campus.* New York: Educational Facilities Laboratory, 1978. (2) (5) (6) (10) (28)

Whitman, Neal A.; Spendlove, David S.; and Clark, Claire A. *Student Stress—Effects and Solutions.* ASHE-ERIC Higher Education Research Report no. 2. Washington, D.C.: Association for Higher Education, 1984. (27)

## Some Higher Education Reports of the 1980's

Carnegie Foundation for the Advancement of Teaching. *Higher Education and the American Resurgence.* Lawrenceville, NJ: Princeton University Press, 1985.

*Equality and Excellence: The Educational Status of Black Americans.* New York: The College Entrance Examination Board, 1985.

*Integrity in the College Curriculum: A Report to the Academic Community.* Washington, D.C.: Association of American Colleges, 1985.

National Endowment for the Humanities. *To Reclaim A Legacy: A Report on the Humanities in Higher Education.* Washington, D.C.: U.S. Government Printing Office, 1984.

National Institute of Education. *Involvement in Learning: Realizing the Potential of American Higher Education.* Washington, D.C.: U. S. Government Printing Office, 1984

# 11

# *Summary*

If you have read and studied the preceding sections of this book and tackled some of the problems and projects, then we have come quite some distance together. It is time to try to see where we have been on this journey and what it might mean in the future.

At the beginning, we learned that values and goals, social forces, human development, learning, and knowledge and cognition should all be considered and interrelated in curriculum planning and the planning of teaching. This process was called a multi-dimensional approach to planning. Knowledge of the theories and research about social forces, human development, learning and learning styles, and knowledge and cognition can provide alternatives and strategies for planning and decision making by curriculum planners and teachers.

Throughout Part I, objectives and the four bases were related to other curriculum criteria, which should be the standards for decision making in curriculum planning. Overall objectives, which constitute the most important curriculum criterion, should contribute to balance and systematic planning and should be developed, in part, through student-teacher planning.

The various levels of social forces were seen as necessary considerations in planning for individual differences, relevance, the teaching of values, self-understanding, and problem solving. Understanding human development offers important guidance in providing for individual differences, relevance, and continuity in learning. Learning theories supply bases for various alternative approaches to planning and to providing flexibility. Knowledge and cognition theories offer still other approaches and thus also contribute to flexibility, relevance, balance, and provision for individual differences. The rationale for Section 6 included a summary of the various theories and theorists that are the potential sources for many of the strategies for curriculum planning.

The rationale for Section 6 also described the stages in curriculum planning, including the identification of the context of the planning or teaching; the formulation of objectives; the selection and implementation of the strategies for achieving the goals; and evaluation. This planning should be recurrent and self-renewing—a continuing process of decision making and strategy selection guided by values and goals, the four bases, and other curriculum criteria. The Section 6 rationale also included several new criteria for planning: *anticipation, participation,* and *values.* The four curriculum bases are the sources of the data needed to plan and select different strategies and alternatives. The preplanned curriculum should also provide strategies and alternatives that the teacher can consider.

In Part II we examined the innovations and trends at each of the curriculum levels—childhood, early adolescence, middle adolescence, late adolescence, adult, and senior citizen. These trends provide the basis for other options, innovations, strategies, and alternatives.

Some of the strategies are person-centered, some are group- or social-centered, and some are knowledge- or skill-centered. Multi-dimensional planning based on objectives and the four bases will result in curricula that attend to individual needs, the society, and knowedge as well. Strategies, alternatives, innovations, and trends should be selected in order to attain goals of self-realization, citizenship, vocation, and critical thinking.

In *Crisis in the Classroom* (New York: Random House, 1970) Charles E. Silberman stated that the most pervasive characteristic of the classroom and schools is mindlessness: failure to think seriously about purpose or consequence. The source of much of this mindlessness is linear thinking. The multi-dimensional approach to planning makes goals of central importance, and provides the means for selecting strategies and alternatives on a professional rather than a random basis.

## TOMORROW'S CURRICULA AND TEACHING

If the implications of our study are fulfilled, what may be some of the likely changes in curricula and teaching? Let us try to name just a few:

1. Programs of education will be characterized by concern for the "hidden curriculum" and moral education, alternative curricula and schools, emphasis on the personal development of learners, the study of personal and social problems, provision for the developmental differences of learners, flexible multi-age grouping, peer teaching, student-teacher planning, continuous learner progress, and programs for *all* learners.
2. The community will be a major focus of learning—an object of study, a setting for instruction, an arena for the development of the skills of future planning, and a source of people with important knowledge to share and skills to impart.
3. Learners will be alert participants in the larger society as observers, advocates, and volunteers in a coming together between adults and young people.

4.  Cultural pluralism, as the source of our continuing social vitality, will characterize educational programs—the academic curricula, the cocurricular activities, and the informal programs.
5.  Humanistically oriented career education will be provided at all age levels, and cooperative education combining school and on-the-job experience will be widely available.
6.  Flexible curricula providing many alternatives will be available to allow youths and adults to "drop in and out."
7.  Early childhood education will be available, involving middle adolescents, parents, and senior citizens.
8.  Curricula and programs that encourage lifelong learning and self-renewal will be generally available.
9.  Teachers will use preplanned curricula as *resources* for their planning. They will demonstrate their professional accountability by basing their planning and selection of multiple teaching strategies on objectives, the four bases, and criteria such as individual differences, relevance, continuity, personalization of instruction and anticipation.
10. Parents, students, and other concerned citizens will participate in planning and evaluating programs of education.

What would you add to this list?

## ADDITIONAL LEARNING ACTIVITIES

### Problems and Projects

1.  You have had an opportunity to examine and analyze over thirty-five articles describing innovations and trends from early childhood through three levels of adolescence and adulthood. Identify the innovations and trends in these programs of education which you think should be common to all age levels. Identify the criteria on which each of these trends is based.
2.  It has been stated that some of the strategies and innovations are person-centered, some are society- or group-centered, and some are knowledge- or skill-centered. Examine the list of trends at any of the age levels and try to classify them according to these three categories. Which of them may be placed in at least two of the categories?
3.  Turn to the beginning of Section 1. To what extent do you feel you have developed the performance competencies listed there by studying this book? What else could you do to develop these competencies? You will have to pay attention to the development and refinement of these competencies throughout your professional career if they are to be attained and maintained.
4.  Review the definitions of curriculum and instruction and the discussion related

to these definitions in Section 1. After studying the rationales, reading the articles, and working through some of the problems or projects in this book, do you agree with these definitions? Try your hand at improving on them. Share your definitions with other students.

5. Often when an educational program is examined in terms of the four bases of the curriculum, it is found that one or more of them has been overlooked or ignored. When this happens, sometimes one or more of the innovations or trends can be used to give greater balance to the program. Examine the lists of trends at the four school levels in order to identify ten trends or innovations for each of the curriculum bases that might foster more attention to social forces, human development, learning, or knowledge and cognition, if it were included in an educational program deficient in one of these areas.

6. The rationale for Section 1 states that "to be professionally accountable means to use the knowledge, methods, and skills that the profession had developed through past experience, theories, and research." Actually, to be professionally accountable one must *demonstrate* that he or she has, in fact, made responsible use of pertinent knowledge in curriculum planning and teaching. Do you agree with this description of accountability? How will you demonstrate your accountability as a result of your study of *Curriculum Planning: A New Approach?*

7. You have been frequently urged in this book to prepare your own set of criteria for curriculum planning. They should reflect your own thinking and area of specialization. Prepare this list now if you have not previously done so, or review and complete what you have done previously. Explain the choices you have made.

8. I believe that the large number of innovations identified at each of the school levels indicates the professional vitality and promise for the future of educational programs, in spite of problems we face. If this is true, how can we capitalize on this professional vitality?

9. In the article "Who Should Plan the Curriculum?" (Section 6), I stated that "the student is the major untapped resource in curriculum planning. Students are in the best position to explain many of the advantages and deficiencies of the present curriculum." I have occasionally received letters from students who have used previous editions of this book and have found them both interesting and helpful. If you are so inclined, I would appreciate your writing to me with your criticisms, comments, and suggestions. The address is Professor Glen Hass, College of Education, University of Florida, Gainesville, Florida 32611.

10. Reference is often made to applying objectives, bases, criteria, and trends to curricula or teaching and suggesting improvements. These same guidelines can be applied to the preparation of teaching materials. Select any curriculum book (this one, for instance), course of study, or study guide and try to determine its objectives and the extent to which the four bases, criteria, and trends were used to guide its preparation. Then suggest improvements. Often the writers of curriculum and other books will state in the preface of the book the criteria or guidelines they used in preparing it.

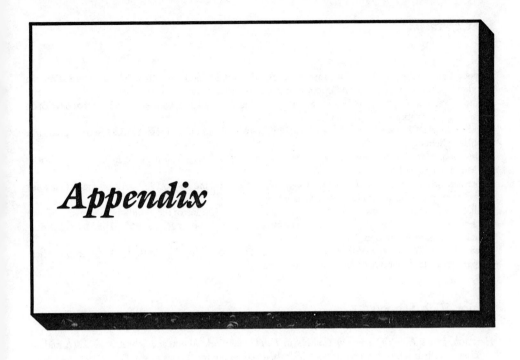

# Appendix

## BOOKS THAT DESCRIBE SCHOOL PROGRAMS

These books are listed because they provide an opportunity to learn about a particular curriculum and its setting in depth. Unfortunately not many books focus on a single curriculum or program; therefore books on this list may be ten or twenty years old. The purpose is to have a curriculum or teaching practices to examine and thus develop the performance competencies related to curriculum planning.

If you wish to use this approach, I hope you can find several of these books in your library. Another avenue might be to select a curriculum that you already know well and make that the basis of your analysis and suggestions for improvement.

Unfortunately I have been unable to find any suitable books that describe middle school, community college, or university programs to include in the list.

### Elementary Schools

DeTurk, Philip H. *P.S. 2001*. Bloomington, Indiana: Phi Delta Kappa, 1974. (The story of the Pasadena Alternative School.)

Hansen, Carl F. *The Amidon School*. Englewood Cliffs, New Jersey: Prentice-Hall, 1962. (A Washington, D.C., elementary school based on organized knowledge and didactic teaching.)

Harris, Lewis E.; and Harris, Rae, *Bootstraps: A Chronicle of a Real Community School*. Cable, Wisconsin: Harris Publications, 1980. (A community education program with adult participation in evening school and an elementary and a secondary curriculum geared to study critical problems in the community. Harris Publications, SR2, Box 123, Cable, Wisconsin 54821.)

Haynes, Carrie Ayers. *Good News on Grape Street*. New York: Citation Press, 1975. (The transformation of a ghetto school from despair and dullness to hope and excitement.)

Hentoff, Nat. *Our Children Are Dying*. New York: Viking Press, 1966. (A school in Harlem that developed an organic relationship with its community.)

Hershey, Myrliss. *Teacher Was a White Witch*. Philadelphia: Westminster Press, 1973. (A second grade in a black ghetto school.)

Holt, John. *How Children Fail*. New York: Pitman Press, 1964. (A fifth grade in Colorado's Rocky Mountain School.)

Lederman, Janet. *Anger and the Rocking Chair*. New York: Viking Press, 1969. (A non-graded class for behavior problems in an elementary school.)

Neill, A. S. *Summerhill*. New York: Hart Publishing Co., 1964. (One of the world's best-known schools.)

Nesbitt, Marion. *A Public School for Tomorrow*. New York: Dell Publishing Co., 1967. (The Maury Elementary School in Richmond, Virginia.)

Rotzel, Grace. *The School in Rose Valley*. Baltimore: The Johns Hopkins Press, 1971. (A school where parents, children, and teachers constantly interact.)

## Junior High Schools

Herndon, James. *How To Survive in Your Native Land*. New York: Simon and Schuster, 1971. (A middle-class suburban junior high school in which the children are the "spoils of war.")

————. *The Way It Spozed to Be*. New York: Simon and Schuster, 1968. (A 98 percent black junior high school in San Fransisco.)

James, Charity. *Young Lives at Stake*. New York: Agathon Press, 1972. (A person-centered school for the education of early adolescents.)

## High Schools

Beggs, D. W. *Decatur-Lakeview High School*. Englewood Cliffs, New Jersey: Prentice-Hall, 1964. (Organizational arrangements intended to individualize learning.)

Bhaerman, Steve; and Denker, Joel. *No Particular Place To Go: The Making of a Free High School*. New York: Simon and Schuster, 1972. (Experiences and problems in teaching in a free school.)

Cox, D. W. *The City as a Schoolhouse*. Valley Forge, Pennsylvania: Judson Press, 1972. (The story of the Parkway Program in Philadelphia.)

Cusick, Philip A. *The Egalitarian Ideal and the American High School: Studies of Three Schools*. New York: Longman, Inc., 1983. (A study of "Factory High," "Urban High," and "Suburban High," all located in an unnamed metropolitan area.)

————. *Inside High School*. New York: Holt, Rinehart and Winston, 1973. (Horatio Gates Senior High School: What does it mean to students?)

Harris, Lewis E.; and Harris, Rae. *Bootstraps: A Chronicle of a Real Community School*. Cable, Wisconsin: Harris Publications, 1980. (A community education program with adult participation in evening school and an elementary and a secondary curriculum geared to study critical problems in the community. Harris Publications, SR 2, Box 123, Cable, Wisconsin 54821.)

Lightfoot, Sara Lawrence. *The Good High School: Portraits of Character and Culture*. New York: Basic Books, Inc., 1983. ("Portraits" of six high schools that are described as good by faculty, students, parents, and communities. The schools have clearly articulated goals and identities.)

Tye, Barbara Benham. *Multiple Realities: A Study of 13 American High Schools*. Lanham, Maryland: University Press of America, Inc., 1985. (Profiles of the thirteen high schools which participated in Goodlad's *The Study of Schooling*, including student perceptions, classroom climates, and recommended policy changes.)

## GENERAL OUTLINE FOR A CASE PROBLEM THAT FOCUSES ON A SCHOOL

I. Introduction

    A. General tone of community and school
    B. Social factors affecting the school and its students

II. The Community

    A. General data that may affect the school
    B. Social groups in the community that may affect the school
    C. Attitudes toward education and the school

III. The School System

IV. The School

    A. The physical plant
    B. The administration
    C. General tone, traditions, etc.
    D. Special advantages or problems

V. The Staff

    A. Teachers
    B. Principal and assistant principals
    C. Resource staff
    D. Aides, etc.

VI. The Students

VII. Curriculum and Curriculum Planning

VIII. Activities

IX. Teaching Practices

X. Questions for Analysis—Use the thirty criterion questions from the first five sections (summarized in Section 6)

XI. Some Sources of Suggestions for Improvement

    A. Which of the curriculum bases is best used in this school or by these teachers?

    B. Which curriculum bases are least effectively used?

    C. Which of the curriculum criteria might be the basis for suggesting changes and improvements?

    D. Which trends are now in use in the curriculum and teaching? Which trends or innovations might be considered?

The case problem might focus on a *student* by including information about the student in appropriate sections of the outline. The same might be done for a *department* that was the focus of a case study.

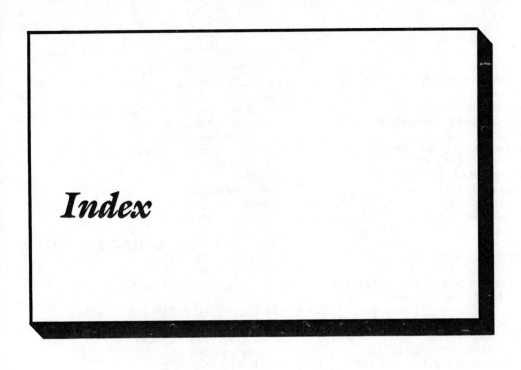

# Index